ANNUAL EDITIONS

American Government 10/11
Fortieth Edition

EDITOR

Bruce Stinebrickner
DePauw University

Bruce Stinebrickner is the Leonard E. and Mary B. Howell Professor of Political Science at DePauw University in Greencastle, Indiana, and has taught American politics at DePauw since 1987. He has also taught at Lehman College of the City University of New York (1974–1976), at the University of Queensland in Brisbane, Australia (1976–1987), and in DePauw programs in Argentina (1990) and Germany (1993). He served fourteen years as chair of his department at DePauw after heading his department at the University of Queensland for two years. He earned his BA *magna cum laude* from Georgetown University in 1968, his MPhil from Yale University in 1972, and his PhD from Yale in 1974.

Professor Stinebrickner is the coauthor (with Robert A. Dahl) of *Modern Political Analysis,* sixth edition (Prentice Hall, 2003), and has published articles on the American presidential selection process, American local governments, the career patterns of Australian politicians, and freedom of the press. He has served as editor of thirty-two earlier editions of this book as well as fourteen editions of its *State and Local Government* counterpart in the McGraw-Hill Contemporary Learning Series. His current research interests focus on government policies involving children (e.g., schooling, child custody, adoption, and foster care). In both his teaching and his writing, Professor Stinebrickner applies insights on politics gained from living, teaching, and lecturing abroad, as well as from serving on the Greencastle, Indiana school board and Redevelopment Commission.

ANNUAL EDITIONS: AMERICAN GOVERNMENT, FORTIETH EDITION

Published by McGraw-Hill, a business unit of The McGraw-Hill Companies, Inc., 1221 Avenue of the Americas, New York, NY 10020. Copyright © 2011 by The McGraw-Hill Companies, Inc. All rights reserved. Previous edition(s) 2008, 2009, 2010. No part of this publication may be reproduced or distributed in any form or by any means, or stored in a database or retrieval system, without the prior written consent of The McGraw-Hill Companies, Inc., including, but not limited to, in any network or other electronic storage or transmission, or broadcast for distance learning.

Some ancillaries, including electronic and print components, may not be available to customers outside the United States.

Annual Editions® is a registered trademark of The McGraw-Hill Companies, Inc.

Annual Editions is published by the **Contemporary Learning Series** group within The McGraw-Hill Higher Education division.

1 2 3 4 5 6 7 8 9 0 WDQ/WDQ 1 0 9 8 7 6 5 4 3 2 1 0

ISBN 978–0–07–805057–2
MHID 0–07–805057–x
ISSN 0891–3390

Managing Editor: *Larry Loeppke*
Developmental Editor: *Debra A. Henricks*
Editorial Coordinator: *Mary Foust*
Editorial Assistant: *Cindy Hedley*
Production Service Assistant: *Rita Hingtgen*
Permissions Coordinator: *Shirley Lanners*
Senior Marketing Manager: *Julie Keck*
Senior Marketing Communications Specialist: *Mary Klein*
Marketing Coordinator: *Alice Link*
Director Specialized Production: *Faye Schilling*
Senior Project Manager: *Joyce Watters*
Design Specialist: *Margarite Reynolds*
Production Supervisor: *Sue Culbertson*
Cover Graphics: *Kristine Jubeck*

Compositor: Laserwords Private Limited
Cover Image: Official White House Photo by Lawrence Jackson (inset); © Getty Images/RF (background)

Library in Congress Cataloging-in-Publication Data
Main entry under title: Annual Editions: American Government 2010/2011.
 1. American Government—Periodicals. I. Stinebrickner, Bruce, *comp.* II. Title: American Government.
658'.05

www.mhhe.com

Editors/Academic Advisory Board

Members of the Academic Advisory Board are instrumental in the final selection of articles for each edition of ANNUAL EDITIONS. Their review of articles for content, level, and appropriateness provides critical direction to the editors and staff. We think that you will find their careful consideration well reflected in this volume.

ANNUAL EDITIONS: American Government 10/11
40th Edition

EDITOR

Bruce Stinebrickner
DePauw University

ACADEMIC ADVISORY BOARD MEMBERS

Oladimeji Adeoye
DePaul University

Alton Alade-Chester
San Bernardino Valley College

Lucas Allen
Michigan State University

David N. Baker
University of Toledo

Ryan J. Barilleaux
Miami University

Larry Berman
University of California—Davis

Kevin Caldwell
Blue Ridge Community College

Steven Campbell
University of South Carolina—Lancaster

Michael Coulter
Grove City College

Jennifer Dillard
Clemson University

Gary Donato
Bentley College

Dean A. Frantsvog
Minot State University

Joe Gaziano
Lewis University

Mitchel Gerber
Southeast Missouri State University

Chris Grill
Empire State College—Latham

Carol L. Guarnieri-Palermo
Rowan University

Michael Harkins
William Rainey Harper College

Margaret Heubeck
University of Virginia—Charlottesville

Jean-Gabriel Jolivet
Southwestern College

John L. Kaczynski
Saginaw Valley State University

Roger Kemp

Jeffrey Kraus
Wagner College

Michael G. Krukones
St. Xavier University

Anne Leonard
Embry-Riddle Aeronautical University

Tal Levy
Marygrove College

Eloise F. Malone
United States Naval Academy

Will Miller
Ohio University

Sherrow O. Pinder
California State University—Chico

Steven Puro
St. Louis University

Andreas W. Reif
Southern New Hampshire

Mark E. Rush
Washington and Lee University

Carlos Scalisi
San Bernardino Valley College

Mack C. Shelley
Iowa State University

David Tabb
San Francisco State University

Pak W. Tang
Chaffey College

Andrew J. Taylor
North Carolina State University—Raleigh

Carole Taylor
Limestone College

Lois Duke Whitaker
Georgia Southern University

Lowell F. Wolf
Dowling College

Preface

In publishing ANNUAL EDITIONS we recognize the enormous role played by the magazines, newspapers, and journals of the public press in providing current, first-rate educational information in a broad spectrum of interest areas. Many of these articles are appropriate for students, researchers, and professionals seeking accurate, current material to help bridge the gap between principles and theories and the real world. These articles, however, become more useful for study when those of lasting value are carefully collected, organized, indexed, and reproduced in a low-cost format, which provides easy and permanent access when the material is needed. That is the role played by ANNUAL EDITIONS.

American Government 10/11 is the fortieth edition in an *Annual Editions* series that has become a mainstay in many introductory courses on the American political system. The educational goal is to provide a readable collection of up-to-date articles that are informative, interesting, and stimulating to students beginning their study of the American political system.

As everyone reading this book knows, in January 2009 Barack Obama was sworn in as president of the United States. That same month the 111th Congress took office, with both houses having substantial Democratic majorities. The forty-fourth president of the United States entered the White House facing a daunting array of challenges. Succeeding Republican George W. Bush, Democrat Obama took office amidst an economic recession that many Americans feared would become a second Great Depression. U.S. military forces had been fighting in Iraq and Afghanistan for most of the decade and many Americans thought it was time to reduce the two wars' toll on American lives and pocketbooks and to try to restore the nation's tattered image in the world. President Obama and the country faced still other major challenges. These included skyrocketing health care costs while millions of Americans were left without insurance and proper medical care, the threat of climate change thought to imperil the entire human race, shortcomings in major financial institutions that had led to the nation's economic woes, the long-simmering problem of millions of undocumented immigrants living in the United States, and large budget deficits and mounting national debt.

No one should be surprised that as I write this preface in November, 2009, President Obama and the 111th Congress have *not* solved all the problems and challenges mentioned in the preceding paragraph. Some of these problems have become worse during 2009 and others have been pushed aside for later consideration; some have been or are being addressed, although with unknown results as of this writing. All in all, the first year of the Obama administration has been extraordinarily interesting, and 2009 may—or may not—turn out to be the starting point of a sustained and successful effort to change the direction(s) in which the country is heading.

Immediately on taking office, President Obama faced decisions about how to spend the remaining $350 billion dollars of Troubled Asset Relief Program (TARP) funds. This amount was left from the TARP law passed in October 2008, a bipartisan attempt to bail out teetering financial institutions that had precipitated the economic crisis. One key TARP decision for Obama was whether—and, if so, how and to what extent—to try to save General Motors and Chrysler, two leading U.S. automakers that had for decades been stalwarts of the American economy but who were on the verge of bankruptcy when President Obama took office. Besides adopting a plan to try to save the two car manufacturers, in time-honored Keynesian fashion President Obama urged quick congressional passage of a mammoth stimulus bill aimed at combating the recession, and in February the president signed into law a $787 billion dollar stimulus package. A week or so later, wearing his commander-in-chief hat, Obama announced an August, 2010, deadline for withdrawing U.S. combat troops from Iraq. In March, he announced a new strategy for U.S. military activities in Afghanistan and in May replaced the U.S. commander in that theatre of war.

In the summer of 2009, Congress began the more public phase of considering major health care reform, supported by the president in this potentially historic endeavor. By October, five different congressional committees had passed five different versions of health care reform. On November 7, the House of Representatives passed its version of health care reform by a five-vote margin, a $1.1 trillion bill that will not reach the president's desk for signature in its current form. How the rest of the health care reform legislative process will play out by the end of the congressional session in late December remains to be seen. At this writing it seems likely, but far from certain, that some version of reform legislation will be passed. Details of a Senate health care reform bill have yet to be worked out (or passed!), and passage of a Senate bill would have to be followed by high-stakes House-Senate negotiations before major health care legislation could be enacted. (Let me emphasize my wording that "at this writing it seems likely . . .", there are no certainties about this matter as I write this preface just after the passage of the House bill.)

In June, 2009, an Obama-supported cap-and-trade bill aimed at restricting greenhouse gas emissions in the United States passed the House of Representatives, and a bill on the same topic was introduced in the Senate in late September. How this particular legislative effort turns out will not be known until 2010, even though the Obama administration's Environmental Protection Agency is preparing regulations to restrict greenhouse gas emissions that may be put into effect without further legislative enactments. President Obama and congressional leaders have publicly agreed to delay addressing the issue of undocumented immigrants living in the United States, but new regulations aimed at preventing the dysfunctions of the financial market that surfaced in the summer of 2008 are being considered in Congress, with the House Financial Services Committee currently taking the lead in that endeavor. The budget deficit for the fiscal year ending 30 September 2009 amounted to the biggest percentage of the nation's economic output since the end of World War II, and huge deficit spending is foreseeable for (at least) several years to come. And, of course, retiring members of the baby boomer generation (the first baby boomers will turn 65 in 2011) will put increasing demands on both the Social Security trust fund and Medicare, a fiscal challenge foreseeable for decades and about which American national government has done relatively little. Last but not least, President Obama has been meeting periodically with his national security advisors since the summer of 2009 to review U.S. military strategy in Afghanistan. The war had taken a turn for the worse while longstanding corruption in the Afghanistan government continued to fester. Many observers seem to agree that U.S. options in Afghanistan range from "bad" to "worse," and it remains to be seen what, if any, change in strategy the commander-in-chief will choose.

A year ago I wrote in the preface to the predecessor of this edition, "Every time I work on the preface for a new edition of this book, I am led to write that the coming year will be another interesting one for students of American politics." The year 2009 has certainly proved no exception to this general rule. Yet, as I have tried to convey, many of the elements in any overall narrative of President Obama's first year in the White House remain incomplete. First and foremost, will President Obama be able to accomplish the sort of fundamental changes that he promised during his campaign? Do the signs of economic recovery that have become apparent signal a return to steady economic growth and satisfactory levels of employment? Will health care reform legislation pass? If passed, will it make quality medical care accessible to all Americans and contain escalating health care costs? Will the United States cooperate with other nations of the world in serious and sustained global efforts to combat climate change? Will reforms designed to prevent the financial markets' excesses of recent years be enacted and be successful in providing greater financial stability for the American economy and the American people?

How will Democratic candidates fare in the congressional elections of November 2010? Will Americans react negatively or positively to the performance of the Democrat-led executive and legislative branches as they cast votes that will elect all 435 members of the House of Representatives and more than one-third of the Senate?

The coming year, 2010, will provide answers or partial answers to many of the questions just posed and others like them. Careful observation of American politics as it unfolds on a day-to-day basis can teach us a great deal about both the regularities and unpredictable aspects of the American political system. The selections in this book should help readers comprehend and even anticipate what will happen in the year to come and, more importantly, enhance their understanding of the characteristic functioning of the contemporary American political system.

The systems approach provides a rough organizational framework for this book. The first unit focuses on ideological and constitutional underpinnings of American politics, from both historical and contemporary perspectives. The second unit treats the major institutions of the national government. The third covers the "input" or "linkage" mechanisms of the system—political parties, elections, interest groups, and media. The fourth and concluding unit shifts the focus to policy choices that confront the government in Washington and resulting "outputs" of the political system.

Each year thousands of articles about American politics appear, and deciding which to reprint in a collection of readings such as this can be difficult. Articles are chosen with an eye toward providing viewpoints from left, right, and center. About half of the selections in this book are new to this year's edition, a reflection of continuing efforts to help keep those who read this book abreast of important contemporary developments in the American political system. Next year will bring another opportunity for change, and you, the reader, are invited to participate in the process. Please complete and return the postage-paid *article rating form* on the last page of the book and let us know what you think.

Bruce Stinebrickner
Editor

Contents

Preface iv
Correlation Guide xiii
Topic Guide xiv
Internet References xvi

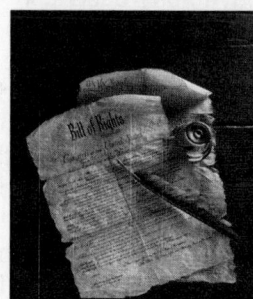

UNIT 1
Foundations of American Politics

Unit Overview xviii

Part A. Basic Documents

1. **The Declaration of Independence,** Thomas Jefferson, *The Declaration of Independence,* 1776
   This document formally announces that 13 former British colonies have become the free and independent United States of America. It eloquently identifies certain **historic principles** on which their claim to independence rests. 2

2. **The History of The Constitution of the United States,** *The Constitution of the U.S.,* 1787
   The Constitution provides an organizational blueprint for the national government and for the **federal** relationship between the national government and the states. In addition, the first 10 amendments, commonly known as the **Bill of Rights,** spell out limits on what the government can do. A commentary accompanying the actual document provides a brief account of the writing of the Constitution and also notes some of its significant features. 4

3. **The Size and Variety of the Union as a Check on Faction: Federalist No. 10,** James Madison, *The Federalist Papers,* 1787
   James Madison argues in support of the union of the 13 states under the new **Constitution.** According to Madison, a system of **representative democracy** governing a large territory and many people will help control the undesirable effects of **"faction."** 15

4. **Checks and Balances: Federalist No. 51,** James Madison, *The Federalist Papers,* 1787
   According to James Madison, both the **separation of powers** among three branches of government and the **division of powers** between the states and the central government will help preserve **representative democracy** under the new **Constitution.** 18

Part B. Contemporary Views and Values

5. **Can America Fail?,** Kishore Mahbubani, *Wilson Quarterly,* Spring 2009
   Kishore Mahbubani identifies **three systemic failures** of **American society.** He argues that Americans must recognize these problems and correct them, or risk the "unthinkable," failure as a society and world power. 20

6. **The Right Bite,** William A. Galston, *Wilson Quarterly*, Winter 2009
   William A. Galston explores **Americans' growing distrust** of their national government over the past four decades and suggests five ways to improve **government's performance.** 25

7. **Progressivism Goes Mainstream,** John Halpin and Ruy Teixeira, *The American Prospect,* May 2009
   John Halpin and Ruy Teixeira report and analyze recent research showing increases in **Americans' progressive inclinations.** 28

The concepts in bold italics are developed in the article. For further expansion, please refer to the Topic Guide.

8. **The Hazard of Moral Hazard,** James K. Glassman, *Commentary,* September 2009

Jame K. Glassman focuses on the phenomenon of *"moral hazard"* and discusses the adverse consequences of United States government efforts to help *financial institutions* that have engaged in overly risky behavior.   **32**

9. **Not So Popular Where It Counts,** Bruce Stokes, *National Journal,* July 25, 2009

Bruce Stokes reports that, while *President Obama* is more popular than his predecessor *George W. Bush* in much of the world, the current president and the United States are viewed unfavorably by the people of key countries such as *Pakistan, Russia, and China.*   **36**

Part C. Constitutional and Legal Matters

10. **It Is Time to Repair the Constitution's Flaws,** Sanford Levinson, *Chronicle of Higher Education,* October 13, 2006

Sanford Levinson assesses the adequacy of the *U.S. Constitution* and observes that many of its structural provisions are obstacles to the practice of *democracy* in the American political system.   **38**

11. **Pursuit of Habeas,** Jack Hitt, *Mother Jones,* September/October 2008

In the context of contemporary detainees at *Guatanamo Bay,* Jack Hitt emphasizes the importance of the legal procedure known as *habeas corpus* and notes that it was among the first great *checks and balances* on *arbitrary government power.*   **41**

12. **Is Judicial Review Obsolete?,** Stuart Taylor Jr., *National Journal,* July 5, 2008

Stuart Taylor argues that *originalism* as a way for judges to interpret the *constitution* is clearly inadequate. Even so, he continues, the *imperial judiciary* will continue to engage in *judicial review.*   **44**

13. **Two Takes: Pulpit Politics Is Free Speech/Campaigns Can Split Churches,** Ron Johnson Jr. and Barry W. Lynn, *U.S. News & World Report,* November 17/24, 2008

Two clergymen debate *church-state relations* in the American political system, with particular emphasis on what restrictions should apply to *political commentary* from the pulpits of *tax-exempt churches.*   **46**

UNIT 2
Structures of American Politics

Unit Overview   **48**

Part A. The Presidency

14. **Misremembering Reagan,** Ramesh Ponnuru, *National Review,* July 6, 2009

Ramesh Ponnuru argues that *President Ronald Reagan* performed differently from the way that conservative admirers remember him today. According to Ponnuru, Reagan was skillfully adaptable in applying *conservative principles* to the problems facing the United States during the time he was president.   **51**

15. **Small Ball after All?,** Jonathan Rauch, *National Journal,* September 20, 2008

Jonathan Rauch reports that many observers consider *George W. Bush* to have been the *worst president* in American history. He argues that Bush's greatest failure was his handing over to his successor many major unsolved problems that already faced the United States when he first became president.   **54**

The concepts in bold italics are developed in the article. For further expansion, please refer to the Topic Guide.

16. **The Founders' Great Mistake,** Garrett Epps, *The Atlantic,* January/February 2009

    Garrett Epps argues that the ***framers of the Constitution*** created a ***dysfunctional and dangerous presidency*** that has caused problems for the United States throughout its history. He offers a number of ***reforms*** relating to the office of chief executive and the interaction of the president with the legislative branch. **60**

17. **Happy Together?,** Donald R. Wolfensberger, *Wilson Quarterly,* Winter 2009

    According to Donald Wolfensberger, whether one party controls the White House and both houses of Congress—***unified party government***—or party control is divided between Republicans and Democrats—***divided party government***—has little effect on the effectiveness or success of American national government. **64**

18. **Veto This!,** Carl M. Cannon, *National Journal,* October 13, 2007

    Carl M. Cannon places ***President Bush's*** infrequent use of the veto in historical context and explores several perspectives on the proper role of the ***president's veto power*** in the operation of the American political system. **67**

19. **A Political Odyssey,** Dan Balz and Haynes Johnson, *The Washington Post,* August 2, 2009

    Dan Balz and Haynes Johnson chronicle ***Barack Obama's*** remarkable campaign to become ***president*** of the United States and discuss what Obama thought were some of the implications of that ***campaign*** for his presidency. **72**

20. **The Shuffle President,** Matt Bai, *The New York Times Magazine,* July 19, 2009

    Matt Bai observes how the early ***presidency of Barack Obama*** seems to have presented an ***untidy political narrative.*** Perhaps because of ***multiple challenges*** facing the United States when he took the oath of office, Bai thinks that President Obama has moved quickly from issue to issue during the first part of his term in office. **77**

Part B. Congress

21. **When Congress Stops Wars: Partisan Politics and Presidential Power,** William G. Howell and Jon C. Pevehouse, *Foreign Affairs,* September/October 2007

    The authors explore the various ways that ***Congress*** can restrict ***presidential war powers.*** They also note that the ***party composition*** of Congress and the ***presidency*** is an important factor in how much influence Congress exerts. **79**

22. **The Case for Congress,** Lee H. Hamilton, *Wilson Quarterly,* Spring 2004

    Lee H. Hamilton defends ***Congress*** against a series of frequently voiced criticisms of the institution and of its individual members. **84**

23. **The Case for Busting the Filibuster,** Thomas Geoghegan, *The Nation,* August 31/September 7, 2009

    Thomas Geoghegan argues that the contemporary ***"procedural filibuster"*** is even worse than its more traditional predecessor, and that members of Congress and citizens should take action to end the ***filibuster*** in the ***Senate*** once and for all. **87**

24. **A Bit of Advice, Madam Speaker,** Charlie Cook, *National Journal,* May 23, 2009

    Charlie Cook identifies strengths and weaknesses of ***House Speaker Nancy Pelosi*** and advises her to play to her ***strengths*** and avoid public appearances that highlight her ***weaknesses.*** **90**

Part C. The Judiciary

25. **Remote Control,** Stuart Taylor Jr., *The Atlantic Monthly,* September 2005

    Stuart Taylor notes that today's ***Supreme Court justices*** have different professional backgrounds than their predecessors, with the result that contemporary justices have lost touch with the real world. **91**

The concepts in bold italics are developed in the article. For further expansion, please refer to the Topic Guide.

26. **Court Approval,** Jeffrey Rosen, *The New Republic,* July 23, 2007

Jeffrey Rosen assesses **Chief Justice John Roberts's** so far unsuccessful quest for more consensus on the **Supreme Court.** He finds that **Associate Justice Stephen Breyer,** usually viewed as a liberal dissenter on the current court, practices **judicial restraint** more consistently than the majority bloc of justices that usually includes Chief Justice Roberts. 93

Part D. Bureaucracy

27. **Marking Time: Why Government Is Too Slow,** Bruce Berkowitz, *The American Interest,* September/October 2007

Bruce Berkowitz addresses why **government bureaucracies** are typically so slow to produce results. He discusses various factors that explain this phenomenon and suggests ways to improve the situation. 95

28. **Worse than You Think,** Peter J. Wallison and Edward Pinto, *National Review,* November 3, 2008

The authors chronicle the **home mortgage crisis** that came to national attention in 2008 and argue that it stemmed from **government policy failures** over several decades, including the **savings-and-loan debacle** in the late 1980s. 102

29. **Teaching a Hippo to Dance,** Amy Wilkinson, *Wilson Quarterly,* Winter 2009

Amy Wilkinson discusses the challenges that American national government faces in attracting and retaining competent employees to work in its **bureaucracy.** She argues that change must come from within and suggests that innovative use of **contemporary technology** might be one way of improving **productivity.** 105

UNIT 3
Process of American Politics

Unit Overview 108

Part A. Political Parties and Voters

30. **Obama's America,** Michael Barone, *National Journal,* July 11, 2009

Michael Barone assesses the **partisan make-up of the American electorate** in the aftermath of **Barack Obama's** comfortable victory over **John McCain** in November 2008. He analyzes the partisan leanings of the contemporary American electorate and Obama's victory over McCain against the background of what seemed a **natural Republican majority** since the **Reagan presidency** in the 1980s. 111

31. **The 'Enduring Majority'—Again,** Jay Cost, *National Review,* June 8, 2009

Jay Cost argues that the Democratic party's ascendance in the 2006 and 2008 national elections should not be taken to mean that the Republican party will continue losing elections for the foreseeable future. He identifies the unusual context in which the 2008 election occurred and says that Republicans and conservatives should not be discouraged. 118

32. **Dr. Dean Regrets Nothing,** James A. Barnes, *National Journal,* January 24, 2009

James A. Barnes reports that **Howard Dean,** who served as **chairman of the Democratic National Committee** from 2001 to early 2005, has no regrets about his controversial **fifty-state strategy** and his emphasis on improving his party's technological capabilities. 122

33. **Direction, Anyone?,** Ramesh Ponnuru, *National Review,* September 7, 2009

Ramesh Ponnuru says that the **Republican party** needs **political entrepreneurs,** but identifies four factors that have led to the scarcity of such individuals among contemporary Republicans politicians. 124

The concepts in bold italics are developed in the article. For further expansion, please refer to the Topic Guide.

Part B. The Conduct of Elections and Nominations

34. America Observed, Robert A. Pastor, *The American Prospect,* January 4, 2005

Robert A. Pastor identifies "dysfunctional decentralization" as the central cause of **problems in America's election system** and compares various dimensions of the system with those of other countries. **126**

35. Can Money Be a Force for Good?, Mark Schmitt, *The American Prospect,* January/February 2009

Mark Schmitt reviews the **staggering sums of money** that **political candidates** raised in the 2008 election cycle and argues that **small-donor democracy** can be a force for good in the American electoral system. **128**

36. Vote or Else, Allison R. Hayward, *The Weekly Standard,* March 21, 2005

Allison R. Hayward proposes a system of **mandatory voting** in the United States and presents the merits of her proposal. **131**

37. The American Presidential Nominating Process: The Beginnings of a New Era, Bruce Stinebrickner, *McGraw-Hill Contemporary Learning Series,* 2008

Bruce Stinebrickner reviews four eras in the history of the **presidential nomination process** and argues that **changes** evident during the first part of the 2008 process suggest that a fifth era is about to begin. **133**

Part C. Interest Groups

38. Still the Chosen One?, Robert Dreyfuss, *Mother Jones,* September/October 2009

Robert Dreyfuss chronicles the great influence that the **American Israel Public Affairs Committee** (AIPAC) has long wielded in **U.S. policy-making in the Middle East** and questions whether that influence will continue during the **Obama administration.** **141**

39. Don't Call Them Lobbyists, Theo Francis and Steve LeVine, *Businessweek,* August 10, 2009

The authors explain that **influence peddlers** in Washington have shifted their tactics and are less inclined to engage in **traditional lobbying** than they used to be. Instead, they serve as **strategists and advisors** for clients who want to shape **public policy.** **146**

40. Born Fighting, Ronald Brownstein, *National Journal,* September 27, 2008

Ronald Brownstein notes the ten-year anniversary of the founding of *MoveOn.org,* a progressive **interest group** that illustrates the rise of the **Internet** as a political force. **148**

41. Why They Lobby, Winter Casey, *National Journal,* May 31, 2008

Winter Casey discusses **lobbyists** who work on behalf of interests such as gambling, alcohol, and tobacco, and he considers the suggestion that they are living on the **"dark side"** of American politics. **150**

Part D. Media

42. The Revolution Will Not Be Published, Clay Shirky, *Utne,* July/August 2009

Clay Shirky assesses the **revolution** currently engulfing **newspapers** as we know them, and discusses how the competition between **electronic and hard-copy news reporting** will eventually play out. On the basis of what happened after Gutenberg's printing press appeared on the scene in the fifteenth century, he expects that the transition from the current communications era to the next era is likely to be chaotic and unpredictable. **153**

43. Build the Wall, David Simon, *Columbia Journalism Review,* July/August 2009

David Simon addresses the publishers of *The New York Times* and *The Washington Post* and urges them to take immediate steps to charge readers for **on-line access** to the **news coverage** that their organizations currently provide free-of-charge. Otherwise, Simon continues, written news coverage of the quality provided by *The Times* and *The Post* will be at risk of disappearing. **156**

The concepts in bold italics are developed in the article. For further expansion, please refer to the Topic Guide.

44. **A See-Through Society,** Micah L. Sifry, *Columbia Journalism Review,* January/February 2009

Micah Sifry makes the case that the American political system is entering *"a new age of political transparency."* He argues that the *Web* is changing the ways that Americans access and consume all sorts of information at all levels of government. **161**

UNIT 4
Products of American Politics

Unit Overview **166**

Part A. Domestic Policy

45. **The Tax-Cut Con,** Paul Krugman, *The New York Times Magazine,* September 14, 2003

Paul Krugman says that a *tax-cut crusade* has dominated the last quarter-century of American politics. He examines the motives of those supporting that crusade and critically assesses its effects on American government both now and in the future. **169**

46. **The Realities of Immigration,** Linda Chavez, *Commentary,* July/August 2006

Linda Chavez tries to set the record straight about *immigration* and *immigration reform,* and uses historical, economic, sociological, and policy perspectives to do so. **176**

47. **The Health of Nations,** Ezra Klein, *The American Prospect,* May 2007

Ezra Klein compares and contrasts *health care delivery* in Canada, France, Britain, Germany, and the *U.S. Veterans Health Administration.* He argues that the presence of the *profit motive* produces adverse consequences in the United States health care system. **182**

48. **The *Real* Infrastructure Crisis,** Burt Solomon, *National Journal,* July 5, 2008

Burt Solomon discusses the state of the nation's *infrastructure* and the American public's interest in spending on roads, bridges, water supply facilities, wastewater plants, and the like. **186**

49. **Speculators, Politicians, and Financial Disasters,** John Steele Gordon, *Commentary,* November 2008

John Steele Gordon surveys the history of government involvement in *banking, credit markets,* and loans, as well as the roles of politicians and speculators since the United States was founded. **192**

50. **A Flimsy Trust: Why Social Security Needs Some Major Repairs,** Allan Sloan, *The Washington Post,* August 2, 2009

Allan Sloan calls attention to the problems facing the country's biggest social program, the *Social Security old-age pension program* that began during the *New Deal.* Sloan understands that other pressing problems besetting the United States today will likely get—and may indeed deserve—more immediate attention, but he argues that Social Security problems will inevitably become greater in the next few years and that *reforms* are urgently needed. **197**

Part B. National and Homeland Security

51. **How Globalization Went Bad,** Steven Weber et al., *Foreign Policy,* January/February 2007

The authors argue that the combination of *globalization* and the status of the United States as the world's *sole superpower* has led to dangerous *instability* in the world. **201**

52. **Are Failed States a Threat to America?,** Justin Logan and Christopher Preble, *Reason* Magazine, July 2006

The authors assert that American *nation-building* efforts have generally been unsuccessful and unwise, and provide evidence and arguments to support their case. **205**

The concepts in bold italics are developed in the article. For further expansion, please refer to the Topic Guide.

xi

53. **Worth Fighting—or Not,** Burt Solomon, *National Journal,* June 13, 2009
    Burt Solomon assesses the *major wars* in which the United States has participated and notes that both *unintended and intended consequences* must be taken into account. **209**

54. **The Abandonment of Democracy,** Joshua Muravchik, *Commentary,* July/August 2009
    Joshua Muravchik criticizes *President Obama* for downplaying considerations of *human rights and freedom* in his *foreign policy* moves during the early part of his presidency. **215**

Test-Your-Knowledge Form **220**
Article Rating Form **221**

The concepts in bold italics are developed in the article. For further expansion, please refer to the Topic Guide.

Correlation Guide

The *Annual Editions* series provides students with convenient, inexpensive access to current, carefully selected articles from the public press. **Annual Editions: American Government 10/11** is an easy-to-use reader that presents articles on important topics in the study of American government. For more information on *Annual Editions* and other *McGraw-Hill Contemporary Learning Series* titles, visit www.mhhe.com/cls.

This convenient guide matches the units in **Annual Editions: American Government 10/11** with the corresponding chapters in three of our best-selling McGraw-Hill American Government textbooks by Harrison et al., Patterson, and Losco/Baker.

Annual Editions: American Government 10/11	American Democracy Now by Harrison et al.	We the People, 8/e by Patterson	AM GOV 2010, 2/e by Losco/Baker
Unit 1: Foundations of American Politics	**Chapter 1:** People, Politics, and Participation **Chapter 2:** The Constitution **Chapter 3:** Federalism **Chapter 4:** Civil Liberties **Chapter 5:** Civil Rights	**Chapter 1:** American Political Culture: Seeking a More Perfect Union **Chapter 2:** Constitutional Democracy: Promoting Liberty and Self-Government **Chapter 3:** Federalism: Forging a Nation **Chapter 4:** Civil Liberties: Protecting Individual Rights **Chapter 5:** Equal Rights: Struggling Toward Fairness	**Chapter 1:** Citizenship in Our Changing Democracy **Chapter 2:** The Constitution: The Foundation of Citizens' Rights **Chapter 3:** Federalism: Citizenship and the Dispersal of Power **Chapter 4:** Civil Liberties: Expanding Citizens' Rights **Chapter 5:** Civil Rights: Toward a More Equal Citizenry
Unit 2: Structures of American Politics	**Chapter 11:** Congress **Chapter 12:** The Presidency **Chapter 13:** The Bureaucracy **Chapter 14:** The Judiciary	**Chapter 11:** Congress: Balancing National Goals and Local Interests **Chapter 12:** The Presidency: Leading the Nation **Chapter 13:** The Federal Bureaucracy: Administering the Government **Chapter 14:** The Judiciary: Applying the Law	**Chapter 11:** Congress: Doing the People's Business **Chapter 12:** The Presidency: Power and Paradox **Chapter 13:** Bureaucracy: Citizens as Owners and Consumers **Chapter 14:** The Courts: Judicial Power in a Democratic Setting
Unit 3: Process of American Politics	**Chapter 6:** Political Socialization and Public Opinion **Chapter 7:** Interest Groups **Chapter 8:** Political Parties **Chapter 9:** Elections, Campaigns, and Voting **Chapter 10:** The Media	**Chapter 6:** Public Opinion and Political Socialization: Shaping the People's Voice **Chapter 7:** Political Participation and Voting: Expressing the Popular Will **Chapter 8:** Political Parties, Candidates, and Campaigns: Defining the Voters' Choice **Chapter 9:** Interest Groups: Organizing for Influence **Chapter 10:** The News Media: Communicating Political Images	**Chapter 6:** Public Opinion: Listening to Citizens **Chapter 7:** Political Participation: Equal Opportunities and Unequal Voices **Chapter 8:** Interest Groups in America **Chapter 9:** Parties and Political Campaigns: Citizens and the Electoral Process **Chapter 10:** Media: Tuning In or Turning Out
Unit 4: Products of American Politics	**Chapter 15:** Economic Policy **Chapter 16:** Domestic Policy **Chapter 17:** Foreign Policy and National Security	**Chapter 15:** Economic and Environmental Policy: Contributing to Prosperity **Chapter 16:** Welfare and Education Policy: Providing for Personal Security and Need **Chapter 17:** Foreign and Defense Policy: Protecting the American Way	**Chapter 15:** Public Policy: Responding to Citizens

Topic Guide

This topic guide suggests how the selections in this book relate to the subjects covered in your course. You may want to use the topics listed on these pages to search the Web more easily.

On the following pages a number of websites have been gathered specifically for this book. They are arranged to reflect the units of this Annual Editions reader. You can link to these sites by going to http://www.mhhe.com/cls.

All the articles that relate to each topic are listed below the bold-faced term.

Bureaucracy
27. Marking Time: Why Government Is Too Slow
28. Worse than You Think
29. Teaching a Hippo to Dance

Bush, George W.
15. Small Ball after All?

Congress
17. Happy Together?
18. Veto This!
21. When Congress Stops Wars: Partisan Politics and Presidential Power
22. The Case for Congress
23. The Case for Busting the Filibuster
24. A Bit of Advice, Madam Speaker

Constitution
2. The History of The Constitution of the United States
3. The Size and Variety of the Union as a Check on Faction: Federalist No. 10
4. Checks and Balances: Federalist No. 51
10. It is Time to Repair the Constitution's Flaws
11. Pursuit of Habeas
12. Is Judicial Review Obsolete?
16. The Founders' Great Mistake

The economy and related matters
5. Can America Fail?
6. The Right Bite
8. The Hazard of Moral Hazard
28. Worse than You Think
49. Speculators, Politicians, and Financial Disasters
50. A Flimsy Trust: Why Social Security Needs Some Major Repairs

Elections and nominations
19. A Political Odyssey
30. Obama's America
31. The 'Enduring Majority'—Again
32. Dr. Dean Regrets Nothing
33. Direction, Anyone?
34. America Observed
35. Can Money Be a Force for Good?
36. Vote or Else
37. The American Presidential Nominating Process: The Beginnings of a New Era

Globalization
51. How Globalization Went Bad

Health care
47. The Health of Nations

Homeland and national security
9. Not So Popular Where It Counts
11. Pursuit of Habeas
21. When Congress Stops Wars: Partisan Politics and Presidential Power

51. How Globalization Went Bad
52. Are Failed States a Threat to America?
53. Worth Fighting—or Not
54. The Abandonment of Democracy

Immigration
46. The Realities of Immigration

Infastructure
48. The *Real* Infrastructure Crisis

Interest groups
38. Still the Chosen One?
39. Don't Call Them Lobbyists
40. Born Fighting
41. Why They Lobby

Internet
32. Dr. Dean Regrets Nothing
40. Born Fighting
42. The Revolution Will Not Be Published
43. Build the Wall
44. A See-Through Society

Iraq war
21. When Congress Stops Wars: Partisan Politics and Presidential Power

Judicial system
11. Pursuit of Habeas
12. Is Judicial Review Obsolete?
25. Remote Control
26. Court Approval

Media
40. Born Fighting
42. The Revolution Will Not Be Published
43. Build the Wall
44. A See-Through Society

Obama, Barack
19. A Political Odyssey
20. The Shuffle President
30. Obama's America

Political parties
7. Progressivism Goes Mainstream
30. Obama's America
31. The 'Enduring Majority'—Again
32. Dr. Dean Regrets Nothing
33. Direction, Anyone?
37. The American Presidential Nominating Process: The Beginnings of a New Era

Presidency
9. Not So Popular Where It Counts
14. Misremembering Reagan
15. Small Ball after All?

16. The Founders' Great Mistake
17. Happy Together?
18. Veto This!
19. A Political Odyssey
20. The Shuffle President
21. When Congress Stops Wars: Partisan Politics and Presidential Power
37. The American Presidential Nominating Process: The Beginnings of a New Era

Presidential election of 2008
7. Progressivism Goes Mainstream
19. A Political Odyssey
32. Dr. Dean Regrets Nothing

Public opinion
7. Progressivism Goes Mainstream
24. A Bit of Advice, Madam Speaker
30. Obama's America

Rights
1. The Declaration of Independence
11. Pursuit of Habeas
12. Is Judicial Review Obsolete?
13. Two Takes: Pulpit Politics Is Free Speech/Campaigns Can Split Churches

September 11, 2001, and its aftermath
11. Pursuit of Habeas

Supreme court
12. Is Judicial Review Obsolete?
25. Remote Control
26. Court Approval

Taxes
45. The Tax-Cut Con

Internet References

The following Internet sites have been selected to support the articles found in this reader. These sites were available at the time of publication. However, because websites often change their structure and content, the information listed may no longer be available. We invite you to visit http://www.mhhe.com/cls for easy access to these sites.

Annual Editions: American Government 10/11

General Sources

John F. Kennedy School of Government
http://www.ksg.harvard.edu

Starting from Harvard University's KSG page, you will be able to click on a huge variety of links to information about American politics and government, ranging from political party and campaign data to debates of enduring issues.

Library of Congress
http://www.loc.gov

Examine this website to learn about the extensive resource tools, library services/resources, exhibitions, and databases available through the Library of Congress in many different subfields of government studies.

National Center for Policy Analysis
http://www.ncpa.org

Through this site, access discussions on an array of topics that are of major interest in the study of American government, from regulatory policy and privatization to economy and income. The Daily Policy Digest is also available.

UNIT 1: Foundations of American Politics

National Archives and Records Administration (NARA)
http://www.archives.gov

This official site, which oversees the management of all federal records, offers easy access to background information for students interested in the policy-making process, including a search of federal documents and speeches, and much more.

Opinion, Inc.: The Site for Conservative Opinion on the Web
http://www.opinioninc.com

Open this site for access to political, cultural, and Web commentary on a number of issues from a conservative political viewpoint. The site is updated frequently.

Smithsonian Institution
http://www.si.edu

This site provides access to the enormous resources of the Smithsonian, which holds some 140 million artifacts and specimens in its trust for "the increase and diffusion of knowledge." Here you can learn about American social, cultural, economic, and political history from a variety of viewpoints.

UNIT 2: Structures of American Politics

Department of State
http://www.state.gov

View this site for understanding of the workings of a major U.S. executive branch department. Links explain exactly what the department does, what services it provides, and what it says about U.S. interests around the world, along with much more information.

Federal Reserve System
http://www.federalreserve.gov

Consult this page to learn the answers to FAQs about the Fed, the structure of the Federal Reserve System, monetary policy, and more. It provides links to speeches and interviews as well as essays and articles presenting different views on the Fed.

Supreme Court/Legal Information Institute
http://supct.law.cornell.edu/supct/index.html

Open this site for current and historical information about the Supreme Court. The LII archive contains many opinions issued since May 1990 as well as a collection of nearly 600 of the most influential decisions of the Court.

United States House of Representatives
http://www.house.gov

This Web page of the House of Representatives will lead you to information about current and past House members and agendas, the legislative process, and more. You can learn about events on the House floor as they happen.

United States Senate
http://www.senate.gov

This U.S. Senate Web page will lead to information about current and past Senate members and agendas, legislative activities, and committees.

UNIT 3: Process of American Politics

The Gallup Organization
http://www.gallup.com

Open this Gallup Organization home page for links to an extensive archive of public opinion poll results and special reports on a variety of topics related to American society, politics, and government.

The Henry L. Stimson Center
http://www.stimson.org

The Stimson Center, a nonprofit and self-described nonpartisan organization, focuses on issues where policy, technology, and politics intersect. Use this site to find assessments of U.S. foreign and domestic policy and other topics.

Influence at Work
http://www.influenceatwork.com

This commercial site focuses on the nature of persuasion, compliance, and propaganda, with many practical examples and applications. Students of such topics as the roles of public opinion and media influence in policy making should find these discussions of interest. The approach is based on the research and methods of influence expert Dr. Robert Cialdini.

LSU Department of Political Science Resources
http://www.lsu.edu/politicalscience

This extensive site will point you to a number of resources for domestic and international political and governmental news, including LSU's Political Science WWW Server, which is maintained by a dedicated group of professionals.

Internet References

NationalJournal.com
http://nationaljournal.com

This is a major site for information on American government and politics. There is discussion of campaigns, the congressional calendar, a news archive, and more for politicians and policymakers. Membership is required, however, to access much of the information.

Poynter Online
http://www.poynter.org

This research site of the Poynter Institute for Media Studies provides extensive links to information and resources about the media, including media ethics and reportage techniques. Many bibliographies and websites are included.

RAND
http://www.rand.org

RAND is a nonprofit institution that works to improve public policy through research and analysis. Links offered on this home page provide for keyword searches of certain topics and descriptions of RAND activities and major research areas.

Real Clear Politics
http://www.realclearpolitics.com

This site presents, in a timely and easily accessible manner, almost all the latest published poll results on a variety of political topics, including, of course, how candidates are faring during election campaigns. There are also commentaries from a range of sources about campaigns and American politics more generally. It is a popular and authoritative source for so-called political junkies.

UNIT 4: Products of American Politics

American Diplomacy
http://www.unc.edu/depts/diplomat/

American Diplomacy is an online journal of commentary, analysis, and research on U.S. foreign policy and its results around the world.

Cato Institute
http://www.cato.org/research/ss_prjct.html

The Cato Institute presents this page to discuss its Project on Social Security Privatization. The site and its links begin from the belief that privatization of the U.S. Social Security system is a positive goal that will empower workers.

Foreign Affairs
http://www.foreignaffairs.org

This home page of the well-respected foreign policy journal is a valuable research tool. It allows users to search the journal's archives and provides indexed access to the field's leading publications, documents, online resources, and more. Links to dozens of other related websites are possible from here.

International Information Programs
http://usinfo.state.gov

This wide-ranging page offered by the State Department provides definitions, related documentation, and a discussion of topics of concern to students of American government. It addresses today's hot topics as well as ongoing issues that form the foundation of the field. Many Web links are provided.

STAT-USA
http://www.stat-usa.gov/stat-usa.html

This essential site, a service of the Department of Commerce, contains daily economic news, frequently requested statistical releases, information on export and international trade, domestic economic news and statistical series, and databases.

Tax Foundation
http://www.taxfoundation.org/index.html

Ever wonder where your taxes go? Consult the site of this self-described "nonprofit, nonpartisan policy research organization" to learn the history of "Tax Freedom Day," tax burdens around the United States, and other information about your tax bill or taxes in general.

UNIT 1
Foundations of American Politics

Unit Selections

1. **The Declaration of Independence,** Thomas Jefferson
2. **The History of The Constitution of the United States,** *The Constitution of the U.S.,* 1787
3. **The Size and Variety of the Union as a Check on Faction: Federalist No. 10,** James Madison
4. **Checks and Balances: Federalist No. 51,** James Madison
5. **Can America Fail?,** Kishore Mahbubani
6. **The Right Bite,** William A. Galston
7. **Progressivism Goes Mainstream,** John Halpin and Ruy Teixeira
8. **The Hazard of Moral Hazard,** James K. Glassman
9. **Not So Popular Where It Counts,** Bruce Stokes
10. **It Is Time to Repair the Constitution's Flaws,** Sanford Levinson
11. **Pursuit of Habeas,** Jack Hitt
12. **Is Judicial Review Obsolete?,** Stuart Taylor Jr.
13. **Two Takes: Pulpit Politics Is Free Speech/Campaigns Can Split Churches,** Ron Johnson Jr. and Barry W. Lynn

Key Points to Consider

- What do you think would surprise the Founders most about the values and ideals held by Americans today?

- Which ideals, ideas, and values seem likely to remain central to American politics, and which seem likely to erode and gradually disappear?

- To what "rights" do you think all Americans are entitled? How, if at all, has September 11 affected Americans' thinking on this matter?

- What makes constitutional interpretation and reinterpretation necessary in the American political system?

- Do you consider yourself a conservative, a liberal, a socialist, a reactionary, or what? Why?

Student Website
www.mhhe.com/cls

Internet References

National Archives and Records Administration (NARA)
http://www.archives.gov

Opinion, Inc.: The Site for Conservative Opinion on the Web
http://www.opinioninc.com

Smithsonian Institution
http://www.si.edu

This unit treats some of the less concrete aspects of the American political system—historic ideals, contemporary ideas and values, and constitutional and legal issues. These dimensions of the system are not immune to change. Instead, they interact with the wider political environment in which they exist, and they are modified accordingly. Usually this interaction is a gradual process, but sometimes events foster more rapid change.

Human beings can be distinguished from other species by their ability to think and reason at relatively high levels of abstraction. In turn, ideas, ideals, values, and principles can and do play important roles in politics. Most Americans value ideals such as democracy, freedom, equal opportunity, and justice. Yet, the precise meanings of these terms and the best ways of implementing them are the subject of much dispute in the political arena. Such ideas and ideals, as well as disputes about their "real" meanings, are important elements in the practice of American politics.

Although the selections in this unit span more than 200 years, they are clearly related to one another. Understanding contemporary political viewpoints is easier if the ideals and principles of the past are also taken into account. In addition, we can better appreciate the significance of historic documents such as the Declaration of Independence and the Constitution if we are familiar with contemporary ideas and perspectives. The interaction of different ideas and values plays an important part in the continuing development of the "foundations" of the American political system.

The first section of this unit includes several historic documents from the eighteenth century. The first is the Declaration of Independence. Written in 1776, it proclaims the Founders' views of why independence from England was justified and, in so doing, identifies certain "unalienable" rights that "all men" are said to possess. The second document, the Constitution of 1787, remains in effect to this day. It provides an organizational blueprint for the structure of American national government, outlines the federal relationship between the national government and the states, and expresses limitations on what government can do. Twenty-seven amendments have been added to the original Constitution in two centuries. In addition to the Declaration of Independence and the Constitution, the first section includes two selections from *The Federalist Papers,* a series of newspaper articles written in support of the proposed new Constitution. Appearing in 1787 and 1788, *The Federalist Papers* treated

© Photodisc/Getty RF

various provisions of the new Constitution and argued that putting the Constitution into effect would bring about good government.

The second section treats contemporary political ideas and viewpoints. As selections in this section illustrate, efforts to apply or act on political beliefs in the context of concrete circumstances often lead to interesting commentary and debate. "Liberal" and "conservative" are two labels often used in American political discussions, but political views and values have far more complexity than can be captured by those two terms.

Selections in the third section show that constitutional and legal issues and interpretations are tied to historic principles as well as to contemporary ideas and values. It has been suggested that throughout American history almost every important political question has, at one time or another, appeared as a constitutional or legal issue.

The historic documents and the other selections in this unit might be more difficult to understand than the articles in other units. Some of them may have to be read and reread carefully to be fully appreciated. But to grapple with the important material treated here is to come to grips with a variety of conceptual blueprints for the American political system. To ignore the theoretical issues raised would be to bypass an important element of American politics today.

Article 1

The Declaration of Independence

THOMAS JEFFERSON

When in the Course of human events, it becomes necessary for one people to dissolve the political bands which have connected them with another, and to assume among the powers of the earth, the separate and equal station to which the Laws of Nature and of Nature's God entitle them, a decent respect to the opinions of mankind requires that they should declare the causes which impel them to the separation.—We hold these truths to be self-evident, that all men are created equal, that they are endowed by their Creator with certain unalienable Rights, that among these are Life, Liberty and the pursuit of Happiness.—That to secure these rights, Governments are instituted among Men, deriving their just powers from the consent of the governed.—That whenever any Form of Government becomes destructive of these ends, it is the Right of the People to alter or to abolish it, and to institute new Government, laying its foundation on such principles and organizing its powers in such form, as to them shall seem most likely to effect their Safety and Happiness. Prudence, indeed, will dictate that Governments long established should not be changed for light and transient causes; and accordingly all experience hath shewn, that mankind are more disposed to suffer, while evils are sufferable, than to right themselves by abolishing the forms to which they are accustomed. But when a long train of abuses and usurpations, pursuing invariably the same Object evinces a design to reduce them under absolute Despotism, it is their right, it is their duty, to throw off such Government, and to provide new Guards for their future security.—Such has been the patient sufferance of these Colonies; and such is now the necessity which constrains them to alter their former Systems of Government. The history of the present King of Great Britain is a history of repeated injuries and usurpations, all having in direct object the establishment of an absolute Tyranny over these States. To prove this, let Facts be submitted to a candid world.—He has refused his Assent to Laws, the most wholesome and necessary for the public good.—He has forbidden his Governors to pass Laws of immediate and pressing importance, unless suspended in their operation till his Assent should be obtained; and when so suspended, he has utterly neglected to attend to them.—He has refused to pass other Laws for the accommodation of large districts of people, unless those people would relinquish the right of Representation in the Legislature, a right inestimable to them and formidable to tyrants only.—He has called together legislative bodies at places unusual, uncomfortable, and distant from the depository of their public Records, for the sole purpose of fatiguing them into compliance with his measures.—He has dissolved Representative Houses repeatedly, for opposing with manly firmness his invasions on the rights of the people.—He has refused for a long time, after such dissolutions, to cause others to be elected; whereby the Legislative powers, incapable of Annihilation, have returned to the People at large for their exercise; the State remaining in the meantime exposed to all the dangers of invasion from without, and convulsions within.—He has endeavoured to prevent the population of these States; for that purpose obstructing the Laws for Naturalization of Foreigners; refusing to pass others to encourage their migrations hither, and raising the conditions of new Appropriations of Lands.—He has obstructed the Administration of Justice, by refusing his Assent to Laws for establishing Judiciary powers.—He has made Judges dependent on his Will alone, for the tenure of their offices, and the amount and payment of their salaries.—He has erected a multitude of New Offices, and sent hither swarms of Officers to harass our people, and eat out their substance. He has kept among us, in times of peace, Standing Armies without the Consent of our legislatures.—He has affected to render the Military independent of and superior to the Civil power.—He has combined with others to subject us to a jurisdiction foreign to our constitution, and unacknowledged by our laws; giving his Assent to their Acts of pretended Legislation:—For quartering large bodies of armed troops among us:—For protecting them, by a mock Trial, from punishment for any Murders which they should commit on the Inhabitants of these States:—For cutting off our Trade with all parts of the world:—For imposing Taxes on us without our Consent:—For depriving us in many cases, of the benefits of Trial by Jury:—For transporting us beyond Seas to be tried for pretended offences:—For abolishing the free System of English Laws in a neighboring Province, establishing therein an Arbitrary government, and enlarging its Boundaries so as to render it at once an example and fit instrument for introducing the same absolute rule into these Colonies:—For taking away our Charters, abolishing our most valuable Laws and altering fundamentally the Forms of our Governments:—For suspending our own Legislatures, and declaring themselves invested with power to legislate for us in all cases whatsoever.—He has abdicated Government here, by declaring us out of his Protection and waging War against us.—He has plundered our seas, ravaged our Coasts, burnt our towns, and destroyed

Article 1. The Declaration of Independence

the lives of our people.—He is at this time transporting large Armies of foreign Mercenaries to compleat the works of death, desolation and tyranny, already begun with circumstances of Cruelty & perfidy scarcely paralled in the most barbarous ages, and totally unworthy the Head of a civilized nation.—He has constrained our fellow Citizens taken Captive on the high Seas to bear Arms against their Country, to become the executioners of their friends and Brethren, or to fall themselves by their Hands.—He has excited domestic insurrections amongst us, and has endeavoured to bring on the inhabitants of our frontiers, the merciless Indian Savages, whose known rule of warfare, is an undistinguished destruction of all ages, sexes and conditions. In every stage of these Oppressions We have Petitioned for Redress in the most humble terms: Our repeated Petitions have been answered only by repeated injury. A Prince, whose character is thus marked by every act which may define a Tyrant, is unfit to be the ruler of a free people. Nor have We been wanting in attentions to our British brethren. We have warned them from time to time of attempts by their legislature to extend an unwarrantable jurisdiction over us. We have reminded them of the circumstances of our emigration and settlement here. We have appealed to their native justice and magnanimity, and we have conjured them by the ties of our common kindred to disavow these usurpations, which would inevitably interrupt our connections and correspondence. They too have been deaf to the voice of justice and of consanguinity. We must, therefore, acquiesce in the necessity, which denounces our Separation, and hold them, as we hold the rest of mankind, Enemies in War, in Peace Friends.—

WE, THEREFORE, the Representatives of the UNITED STATES OF AMERICA, in General Congress, Assembled, appealing to the Supreme Judge of the world for the rectitude of our intentions, do, in the Name, and by Authority of the good People of these Colonies, solemnly publish and declare, That these United Colonies are, and of Right ought to be FREE AND INDEPENDENT STATES; that they are Absolved from all Allegiance to the British Crown, and that all political connection between them and the State of Great Britain, is and ought to be totally dissolved; and that as Free and Independent States, they have full Power to levy War, conclude Peace, contract Alliances, establish Commerce, and to do all other Acts and Things which Independent States may of right do.—And for the support of this Declaration, with a firm reliance on the protection of divine Providence, we mutually pledge to each other our Lives, our Fortunes and our sacred Honor.

Article 2

The History of The Constitution of the United States

Constitution of the United States. The Articles of Confederation did not provide the centralizing force necessary for unity among the new states and were soon found to be so fundamentally weak that a different political structure was vital. Conflicts about money and credit, trade, and suspicions about regional domination were among the concerns when Congress on February 21, 1787, authorized a Constitutional Convention to revise the Articles. The delegates were selected and assembled in Philadelphia about three months after the call. They concluded their work by September.

The delegates agreed and abided to secrecy. Years afterward James Madison supported the secrecy decision writing that "no man felt himself obliged to retain his opinions any longer than he was satisfied of their propriety and truth, and was open to the force of argument." Secrecy was not for all time. Madison, a delegate from Virginia, was a self-appointed but recognized recorder and took notes in the clear view of the members. Published long afterward, Madison's Journal gives a good record of the convention.

The delegates began to assemble on May 14, 1787, but a majority did not arrive until May 25. George Washington was elected President of the Convention without opposition. The lag of those few days gave some of the early arrivals, especially Madison, time to make preparations on substantive matters, and Gov. Edmund Jennings Randolph presented a plan early in the proceedings that formed the basis for much of the convention deliberations. The essentials were that there should be a government adequate to prevent foreign invasion, prevent dissension among the states, and provide for general national development, and give the national government power enough to make it superior in its realm. The decision was made not merely to revise the articles but to create a new government and a new constitution.

One of the most crucial decisions was the arrangement for representation, a compromise providing that one house would represent the states equally, the other house to be based on popular representation (with some modification due to the slavery question). This arrangement recognized political facts and concessions among men with both theoretical and practical political knowledge.

Basic Features. Oliver Wendell Holmes, Jr., once wrote that the provisions of the Constitution were not mathematical formulas, but "organic living institutions [sic] and its origins and growth were vital to understanding it." The constitution's basic features provide for a supreme law—notwithstanding any other legal document or practice, the Constitution is supreme, as are the laws made in pursuance of it and treaties made under the authority of the United States.

The organizational plan for government is widely known. Foremost is the separation of powers. If the new government were to be limited in its powers, one way to keep it limited would have been executive, legislative, and judicial power [given] to three distinct and non-overlapping branches. A government could not actually function, however, if the separation meant the independence of one branch from the others. The answer was a design to insure cooperation and the sharing of some functions. Among these are the executive veto and the power of Congress to have its way if it musters a super-majority to override that veto. The direction of foreign affairs and the war power are both dispersed and shared. The appointing power is shared by the Senate and the president; impeaching of officers and financial controls are powers shared by the Senate and the House.

A second major contribution by the convention is the provision for the judiciary, which gave rise to the doctrine of judicial review. There is some doubt that the delegates comprehended this prospect but Alexander Hamilton considered it in *Federalist* No. 78: "The interpretation of the laws is a proper and peculiar province of the Courts. . . . Wherever a particular statute contravenes the Constitution, it will be the duty of the judicial tribunals to adhere to the latter and disregard the former."

Another contribution is the federal system, an evolution from colonial practice and the relations between the colonies and the mother country. This division of authority between the new national government and the states recognized the doctrine of delegated and reserved powers. Only certain authority was to go to the new government; the states were not to be done away with and much of the Constitution is devoted to insuring that they were to be maintained even with the stripping of some of their powers.

It is not surprising, therefore, that the convention has been called a great political reform caucus composed of both revolutionaries and men dedicated to democracy. By eighteenth-century standards the Constitution was a democratic document, but standards change and the Constitution has changed since its adoption.

Change and Adaptation. The authors of the Constitution knew that provision for change was essential and provided for it in Article V, insuring that a majority could amend, but being restrictive enough that changes were not likely for the "light and transient" causes Jefferson warned about in the Declaration of Independence.

During the period immediately following the presentation of the Constitution for ratification, requiring assent of nine states to be effective, some alarm was expressed that there was a major defect: there was no bill of rights. So, many leaders committed themselves to the presentation of constitutional amendments for the purpose. Hamilton argued that the absence of a bill of rights was not a defect; indeed, a bill was not necessary. "Why," he wrote, in the last of *The Federalist Papers,* "declare things that shall not be done which there is no power to do?" Nonetheless, the Bill of Rights was presented in the form of amendments and adopted by the states in 1791.

Since 1791 many proposals have been suggested to amend the Constitution. By 1972 sixteen additional amendments had been adopted. Only one, the Twenty-first, which repealed the Eighteenth, was ratified by state conventions. All the others were ratified by state legislatures.

Even a cursory reading of the later amendments shows they do not alter the fundamentals of limited government, the separation of powers, the federal system, or the political process set in motion originally. The Thirteenth, Fourteenth, Fifteenth, and Nineteenth amendments attempt to insure equality to all and are an extension of the Bill of Rights. The others reaffirm some existing constitutional arrangements, alter some procedures, and at least one, the Sixteenth, states national policy.

Substantial change and adaptation of the Constitution beyond the formal amendments have come from national experience, growth, and development. It has been from the Supreme Court that much of the gradual significant shaping of the Constitution has been done.

Government has remained neither static nor tranquil. Some conflict prevails continually. It may be about the activities of some phase of government or the extent of operations, and whether the arrangement for government can be made responsive to current and prospective needs of society. Conflict is inevitable in a democratic society. Sometimes the conflict is spirited and rises to challenge the continuation of the system. Questions arise whether a fair trial may be possible here or there; legislators are alleged to be indifferent to human problems and pursue distorted public priorities. Presidents are charged with secret actions designed for self-aggrandizement or actions based on half-truths. Voices are heard urging revolution again as the only means of righting alleged wrongs.

The responses continue to demonstrate, however, that the constitutional arrangement for government, the allocation of powers, and the restraints on government all provide the needed flexibility. The Constitution endures.

Adam C. Breckenridge, University of Nebraska-Lincoln

The Constitution of the United States

We the People of the United States, in Order to form a more perfect Union, establish Justice, insure domestic Tranquility, provide for the common defence, promote the general Welfare, and secure the Blessings of Liberty to ourselves and our Posterity, do ordain and establish this Constitution for the United States of America.

Article. I.

SECTION. 1. All legislative Powers herein granted shall be vested in a Congress of the United States, which shall consist of a Senate and House of Representatives.

SECTION. 2. The House of Representatives shall be composed of Members chosen every second Year by the People of the several States, and the Electors in each State shall have the Qualifications requisite for Electors of the most numerous Branch of the State Legislature.

No Person shall be a Representative who shall not have attained to the age of twenty five Years, and been seven Years a Citizen of the United States, and who shall not, when elected, be an Inhabitant of that State in which he shall be chosen.

Representatives and direct Taxes shall be apportioned among the several States which may be included within this Union, according to their respective Numbers, which shall be determined by adding to the whole Number of free Persons, including those bound to Service for a Term of Years, and excluding Indians not taxed, three fifths of all other Persons. The actual Enumeration shall be made within three Years after the first Meeting of the Congress of the United States, and within every subsequent Term of ten Years, in such Manner as they shall by Law direct. The Number of Representatives shall not exceed one for every thirty Thousand, but each State shall have at Least one Representative; and until such enumeration shall be made, the State of New Hampshire shall be entitled to chuse three, Massachusetts eight, Rhode-Island and Providence Plantations one, Connecticut five, New York six, New Jersey four, Pennsylvania eight, Delaware one, Maryland six, Virginia ten, North Carolina five, South Carolina five, and Georgia three.

When vacancies happen in the Representation from any State, the Executive Authority thereof shall issue Writs of Election to fill such Vacancies.

The House of Representatives shall chuse their Speaker and other Officers; and shall have the sole Power of Impeachment.

SECTION. 3. The Senate of the United States shall be composed of two Senators from each State, chosen by the Legislature thereof, for six years; and each Senator shall have one Vote.

Immediately after they shall be assembled in Consequence of the first Election, they shall be divided as equally as may be into three Classes. The Seats of the Senators of the first Class shall be vacated at the Expiration of the second Year, of the second Class at the Expiration of the fourth Year, and of the third Class at the Expiration of the sixth Year, so that one third may be chosen every second year; and if Vacancies happen by Resignation, or otherwise, during the Recess of the Legislature of any State, the Executive thereof may make temporary Appointments until the next Meeting of the Legislature, which shall then fill such Vacancies.

No Person shall be a Senator who shall not have attained to the Age of thirty Years, and been nine Years a Citizen of the United States, and who shall not, when elected, be an Inhabitant of that State for which he shall be chosen.

The Vice President of the United States shall be President of the Senate, but shall have no Vote, unless they be equally divided.

The Senate shall chuse their other Officers, and also a President pro tempore, in the Absence of the Vice President, or when he shall exercise the Office of President of the United States.

The Senate shall have the sole Power to try all Impeachments. When sitting for that Purpose, they shall be on Oath or Affirmation. When the President of the United States is tried the Chief Justice shall preside: And no Person shall be convicted without the Concurrence of two thirds of the Members present.

Judgment in Cases of Impeachment shall not extend further than to removal from Office, and disqualification to hold and enjoy any Office of honor, Trust or Profit under the United States: but the Party convicted shall nevertheless be liable and subject to Indictment, Trial, Judgment and Punishment, according to Law.

SECTION. 4. The Times, Places and Manner of holding Elections for Senators and Representatives, shall be prescribed in each State by the Legislature thereof; but the Congress may at any time by Law make or alter such Regulations, except as to the Places of chusing Senators.

The Congress shall assemble at least once in every Year, and such Meeting shall be on the first Monday in December, unless they shall by Law appoint a different Day.

SECTION. 5. Each House shall be the Judge of the Elections, Returns and Qualifications of its own Members, and a Majority of each shall constitute a Quorum to do Business; but a smaller Number may adjourn from day to day, and may be authorized to compel the Attendance of absent Members, in such Manner, and under such Penalties as each House may provide.

Each House may determine the Rules of its Proceedings, punish its Members for disorderly Behaviour, and, with the Concurrence of two thirds, expel a Member.

Each House shall keep a Journal of its Proceedings, and from time to time publish the same, excepting such Parts as may in their Judgment require Secrecy; and the Yeas and Nays of the Members of either House on any question shall, at the Desire of one fifth of those Present, be entered on the Journal.

Neither House, during the Session of Congress, shall, without the Consent of the other, adjourn for more than three days, nor to any other Place than that in which the two Houses shall be sitting.

SECTION. 6. The Senators and Representatives shall receive a Compensation for their Services, to be ascertained by Law, and paid out of the Treasury of the United States. They shall in all Cases, except Treason, Felony and Breach of the Peace, be privileged from Arrest during their Attendance at the Session of their respective Houses, and in going to and returning from the same; and for any Speech or Debate in either House, they shall not be questioned in any other Place.

No Senator or Representative shall, during the Time for which he was elected, be appointed to any civil Office under the Authority of the United States, which shall have been created, or the Emoluments whereof shall have been encreased during such time; and no Person holding any Office under the United States, shall be a Member of either House during his Continuance in Office.

SECTION. 7. All Bills for raising Revenue shall originate in the House of Representatives; but the Senate may propose or concur with amendments as on other Bills.

Every Bill which shall have passed the House of Representatives and the Senate, shall, before it become a Law, be presented to the President of the United States; If he approve he shall sign it, but if not he shall return it, with his Objections to that House in which it shall have originated, who shall enter the Objections at large on their Journal, and proceed to reconsider it. If after such Reconsideration two thirds of that House shall agree to pass the Bill, it shall be sent, together with the Objections, to the other House, by which it shall likewise be reconsidered, and if approved by two thirds of that House, it shall become a Law. But in all such Cases the Votes of both Houses shall be determined by Yeas and Nays, and the Names of the Persons voting for and against the Bill shall be entered on the Journal of each House respectively. If any Bill shall not be returned by the President within ten Days (Sundays excepted) after it shall have been presented to him, the Same shall be a Law, in like Manner as if he had signed it, unless the Congress by their Adjournment prevent its Return, in which Case it shall not be a Law.

Every Order, Resolution, or Vote to which the Concurrence of the Senate and House of Representatives may be necessary (except on a question of Adjournment) shall be presented to the President of the United States; and before the Same shall take Effect, shall be approved by him, or being disapproved by him, shall be repassed by two thirds of the Senate and House of Representatives, according to the Rules and Limitations prescribed in the Case of a Bill.

SECTION. 8. The Congress shall have Power To lay and collect Taxes, Duties, Imposts and Excises, to pay the Debts and provide for the common Defence and general Welfare of the United States; but all Duties, Imposts and Excises shall be uniform throughout the United States;

To borrow Money on the credit of the United States;

To regulate Commerce with foreign Nations, and among the several States, and with the Indian Tribes;

To establish an uniform Rule of Naturalization, and uniform Laws on the subject of Bankruptcies throughout the United States;

To coin Money, regulate the Value thereof, and of foreign Coin, and fix the Standard of Weights and Measures;

To provide for the Punishment of counterfeiting the Securities and current Coin of the United States;

To establish Post Offices and post Roads;

To promote the Progress of Science and useful Arts, by securing for limited Times to Authors and Inventors the exclusive Right to their respective Writings and Discoveries;

To constitute Tribunals inferior to the supreme Court;

To define and punish Piracies and Felonies committed on the high Seas, and Offences against the Law of Nations;

To declare War, grant Letters of Marque and Reprisal, and make Rules concerning Captures on Land and Water;

To raise and support Armies, but no Appropriation of Money to that Use shall be for a longer Term than two Years;

To provide and maintain a Navy;

To make Rules for the Government and Regulation of the land and naval Forces;

To provide for calling forth the Militia to execute the Laws of the Union, suppress Insurrections and repel Invasions;

To provide for organizing, arming, and disciplining, the Militia, and for governing such Part of them as may be employed in the Service of the United States, reserving to the States respectively, the Appointment of the Officers, and the Authority of training the Militia according to the discipline prescribed by Congress;

To exercise exclusive Legislation in all Cases whatsoever, over such District (not exceeding ten Miles square) as may, by Cession of Particular States, and the Acceptance of Congress, become the Seat of the Government of the United States, and to exercise like Authority over all Places purchased by the Consent of the Legislature of the State in which the Same shall be, for the Erection of Forts, Magazines, Arsenals, dock-Yards, and other needful Buildings;—And

To make all Laws which shall be necessary and proper for carrying into Execution the foregoing Powers, and all other Powers vested by this Constitution in the Government of the United States, or in any Department or Officer thereof.

SECTION. 9. The Migration or Importation of such Persons as any of the States now existing shall think proper to admit, shall not be prohibited by the Congress prior to the Year one thousand eight hundred and eight, but a Tax or duty may be imposed on such Importation, not exceeding ten dollars for each Person.

The Privilege of the Writ of Habeas Corpus shall not be suspended, unless when in Cases of Rebellion or Invasion the public Safety may require it.

No Bill of Attainder or ex post facto Law shall be passed.

No Capitation, or other direct, Tax shall be laid, unless in Proportion to the Census or Enumeration herein before directed to be taken.

No Tax or Duty shall be laid on Articles exported from any State.

No Preference shall be given by any Regulation or Commerce or Revenue to the Ports of one State over those of another; nor shall Vessels bound to, or from, one State, be obliged to enter, clear or pay Duties in another.

No Money shall be drawn from the Treasury, but in Consequence of Appropriations made by Law; and a regular Statement and Account of the Receipts and Expenditures of all public Money shall be published from time to time.

No Title of Nobility shall be granted by the United States: And no Person holding any Office of Profit or Trust under them, shall, without the Consent of the Congress, accept of any present Emolument, Office, or Title, of any kind whatever, from any King, Prince, or foreign State.

SECTION. 10. No State shall enter into any Treaty, Alliance, or Confederation; grant Letters of Marque and Reprisal; coin Money; emit Bills of Credit; make any Thing but gold and silver Coin a Tender in Payment of Debts; pass any Bill of Attainder, ex post facto Law, or Law impairing the Obligation of Contracts, or grant any Title of Nobility.

No State shall, without the Consent of the Congress, lay any Imposts or Duties on Imports or Exports, except what may be absolutely necessary for executing its inspection Laws: and the net Produce of all Duties and Imposts, laid by any State on Imports or Exports, shall be for the Use of the Treasury of the United States; and all such Laws shall be subject to the Revision and Controul of the Congress.

No state shall, without the Consent of Congress, lay any Duty of Tonnage, keep Troops, or Ships of War in time of Peace, enter into any Agreement or Compact with another State, or with a foreign Power, or engage in War, unless actually invaded, or in such imminent Danger as will not admit of delay.

Article. II.

SECTION. 1. The executive Power shall be vested in a President of the United States of America. He shall hold his Office during the Term of four Years, and, together with the Vice President, chosen for the same Term, be elected as follows.

Each State shall appoint, in such Manner as the Legislature thereof may direct, a Number of Electors, equal to the whole Number of Senators and Representatives to which the State may be entitled in the Congress: but no Senator or Representative, or Person holding an Office of Trust or Profit under the United States, shall be appointed an Elector.

The Electors shall meet in their respective States, and vote by Ballot for two Persons, of whom one at least shall not be an Inhabitant of the same State with themselves. And they shall make a List of all the persons voted for, and of the Number of Votes for each; which List they shall sign and certify, and transmit sealed to the Seat of Government of the United States, directed to the President of the Senate. The President of the Senate shall, in the Presence of the Senate and House of Representatives, open all the Certificates, and the Votes shall then be counted. The Person having the greatest Number of Votes shall be the President, if such Number be a Majority of the whole Number of Electors appointed; and if there be more than one who have such Majority, and have an equal Number of Votes, then the House of Representatives shall immediately chuse by Ballot one of them for President; and if no Person have a Majority, then from the five highest on the List the said House shall in like Manner chuse the President. But in chusing the President, the Votes shall be taken by States, the Representation from each State having one Vote; a quorum for this Purpose shall consist of a Member or Members from two thirds of the States, and a Majority of all the States shall be necessary to a Choice. In every Case, after the Choice of the President, the Person having the greatest Number of Votes of the Electors shall be the Vice President. But if there should remain two or more who have equal Votes, the Senate shall chuse from them by Ballot the Vice President.

The Congress may determine the Time of chusing the Electors, and the Day on which they shall give their Votes; which Day shall be the same throughout the United States.

No Person except a natural born Citizen, or a Citizen of the United States, at the time of the Adoption of this Constitution, shall be eligible to the Office of President; neither shall any person be eligible to that Office who shall not have attained to the Age of thirty five Years, and been fourteen Years a Resident within the United States.

In Case of the Removal of the President from Office, or of his Death, Resignation, or Inability to discharge the Powers and Duties of the said Office, the Same shall devolve on the Vice President, and the Congress may by Law provide for the Case of Removal, Death, Resignation or Inability, both of the President and Vice President, declaring what Officer shall then act as President, and such Officer shall act accordingly, until the Disability be removed, or a President shall be elected.

The President shall, at stated Times, receive for his Services, a Compensation, which shall neither be encreased nor diminished during the Period for which he shall have been elected, and he shall not receive within that period any other Emolument from the United States, or any of them.

Before he enter on the Execution of his Office, he shall take the following Oath or Affirmation:—"I do solemnly swear (or affirm) that I will faithfully execute the Office of President of the United States, and will to the best of my Ability, preserve, protect and defend the Constitution of the United States."

SECTION. 2. The President shall be Commander in Chief of the Army and Navy of the United States, and of the Militia of the several States, when called into the actual Service of the United States; he may require the Opinion, in writing, of the principal Officer in each of the executive Departments, upon any Subject relating to the Duties of their respective Offices, and he shall have Power to grant Reprieves and Pardons for Offences against the United States, except in Cases of Impeachment.

He shall have Power, by and with the Advice and Consent of the Senate, to make Treaties, provided two thirds of the Senators present concur; and he shall nominate, and by and with the Advice and Consent of the Senate, shall appoint Ambassadors, other public Ministers and Consuls, Judges of the supreme Court, and all other Officers of the United States, whose Appointments are not herein otherwise provided for, and which shall be established by Law: but the Congress may by Law vest the Appointment of such inferior Officers, as they think proper, in the President alone, in the Courts of Law, or in the Heads of Departments.

The President shall have Power to fill up all Vacancies that may happen during the Recess of the Senate, by granting

Commissions which shall expire at the End of their next Session.

SECTION. 3. He shall from time to time give to the Congress Information of the State of the Union, and recommend to their Consideration such Measures as he shall judge necessary and expedient; he may, on extraordinary Occasions, convene both Houses, or either of them, and in Case of Disagreement between them, with Respect to the Time of Adjournment, he may adjourn them to such Time as he shall think proper; he shall receive Ambassadors and other public Ministers; he shall take Care that the Laws be faithfully executed, and shall Commission all the Officers of the United States.

SECTION. 4. The President, Vice President and all civil Officers of the United States, shall be removed from Office on Impeachment for, and Conviction of, Treason, Bribery, or other high Crimes and Misdemeanors.

Article. III.

SECTION. 1. The judicial Power of the United States, shall be vested in one supreme Court, and in such inferior Courts as the Congress may from time to time ordain and establish. The Judges, both of the supreme and inferior Courts, shall hold their Offices during good Behaviour, and shall, at stated Times, receive for their Services, a Compensation, which shall not be diminished during their Continuance in Office.

SECTION. 2. The judicial Power shall extend to all Cases, in Law and Equity, arising under this Constitution, the Laws of the United States, and Treaties made, or which shall be made, under their Authority;—to all Cases affecting Ambassadors, other public Ministers and Consuls;—to all Cases of admiralty and maritime Jurisdiction;—to Controversies to which the United States shall be a Party;—to Controversies between two or more States;—between a State and Citizens of another State;—between Citizens of different States;—between Citizens of the same State claiming Lands under Grants of different States, and between a State, or the Citizens thereof, and foreign States, Citizens or Subjects.

In all Cases affecting Ambassadors, other public Ministers and Consuls, and those in which a State shall be Party, the supreme Court shall have original Jurisdiction. In all the other Cases before mentioned, the supreme Court shall have appellate Jurisdiction, both as to Law and Fact, with such Exceptions, and under such Regulations as the Congress shall make.

The Trial of all Crimes, except in Cases of Impeachment, shall be by Jury; and such Trial shall be held in the State where the said Crimes shall have been committed; but when not committed within any State, the Trial shall be at such Place or Places as the Congress may by Law have directed.

SECTION. 3. Treason against the United States, shall consist only in levying War against them, or in adhering to their Enemies, giving them Aid and Comfort. No Person shall be convicted of Treason unless on the Testimony of two Witnesses to the same overt Act, or on Confession in open Court.

The Congress shall have Power to declare the Punishment of Treason, but no Attainder of Treason shall work Corruption of Blood, or Forfeiture except during the Life of the Person attained.

Article. IV.

SECTION. 1. Full Faith and Credit shall be given in each State to the public Acts, Records, and judicial Proceedings of every other State. And the Congress may by general Laws prescribe the Manner in which such Acts, Record and Proceedings shall be proved, and the Effect thereof.

SECTION. 2. The Citizens of each State shall be entitled to all Privileges and Immunities of Citizens in the several States.

A Person charged in any State with Treason, Felony, or other Crime, who shall flee from Justice, and be found in another State, shall on Demand of the executive Authority of the State from which he fled, be delivered up, to be removed to the State having Jurisdiction of the Crime.

No Person held to Service or Labour in one State, under the Laws thereof, escaping into another, shall, in Consequence of any Law or Regulation therein, be discharged from such Service or Labour, but shall be delivered up on Claim of the Party to whom such Service or Labour may be due.

SECTION. 3. New States may be admitted by the Congress into this Union; but no new State shall be formed or erected within the Jurisdiction of any other State; nor any State be formed by the Junction of two or more States, or Parts of States, without the Consent of the Legislatures of the States concerned as well as of the Congress.

The Congress shall have Power to dispose of and make all needful Rules and Regulations respecting the Territory or other Property belonging to the United States; and nothing in this Constitution shall be so construed as to Prejudice any Claims of the United States, or of any particular State.

SECTION. 4. The United States shall guarantee to every State in this Union a Republican Form of Government, and shall protect each of them against Invasion; and on Application of the Legislature, or of the Executive (when the Legislature cannot be convened) against domestic Violence.

Article. V.

The Congress, whenever two thirds of both Houses shall deem it necessary, shall propose Amendments to this Constitution, or, on the Application of the Legislature of two thirds of the several States, shall call a Convention for proposing Amendments, which, in either Case, shall be valid to all Intents and Purposes, as Part of this Constitution, when ratified by the Legislatures of three fourths of the several States, or by Conventions in three fourths thereof, as the one or the other Mode of Ratification may be proposed by the Congress; Provided that no Amendment which may be made prior to the Year One thousand eight hundred and eight shall in any Manner affect the first and fourth Clauses in the Ninth Section of the first Article; and that no State, without its Consent, shall be deprived of its equal Suffrage in the Senate.

Article. VI.

All Debts contracted and Engagements entered into, before the Adoption of this Constitution, shall be as valid against the United States under this Constitution, as under the Confederation.

This Constitution, and the Laws of the United States which shall be made in Pursuance thereof; and all Treaties made, or which shall be made, under the Authority of the United States, shall be the supreme Law of the Land; and the Judges in every State shall be bound thereby, any Thing in the Constitution or Laws of any State to the Contrary notwithstanding.

The Senators and Representatives before mentioned, and the Members of the several State Legislatures, and all executive and judicial Officers, both of the United States and of the several States, shall be bound by Oath or Affirmation, to support this Constitution; but no religious Test shall ever be required as a Qualification to any Office or public Trust under the United States.

Article. VII.

The Ratification of the Conventions of nine States, shall be sufficient for the Establishment of this Constitution between the States so ratifying the Same.

Done in Convention by the Unanimous Consent of the States present the Seventeenth Day of September in the Year of our Lord one thousand seven hundred and Eighty seven and of the Independence of the United States of America the Twelfth In witness whereof We have hereunto subscribed our Names,

Go. WASHINGTON—Presidt. and deputy from Virginia

In Convention Monday, September 17th 1787.

Present The States of

New Hampshire, Massachusetts, Connecticut, Mr. Hamilton from New York, New Jersey, Pennsylvania, Delaware, Maryland, Virginia, North Carolina and Georgia.

Resolved,

That the preceeding Constitution be laid before the United States in Congress assembled, and that it is the Opinion of this Convention, that it should afterwards be submitted to a Convention of Delegates, chosen in each State by the People thereof, under the Recommendation of its Legislature, for their Assent and Ratification; and that each Convention assenting to, and ratifying the Same, should give Notice thereof to the United States in Congress assembled. Resolved, That it is the Opinion of this Convention, that as soon as the Conventions of nine States shall have ratified this Constitution, the United States in Congress assembled should fix a Day on which Electors should be appointed by the States which shall have ratified the same, and a Day on which the Electors should assemble to vote for the President, and the Time and Place for commencing Proceedings under this Constitution. That after such Publication the Electors should be appointed, and the Senators and Representatives elected: That the Electors should meet on the Day fixed for the Election of the President, and should transmit their Votes certified, signed, sealed and directed, as the Constitution requires, to the Secretary of the United States in Congress assembled, that

New Hampshire	JOHN LANGDON
	NICHOLAS GILMAN
Massachusetts	NATHANIEL GORHAM
	RUFUS KING
Connecticut	Wm. SAML JOHNSON
	ROGER SHERMAN
New York . . .	ALEXANDER HAMILTON
New Jersey	WIL: LIVINGSTON
	DAVID BREARLEY
	Wm. PATERSON
	JONA: DAYTON
Pennsylvania	B FRANKLIN
	THOMAS MIFFLIN
	ROBt MORRIS
	GEO. CLYMER
	THOs. FITZSIMONS
	JARED INGERSOLL
	JAMES WILSON
	GOUV MORRIS
Delaware	GEO: READ
	GUNNING BEDFORD jun
	JOHN DICKINSON
	RICHARD BASSETT
	JACO: BROOM
Maryland	JAMES McHENRY
	DAN OF St THOs. JENIFER
	DANL CARROLL
Virginia	JOHN BLAIR
	JAMES MADISON Jr.
North Carolina	Wm. BLOUNT
	RICHd. DOBBS SPAIGHT
	HU WILLIAMSON
South Carolina	J. RUTLEDGE
	CHARLES COTESWORTH PINCKNEY
	CHARLES PINCKNEY
	PIERCE BUTLER
Georgia	WILLIAM FEW
	ABR BALDWIN

Ratification of the Constitution

State	Date of Ratification
Delaware	Dec 7, 1787
Pennsylvania	Dec 12, 1787
New Jersey	Dec 19, 1787
Georgia	Jan 2, 1788
Connecticut	Jan 9, 1788
Massachusetts	Feb 6, 1788
Maryland	Apr 28, 1788
South Carolina	May 23, 1788
New Hampshire	June 21, 1788
Virginia	Jun 25, 1788
New York	Jun 26, 1788
Rhode Island	May 29, 1790
North Carolina	Nov 21, 1789

Article 2. The History of The Constitution of the United States

the Senators and Representatives should convene at the Time and Place assigned; that the Senators should appoint a President of the Senate, for the sole Purpose of receiving, opening and counting the Votes for President; and, that after he shall be chosen, the Congress, together with the President, should, without Delay, proceed to execute this Constitution.

By the Unanimous Order of the Convention
Go. WASHINGTON—Presidt.
W. JACKSON Secretary.

ARTICLES IN ADDITION TO, AND AMENDMENT OF, THE CONSTITUTION OF THE UNITED STATES OF AMERICA, PROPOSED BY CONGRESS, AND RATIFIED BY THE SEVERAL STATES, PURSUANT TO THE FIFTH ARTICLE OF THE ORIGINAL CONSTITUTION.

Amendment I.

Congress shall make no law respecting an establishment of religion, or prohibiting the free exercise thereof; or abridging the freedom of speech, or of the press; or the right of the people peaceably to assemble, and to petition the Government for a redress of grievances.

Amendment II.

A well regulated Militia, being necessary to the security of a free State, the right of the people to keep and bear Arms, shall not be infringed.

Amendment III.

No Soldier shall, in time of peace be quartered in any house, without the consent of the Owner, nor in time of war, but in a manner to be prescribed by law.

Amendment IV.

The right of the people to be secure in their persons, houses, papers, and effects, against unreasonable searches and seizures, shall not be violated, and no Warrants shall issue, but upon probable cause, supported by Oath or affirmation, and particularly describing the place to be searched, and the persons or things to be seized.

Amendment V.

No person shall be held to answer for a capital, or otherwise infamous crime, unless on a presentment or indictment of a Grand Jury, except in cases arising in the land or naval forces, or in the Militia, when in actual service in time of War or public danger; nor shall any person be subject for the same offence to be twice put in jeopardy of life or limb; nor shall be compelled in any criminal case to be a witness against himself, nor be deprived of life, liberty, or property, without due process of law; nor shall private property be taken for public use, without just compensation.

Amendment VI.

In all criminal prosecutions, the accused shall enjoy the right to a speedy and public trial, by an impartial jury of the State and district wherein the crime shall have been committed, which district shall have been previously ascertained by law, and to be informed of the nature and cause of the accusation; to be confronted with the witnesses against him; to have compulsory process for obtaining witnesses in his favor, and to have the Assistance of Counsel for his defence.

Amendment VII.

In Suits at common law, where the value in controversy shall exceed twenty dollars, the right of trial by jury shall be preserved, and no fact tried by a jury, shall be otherwise re-examined in any Court of the United States, than according to the rules of the common law.

Amendment VIII.

Excessive bail shall not be required, nor excessive fines imposed, nor cruel and unusual punishments inflicted.

Amendment IX.

The enumeration in the Constitution, of certain rights, shall not be construed to deny or disparage others retained by the people.

Amendment X.

The powers not delegated to the United States by the Constitution, nor prohibited by it to the States, are reserved to the States respectively, or to the people.

Amendment XI.
(Adopted Jan. 8, 1798)

The Judicial power of the United States shall not be construed to extend to any suit in law or equity, commenced or prosecuted against one of the United States by Citizens of another State, or by Citizens or Subjects of any Foreign State.

Amendment XII.
(Adopted Sept. 25, 1804)

The Electors shall meet in their respective states and vote by ballot for President and Vice-President, one of whom, at least, shall not be an inhabitant of the same state with themselves; they shall name in their ballots the person voted for as President, and in distinct ballots the person voted for as Vice-President, and they shall make distinct lists of all persons voted for as President, and of all persons voted for as Vice-President, and of the number of votes for each, which lists they shall sign and certify, and transmit sealed to the seat of the government of the United States, directed to the President of the Senate;—The President of the Senate shall, in the presence of the Senate and House of Representatives, open all the certificates and the votes shall then be counted;—The person having the greatest number of votes for President, shall be the President, if such number be a majority of the whole number of Electors appointed; and if no person have such majority, then from the persons having the highest numbers not exceeding three on the list of those voted for as President, the House of Representatives shall choose immediately, by ballot, the President. But in choosing the President, the votes shall be taken by states, the representation from each state having one vote; a quorum for this purpose shall consist of a member or members from two-thirds of the states, and a majority of all the states shall be necessary to a choice. And if the House of Representatives shall not choose a President whenever the right of choice shall devolve upon them, before the fourth day of March next following, then the Vice-President shall act as President, as in the case of the death or other constitutional disability of the President.—The person having the greatest number of votes as Vice-President, shall be the Vice-President, if such number be a majority of the whole number of Electors appointed, and if no person have a majority, then from the two highest numbers on the list, the Senate shall choose the Vice-President; a quorum for the purpose shall consist of two-thirds of the whole number of Senators, and a majority of the whole number shall be necessary to a choice. But no person constitutionally ineligible to the office of President shall be eligible to that of Vice-President of the United States.

Amendment XIII.

(Adopted Dec. 18, 1865)

SECTION 1. Neither slavery nor involuntary servitude, except as a punishment for crime whereof the party shall have been duly convicted, shall exist within the United States, or any place subject to their jurisdiction.

SECTION 2. Congress shall have power to enforce this article by appropriate legislation.

Amendment XIV.

(Adopted July 28, 1868)

SECTION 1. All persons born or naturalized in the United States and subject to the jurisdiction thereof, are citizens of the United States and of the State wherein they reside. No State shall make or enforce any law which shall abridge the privileges or immunities of citizens of the United States; nor shall any State deprive any person of life, liberty, or property, without due process of law; nor deny to any person within its jurisdiction the equal protection of the laws.

SECTION 2. Representatives shall be apportioned among the several States according to their respective numbers, counting the whole number of persons in each State, excluding Indians not taxed. But when the right to vote at any election for the choice of electors for President and Vice President of the United States, Representatives in Congress, the Executive and Judicial officers of a State, or the members of the Legislature thereof, is denied to any of the male inhabitants of such State, being twenty-one years of age, and citizens of the United States, or in any way abridged, except for participation in rebellion, or other crime, the basis of representation therein shall be reduced in the proportion which the number of such male citizens shall bear to the whole number of male citizens twenty-one years of age in such State.

SECTION 3. No person shall be a Senator or Representative in Congress, or elector of President and Vice President, or hold any office, civil or military, under the United States, or under any State, who, having previously taken an oath, as a member of Congress, or as an officer of the United States, or as a member of any State legislature, or as an executive or judicial officer of any State, to support the Constitution of the United States, shall have engaged in insurrection or rebellion against the same, or given aid or comfort to the enemies thereof. But Congress may by a vote of two-thirds of each House, remove such disability.

SECTION 4. The validity of the public debt of the United States, authorized by law, including debts incurred for payment of pensions and bounties for services in suppressing insurrection or rebellion, shall not be questioned. But neither the United States nor any State shall assume or pay any debt or obligation incurred in aid of insurrection or rebellion against the United States, or any claim for the loss or emancipation of any slave; but all such debts, obligations and claims shall be held illegal and void.

SECTION 5. The Congress shall have power to enforce, by appropriate legislation, the provisions of this article.

Amendment XV.

(Adopted March 30, 1870)

SECTION 1. The right of citizens of the United States to vote shall not be denied or abridged by the United States or by any State on account of race, color, or previous condition of servitude.

SECTION 2. The Congress shall have power to enforce this article by appropriate legislation.

Amendment XVI.

(Adopted Feb. 25, 1913)

The Congress shall have power to lay and collect taxes on incomes, from whatever source derived, without apportionment among the several States, and without regard to any census or enumeration.

Amendment XVII.

(Adopted May 31, 1913)

The Senate of the United States shall be composed of two Senators from each State, elected by the people thereof, for six years; and each Senator shall have one vote. The electors in each State shall have the qualifications requisite for electors of the most numerous branch of the State legislatures.

When vacancies happen in the representation of any State in the Senate, the executive authority of such State shall issue writs of election to fill such vacancies: Provided, That the legislature of any State may empower the executive thereof to make temporary appointments until the people fill the vacancies by election as the legislature may direct.

This amendment shall not be so construed as to affect the election or term of any Senator chosen before it becomes valid as part of the Constitution.

Amendment XVIII.

(Adopted Jan. 29, 1919)

SECTION 1. After one year from the ratification of this article the manufacture, sale or transportation of intoxicating liquors within, the importation thereof into, or the exportation thereof from the United States and all territory subject to the jurisdiction thereof for beverage purposes is hereby prohibited.

SECTION 2. The Congress and the several States shall have concurrent power to enforce this article by appropriate legislation.

SECTION 3. This article shall be inoperative unless it shall have been ratified as an amendment to the Constitution by the legislatures of the several States, as provided in the Constitution, within seven years from the date of the submission hereof to the States by the Congress.

Amendment XIX.

(Adopted Aug. 26, 1920)

The right of citizens of the United States to vote shall not be denied or abridged by the United States or by any State on account of sex.

Congress shall have power to enforce this article by appropriate legislation.

Amendment XX.

(Adopted Feb. 6, 1933)

SECTION 1. The terms of the President and Vice President shall end at noon on the 20th day of January, and the terms of Senators and Representatives at noon on the 3d day of January, of the years in which such terms would have ended if this article had not been ratified; and the terms of their successors shall then begin.

SECTION 2. The Congress shall assemble at least once in every year, and such meeting shall begin at noon on the 3d day of January, unless they shall by law appoint a different day.

SECTION 3. If, at the time fixed for the beginning of the term of the President, the President elect shall have died, the Vice President elect shall become President. If a President shall not have been chosen before the time fixed for the beginning of his term, or if the President elect shall have failed to qualify, then the Vice President elect shall act as President until a President shall have qualified; and the Congress may by law provide for the case wherein neither a President elect nor a Vice President elect shall have qualified, declaring who shall then act as President, or the manner in which one who is to act shall be selected, and such person shall act accordingly until a President or Vice President shall have qualified.

SECTION 4. The Congress may by law provide for the case of the death of any of the persons from whom the House of Representatives may choose a President whenever the right of choice shall have devolved upon them, and for the case of the death of any of the persons from whom the Senate may choose a Vice President whenever the right of choice shall have devolved upon them.

SECTION 5. Sections 1 and 2 shall take effect on the 15th day of October following the ratification of this article.

SECTION 6. This article shall be inoperative unless it shall have been ratified as an amendment to the Constitution by the legislatures of three-fourths of the several States within seven years from the date of its submission.

Amendment XXI.

(Adopted Dec. 5, 1933)

SECTION 1. The eighteenth article of amendment to the Constitution of the United States is hereby repealed.

SECTION 2. The transportation or importation into any State, Territory, or possession of the United States for delivery or use therein of intoxicating liquors, in violation of the laws thereof, is hereby prohibited.

SECTION 3. This article shall be inoperative unless it shall have been ratified as an amendment to the Constitution by conventions in the several States, as provided in the Constitution, within seven years from the date of the submission hereof to the States by the Congress.

Amendment XXII.

(Adopted Feb. 27, 1951)

SECTION 1. No person shall be elected to the office of the President more than twice, and no person who has held the office of President, or acted as President, for more than two years of a term to which some other person was elected President shall be elected to the office of the President more than once. But this Article shall not apply to any person holding the office of President when this Article was proposed by the Congress, and shall not prevent any person who may be holding the office of President, or acting as President, during the term within which this Article becomes operative from holding the office of President or acting as President during the remainder of such term.

SECTION 2. This Article shall be inoperative unless it shall have been ratified as an amendment to the Constitution by the legislatures of three-fourths of the several States within seven years from the date of its submission to the States by the Congress.

Amendment XXIII.
(Adopted Mar. 29, 1961)

SECTION 1. The District constituting the seat of Government of the United States shall appoint in such manner as the Congress may direct:

A number of electors of President and Vice President equal to the whole number of Senators and Representatives in Congress to which the District would be entitled if it were a State, but in no event more than the least populous State; they shall be in addition to those appointed by the States, but they shall be considered, for the purposes of the election of President and Vice President, to be electors appointed by a State; and they shall meet in the District and perform such duties as provided by the twelfth article of amendment.

SECTION 2. The Congress shall have power to enforce this article by appropriate legislation.

Amendment XXIV.
(Adopted Jan. 23, 1964)

SECTION 1. The right of citizens of the United States to vote in any primary or other election for President or Vice President, for electors for President or Vice President, or for Senator or Representative in Congress, shall not be denied or abridged by the United States or any State by reason of failure to pay any poll tax or other tax.

SECTION 2. The Congress shall have the power to enforce this article by appropriate legislation.

Amendment XXV.
(Adopted Feb. 10, 1967)

SECTION 1. In case of the removal of the President from office or of his death or resignation, the Vice President shall become President.

SECTION 2. Whenever there is a vacancy in the office of the Vice President, the President shall nominate a Vice President who shall take the office upon confirmation by a majority vote of both houses of Congress.

SECTION 3. Whenever the President transmits to the President pro tempore of the Senate and the Speaker of the House of Representatives his written declaration that he is unable to discharge the powers and duties of his office, and until he transmits to them a written declaration to the contrary, such powers and duties shall be discharged by the Vice President as Acting President.

SECTION 4. Whenever the Vice President and a majority of either the principal officers of the executive departments or of such other body as Congress may by law provide, transmit to the President pro tempore of the Senate and the Speaker of the House of Representatives their written declaration that the President is unable to discharge the powers and duties of his office, the Vice President shall immediately assume the powers and duties of the office as Acting President.

Thereafter, when the President transmits to the President pro tempore of the Senate and the Speaker of the House of Representatives his written declaration that no inability exists, he shall resume the powers and duties of his office unless the Vice President and a majority of either the principal officers of the executive department or of such other body as Congress may by law provide, transmit within four days to the President pro tempore of the Senate and the Speaker of the House of Representatives their written declaration that the President is unable to discharge the powers and duties of his office. Thereupon Congress shall decide the issue, assembling within forty-eight hours for that purpose if not in session. If the Congress within twenty-one days after receipt of the latter written declaration, or, if Congress is not in session, within twenty-one days after Congress is required to assemble, determines by two-thirds vote of both Houses that the President is unable to discharge the powers and duties of his office, the Vice President shall continue to discharge the same as Acting President; otherwise, the President shall resume the powers and duties of his office.

Amendment XXVI.
(Adopted June 30, 1971)

SECTION 1. The right of citizens of the United States, who are 18 years of age or older, to vote shall not be denied or abridged by the United States or by any state on account of age.

SECTION 2. The Congress shall have the power to enforce this article by appropriate legislation.

Amendment XXVII.
(Adopted May 7, 1992)

No law, varying the compensation for the services of the Senators and Representatives, shall take effect, until an election of Representatives shall have intervened.

Article 3

The Size and Variety of the Union as a Check on Faction
Federalist No. 10

JAMES MADISON

To the People of the State of New York:

Among the numerous advantages promised by a well-constructed Union, none deserves to be more accurately developed than its tendency to break and control the violence of faction. The friend of popular governments never finds himself so much alarmed for their character and fate, as when he contemplates their propensity to this dangerous vice. He will not fail, therefore, to set a due value on any plan which, without violating the principles to which he is attached, provides a proper cure for it. The instability, injustice, and confusion introduced into the public councils, have, in truth, been the mortal diseases under which popular governments have everywhere perished; as they continue to be the favorite and fruitful topics from which the adversaries to liberty derive their most specious declamations. The valuable improvements made by the American constitutions on the popular models, both ancient and modern, cannot certainly be too much admired; but it would be an unwarrantable partiality, to contend that they have as effectually obviated the danger on this side, as was wished and expected. Complaints are everywhere heard from our most considerate and virtuous citizens, equally the friends of public and private faith, and of public and personal liberty, that our governments are too unstable, that the public good is disregarded in the conflicts of rival parties, and that measures are too often decided, not according to the rules of justice and the rights of the minor party, but by the superior force of an interested and overbearing majority. However anxiously we may wish that these complaints had no foundation, the evidence of known facts will not permit us to deny that they are in some degree true. It will be found, indeed, on a candid review of our situation, that some of the distresses under which we labor have been erroneously charged on the operation of our governments; but it will be found, at the same time, that other causes will not alone account for many of our heaviest misfortunes; and, particularly, for that prevailing and increasing distrust of public engagements, and alarm for private rights, which are echoed from one end of the continent to the other. These must be chiefly, if not wholly, effects of the unsteadiness and injustice with which a factious spirit has tainted our public administrations.

By a faction, I understand a number of citizens, whether amounting to a majority or minority of the whole, who are united and actuated by some common impulse of passion, or of interest, adverse to the rights of other citizens, or to the permanent and aggregate interests of the community.

There are two methods of curing the mischiefs of faction: the one, by removing its causes; the other, by controlling its effects.

There are again two methods of removing the causes of faction: the one, by destroying the liberty which is essential to its existence; the other, by giving to every citizen the same opinions, the same passions, and the same interests.

It could never be more truly said than of the first remedy, that it was worse than the disease. Liberty is to faction what air is to fire, an aliment without which it instantly expires. But it could not be less folly to abolish liberty, which is essential to political life, because it nourishes faction, than it would be to wish the annihilation of air, which is essential to animal life, because it imparts to fire its destructive agency.

The second expedient is as impracticable as the first would be unwise. As long as the reason of man continues fallible, and he is at liberty to exercise it, different opinions will be formed. As long as the connection subsists between his reason and his self-love, his opinions and his passions will have a reciprocal influence on each other; and the former will be objects to which the latter will attach themselves. The diversity in the faculties of men, from which the rights of property originate, is not less an insuperable obstacle to a uniformity of interests. The protection of these faculties is the first object of government. From the protection of different and unequal faculties of acquiring property, the possession of different degrees and kinds of property immediately results; and from the influence of these on the sentiments and views of the respective proprietors, ensues a division of the society into different interests and parties.

The latent causes of faction are thus sown in the nature of man; and we see them everywhere brought into different degrees of activity, according to the different circumstances of civil society. A zeal for different opinions concerning religion, concerning government, and many other points, as well of speculation as of practice; an attachment to different leaders ambitiously contending for pre-eminence and power; or to persons of other descriptions whose fortunes have been interesting to the human passions, have, in turn, divided mankind into parties, inflamed them with mutual animosity, and rendered them much more disposed to vex and oppress each other than to co-operate for their common good. So strong is this propensity of mankind to fall into mutual animosities, that where no substantial occasion presents itself, the most frivolous and fanciful distinctions have been sufficient to kindle their unfriendly passions and excite their most violent conflicts. But the most common and durable source of factions has been the various and unequal distribution of property. Those who hold and those who are without property have ever formed distinct interests in society.

Those who are creditors, and those who are debtors, fall under a like discrimination. A landed interest, a manufacturing interest, a mercantile interest, a moneyed interest, with many lesser interests, grow up of necessity in civilized nations, and divide them into different classes, actuated by different sentiments and views. The regulation of these various and interfering interests forms the principal task of modern legislation, and involves the spirit of party and faction in the necessary and ordinary operations of the government.

No man is allowed to be a judge in his own cause, because his interest would certainly bias his judgment, and, not improbably, corrupt his integrity. With equal, nay with greater reason, a body of men are unfit to be both judges and parties at the same time; yet what are many of the most important acts of legislation, but so many judicial determinations, not indeed concerning the rights of single persons, but concerning the rights of large bodies of citizens? And what are the different classes of legislators but advocates and parties to the causes which they determine? Is a law proposed concerning private debts? It is a question to which the creditors are parties on one side and the debtors on the other. Justice ought to hold the balance between them. Yet the parties are, and must be, themselves the judges; and the most numerous party, or, in other words, the most powerful faction must be expected to prevail. Shall domestic manufactures be encouraged, and in what degree, by restrictions on foreign manufactures? are questions which would be differently decided by the landed and the manufacturing classes, and probably by neither with a sole regard to justice and the public good. The apportionment of taxes on the various descriptions of property is an act which seems to require the most exact impartiality; yet there is, perhaps, no legislative act in which greater opportunity and temptation are given to a predominant party to trample on the rules of justice. Every shilling with which they overburden the inferior number, is a shilling saved to their own pockets.

It is in vain to say that enlightened statesmen will be able to adjust these clashing interests, and render them all subservient to the public good. Enlightened statesmen will not always be at the helm. Nor, in many cases, can such an adjustment be made at all without taking into view indirect and remote considerations, which will rarely prevail over the immediate interest which one party may find in disregarding the rights of another or the good of the whole.

The inference to which we are brought is, that the *causes* of faction cannot be removed, and that relief is only to be sought in the means of controlling its *effects*.

If a faction consists of less than a majority, relief is supplied by the republican principle, which enables the majority to defeat its sinister views by regular vote. It may clog the administration, it may convulse the society; but it will be unable to execute and mask its violence under the forms of the Constitution. When a majority is included in a faction, the form of popular government, on the other hand, enables it to sacrifice to its ruling passion or interest both the public good and the rights of other citizens. To secure the public good and private rights against the danger of such a faction, and at the same time to preserve the spirit and the form of popular government, is then the great object to which our inquiries are directed. Let me add that it is the great desideratum by which this form of government can be rescued from the opprobrium under which it has so long labored, and be recommended to the esteem and adoption of mankind.

By what means is this object attainable? Evidently by one of two only. Either the existence of the same passion or interest in a majority at the same time must be prevented, or the majority, having such coexistent passion or interest, must be rendered, by their number and local situation, unable to concert and carry into effect schemes of oppression. If the impulse and the opportunity be suffered to coincide, we well know that neither moral nor religious motives can be relied on as an adequate control. They are not found to be such on the injustice and violence of individuals, and lose their efficacy in proportion to the number combined together, that is, in proportion as their efficacy becomes needful.

From this view of the subject it may be concluded that a pure democracy, by which I mean a society consisting of a small number of citizens, who assemble and administer the government in person, can admit of no cure for the mischiefs of faction. A common passion or interest will, in almost every case, be felt by a majority of the whole; a communication and concert result from the form of government itself; and there is nothing to check the inducements to sacrifice the weaker party or an obnoxious individual. Hence it is that such democracies have ever been spectacles of turbulence and contention; have ever been found incompatible with personal security or the rights of property; and have in general been as short in their lives as they have been violent in their deaths. Theoretic politicians, who have patronized this species of government, have erroneously supposed that by reducing mankind to a perfect equality in their political rights, they would, at the same time, be perfectly equalized and assimilated in their possessions, their opinions, and their passions.

A republic, by which I mean a government in which the scheme of representation takes place, opens a different prospect, and promises the cure for which we are seeking. Let us examine the points in which it varies from pure democracy, and

Article 3. The Size and Variety of the Union as a Check on Faction

we shall comprehend both the nature of the cure and the efficacy which it must derive from the Union.

The two great points of difference between a democracy and a republic are: first, the delegation of the government, in the latter, to a small number of citizens elected by the rest; secondly, the greater number of citizens, and greater sphere of country, over which the latter may be extended.

The effect of the first difference is, on the one hand, to refine and enlarge the public views, by passing them through the medium of a chosen body of citizens, whose wisdom may best discern the true interest of their country, and whose patriotism and love of justice will be least likely to sacrifice it to temporary or partial considerations. Under such a regulation, it may well happen that the public voice, pronounced by the representatives of the people, will be more consonant to the public good than if pronounced by the people themselves, convened for the purpose. On the other hand, the effect may be inverted. Men of factious tempers, of local prejudices, or of sinister designs, may, by intrigue, by corruption, or by other means, first obtain the suffrages, and then betray the interests, of the people. The question resulting is, whether small or extensive republics are more favorable to the election of proper guardians of the public weal; and it is clearly decided in favor of the latter by two obvious considerations.

In the first place, it is to be remarked that, however small the republic may be, the representatives must be raised to a certain number, in order to guard against the cabals of a few; and that, however large it may be, they must be limited to a certain number, in order to guard against the confusion of a multitude. Hence, the number of representatives in the two cases not being in proportion to that of the two constituents, and being proportionally greater in the small republic, it follows that, if the proportion of fit characters be not less in the large than in the small republic, the former will present a greater option, and consequently a greater probability of a fit choice.

In the next place, as each representative will be chosen by a greater number of citizens in the large than in the small republic, it will be more difficult for unworthy candidates to practise with success the vicious arts by which elections are too often carried; and the suffrages of the people being more free, will be more likely to centre in men who possess the most attractive merit and the most diffusive and established characters.

It must be confessed that in this, as in most other cases, there is a mean, on both sides of which inconveniences will be found to lie. By enlarging too much the number of electors, you render the representative too little acquainted with all their local circumstances and lesser interests; as by reducing it too much, you render him unduly attached to these, and too little fit to comprehend and pursue great and national objects. The federal Constitution forms a happy combination in this respect; the great and aggregate interests being referred to the national, the local and particular to the State legislatures.

The other point of difference is, the greater number of citizens and extent of territory which may be brought within the compass of republican than of democratic government; and it is this circumstance principally which renders factious combinations less to be dreaded in the former than in the latter. The smaller the society, the fewer probably will be the distinct parties and interests composing it; the fewer the distinct parties and interests, the more frequently will a majority be found of the same party; and the smaller the number of individuals composing a majority, and the smaller the compass within which they are placed, the more easily will they concert and execute their plans of oppression. Extend the sphere and you take in a greater variety of parties and interests; you will make it less probable that a majority of the whole will have a common motive to invade the rights of other citizens; or if such a common motive exists, it will be more difficult for all who feel it to discover their own strength, and to act in unison with each other. Besides other impediments, it may be remarked that, where there is a consciousness of unjust or dishonorable purposes, communication is always checked by distrust in proportion to the number whose concurrence is necessary.

Hence, it clearly appears, that the same advantage which a republic has over a democracy, in controlling the effects of faction, is enjoyed by a large over a small republic,—is enjoyed by the Union over the States composing it. Does the advantage consist in the substitution of representatives whose enlightened views and virtuous sentiments render them superior to local prejudices and to schemes of injustice? It will not be denied that the representation of the Union will be most likely to possess these requisite endowments. Does it consist in the greater security afforded by a greater variety of parties, against the event of any one party being able to outnumber and oppress the rest? In an equal degree does the increased variety of parties comprised within the Union, increase this security. Does it, in fine, consist in the greater obstacles opposed to the concert and accomplishment of the secret wishes of an unjust and interested majority? Here, again, the extent of the Union gives it the most palpable advantage.

The influence of factious leaders may kindle a flame within their particular States, but will be unable to spread a general conflagration through the other States. A religious sect may degenerate into a political faction in a part of the Confederacy; but the variety of sects dispersed over the entire face of it must secure the national councils against any danger from that source. A rage for paper money, for an abolition of debts, for an equal division of property, or for any other improper or wicked project, will be less apt to pervade the whole body of the Union than a particular member of it; in the same proportion as such a malady is more likely to taint a particular county or district, than an entire State.

In the extent and proper structure of the Union, therefore, we behold a republican remedy for the diseases most incident to republican government. And according to the degree of pleasure and pride we feel in being republicans, ought to be our zeal in cherishing the spirit and supporting the character of Federalists.

PUBLIUS

Federalist No. 10, from *The Federalist Papers*, 1787.

Article 4

Checks and Balances
Federalist No. 51

JAMES MADISON

To the People of the State of New York:

To what expedient, then, shall we finally resort, for maintaining in practice the necessary partition of power among the several departments, as laid down in the Constitution? The only answer that can be given is, that as all these exterior provisions are found to be inadequate, the defect must be supplied, by so contriving the interior structure of the government as that its several constituent parts may, by their mutual relations, be the means of keeping each other in their proper places. Without presuming to undertake a full development of this important idea, I will hazard a few general observations, which may perhaps place it in a clearer light, and enable us to form a more correct judgment of the principles and structure of the government planned by the convention.

In order to lay a due foundation for that separate and distinct exercise of the different powers of government, which to a certain extent is admitted on all hands to be essential to the preservation of liberty, it is evident that each department should have a will of its own; and consequently should be so constituted that the members of each should have as little agency as possible in the appointment of the members of the others. Were this principle rigorously adhered to, it would require that all the appointments for the supreme executive, legislative, and judiciary magistracies should be drawn from the same fountain of authority, the people, through channels having no communication whatever with one another. Perhaps such a plan of constructing the several departments would be less difficult in practice than it may in contemplation appear. Some difficulties, however, and some additional expense would attend the execution of it. Some deviations, therefore, from the principle must be admitted. In the constitution of the judiciary department in particular, it might be inexpedient to insist rigorously on the principle: first, because peculiar qualifications being essential in the members, the primary consideration ought to be to select that mode of choice which best secures these qualifications; secondly, because the permanent tenure by which the appointments are held in that department, must soon destroy all sense of dependence on the authority conferring them.

It is equally evident, that the members of each department should be as little dependent as possible on those of the others, for the emoluments annexed to their offices. Were the executive magistrate, or the judges, not independent of the legislature in this particular, their independence in every other would be merely nominal.

But the great security against a gradual concentration of the several powers in the same department, consists in giving to those who administer each department the necessary constitutional means and personal motives to resist encroachments of the others. The provision for defence must in this, as in all other cases, be made commensurate to the danger of attack. Ambition must be made to counteract ambition. The interest of the man must be connected with the constitutional rights of the place. It may be a reflection on human nature, that such devices should be necessary to control the abuses of government. But what is government itself, but the greatest of all reflections on human nature? If men were angels, no government would be necessary. If angels were to govern men, neither external nor internal controls on government would be necessary. In framing a government which is to be administered by men over men, the great difficulty lies in this: you must first enable the government to control the governed; and in the next place oblige it to control itself. A dependence on the people is, no doubt, the primary control on the government; but experience has taught mankind the necessity of auxiliary precautions.

This policy of supplying, by opposite and rival interests, the defect of better motives, might be traced through the whole system of human affairs, private as well as public. We see it particularly displayed in all the subordinate distributions of power, where the constant aim is to divide and arrange the several offices in such a manner as that each may be a check on the other—that the private interest of every individual may be a sentinel over the public rights. These inventions of prudence cannot be less requisite in the distribution of the supreme powers of the State.

But it is not possible to give to each department an equal power of self-defence. In republican government, the legislative authority necessarily predominates. The remedy for this inconveniency is to divide the legislature into different branches; and to render them, by different modes of election and different

Article 4. Checks and Balances

principles of action, as little connected with each other as the nature of their common functions and their common dependence on the society will admit. It may even be necessary to guard against dangerous encroachments by still further precautions. As the weight of the legislative authority requires that it should be thus divided, the weakness of the executive may require, on the other hand, that it should be fortified. An absolute negative on the legislature appears, at first view, to be the natural defence with which the executive magistrate should be armed. But perhaps it would be neither altogether safe nor alone sufficient. On ordinary occasions it might not be exerted with the requisite firmness, and on extraordinary occasions it might be perfidiously abused. May not this defect of an absolute negative be supplied by some qualified connection between this weaker department and the weaker branch of the stronger department, by which the latter may be led to support the constitutional rights of the former, without being too much detached from the rights of its own department?

If the principles on which these observations are founded be just, as I persuade myself they are, and they be applied as a criterion to the several State constitutions, and to the federal Constitution, it will be found that if the latter does not perfectly correspond with them, the former are infinitely less able to bear such a test.

There are, moreover, two considerations particularly applicable to the federal system of America, which place that system in a very interesting point of view.

First. In a single republic, all the power surrendered by the people is submitted to the administration of a single government; and the usurpations are guarded against by a division of the government into distinct and separate departments. In the compound republic of America, the power surrendered by the people is first divided between two distinct governments, and then the portion allotted to each subdivided among distinct and separate departments. Hence a double security arises to the rights of the people. The different governments will control each other, at the same time that each will be controlled by itself.

Second. It is of great importance in a republic not only to guard the society against the oppression of its rulers, but to guard one part of the society against the injustice of the other part. Different interests necessarily exist in different classes of citizens. If a majority be united by a common interest, the rights of the minority will be insecure. There are but two methods of providing against this evil: the one by creating a will in the community independent of the majority—that is, of the society itself; the other, by comprehending in the society so many separate descriptions of citizens as will render an unjust combination of a majority of the whole very improbable, if not impracticable. The first method prevails in all governments possessing an hereditary or self-appointed authority. This, at best, is but a precarious security; because a power independent of the society may as well espouse the unjust views of the major, as the rightful interests of the minor party, and may possibly be turned against both parties. The second method will be exemplified in the federal republic of the United States. Whilst all authority in it will be derived from and dependent on the society, the society itself will be broken into so many parts, interests and classes of citizens, that the rights of individuals, or of the minority, will be in little danger from interested combinations of the majority. In a free government the security for civil rights must be the same as that for religious rights. It consists in the one case in the multiplicity of interests, and in the other in the multiplicity of sects. The degree of security in both cases will depend on the number of interests and sects; and this may be presumed to depend on the extent of country and number of people comprehended under the same government. This view of the subject must particularly recommend a proper federal system to all the sincere and considerate friends of republican government, since it shows that in exact proportion as the territory of the Union may be formed into more circumscribed Confederacies, or States, oppressive combinations of a majority will be facilitated; the best security, under the republican forms, for the rights of every class of citizens, will be diminished; and consequently the stability and independence of some member of the government, the only other security, must be proportionally increased. Justice is the end of government. It is the end of civil society. It ever has been and ever will be pursued until it be obtained, or until liberty be lost in the pursuit. In a society under the forms of which the stronger faction can readily unite and oppress the weaker, anarchy may as truly be said to reign as in a state of nature, where the weaker individual is not secured against the violence of the stronger; and as, in the latter state, even the stronger individuals are prompted, by the uncertainty of their condition, to submit to a government which may protect the weak as well as themselves; so, in the former state, will the more powerful factions or parties be gradually induced, by a like motive, to wish for a government which will protect all parties, the weaker as well as the more powerful. It can be little doubted that if the State of Rhode Island was separated from the Confederacy and left to itself, the insecurity of rights under the popular form of government within such narrow limits would be displayed by such reiterated oppressions of factious majorities that some power altogether independent of the people would soon be called for by the voice of the very factions whose misrule had proved the necessity of it. In the extended republic of the United States, and among the great variety of interests, parties, and sects which it embraces, a coalition of a majority of the whole society could seldom take place on any other principles than those of justice and the general good; whilst there being thus less danger to a minor from the will of a major party, there must be less pretext, also, to provide for the security of the former, by introducing into the government a will not dependent on the latter, or, in other words, a will independent of the society itself. It is no less certain than it is important, notwithstanding the contrary opinions which have been entertained, that the larger the society, provided it lie within a particular sphere, the more duly capable it will be of self-government. And happily for the *republican cause,* the practicable sphere may be carried to a very great extent, by a judicious modification and mixture of the *federal principle.*

PUBLIUS

Federalist No. 51, from *The Federalist Papers,* 1787.

Can America Fail?

A sympathetic critic issues a wake-up call for an America mired in groupthink and blind to its own shortcomings.

KISHORE MAHBUBANI

In 1981, Singapore's long-ruling People's Action Party was shocked when it suffered its first defeat at the polls in many years, even though the contest was in a single constituency. I asked Dr. Goh Keng Swee, one of Singapore's three founding fathers and the architect of its economic miracle, why the PAP lost. He replied, "Kishore, we failed because we did not even conceive of the possibility of failure."

The simple thesis of this essay is that American society could also fail if it does not force itself to conceive of failure. The massive crises that American society is experiencing now are partly the product of just such a blindness to potential catastrophe. That is not a diagnosis I deliver with rancor. Nations, like individuals, languish when they only have uncritical lovers or unloving critics. I consider myself a loving critic of the United States, a critic who wants American society to succeed. America, I wrote in 2005 in *Beyond the Age of Innocence: Rebuilding Trust Between America and the World*, "has done more good for the rest of the world than any other society." If the United States fails, the world will suffer too.

The first systemic failure America has suffered is groupthink. Looking back at the origins of the current financial crisis, it is amazing that American society accepted the incredible assumptions of economic gurus such as Alan Greenspan and Robert Rubin that unregulated financial markets would naturally deliver economic growth and serve the public good. In 2003, Greenspan posed this question: "The vast increase in the size of the over-the-counter derivatives markets is the result of the market finding them a very useful vehicle. And the question is, should these be regulated?" His own answer was that the state should not go beyond regular banking regulation because "these derivative transactions are transactions among professionals." In short, the financial players would regulate themselves.

This is manifest nonsense. The goal of these financial professionals was always to enhance their personal wealth, not to serve the public interest. So why was Greenspan's nonsense accepted by American society? The simple and amazing answer is that most Americans assumed that their country has a rich and vibrant "marketplace of ideas" in which all ideas are challenged. Certainly, America has the finest media in the world. No subject is taboo. No sacred cow is immune from criticism. But the paradox here is that the *belief* that American society allows every idea to be challenged has led Americans to assume that every idea *is* challenged. They have failed to notice when their minds have been enveloped in groupthink. Again, failure occurs when you do not conceive of failure.

The second systemic failure has been the erosion of the notion of individual responsibility. Here, too, an illusion is at work. Because they so firmly believe that their society rests on a culture of individual responsibility—rather than a culture of entitlement, like the social welfare states of Europe—Americans cannot see how their individual actions have undermined, rather than strengthened, their society. In their heart of hearts, many Americans believe that they are living up to the famous challenge of President John F. Kennedy, "Ask not what your country can do for you—ask what you can do for your country." They believe that they give more than they take back from their own society.

There is a simple empirical test to see whether this is true: Do Americans pay more in taxes to the government than they receive in government services? The answer is clear. Apart from a few years during the Clinton administration, the United States has had many more federal budget deficits than surpluses—and the ostensibly more fiscally responsible Republicans are even guiltier of deficit financing than the Democrats.

The recently departed Bush administration left America with a national debt of more than $10 trillion, compared with the $5.7 trillion left by the Clinton administration. Because of this large debt burden, President Barack Obama has fewer bullets to fire as he faces the biggest national economic crisis in almost a century. The American population has taken away the ammunition he could have used, and left its leaders to pray that China and Japan will continue to buy U.S. Treasury bonds.

How did this happen? Americans have justified the erosion of individual responsibility by demonizing taxes. Every candidate for political office in America runs against taxes. No American politician—including

Article 5. Can America Fail?

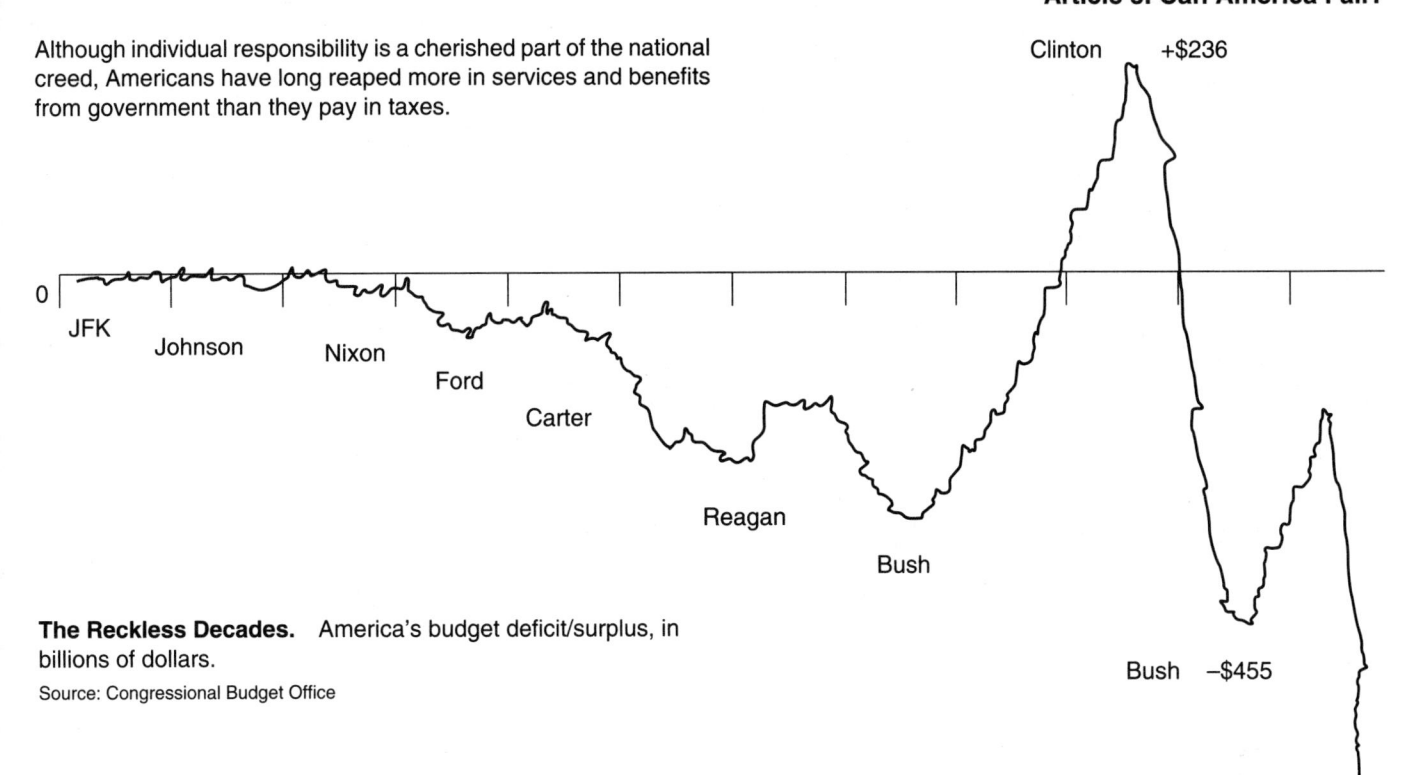

Although individual responsibility is a cherished part of the national creed, Americans have long reaped more in services and benefits from government than they pay in taxes.

Clinton   +$236

JFK
Johnson
Nixon
Ford
Carter
Reagan
Bush

Bush   −$455

Obama
−$1,2
(projected)

The Reckless Decades. America's budget deficit/surplus, in billions of dollars.
Source: Congressional Budget Office

President Obama—dares to tell the truth: that no modern society can function without significant taxes. In some cases, taxes do a lot of good. If Americans were to impose a $1 per gallon tax on gasoline (which they could easily afford), they would begin to solve many of their problems, reducing greenhouse-gas emissions, dependence on Middle East oil, and the production of fuel-inefficient cars and trucks.

The way Americans have dealt with the tax question shows that there is a sharp contradiction between their belief that their society rests on a culture of individual responsibility and the reality that it has been engulfed by a culture of individual irresponsibility. But beliefs are hard to change. Many American myths come from the Wild West era, when lone cowboys struggled and survived supposedly through individual ingenuity alone, without the help of the state. Americans continue to believe that they do not benefit from state support. The reality is that many do.

The third systemic failure of American society is its failure to see how the abuse of American power has created many of the problems the United States now confronts abroad. The best example is 9/11. Americans believe they were innocent victims of an evil attack by Osama bin Laden and Al Qaeda. And there can be no doubt that the victims of 9/11 were innocent. Yet Americans tend to forget the fact that Osama bin Laden and Al Qaeda were essentially created by U.S. policies. In short, a force launched by the United States came back to bite it.

During the Cold War, the United States was looking for a powerful weapon to destabilize the Soviet Union. It found it when it created a pan-Islamic force of mujahideen fighters, drawn from countries as diverse as Algeria and Indonesia, to roll back the Soviet invasion of Afghanistan after 1979. For a time, American interests and the interests of the Islamic world converged, and the fighters drove the Soviets out and contributed to the collapse of the Soviet Union. At the same time, however, America also awakened the sleeping dragon of Islamic solidarity.

Yet when the Cold War ended, America thoughtlessly disengaged from Afghanistan and the powerful Islamic forces it had supported there. To make matters worse, it switched its Middle East policy from a relatively evenhanded one on the Israel-Palestine issue to one heavily weighted toward the Israelis. Aaron David Miller, a longtime U.S. Middle East negotiator who served under both the Clinton and George W. Bush administrations (and is now a public-policy scholar at the Woodrow Wilson Center), wrote recently that both administrations "scrupulously" road-tested every idea and proposal with Israel before bringing it to the Palestinians.

Americans seem only barely aware of the pain and suffering of the Palestinian people, and the sympathy their plight stirs in the world's 1.2 billion Muslims, who hold America responsible for the Palestinians' condition. And tragically, in the long run, a conflict between six million Israelis and 1.2 billion Muslims would bring grief to Israel. Hence, Americans should seriously review their Middle East policies.

The Middle East is only one of many areas in which American policies have harmed the world. From U.S. cotton subsidies, which have hurt poor African farmers, to the invasion of Iraq; from Washington's double standard on nuclear proliferation—calling on non-nuclear states to abide by the Nuclear Non-Proliferation Treaty while ignoring its own obligations—to its decision to walk away from the Kyoto Protocol without providing an alternate approach to global warming, many American policies have injured the 6.5 billion other people who inhabit the world.

Why aren't Americans aware of this? The reason is that virtually all analysis by American intellectuals rests on the assumption that *problems* come from outside America and America provides only *solutions*. Yet the rest of the world can see clearly that American power has created many of the world's major problems. American thinkers and policymakers cannot see this because they are engaged in an incestuous, self-referential, and self-congratulatory discourse. They have lost the ability to listen to other voices on the planet because they cannot conceive of the possibility that they are not already listening. But until they begin to open their ears, America's problems with the world will continue.

American thinkers and policy-makers have lost the ability to listen to other voices on the planet.

It will not be easy for America to change course, because many of its problems have deep structural causes. To an outsider, it is plain to see that structural failures have developed in America's governance, in its social contract, and in its response to globalization. Many Americans still cannot see this.

When Americans are asked to identify what makes them proudest of their society, they inevitably point to its democratic character. And there can be no doubt that America has the most successful democracy in the world. Yet it may also have some of the most corrupt governance in the world. The reason more Americans are not aware of this is that most of the corruption is legal.

In democracies, the role of government is to serve the public interest. Americans believe that they have a government "of the people, by the people, and for the people." The reality is more complex. It looks more like a government "of the people, by special-interest groups, and for special-interest groups." In the theory of democracy, corrupt and ineffective politicians are thrown out by elections. Yet the fact that more than 90 percent of incumbents who seek reelection to the U.S. House of Representatives are reelected provides a clear warning that all is not well. In *The Audacity of Hope* (2006), Barack Obama himself describes the corruption of the political system and the public's low regard for politicians. "All of which leads to the conclusion that if we want anything to change in Washington, we'll need to throw the rascals out. And yet year after year we keep the rascals right where they are, with the reelection rate for House members hovering at around 96 percent," Obama writes. Why? "These days, almost every congressional district is drawn by the ruling party with computer-driven precision to ensure that a clear majority of Democrats or Republicans reside within its borders. Indeed, it's not a stretch to say that most voters no longer choose their representatives; instead, representatives choose their voters."

The net effect of this corruption is that American governmental institutions and processes are now designed to protect special interests rather than public interests. As the financial crisis has revealed with startling clarity, regulatory agencies such as the Securities and Exchange Commission and the Commodity Futures Trading Commission have been captured by the industries they are supposed to regulate. And when Congress opens the government's purse, the benefits flow to special interests rather than the public interest. Few Americans are aware how severely special interests undermine their own national interests, both at home and abroad. The latest two world trade negotiating rounds (including the present Doha Round), for example, have been held hostage by the American agricultural lobbies. To protect 25,000 rich American cotton farmers, the United States has jeopardized the interests of the rest of the 6.8 billion people in the world.

When congress opens the government's purse, the benefits flow to special interests rather than the public interest.

Normally, a crisis provides a great opportunity to change course. Yet the current crisis has elicited tremendous delay, obfuscation, and pandering to special interests. From afar, America's myopia is astounding and incomprehensible. When the stimulus packages of the Chinese and U.S. governments emerged at about the same time, I scanned American publications in search of attempts to compare the two measures. I could not find any. This confirmed my suspicion that American intellectuals and policymakers could not even conceive of the possibility that the Chinese effort may be smarter or better designed than the American one.

An even bigger structural failure that American society may face is the collapse of its social contract. The general assumption in the United States is that American society remains strong and cohesive because every citizen has an equal chance to succeed. Because most Americans believe they have had the same opportunity, there is little resentment when a Bill Gates or a Sergey Brin amasses a great fortune.

This ideal of equal opportunity is a useful national myth. But when the gap between myth and reality becomes too wide, the myth cannot be sustained. Today, research shows that social mobility in the United States has declined significantly. In the 2008 report *The Measure of America*, a research group, the American Human Development Project, notes that "the average income of the top fifth of U.S. households in 2006 was almost 15 times that of those in the lowest fifth—or $168,170 versus $11,352." The researchers also observe that "social mobility is now less fluid in the United States than in other affluent nations. Indeed, a poor child born in Germany, France, Canada, or one of the Nordic countries has a better chance to join the middle class in adulthood than an American child born into similar circumstances."

Behind these statistics are some harsh realities. Nearly one in five American children lives in poverty, and more than one in 13 lives in extreme poverty. African-American babies are more than twice as likely as white or Latino babies to die before reaching their first birthday. People in more than half a million households experience hunger, data from the U.S. Department of Agriculture indicate. The education system is both inegalitarian and ineffective. In a recent international assessment of subject-matter literacy in 57 countries, America's 15-year-olds ranked 24th in mathematics and 17th in science. It should come as no surprise that though the United States ranks second among 177 countries in per capita income, it ranks only 12th in terms of human development.

More dangerously, many of those who have grown wealthy in the past few decades have added little of real economic value to society. Instead, they have created "financial weapons of mass destruction," and now they continue to expect rich bonuses even after they delivered staggering losses. Their behavior demonstrates a remarkable decline of American values and, more important, the deterioration of the implicit social contract between the wealthy and the rest of society. It would be fatal for America if the wealthy classes were to lose the trust and confidence of the broader American body politic. But many of America's wealthy cannot even conceive of this possibility. This explains why so few of the Richard Fulds and John Thains have apologized with any sincerity for the damage they have done.

America's latest responses to globalization also reveal symptoms of a structural failure. Hitherto, Americans have been champions of globalization because they have believed that their own economy, the most competitive in the world, would naturally triumph as countries lowered their trade and tariff barriers. This belief has been an important force driving the world trading system toward greater openness.

Today, in a sign of great danger for the United States and for the world, the American people are losing confidence in their ability to compete with Chinese and Indian workers. More and more American politicians are jumping on the protectionist bandwagon (although almost all of them dishonestly claim they are not protectionists). Even the American intelligentsia is retreating from its once stout defense of free trade. Paul Krugman of Princeton and The *New York Times,* who won the Nobel Prize for Economics in 2008, showed which way the wind was blowing when he wrote, "It's hard to avoid the conclusion that growing U.S. trade with Third World countries reduces the real wages of many and perhaps most workers in this country. And that reality makes the politics of trade very difficult."

At the moment of their country's greatest economic vulnerability in many decades, few Americans dare to speak the truth and say that the United States cannot retreat from globalization. Both the American people and the world would be worse off. However, as globalization and global capitalism create new forces of "creative destruction," America will have to restructure its economy and society in order to compete. It will need to confront its enormously wasteful and inefficient health care policies and the deteriorating standards of its public education system. It must finally confront its economic failures as well, and stop rewarding them. If General Motors, Chrysler, and Ford cannot compete, it will be futile to protect them. They, too, have failed because they could not conceive of failure.

Every problem has a solution. This has always been the optimistic American view. It is just as true in bad times as in good times. But painful problems do not often have painless solutions. This is equally true of the current economic crisis. To deal with it, American leaders must add an important word when they speak the truth to the American people. The word is *sacrifice*. There can be no solution to America's problems without sacrifice.

One paradox of the human condition is that the most logical point at which to undertake painful reform is in good times. The pain will be less then. But virtually no society, and especially no democratic society, can administer significant pain in good times. It takes a crisis to make change possible. Hence, there is a lot of wisdom in the principle, "never waste a crisis."

Let me suggest for purely illustrative purposes three painful reforms the United States should consider now. The goal of these suggestions is to trigger a serious discussion of reform in American discourse.

First, there is a silver bullet that can dispel some of the doom and gloom enveloping the world and admit a little hope. And hope is what we need to get the economic wheels turning in the right direction. As Amartya Sen, another Nobel laureate in economics, said recently, "Once an economy is in the grip of pessimism, you cannot change it just by changing the objective circumstance, because the lack of confidence in people makes the economy almost unrescuable. You have to address the confidence thing, and that requires a different type of agenda than we have." The completion of the Doha Round of world trade talks would go a long way toward restoring that confidence. The good news is that the deal is almost 95 percent cooked. But the last five percent is the most difficult.

One of the key obstacles to the completion of the Doha Round is the resistance of those 25,000 rich American cotton farmers. Millions of their poor West African counterparts will not accept a Doha Round agreement without a removal of the U.S. cotton subsidies that unfairly render their own crops uncompetitive. In both moral and rational terms, the decision should be obvious. The interests of the 6.8 billion people who will benefit from a successful Doha Round are more important than the interests of 25,000 American farmers. This handful of individuals should not be allowed to veto a global trade deal.

America's rich cotton farmers are also in the best position to make a sacrifice. Collectively, they have received more than $3 billion a year in subsidies over the last eight years, a total of about $1 million each. If they cannot make a sacrifice, who in America can? Where is the American politician with the courage to say this?

America has a second silver bullet it can use: a $1 per gallon tax on gasoline. To prevent the diversion of the resulting revenues into pork barrel projects, the money should be firewalled and used only to promote energy efficiency and address the challenge of climate change. Last year, the United States consumed more than 142 billion gallons of gas. Hence, even allowing for a change in consumption, a gas tax could easily raise more than $100 billion per year to address energy challenges.

This sounds like a painful sacrifice, one that America's leaders can hardly conceive of asking, yet it is surprising that Americans did not complain when they effectively paid a tax of well over $1 per gallon to Saudi Arabia and other oil producers when oil prices surged last year. Then, the price at the pump was more than $4 a gallon. Today, with world oil prices hovering around only $40 a barrel, the price per gallon is around half its peak price. A $1 tax would still leave gas relatively cheap.

This brings me to the third silver bullet: Every American politician should declare that the long-term interests of the country are more important than his or her personal political career. As leaders, they should be prepared to make the ultimate political sacrifice in order to speak the truth: The time has come for Americans to spend less and work harder. This would be an extraordinary commitment for politicians anywhere in the world, but it is precisely politics as usual that led the United States to today's debacle.

The latest budget presented to Congress by President Obama offers a great opportunity for change. Instead of tearing the budget apart in pursuit of narrow interests and larding it with provisions for special interests, Congress has the opportunity to help craft a rational plan to help people at the bottom, promote universal health care, and create incentives to enhance American competitiveness.

I know that such a rational budget is almost totally inconceivable to the American body politic. The American political system has become so badly clogged with special interests that it resembles a diseased heart. When an individual develops coronary blockages, he or she knows that the choices are massive surgery or a massive heart attack. The fact that the American body politic cannot conceive of the possibility that its clogged political arteries could lead to a catastrophic heart attack is an indication that American society cannot conceive of failure. And if you cannot conceive of failure, failure comes.

KISHORE MAHBUBANI, dean of the Lee Kuan Yew School of Public Policy at the National University of Singapore, is the author most recently of *The New Asian Hemisphere: The Irresistible Shift of Global Power to the East* (2008).

From *The Wilson Quarterly*, Spring 2009, pp. 48–54. Copyright © 2009 by Kishore Mahbubani. Reprinted by permission of Kishore Mahbubani.

The Right Bite

There are five maxims the federal government can follow to regain the public confidence it has lost over the past four decades.

WILLIAM A. GALSTON

One of the puzzles of our age is why Americans distrust their own government so deeply. Against the inescapable and well-publicized cases of failure by the federal government must be weighed a remarkable half-century record of accomplishment. The federal government has cleaned up our air and water, improved safety in the workplace, spurred immense amounts of scientific and medical research, and underwritten technological innovations, such as the computer and the Internet, that have transformed our society. It has dramatically reduced poverty among the elderly while ensuring their access to medical care. It has expanded both individual freedom and social inclusion—for women, racial and ethnic minorities, and people with disabilities, among others. The list goes on. Yet despite this record, trust in the federal government now stands at the lowest level ever recorded. That is not merely a riddle for academicians. Without the public's confidence it becomes ever more difficult for government to do its job effectively.

We might be tempted to seek an explanation in recent failures, such as an unpopular war, economic crisis, and the monumentally botched response to Hurricane Katrina. But the decline began long ago. As recently as the mid-1960s, about 70 percent of Americans reported that they trusted the federal government. That number then dropped steadily, with only modest interruptions, before bottoming out at 21 percent in the early 1990s. The peace and prosperity of the Clinton years brought it back up, but only to about 40 percent—little more than half its post–World War II peak. After another rise early in George W. Bush's first term, it has steadily declined and now stands at 17 percent. We are mired, it seems, in a long cycle of diminished trust, decoupled—at least in part—from government's performance. The question is why.

One possibility is that the two decades after World War II are a misleading baseline. Compared with those of other advanced societies, America's public culture is basically antistatist, skeptical at best about concentrated public power. Government's successful response to the Great Depression and the fascist threat shifted the mainstream, this argument goes, but only temporarily. As memories of crisis faded and a generation reached maturity, public sentiment would inevitably have reverted to its deeply rooted default setting, a process accelerated by the Vietnam War, Watergate, and the "Great Inflation" of the 1970s. As Hugh Heclo, a leading scholar of political institutions, puts it, "We are disposed to distrust institutions. That is the basic fact of life we share as modern people. . . . We are compelled to live in a thick tangle of institutions while believing that they do not have our best interests at heart."

While we cannot dismiss this hypothesis out of hand, we must consider that trust in state and local government remained relatively stable even as trust in the federal government plunged. We cannot explain this divergence as a response to the sheer growth of federal activities: By many measures, state and local governments have expanded at least as fast. Nor can it be said that state and local governments are more honest, less self-dealing, or less corrupt. Heclo himself notes that the most logical consequence of America's quasi-libertarian tradition is skepticism about the federal government, not the cynicism that prevails today. It is the move from skepticism to outright cynicism that needs explaining.

One possibility is that the news media's turn from supportive to adversarial during the 1970s exacerbated mistrust by bringing to light mistakes and misdeeds in Washington that would have remained hidden in earlier times. There's something to this, but the withdrawal of public trust was under way well before Bob Woodward and Carl Bernstein broke the Watergate story and made investigative journalism fashionable. The public's response to events—real or perceived—changed the tone of public life and created an opportunity that journalists alertly filled.

The remaining possibility is that something about the qualitative expansion of federal power—about the additional responsibilities the federal government has taken on and the way in which it discharges them—is the reason for its diminished standing. Here there is much to say.

Since the New Deal, Americans have held the federal government accountable for the performance of the economy. In the quarter-century after World War II, this expanded responsibility seemed unproblematic: The economy grew steadily, with low inflation, and Americans at every income level experienced rising living standards. Among officials and citizens alike, confidence grew that Keynesian economics offered the tools needed to mute the inevitable downturns and spur non-inflationary growth whose fruits would be widely shared. But at the moment that complacency peaked (Richard M. Nixon famously declared that "we are all Keynesians now"), new developments—slower growth, higher inflation, increasing inequality, and threats to U.S. manufacturing supremacy—challenged government competence and eroded public confidence.

At roughly the same time, the elite consensus on fundamentals was breaking down. Liberals and conservatives parted ways on economics and foreign policy, and the duopoly that had kept most racial and cultural issues off the federal government's agenda gave way to national action and contestation. When combined with government's expanded reach, rancorous and prolonged disputes among elites further weakened public confidence.

Some have argued that starting with the civil rights and voting rights legislation of the mid-1960s, the federal government's efforts to advance racial equality led to a withdrawal of trust among white Americans. The facts do not support this view. Whites and blacks expressed trust in the federal government at equal (and high) rates until 1968, after which trust declined more rapidly among blacks than among whites for a number of years before measures for the two groups converged again in the late 1970s. It may well be the case, however, that public controversy over government's role in race relations exacerbated the decline across the board.

In civil rights and many other areas, expanding government bypassed the tiered constraints of the federal system and established direct links between Washington and localities, or with the people themselves. The federal government not only created new conflicts with mayors and governors but also assumed responsibilities that often exceeded its ability to act effectively. Although the Elementary and Secondary Education Act of 1965 aimed to reduce inequalities between rich and poor districts, the federal government provided less than 10 percent of total funding for the nation's public schools and had limited authority, at most, to alter local school practices. A gap between promise and performance was inevitable. All too often, the federal government used legislative authorizations to proclaim expansive good intentions while proving unable or unwilling to back up those intentions with commensurate resources.

During the New Deal, a new kind of governance had arisen, as Congress increasingly set only general goals in legislation, leaving it to government agencies to give form and substance to national policies through regulations and other administrative tools. The presidencies of Lyndon B. Johnson and Richard Nixon expanded this strategy into a host of new areas, from workplace safety and racial equity to environmental regulation. While yielding some real accomplishments, the new "administrative state," as political scientists called it, produced unintended harmful consequences. As former Harvard president Derek Bok has argued, federal agencies tended to develop regulations without adequately consulting the people they affected, generating charges that elites and "faceless bureaucrats" were running roughshod over democracy. Litigation surged, slowing the translation of purposes into policy. As agencies with overlapping jurisdictions issued conflicting directives, compliance costs rose. And many citizens experienced regulations—for example, limiting construction on their property to preserve wetlands—as invasions of what they had long considered their personal rights and liberties.

This was but one instance of a more general problem: As government activities ramified through society, interactions between citizens and the federal government multiplied. All too often, in areas ranging from drivers' licenses and home improvement permits to voter registration, government was slow moving, unresponsive, and maddeningly hard to navigate. Interaction often bred dissatisfaction. As the private sector deployed new technologies to improve customer service, government suffered by comparison.

Even at its best, however, government could not hope to be as flexible as the private sector at its best can be. In the first place, the exercise of public power requires public authorization, direct or indirect, a process that is bound to be more cumbersome than everyday corporate decision-making. Second, government is committed to norms of procedural fairness that tug against efficiency. This fact reflects Americans' historic aversion to concentrated power as well as a more recent mistrust of unchecked administrative discretion. Public infrastructure projects, for example, now must run a gauntlet of public meetings, environmental impact statements, and multilayered policy reviews that can last for a decade—longer than the entire New Deal era. Unless citizens are prepared to relax their guard, they will have to accept a government that moves more slowly than the private sector in making decisions; implementing, reviewing, and adjusting those decisions; and firing incompetent or redundant employees.

Many of the federal government's new responsibilities strained against the limits of its effectiveness. The key issue, however, turned out to be qualitative, not quantitative. For example, though large and increasingly costly, Social Security proved relatively straightforward to administer: Government collected payroll taxes at a flat rate, kept records of contributions, and made payments to retirees based on a clear formula that left little room for bureaucratic discretion. Every month, the Social Security Administration, with only 62,000 employees, efficiently dispenses billions of dollars in benefits to 55 million Americans. To the extent that it involved more than writing checks, winning the Johnson-era "war on poverty" turned out to be far more difficult. And it proved impossible to honor the new commitment to eliminate racial segregation in public education; residential mobility defeated efforts of bureaucrats and courts to establish and maintain racially balanced jurisdictions.

Government is now called upon to exercise a degree of foresight that exceeds its competence.

Citizens' enlarged expectations make matters worse. Government is now called upon to exercise a degree of foresight—about the performance of the economy, the future costs of present commitments, the behavior of adversaries, and much else—that exceeds its competence (indeed, anyone's competence). Contingency and risk are built into social life. Beyond a certain point, the effort to increase security becomes futile, even self-defeating.

Nor is it possible wholly to avoid administrative error, a fact that legislators and the news media often overlook. When officials fear that they will be pilloried for isolated mistakes, they will manage defensively, impairing government innovation and effectiveness. Although the cost of excessive caution is harder to measure than that of recklessness, it is no less real. After a period in which home loan standards were relaxed to an absurd degree, we are in danger of lurching to the other extreme, making mortgages inaccessible to all but gold-plated borrowers. We would do well to remember the old maxim that a loan officer who never makes a bad loan is a bad loan officer, and adapt it to government: An administrator who never makes a mistake is probably too cautious.

So what is to be done? There is no manual for improving government's performance, let alone the public's assessment of it. But heeding a few simple (at least simple to state) maxims would make matters better over time.

The first is to focus on the basics. The people expect the national government to keep the economy on an even keel, exercise a measure of foresight, win the wars it decides to wage, and deal effectively with disasters. In recent years, government has done poorly in all these areas. The new administration and Congress must do better.

Second, federal officials in every branch of government must be more conscious of the need to align their promises with the limits of feasible performance. While we can reasonably hope to move our transportation system away from fossil fuels during the next generation, "energy independence" is beyond reach. The constant use of that phrase does nothing to reduce public cynicism.

Third, leaders must be more honest about the costs as well as benefits of the measures they support. In the debate over how to reduce greenhouse-gas emissions, for example, many elected officials prefer a "cap-and-trade" strategy rather than a carbon tax because they think the public would rebel against a new tax. But most specialists agree that a cap-and-trade system would drive up consumers' costs just as much as the tax, albeit indirectly, and might also invite corruption in the distribution of pollution quotas. The deliberate attempt to obscure the link between a policy decision and its consequences will exacerbate mistrust without improving performance.

Fourth, pay attention to institutional design. After the end of the Cold War, Washington reduced the effectiveness of our public diplomacy by abolishing the independent U.S. Information Agency and folding its functions into the State Department, where its old mission of promoting American ideas and values conflicted with Foggy Bottom's culture of conflict avoidance and diplomacy. Incorporating the Federal Emergency Management Agency into the new, behemoth Department of Homeland Security contributed to the federal government's disastrous response to Hurricane Katrina. Conversely, as the United States imports increasing quantities of food from countries around the world, the failure to establish a single, unified agency to oversee food safety has been steadily increasing risks, some of which are already becoming realities. High-profile consternation over the adulteration of Chinese-manufactured powdered milk is a warning sign that we should not ignore.

Fifth, as Elaine Kamarck, the director of the National Performance Review during the Clinton administration, has argued, policies should be designed with effective implementation firmly in mind: Pick the right means to each end. For any particular initiative, policymakers can choose to use reformed bureaucracies, networks, or market mechanisms to accomplish their goals. For some purposes, moving away from public institutions to contracts with the private sector or nonprofit institutions may work best. (This is one of the principal arguments in favor of President George W. Bush's faith-based initiative, which President Barack Obama has pledged to continue.) For others—environmental regulation and health insurance are frequently cited examples—it may make sense to use public power to create market mechanisms. In every case, however, employing public power and resources requires effective mechanisms of oversight and accountability. "Contracting out" will not achieve its intended purpose if contract recipients misappropriate funds or do shoddy work, and public confidence will be further weakened.

Policymakers must stop the vicious circle in which mistrust breeds inaction and thus exacerbates mistrust. We need to set in motion a virtuous circle of reform.

Public policies cannot succeed in democracies without sustainable public support. In order to restore public confidence in government, policymakers must stop the vicious circle in which mistrust breeds inaction and thus exacerbates mistrust. We need to set in motion a virtuous circle of reform. That means adopting measures that make people's lives better, step by step, without violating their intuitive sense of how much government should try to do and how it should go about doing it.

WILLIAM A. GALSTON is a senior fellow at the Brookings Institution, where he holds the Ezra Zilkha Chair in Governance Studies. A former deputy assistant for domestic policy to President Bill Clinton, he is the author most recently of *Public Matters: Politics, Policy, and Religion in the 21st Century* (2005).

From *The Wilson Quarterly*, Winter 2009, pp. 50–54. Copyright © 2009 by William A. Galston. Reprinted by permission of William A. Galston.

Progressivism Goes Mainstream

New research on ideology refutes the conservative myth that America is a "center right" nation.

JOHN HALPIN AND RUY TEIXEIRA

President Barack Obama's stimulus package, his joint address to Congress, and his 2010 budget have sent conservatives into fits of indignation over the supposed radicalism of the new president's agenda. Dusting off red-scare rhetoric from the early years of Franklin Roosevelt's presidency, Minority Leader John Boehner declared Obama's initiatives on energy, health care, and education to be "one big down payment on a new American socialist experiment." At the Conservative Political Action Conference held at the end of February, Sen. Jim DeMint of South Carolina implored the young activists to "take to the streets to stop America's slide into socialism." Former presidential candidate Mike Huckabee added, "The Union of Soviet Socialist Republics may be dead, but the Union of American Socialist Republics is being born!" *National Review*, taking a slightly more measured tone in confronting the specter of collectivist tyranny, asked historians and other academics, "Is Ayn Rand freshly relevant in the Age of Obama?"

How do we make sense of all this righteous anger? Are conservatives tapping into a deep-seated aversion to progressive government among the electorate? Hardly. Not unlike the characters in Rand's various fantasies of libertarian anarchy, conservatives today are living in an alternative universe. And the sooner they wake up to this reality the better off they will be.

The 2008 presidential election not only solidified partisan shifts to the Democratic Party, it also marked a significant transformation in the ideological and electoral landscape of America. In two major studies of American beliefs and demographic trends—the *State of American Political Ideology, 2009* and *New Progressive America*, both conducted by the Progressive Studies Program at the Center for American Progress—we found that the president's agenda reflects deep and growing consensus among the American public about the priorities and values that should guide our government and society. Not surprisingly, conservatives are the ones who are out of line with the values of most Americans.

The rise of progressivism in America today is reflected most directly in public ratings of various ideological approaches. Today more than two-thirds of Americans rate a "progressive" approach to politics favorably, a 25-point increase in favorability over the last five years, with gains coming primarily from those who were previously unaware of the term. "Progressive" now equals "conservative" in terms of overall public favorability (67 percent, respectively). Both the "liberal" and "libertarian" labels enjoy much lower overall favorability, with only a plurality of Americans rating each positively. (As a side note, conservative elites might want to rethink their Ayn Rand obsession: a mere 35 percent of self-identified conservatives rate the term "libertarian" favorably, only 10-points higher than their rating of "liberal.")

Employing an innovative measurement of Americans' ideological self-identification, our study expanded the traditional liberal-moderate-conservative test with a five-point measure that more accurately reflects the dominant ideologies in politics today. Under this approach, roughly a third of Americans classify themselves as "progressive" or "liberal," a third are self-described "moderate" or "other," and just over a third label themselves "conservative" or "libertarian." After a follow-up question that pushes moderates to choose between the other ideological approaches, a roughly even left-right breakdown surfaces: 47 percent of Americans are "progressive" or "liberal" and 48 percent are "conservative" or "libertarian." The notion that we are a center-right nation is certainly exaggerated.

On a more substantive level, beyond ideological labels, we presented Americans with a series of 40 statements, split evenly between progressive and conservative ideas. Examining the results, it is clear that public acceptance of the Reagan-Bush model of conservatism—limited government, tax cuts, traditional values, and military strength—has given way to a broad and deep cross section of the American public now holding solidly progressive attitudes about government and society.

Nearly 80 percent of Americans agree that "government investments in education, infrastructure, and science are necessary to ensure America's long-term economic growth." Overall, the unanimity of opinion found on this issue is rare, showing that conservatives are out of step with the rest of the country in opposing new government investments. More than two in three Americans agree that "government has a responsibility to provide financial support for the poor, the sick, and the elderly,"

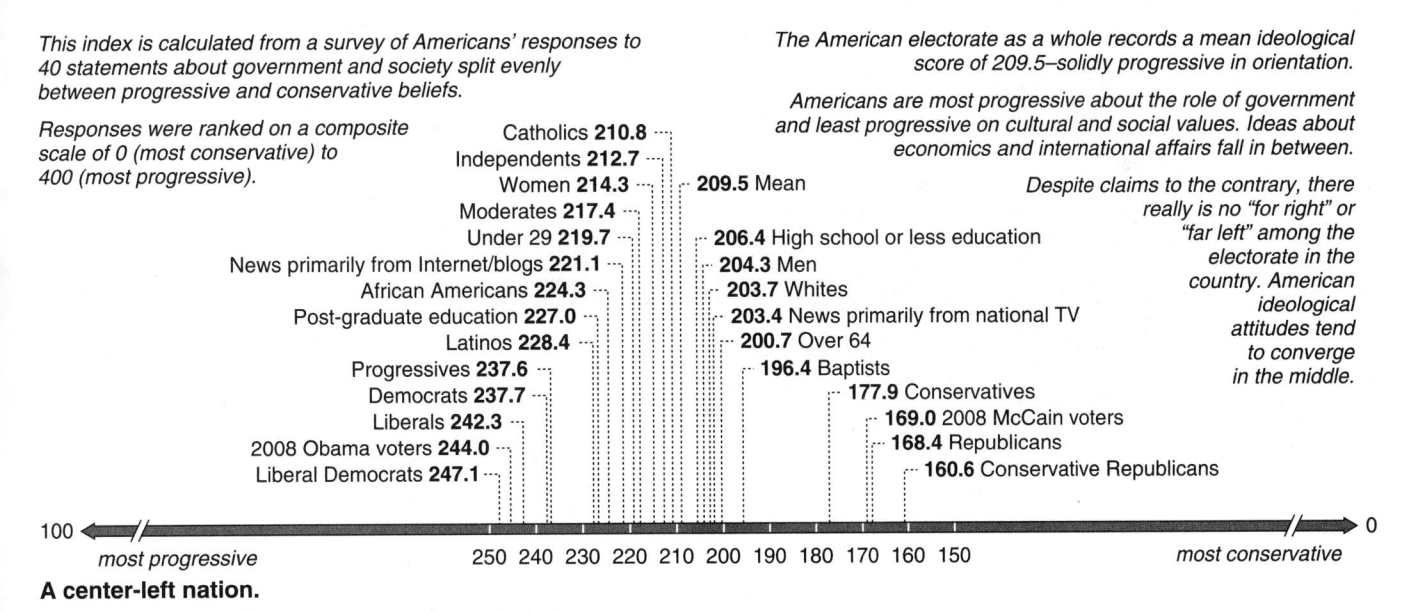

Article 7. Progressivism Goes Mainstream

This index is calculated from a survey of Americans' responses to 40 statements about government and society split evenly between progressive and conservative beliefs.

Responses were ranked on a composite scale of 0 (most conservative) to 400 (most progressive).

The American electorate as a whole records a mean ideological score of 209.5–solidly progressive in orientation.

Americans are most progressive about the role of government and least progressive on cultural and social values. Ideas about economics and international affairs fall in between.

Despite claims to the contrary, there really is no "for right" or "far left" among the electorate in the country. American ideological attitudes tend to converge in the middle.

Catholics **210.8**
Independents **212.7**
Women **214.3** — **209.5** Mean
Moderates **217.4**
Under 29 **219.7** — **206.4** High school or less education
News primarily from Internet/blogs **221.1** — **204.3** Men
African Americans **224.3** — **203.7** Whites
Post-graduate education **227.0** — **203.4** News primarily from national TV
Latinos **228.4** — **200.7** Over 64
Progressives **237.6** — **196.4** Baptists
Democrats **237.7** — **177.9** Conservatives
Liberals **242.3** — **169.0** 2008 McCain voters
2008 Obama voters **244.0** — **168.4** Republicans
Liberal Democrats **247.1** — **160.6** Conservative Republicans

100 ← most progressive   250 240 230 220 210 200 190 180 170 160 150   most conservative → 0

A center-left nation.

Source: Progressive studies program measure of composite ideology

---

while 15 percent are neutral and another 15 percent disagree. Democrats remain almost unanimously supportive, and independents lean strongly toward this progressive position. A slim majority of Republicans similarly agree.

While conservative elites have long held government regulation as an impediment to economic growth, nearly three in four Americans disagree, believing instead that "government regulations are necessary to keep businesses in check and protect workers and consumers." Once again, there is surprising partisan and ideological harmony among Americans, with agreement topping 60 percent among both Republicans and conservatives. Seventy-six percent of Americans also agree with the president's argument that "America's economic future requires a transformation away from oil, gas, and coal to renewable energy sources such as wind and solar," with 12 percent neutral and just 11 percent who say such a transformation is not needed. A major pillar of Obama's economic vision, and the key to his cost-containment strategies, is ensuring affordable health coverage for all Americans. Nearly 65 percent of Americans are on board with this goal, including 44 percent who strongly agree that "the federal government should guarantee affordable health coverage for every American."

Complementing these consensus political values are significant demographic and electoral shifts that favor progressives. Obama's 53 percent of the popular vote in 2008 represents the largest share of the popular vote received by any presidential candidate in 20 years. The last candidate to register that level of support was George H. W. Bush, who won by an identical 53 percent-to-46 percent margin in 1988. Separated by 20 years, the two elections are mirror images of one another, but with conservatives on the winning end of the first and progressives on the winning end of the second.

What happened to create such a reversal? In those intervening 20 years, a new progressive America has emerged, with a new demography, a new geography, and a new agenda. The share of black, Asian, and Hispanic voters in presidential elections has risen by 11 percentage points, while the share of increasingly progressive, white, college-graduate voters has risen by four points. But the share of white working-class voters, who have remained conservative in their orientation, has plummeted by 15 points. This pattern is repeated in state after state, helping to send these areas in a progressive direction. For example, in Pennsylvania the white working-class population declined by 25 points between 1988 and 2008, while white college graduates rose by 16 points and people of color rose by 8 points. And in Nevada, the white working class is down 24 points over the same time period, while voters of color are up an astounding 19 points and white college graduates are up by 4 points.

This shift strengthens the progressive agenda and will continue to strengthen it in the future as the decline of the white working class and the rise in more progressive populations continues. By 2050, the country will be 54 percent people of color as Hispanics double from 15 percent to 30 percent of the population, Asians increase from 5 percent to 9 percent, and African Americans move from 14 percent to 15 percent.

Other key progressive constituencies are expected to grow as well. The millennial generation—those born between 1978 and 2000—gave Obama a stunning 66 percent-to-32 percent margin in 2008. Between now and 2018, millennials of voting age will increase by 4.5 million a year. Professionals, single women, and college-educated women are other growing groups that heavily favor progressives.

Geographic trends are equally important. Progressive gains since 1988 have been heavily concentrated in not just the urbanized cores of large metro areas but also the growing suburbs around them. Even in exurbia, progressives have made big gains. Only in the smallest metro areas and in rural America were progressive gains minimal. And only in the most isolated, least populated rural counties did progressives actually lose ground.

Central 207.2
East 217.6
West 213.0
South 204.6

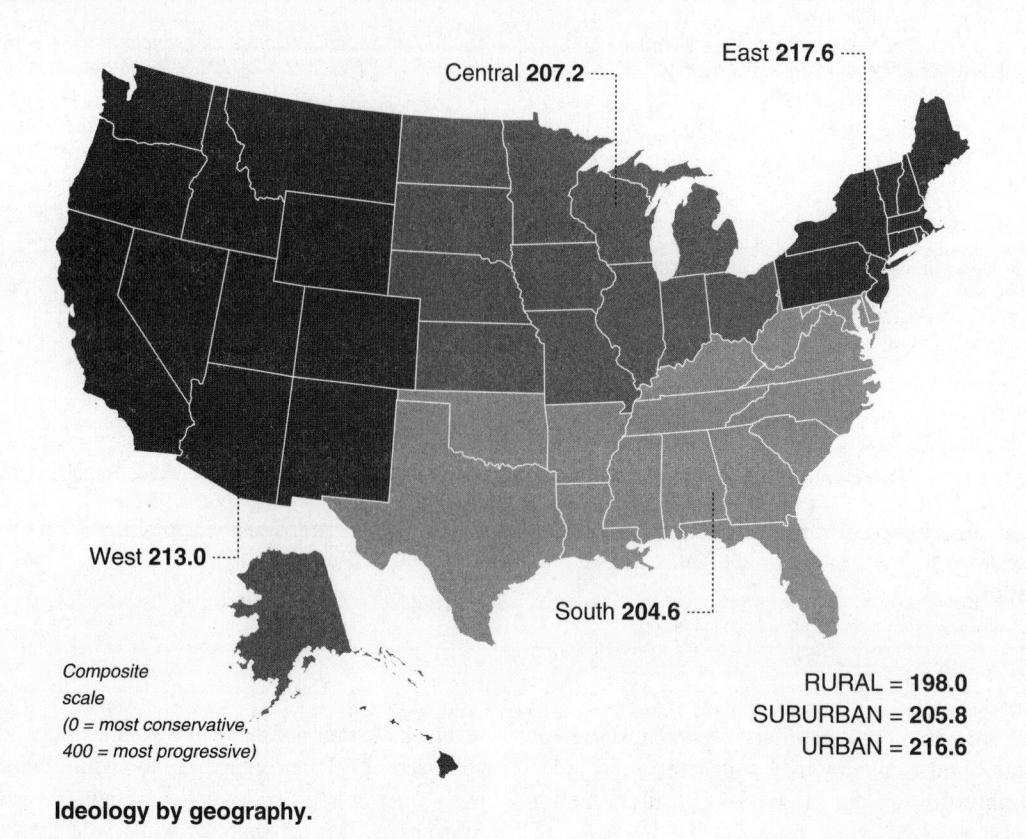

Composite scale
(0 = most conservative, 400 = most progressive)

RURAL = 198.0
SUBURBAN = 205.8
URBAN = 216.6

Ideology by geography.

Within states, there is a persistent pattern of strong progressive shifts in fast-growing metropolitan areas. In Colorado, Obama improved over Kerry's margin by 14 points in the fast-growing Denver metro area and made his greatest gains in the even-faster-growing Denver suburbs. In Nevada, Obama carried the Las Vegas metro area by 19 points, which was 14 points better than Kerry did in 2004 and 35 points better than Michael Dukakis did in 1988. In Florida, Obama won the Orlando metro area by 9 points, a 17-point gain over 2004 and an amazing 48-point shift since 1988. In Virginia, Obama dominated the D.C. suburbs, the growth engine of the state, by 19 points—15 points more than Kerry and 38 points more than Dukakis. The story is the same in state after state: Where America is growing the most, progressives are gaining strength and gaining it fast.

> **Culture-war issues, which so conspicuously failed to move many voters in the last couple of elections, will lose even more force in years to come.**

As the country is evolving, so are the American people's views on what government can and should do. Start with the likely diminution in the culture wars that have bedeviled American politics for so long. While cultural disagreements remain, their political influence is being undermined by the rise of the millennial generation, increasing religious and family diversity, and the decline of the culturally conservative white working class. Culture-war issues such as abortion and gay marriage, which so conspicuously failed to move many voters in the last couple of elections, will lose even more force in years to come.

Instead, we are likely to see more attention paid to health care, energy, and education—issues Americans care about and in which government has a positive role to play. The public holds distinctly progressive views in each of these areas, supporting health care for all, a transition to clean energy, and building a 21st-century education system, including a major infusion of resources to improve K–12 education and college access. The public's commitment to these progressive goals is only likely to intensify, since rising demographic groups tend to be especially supportive.

Although these attitudinal and demographic trends strongly suggest a rising progressive America, the emergence of this new coalition and agenda is neither assured nor automatic. Conservatives are not out of the ideological hunt altogether. Majorities of Americans, ranging from 55 percent to 58 percent, agree with a cluster of conservative ideas about the role of markets, taxes, Social Security, and limited government. Nearly two-thirds of Americans agree with the conservative stance on free trade, and another six in 10 support the conservative view that "government spending is almost always wasteful and inefficient."

Similarly, recent political history from both the Clinton and Bush years shows us that voters are often fickle and prone to significant shifts in opinion if their demands and desires are not met or if leaders fall short of their expectations. Voter antipathy toward Bush and conservatives could easily shift toward Obama and progressives if they are not careful. The economy, public spending, and the financial bailouts are the most likely issues to trip up progressives; they are areas where our study found clear undercurrents of anti-corporate, anti-bailout populism across many segments of the electorate.

The research also reveals an interesting complexity in American ideology that could alter the political calculus in important ways. For example, we find that majorities of self-identified conservatives agree with four out of five progressive perspectives on the role of government, while majorities of self-identified progressives and liberals agree with conservative economic positions on trade and Social Security.

Conservatives could possibly take advantage of these ideological complexities with a leader who reconfigured the Republican Party to better address progressive goals through conservative means, as has David Cameron, leader of the Conservative Party in Britain. However, given the ideological sentiments enveloping the GOP today, this transformation seems unlikely in the short term. Unless and until conservatives recognize the depth of affinity between Obama's ideological progressivism and that of the American electorate, conservative ideas likely will remain in secondary status for years to come.

As for progressives, they have a marvelous opportunity. If Obama and his supporters can deliver on his ambitious agenda, with the very real changes that it would bring to our country, these changes will reinforce the progressive values that are now ascendant. This reinforcement of progressive beliefs, bolstered by ongoing demographic trends, would, in turn, create the possibility of more progressive change. Such a virtuous circle could lead to a real and durable political realignment.

JOHN HALPIN and **RUY TEIXEIRA** are senior fellows and co-directors of the Progressive Studies Program at the Center for American Progress.

From *The American Prospect,* May 2009, pp. 26–28. Copyright © 2009. Reprinted with permission from John Halpin and Ruy Teixeira and The American Prospect, Washington, DC. All rights reserved. www.prospect.org

The Hazard of Moral Hazard

Intervention to save the economy may be endangering it.

JAMES K. GLASSMAN

When someone insures you against the consequences of a nasty event, oddly enough, he raises the incentives for you to behave in a way that will cause the event. So if your diamond ring is insured for $50,000, you are more likely to leave it out of the safe. Economists call this phenomenon "moral hazard," and if you look around, you will see it everywhere. "With automobile collision insurance, for example, one is more likely to venture forth on an icy night," writes Harvard economist Richard Zeckhauser. "Federal deposit insurance made S&Ls more willing to take on risky loans. Federally subsidized flood insurance encourages citizens to build homes on flood plains."

In 1963 the Nobel Prize winner Kenneth Arrow, who happens to be the uncle of President Obama's top economic adviser, Larry Summers, wrote a paper for the *American Economic Review* titled "Uncertainty and the Economics of Medical Care." Arrow argued strenuously for vastly increasing health insurance, even if the government had to supply some of it, but he also recognized the dangers of moral hazard that health insurance causes. The ideal case for insurance, Arrow wrote, is "that the event against which insurance is taken be out of the control of the individual" who is insured—like, say, insurance against damage from a meteor crashing into your house. In health care, people who are insured (especially if the premiums are being paid by their employers) have greater incentives to risk their health by, for example, smoking than they would if they had to pay the bill for their lung-cancer treatment themselves.[1] Insurers struggle to mitigate moral hazard by making people pay part of the cost of their care or, in the case of life insurance, by raising premiums on smokers or denying coverage to skydivers.

The most dangerous kind of moral hazard is produced not from explicit insurance policies (on which, after all, the insurer can raise premiums) but from *implicit* ones. If your teenager thinks you will bail him out of jail or fix it with the judge if he gets arrested, then he will be more apt to drive drunk. More broadly, in the jargon of Alcoholics Anonymous, your behavior would be called "enabling." By rescuing an alcoholic from the consequences of his actions, you are encouraging him to drink because he figures you will rescue him the next time.

Over the past three decades, the world has been awash in just this kind of moral hazard, as governments have become more adept at economic rescue and as practitioners of the art have won praise for seeming to pull the world back from the abyss.

Consider the three government officials—Summers, then deputy secretary of the Treasury; Robert Rubin, his boss at Treasury; and Alan Greenspan, chairman of the Federal Reserve—who stared out from the February 15, 1999, cover of *Time,* which called them, with no irony, "The Committee to Save the World." With help from the International Monetary Fund and the World Bank, the three, we were told, had averted global disasters, from the vaporizing of the Thai baht, the default of Russian bonds, and the near collapse of Long-Term Capital Management (a huge Greenwich, Connecticut, hedge fund cofounded by two Nobel economists).

A few years later, the Fed chairman would appear to save the world once more by dramatically cutting U.S. interest rates after 9/11, in the process reinforcing what Wall Street called the Greenspan "put." Ever since the 1987 stock-market crash, in bad times—the start of the Gulf War of 1990–91, the Mexican credit crisis of 1994, the Asian and Russian blights of the late 1990s, and the popping of the tech bubble in 2000—the Fed has pumped liquidity (that is, available money) into the financial system, saving investors from greater horrors by keeping stock prices buoyant.

As a result, investors began to believe that if they bought stocks, the Fed was offering them an implicit put option, which protected the price of their shares through thick and thin. "There has been a sense that participants in the market may think there is this cushion if things get ugly," said Michael Prell, a former research director at the Fed, in an article in the *Financial Times* headlined "Greenspan Put May Be Encouraging Complacency." The date was December 8, 2000.

Eight years later, the global economy faced a crisis caused by lenders who flamboyantly disregarded the creditworthiness of borrowers. In response, government rescuers instituted policies that made the efforts of *Time*'s Committee to Save the World seem quaint. In the committee's heyday, the Asians got $40 billion in help, the Russians $23 billion, and the Greenwich hedge-fund guys $4 billion. But in 2008 and 2009, just two programs in one country—America's Troubled Assets Relief Program (TARP) and its stimulus package—together total more than $1.5 *trillion.*

Meanwhile, the Fed cut short-term interest rates to zero, and the White House and Congress decided to save the country's largest insurance company (American International Group, or AIG), its largest and second-largest automakers (General Motors and Chrysler), its two largest providers of mortgage-financing (Fannie Mae and Freddie Mac), and various gigantic commercial and investment banks and finance companies. The creeping dread is that previous rescue policies had induced the moral hazard that made the 2008–09 crisis not only inevitable but also far worse in scale than the economic disruptions that had come before—and that the 2008–09 rescue will induce a disaster worse still.

The financial historian Charles Kindleberger, in his classic *Manias, Panics, and Crashes*, had it right more than 30 years ago when he described "the moral hazard that the more interventionist the authorities are with respect to the current crisis, the more intense the next bubble will be, because many of the market participants will believe that their possible losses will be limited by government measures."

How much moral hazard is sloshing around the world? That can't be measured, but Peter L. Bernstein, one of the great historians of economic risk, wrote in June: "The moral hazard imposed on the system in recent months is truly mind-boggling in scale and scope. Across the globe the banks and insurers whose errors of judgment created the bubbles have been bailed out without hesitation."

Bernstein, who died in June at 91, wrote those words in a short cri de coeur published posthumously by the *Harvard Business Review*. He argued not just that there is a great deal of moral hazard around but also that, unlike in the past, few people seem worried about it. He was certainly a lonely voice. "I am disturbed," he wrote, "by the almost complete absence of a dissenting conservative view"—that is, the view that "overprotectedness on the part of government officials . . . only encouraged more reckless risk-taking."

Policymakers have responded that they had, and have, no choice. "The problem we have is that in a financial crisis, if you let the big firms collapse in a disorderly way, they'll bring down the whole system," Ben Bernanke, the current Fed chairman, said in July. "When the elephant falls down, all the grass gets crushed as well." President Obama's own favorite metaphor is the burning house:[2] The fire could not be allowed simply to burn itself out, because the flames might jump to the next house and the next. So government, at whatever cost, had to douse the flames and stop the contagion—even if its actions would encourage people to build firetraps and smoke cigarettes in bed. Obama's was a policy very different from what Treasury Secretary Andrew Mellon prescribed (and his president, Herbert Hoover, rejected) for the Great Depression: "Liquidate labor, liquidate stocks, liquidate the farmers, liquidate real estate."

Liquidate Lehman Brothers? That, it turned out, was OK—but what government would have the courage to let General Motors fail? Or Citigroup? Wily policymakers recognize moral hazard, but like wily health insurers, they think they have a way to mitigate it. In a May 2008 speech, Bernanke said:

Central banks face a tradeoff when deciding to provide extraordinary liquidity support. . . . If market participants come to believe that the Federal Reserve or other central banks will take such measures whenever financial stress develops, financial institutions and their creditors would have less incentive to pursue suitable strategies for managing liquidity risk and more incentive to take such risks.

Lately, of course, the Fed *has* taken such measures. But in that May 2008 speech, Bernanke told us not to worry, there was an answer:

The problem of moral hazard can perhaps be most effectively addressed by prudential supervision and regulation that ensures that financial institutions manage their liquidity risks effectively in advance of the crisis.

At the time Bernanke spoke, of course, the Dow Jones Industrial Average was floating along at 12,900, and the Fed had just pumped emergency cash into Bear Stearns as part of its forced sale to JPMorgan Chase. There was still widespread faith that the formula of "extraordinary liquidity support" plus "prudential regulation" could overcome any problems caused by moral hazard.

Clearly, the formula didn't work.

Nor should we have expected it to. For the dirty little secret is that regulation can *enhance* moral hazard, not dampen it. When people expect regulations to protect them, they lose the incentive to protect themselves.

The dirty little secret is that regulation can enhance moral hazard, not dampen it. When people expect regulations to protect them, they lose the incentive to protect themselves.

Can regulators adequately police the 8,400 banks that are insured by the Federal Deposit Insurance Corporation? Of course not. Nor can the Securities and Exchange Commission (SEC) protect investors against fraud. As Arthur Levitt, the longest-serving chairman in the history of the SEC, puts it, "A very skillful criminal can almost always outfox the regulator or the overseer." When investors rely on regulators, they let their own guards down and are more likely to make mistakes. In rejecting self-reliance in favor of confidence in government, investors disregard actions that will truly protect them—like diversifying their portfolios or just using their own good common sense.

Regulations cannot protect against every contingency. To echo the opening line of *Anna Karenina*, each period of financial excess is excessive in its own way. Financial regulators are too busy protecting against the last disaster to think about the next one. And businesses, especially those in the financial sector, apply high-priced brainpower to finding ways to evade regulation through means such as the off-balancesheet partnerships that made it appear as though Enron was not going bankrupt.

Only tens of millions of investors can apply the necessary vigilance for effective deterrence. But if those investors think that they're being protected by the SEC or the FTC or the new Consumer Financial Protection Agency that Obama wants to create, they grow complacent or, worse, feel they have license to engage in risky behavior themselves: *If the FDIC is insuring my bank deposits, I can afford to take a flier in penny gold-mining stocks.*

The economist Sam Peltzman of the University of Chicago first recognized this phenomenon in 1975. The "Peltzman Effect" holds that people often react to safety regulations by increasing their risky behavior. A law requiring seat-belt use, for example, leads to an increase in speeding.[3] "The greater protection," wrote Peltzman, "had reduced the price of risky driving . . . by reducing the consequences you could expect if you got into an accident." So people found their risks somewhere else.

Is regulation futile? Not completely, but if policies increase moral hazard and promote dangerously risky behavior by businesses, you can't expect regulation to balance the adverse effects. A better approach might be termed organic. We must find ways to make sensible risk aversion second nature, ingrained, reflexive. One antidote would be to increase the personal exposure of financial risk takers. That exposure was greatly reduced starting in 1981—right before the moral-hazard problem began to burgeon with the Latin American "debt bomb" economic crisis—when Wall Street's investment firms, starting with Salomon Brothers, switched from being organized as partnerships to becoming corporations after a ruling by the New York Stock Exchange made that possible.

In a partnership, the owners are on the hook personally for the firm's liabilities; in a corporation, the personal holdings of owners are walled off from the risks they take.[4] To be sure, the corporation was a great invention. After all, we want entrepreneurs to take risks. Without corporations—and bankruptcy, for that matter—the "animal spirits" that John Maynard Keynes recognized as critical to economic growth would be suppressed. Academic research has found, for instance, that states with the most forgiving bankruptcy laws are home to the most entrepreneurial activity.

The external effects of a bank's failure are not nearly so terrible as Obama's fire metaphor makes them seem, but they are far worse than, say, a retailer shutting its doors.

But finance is different. The external effects of a bank's failure are not nearly so terrible as Obama's fire metaphor makes them seem, but they are far worse than, say, a retailer shutting its doors. Kevin Dowd, an economist who specializes in risk management, wrote recently about the banking crisis in the *Cato Journal*, "The root problem is limited liability, which allows investors and executives the full upside benefit of their risk-taking, while limiting their downside exposure." Dowd quoted Adam Smith's warning about corporations in *The Wealth of Nations*:

The directors of such companies . . . being the managers of other people's money than their own, it cannot well be expected that they should watch over it with the same anxious vigilance. . . . Negligence . . . must always prevail, more or less, in the management of such a company.

If the managers of Bear Stearns had been required to be owners, and if they had faced losing their bank accounts, their cars, and their second homes, then they would have been far less likely to take enormous risks in, for instance, subprime mortgage securities.

Another example of the organic approach would be to reduce, rather than increase, government's role in protecting consumers. Consider federal deposit insurance, which was instituted in 1934 to prevent runs on banks. Originally, deposits were insured up to $10,000; today the limit is $250,000. In practice, as Kindleberger points out, the federal government protects all depositors in insured banks. The effect, he writes, is that insurance "encouraged banks to make riskier loans since they were confident that they were protected against runs—if these loans proved profitable, the owners of the banks would benefit." If the government cut the limit on insurance to, say, $20,000, that single act would send a strong signal to consumers (put your money in a strong bank rather than a weak one) and to bankers (shore up your balance sheet or you won't get deposits). That this is not likely to happen, to put it mildly, has nothing to do with whether it *should* happen.

The best way to dampen moral hazard is to resist the urge to act. Repeated economic crises are caused, in large part, by the expectations raised by the interventions themselves.

The best way to dampen moral hazard, however, is for politicians and regulators to resist the urge to act, act, act. They do have to maintain confidence in financial markets, but that confidence is being undermined by repeated economic crises that are caused, in large part, by the expectations raised by the interventions themselves. Never have expectations been raised so high. "Bad as the increased debt and subversion of the Fed may be," Bernstein wrote, "their impact on our economic well-being pales in comparison with what could happen if the bailouts lessen our aversion to risk."

At the very least, policymakers need to take moral hazard—in all its permutations—into their calculations. They did so in the past. Bernstein refers to the "hue and cry" that used to arise when "governments took steps to cushion the adverse consequences of bubbles for particular companies or sectors of the economy." Today alarms are being raised about cost. But about the impact on behavior there is barely a peep. In fact, there is blithe indifference to the future effects of today's policies and a kind of smug congratulatory air redolent of that 1999 *Time* magazine cover celebrating the Committee to Save the World. "The fire is out now," said President Obama in July, reverting to his economic metaphor. Perhaps. But the embers are still glowing, waiting for the next gust of wind—or dose of kerosene—to ignite them.

Notes

1. An academic paper published by the National Bureau of Economic Research in July asked the question "Does Health Insurance Make You Fat?" The authors, economists Jay Bhattacharya and Kate Bundorf of Stanford and two colleagues, found in the affirmative: "Our estimates suggest that, by insulating people from the costs of obesity-related medical care expenditures, insurance coverage creates moral hazard in behaviors related to body weight. These effects are larger in public insurance programs where premiums are not risk adjusted and smaller in private insurance markets where [the] obese might pay for incremental medical care costs in the form of lower wages."

2. Fire metaphors have long been popular in discussions of financial crises. Unlike Obama, Thomas Joplin, in a contemporary letter about the British panic of 1825, argued that "the fire can be left to burn itself out" ("Case for Parliamentary Inquiry into the Circumstances of the Panic," cited by Kindleberger).

3. Stephen J. Dubner, co-author of *Freakonomics,* wrote of the Peltzman Effect in the *New York Times:* "My favorite version of this theory is what I call the Lipitor Effect: if your daily diet includes 20 mg of the anti-cholesterol drug Lipitor, it can also include a pastrami sandwich."

4. I first laid out this idea in "Bankers Need More Skin in the Game," co-authored with William T. Nolan, in the *Wall Street Journal,* Feb. 25, 2009. The op-ed cited Brown Brothers Harriman as the only major investment bank that remains a partnership and argued that it was no coincidence that the firm had avoided the excesses of its corporate peers.

JAMES K. GLASSMAN, former Undersecretary of State for Public Diplomacy and Public Affairs, is president of the World Growth Institute.

From *Commentary,* September 2009, pp. 28–32. Copyright © 2009 by Commentary. Reprinted by permission of Commentary and James K. Glassman.

Not So Popular Where It Counts

In nations the U.S. needs cooperation from on a host of crises, antipathy to America and Barack Obama remains high.

BRUCE STOKES

Obamamania is alive and well from Germany to Japan to Brazil. Overwhelmingly, people all over the world have more confidence in President Obama than they did in his predecessor, George W. Bush. Anti-Americanism has all but disappeared in many places, according to the new Pew Global Attitudes Survey by the Washington-based Pew Research Center for the People and the Press.

The collective sense of relief that these data undoubtedly bring to Foggy Bottom and the White House should be tempered, however, by sobering evidence from key hot spots of continued antipathy toward America, doubts about Obama's leadership, lack of willingness to work with the United States, and outright opposition to the president's initiatives.

That America and its leadership are once again widely trusted facilitates Obama's pursuit of U.S. interests abroad. But in the places that embody the toughest foreign-policy challenges and that will define the Obama presidency—Afghanistan, Pakistan, China, Russia, the Middle East, and Mexico—the United States still must earn the respect and cooperation of many key players.

Opinion about the United States has improved this year in 17 of the 20 countries for which Pew has comparable data from last year. And an "Obama bounce," defined as an increase in the percentage of people who say they have more confidence in Obama than they did in Bush last year, is evident in 23 of the 24 foreign countries that Pew surveyed.

But Obama's increase of troops in Afghanistan, his signature foreign-policy initiative to date, garners disapproval in 20 of 24 Pew survey nations, including all seven NATO countries polled.

And even if Obama's Afghanistan headache can be explained away as a Bush hangover, troubled Pakistan is Obama's impending migraine. A mere 16 percent of the Pakistani people have a favorable view of the United States. Only 13 percent of Pakistanis trust the president to do the right thing in world affairs. Just 24 percent support the U.S.-led fight against terrorism. A paltry 9 percent of Pakistanis see Uncle Sam as a partner. And four in five fear that the United States could pose a military threat one day. Finding common ground with Islamabad to stabilize this disintegrating country may prove beyond Obama's formidable skills.

In the Middle East, only 15 percent of Palestinians are pro-American, 23 percent have confidence in Obama's handling of foreign policy, and just 5 percent view the United States as a partner. Israeli sentiment is much more positive, but the Jewish state is the only traditional U.S. ally in which the Obama presidency has prompted stagnating or declining support for the United States and American foreign-policy leadership.

In longtime adversary China, confidence in Obama's handling of world affairs is double Bush's level of support, and anti-Americanism is down slightly from last year. But disturbingly, only one in 15 Chinese view the United States as a potential collaborator. Pew found a significant Obama bounce in Russia, America's other traditional rival, but even so, barely a third of Russians believe in the president's handling of foreign policy. Just over one-quarter of Russians see Washington as a partner.

Moscow and Beijing certainly cannot be counted on to follow the Obama playbook. But on issues of mutual interest, such as the fight against terrorism, popular support for U.S.-led efforts is rebounding in both countries, offering opportunities for cooperation.

Mexico has not been a foreign-policy problem for Washington since the days of Pancho Villa. But as escalating drug-war violence ravages that country, it classifies

Hearts and Minds Yet to Be Won

Although President Obama generally elicits significantly more-favorable feelings abroad than his predecessor, a Pew survey reveals that there's still room for improvement—especially among a group of countries the U.S. may find itself at odds with in the future.

	Favorable view of U.S.	Confidence Obama will do the right thing with regard to world affairs	Think of U.S. as a partner to their country
Palestinian Ter.	15%	23%	5%
Pakistan	16	13	9
Russia	44	37	27
China	47	62	6
Mexico	69	55	64
Israel	71	56	84
Global Median	62	67	44

Source: Pew Global Attitudes Survey.

as a looming hot spot. Fortunately for the Obama administration, Mexico is one potential crisis area where working with the United States is no longer anathema. U.S. favorability is up significantly among Mexicans, back to levels of support during President Clinton's era. A majority of Mexicans trust Obama's handling of foreign policy. And nearly two in three see Uncle Sam as a partner.

Obama's personal charisma will carry U.S. foreign policy only so far. Ultimately, his international legacy will be determined by his handling of a few strategic issues. And on many of those challenges, the president still lacks the support of pivotal foreign publics.

bstokes@nationaljournal.com

Reprinted by permission from *National Journal*, July 25, 2009, p. 23. Copyright © 2009 by National Journal Group Inc. All rights reserved.

Article 10

It Is Time to Repair the Constitution's Flaws

SANFORD LEVINSON

In 1987 I went to a marvelous exhibit in Philadelphia commemorating the bicentennial of the drafting of the U.S. Constitution. The exhibit concluded with two scrolls, each with the same two questions: First, "Will You Sign This Constitution?" And then, "If you had been in Independence Hall on September 17, 1787, would you have endorsed the Constitution?" The second question emphasized that we were being asked to assess the 1787 Constitution. That was no small matter inasmuch as the document did not include *any* of the subsequent amendments, including the Bill of Rights. Moreover, the viewer had been made aware in the course of the exhibit that the Constitution included several terrible compromises with slavery.

Even in 1987, because of those compromises I tended to regard the original Constitution as what the antislavery crusader William Lloyd Garrison so memorably called "a covenant with death and an agreement with hell." So why did I choose to sign the scroll? I was impressed that Frederick Douglass, the great black abolitionist, after an initial flirtation with Garrison's rejectionism, endorsed even the antebellum Constitution. He argued that, correctly understood, it was deeply antislavery at its core.

The language of the Constitution—including, most importantly, its magnificent preamble—allows us to mount a critique of slavery, and much else, from within. The Constitution offers us a language by which we can protect those rights that we deem important. We need not reject the Constitution in order to carry on such a conversation. If the Constitution, at the present time, is viewed as insufficiently protective of such rights, that is because of the limited imagination of those interpreters with the most political power, including members of the Supreme Court. So I added my signature to the scroll endorsing the 1787 Constitution.

On July 3, 2003, I was back in Philadelphia to participate in the grand opening of the National Constitution Center. The exhibit culminated in Signers' Hall, which featured life-size (and lifelike) statues of each of the delegates to the constitutional convention. As one walked through the hall and brushed against James Madison, Alexander Hamilton, and other giants of our history, one could almost feel the remarkable energy that must have impressed itself on those actually in Independence Hall.

As was true in 1987, the visitor was invited to join the signers by adding his or her own signature to the Constitution. Indeed, the center organized a major project during September 2003 called "I Signed the Constitution." Sites in all 50 states were available for such a signing. Both the temporary 1987 exhibit and the permanent one that remains at the National Constitution Center leave little doubt about the proper stance that a citizen should take toward our founding document.

This time, however, I rejected the invitation to re-sign the Constitution. I had not changed my mind that in many ways it offers a rich, even inspiring, language to envision and defend a desirable political order. Nor did my decision necessarily mean that I would have preferred that the Constitution go down to defeat in the ratification votes of 1787–88. Rather, I treated the center as asking me about my level of support for the Constitution *today* and, just as important, whether I wished to encourage my fellow citizens to reaffirm it in a relatively thoughtless manner. As to the first, I realized that I had, between 1987 and 2003, become far more concerned about the inadequacies of the Constitution. As to the second, I had come to think that it is vitally important to engage in a national conversation about its adequacy rather than automatically to assume its fitness for our own times.

My concern is only minimally related to the formal rights protected by the Constitution. Even if, as a practical matter, the Supreme Court reads the Constitution less protectively with regard to certain rights than I do, the proper response is not to reject the Constitution but to work within it by trying to persuade fellow Americans to share our views of constitutional possibility and by supporting presidential candidates who will appoint (and get through the Senate) judges who will be more open to better interpretations. Given that much constitutional interpretation occurs outside the courts, one also wants public officials at all levels to share one's own visions of constitutional possibility—as well, of course, as of constitutional constraints. And that is true even for readers who disagree with me on what specific rights are most important.

So what accounts for my change of views since 1987? The brief answer is that I have become ever more despondent about many structural provisions of the Constitution that place almost insurmountable barriers in the way of any acceptable contemporary notion of democracy. I put it that way to acknowledge that "democracy" is most certainly what political theorists call an "essentially contested concept." It would be tendentious to claim that there is only one understanding—such as "numerical majorities always prevail"—that is consistent with "democracy." Liberal constitutionalists, for example, would correctly place certain constraints on what majorities can do to vulnerable minorities.

That being said, I believe that it is increasingly difficult to construct a theory of democratic constitutionalism, *applying our own 21st-century norms,* that vindicates the Constitution under which we are governed today. Our 18th-century ancestors had little trouble integrating slavery and the rank subordination of women into their conception of a "republican" political order. *That* vision of politics is blessedly long behind us, but the Constitution is not. It does not deserve rote support from Americans who properly believe that majority rule, even if tempered by the recognition of minority rights, is integral to "consent of the governed."

I invite you to ask the following questions:

1. Even if you support having a Senate in addition to a House of Representatives, do you support as well giving Wyoming the same number of votes as California, which has roughly 70 times the population? To the degree that Congress is in significant ways *unrepresentative,* we have less reason to respect it. It is not a cogent response, incidentally, to say that any such inequalities are vitiated by the fact that the House of Representatives is organized on the basis of population, putting to one side issues raised by partisan gerrymandering. The very nature of our particular version of bicameralism, after all, requires that both houses assent to any legislation. By definition, that means that the *Senate can exercise the equivalent of an absolute veto power* on majoritarian legislation passed by the House that is deemed too costly to the interests of the small states that are overrepresented in the Senate, especially those clustered together in the Rocky Mountain area and the upper Midwest.

2. Are you comfortable with an Electoral College that, among other things, has since World War II placed in the White House five candidates—Truman, Kennedy, Nixon (1968), Clinton (1992 and 1996), and Bush (2000)—who did not get a majority of the popular vote? In at least two of those elections—in 1960, for which evidence exists that Nixon would have won a recount, and in 2000—the winners did not even come in first in the popular vote. The fact is that presidential candidates and their campaign managers are not necessarily trying to win the popular vote, except as an afterthought. Instead they are dedicated to putting together a coalition of states that will provide a majority of the electoral votes.

3. Are you concerned that the president might have too much power, whether to spy on Americans without any Congressional or judicial authorization or to frustrate the will of a majority of both houses of Congress by vetoing legislation with which he disagrees on political, as distinguished from constitutional, grounds? At the very least, it should be clear from recent controversies that the present Constitution does not offer a clear understanding of the limits of presidential power, particularly during times of presidentially perceived emergencies.

4. Are you concerned about whether the country is well served by the extended hiatus between election day and the presidential inauguration some 10 weeks later, during which lame-duck presidents retain full legal authority to make often controversial decisions? Imagine if John Kerry had won the 2004 election, and President Bush had continued to make decisions about policy on Iraq, Iran, and North Korea that would have greatly affected his administration. Much of the hiatus is explicable only with regard to the need for the Electoral College to operate (which serves as an additional reason to eliminate that dysfunctional institution).

5. Are you satisfied with a Constitution that, in effect, maximizes the baleful consequences of certain kinds of terrorist attacks on the United States? If a successor to United Flight 93 were to succeed in a catastrophic attack on the House of Representatives and the Senate, we could find ourselves in a situation where neither institution could operate—because the Constitution makes it impossible to replace disabled (as distinguished from dead) senators or to fill House vacancies by any process other than an election. That would contribute to the overwhelming likelihood of a presidential dictatorship. The Constitution is written for what is termed "retail" vacancies, which occur only occasionally and are easily subject to being handled by the existing rules. Should "wholesale" vacancies occur, however, the present Constitution is nothing less than a ticking time bomb.

6. Do you really want justices on the Supreme Court to serve up to four decades and, among other things, to be able to time their resignations to mesh with their own political preferences as to their successors?

7. Finally, do you find it "democratic" that 13 legislative houses in as many states can block constitutional amendments desired by the overwhelming majority of Americans as well as, possibly, 86 out of the 99 legislative houses in the American states? No other country—nor, for that matter, any of the 50 American states—makes it so difficult to amend its constitution. Article V of our Constitution constitutes an iron cage with regard to changing some of the most important aspects of our political system. But almost as important is the way that it also constitutes an iron cage with regard to our imagination. Because it is so difficult to amend the Constitution—it seems almost utopian to suggest the possibility, with regard to anything that is truly important—citizens are encouraged to believe that change is almost never desirable, let alone necessary.

One might regard those questions as raising only theoretical, perhaps even "aesthetic," objections to our basic institutional structures *if* we feel truly satisfied by the outcomes generated by our national political institutions. But that is patently not the case. Consider the results when samples of Americans are asked whether they believe the country is headed in the right or the wrong direction. In April 2005, a full 62 percent of the respondents to a CBS poll indicated that they believed that the country was headed in "the wrong direction." A year later, a similar CBS poll found that 71 percent of the respondents said that the country was "on the wrong track," with unfavorable ratings for Congress and the president, and only a slim majority approving of the Supreme Court. Surely that comprehensive sense of dissatisfaction is related for most Americans to a belief that our political institutions are *not* adequately responding to the issues at hand. Serious liberals and conservatives increasingly share an attitude of profound disquiet about the capacity of our institutions to meet the problems confronting us as a society.

To be sure, most Americans still seem to approve of their particular members of Congress. The reason for such approval, alas, may be the representatives' success in bringing home federally financed pork, which scarcely relates to the great national and international issues that we might hope that Congress could confront effectively. In any event, we should resist the temptation simply to criticize specific inhabitants of national offices. An emphasis on the deficiencies of particular officeholders suggests that the cure for what ails us is simply to win some elections and replace those officeholders with presumptively more virtuous officials. But we are deluding ourselves if we believe that winning elections is enough to overcome the deficiencies of the American political system.

We must recognize that substantial responsibility for the defects of our polity lies in the Constitution itself. A number of wrong turns were taken at the time of the initial drafting of the Constitution, even if for the best of reasons given the political realities of 1787. Even the most skilled and admirable leaders may not be able to overcome the barriers to effective government constructed by the Constitution. In many ways, we are like the police officer in Edgar Allen Poe's classic *The Purloined Letter,* unable to comprehend the true importance of what is clearly in front of us.

If I am correct that the Constitution is both insufficiently democratic, in a country that professes to believe in democracy, and significantly dysfunctional, in terms of the quality of government that we receive, then it follows that we should no longer express our blind devotion to it. It is not, as Thomas Jefferson properly suggested, the equivalent of the Ark of the Covenant. It is a human creation open to criticism and even to rejection. You should join me in supporting the call for a new constitutional convention.

SANFORD LEVINSON is a professor of law at the University of Texas Law School. This essay is adapted from *Our Undemocratic Constitution: Where the Constitution Goes Wrong (And How We the People Can Correct It),* by Oxford University Press. Copyright © 2006 by Oxford University Press.

As seen in *Chronicle of Higher Education,* Vol. 53, Iss. 8, October 13, 2006, p. B10; adapted from *Our Undemocratic Constitution: Where the Constitution Goes Wrong (And How We the People Can Correct It),* by Sanford Levinson, Oxford University Press, 2006. Copyright © 2006 by Oxford University Press, Ltd. Reprinted by permission.

Article 11

Pursuit of Habeas

To justify Gitmo, the Bushies kept monkeying around with the Constitution. But by trying to kill the right of habeas corpus, they only made it stronger.

JACK HITT

The era of Guantanamo Bay will come to an end, according to Joseph Margulies, a lawyer who has represented some of the detainees, when a judge utters the following words to George W. Bush: "Call your first witness."

Margulies is not alone in believing that the only thing administration officials are more zealous about than fighting the Global War on Terrorism is any attempt to make public the murky processes they've cobbled together to wage it. The intricate legal scaffolding constructed by the Bush administration replaced something simple, basic, and beautiful: habeas corpus. Most Americans probably don't know the meaning of that creaky Latin phrase and have been left with the impression that it is some boutique legalism that just ends up coddling terrorists. Actually, habeas is perfectly straightforward. It is the ancient right of anyone seized by the king to cry out from the dungeon and say, "I've been wrongly jailed!" Then you get a chance to prove your claim before a neutral judge, or back to the pokey you go. Habeas puts a basic check on the most fearsome power of the state and any citizen's most primal fear—being locked away and forgotten, the civil equivalent of being buried alive.

This fundamental right was most famously codified in 1215 when, in the meadow of Runnymede, King John was forced to set his royal seal upon the Magna Carta, the seminal document that declared the rule of law above any man, including the king. The habeas hearing was among the first checks and balances. Habeas is an affront to the royalist impulse to consolidate all power under one king, or as Beltway ideologues call it these days, "the unitary executive."

The problem with opposing habeas corpus now is no different than it was eight centuries ago: You're siding with the Sheriff of Nottingham.

The problem with opposing habeas now is no different than it was eight centuries ago: You're siding with the Sheriff of Nottingham.

Since 9/11, Bush's officials have played a seven-year game of legal keep-away: filing new motions, changing jurisdictions, improvising legal proceedings on the fly, stalling, appealing, amending, and then appealing some more. So much so that the matter of habeas has now become a hot-button issue on the presidential trail. Barack Obama applauded the high court's recent decision to extend habeas to detainees in Guantanamo; former POW John McCain said it was "one of the worst decisions in the history of this country."

Many defenders of the Bush administration point out that detainees at Gitmo shouldn't be receiving a habeas hearing because they are foreign combatants. To the Supreme Court, however, the key issue is not the rights of aliens but separation of powers. It challenged Congress' audacity to limit this basic judicial power when the Constitution is clear that habeas can be suspended in only two situations—rebellion or invasion.

Another reason why habeas is being debated goes back to the original sin of the Bush administration's catastrophic decisions on the battlefield. Ever since World War II, when the military has rounded up people after a battle, it has held brief hearings to determine if a prisoner was a legitimate POW or somebody picked up in error. Lots of mistakes get made in wartime, and commanders typically don't want to be burdened with unnecessary detainees, so dealing with this matter right away—separating those who've taken up arms from those who got caught up in a raid—is essential. In the wake of the Geneva Conventions these battlefield tribunals have been referred to as Article 5 hearings.

In Vietnam, Article 5 hearings were typically held right there in the jungle. In the first Gulf War, 1,196 Article 5 hearings were held and only 310 detainees were classified as POWs. And that's typical. But not after 9/11.

Early on, White House Counsel Alberto Gonzales dismissed the Geneva Conventions as "quaint." So everybody swept up was sent en masse to the camps. Then, the civilian leadership of the Pentagon made matters even more difficult. We bloated the enemy combatant population with a new technique: We started *buying* combatants.

We dropped leaflets out of planes, offering Afghans and Pakistanis as much as $25,000 to turn in Taliban and Al Qaeda fighters. Many of these leaflets landed in areas where an annual salary might be a few hundred dollars. This made it very tempting to turn in that neighbor whose goats always harassed your sheep. And that kind of feud settling happened. It will probably be years before we entirely understand just what kind of mishmash we made of our prisoner population by turning the fire hose of turbocapitalism on the Afghan outback.

Yet from the beginning, we've always had a clue. Donald Rumsfeld announced that the detainees were the "worst of the worst," and General Richard Myers warned they "would gnaw hydraulic lines in the back of a C-17 to bring it down." But as early as 2002, the commander at Gitmo, Maj. General Michael Dunlavey, complained that he was receiving too many "Mickey Mouse" prisoners. A 2004 *New York Times* investigation found numerous officials who said that of the 595 detainees then held at Gitmo, maybe two dozen possessed any useful information. In 2006, a study of Pentagon filings on 517 detainees led by Seton Hall law professor Mark Denbeaux quantified it with hard numbers: Only 5 percent of the men at Gitmo had been scooped up by US forces, and only 8 percent were fighters of any kind.

Overstating the number of hydraulic-line chewers at Gitmo has been a routine rhetorical tactic of Bush apologists. In his dissent in the latest case, Justice Antonin Scalia (who can't get over the fact that other people can't get over *Bush v. Gore*) hysterically noted that at least 30 released detainees "have returned to the battlefield." Seton Hall's Denbeaux looked at the evidence behind that number and found that the Pentagon counted as "returning to the battlefield" detainees who had participated in the documentary *The Road to Guantanamo* or had written a pro-habeas op-ed in the *New York Times*. When you narrow it down to those who've left Gitmo and actually taken up arms against the United States, according to Denbeaux, the number is five. And among those, it would be interesting to examine the use of the word "return." What evidence does Scalia have that they weren't goatherds radicalized by years of undeserved dungeon time?

Of course, there's no better confirmation than the actions of the Pentagon itself. Even without abiding by habeas, the Pentagon has quietly released some 500 of the 770 detainees held at Guantanamo.

Over the years, as the courts have ordered the Bush administration to provide some kind of habeas-like hearing to the remaining detainees, the government's lawyers ginned up something called a "combatant status review tribunal." During a CSRT, however, you can't have a lawyer, know the evidence against you, or call witnesses except those "reasonably available." The result? Hearings that are simply bizarre. Take the case of German-born detainee Murat Kurnaz, picked up in 2001. (See "Inside Gitmo With Detainee 061") At his CSRT, he learned that one of the official reasons for holding him was because two years *after* he was seized a friend blew himself up, except that because of bureaucratic incompetence, it wasn't his friend at all, who was alive and well and living nonterroristically back in Germany.

Paging Terry Gilliam.

The CSRTs have become such a fiasco that one-fourth of the division of Justice Department lawyers charged with executing these tribunals have opted out. In the case of actual military commissions (the improvised "trials" that follow a CSRT hearing), last year the chief prosecutor, Colonel Morris Davis, denounced the commissions as rigged, quit his job, and offered to testify on behalf of a detainee.

The reasoning for these complicated, shadowy processes—seizing prisoners in unorthodox ways, isolating them outside US jurisdiction, never bringing charges, then offering makeshift legal proceedings—is usually explained with the argument that 9/11 changed everything. Actually, Guantanamo is a case of history repeating itself.

Habeas corpus was the law of the land in England until the mid-17th century when royalist Cavaliers found themselves in a holy war with Protestant Roundheads. To the royalists it appeared that England was beset with terrorists, crazy fundamentalists who had no regard for human life—a.k.a. the Puritans. We remember them as folksy pilgrims with a garish taste in buckles. The British had other impressions. Even though the royalists themselves didn't much care for Charles I, the idea of publicly executing the king was seen as an act of bloodthirsty terrorism on a par with, say, crashing a plane into a tower. When the pendulum swung back to royalism more than a decade later, King Charles II ascended the throne. Needless to say, the king's lord chancellor—the head of day-to-day governing—a man named Edward Hyde, Earl of Clarendon, was suspicious of Puritans, suspicious of everybody. Terrorism makes you that way. So he seized anyone he fancied to be a potential threat and held them at detainment camps. And in order to avoid the bother of habeas hearings, he put them on an island off the British shore—some historians say it was the isle of Jersey—in order to deprive them of the protection of English common law.

Sound familiar?

In the end, Clarendon was impeached and fled in disgrace. Parliamentarians who thought Clarendon had gone too far—particularly one Lord Shaftesbury—passed the Habeas Corpus Act of 1679, reestablishing a balance between an executive who must make arrests in order to keep the peace and the individual's right to challenge that arrest in court. Having learned the lessons of Guantanamo Bay more than 300 years ago, the 1679 act forbade the king from removing a prisoner to "Scotland, Ireland, Jersey, Guernsey, Tangier, or into Parts, Garrisons, Islands or Places beyond the Seas, which are or at any time hereafter shall be within or without the Dominions of his Majesty."

And that was our inherited position, until George W. Bush became president. But the assault on habeas will end. Other Bush-era presidential powers will be challenged and debated. But not only will habeas be fully restored as a centerpiece of American jurisprudence, one might ultimately credit Bush indirectly for internationalizing the right, since that is a likely long-term outcome of his attempt to subvert it. The most recent court ruling broadened the reach of habeas—suggesting that no democracy should leave home without it.

Habeas is among the first great checks and balances in the very system of powers that we are said to be fighting for. With each Supreme Court reversal, with each appellate court smackdown, America walks the issue back, back to this elegant idea, back to this ancient right, back to habeas corpus. Even some of our most conservative judges have stepped up to affirm it. It's only a matter of time before Congress does the same, restraining future presidents from ever again sending prisoners "into Parts, Garrisons, Islands or Places beyond the Seas."

From *Mother Jones,* September/October 2008, pp. 37–39. Copyright © 2008 by Mother Jones. Reprinted by permission of the Foundation for National Progress.

Article 12

Is Judicial Review Obsolete?

STUART TAYLOR JR.

The big decision on June 26 that the Second Amendment protects an individual right to keep a loaded handgun for self-defense at home is the high-water mark of the "original meaning" approach to constitutional interpretation championed by Justice Antonin Scalia and many other conservatives. At the same time, the decision may show "originalism" to be a false promise.

Scalia's 64-page opinion for the five-justice majority was a tour de force of originalist analysis. Without pausing to ask whether gun rights is good policy, Scalia parsed the Second Amendment's 27 words one by one while consulting 18th-century dictionaries, early American history, the 1689 English Bill of Rights, 19th-century treatises, and other historical material.

And even the lead dissent for the Court's four liberals—who are accustomed to deep-sixing original meaning on issues ranging from the death penalty to abortion, gay rights, and many others—all but conceded that this case should turn mainly on the original meaning of the 217-year-old Second Amendment. They had little choice, given the unusual absence of binding precedent.

But in another sense, *District of Columbia v. Heller* belies the two great advantages that originalism has been touted as having over the liberals' "living Constitution" approach. Originalism is supposed to supply first principles that will prevent justices from merely voting their policy preferences and to foster what Judge Robert Bork once called "deference to democratic choice." But the gun case suggests that originalism does neither.

Even though all nine justices claimed to be following original meaning, they split along liberal-conservative lines perfectly matching their apparent policy preferences.

First, even though all nine justices claimed to be following original meaning, they split angrily along liberal-conservative lines perfectly matching their apparent policy preferences, with the four conservatives (plus swing-voting Anthony Kennedy) voting for gun rights and the four liberals against.

These eight justices cleaved in *exactly* the same way—with Kennedy tipping the balance from case to case—in the decision the same day striking down a campaign finance provision designed to handicap rich, self-funded political candidates; the June 25 decision barring the death penalty for raping a child; the June 12 decision striking down the elected branches' restrictions on judicial review of Guantanamo detainees' petitions for release; and past decisions on abortion, affirmative action, gay rights, religion, and more.

This pattern does not mean that the justices are *insincerely* using legal doctrines as a cover for politically driven votes. Rather, it shows that ascertaining the original meaning of provisions drafted more than 200 years ago, in a very different society, is often a subjective process on which reasonable people disagree—and often reach conclusions driven consciously or subconsciously by their policy preferences. And some of us have trouble coming to confident conclusions either way.

I wrote approvingly of the federal Appeals Court opinion striking down the District of Colombia's strict handgun ban 15 months ago, and found Scalia's argument for the same result equally persuasive. But then I studied the dissents by liberal Justices John Paul Stevens and Stephen Breyer, and found them pretty persuasive too. Scalia and the two dissenters all made cogent arguments while papering over weaknesses in their positions. I think that Scalia may have won on points. But more study might tip me the other way.

The reason is that the justices' exhaustive analyses of the text and relevant history do not definitively resolve the ambiguity inherent in the amendment's curious wording: "A well-regulated militia, being necessary to the security of a free state, the right of the people to keep and bear arms, shall not be infringed."

And even if there is a clear right answer evident to people more discerning than I, the voting pattern suggests that conservative and liberal justices will never agree on what it is. More broadly, even when there is no dispute as to original meaning, it is often intolerable to liberals and conservatives alike. For example, no constitutional provision or amendment was ever designed to prohibit the federal government from discriminating based on race (or sex). This has not stopped conservatives from voting to strike down federal racial preferences for minorities (by seeking to extend liberal precedents) any more than it stopped liberals from striking down the federal laws that once discriminated against women.

Second, the notion that originalists would defer more to democratic choices than would the loosey-goosey liberals has come to ring a bit hollow. The originalists began with a compelling critique of the liberals' invention of new constitutional rights to strike down all state abortion and death-penalty laws, among others. But the current conservative justices have hardly been models of judicial restraint.

They have used highly debatable interpretations of original meaning to sweep aside a raft of democratically adopted laws. These include federal laws regulating campaign money and imposing monetary liability on states. And in last year's 5-4 decision striking down two local school-integration laws, the conservative majority came close to imposing a "colorblind Constitution" vision of equal protection that may be good policy but which is hard to find in the 14th Amendment's original meaning.

In the gun case, as Justice Breyer argued, "the majority's decision threatens severely to limit the ability of more knowledgeable, democratically elected officials to deal with gun-related problems." (Of course, Breyer's solicitude for elected officials disappears when the issue is whether they should be able to execute rapists of children or ban an especially grisly abortion method.)

If originalism does not deliver on its promises to channel judicial discretion and constrain judicial usurpations of elected officials' power, what good is it?

Indeed, it seems almost perverse to be assessing what gun controls do allow based not on examining how best to save lives but on seeking to read the minds of the men who ratified the Bill of Rights well over 200 years ago.

The originalist approach seems especially odd when it comes down to arguing over such matters as whether 18th-century lawyers agreed (as Scalia contends) that "a prefatory clause does not limit or expand the scope of the operative clause" and whether (as Stevens contends) the phrase "'bear arms' most naturally conveys a military meaning" and "the Second Amendment does not protect a 'right to keep *and* to bear arms,' but rather 'a right to keep and bear arms'" (emphasis in original). The justices may as well have tried reading the entrails of dead hamsters.

Is the answer to embrace liberals' "living Constitution" jurisprudence, which roughly translates to reading into the 18th-century document whichever meaning and values the justices consider most fundamental?

By no means. Rather, in the many cases in which nothing close to consensus about the meaning of the Constitution is attainable, the justices should leave the lawmaking to elected officials. To borrow from an article I wrote in 1986: "Those who work so hard to prove that the Constitution cannot supply the values for governance of modern society seem to think that judges must do it, with a little help from their friends in academia. But the argument rebounds against the legitimacy of judicial review itself. Bork poses a question for which they have no good answer: 'If the Constitution is not law [that] tells judges what to do and what not to do—. . . what authorizes judges to set at naught the majority judgment of the American people?'"

Now it seems that the originalist view of the Constitution is indeed incapable of telling today's judges what to do—not, at least, with any consistency from one judge to the next. So is judicial review itself obsolete?

Not quite. Judicial review remains valuable, perhaps indispensable, because it helps provide the stability and protection for liberty inherent in our tripartite separation of powers, with the legislative, executive, and judicial branches serving as the three legs of a stool and with each potent enough to check abuses and excesses by the others.

The June 12 decision rebuffing President Bush's (and Congress's) denial of fair hearings to Guantanamo detainees proclaiming their innocence is a case in point. But the broad wording of Kennedy's majority opinion, joined by the four liberals, went too far by flirting with a hubristic vision of unprecedented judicial power to intrude deeply into the conduct of foreign wars. *(See my column, 6/21/08, p. 15.)*

For better or worse, what Scalia has called the imperial judiciary—sometimes liberal, sometimes conservative—seems here to stay.

Indeed, not one of the nine justices seems to have a modest understanding of his or her powers to set national policy in the name of enforcing the Constitution. But the other branches, and most voters, seem content with raw judicial policy-making—except when they don't like the policies. For better or worse, what Scalia has called "the imperial judiciary"—sometimes liberal, sometimes conservative—seems here to stay.

Given this, the best way to restrain judicial imperialism may be for the president and the Senate to worry less about whether prospective justices are liberal or conservative and more about whether they have a healthy sense of their own fallibility.

Reprinted by permission from *National Journal*, July 5, 2008, pp. 10–11. Copyright © 2008 by National Journal Group Inc. All rights reserved.

Article 13

Two Takes
Pulpit Politics Is Free Speech

To what extent should religious leaders be able to incorporate political endorsements into their preaching? Some pastors are protesting IRS restrictions preventing them from backing specific candidates. Should religious leaders be allowed to endorse candidates from their pulpits?

RON JOHNSON JR.

Pro Who is in charge of the pulpit? The church or the IRS? That is the question that recently led me and other pastors to deliver sermons on the subject of the upcoming elections, despite tax rules used to stifle speech about candidates. The sermons were part of a broader effort, the Alliance Defense Fund's Pulpit Initiative, which is designed to protect pastors' First Amendment rights.

I wish to be clear from the outset. I have no desire to turn my pulpit into a Christian version of the Chicago political machine. My church will not be writing large checks to candidates, or to anyone else for that matter. We have plenty to do educating Christians about tithing to support the church, let alone political campaigns.

I have no intention of selecting my sermon topics by watching CNN or Fox News. I have no secret dream of becoming president or even running for dogcatcher. To suggest, as some have, that somehow we are being seduced by political power or that we are looking to government to be America's "savior" is silliness. And no, the Pulpit Initiative is not about encouraging pastors to endorse candidates from the pulpit.

Free speech. The purpose of the Pulpit Initiative is to restore the right of pastors to speak freely from the pulpit without fear of punishment by the government for doing what churches do: speak on any number of cultural and societal issues from a biblical perspective. Christians believe that civil government owes its existence to God and is therefore accountable to him to behave righteously in serving the common good. A significant role of the church is—and always has been—to encourage the civil magistrate to do what is good and not what is evil.

"Why does the IRS get to judge the political content of a pastor's sermon?"

—Ron Johnson Jr. is the senior associate pastor of the Living Stones Fellowship Church in Crown Point, Ind.

The Internal Revenue Service has placed itself in the role of evaluating the content of a pastor's sermon to determine if the message is "political." We need to ask: Where did this authority come from? And why should Americans be willing to submit to this unconstitutional power grab without even a whimper? Why are pastors the only people who have allowed the IRS to censor their First Amendment rights for a tax exemption they have enjoyed since the founding of our nation—a tax exemption that existed long before the IRS did?

Erik Stanley, the head of the Pulpit Initiative, has rightly pointed out that pastors spoke freely about the policy positions of candidates for elective office throughout American history, even endorsing or opposing candidates from the pulpit, without anyone ever questioning whether churches should remain tax exempt. It was common-place—even expected—for pastors to speak in support of or in opposition to candidates until the tax code was amended in 1954 with no legislative analysis or debate.

Churches are tax exempt because they are churches, not because the government decided to bless them with a "subsidy." The church is not a profit-making business or individual. It is not getting a pass on taxes; it is simply outside the government's appropriate tax base.

Secularists often create a false sacred/secular dichotomy that conveniently silences our message. While it's true that pastors need to stop letting others tell us to keep Jesus inside of the church and out of the world he died to redeem, this particular battle is about whether we as pastors even have the right to speak as we feel led to within our own four walls.

The Pulpit Initiative is not about promoting political parties or agendas or establishing a "theocracy." It's about our right to bring kingdom principles and solutions to bear on contemporary social problems if we so choose. A pastor may choose not to, but it's the pastor's choice, not the choice of the IRS.

If we cannot discuss any and all topics, including those the IRS may deem "political," even within our communities of faith, we will become what Martin Luther King Jr. called an "irrelevant social club without moral or spiritual authority."

Simply put, it's time for the church to be the church.

Article 13. Two Takes

Campaigns Can Split Churches

REV. BARRY W. LYNN

Con Most Americans who go to church expect to hear about salvation, morality, and scripture. They don't anticipate hard-ball political endorsements.

Congress made it clear in 1954 that nonprofit groups, religious or secular, may not endorse or oppose any candidate for public office.

That doesn't mean pastors, priests, rabbis, or imams cannot criticize government policies. It doesn't mean clergy cannot express views on specific pieces of legislation or ballot initiatives. Nor does it even mean they cannot participate in partisan political activities in their own personal capacity.

What it does signify is that pastors cannot make declarations to favor or oppose any candidate from the pulpit. They cannot take money from the collection plate and give it to support a candidate. And if they want to participate in any partisan activity in their personal capacity, they must make sure it is done in a manner indicating it is separate from their religious institution.

Put simply, the tax code prevents religious institutions from serving as political machines, a concept in keeping with the separation of church and state our founding fathers envisioned.

Now a group called the Alliance Defense Fund is working to alter that vision. The group recently urged pastors around the country to violate tax law and promote candidates from the pulpit. Thirty-three pastors participated. But we all know churches in America are already free to engage in religious speech. Tax law doesn't take that freedom away.

We know this because the Revs. Jerry Falwell (on the right) and William Sloane Coffin (on the left) weren't silenced from speaking from the pulpit on moral issues. And the regulation never prohibited the Rev. Martin Luther King Jr. from speaking passionately of the need for social change in our country—while never once endorsing a candidate from the pulpit.

"The law affords an astounding amount of freedom for the clergy to preach."

—Barry W. Lynn of Americans United for Separation of Church and State is an ordained minister in the United Church of Christ.

It's clear that the law as it is provides those of us in the clergy with an astounding amount of freedom to express a wide array of opinions from the pulpit. But we cannot turn sermons into political ads for candidates, nor should we have that "freedom." In a recent survey on this issue, 87 percent of Americans agreed that pastors shouldn't endorse candidates during worship services. Americans clearly see that churches should not become cogs in anybody's political machine.

Church schisms. Americans also recognize politics can split congregations.

Take, for example, the church in Waynesville, N.C., where the Rev. Chan Chandler told congregants during a sermon in October 2004, "If you vote for John Kerry this year, you need to repent or resign." This comment tore apart the congregation, initially leading to the ouster of nine Democratic members. Following a congregational meeting, they were invited back to the church and Chandler was forced to resign.

More recently at High Point Church in Arlington, Texas, Pastor Gary Simons showed a video that depicted the views of Barack Obama and John McCain on abortion. His sermon gave God's alleged view on abortion and told the congregation how to vote accordingly. Some congregants said the pastor seemed to be comparing Obama to King Herod, the biblical monarch who ordered the mass murder of infants. Several members just walked out.

Frankly, a tax exemption is a privilege, not a right. The IRS can strip a church of its tax exemption for egregious violations of law. It did just that to the Church at Pierce Creek in Binghamton, N.Y. In 1992, the church spent $44,000 on an ad in *USA Today* that called Bill Clinton a sinner and warned Christians against voting for him. The congregation contested the revocation in court but lost at every level. Not one judge agreed the church had some sort of "free speech" or "free exercise" right to engage in partisan activities.

This is not a First Amendment concern but a ploy for groups like the Alliance Defense Fund to use churches to push a political agenda. If a church doesn't want to follow IRS law, it can refuse the tax exemption. But churches that want this privilege have to play by the same rules as everyone else.

From *U.S. News & World Report*, November 17/24, 2008, pp. 10–11. Copyright © 2008 by U.S. News & World Report. Reprinted by permission.

UNIT 2

Structures of American Politics

Unit Selections

14. **Misremembering Reagan,** Ramesh Ponnuru
15. **Small Ball after All?,** Jonathan Rauch
16. **The Founders' Great Mistake,** Garrett Epps
17. **Happy Together?,** Donald R. Wolfensberger
18. **Veto This!,** Carl M. Cannon
19. **A Political Odyssey,** Dan Balz and Haynes Johnson
20. **The Shuffle President,** Matt Bai
21. **When Congress Stops Wars: Partisan Politics and Presidential Power,** William G. Howell and Jon C. Pevehouse
22. **The Case for Congress,** Lee H. Hamilton
23. **The Case for Busting the Filibuster,** Thomas Geoghegan
24. **A Bit of Advice, Madam Speaker,** Charlie Cook
25. **Remote Control,** Stuart Taylor Jr.
26. **Court Approval,** Jeffrey Rosen
27. **Marking Time: Why Government Is Too Slow,** Bruce Berkowitz
28. **Worse than You Think,** Peter J. Wallison and Edward Pinto
29. **Teaching a Hippo to Dance,** Amy Wilkinson

Key Points to Consider

- Read Articles I, II, and III of the U.S. Constitution to get a picture of the legislative, executive, and judicial branches as painted by the words of the Framers. How does that picture compare with the reality of the three branches as they operate today?

- How might the presidency and Congress change in the next 100 years? What about the judicial branch?

- What advantages and disadvantages do each of the following have for getting things done: The president? The vice president? A cabinet member? The speaker of the House of Representatives? The Senate majority leader? The chief justice? A top-ranking bureaucrat in an executive branch agency? A congressional aide?

- Which position in American government would you most like to hold? Why?

Student Website
www.mhhe.com/cls

Internet References

Department of State
http://www.state.gov

Federal Reserve System
http://www.federalreserve.gov

Supreme Court/Legal Information Institute
http://supct.law.cornell.edu/supct/index.html

United States House of Representatives
http://www.house.gov

United States Senate
http://www.senate.gov

James Madison, one of the primary architects of the American system of government, observed that the three-branch structure of government created at the Constitutional Convention of 1787 pitted the ambitions of some individuals against the ambitions of others. Nearly two centuries later, political scientist Richard Neustadt wrote that the structure of American national government is one of "separated institutions sharing powers." These two eminent students of American politics suggest an important proposition: the very design of American national government contributes to the struggles that occur among government officials who have different institutional loyalties and potentially competing goals.

This unit is divided into four sections. The first three treat the three traditional branches of American government, and the last one treats the bureaucracy. One point to remember when studying these institutions is that the Constitution provides only a bare skeleton of the workings of the American political system. The flesh and blood of the presidency, Congress, judiciary, and bureaucracy are derived from decades of experience and the shared expectations of today's political actors.

A second relevant point is that the way a particular institution functions is partly determined by the identities of those who occupy relevant offices. The presidency operates differently with Barack Obama in the White House than it did when George W. Bush was president. Similarly, Congress and the Supreme Court function differently according to who serve as members and who hold leadership positions within the institutions. There were significant changes in the House of Representatives after Democrat Nancy Pelosi succeeded Republican Dennis Hastert as speaker in 2007 and, before that, when Hastert took over from Newt Gingrich in 1999. In the Senate, over a two-year period beginning in January 2001, Republican majority leader Trent Lott was succeeded by Democrat Tom Daschle, who in turn was succeeded by Republican Bill Frist. These changes in leadership brought obvious changes in the operation of the Senate. Changes were evident once again when Democrat Harry Reid succeeded Frist in 2007.

A third point about today's American political system is that in recent decades traditional branch-vs.-branch conflict has been accompanied, and perhaps even overshadowed, by increasing partisanship between the two major parties. In the first six years of George W. Bush's presidency, Republican members of Congress seemed to be substantially more influenced by the party affiliation that they shared with President Bush than the institutional loyalties that, in Madison's eyes, would and should pit Congress against the president. In turn, many observers think that during the first six years of the twenty-first century, Congress did not satisfactorily perform its traditional function of "checking" and "balancing" the executive branch.

The November 2006 elections brought Democratic majorities to both houses of Congress. For Democrats in the 110th Congress, party affiliation and a belief in institutional or branch prerogatives reinforced one another. Both their party differences with President Bush *and* their belief that Congress is and should be co-equal to the executive branch fueled opposition to the Iraq war and to other Bush initiatives. And President Bush no doubt had both party loyalties and executive branch prerogatives in mind as he contended with Democratic leaders and Democratic majorities in the 110th Congress. The 2008 elections brought Democratic control to all three elective institutions of the national government (Presidency, House of Representatives, and Senate), a situation that political scientists call "unified government." Some observers of the American political system, Woodrow Wilson among them, have argued that "unified government" is likely to be more effective and efficient than its counterpart, "divided government" (in which neither major party controls all three elective institutions). Others, most notably Professor David Mayhew of Yale University, arguably the most respected contemporary political scientist specializing in the study of American politics, have concluded that "unified governments" vary very little, if at all, from "divided governments" in what they accomplish. For nearly two-thirds of the six decades since World War II, Americans have lived under "divided government." But in January 2009, a new period of "unified government" (under Democratic control) began, and time will tell how well the country is served.

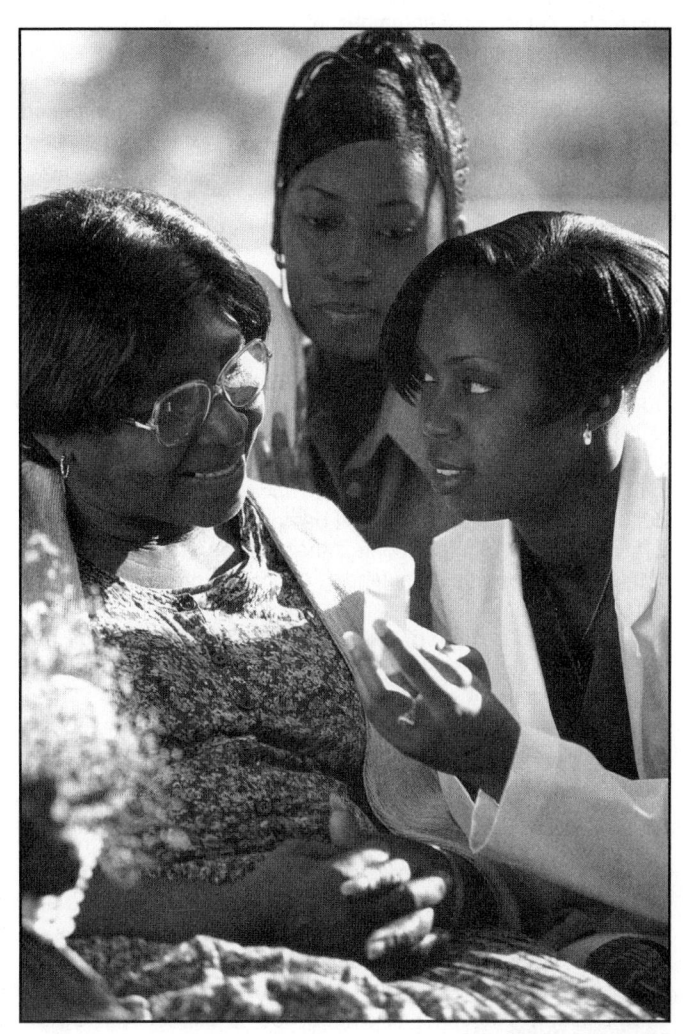

© Creatas/PunchStock RF

The first section of this unit contains articles on the contemporary presidency. They include both retrospective assessments of the presidency of George W. Bush, and articles appearing after Barack Obama had served a few months in office. Eight months after Bush became president in the aftermath of the controversial 2000 election, terrorist attacks on the World Trade Center and the Pentagon on September 11, 2001, abruptly transformed the context of his presidency. Americans of both parties rallied around President Bush in his efforts to respond decisively to the attacks, and Congress passed a resolution that authorized President Bush to invade Iraq. The resulting war in Iraq began in early 2003, and within a few weeks President Bush triumphantly declared the success of the invasion that had overthrown the regime of Iraqi president Saddam Hussein.

But the situation in Iraq grew worse instead of better in the next few years, and by the start of 2006, the majority of Americans opposed the Iraq war and disapproved of Bush's performance as president. The 2006 congressional elections gave voters the chance to express their views forcefully on the Bush administration and they did so, handing majority control of both houses of Congress to the Democrats. In November 2008, of course, Democrat Barack Obama won the presidency over Republican John McCain, with widespread disapproval of Bush's performance as president being a key factor in that electoral outcome. It is in this context that articles in the first section of this unit assess the presidencies of both George W. Bush and Barack Obama.

The second section of this unit treats Congress, which has undergone noteworthy changes in the past four decades after over a half-century of relative stability anchored by an enormously powerful seniority system instituted in the early twentieth century. In the 1970s, reforms in that seniority system and the budgetary process brought an enormous degree of decentralization to Capitol Hill. The unexpected Republican takeover of the House of Representatives as a result of the 1994 congressional elections brought even more changes. The new Republican speaker, Newt Gingrich, reduced the power of committees and the importance of the seniority system, imposed term limits on committee chairs, consolidated power in the Speaker's office, and became a prominent figure on the national scene. The 2006 congressional elections, of course, led to Democrats regaining majority control of both houses. A woman, Representative Nancy Pelosi of California, became Speaker of the House for the first time in history, and Republicans controlled neither house of Congress for the first time in a dozen years. Democrats increased their majorities in both houses of Congress in the 2008 elections, and, of course, a fellow Democrat, Barack Obama, won the White House. As mentioned above, it remains to be seen whether the first instance of "unified government" under Democratic control since the first two years of the Clinton administration in the early 1990s will lead to noteworthy accomplishments.

The Supreme Court sits at the top of the U.S. court system and is the focus of the third section in this unit. The Court is not merely a legal institution; it is a policymaker whose decisions can affect the lives of millions of citizens. The Court's decisive role in determining the outcome of the 2000 presidential election showed its powerful role in the American political system. Like all people in high government offices, Supreme Court justices have policy views of their own, and observers of the Court pay careful attention to the way the nine justices interact with one another in shaping decisions of the Court.

Membership of the nine-member Court—and, in turn, operation of the institution as a whole—was unusually stable between 1994 and 2005, one of the longest periods in American history during which no Supreme Court vacancies occurred. In July 2005, Associate Justice Sandra Day O'Connor announced her intention to resign and a few months later Chief Justice William Rehnquist died. President Bush's nominees to fill the two vacancies, John Roberts and Samuel Alito, became Chief Justice and Associate Justice, respectively. Less than four months into Barack Obama's presidency, Associate Justice David Souter announced his retirement. President Obama nominated Sonia Sontomayor to replace Souter, and she became the first Hispanic woman to sit on the Court. Most observers expect more vacancies to occur during the Obama presidency and the new president is expected to continue to nominate individuals with quite different judicial and policy views from those of Bush's two nominees.

The bureaucracy of the national government, the subject of the fourth and last section in this unit, is responsible for carrying out policies determined by top-ranking officials. Yet the bureaucracy is not merely a neutral administrative instrument, and it is often criticized for waste and inefficiency. Even so, government bureaucracies must be given credit for many of the accomplishments of American government.

As a response to the September 11 terrorist attacks, Congress in 2002 passed a bill establishing the Department of Homeland Security, the biggest reorganization of the executive branch since the Department of Defense was founded in the aftermath of World War II. In the summer of 2004, the 9/11 Commission issued its report recommending the restructuring of the government's intelligence community. In response, Congress passed a bill in December 2004, establishing the position of Director of National Intelligence in an attempt to bring a clearer hierarchy and better communication to the government's intelligence establishment. More effective and efficient functioning of the bureaucracy has clearly become an important concern since the destruction of the World Trade Center, and efforts to improve government bureaucracy's performance in the areas of homeland security and intelligence gathering are continuing.

Some observers have attributed the home mortgage crisis and related credit and banking problems that signaled a dramatic economic downturn in 2008 to ineptly functioning bureaucracies of the national government. Fannie Mae and Freddie Mac, two relatively obscure government-related agencies, began to receive unfavorable scrutiny as the nation's home mortgage system faltered, with catastrophic consequences for Wall Street and the economy as a whole. Critics suggested that too generous lending by banks under the auspices of Fannie Mae and Freddie Mac was responsible for the credit problems that touched off the global economic downturn.

Misremembering Reagan

The Gipper still has lessons to teach—just not the ones we usually hear.

RAMESH PONNURU

"Republicans have attempted to lead with one eye on the rear-view mirror, gazing at the fading reflection of Ronald Reagan.... But Ronald Reagan cannot win the victory for Republicans in [the next election], and the party had best get busy finding fresh ideas and new leaders." Ralph Reed wrote those words after the Republicans lost the election—the election of 1998.

Since then, Reagan's reflection has faded still more. Yet the tendency Reed lamented has only gotten stronger. Reagan's death, the reevaluation of his presidency by historians (including liberal historians), and, above all, the political failure of George W. Bush have made conservatives cling to Reagan's memory more fiercely. In 2008, during the first presidential-primary campaign since Reagan died, each of the Republican candidates presented himself as his reincarnation. After Republicans lost the election, conservative activist Phyllis Schlafly offered familiar advice: "Republicans should follow Ronald Reagan's example." Conservative congressman Patrick McHenry is running a PAC that seeks "to return the Republican party to its Ronald Reagan roots." The Heritage Foundation's website seeks to resolve today's policy debates by asking, "What would Reagan do?"

Much of the debate over the Republican party's future concerns Reagan. Should the party return to Reaganism, as the "traditionalists" argue, or move beyond it, as the "reformers" say? At a recent party gathering, Jeb Bush was reported to have thrown in his lot with the reformers and urged the party to let go of Reagan's memory. (There are conflicting accounts of what Bush said.) Several conservatives who had previously been fans of the former Florida governor attacked him lustily and in public for the alleged slight.

Liberals deride the Right's fixation with Reagan, and even some conservatives roll their eyes about it. When invoking Reagan, conservatives are prone to two characteristic vices: hero-worship and nostalgia. To hear some conservatives talk, you would forget that Reagan was a human being who made mistakes, including in office. You would certainly forget that movement conservatives were frequently exasperated with Reagan's administration.

Nostalgia is the more serious charge. Conservatives may be looking for a presidential candidate to present himself as "the next Reagan"—the Republican field in 2008 certainly thought so—but the public at large is not. It has, after all, been more than 20 years since Reagan held office. The country has changed, and many observers say that his agenda and even his political vision are now obsolete. "I love Reagan too," Republican strategist Mike Murphy recently wrote in *Time*. "But demographics no longer do."

Liberals may disdain what they call the "cult of Reagan," but Republicans' affection and respect for the man who won the Cold War seems a lot less cultish than their own infatuation with President Obama. Reagan was the most consequential president of the last 35 years, the most successful Republican president of the last century, and the president most associated with the conservative movement. Of course conservatives should try to learn from his example.

If, that is, they can decide which Reagan to learn from. There are quite a few on offer. There is the sunny, irenic Reagan. At a reception following the unveiling of a statue of Reagan in the Capitol, RNC chairman Michael Steele said, "You never heard a harsh word come out of his mouth." (What about the "evil empire" and "welfare queens"?) There is the libertarian Reagan: Former congressman and media personality Joe Scarborough recently complained that Republicans had gone astray by forgetting the maxim, which he attributed to Reagan, that the government is best that governs least. (This was right after Scarborough complained that Republicans had gone too far in deregulating Wall Street.) The liberals' Reagan, meanwhile, is defined less by his principles than by the compromises he made to them: less by the large tax cuts he won than by the smaller tax increases he accepted.

The conservatives who summon Reagan's ghost for use in today's arguments usually use him as a stand-in for doctrinal purity. He illustrates the alleged axiom that true-blue conservatism—these days we would probably have to say true-red—wins elections. His leadership of his party was bookended by moderate-Republican failure. Presidents Nixon and Ford brought their party so low that in their aftermath it considered changing its name. The elder President Bush wasn't just a one-termer; his vote in successive elections dropped more than that of any president since Hoover (another moderate Republican, as historically minded conservatives will inform you). Many conservatives draw the lesson that the GOP is better-off without its non-Reaganite politicians, now dubbed RINOs, for "Republicans in name only."

Such Republicans regularly put up roadblocks in President Reagan's path, and he was frequently tart about them in his diaries. Yet he never supported primary campaigns against them. He challenged an incumbent Republican in a primary himself, of course, in 1976. But he did not support his former aide Jeffrey Bell in his 1978 primary against New Jersey senator Clifford Case. His White House even supported Jim Jeffords of Vermont. After he won the battle over the basic direction of the party, he seems to have concluded in practice that further intra-party fighting was counterproductive. He may have been on to something. It is melancholy for conservatives to contemplate that yesterday's liberal Republican senators have been replaced far more often by liberal Democrats than by conservative Republicans.

Reagan's practice ran counter to our superficial impressions of him in other respects, too. "It's true hard work never killed anyone," he famously quipped, "but I figure, why take the chance?" Reagan had his reasons for wanting his political career to seem effortless. It can be useful for a politician to be underestimated, and for his utterances to sound like pure expressions of common sense. But we now have an extensive documentary record that shows that Reagan worked extremely hard both on his policies and on his rhetoric.

As a conservative spokesman, the governor of the largest state, and then a presidential-candidate-in-waiting, Reagan had taken and defended positions on a multitude of issues. Compared with some later Republican leaders, such as the first Bush and Sen. John McCain, Reagan cared about a broader range of policies and knew more about them. He didn't make up positions on the fly or go with his gut. He had also honed his explanations of why he sought some reforms and rejected other proposals. Steven Hayward, the second volume of whose excellent history *The Age of Reagan* appears this summer, points out that it took practice and attention as well as talent for Reagan to become the Great Communicator. Reagan could ramble through responses to questions and even occasionally flub his lines. But he concentrated on getting his most important messages across, and doing it succinctly.

Are Reagan's would-be successors willing to follow this example? Bush, Dole, Bush, and McCain didn't. None of them could talk, and some of them seemed to disdain the enterprise. One hopes that Sarah Palin is doing her homework on national policy issues behind the scenes, prepared to reemerge with an unquestioned mastery of them. In her career in national politics, she has given one fine speech, at last year's party convention. Nothing as good has followed.

Contemporary Republican politicians might find two features of Reagan's rhetoric instructive. The first is that when he was not appearing before movement audiences, his conservatism was rarely explicit. He did not advertise his conformity to a school of thought even when he did, in fact, conform. He did not, that is, sell his policies on the basis of their conservatism. Rather the reverse: He used attractive policies to get people to give his conservatism a look. Hayward notes that Reagan's televised speech on behalf of Barry Goldwater's presidential campaign was "quite ideological," but that Reagan presented the choice before Americans as "up or down" rather than "left or right."

The second is that the American Founding loomed large in Reagan's rhetoric. The political scientist Andrew Busch has found that during his presidency Reagan mentioned the Founders more than his four immediate predecessors combined. He mentioned the Constitution ten times in his memoirs, compared with zero for those predecessors. Those of us who believe that our political inheritance from the Founders is what conservatives ought to be trying to conserve will naturally find this fact heartening. No serious student of Reagan can believe that his constitutionalism was other than sincere. It also served him well politically. It promoted unity among his sometimes fractious supporters. It rooted him in American tradition even as his opponents called him a radical. It provided a connective thread, a coherence, a seriousness, and even a nobility to his politics that it might otherwise have lacked.

Reagan's constitutionalism puts him squarely in the "traditionalist" camp of today's intra-conservative debates. Taken in full, though, his record shows how misconceived those debates are. Some of his current admirers make him out to be a supremely gifted exponent of a timeless conservative platform, as though he were merely Barry Goldwater with better public-relations skills. Yet Reagan differed in both his program and, especially, his emphases.

John O'Sullivan has written that "Reaganism was not an innovation in political thought":

> It was conservative common sense applied to the problems that had developed in the 1960s and 1970s. To the stagflation of the economy, it applied tax cuts and the monetary control of inflation; to the market-sharing cartel of OPEC, it applied price decontrol and the "magic of the marketplace"; and to the revived threat from the Soviet Union it applied a military build-up and economic competition.
>
> These policies were what most conservatives would have recommended as answers to these problems at most times in [the 20th] century. The only novel thing about them is that they were actually carried out.

That is not quite right. Reagan was an innovator in key respects. It is true, for example, that most conservatives harbored a preference for lower spending and lower taxes. But the previous conservative orthodoxy was content to wait until some future day when spending was lowered to embark on tax cuts. Hence Goldwater voted against Kennedy's tax reductions. Reagan redefined the conservative orthodoxy on this issue.

I quote O'Sullivan at length because he nonetheless grasps something that other admirers of Reagan have scanted: Reaganism succeeded as state craft because it applied characteristically conservative insights to the challenges of his time. Reagan wanted to reform entitlement programs, just as Goldwater did; but he saw that the country had more pressing needs, such as for tax reduction. The tight connection between Reagan's agenda and the nation's circumstances tends to elude us these days—so much so that we misquote one of his signature lines. Everyone remembers that he said in his first inaugural address that "government is not the solution, government is the problem." Everyone forgets that the line began "In this present crisis." He wasn't saying that government was always "the problem," let alone that it would always be the problem in the same way that it was in 1981.

It is thus a mistake to assume that keeping true to the spirit of Reaganism requires contemporary conservatives to press forward with his administration's program: to keep trying to reduce the top income-tax rate, for example, with the same urgency he brought to the task. A conservative today should share Reagan's conservative preference for lower taxes and a less socially harmful tax code. But he might conclude that, in part because Reagan changed our circumstances, the tax that most needs lowering today is the payroll tax. Or he might conclude that a free-market reform of health care is more important now than any changes to the tax code.

Gov. Mitch Daniels of Indiana says that Republicans must be the party of hope, not the party of memory. Reagan managed to lead both parties simultaneously. George Will, correcting a widespread misunderstanding at the time Reagan took office, said that he did not wish to take the country back to the past: He wanted to restore the past's way of facing the future. Conservatism must constantly adapt. Burke knew it. So did Reagan. He was simultaneously a traditionalist and a reformer. Let all conservatives be so.

From *The National Review,* July 6, 2009, pp. 33–34. Copyright © 2009 by National Review, Inc, 215 Lexington Avenue, New York, NY 10016. Reprinted by permission.

Small Ball after All?

Both supporters and critics of George W. Bush tend to view him as a game-changing president. But it's possible he may be remembered another way—as a comparatively minor figure.

JONATHAN RAUCH

"Worst. President. Ever." That succinct judgment, received not long ago via e-mail from a political scientist, sums up a good deal of what conventional wisdom has to say about President Bush. In an unscientific online poll of 109 historians conducted in April and published by the History News Network at www.hnn.us, more than 60 percent rated Bush's presidency as the worst in U.S. history. In his 2007 book, *Second Chance: Three Presidents and the Crisis of American Superpower,* former National Security Adviser Zbigniew Brzezinski titles his chapter on Bush "Catastrophic Leadership." "A calamity," Brzezinski wrote. "A historical failure."

And he was referring to just the Iraq war. The litany of disasters and failures commonly attributed to Bush has grown familiar enough to summarize in checklist format: WMD; Guantanamo; Abu Ghraib; waterboarding; wiretapping; habeas corpus; "Osama bin Forgotten"; anti-Americanism; deficits; spending; Katrina; Rumsfeld; Cheney; Gonzales; Libby. In this view, George W. Bush is at least as destructive as was Richard Nixon, a president whose mistakes and malfeasances took decades to undo.

Though a smaller band, Bush's defenders parry that he will look to history more like Harry Truman, a president whose achievements took decades to appreciate. In this view, Bush will be remembered as the president who laid the strategic groundwork for an extended struggle against Islamist terrorism; who made democratization the centerpiece of foreign policy; who transformed the federal-state relationship in education; who showed that a candidate can touch the "third rail" of Social Security and still get elected (twice).

Antithetical as these two views are, notice what they assume in common: Bush has been a game-changing president. For better or worse, he has succeeded in his ambition of being a transformative figure rather than one who plays "small ball," in Bush's own disdainful phrase. Hasn't he?

Perhaps not. Today's debate overlooks another possibility: Bush may go down in history as a transitional and comparatively minor figure. His presidency, though politically traumatic, may leave only a modest policy footprint. In that sense—though by no means substantively or stylistically—Bush's historical profile may resemble Jimmy Carter's more than Truman's or Nixon's. Recall that in 1980 many people wondered if the country would ever recover from Carter. Five years later, he was all but forgotten.

In other words, Bush may have accomplished something that seemed out of the question in January 2002, when he touched greatness, and in January 2007, when he touched bottom. Bush may have achieved mediocrity.

If that hypothesis sounds snide, it is not intended to. Had Bush left office at the beginning of last year, his tenure might indeed have gone down as calamitous. Winding up in the middling ranks, then, would be no mean accomplishment. Far from being happenstance, such a finish would reflect an unusual period of course correction that might be thought of as Bush's third term.

From Uniter to Divider

Odd as it may sound today, this president entered office as a proponent of bipartisanship. In his December 13, 2000, victory speech after Vice President Gore conceded the election, Bush called for a new politics of conciliation. Speaking from the chamber of the Texas House of Representatives, he said, "The spirit of cooperation I have seen in this hall is what is needed in Washington, D.C."

To be sure, Bush was capable of aggressive partisanship and brusque unilateralism, as when in 2001 he pushed through large tax cuts with little Democratic support and tore up an assortment of treaties. But in the early days, he also brought off a bipartisan education reform, and after the September 11 terrorist attacks, he did what even his critics agreed was a masterful job of rallying the country. His public approval rose to a dizzying 90 percent.

The fruits of this early period of two-party government were considerable: a new campaign finance law, the USA PATRIOT Act's revisions to domestic-security law, the Sarbanes-Oxley corporate accountability law, the creation of the Homeland

Security Department, and more. "Seventeen major legislative acts were passed in the first two years of the Bush presidency—the second-highest among first-term presidents in the post–World War II period," writes Charles O. Jones, a presidential historian.

Had Bush left office in January 2003, his reputation as our era's Truman might have been assured. His successor would have inherited not only the aforementioned laws but also a successful military campaign in Afghanistan, a set of broadly accepted policies for combating terrorism, and a United Nations still following America's lead in efforts to confront Iraq's Saddam Hussein.

But 2002 also marked the Bush administration's transition to a more rigidly partisan governing style. That January, Karl Rove, Bush's top political adviser, signaled that Republicans would "make the president's handling of the war on terrorism the centerpiece of their strategy to win back the Senate," as *The Washington Post* reported. This represented a distinct change in tone: "Until now," *The Post* noted, "Bush has stressed that the fight against terrorism is a bipartisan and unifying issue for the country."

It was in this period, says Steven Schier, a political scientist at Carleton College and the author of a forthcoming book on Bush's presidency, that "you get the idea of permanent political advantage based on national security, which becomes intoxicating to Republicans." That year's midterm election, which gave Republicans control of the Senate and consolidated their margin in the House, vindicated their strategy but also trapped the party within it.

In firm control of both branches, Bush and congressional Republicans embarked on an experiment in one-party government. Thanks to superbly honed party discipline, the plan worked for a while, but the price was high. Republicans had to govern from the center of their party, rather than the center of the country; Democrats were absolved from responsibility for the results.

What followed was a period of substantive excess and stylistic harshness that came to define Bush's presidency in the public's mind, obliterating memories of the "compassionate conservative." The list of setbacks in this period is long, merely beginning with Iraq's disintegration, North Korea's test of a nuclear bomb, and Iran's growing boldness and influence.

At home, profligate spending and a major Medicare expansion disgusted conservatives. Rising deficits troubled centrists, as did Bush's (unsuccessful) intervention in a dispute over ending the life of Terri Schiavo. His efforts to reform Social Security and immigration policy collapsed embarrassingly; his sluggish response to Hurricane Katrina cratered Americans' faith in his competence. Abroad, Abu Ghraib, Guantanamo, waterboarding, and extrajudicial detentions called the country's basic decency into question. One could go on.

Whatever you may think of the administration's policies on those issues individually, their cumulative effect on Bush and his party are not in doubt. By 2006, the president's approval rating was in the 30 percent range and falling. The Democrats swept control of Congress in November. If Bush's presidency had ended in January 2007, his reputation as our era's Nixon might have been assured.

But, of course, Bush did not leave office then. Instead he embarked on what history may come to regard as the most surprising and interesting period of his presidency. Many presidents have had good first terms and troubled second ones; the pattern is conventional, and Bush's presidency approximately fits it. But Bush has used his last two years as, in effect, a third term, behaving as if he were his own successor.

Bush's Third Term

He began with some significant personnel changes. In 2006, Bush replaced the second of two mediocre Treasury secretaries with Henry Paulson Jr., whose performance has been lauded by the likes of House Financial Services Committee Chairman Barney Frank, D-Mass., and New York City Mayor Michael Bloomberg—neither of them Bush fans.

Shortly afterward, ending what seemed an interminable wait, Bush got around to replacing the dysfunctional Donald Rumsfeld at the Defense Department with the far more adept Robert Gates. At Justice, Michael Mukasey, a respected federal judge, set about re-professionalizing a department whose independence and credibility had been compromised under Alberto Gonzales. At State, the president gave Condoleezza Rice her head, a trust that her predecessor, Colin Powell, had never been allowed.

"There was unquestionably a sharp change in their approach to the world and in their policies," says Kenneth Pollack, a senior fellow at the Brookings Institution's Saban Center for Middle East Policy. Frequently cited examples include:

- **The Iraq surge.** Against conventional wisdom, the administration sent more troops to Iraq and gave them a new commander with a new strategy. Even Bush's critics now acknowledge that Iraq is in far better shape than it was two years ago. The gains may or may not be sustainable, but if they can be preserved, Iraq has a shot at peace and stability. That seemed a pipe dream before the surge.
- **Iran.** Bush has been patient but, many critics have said, rigid in his dealings with this charter "axis of evil" member. Lately, however, he has softened his posture and attempted to cultivate new openings, notably by authorizing what *The New York Times* called "the most significant American diplomatic contact with Iran since the Islamic revolution in 1979."
- **The Israeli-Palestinian conflict.** After years of keeping his distance from what he seemed to regard as a morass, Bush changed course in 2007, authorizing Rice to pursue diplomacy vigorously and presiding over a relaunch of Israeli-Palestinian peace talks last November.
- **North Korea.** Over hawks' objections, Bush struck a denuclearization deal with Pyongyang much like the one that conservatives, including some Bushies, derided the Clinton administration for making. "That

is the really dramatic example of Bush doing toward the end of his presidency something he would never have contemplated or tolerated early on," says Strobe Talbott, who was deputy secretary of State in the Clinton administration and is now the president of Brookings.
- **Global warming.** Repudiating the Kyoto climate treaty was among Bush's first presidential acts, and he maintained his disengagement from the issue through most of his presidency. But in July he joined the other major industrial countries in promising to halve greenhouse-gas emissions by 2050. A European environmental official told *The Washington Post,* "President Bush has moved considerably over the past one to two years."

What changed? "I think we learned a bit," Stephen Hadley, Bush's national security adviser, told reporters in June. He was speaking of U.S. forbearance in dealing with the always obstreperous North Koreans, but to outsiders the statement appears to have broader applicability. Liberals say that the administration became more flexible because it ran out of alternatives, conservatives that its resolve weakened, Kremlinologists that (as one aide told Carla Anne Robbins of *The New York Times*) "Condi wins."

Ever protective of Bush's trademark steadfastness, the White House takes issue with any talk of U-turns. "I think there's actually remarkable continuity," says Tony Fratto, the deputy press secretary. He asserts that reality has caught up with the administration rather than the other way around. It took time to draw China, India, and other major emerging economies into global-warming negotiations, a prerequisite for any ambitious U.S. commitment; it took time to persuade China to lean on the North Koreans to make a nuclear deal; it took time to weather leadership changes and factional struggles so that Middle East peace negotiations could resume. The surge in Iraq, Fratto says, "was clearly a change of course. It was a new strategy." Elsewhere, he argues, the administration has been reaping the fruits of patient effort.

Whatever the explanation (the various versions may all be partially right), in the past couple of years Bush has significantly changed the starting point for his successor. He now hands President McCain or President Obama a healing rather than a broken Iraq, diplomatic processes rather than deadlocks in the Middle East and the Korean Peninsula, and a position on global warming that is widely viewed as moving the United States past obstructionism. Both Republican John McCain and Democrat Barack Obama, it seems fair to guess, would rather follow than precede Bush's late-term adjustments. Whatever you may think of Bush's abilities as a sailor, he has proved pretty good at bailing.

Meanwhile, despite his abysmal popularity and the Democrats' control of Congress, Bush managed to win approval, on essentially his own terms, of a new wiretapping law and funding for the war in Iraq, the last things anyone expected a Democratic Congress to give him. "I think what you see here is a guy who has learned to be as effective as possible in reduced circumstances," says Schier, the Carleton College political scientist. Paradoxically, this chief executive who prided himself on assertive, even aggressive, leadership proved to be a weak strong president but a surprisingly strong weak one.

Back to the Future

To what end?

That Bush has improved his legacy over the past couple of years is an easy case to make. True, the economy has declined, oil prices have risen, and the mortgage crisis has loosed a Category 4 storm on Wall Street. But the economy and oil prices are not under Bush's control, and both he and Congress have leaned aggressively into the financial gale, adopting a bipartisan stimulus package and intervening forcefully to support the mortgage market. With unemployment rising and Wall Street wondering where the mortgage fallout may end, no one much likes the economy's condition today, but not many people would trade the *policies* of late 2008 for the *policies* of late 2006.

The harder question is where Bush will leave matters after eight years, not after just the past two. The only honest answer is: It depends. What do you measure? How do you think a President Gore would have done? Those are the sorts of questions that keep historians and journalists in business. You will find no definitive answers here.

But you will find a hypothesis, one at odds with the prevailing wisdom that Bush, whatever you think of him, has been a president of major consequence. Consider, again, the five problems mentioned earlier, this time comparing their likely status in January 2009 with where things stood in January 2001.

- **Iraq.** The situation in January 2001 was unstable and dangerous but not critical. Then, for a time, affairs in Iraq became critical, verging on catastrophic. Now the situation is again unstable and dangerous but not critical. Obviously, Iraq today is a very different kind of problem than it was eight years ago, one more pregnant with both promise and risk. But the U.S. preoccupation with Iraq that Bush inherited in 2001, and that he intended to dispose of once and for all, will instead continue into its fourth presidency, if not beyond. (Iraq will soon have been a sinkhole for U.S. foreign-policy energy for 20 years, almost half the length of the Cold War.)
- **Iran.** This rogue nation was a problem in 2001 and remains a problem now. In the interim, Iran has raced ahead with uranium enrichment, elevated an apocalyptic demagogue to its second-highest office, and expanded its regional influence. At the same time, however, Western powers have edged toward a consensus on confronting Iran, and the United Nations has imposed several sets of sanctions, some of which—the financial ones—appear to be biting.
- **The Israeli-Palestinian conflict.** As Bill Clinton left office, the United States was struggling against long odds to broker a peace deal; as George W. Bush leaves office, the United States is struggling against long odds to broker a peace deal. Whether the situation is more

intractable today than it was eight years ago is an open question, but Bush's reluctant conclusion that the U.S. must mediate an agreement all but guarantees that no future president will try to walk away from the problem. If Bush couldn't walk away, no one can.

- **North Korea.** A tenuous denuclearization agreement was in place eight years ago; a tenuous denuclearization agreement is in place again today. Now, as then, the agreement may or may not be worth the paper it is written on. In the interim, Pyongyang acquired a few more nuclear bombs and tested one, but the two sides are still playing the same game.
- **Global warming.** Eight years ago, the United States had committed itself to reducing greenhouse-gas emissions, though rhetorically rather than substantively; today the United States has again committed itself to reducing greenhouse-gas emissions, though rhetorically rather than substantively. As with the Israeli-Palestinian conflict, Bush's attempt to disengage from the climate-change issue merely established that the United States cannot do so. The next president will pick up more or less where the Clinton-era Kyoto Protocol left off.

Bush may have made these problems harder or easier to solve, a question that partisans can contest to their hearts' delight. What is clear, however, is that all five were large and difficult challenges in 2000 and all five remain large and difficult challenges in 2008.

Two other areas, the war on terrorism and fiscal policy, deserve a closer look. Bush's defenders stake their claims heavily on the former, his detractors on the latter. Has Bush built a lasting architecture for the "long war"? Has he wrecked the country's finances?

The War on Terrorism

September 11, 2001, it is often said, "changed everything." It certainly changed Americans' attitudes, convincing the public that Al Qaeda and its affiliates are a threat rather than a nuisance, and that the United States must apply military as well as civilian tools to confront terrorism. September 11 thereby triggered a cascade of policy changes, ranging from the PATRIOT Act to the Iraq war.

The threat was pre-existing, however, as Bush's supporters tirelessly repeat (adding that the Clinton administration failed to deal with it). The Qaeda-Taliban-jihadi nexus has relocated its headquarters from Afghanistan to the nearby borderlands of Pakistan, but whether and how much it has been weakened is hard to say. The absence of attacks on the American homeland is to the Bush administration's credit, but it seems only fair to guess that a Gore administration would have worked domestic security just as hard. And to the extent that the United States is safer because jihadists shifted their attention to the softer targets of Iraq and Afghanistan, that is not altogether reassuring. Might a different administration have attained better results with less damage to the American brand overseas? Maybe.

A more intellectually interesting question is whether Bush, like Truman, has set up a lasting strategic and institutional architecture for managing the conflict. Bush's defenders argue that a return to either the pinprick responses of the 1990s or the cynical realism of the Cold War is inconceivable. "If we wait for threats to fully materialize, we will have waited too long," Bush said in June 2002. That statement, the core of the Bush Doctrine, is hardly controversial today.

"None of the key elements of the Bush Doctrine—[U.S.] primacy, prevention [of terrorist attacks], coalitions of the willing, and democracy promotion—will be abandoned in practice by successor administrations, whatever their rhetorical recalibrations and tactical adjustments," write Timothy J. Lynch and Robert S. Singh in their new book, *After Bush: The Case for Continuity in American Foreign Policy*. Similarly, the Detainee Treatment Act, the Military Commissions Act, the PATRIOT Act, and the new Foreign Intelligence Surveillance Act have put in place mechanisms that subsequent presidents may revise but will not repudiate.

Such is the strongest upside case for Bush as a turning-point president, and it may well prove correct. The retort, however, is also strong: What was most striking about Bush's attitude toward the long war was his perverse *reluctance* to create a sustainable institutional architecture. In marked contrast to Truman, Bush treated Congress and U.S. allies as afterthoughts, running the war on jihadism as a permanent emergency in which the president could single-handedly make up the rules as he went along. He regarded the war as an opportunity to build a political base, not an institutional one.

Result: It took nearly seven years to finish the first trial of a Guantanamo detainee. The courts have shredded Bush's claim that he could detain almost anyone practically forever, leaving the presidency, in some respects, with less power than it had before. (George H.W. Bush and Bill Clinton both used Guantanamo Bay to hold detainees without judicial oversight; the Supreme Court recently revoked that authority.) The country still lacks coherent and indisputably constitutional structures governing the detention and treatment of terrorism suspects. The sad fact, in this view, is that it will be largely up to the next president to construct the durable, consensus-based structures for the war on terrorism that Bush could and should have built.

As for strategy, this retort continues, what is new about the Bush Doctrine is not sustainable, and what is sustainable is not new. President Gore would likely have moved toward preemption and democratization, but without the rhetorical and military excesses that have widely discredited both approaches. Indeed, Bush has been forced to become a reluctant realist, collaborating with exactly the sorts of tyrannies—in the Middle East, Africa, and Asia—that he has condemned. The Bush Doctrine's worst enemy, in this view, has been Bush.

This argument can't be settled any time soon, if ever. What seems fairly clear, however, is that the jihadist threat is still very much present and that Bush's role has been ambiguous, erecting while also partially discrediting a militarily focused, executive-driven approach that may prove more vigorous than sustainable.

ANNUAL EDITIONS

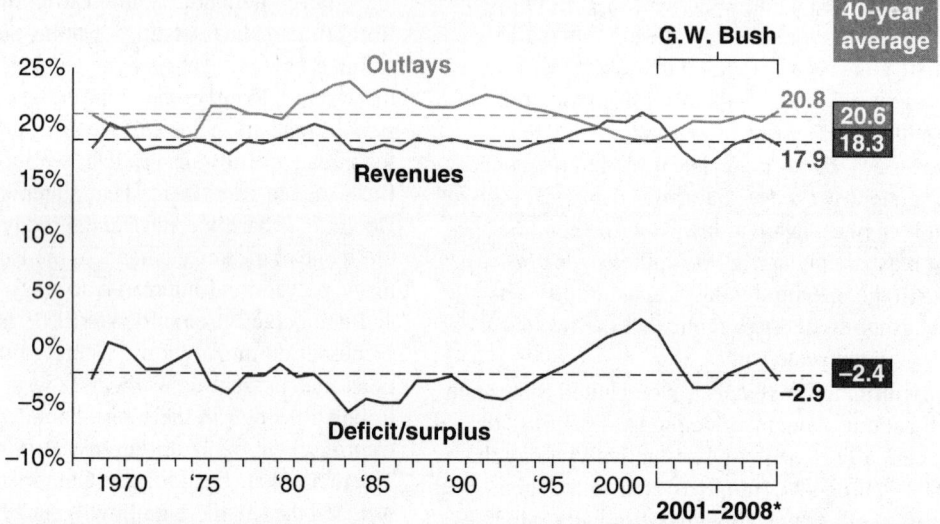

Only Average Federal outlays, revenues and deficit, 1968–2008 (percentage of GDP).
Source: Congressional Budget Office.

Red Ink Rising

Bush's critics, meanwhile, argue that he trashed the country's finances. He cut taxes steeply, waged an expensive war without paying for it, engineered a costly expansion of Medicare (also without paying for it), and untethered federal spending, thus turning healthy surpluses into chronic deficits—all while failing to come to grips with an imminent crisis in entitlement programs.

"We're in much worse fiscal shape today than we were in 2001," says David Walker, who until recently headed the Government Accountability Office and is now president of the Peter G. Peterson Foundation. According to GAO figures, the country's fiscal exposure—the long-term shortfall in its finances, in present-value terms—more than doubled between 2000 and 2007 from $20.4 trillion to $52.7 trillion. Walker says, moreover, "Our $53 trillion hole grows $2 trillion to $3 trillion a year even with a balanced budget," because of rising health care costs, demographic changes (fewer workers supporting more retirees), and accumulating interest on the national debt.

Fiscal recklessness is probably the strongest downside case for Bush as a turning-point president. Here again, however, there is a challenging counterargument.

Thanks mainly to a growing economy, but also partly to tighter budgets, the deficit shrank relative to the economy in Bush's second term. *(See Chart, this page.)* In fiscal 2007, the deficit was 1.2 percent of gross domestic product, which was below the average of the last 40 years. The 2008 deficit will rise to about 2.9 percent of GDP, according to administration projections; but that is still only slightly above the 40-year average, and the cause is primarily cyclical rather than structural, because the economy is slowing down.

For all the talk of runaway spending, moreover, outlays are also right at the 40-year norm. The exceptional federal spending policies were Ronald Reagan's and Bill Clinton's, not Bush's.

As for Bush's tax cuts, viewed in historical perspective they were a blip, not a turning point. Overall, taxes went down early in this decade but then bobbed back up again, though not all the way. In 2007, federal receipts were 18.8 percent of GDP, slightly *above* the 40-year average of 18.3 percent. Even assuming that Bush's tax cuts are all extended when they expire after 2010, *and* assuming that Congress "fixes" the alternative minimum tax by permanently stopping its upward creep, the Congressional Budget Office forecasts that taxes will stay at about 19 percent of GDP.

Bush and Congress, then, didn't smash the revenue base; they just returned it to its well-worn groove. That groove seems to track the public's comfort zone, as suggested by the nonpartisan Tax Policy Center's recent report that Obama's tax program would keep revenues at about 18.4 percent of GDP through 2018—again, right at the historical norm.

As for how the tax burden is allocated, Obama promises to cut taxes at the bottom and increase them at the top. He would raise the top income-tax rate to 39.5 percent, right back where Bill Clinton left it. You can make a plausible case that the end result would approximate what would have been President Gore's tax code.

No question about it: Bush failed to deal with the long-term entitlement problem. He left the ledger in worse shape than he found it, and his botched effort to reform Social Security may have made entitlement reform more difficult politically. "I think we've lost a tremendous opportunity during the Bush period and, really, over the last part of the Clinton period," says Stuart Butler, an analyst at the Heritage Foundation.

Still, as Butler's comment implies, Bush's failure in this regard is not unique. His predecessors ducked the entitlement problem and his would-be successors are all but promising to do the same. McCain's pledges to reduce taxes, and Obama's to increase spending, would likely make the problem worse.

Bush's fiscal failing, in short, arguably lies not in being exceptional but in being all too ordinary.

Disaster, or Detour?

The point of this article is not that the Bush years were uneventful or barren. Far from it. In the realm of foreign policy, the last eight years have seen a nuclear pact with India, a passel of bilateral trade agreements, a redoubled commitment to fight HIV/AIDS, and an innovative foreign-aid program (the Millennium Challenge Account). In social policy, the Bush presidency has brought education reform, restrictions on embryonic-stem-cell research, and incentives for faith-based programs. In finance, the 2002 Sarbanes-Oxley law and the government's current scramble to contain the mortgage-market turmoil have arguably done more to extend Washington's control over Wall Street than anything since the Depression era. The creation of the Homeland Security Department represents the biggest bureaucratic reorganization that Washington has seen in two generations. Bush's two Supreme Court appointments have nudged the Court to the right.

None of those changes is trivial. But few if any are outside the boundaries of ordinary policy-making in an eventful eight-year presidency. It seems fair to guess that most will get sentences or paragraphs, rather than chapters, in the history books.

Indeed, what is most striking about the Bush presidency is not the new problems it has created (though Iraq may yet change that verdict) or the old problems it has solved (though Iraq may yet change that verdict, too). What is striking, rather, is that Bush will pass on to his successor all the major problems and preoccupations he inherited: Iraq, Iran, Israel and the Palestinians, North Korea, global warming, Islamist terrorism, nuclear proliferation, health care, entitlement costs, immigration. What is remarkable, in other words, is not how much Bush has done to reshape the agenda but how little.

Reagan removed inflation from the agenda; he and George H.W. Bush (still sadly underrated) removed the Cold War; Clinton removed welfare and the deficit. Bush, as of now, ends up more or less where he started—not exactly, of course (he resurrected the deficit, for example), but about as close as history's turbulence allows. The biggest surprise of the Bush presidency is its late-breaking bid to join the middling ranks of administrations that are judged not by their triumph or tragedy but by their opportunity cost: What might a greater or lesser president have done with Bush's eight years?

In his recent book *The Bush Tragedy,* Jacob Weisberg, the editor-in-chief of the Washington Post Co.'s Slate Group, mentions the he was "originally going to call this book *The Bush Detour,* thinking of the Bush presidency simply as lost time for the country." His original title may have been closer to the mark. If so, history's ironic judgment on this singularly ambitious president will be that his legacy was small ball, after all.

Reprinted by permission from *National Journal,* September 20, 2008, pp. 22–28. Copyright © 2008 by National Journal Group Inc. All rights reserved.

Article 16

The Founders' Great Mistake

Who is responsible for the past eight years of dismal American governance? "George W. Bush" is a decent answer. But we should reserve some blame for the Founding Fathers, who created a presidential office that is ill-considered, vaguely defined, and ripe for abuse. Here's how to fix what the Founders got wrong—before the next G. W. Bush enters the Oval Office.

GARRETT EPPS

For the past eight years, George W. Bush has treated the White House much as Kenneth Grahame's Mr. Toad treated a new automobile—like a shiny toy to be wrecked by racing the motor, spinning smoke from the tires, and smashing through farmyards until the wheels come off. Bush got to the Oval Office despite having lost the popular vote, and he governed with a fine disdain for democratic and legal norms—stonewalling congressional oversight; detaining foreigners and U.S. citizens on his "inherent authority"; using the Justice Department as a political cudgel; ordering officials to ignore statutes and treaties that he found inconvenient; and persisting in actions, such as the Iraq War, that had come to be deeply unpopular in Congress and on Main Street.

Understandably, most Americans today are primarily concerned with whether Barack Obama can clean up Bush's mess. But as Bush leaves the White House, it's worth asking why he was able to behave so badly for so long without being stopped by the Constitution's famous "checks and balances." Some of the problems with the Bush administration, in fact, have their source not in Bush's leadership style but in the constitutional design of the presidency. Unless these problems are fixed, it will only be a matter of time before another hot-rodder gets hold of the keys and damages the country further.

The historian Jack N. Rakove has written, "The creation of the presidency was [the Framers'] most creative act." That may be true, but it wasn't their best work. The Framers were designing something the modern world had never seen—a republican chief executive who would owe his power to the people rather than to heredity or brute force. The wonder is not that they got so much wrong, but that they got anything right at all.

According to James Madison's *Notes of Debates in the Federal Convention of 1787*, the executive received surprisingly little attention at the Constitutional Convention in Philadelphia. Debate over the creation and workings of the new Congress was long and lively; the presidency, by contrast, was fashioned relatively quickly, after considerably less discussion. One important reason for the delegates' reticence was that George Washington, the most admired man in the world at that time, was the convention's president. Every delegate knew that Washington would, if he chose, be the first president of the new federal government—and that the new government itself would likely fail without Washington at the helm. To express too much fear of executive authority might have seemed disrespectful to the man for whom the office was being tailored.

Washington's force of personality terrified almost all of his contemporaries, and although he said little as presiding officer, he was not always quiet. Once, when an unknown delegate left a copy of some proposed provisions lying around, Washington scolded the delegates like a headmaster reproving careless prep-schoolers, and then left the document on a table, saying, "Let him who owns it take it." No one did.

Even when Washington remained silent, his presence shaped the debate. When, on June 1, James Wilson suggested that the executive power be lodged in a single person, no one spoke up in response. The silence went on until Benjamin Franklin finally suggested a debate; the debate itself proceeded awkwardly for a little while, and was then put off for another day.

Many of the conversations about presidential authority were similarly awkward, and tended to be indirect. Later interpreters have found the original debates on the presidency, in the words of former Supreme Court Justice Robert H. Jackson, "almost as enigmatic as the dreams Joseph was called upon to interpret for Pharaoh."

In the end, the Framers were artfully vague about the extent and limits of the president's powers. Article I, Section 8 of the Constitution, which empowers Congress, runs 429 words; Article II, Section 2, the presidential equivalent, is about half as long. The powers assigned to the president alone are few: he can require Cabinet members to give him their opinions in writing; he can convene a special session of Congress "on extraordinary occasions," and may set a date for adjournment if the two houses cannot agree on one; he receives ambassadors and is commander in chief of the armed forces; he has a veto on legislation (which Congress can override); and he has the power to pardon.

The president also *shares* two powers with the Senate—to make treaties, and to appoint federal judges and other "officers of the United States," including Cabinet members. And, finally, the president has two specific *duties*—to give regular reports on the state of the union, and to "take care that the laws be faithfully executed."

Article 16. The Founders' Great Mistake

All in all, the text of Article II, while somewhat ambiguous—a flaw that would be quickly exploited—provided little warning that the office of president would become uniquely powerful. Even at the convention, Madison mused that it "would rarely if ever happen that the executive constituted as ours is proposed to be would have firmness enough to resist the legislature." In fact, when citizens considered the draft Constitution during the ratification debates in 1787 and 1788, many of their concerns centered on the possibility that the Senate would make the president its cat's-paw. Few people foresaw the modern presidency, largely because the office as we know it today bears so little relation to that prescribed by the Constitution.

The modern presidency is primarily the intellectual handiwork not of "the Framers" but of one Framer—Alexander Hamilton. Hamilton's idea of the presidency can be found in a remarkable speech he gave to the convention, on June 18, 1787. In it, Hamilton argued that the president should serve for life, name Cabinet members without Senate approval, have an absolute veto on legislation, and have "the direction of war" once "authorized or begun." The president would be a monarch, Hamilton admitted, but an "elective monarch."

Hamilton's plan was so far from the mainstream of thought at the convention that none of its provisions was ever seriously discussed. Nonetheless, Hamilton was and remains the chief theorist of the presidency, first in writing his essays for *The Federalist* and then in serving as George Washington's secretary of the Treasury. In this latter role, acting as Washington's de facto prime minister, Hamilton took full advantage of the vagueness and brevity of Article II, laying the groundwork for an outsize presidency while the war-hero Washington was still in office.

In *The Federalist*, Hamilton had famously proclaimed that "energy in the executive is a leading character in the definition of good government." Just how much energy he favored became clear during America's first foreign crisis, the Neutrality Proclamation controversy of 1793. When Britain and France went to war, many Americans wanted to aid their Revolutionary ally. But Washington and the Federalists were rightly terrified of war with the powerful British Empire. Washington unilaterally proclaimed that the United States would be neutral.

France's American supporters, covertly aided by Thomas Jefferson, fiercely attacked Washington for exceeding his constitutional authority. The power to make treaties, they said, was jointly lodged in the president and the Senate; how could Washington unilaterally interpret or change the terms of the treaty of alliance with France?

Under the pen name "Pacificus," Hamilton wrote a defense of Washington's power to act without congressional sanction. The first Pacificus essay is the mother document of the "unitary executive" theory that Bush's apologists have pushed to its limits since 2001. Hamilton seized on the first words of Article II: "The executive power shall be vested in a President of the United States of America." He contrasted this wording with Article I, which governs Congress and which begins, "All legislative powers herein granted shall be vested in a Congress of the United States." What this meant, Hamilton argued, was that Article II was "a general grant of . . . power" to the president. Although Congress was limited to its enumerated powers, the executive could do literally anything that the Constitution did not expressly forbid. Hamilton's president existed, in effect, outside the Constitution.

That's the Bush conception, too. In 2005, John Yoo, the author of most of the administration's controversial "torture memos," drew on Hamilton's essay when he wrote, "The Constitution provides a general grant of executive power to the president." Since Article I vests in Congress "only those legislative powers 'herein granted,'" Yoo argued, the more broadly stated Article II must grant the president "an unenumerated executive authority."

Hamilton's interpretation has proved durable even though there is little in the record of constitutional framing and ratification to suggest that anyone else shared his view. In times of crisis, power flows to the executive; too rarely does it flow back. And while Washington himself used his power wisely (Jeffersonians found out in 1812 that pulling the British lion's tail was poor policy), it was during his administration that the seeds of the "national-security state" were planted.

The system that the Framers developed for electing the president was, unfortunately, as flawed as their design of the office itself. When Madison opened discussion on presidential election in Philadelphia, he opined that "the people at large" were the "fittest" electorate. But he immediately conceded that popular election would hurt the South, which had many slaves and few voters relative to the North. To get around this "difficulty" he proposed using state electors. Electoral-vote strength was based on a state's total population, not on its number of voters—and the South received representation for three-fifths of its slaves both in the House of Representatives and in the Electoral College.

Scholars still debate whether the Framers foresaw the prospect of a contested presidential election, followed by a peaceful shift of power. (Remember that, as Shakespeare pointed out in *Richard II*, kings left office feet first.) Some members of the founding generation believed that a duly elected president would simply be reelected until his death, at which point the vice president would take his place, much like the Prince of Wales ascending to the throne.

Perhaps as a result, the mechanics of presidential election laid out in the Constitution quickly showed themselves to be utterly unworkable. The text of Article II contained no provision for a presidential ticket—with one candidate for president and one for vice president. Instead, each elector was supposed to vote for any two presidential candidates; the candidate who received the largest majority of votes would be president; the runner-up would be vice president. In 1800, this ungainly system nearly brought the country to civil war. Thomas Jefferson and Aaron Burr ran as a team; their electors were expected to vote for both of them. Jefferson assumed that one or two would drop Burr's name from the ballot. That would have given Jefferson the larger majority, with Burr winning the vice presidency. But due to a still-mysterious misunderstanding, all the electors voted for both candidates, producing a tie in the electoral vote and throwing the election to a House vote.

The ensuing drama lasted six days and 36 ballots before Hamilton threw Federalist support to Jefferson (as much as he despised Jefferson, he regarded Burr as "an embryo-Caesar"). This choice began the chain of events that led to Hamilton's death at Burr's hands three years later. More important, the imbroglio exposed the fragility of the election procedure.

In 1804, the Electoral College was "repaired" by the Twelfth Amendment; now the electors would vote for one candidate for president and another for vice president. This was the first patch on Article II, but far from the last—the procedures for presidential election and succession were changed by constitutional amendment in 1933, 1951, 1961, and 1967. None of this fine-tuning has been able to fix the system. In 1824, 1876, 1888, and 2000, the Electoral College produced winners who received fewer popular votes than the losers, and it came startlingly close to doing so again in 2004; in 1824, 1876, and 2000, it also produced prolonged uncertainty and the prospect of civil unrest—or the fact of it.

Even when the election system works passably, a president-elect must endure another indefensible feature of the succession process. In England, a new prime minister takes office the day after parliamentary elections; in France, a newly elected president is inaugurated within a week or two. But when Americans choose a new leader, the victor waits weeks—nearly a quarter-year—to assume office. The presidential interregnum is a recurrent period of danger.

Originally, a new president didn't take office until March 4. This long delay nearly destroyed the nation after the 1860 election. During the disastrous "secession winter," Abraham Lincoln waited in Illinois while his feckless predecessor, James Buchanan, permitted secessionists to seize federal arsenals and forts. By March 1861, when Lincoln took office, the Civil War was nearly lost, though officially it had not even begun.

In 1932, Franklin Roosevelt crushed the incumbent, Herbert Hoover, but had to wait four months to take office. During that period, Hoover attempted to force the president-elect to abandon his proposals for economic reform. Roosevelt refused to commit himself, but the resulting uncertainty led the financial system to the brink of collapse.

The Twentieth Amendment, ratified in 1933, cut the interregnum nearly in half, but 11 weeks is still too long. After his defeat in 1992, President George H. W. Bush committed U.S. troops to a military mission in Somalia. The mission turned toxic, and Bill Clinton withdrew the troops the following year. Clinton was criticized for his military leadership, perhaps rightly—but the Constitution should not have permitted a repudiated president to commit his successor to an international conflict that neither the new president nor Congress had approved.

As the elder Bush did, an interregnum president retains the power of life or death over the nation. As Clinton did, an interregnum president may issue controversial or corrupt pardons. In either case, the voters have no means of holding their leader accountable.

The most dangerous presidential malfunction might be called the "runaway presidency." The Framers were fearful of making the president too dependent on Congress; short of impeachment—the atomic bomb of domestic politics—there are no means by which a president can be reined in politically during his term. Taking advantage of this deficiency, runaway presidents have at times committed the country to courses of action that the voters never approved—or ones they even rejected.

John Tyler, who was never elected president, was the first runaway, in 1841. William Henry Harrison had served only a few weeks; after his death, the obscure Tyler governed in open defiance of the Whig Party that had put him on the ticket, pressing unpopular proslavery policies that helped set the stage for the Civil War.

Andrew Johnson was the next unelected runaway. Politically, he had been an afterthought. But after Lincoln's assassination, Johnson adopted a pro-Southern Reconstruction policy. He treated the party that had nominated him with such scorn that many contemporaries came to believe he was preparing to use the Army to break up Congress by force. After Johnson rebuffed any attempt at compromise, the Republican House impeached him, but the Senate, by one vote, refused to remove him from office. His obduracy crippled Reconstruction; in fact, we still haven't fully recovered from that crisis.

American political commentators tend to think loosely about exertions of presidential authority. The paradigm cases are Lincoln rallying the nation after Fort Sumter, and Roosevelt, about a year before Pearl Harbor, using pure executive power to transfer American destroyers to embattled Britain in exchange for use of certain British bases. Because these great leaders used their authority broadly, the thinking goes, assertions of executive prerogative are valid and desirable.

Certainly there are times when presidential firmness is better than rapid changes in policy to suit public opinion. Executive theorists in the United States often pose the choice that way—steady, independent executive leadership or feckless, inconstant pursuit of what Hamilton called "the temporary delusion" of public opinion. But not all shifts in public opinion are delusive or temporary. An executive should have some independence, but a presidency that treats the people as irrelevant is not democratic. It is authoritarian.

Lincoln and Roosevelt asserted emergency powers while holding popular mandates. Lincoln had just won an election that also provided him with a handy majority in Congress; Roosevelt was enormously popular, and in 1940 his party outnumbered the opposition 3-to-1 in the Senate and by nearly 100 seats in the House.

But sometimes a president with little or no political mandate uses the office to further a surprising, obscure, or discredited political agenda. Under these circumstances, what poses as bold leadership is in fact usurpation. The most egregious case arises when a president's policy and leadership have been repudiated by the voters, either by a defeat for reelection or by a sweeping rejection of his congressional allies in a midterm election. When that happens, presidents too often do what George Bush did in 2006—simply persist in the conduct that has alienated the country. Intoxicated by the image of the hero-president, unencumbered by any direct political check, stubborn presidents in this situation have no incentive to change course.

When the voters turn sharply against a president mid-term, his leadership loses some or all of its legitimacy, and the result can be disastrous. Clinton was decisively repudiated in November 1994. After the election, the administration and the new Republican Congress remained so far apart on funding decisions that the government had to shut down for 26 days in 1995 and 1996. This episode is now remembered for Clinton's political mastery, but it was actually a dangerous structural failure. (Imagine that the al-Qaeda attacks of September 11, 2001, had happened instead on December 20, 1995, when the stalemate had forced the executive branch to send most of its "nonessential" employees home.)

To sum up, while George W. Bush may have been a particularly bad driver, the presidency itself is, and always has been, an unreliable vehicle—with a cranky starter, an engine too big for the chassis, erratic steering, and virtually no brakes. It needs an overhaul, a comprehensive redo of Article II.

Constitutional change is a daunting prospect. But consider how often we have already changed the presidency; it is the Constitution's most-amended feature. And this is the moment to think of reform—the public's attention is focused on the Bush disaster, and ordinary people might be willing to look at the flaws in the office that allowed Bush to do what he did.

So how should the presidency be changed?

First, voters should elect presidents directly. And once the vote is counted, the president-elect (and the new Congress) should take office within a week. Americans accustomed to the current system will object that this would not allow enough time to assemble a Cabinet—but in England and France, the new chief executive considers ministerial nominations before the election. A shorter interregnum would force the creation of something like the British shadow cabinet, in which a candidate makes public the names of his key advisers. That would give voters important information, and provide the president with a running start.

Next, Article II should include a specific and limited set of presidential powers. The "unitary executive" theorists should no longer be allowed to spin a quasi-dictatorship out of the bare phrase *executive power;* like the responsibilities of Congress, those of the president should be clearly enumerated.

It should be made clear, for example, that the president's powers as commander in chief do not crowd out the power of Congress to start—and stop—armed conflict. Likewise, the duty to "take care that the laws be faithfully executed" needs to be clarified: it is not the power to decide which laws the president wants to follow, or to rewrite new statutes in "signing statements" after Congress has passed them; it is a duty to uphold the Constitution, valid treaties, and congressional statutes (which together, according to the Constitution, form "the supreme law of the land").

After a transformative midterm election like that of 1994 or 2006, the nation should require a compromise between the rejected president and the new Congress. A president whose party has lost some minimum number of seats in Congress should be forced to form the equivalent of a national-unity government. This could be done by requiring the president to present a new Cabinet that includes members of both parties, which the new Congress would approve or disapprove as a whole—no drawn-out confirmation hearings on each nominee. If the president were unwilling to assemble such a government or unable to get congressional approval after, say, three tries, he would have to resign.

This would not give Congress control of the executive branch. A resigning president would be replaced by the vice president, who would not be subject to the new-Cabinet requirement. This new president might succeed politically where the previous one had failed (imagine Al Gore becoming president in 1995, and running in 1996—and perhaps in 2000—as an incumbent). And that possibility would discourage the new congressional majority from simply rejecting the compromise Cabinet. Resignation might be worse for them than approval.

As a final reform, we should reconsider the entire Hamiltonian concept of the "unitary executive." When George Washington became president, he left a large organization (the Mount Vernon plantation) to head a smaller one (the federal government). But today, the executive branch is a behemoth, with control over law enforcement, the military, economic policy, education, the environment, and most other aspects of national life. That behemoth is responsible to one person, and that one person, as we have seen, is only loosely accountable to the electorate.

In other areas, the Framers solved this problem neatly: they divided power in order to protect against its abuse. Congress was split into the House and the Senate to ensure that the legislative process would not be so efficient as to absorb powers properly belonging to the other branches. The problem now is not an overweening Congress but an aggrandized executive branch; still, the remedy is the same. We should divide the executive branch between two elected officials—a president, and an attorney general who would be voted in during midterm elections.

As we are learning from the ongoing scandal of the torture memos, one of the drawbacks of a single executive is that Justice Department lawyers may consider it their job to twist the law to suit the White House. But the president is not their client; the United States is. Justice Department lawyers appointed by an elected attorney general would have no motive to distort law and logic to empower the president, while the White House counsel's office, which does represent the president, would have every incentive to monitor the Justice Department to ensure that it did not tilt too strongly against the executive branch. The watchmen would watch each other.

This arrangement would hardly be unprecedented: most state governments elect an attorney general. The new Article II could make clear that the president has the responsibility for setting overall legal policy, just as governors do today.

None of these changes would erode the "separation of powers." That happens only when a change gives one branch's prerogatives to another branch. These changes refer in each instance back to the people, who are the proper source of all power. The changes would still leave plenty of room for "energy in the executive" but would afford far less opportunity for high-handedness, secrecy, and simple rigidity. They would allow presidential firmness, but not at the expense of democratic self-governance.

It's not surprising that the Framers did not understand the perils of the office they designed. They were working in the dark, and they got a lot of things right. But we should not let our admiration for the Framers deter us from fixing their mistakes.

Our government is badly out of balance. There is a difference between executive energy and autocratic license; between leadership and authoritarianism; between the democratic firmness of a Lincoln and the authoritarian rigidity of a Bush. The challenge we face today is to find some advantage in Bush's sorry legacy. Reform of the executive branch would be a good place to start.

From *The Atlantic*, January/February 2009, pp. 68, 70–73. Copyright © 2009 by Atlantic Monthly Group. Reprinted by permission of TMS Reprints.

Happy Together?

Americans love to complain about gridlock in Washington and partisan warfare between presidents and Congress. Yet the record suggests that unified party government is no panacea.

DONALD R. WOLFENSBERGER

On the campaign trail, Barack Obama promised to bring change to Washington and a post-partisan, non-ideological approach to governing. In his first post-election press conference on November 7, he reiterated this hope: "I know we will succeed if we put aside partisanship and politics and work together as one nation."

These snowflakes of soothing rhetoric drift slowly down on a Capitol Hill power plant fueled by partisanship and politics. What will happen when the snow hits the furnace—where majority Democrats and their allied interest groups have long been denied their wishes by Republican presidents and Congresses? The question is not whether President Obama can forge an extrapolitical national consensus to solve problems, but how effectively he will be able to govern with his own party in the majority in Congress.

One should not assume that Obama will get everything he wants from congressional Democrats any more than they will succeed in getting him to sign off on all their pent-up demands. Not only does the spike in deficits from the financial bailout and economic recession impose severe constraints, but the history of unified party government suggests that it is no more a guarantor of success than divided government is of failure. Indeed, American chief executives from Harry S Truman to Ronald Reagan enjoyed some of their greatest successes in periods of divided government. In the end, what the people want and are willing to speak up for usually matters more than all the frantic maneuvering in Washington.

One of the features of the American system that most baffles visitors from parliamentary democracies is the paradox that it can create unified party government without total party unity. They find it hard to believe that our system was intentionally designed with internal checks and balances precisely in order to prevent hasty action and the concentration of too much power in any one place. As James Madison put it, "Ambition must be made to counteract ambition." And the Pennsylvania Avenue axis of power between the White House and the Capitol is aswirl with ambition. Even when politicians belong to the same party, they represent different geographic and demographic constituencies that often put them at odds with one another and their own party's president. The system was not designed for action. It typically reacts only when required by events, public opinion, and presidential prodding.

That is why the young scholar Woodrow Wilson dismissed the Madisonian system as outmoded. "As at present constituted," he wrote in his 1885 doctoral dissertation, *Congressional Government,* "the federal government lacks strength because its powers are divided, lacks promptness because its authorities are multiplied, lacks wieldiness because its processes are roundabout, lacks efficiency because its responsibility is indistinct and its action without competent direction."

As president, Wilson would reconcile himself to Madison's Constitution as a "living" and "evolving" document. Building on his admiration for the British system of responsible party government, Wilson gave us the first "legislative presidency" as he moved his New Freedom agenda through a Democratic Congress in his first two years. He did so by addressing joint sessions of Congress (a record 22 appearances over eight years); traveling frequently to Capitol Hill to meet with Democratic leaders and their committee lieutenants; holding informal press conferences; and even scheduling forums in the White House on whether he should sign legislation sent to him by Congress.

But the Capitol Hill experiences of the Obama administration are not likely to resemble those of Wilson, nor of the other great examples of "unified" party government, which gave us Franklin D. Roosevelt's New Deal and Lyndon B. Johnson's Great Society.

FDR's presidency occurred under very unusual circumstances (notwithstanding some parallels to today's economic troubles). President Johnson's Great Society successes were made possible in part by the emotional backwash from the assassination of President John F. Kennedy and in part by LBJ's unique mastery of congressional procedures and personalities.

Moreover, Congress as an institution has changed considerably since those periods of presidential dominance. Compared with earlier times, when powerful, autonomy-minded committee chairmen ruled the Hill, the political parties and their leaders in Congress play a much greater role today in directing legislative policy-making. Congress entered this new age in the early 1970s as a result of congressional reforms that produced a resurgence of internal party cohesion and activity to levels not witnessed since the turn of the 20th century. Inspired in part by opposition to the Nixon administration, the Democratically controlled Congress and its members became more assertive, entrepreneurial, and independent of the executive branch.

The more relevant examples of unified party government are the presidencies of Jimmy Carter, Bill Clinton, and George W. Bush—all of whom came to the White House from the governorships of southern states, and all of whom promised to change the way Washington worked. All three experiences provide highly cautionary lessons.

Carter was elected in 1976 after the contentious Nixon years. Although he had a firm working majority of Democrats in both houses—292–143 in the House and 61–38 in the Senate—he never had a firm working partnership with Democrats on the Hill. His arrogant and dismissive attitude toward the Capital establishment offended his own party's leaders in Congress, as did his appointment of Washington neophytes to key staff positions in the White House. (After being refused a common courtesy by the White House, Speaker of the House Thomas "Tip" O'Neill [D.-Mass.] derisively referred to Carter aide Hamilton Jordan as "Hannibal Jerkin.") And Carter's attempt to eliminate pork barrel projects did not endear him to those members of Congress with a taste for that "other white meat."

Carter had a tendency to overload Congress's circuits by submitting many legislative proposals simultaneously, generating sparks and committee power outages. He sent his welfare reform proposal to the Hill, for instance, when the House Ways and Means Committee was already bogged down with his energy and tax reform initiatives. His attempt to enact a comprehensive energy plan faltered in Congress as special interests picked it apart, and it emerged much diminished. Four years of unified party government ended with the economy in dreadful condition and a hostage crisis in Iran (which was beyond Carter's control). The Democrats lost the White House and the Senate.

Bill Clinton took office in 1993 determined not to repeat Carter's mistakes. He made a point to meet with Democratic leaders in Congress prior to his inauguration to map out legislative priorities. He was persuaded to delay his campaign pledge to "eliminate welfare as we know it," and reluctant congressional Democrats agreed to move forward on a deficit reduction package to reassure financial markets in return for his backing of an economic stimulus package.

Clinton eked out narrow victories in both houses on his deficit package after being forced to abandon a hefty BTU energy tax proposal and settle instead for a 4.3-cents-per-gallon gasoline tax increase. His $16 billion economic stimulus club was whittled down in the Senate to a scrawny $840 million twig. The first lady's secret healthcare task force produced a bulky plan that couldn't get off the ground in either house as key congressional committee chairmen who had been shut out of the plan's development were unable to reach consensus.

The Clinton-era experiment with unified government ended ignominiously in 1994 with a Republican electoral sweep of both houses of Congress—which included the first GOP majority in the lower house in 40 years. Some of Clinton's signal achievements, however, were still to come. Even before the GOP takeover, his victory in passing the North American Free Trade Agreement in 1993 depended heavily on Republican support to offset large Democratic defections. Once Republicans took control of Congress, Clinton built on this tactic of "triangulating" between the two caucuses to enact welfare reform and balanced budget legislation.

George W. Bush came to office in 2001 after losing the popular vote and narrowly winning the Electoral College bowl in a sudden-death overtime refereed by the Supreme Court. Notwithstanding widespread press assertions that he had no mandate, he proceeded as if he did, assiduously courting members of both parties to pave the way for his priorities. Even though the Senate flipped to Democratic control in mid-2001 with the defection of Vermont Republican James Jeffords, the GOP still controlled the House. By the end of the year Bush managed to enact his No Child Left Behind education reform with bipartisan support, and his tax cuts with only minimal Democratic support.

Bush failed to achieve two other priorities of his administration, Social Security reform and immigration reform, but it was less party rivalry in Congress than a lack of firm support in the country that did them in. Democrats artfully played his proposal for private accounts in Social Security as an attempt to "privatize" the system, frightening seniors and forcing even Republicans to abandon it. Immigration reform was shot down by members of Bush's own party in Congress, aided by radio and cable shock jocks who claimed he was giving "amnesty" to "illegals."

The Bush presidency was at its apex in the wake of the September 11, 2001, terrorist attacks, when a divided Congress worked together to produce a blizzard of legislation in response. The president's job approval rating shot up to 90 percent, and even Congress briefly enjoyed an unprecedented 84 percent approval rating (more than double its customary level). Five years later, however, in the 2006 elections, Democrats retook control of both houses of Congress as public opinion turned against the Iraq war.

Within Congress itself, unified party government has generally had two less than salutary characteristics. The legislative branch tends to spend more money than it does under divided party government. It is generally more demanding, and presidents more giving (an arrangement that provides new meaning to the term normally used to describe the final review of legislative text before passage—"bill markup"). At the same time, Congress tends to slack off on its oversight responsibilities when its majorities share the president's party label. Under divided party government, however, it is suddenly able to juggle numerous high-level investigative oversight hearings into executive branch activities simultaneously.

Where might an Obama presidency fit in this historical mosaic of unified party governments? Unlike four of the last five presidents, who were governors, Obama is not a stranger to Washington's ways. His four years in the Senate count for something (though he spent most of the last two years running for president). His early picks of experienced hands to run his White House, cabinet departments, and legislative affairs office bode well for his success. But it will not be enough to have the best people giving the best advice in the White House and cabinet. It will ultimately depend on the president himself to show he can work with an independent, coequal branch made up of diverse personalities, interests, and ideologies—a branch that enjoys bipartisan unanimity on at least one principle: It is not about to abandon politics. Politics, after all, is simply a process of working through problems to build a consensus around mutually agreeable solutions—sometimes known as deliberative democracy.

If there is any conclusion to be drawn from recent history on the relative benefits of unified versus divided party government in the United States, it is this: The American system is capable of monumental accomplishments in times of crisis regardless of which party is in control of what lever of government, but the system can be just as incapable of doing anything when the people are not behind it—even with unified party control.

The American system is capable of monumental accomplishments in times of crisis regardless of which party is in control of what lever of government.

President Abraham Lincoln said as much when he observed, "With public sentiment, nothing can fail; without it, nothing can succeed." The success or failure of the Obama presidency will ultimately depend on the extent to which the people rally behind the plans and programs the new president and Congress are able to develop together as they work to address some of the most difficult problems this country has ever faced.

DONALD R. WOLFENSBERGER is director of the Congress Project at the Woodrow Wilson Center and author of *Congress and the People: Deliberative Democracy on Trial* (2000). His 28-year career as a staff member in the U.S. House of Representatives culminated in his position as chief of staff of the House Rules Committee.

From *The Wilson Quarterly*, Winter 2009, pp. 63–66. Copyright © 2009 by Donald R. Wolfensberger. Reprinted by permission of Donald R. Wolfensberger and Woodrow Wilson International Center for Scholars.

Article 18

Veto This!

When presidents veto a bill, they're exercising strength—or showing weakness. They usually win the override battles but sometimes lose the war for public approval.

CARL M. CANNON

The first presidential veto in American history was exercised, fittingly enough, by George Washington. He informed Congress in writing on April 5, 1792, that having "maturely considered the Act passed by the two Houses," he felt obligated to send it back on the grounds that it was unconstitutional. The legislation had to do with the number of citizens that each member of the House would represent. Having defeated the British on the field of battle—thereby giving the members of Congress their jobs to begin with—President Washington was accorded a high level of deference. No serious attempt to override the veto transpired, and Congress rewrote the measure to satisfy his objections.

Washington issued a single veto in his second term as well. This time, the dispute was on policy grounds, as the former general didn't cotton to the minutiae of a congressional plan for reorganizing the armed forces. He issued that veto on February 28, 1797; again, the veto stood. With these two actions, Washington initiated a tug-of-war between the executive and legislative branches of the federal government that persists to this day. The veto, a forgotten power during George W. Bush's first term, has now emerged as a prime battleground in the twilight months of his presidency.

"One thing that needs to be underscored is that because President Bush is a 'lame-duck' president, it doesn't mean that he is no longer powerful," said Chris Kelley, a political science professor at the University of Miami in Ohio. "The veto is a powerful weapon that the president simply must use from time to time."

Alexander Hamilton would have agreed. At the dawn of the Republic, Hamilton told his fellow Founders that the presidential veto (Latin for "I forbid") was "a qualified negative" that would serve as a brake on the passions of a popularly elected legislature. For five years, Bush did not avail himself of this authority, making him the only president except for John Quincy Adams to go an entire four-year term without vetoing anything that Congress sent him.

Was Bush practicing good government, or bad government? The answers to that question—and to the questions about Bush's newfound fondness for the veto—are partly political, partly theoretical. The political portion of the question is the voters' to answer. It will be addressed on the 2008 campaign trail, where presidential and congressional candidates from both parties are parsing Bush's recent vetoes to boost their candidacies. The theoretical component has even more movable parts and is the continuation of an argument more than 200 years old.

The first U.S. president to use the prerogative to veto *major* legislation solely over policy objections was Andrew Jackson. He was also the first to see the veto's potential as a political tool: In 1832, Jackson vetoed the enabling legislation to extend the charter of the villified Second Bank of the United States. Although his economic reasoning was specious, his political antenna was flawless, and the 1832 bank veto helped to assure Jackson's re-election.

For the better part of two centuries, political scientists and constitutional scholars have debated the propriety of Jackson's willingness to use the veto as a political tool, even while the principle became the standard for all subsequent presidents. Two rival theories of what constitutes a good-government use of the veto emerged.

The first, in the words of Stephen Skowronek, a political science professor at Yale University, is that the Jackson veto precedent "made a mockery of the premier operating principle" of Jeffersonian democracy, that is, deference to people's representatives in Congress. Jackson's veto was an artifice, these critics have said over the years, that short-circuited the separation of powers and contributed to the rise of the "imperial presidency" so disfavored by the Founders. In substituting the whims of one person for the will of the people, the veto also—and inevitably—soured relations between the branches of government.

"The veto tilts the balance of power in Washington too far toward the status quo."

—Sanford Levinson,
University of Texas professor

This was the precise complaint leveled against Bush last week when he vetoed a $35 billion, five-year expansion of the State Children's Health Insurance Program that passed both chambers of Congress with comfortable majorities and enjoyed bipartisan support.

"You [had] consensus across party and ideology, and a unity on the most important domestic issue, health care," Rep. Rahm Emanuel, D-Ill., said. "Except for one person."

But one person is all it takes—if that person is the president. "I think that this is probably the most inexplicable veto in the history of the country," Sen. Edward Kennedy, D-Mass., declared on the Senate floor. "It is incomprehensible: It is intolerable. It's unacceptable."

But accept it Congress must—unless Democrats can muster a two-thirds vote in each chamber to override. And that's where critics of the veto say that the system goes off the rails. "Put simply, the veto tilts the balance of power in Washington too far toward the status quo," says Sanford Levinson, professor of law and government at the University of Texas (Austin).

Levinson, author of a recent book, *Our Undemocratic Constitution: Where the Constitution Goes Wrong (and How We the People Can Correct It)*, asserts that anyone who thinks that judicial review of legislation passed by majorities has an autocratic tinge to it ought to be more worried about the presidential veto. He says that the Supreme Court has invalidated some 165 laws throughout U.S. history, while presidents have vetoed about 2,550 bills—only 106 of which Congress has managed to override. "If judicial activism is anti-democratic," he wrote recently, "then the presidential veto is, well, *very* anti-democratic."

There is, however, a second school of thought, represented by such scholars as Ronald C. Moe and Louis Fisher, who wrote about separation-of-powers issues for the Congressional Research Service. In this view, the presidential veto has a positive impact on the political process. For starters, the threat of a veto gives Congress an incentive to draw legislation more carefully, encouraging compromise. The veto can serve, as Alexander Hamilton suggested it might, as an additional brake against "improper laws" passed in the heat of the moment. "It establishes a salutary check upon the legislative body, calculated to guard the community against the effects of faction, precipitancy, or of any impulse unfriendly to the public good, which may happen to influence a majority of that body," Hamilton wrote.

Implicit in this view of checks and balances is a sophisticated notion: namely, that bad ideas, once signed into law, are more difficult to repeal than they were to enact. A contemporary illustration of Hamilton's fear may be the innocent sounding "Anti-Drug Abuse Act." Congress passed it hurriedly in 1986 without hearings, partially as a response to the cocaine-induced death of University of Maryland basketball star Len Bias. Coming as cheap crack, cocaine was turning urban streets into shooting galleries, the law prescribed far harsher sentences for possessing or dealing crack than it did for having powder cocaine.

That provision has put tens of thousands of young African-Americans in federal prison for far longer terms than white drug abusers, who tend to traffic in powder cocaine. President Reagan signed the law a week before the 1986 election. Eric Sterling, then a Democratic House aide who helped to draft the bill, wistfully recalls wishing that Reagan had vetoed it. Sterling, who now heads the Criminal Justice Policy Foundation, has been trying for the better part of two decades to persuade Congress to repeal the 1986 statute that mandates harsh terms for low-level cocaine dealers. "The Framers would have offered this law as a perfect example of the proper use of the presidential veto," Sterling said. "The problem is that by virtue of [these laws'] popularity, they are the hardest vetoes to cast."

Who's in Charge?

Mirroring the ongoing philosophical discussion about the proper role of presidential vetoes, another conversation is taking place on a more practical political level: Are vetoes a sign of strength or weakness in a chief executive? Does it help a president to issue vetoes, or hurt him and his party? These, as Bush and his suddenly fractious Republicans are discovering during the current term of Congress, are not academic questions. Once again, there are two sides to the equation; and once again, it is clear that the dispute won't be settled in Bush's presidency.

Let's call the first viewpoint the Rodney King school of thought. Why *can't* we all get along? This argument holds that presidential vetoes are, almost by definition, a sign that the chief executive lacks power, leadership ability, and a large enough following to shape events. In other words, a president who has to veto has failed to persuade, can't compromise, can't get the White House's own legislation through Congress, and is unable to take the issue over the heads of Congress to the people.

"A strong president needs fewer vetoes because he's able to exercise sufficient control over the congressional agenda, whether through decisive influence over legislative formulation or judicious use of veto threats that make it unlikely bills the president would oppose would land on his desk," says Robert Spitzer, professor of political science at the State University of New York (Cortland).

Framed this way, Capitol Hill has more say-so in setting the veto-agenda than is generally acknowledged these days in Washington. In an influential 1978 book on the politics of the veto, political scientists Thomas Romer and Howard Rosenthal explored this point. The authors outlined a "monopoly agenda control model" in which Congress, not the president, determines the fate of veto threats. In their theory, the agenda-setter is the pivotal legislator on any given issue, who presents the White House with take-it-or-leave-it proposals. Thus, the president is essentially in a reactive, and therefore, subordinate, position. This is something of a postmodern (or, at least, post–Franklin Roosevelt) view, and it probably is not a coincidence that Romer and Rosenthal were doing their research when Gerald Ford was president.

Ford was a creature of the House, but as president he was also a captive of the huge Democratic majorities he inherited as voters in 1974 reacted against the Republican Party of Richard Nixon, Spiro Agnew, and Watergate. Despite serving as president for barely half a term, Ford has the distinction of tying for second place on the all-time list of presidential vetoes that were overridden by Congress. Ford, overridden 12 times, shares that dubious silver medal with President Truman, who recorded the lowest Gallup Poll job-approval rating in history. The record-holder is Andrew Johnson, overridden 15 times, who was impeached by the House and nearly convicted in the Senate. The precipitating act of impeachment was Johnson's veto of a bill he believed—correctly, the Supreme Court later ruled—was unconstitutional.

"Many conventional presidency scholars argue that the use of a veto indicates a weak president, since the power of the presidency resides in his ability to bargain and persuade the Congress to go along with his policies," Kelley said. "Thus if he uses a veto, it means that his credibility with the Congress is low. Those who point to Ford as a failed president often will examine both his vetoes and the overrides."

Nolan McCarty, acting dean of the Woodrow Wilson School of Public and International Affairs at Princeton University, has described two other models for vetoes. In one, the White House and Congress have incomplete information about exactly what will precipitate a veto. Bush, for example, threatened to veto an expansion of the student loan program, but then didn't, perhaps leading wishful Democrats to believe that he would feel

Presidents Usually Win

Congress is rarely able to muster the two-thirds majority of votes in both chambers to override a presidential veto. This list, based on a compilation by the Congressional Research Service, does not include pocket vetoes after Congress adjourned.

President	Vetoes	Overrides	Vetos that Stuck	Major Overrides
TRUMAN	180	12	Natural-gas deregulation 1950 Coastal tidelands 1946, 1952	Taft-Hartley labor relations 1947 Income-tax cuts 1947, 1948 McCarran Internal Security 1950 McCarran-Walter immigration quotas 1952
EISENHOWER	73	2	Natural gas 1956 Farm spending 1956, 1958 Housing programs 1959 Pollution control 1960	TVA spending 1959 Federal pay 1960
KENNEDY	12	0	Federal pensions 1961	
JOHNSON	16	0	Cotton quotas 1968	
NIXON	26	7	Minimum-wage increase 1973	Water Pollution Control 1972 War Powers Act 1973
FORD	48	12	Oil price controls 1975	Freedom of Information Act 1974
CARTER	13	2	Nuclear reactor 1977	Oil import fee 1980
REAGAN	39	9	Textile quotas 1988	South Africa sanctions 1986 Water projects 1987 Highway funding 1987
G.H.W. BUSH	29	1	Minimum-wage increase 1989 Job discrimination 1990 China trade status 1992 Family-medical leave 1990, 1992 Taxes 1992 Stem-cell research 1992 Campaign finance 1992	Cable TV 1992
CLINTON	36	2	Spending reductions 1995 Appropriations 1995 Bosnia arms embargo 1995 "Partial-birth" abortion 1996, 1997 Product liability 1996 Tax culs 1999 Estate-tax repeal 2000	Line-item vetoes 1998 Securities litigation 1995
G.W. BUSH	4	0	Stem-cell research 2006, 2007 Iraq war limits 2007	

pressured to sign the SCHIP bill. The absence of a dominant legislative actor is what leads to the impasse. "When there is such uncertainty," McCarty wrote, "vetoes may occur because the Legislature overestimates its ability to extract concessions from the president."

In the wake of Bush's SCHIP veto, perhaps the nation's capital finds itself in that fluid state of affairs—meaning that, eventually, compromise legislation will emerge. The president has left the door open, and Congress is home to a handful of moderate Republicans who hope that Bush and the Democrats will walk through that door together. Of course, there is another, less pleasant, place to be. McCarty describes this model as "Blame-Game Vetoes."

When one party accuses the other of making "war on children," it is a safe bet that partisan advantage, not meaningful negotiation, is at the frontal cortex of the party's collective brain. Not that the Democrats tried to hide it. "We're not going to compromise," Senate Majority Leader Harry Reid said flatly after Bush's recent veto. House Speaker Nancy Pelosi vowed that Democrats would try to override and to make the issue "a hard vote for Republicans." New Jersey's Democratic governor, Jon Corzine, said, "I hope we override the veto before we start worrying about compromise."

To produce legislation, the process usually needs to work the other way around. But this is the blame game. SCHIP "has got to be up there with motherhood and apple pie," Rep. Jim Cooper, D-Tenn., told the *Los Angeles Times,* apparently with a straight face. "This is Tiny Tim. And who is against Tiny Tim? The only person in all of literature was Ebenezer Scrooge."

So who is winning the blame game? The early signs were a thumbs-down for George W. Scrooge and a thumbs-up for the Democrats. Public opinion polls showed that the voters, egged on by Democrats and media editorialists, thought that Bush's veto was wrongheaded, if not heartless. Eventually, White House aides and a few Republicans joined the fray, raising various arguments to support Bush's position: Some of the "children" covered under this bill would be nearly 25 years of age; the earning power of some eligible families tops $80,000 a year; some people opting into the program already have private health insurance; the Democrats' plan would be funded with a regressive $1-a-pack tax on cigarettes—that kind of thing. There was truth (or some truth, anyway) to all of these assertions, but Bush did not make them in the days leading up to the veto. Speaking to reporters at the White House, Bush simply said he had "philosophical" differences with the Democrats.

That was code, pure and simple, intended for the ears of fiscal conservatives, who have grown disenchanted with the GOP leader who has run up huge budget deficits in each year of his presidency. Translated, Bush's words meant: "OK, OK, I'll quit spending tax dollars like a drunken sailor."

In this new spirit, Bush has threatened to veto 10 of 11 pending appropriations bills. Until now, nobody knew for sure whether he was serious. In his first term, Bush vetoed nothing. In year five of his presidency, despite threatening 133 vetoes, Bush issued a single one, on embryonic-stem-cell research. This year, he vetoed a similar stem-cell bill, along with a spending measure aimed at curbing escalation of the Iraq war. Now Bush has issued his fourth veto. Has he found his groove? Perhaps. But some believe that he waited too long.

"It's an hour too late," says Frank Luntz, the Republican communications guru who helped fashion the 1994 Contract with America. "And a dollar too short."

Situational Ethics

Until Democrats reclaimed Congress in the 2006 elections, the premium in Bushworld was indeed on getting along. Rodney King would have approved. In the first term, Nicholas Calio, then-White House director of legislative affairs, told *National Journal* that the two top Republicans in the House, Speaker Dennis Hastert and Majority Leader Tom DeLay, made it a point of pride to send no bill to 1600 Pennsylvania Avenue that would be vetoed. "It's a real principle with the speaker and DeLay," Calio said. John Feehery, Hastert's spokesman at the time, went further, asserting that his boss believed that to invite a presidential veto signaled "a breakdown in the system."

"We don't want to make political points with this president," Feehery added, "because we agree with him on almost everything." Congressional Republicans challenged Bush's veto threats only once, in 2002, on a campaign finance overhaul. Bush didn't like the bill, but he put his signature on it anyway, the overt evidence of his displeasure was that he didn't invite one of its principal authors, Sen. John McCain, R-Ariz., to the signing ceremony.

Another reason that Bush hasn't relied on the veto is that he routinely uses "signing statements" to assert that he will implement new legislation in ways that conform with his thinking and that of White House lawyers and policy makers. On other occasions, particularly as regards national security, this president hasn't even given that much deference to congressional intent: If White House lawyers deem a law, such as the statutes regarding the wiretapping of suspected foreign terrorists, to be technologically out-of-date, well, this administration just writes its own hall pass.

Thus, Bush's first term featured an odd combination of co-operating closely with Capitol Hill Republicans on some occasions and simply ignoring Congress on others. Along the way, Team Bush overlooked historic examples showing that sometimes a veto—along with a healthy dose of chutzpah—is just what it takes to make a president look strong. Truman, in his first term, lamented during several crippling national strikes that he lacked the executive authority to force trade union leaders to the bargaining table. Congress gave Truman that power in the Taft-Hartley Act. He promptly vetoed it, putting himself at long last in organized labor's good graces. Congress overrode the president's veto, and Truman happily used the power vested in him some dozen times. Moreover, he turned around and won re-election in 1948, with, yes, the help of labor. For a president, this is as good as it gets—veto nirvana.

Republicans were in charge of both ends of Pennsylvania Avenue during most of the first six years of Bush's presidency, so the chances for such showdowns were small. But Democrats ran the show when Franklin Roosevelt was president—and he vetoed 635 of their bills. According to presidential scholar William Leuchtenburg, Roosevelt would instruct White House aides to look for legislation that he could veto, "in order to remind Congress that it was being watched."

Alan Greenspan, who is old enough to remember FDR, believes that Bush—and the country—would have been well served if this president had done the same. "My biggest frustration remained the president's unwillingness to wield his veto against out-of-control spending," Greenspan wrote in his new book, *The Age of Turbulence: Adventures in a New World*. "Not exercising the veto power became a hallmark of the Bush presidency.... To my mind, Bush's collaborate-don't-confront approach was a major mistake."

Many movement conservatives couldn't agree more. They think that Bush's belated embrace of the veto might save the GOP's soul and give the Republican base a principle to be excited about. "The GOP needs to regain its brand on spending," says Grover Norquist, president of Americans for Tax Reform. "The Democrats are acting now in 2007 and 2008 as they did in 1993 and 1994: taxing, spending. And here the GOP can highlight its differences with vetoes and veto-upholding. It is a truly selfless act by Bush as he isn't running, but the GOP House and Senate guys are, and they need their brand back. This autumn's fight, which I hope to be long and drawn out and repetitive, will do for the GOP what they should have been doing over the past six years."

Other Republicans, most notably moderates who face tough re-election fights next year, are unnerved by Bush's newfound fiscal conservatism, and especially by his willingness to veto a children's health bill to prove it. "I believe this is an irresponsible use of the veto pen," said Sen. Gordon Smith, an Oregon Republican who faces a spirited challenge in 2008. "It's the White House that needs to give," added another Senate GOP centrist, Susan Collins of Maine.

The noises emanating from the White House don't give these worried Republicans much reassurance. "Good policy is good politics," said White House spokesman Tony Fratto last week. "If members stand on principle, they'll be just fine."

Principles can be in the eye of the beholder, however, especially in Washington, where situational ethics are routinely on display. Dan Mitchell of the libertarian Cato Institute points out that the money at stake in the health care initiative is small compared with the excess spending that Bush accepted when Republicans controlled Congress. "There certainly does seem to be a legitimate argument that the president only objects to new spending when Democrats are doing it," Mitchell said.

Bush might have more moral sway had he, back in 2002, vetoed a bipartisan and pork-laden $190 billion farm bill. Half a century ago, Dwight Eisenhower did just that. The Democrats pounced, thinking they had Ike right where they wanted him. "The veto of the farm bill," then-Senate Majority Leader Lyndon Johnson said, "can be described only as a crushing blow to the hopes and the legitimate desires of American agriculture." That was one description. Another was "fiscal restraint," something that Eisenhower had managed to make sexy—with his veto pen.

By the end of the 1959 Christmas recess, an unnamed White House aide was telling *Time* magazine, "When those congressmen come back in January, they're going to be so anxious to find something to cut that they'll cut their own wrists if necessary." On his way out of office, with high approval ratings and a federal budget nearly in balance, Eisenhower was *Time's* "Man of the Year."

Similar battle lines are drawn for the upcoming year, during which Democrats will try to hold their congressional majorities and recapture the White House. Will they succeed? They will if Sen. Hillary Rodham Clinton has anything to say about it. "With the stroke of a pen, President Bush has robbed nearly 4 million uninsured children of the chance for a healthy start in life and the health coverage they need but can't afford," the New York Democrat and 2008 presidential front-runner said after Bush's veto.

"This is vetoing the will of the American people," Clinton added. "I was proud to help create the Children's Health Insurance Program during the Clinton administration, which today provides health insurance for 6 million children."

Hillary Clinton was right about her role in SCHIP. The part of the story that she may be forgetting, however, is that her husband got traction as president after the Republicans took over Congress and he began wielding his veto pen—36 times before leaving office.

"Clinton's skillful and aggressive use of the veto was a hallmark of his domestic presidency after the Republicans gained control of Congress in 1994," wrote Charles Cameron, a political science professor at Princeton and the author of *Veto Bargaining: Presidents and the Politics of Negative Power*. "In some respects, he was more successful opposing Congress than he had been leading it, when the Democrats controlled the institution."

Reagan faced a House controlled by the opposition party and he, too, issued a spate of vetoes, 78 (half of them pocket vetoes). Congress overrode nine—matching Roosevelt's tally. The overrides didn't hurt either man's legacy. At least one of the 2008 presidential candidates has apparently taken this lesson to heart. Republican Mitt Romney, who as Massachusetts governor faced an overwhelmingly Democratic Legislature for four years, boasts of vetoing hundreds of appropriations while serving in Boston—and says he'd happily do it all over again in Washington.

"If I'm elected president, I'm going to cap nondefense discretionary spending at inflation minus 1 percent," he said recently. "And if Congress sends me a budget that exceeds that cap, I will veto that budget. And I know how to veto. I like vetoes."

ccannon@nationaljournal.com.

Reprinted by permission from *National Journal*, October 13, 2007, pp. 32–38. Copyright © 2007 by National Journal Group Inc. All rights reserved.

Article 19

A Political Odyssey

How Obama's team forged a path that surprised everyone, even the candidate.

DAN BALZ AND HAYNES JOHNSON

"I think the whole election was a novel," Barack Obama said.

It was mid-December 2008. The president-elect was seated in his transition headquarters in the federal building in downtown Chicago. Next to him were a football, and a basketball with an "Obama '08" insignia. Bulletproof panels had been placed along floor-to-ceiling windows.

Obama was welcoming and upbeat, although later that day he would learn during a meeting with his economic advisers that the fiscal crisis was even worse than they had believed. Escorting us to his office, he expressed mock dismay at the mess around the desk of his personal assistant, Reggie Love. Eyeing an open bag of potato chips and papers strewn on the floor, he exclaimed that this was no way for the president-elect's space to look. "Reggie!" he shouted, but Love was nowhere to be seen.

As Obama settled into his sofa, drinking bottled tea and munching almonds, he grew more and more reflective, offering his most expansive rumination on the election to date. He spoke candidly about his competitors, his own failings, his controversial former pastor and how he hoped to govern, providing insight that is useful today as Americans observe a president struggling with the nation's enormous challenges.

"I don't think I was the most interesting character in the election," he said, noting "a whole cast of characters at the beginning who are fascinating in their own right, in some ways compelling just from a human perspective: John Edwards, [Mike] Huckabee. And then comes the general election [and] you get Sarah Palin and Joe the Plumber. You've got Reverend Wright, Bill Ayers. It's a pretty fascinating slice of Americana."

He was asked how the writer in him would spin the tale of what ultimately happened in 2008. "The way I would tell the story would really have to do with what this campaign said about America and where we've traveled," Obama said. "The fact that just a little over 40 years after the passage of the Voting Rights Act, that I can run. That just a few decades after women were admitted to professions like law or medicine in any meaningful numbers, that Hillary could run in a credible way. The generational changes between John McCain's era and our own, and sort of the vestiges of Vietnam, the shift that's taken place in the salience of some of the culture wars that emerged in the '60s that really were the dominant force in our politics, starting with Ronald Reagan, and how that had less power. Which, by the way, includes why the issue of Reverend Wright or Bill Ayers never caught as powerfully as it might have 15 or 20 years ago. The way the Internet served our campaign in unprecedented ways."

Six months into his presidency, there are questions about whether Obama can deliver on the promises of his campaign. His health-care initiative continues to meet difficulty in Congress. Increasing unemployment has raised doubts about his economic stimulus package. His energy plan faces real resistance on Capitol Hill.

As a candidate, Obama confronted similar questions and doubts: Was he too inexperienced, was he strong enough to lead the country, were his governing instincts liberal or moderate, was his commitment to bipartisanship achievable? Those questions were on the table in the late fall of 2006, as Obama and his advisers deliberated a presidential run.

David Axelrod knew his candidate as well as anyone in the inner circle. The transplanted New Yorker was a political reporter turned political consultant and strategist. He helped Obama win election to the Senate in 2004 and was at Obama's side as the presidential campaign took root.

In the days leading up to Obama's decision to run, Axelrod prepared a private strategy memo—dated Nov. 28, 2006—that has never been published before. He wrote that an outgoing president nearly always defines the next election and argued that people almost never seek a replica—certainly not after the presidency of George W. Bush. In 2008, people were going to be looking for a replacement, someone who represented different qualities. In Axelrod's opinion, Obama's profile fit this historical moment far better than did Hillary Rodham Clinton's. If he was right, Obama could spark a political movement and prevail against sizable odds. He also counseled Obama against waiting for a future opportunity to run for president. "History is replete with potential candidates for the presidency who waited too long rather than examples of people who ran too soon. . . . You will never be hotter than you are right now."

The second half of the Axelrod memo was more personal and pointed. "We should not get into a White Paper war with the Clintons, or get twisted into knots by the elites," he wrote. He argued that the issue of experience was overrated but said strength was not, and he conceded that Clinton, because of all she had weathered, was seen by voters as a candidate of strength. "But," he added, "the campaign itself also is a proving ground for strength."

Clinton, he wrote, "will try to command the race early. . . . Her goal will be two: to suggest that she has the beef, while we offer only sizzle; and that she is not about the past but the future. But for all her advantages, she is not a healing figure. As much as she tacks to the right, she will have a hard time escaping the well-formulated perceptions of her among swing voters as a left-wing ideologue."

Axelrod also warned that Obama's confessions of youthful drug use, described in his memoir, "Dreams From My Father," would be used against him. "This is more than an unpleasant inconvenience," he wrote. "It goes to your willingness and ability to put up with something you have never experienced on a sustained basis: criticism. At the risk of triggering the very reaction that concerns me, I don't know if you are Muhammad Ali or Floyd Patterson when it comes to taking a punch. You care far too much what is written and said about you. You don't relish combat when it becomes personal and nasty. When the largely irrelevant Alan Keyes attacked you, you flinched," he said of Obama's 2004 U.S. Senate opponent.

Axelrod's memo proved prescient in many respects, particularly about the confluence of public mood and Obama's innate political appeal and how that could be more compelling than the experience and network of Hillary Clinton. He also rightly judged that the campaign would be an opportunity for Obama to demonstrate that he had the strength and toughness. Now, as Obama grapples with the huge demands of his presidency, the question is whether the experience of the campaign provides a reliable indicator of his performance as chief executive.

One day in late September 2008, aboard his chartered flight from North Carolina to Chicago, Obama talked about what pushed him into the presidential race after only two years in the Senate. "Objectively you've got to say there's a certain megalomania there that's unhealthy. Right?" he said with a chuckle. "Axelrod said this to me, and he always reminds me of this. One of the things he said to me is he wasn't sure I would be a good candidate because I might be too normal. Which is why it's amusing, during the course of this campaign, the evolving narrative about me being aloof and elitist.

"Axelrod's right," he continued. "I'm not somebody who actually takes myself that seriously. I'm pretty well adjusted. You know, you can psychoanalyze my father leaving and this and that, but a lot of those things I resolved a long time ago. I'm pretty happy with my life. So there's an element, I think, of being driven that might have operated a little differently with me than maybe some other candidates. The way I thought about it was more of a sense of duty, in this sense. I thought to myself: There aren't that many people put in the position I'm put in. Some of it's just dumb luck. Some of it maybe has to do with me embodying some characteristics that are interesting for the time that we're in. But when I made the decision to do this, it wasn't with the certainty that I was the right person for the job. It was more the sense of, given what's been given to me, I should probably just give it a shot and see whether in fact there's something real there.

'I gave myself 25 percent odds . . . maybe 30' to win.

"But I went into it with some modesty, thinking to myself: It may be that this really is all hype, and once people get a sense of my ideas and what's going on there that they think I'm some callow youth or full of hot air, and if that turned out to be the case, that was okay. I think for me it was more of a sense of being willing to do this, understanding that the odds were probably—I gave myself 25 percent odds, you know, maybe 30—which are pretty remarkable odds to be president of the United States, if you're a gambling man."

Still, there was no doubting Obama's driving ambition and sense of self-confidence, no matter what odds he had given himself at the beginning of his campaign.

Yet his early days as a candidate were difficult, and Obama knew it. There was a disastrous appearance at a health-care forum in Las Vegas, poor performances before several union audiences in Washington, and the physical and mental taxation that went with the grueling schedule he was keeping. By the end of the first quarter of 2007, he was exhausted and down, aides said.

"I'm actually always sort of a slow starter," Obama said. "The same thing happened during my U.S. Senate race. My stump speeches tend to come to me organically. I try a bunch of things out. And sometimes they work and sometimes they don't. So in those first couple of months, I wasn't operating on this tight script." He recalled the opening months of the Senate campaign. "I'd be talking to an audience of 30 people in a living room somewhere or in a diner or a VFW hall. So you're off-Broadway and nobody's paying attention," he said. "But the problem for us was, we were already on Broadway. The media was following us nonstop. In April of 2007, we had 23,000 people show up in Austin, Texas. So suddenly you've got these enormous crowds, huge spotlight, and I'm still sort of working out my riff."

Aides worried that Obama's low morale might infect others in the campaign and spoke to him about it. They tried to buck him up, but at points in the spring and early summer of 2007, he was deeply frustrated—with his own performance and with that of much of his campaign. On July 15, he met with his senior staff at the home of Valerie Jarrett, a close friend and confidante to both Obama and his wife, Michelle. One adviser recalled it as the moment Obama began to take a more direct role in the operations of his campaign. He was blunt in his critique, and the exchanges among some of his advisers became testy. Beyond fundraising and the operation overseeing the Internet and new media, the campaign was not performing well, Obama said. The message still wasn't where it should be. The political operation wasn't up to speed. The campaign lacked crispness and good execution. He thought it was becoming too insular, and he wanted new people added to the inner circle. He told his team members they were all doing B-level work. If they continued on that course, they would come in a respectable second.

"Second is not good enough," he said.

Obama's struggles continued. In October, Jarrett traveled to Iowa with him for a meeting with members of his national finance committee, who were peppering the candidate's advisers with doubts and complaints. Obama was well aware of the concerns, and what he said that day stayed with Jarrett for months afterward. "He said, 'I know you guys are nervous, I know it's much bumpier than you thought it would be, but I'll hold your hand and we'll get through this,'" she said. "He said, 'I'll hold your hand if you're nervous, I'll be right there with you, but we're going to get through this, we're going to do this together.'"

Obama said that trip was an important moment of confidence-building. "I just told people—I said, 'If you guys thought this was going to be easy, you must have not been listening to us. We always knew this was hard and that I'm the underdog, but we can win this thing if you don't waver.'"

The real turnaround came a month later at the Iowa Democratic Party's Jefferson-Jackson dinner, which featured all the presidential candidates. Obama delivered a rousing speech that, without mentioning Clinton, drew a sharp contrast with her and better defined his own candidacy. That speech gave Obama's well-organized Iowa operation the boost needed to propel him to win the caucuses on Jan. 3, 2008. A stunned Clinton finished third, behind John Edwards. The moment of victory spawned a movement.

If Iowa launched his candidacy, New Hampshire the next week almost ended it. Clinton's come-from-behind triumph was a moment of crushing disappointment for Obama and his team. The candidate took the news stoically when his advisers came to tell him that she would win after everyone had counted her out. To aides, he quoted Frederick Douglass, who had said that if there is no struggle, there is no progress, that power concedes nothing without a demand.

We asked Obama what had happened in New Hampshire. "What our pollsters told me was every undecided woman swung to Hillary that last three days," he said. "All of them. Which just doesn't usually happen. I think the combination of her choking up; an inartful comment by me during the debate that wasn't intended in any way the way it came out, but I understood it came out as sort of dismissive; John Edwards doing a weird thing and kind of ganging up on her, despite the fact that I had won [Iowa].... And I just think the sense that, 'Gosh, you know, we shouldn't just hand it to this guy, and she's really fighting for this thing and has paid her dues.' I think all those things just converged for people to say to themselves, 'Let's keep this going a little bit.'"

There would be other losses ahead, disappointing setbacks in Ohio and Texas that would prolong the nomination battle for three more months. "After Ohio and Texas, my attitude was: We will win this thing, but it will be painful, and let's figure out what we need to do to execute and win," Obama said, adding that he told his staff and supporters that "it probably shouldn't be this easy for me to win, that we probably do need to earn this thing, because we're going to have a tough time, should we get the nomination, against Republicans and we need to have one of these under our belts."

There was no greater threat to Obama's chances of winning the presidency than the controversy that erupted over the Rev. Jeremiah Wright, his former longtime pastor. In early April 2008, ABC News aired a report about Wright's incendiary sermons, particularly one that came shortly after Sept. 11, 2001, in which he thundered from the pulpit, "God *damn* America!" The preacher in the videos was not the benign and fatherly figure Obama had described as his spiritual adviser and inspiration for the title of his second book, "The Audacity of Hope." This pastor was divisive and offensive, filled with resentment toward white America and the national government Obama was seeking to lead.

In our December interview in Chicago, we asked Obama what had made him believe that the country was ready for an African American president. He cited his run for the Senate in 2004, saying the experience had given him confidence that his race would not be an insurmountable obstacle. "Illinois is a pretty good microcosm of the country, and when I started my U.S. Senate race everybody said a guy with your name, African American, can't win a U.S. Senate race. And we won," he said. "And my approval ratings, I think, when I announced for the presidency here in Illinois, were like 70 percent. So I thought to myself, If I'm in a big industrial state with 12 percent African American population and people seem to not be concerned about my race and much more concerned with my performance, why would [that not hold true] across the country?"

He never lost confidence that he could overcome racial barriers, though the Rev. Wright flap had severely tested that belief. Race, the topic that Obama had tried to transcend, now dominated the discussion about him. He wanted to be a post-racial candidate, not an extension of the civil rights generation, and he suddenly found himself at the center of a controversy that highlighted the gulf that still divided blacks and whites. "What you had was a moment where all the suspicions and misunderstandings that are embedded in our racial history were suddenly laid bare," he said during one of our interviews. He knew there was no way to dodge this crisis. "If we had not handled the Reverend Wright episode properly," he said, "I think we could have lost."

The Wright controversy led to perhaps Obama's most important speech of the campaign, his discussion of race before an audience in Philadelphia. "I thought it was very important at that point for me to help translate the experiences both of Reverend Wright but also how the ordinary white American might feel in hearing Reverend Wright and how both sets of experiences were an outgrowth of our history and had to be acknowledged and dealt with instead of just papered over or reduced to a caricature. And I think that the speech in Philadelphia succeeded in doing that."

The speech did not end the controversy over Wright. His reappearance later in the spring, in a series of events in which he declined to take back his most controversial statements, brought a new test for the candidate. "The second [Wright eruption] was in some ways more painful because I felt that was a personal breach on the part of Reverend Wright," Obama said.

He added: "He's a great preacher . . . but Reverend Wright remained rooted in the rhetoric of the '60s. . . . What he was saying was not considered in any way exceptional in the African American community for his generation. He never updated or refreshed that worldview to accommodate the changes that were taking place in America. And what you were seeing in Reverend Wright and those statements were not only offensive to everybody in many ways, but it also showed an anger and bitterness . . . that may be more acceptable in some circles in the African American community but is never acceptable in mainstream America. And so you had that sudden, really volatile potential clash of visions."

Wright's reappearance came the week before two crucial May 6 primaries in Indiana and North Carolina. The evening before the primaries, Obama was in Indiana and had some time to relax before a late-night visit to a factory. As was often the case in moments of stress or relaxation, he was joined by friends Valerie Jarrett, Eric Whitaker and Marty Nesbitt. Jarrett remembers Obama despondent, worried that the Wright controversy might undo all his campaign had accomplished. She said she had never seen him as down as he was that night.

"We had lost Pennsylvania and now we're going into a couple of pretty tough states," Obama told us, recalling that moment. "We [were] just getting our groove back and suddenly this [Wright] thing pops up again. And you felt like, well, maybe we're just not going to survive this. Maybe people are just going to feel too skittish or just feel that I was mortally wounded and that I wouldn't be able to survive a general election, and that could start changing how delegates think."

In fact, the primaries in Indiana and North Carolina proved to be effectively the end of Clinton's campaign. Obama easily won North Carolina and barely lost Indiana. Now there was no way for Clinton to amass enough delegates to win. A month later, on June 3, Obama celebrated the end of the primaries and his nomination at a rally in St. Paul, Minn. During our September 2008 interview, we asked whether, on that night, he felt caught up in the emotion of making history as the first African American nominated for president by a major party.

"I am very glad that there are people who have been inspired by this race. But I did not begin this race to run a symbolic contest. I ran to win," he said. "And what I thought, and this is the honest truth—I said this to Axelrod—having won against a very formidable opponent, my main thought was, I'd better win the general election. Because this should be a Democratic year and I beat somebody who would have been a good general-election candidate, so we'd better get our act together now."

But history-in-the-making was always part of the Obama campaign, and in the hours before he was to give his acceptance speech before 80,000 people at Denver's Invesco Field during the Democratic National Convention, even the candidate was overwhelmed by it. It happened in a hotel room during his late-afternoon rehearsal before Axelrod and speechwriter Jon Favreau. When he got to the passage in the speech in which he was going to refer to the historic address the Rev. Martin Luther King Jr. gave 45 years earlier on the steps of the Lincoln Memorial, Obama suddenly was overcome.

"I started reading it and I got to the section right at the end when it talks about, you know, this young preacher from Georgia. And . . . I had to stop. I choked up," Obama said. He went into the bathroom and closed the door. He returned composed and ready to continue.

As he reviewed the campaign from his transition headquarters in mid-December, Obama offered a frank assessment of his two main competitors: Clinton and John McCain. "I was sure that my toughest race was Hillary," he said. "Hillary was just a terrific candidate, and she really found her voice in the last part of the campaign. After Texas and Ohio she just became less cautious and was out there and was working hard and I think connecting with voters really well. She was just a terrific candidate. And [the Clinton campaign] operation was not as good as ours and not as tight as ours, but they were still plenty tough. Their rapid response, how they messaged in the media was really good. So we just always thought they were our most formidable challenge. That isn't to say that we underestimated John McCain; it's just that we didn't think that their campaign operation was as good. And one of the hardest things for me, during the primary, was finding differences with Hillary. I mean, a lot of the differences between us, substantively, were pretty modest. . . .

"Going into the general election, I just felt liberated, because there was such a stark contrast between John and myself. . . . They made a strategic decision early on to flip on the Bush tax cuts, and in fact double down on them, which locked them into a domestic agenda that was very difficult to separate from George Bush's domestic agenda. So that just gave us a lot of running room on the issues."

Did he believe that his election marked the end of the Reagan era?

"What Reagan ushered in was a skepticism toward government solutions to every problem, a suspicion of command-and-control, top-down social engineering," he said. "I don't think that has changed. I think that's a lasting legacy of the Reagan era and the conservative movement, starting with Goldwater. But I do think [what we're seeing] is an end to the knee-jerk reaction toward the New Deal and big government."

Added Obama: "What we don't know yet is whether my administration and this next generation of leadership is going to be able to hew to a new, more pragmatic approach that is less interested in whether we have big government or small government, [but is] more interested in whether we have a smart, effective government."

And what had he learned about the American people from his campaign?

"I have to tell you," he said, "and this is in no way an indication of overconfidence—I was not surprised by the campaign. I felt that, and I said this on the stump, I felt vindicated in my faith in the American people."

Drawing on his legal background, he offered "a theory of the case" that he said guided his campaign. "For at least a decade, maybe longer," he said, Americans have been "frustrated with a government that was unresponsive; that their economic life was becoming more difficult despite the surface prosperity; that wages and incomes had flat-lined and that in this new globalized world people were feeling more and more insecure; that we had never replaced or updated the structures for security that the New Deal had provided with something that made sense for this new economy; that people were weary of culture wars as a substitute for policy; that people were tired of only focusing on what divides instead of what brought us together; that the 50-plus-one electoral strategies that were generally pursued in national elections were completely inadequate to solve big problems like health care and energy that would require a broader consensus; that people were embarrassed by the decline in America's standing in the eyes of the world and that that would have political relevance to voters who normally might not care that much about foreign policy; and that the American people were decent and good and would be open to a different tone to politics.

"So that was the theory that we started with. What was remarkable in my mind about our campaign was we never really changed our theory. You could read the speech we gave the day I announced and then read my speech on election night, and it was pretty consistent."

It was time to leave, but not before raising one last subject. Obama started his campaign in the shadow of the Old State Capitol in Springfield, Ill., where Lincoln had delivered his famous "House Divided" speech, warning that the nation could not survive half slave and half free. Now, as he prepared to return to Washington, his transition team had announced plans for him to follow the last part of Lincoln's train ride to Washington before his inauguration. We wondered how Lincoln, an Illinois lawyer with little national experience, affected Obama's thoughts about his own presidency as another young Illinois lawyer with limited national experience soon to take his oath of office.

"Lincoln's my favorite president and one of my personal heroes," he answered. "I have to be very careful here that in no way am I drawing equivalence between my candidacy, my life experience, or what I face and what he went through. I just want to put that out there so you don't get a bunch of folks saying I'm comparing myself to Lincoln."

He paused. "What I admire so deeply about Lincoln—number one, I think he's the quintessential American because he's self-made. The way Alexander Hamilton was self-made or so many of our great iconic Americans are, that sense that you don't accept limits, that you can shape your own destiny. That obviously has appeal to me, given where I came from. That American spirit is one of the things that is most fundamental to me, and I think he embodies that.

"But the second thing that I admire most in Lincoln is that there is just a deep-rooted honesty and empathy to the man that allowed him to always be able to see the other person's point of view and always sought to find that truth that is in the gap between you and me. Right? That the truth is out there somewhere and I don't fully possess it and you don't fully possess it and our job then is to listen and learn and imagine enough to be able to get to that truth.

"If you look at his presidency, he never lost that. Most of our other great presidents, there was that sense of working the angles and bending other people to their will. FDR being the classic example. And Lincoln just found a way to shape public opinion and shape people around him and lead them and guide them without tricking them or bullying them, but just through the force of what I just talked about: that way of helping to illuminate the truth. I just find that to be a very compelling style of leadership.

"It's not one that I've mastered, but I think that's when leadership is at its best."

Adapted from "The Battle for America 2008: The Story of an Extraordinary Election".

As seen in *The Washington Post,* August 2, 2009, pp. A1, A10–A11. Adapted from: *The Battle for America 2008: The Story of an Extraordinary Election* by Haynes Johnson and Dan Balz (Viking Adult Books, 2009). Copyright © 2009 by Dan Balz and Haynes Johnson. Reprinted by permission from Penguin Group (USA) Inc.

The Shuffle President

Matt Bai

Like romantic comedies and superhero blockbusters, the modern presidency has evolved into a reliable form of dramatic narrative. A candidate comes into office brandishing a broad theme—a vow to clean up government, perhaps, or to fearlessly prune it back—and then lays out one or two big proposals to make it real. In time, of course, a presidency tends to sprawl as events intrude. Bill Clinton couldn't have imagined he would spend so much of his two terms fending off resurgent Republicans, just as George W. Bush didn't envision going to war. But at least for those first several months, while the White House controls its own fate, the presidency is supposed to unfold in discrete chapters, each building atop the last. Both Ronald Reagan and Bush began with an almost single-minded push for tax cuts during their opening months, while Clinton opened with an economic program and then a monthslong drive for health care reform. The simple premise here is that every new presidency is a story; the more muddled and erratic the storyline, the harder it is for the public to follow along and the less likely the chances of reaching a satisfying end.

Barack Obama is a born storyteller, which makes it all the more confounding that as president he refuses to inhabit a neat political narrative. Obama's themes are clear enough (salvaging the American economy, reversing the Bush years), but his legislative priorities seem to rotate in and out like so many suitcases on a conveyor belt. One day his presidency hinges on health care, then he's lobbying for a cap-and-trade plan to reduce carbon emissions and then he's out there trying to re-regulate the financial world or sell a new treaty with the Russians. "An administration about everything is an administration about nothing" is the way the conservative columnist Peggy Noonan put it in *The Wall Street Journal*. Colin Powell made a similar point, telling John King of CNN, "I think one of the cautions that has to be given to the president—and I've talked to some of his people about this—is that you can't have so many things on the table that you can't absorb it all."

Some of this itinerary must be attributed to the sheer scope of the wreckage Obama inherited. When you've got failing banks and corporate giants, two ongoing wars, melting icecaps and mountainous health care costs, it's hard to see what gets pushed to the margins. It's also true, though, that Obama's style reflects, whether he means it to or not, a cultural shift on the importance of narrative. Americans acclimated to clicking around hundreds of cable channels or Web pages experience the world less chronologically than their parents did. The most popular books now—business guides like "Good to Great" or social explorations like "The Tipping Point"—allow the casual reader to absorb their insights in random order or while skimming whole chapters.

Once we listened to cohesive albums like, say, Bob Dylan's "Highway 61 Revisited," which kicked off with the snare hit of "Like a Rolling Stone," almost like a starter pistol, and worked its way toward the melancholy postscript of "Desolation Row." Now your iPod might jump mindlessly from "Desolation Row" to "Tombstone Blues," or from Dylan to Rihanna. The shrink-wrapped record has given way to the downloaded single. Wasn't this one reason for all the tributes to Michael Jackson? It's not that "Thriller" was really as singularly awesome as so many of us thought it was in high school. It's more that we know there may never be an album that epic again.

Obama is the nation's first shuffle president. He's telling lots of stories at once, and in no particular order. His agenda is fully downloadable. If what you care most about is health care, then you can jump right to that. If global warming gets you going, then click over there. It's not especially realistic to imagine that politics could cling to a linear way of rendering stories while the rest of American culture adapts to a more customized form of consumption. Obama's ethos may disconcert the older guard in Washington, but it's probably comforting to a lot of younger voters who could never be expected to listen to successive tracks, in the same order, over and over again.

Such an approach does, however, invite significant peril. Random play may popularize your music in the aggregate, but it doesn't foster the same kind of investment in the songs themselves. U2 may have more fans than ever, but that doesn't mean these listeners can name half the tracks on the band's latest release.

Similarly, Obama retains higher favorability ratings than any of his recent predecessors—about 60 percent, according to an NBC/*Wall Street Journal* poll conducted last month. But only 46 percent in the same poll were either "quite" or "extremely" confident that Obama had the right policies to revive the economy, and only 33 percent volunteered support for his health care plan. That last number grew to 55 percent when the broad plan was explained to voters, which means that even the outlines of what is arguably Obama's most important proposal haven't been absorbed by the public. In other words, most Americans seem to like the president, but they're not engaged with the specific arguments he's making.

And should the president prevail on one or another of his proposals, he might find that acclaim, in this digital moment, can be ephemeral. Landmark legislative proposals, like hit singles, can come to seem interchangeable and dispensable. Creating a new health care framework, after more than a half-century of talking about it, would be a monumental achievement for any president, but even that might seem somehow small when viewed as only one in a series of competing storylines. What about carbon emissions? How about reining in Wall Street? Too much comes at us now, too devoid of context, for any one thing to matter as much as it probably should. In a society on shuffle, we're always left to wonder what's next.

MATT BAI, who covers politics for the magazine, is the author of "The Argument: Inside the Battle to Remake Democratic Politics."

From *The New York Times Magazine*, July 19, 2009. Copyright © 2009 by Matt Bai. Distributed by The New York Times Special Features. Reprinted by permission.

When Congress Stops Wars
Partisan Politics and Presidential Power

WILLIAM G. HOWELL AND JON C. PEVEHOUSE

For most of George W. Bush's tenure, political observers have lambasted Congress for failing to fulfill its basic foreign policy obligations. Typical was the recent *Foreign Affairs* article by Norman Ornstein and Thomas Mann, "When Congress Checks Out," which offered a sweeping indictment of Congress' failure to monitor the president's execution of foreign wars and antiterrorist initiatives. Over the past six years, they concluded, Congressional oversight of the White House's foreign and national security policy "has virtually collapsed." Ornstein and Mann's characterization is hardly unique. Numerous constitutional-law scholars, political scientists, bureaucrats, and even members of Congress have, over the years, lamented the lack of legislative constraints on presidential war powers. But the dearth of Congressional oversight between 2000 and 2006 is nothing new. Contrary to what many critics believe, terrorist threats, an overly aggressive White House, and an impotent Democratic Party are not the sole explanations for Congressional inactivity over the past six years. Good old-fashioned partisan politics has been, and continues to be, at play.

It is often assumed that everyday politics *stops* at the water's edge and that legislators abandon their partisan identities during times of war in order to become faithful stewards of their constitutional obligations. But this received wisdom is almost always wrong. The illusion of Congressional wartime unity misconstrues the nature of legislative oversight and fails to capture the particular conditions under which members of Congress are likely to emerge as meaningful critics of any particular military venture.

The partisan composition of Congress has historically been the decisive factor in determining whether lawmakers will oppose or acquiesce in presidential calls for war. From Harry Truman to Bill Clinton, nearly every U.S. president has learned that members of Congress, and members of the opposition party in particular, are fully capable of interjecting their opinions about proposed and ongoing military ventures. When the opposition party holds a large number of seats or controls one or both chambers of Congress, members routinely challenge the president and step up oversight of foreign conflicts; when the legislative branch is dominated by the president's party, it generally goes along with the White House. Partisan unity, not institutional laziness, explains why the Bush administration's Iraq policy received such a favorable hearing in Congress from 2000 to 2006.

The dramatic increase in Congressional oversight following the 2006 midterm elections is a case in point. Immediately after assuming control of Congress, House Democrats passed a resolution condemning a proposed "surge" of U.S. troops in Iraq and Senate Democrats debated a series of resolutions expressing varying degrees of outrage against the war in Iraq. The spring 2007 supplemental appropriations debate resulted in a House bill calling for a phased withdrawal (the president vetoed that bill, and the Senate then passed a bill accepting more war funding without withdrawal provisions). Democratic heads of committees in both chambers continue to launch hearings and investigations into the various mishaps, scandals, and tactical errors that have plagued the Iraq war. By all indications, if the government in Baghdad has not met certain benchmarks by September, the Democrats will push for binding legislation that further restricts the president's ability to sustain military operations in Iraq.

Neither Congress' prior languor nor its recent awakening should come as much of a surprise. When they choose to do so, members of Congress can exert a great deal of influence over the conduct of war. They can enact laws that dictate how long military campaigns may last, control the purse strings that determine how well they are funded, and dictate how appropriations may be spent. Moreover, they can call hearings and issue public pronouncements on foreign policy matters. These powers allow members to cut funding for ill-advised military ventures, set timetables for the withdrawal of troops, foreclose opportunities to expand a conflict into new regions, and establish reporting requirements. Through legislation, appropriations, hearings, and public appeals, members of Congress can substantially increase the political costs of military action—sometimes forcing presidents to withdraw sooner than they would like or even preventing any kind of military action whatsoever.

The Partisan Imperative

Critics have made a habit of equating legislative inactivity with Congress' abdication of its foreign policy obligations. Too often, the infrequency with which Congress enacts restrictive statutes is seen as prima facie evidence of the institution's failings. Sometimes it is. But one cannot gauge the health of the U.S. system of governance strictly on the basis of what Congress does—or does not do—in the immediate aftermath of presidential initiatives.

After all, when presidents anticipate Congressional resistance they will not be able to overcome, they often abandon the sword as their primary tool of diplomacy. More generally, when the White House knows that Congress will strike down key provisions of a policy initiative, it usually backs off. President Bush himself has relented, to varying degrees, during the struggle to create the Department of Homeland Security and during conflicts over the design of military tribunals and the prosecution of U.S. citizens as enemy combatants. Indeed, by most accounts, the administration recently forced the resignation of the chairman of the Joint Chiefs of Staff, General Peter Pace, so as to avoid a clash with Congress over his reappointment.

To assess the extent of Congressional influence on presidential war powers, it is not sufficient to count how many war authorizations are enacted or how often members deem it necessary to start the "war powers clock"—based on the War Powers Act requirement that the president obtain legislative approval within 60 days after any military deployment. Rather, one must examine the underlying partisan alignments across the branches of government and presidential efforts to anticipate and preempt Congressional recriminations.

During the past half century, partisan divisions have fundamentally defined the domestic politics of war. A variety of factors help explain why partisanship has so prominently defined the contours of interbranch struggles over foreign military deployments. To begin with, some members of Congress have electoral incentives to increase their oversight of wars when the opposing party controls the White House. If presidential approval ratings increase due to a "rally around the flag" effect in times of war, and if those high ratings only benefit the president's party in Congress, then the opposition party has an incentive to highlight any failures, missteps, or scandals that might arise in the course of a military venture.

After all, the making of U.S. foreign policy hinges on how U.S. national interests are defined and the means chosen to achieve them. This process is deeply, and unavoidably, political. Therefore, only in very particular circumstances—a direct attack on U.S. soil or on Americans abroad—have political parties temporarily united for the sake of protecting the national interest. Even then, partisan politics has flared as the toll of war has become evident. Issues of trust and access to information further fuel these partisan fires. In environments in which information is sparse, individuals with shared ideological or partisan affiliations find it easier to communicate with one another. The president possesses unparalleled intelligence about threats to national interests, and he is far more likely to share that information with members of his own political party than with political opponents. Whereas the commander in chief has an entire set of executive-branch agencies at his beck and call, Congress has relatively few sources of reliable classified information. Consequently, when a president claims that a foreign crisis warrants military intervention, members of his own party tend to trust him more often than not, whereas members of the opposition party are predisposed to doubt and challenge such claims. In this regard, Congressional Democrats' constant interrogations of Bush administration officials represent just the latest round in an ongoing interparty struggle to control the machinery of war.

Congressional Influence and Its Limits

Historically, presidents emerging from midterm election defeats have been less likely to respond to foreign policy crises aggressively, and when they have ordered the use of force, they have taken much longer to do so. Our research shows that the White House's propensity to exercise military force steadily declines as members of the opposition party pick up seats in Congress. In fact, it is not even necessary for the control of Congress to switch parties; the loss of even a handful of seats can materially affect the probability that the nation will go to war.

The partisan composition of Congress also influences its willingness to launch formal oversight hearings. While criticizing members for their inactivity during the Bush administration, Ornstein and Mann make much of the well-established long-term decline in the number of hearings held on Capitol Hill. This steady decline, however, has not muted traditional partisan politics. According to Linda Fowler, of Dartmouth College, the presence or absence of unified government largely determines the frequency of Congressional hearings. Contrary to Ornstein and Mann's argument that "vigorous oversight was the norm until the end of the twentieth century," Fowler demonstrates that during the post–World War II era, when the same party controlled both Congress and the presidency, the number of hearings about military policy decreased, but when the opposition party controlled at least one chamber of Congress, hearings occurred with greater frequency. Likewise, Boston University's Douglas Kriner has shown that Congressional authorizations of war as well as legislative initiatives that establish timetables for the withdrawal of troops, cut funds, or otherwise curtail military operations critically depend on the partisan balance of power on Capitol Hill.

Still, it is important not to overstate the extent of Congressional influence. Even when Congress is most aggressive, the executive branch retains a tremendous amount of power when it comes to military matters. Modern presidents enjoy extraordinary advantages in times of war, not least of which the ability to act unilaterally on military matters and thereby place on Congress (and everyone else) the onus of coordinating a response. Once troops enter a region, members of Congress face the difficult choice of either cutting funds and then facing the charge of undermining the troops or keeping the public coffers open and thereby aiding a potentially ill-advised military operation.

On this score, Ornstein and Mann effectively illustrate Bush's efforts to expand his influence over the war in Iraq and the war on terrorism by refusing to disclose classified information, regularly circumventing the legislative process, and resisting even modest efforts at oversight. Similarly, they note that Republican Congressional majorities failed to take full advantage of their institution's formal powers to monitor and influence either the formulation or the implementation of foreign policy during the first six years of Bush's presidency. Ornstein and Mann, however, mistakenly attribute such lapses in Congressional oversight to a loss of an "institutional identity" that was ostensibly forged during a bygone era when "tough oversight of the executive was common, whether or not different parties controlled the White House and Congress" and when members' willingness to challenge presidents had less to do with partisan allegiances and more to do with a shared sense of institutional responsibility. In the modern era, foreign-policy making has rarely worked this way. On the contrary, partisan competition has contributed to nearly every foreign policy clash between Capitol Hill and the White House for the past six decades.

Divided We Stand

Shortly after World War II—the beginning of a period often mischaracterized as one of "Cold War consensus"—partisan wrangling over the direction of U.S. foreign policy returned to Washington, ending a brief period of wartime unity. By defining U.S. military involvement in Korea as a police action rather than a war, President Truman effectively freed himself from the constitutional requirements regarding war and established a precedent for all subsequent presidents to circumvent Congress when sending the military abroad. Although Truman's party narrowly controlled both chambers, Congress hounded him throughout the Korean War, driving his approval ratings down into the 20s and paving the way for a Republican electoral victory in 1952. Railing off a litany of complaints about the president's firing of General Douglas MacArthur and his meager progress toward ending the war, Senator Robert Taft, then a Republican presidential candidate, declared that "the greatest failure of foreign policy is an unnecessary war, and we have been involved in such a war now for more than a year. . . . As a matter of fact, every purpose of the war has now failed. We are exactly where we were three years ago, and where we could have stayed."

On the heels of the Korean War came yet another opportunity to use force in Asia, but facing a divided Congress, President Dwight Eisenhower was hesitant to get involved. French requests for assistance in Indochina initially fell on sympathetic ears in the Eisenhower administration, which listed Indochina as an area of strategic importance in its "new look" defense policy. However, in January 1954, when the French asked for a commitment of U.S. troops, Eisenhower balked. The president stated that he "could conceive of no greater tragedy than for the United States to become involved in an all-out war in Indochina." His reluctance derived in part from the anticipated fight with Congress that he knew would arise over such a war. Even after his decision to provide modest technical assistance to France, in the form of B-26 bombers and air force technicians, Congressional leaders demanded a personal meeting with the president to voice their disapproval. Soon afterward, Eisenhower promised to withdraw the air force personnel, replacing them with civilian contractors.

Eventually, the United States did become involved in a ground war in Asia, and it was that war that brought Congressional opposition to the presidential use of force to a fever pitch. As the Vietnam War dragged on and casualties mounted, Congress and the public grew increasingly wary of the conflict and of the power delegated to the president in the 1964 Gulf of Tonkin resolution. In 1970, with upward of 350,000 U.S. troops in the field and the war spilling over into Cambodia, Congress formally repealed that resolution. And over the next several years, legislators enacted a series of appropriations bills intended to restrict the war's scope and duration. Then, in June 1973, after the Paris peace accords had been signed, Congress enacted a supplemental appropriations act that cut off all funding for additional military involvement in Southeast Asia, including in Cambodia, Laos, North Vietnam, and South Vietnam. Finally, when South Vietnam fell in 1975, Congress took the extraordinary step of formally forbidding U.S. troops from enforcing the Paris peace accords, despite the opposition of President Gerald Ford and Secretary of State Henry Kissinger.

Three years later, a Democratic Congress forbade the use of funds for a military action that was supported by the president—this time, the supply of covert aid to anticommunist forces in Angola. At the insistence of Senator Dick Clark (D-Iowa), the 1976 Defense Department appropriations act stipulated that no monies would be used "for any activities involving Angola other than intelligence gathering." Facing such staunch Congressional opposition, President Ford suspended military assistance to Angola, unhappily noting that the Democratic-controlled Congress had "lost its guts" with regard to foreign policy.

In just one instance, the case of Lebanon in 1983, did Congress formally start the 60-day clock of the 1973 War Powers Act. Most scholars who call Congress to task for failing to fulfill its constitutional responsibilities make much of the fact that in this case it ended up authorizing the use of force for a full 18 months, far longer than the 60 days automatically allowed under the act. However, critics often overlook the fact that Congress simultaneously forbade the president from unilaterally altering the scope, target, or mission of the U.S. troops participating in the multinational peacekeeping force. Furthermore, Congress asserted its right to terminate the venture at any time with a one-chamber majority vote or a joint resolution and established firm reporting requirements as the U.S. presence in Lebanon continued.

During the 1980s, no foreign policy issue dominated Congressional discussions more than aid to the contras in Nicaragua, rebel forces who sought to topple the leftist Sandinista regime. In 1984, a Democratic-controlled House enacted an appropriations bill that forbade President Ronald Reagan from supporting the contras. Reagan appeared undeterred. Rather than abandon the project, the administration instead diverted funds from Iranian arms sales to support the contras, establishing the basis for the most serious presidential scandal since Watergate. Absent Congressional opposition on this issue, Reagan may well have intervened directly, or at least directed greater, more transparent aid to the rebels fighting the Nicaraguan government.

Regardless of which party holds a majority of the seats in Congress, it is almost always the opposition party that creates the most trouble for a president intent on waging war. When, in the early 1990s, a UN humanitarian operation in Somalia devolved into urban warfare, filling nightly newscasts with scenes from Mogadishu, Congress swung into action. Despite previous declarations of public support for the president's actions, Congressional Republicans and some Democrats passed a Department of Defense appropriations act in November 1993 that simultaneously authorized the use of force to protect UN units and required that U.S. forces be withdrawn by March 31, 1994.

A few years later, a Republican-controlled Congress took similar steps to restrict the use of funds for a humanitarian crisis occurring in Kosovo. One month after the March 1999 NATO air strikes against Serbia, the House passed a bill forbidding the use of Defense Department funds to introduce U.S. ground troops into the conflict without Congressional authorization. When President Clinton requested funding for operations in the Balkans, Republicans in Congress (and some hawkish Democrats) seized on the opportunity to attach additional monies for unrelated defense programs, military personnel policies, aid to farmers, and hurricane relief and passed a supplemental appropriations bill that was considerably larger than the amount requested by the president. The mixed messages sent by the Republicans caught the attention of Clinton's Democratic allies. As House member Martin Frost (D-Tex.) noted, "I am at a loss to explain how the Republican Party can, on one hand, be so irresponsible as to abandon our troops in the midst of a military action to demonstrate its visceral hostility toward the commander in chief, and then, on the other, turn around and double his request for money for what they call 'Clinton's war.'" The 1999 debate is remarkably similar to the current wrangling over spending on Iraq.

Legislating Opinion

The voice of Congress (or lack thereof) has had a profound impact on the media coverage of the current war in Iraq, just as it has colored public perceptions of U.S. foreign policy in the past. Indeed, Congress' ability to influence executive-branch decision-making extends far beyond its legislative and budgetary powers. Cutting funds, starting the war powers clock, or forcing troop withdrawals are the most extreme options available to them. More frequently, members of Congress make appeals designed to influence both media coverage and public opinion of a president's war. For example, Congress' vehement criticism of Reagan's decision to reflag Kuwaiti tankers during the Iran-Iraq War led to reporting requirements for the administration. Similarly, the Clinton administration's threats to invade Haiti in 1994 were met with resistance by Republicans and a handful of skeptical Democrats in Congress, who took to the airwaves to force Clinton to continually justify placing U.S. troops in harm's way.

Such appeals resonate widely. Many studies have shown that the media regularly follow official debates about war in Washington, adjusting their coverage to the scope of the discussion among the nation's political elite. And among the elite, members of Congress—through their own independent initiatives and through journalists' propensity to follow them—stand out as the single most potent source of dissent against the president. The sheer number of press releases and direct feeds that members of Congress produce is nothing short of breathtaking. And through carefully staged hearings, debates, and investigations, members deliberately shape the volume and content of the media's war coverage. The public posturing, turns of praise and condemnation, rapid-fire questioning, long-winded exhortations, pithy Shakespearean references, graphs, timelines, and pie charts that fill these highly scripted affairs are intended to focus media attention and thereby sway the national conversation surrounding questions of war and peace. Whether the media scrutinize every aspect of a proposed military venture or assume a more relaxed posture depends in part on Congress' willingness to take on the president.

Indeed, in the weeks preceding the October 2002 war authorization vote, the media paid a tremendous amount of attention to debates about Iraq inside the Beltway. Following the vote, however, coverage of Iraq dropped precipitously, despite continued domestic controversies, debates at the United Nations, continued efforts by the administration to rally public support, and grass-roots opposition to the war that featured large public protests. Congress helped set the agenda for public discussion, influencing both the volume and the tone of the coverage granted to an impending war, and Congress' silence after the authorization was paralleled by that of the press.

Crucially, Congressional influence over the media extended to public opinion as well. An analysis of local television broadcast data and national public-opinion surveys from the period reveals a strong relationship between the type of media coverage and public opinion regarding the war. Even when accounting for factors such as the ideological tendencies of a media market (since liberal markets tend to have liberal voters and liberal media, while conservative districts have the opposite), we found that the airing of more critical viewpoints led to greater public disapproval of the proposed war, and more positive viewpoints buoyed support for the war. As Congress speaks, it would seem, the media report, and the public listens.

As these cases illustrate, the United States has a Congress with considerably more agenda-setting power than most analysts presume and a less independent press corps than many would like. As the National Journal columnist William Powers observed during the fall of 2006, "Journalists like to think they are reporting just the facts, straight and unaffected by circumstance." On the contrary, he recognized, news is a product of the contemporary political environment, and the way stories are framed and spun has little to do with the facts. In Washington, the party that controls Congress also determines the volume and the tone of the coverage given to a president's war. Anticipating a Democratic Congressional sweep in November 2006, Powers correctly predicted that "if Bush suffers a major political setback, the media will feel freed up to tear into this war as they have never done before."

With the nation standing at the precipice of new wars, it is vital that the American public understand the nature and extent of Congress' war powers and its members' partisan motivations for exercising or forsaking them. President Bush retains extraordinary institutional advantages over Congress, but with the Democrats now in control of both houses, the political costs of pursuing new wars (whether against Iran, North Korea, or any other country) and prosecuting ongoing ones have increased significantly.

Congress will continue to challenge the president's interpretation of the national interest. Justifications for future deployments will encounter more scrutiny and require more evidence. Questions of appropriate strategy and implementation will surface more quickly with threats of Congressional hearings and investigations looming. Oversight hearings will proceed at a furious pace. Concerning Iraq, the Democrats will press the administration on a withdrawal timetable, hoping to use their agenda-setting power with the media to persuade enough Senate Republicans to defect and thereby secure the votes they need to close floor debate on the issue.

This fall, the Democrats will likely attempt to build even more momentum to end the war in Iraq, further limiting the president's menu of choices. This is not the first instance of heavy Congressional involvement in foreign affairs and war, nor will it be the last. This fact has been lost on too many political commentators convinced that some combination of an eroding political identity, 9/11, failures of leadership, and dwindling political will have made Congress irrelevant to deliberations about foreign policy.

On the contrary, the new Democratic-controlled Congress is conforming to a tried-and-true pattern of partisan competition between the executive and legislative branches that has characterized Washington politics for the last half century and shows no signs of abating. Reports of Congress' death have been greatly exaggerated.

WILLIAM G. HOWELL and **JON C. PEVEHOUSE** are Associate Professors at the Harris School of Public Policy at the University of Chicago and the authors of *While Dangers Gather: Congressional Checks on Presidential War Powers.*

From *Foreign Affairs*, September/October 2007. Copyright © 2007 by Council on Foreign Relations. Reprinted by permission. www.ForeignAffairs.com

The Case for Congress

According to opinion polls, Congress is one of the least esteemed institutions in American life. While that should come as a shock, today it's taken for granted. What can't be taken for granted is the health of representative democracy amid this corrosive— and often unwarranted—distrust of its central institution.

LEE H. HAMILTON

Several years ago, I was watching the evening news on television when the anchorman announced the death of Wilbur Mills, the legendary former chairman of the House Ways and Means Committee. There was a lot the newscaster could have said. He might have recounted the central role Mills had played in creating Medicare. Or he might have talked about Mills's hand in shaping the Social Security system and in drafting the tax code. But he did not. Instead, he recalled how Mills's career collapsed after he was found early one morning with an Argentine stripper named Fanne Foxe. And then the anchorman moved on to the next story.

One of the perks of being chairman of an influential committee in Congress, as I was at the time, is that you can pick up the telephone and get through to a TV news anchor. Which I did. I chided the fellow for summing up Mills's career with a scandal. And much to my surprise, he apologized.

Americans of all stripes like to dwell on misbehavior by members of Congress. They look at the latest scandal and assume that they're seeing the *real* Congress. But they're not. They hear repeatedly in the media about missteps, but very little about the House leader who goes home on weekends to pastor his local church, or the senator who spends one day a month working in a local job to better understand the needs of constituents, or the many members who labor behind the scenes in a bipartisan way to reach the delicate compromises needed to make the system work.

I don't want to claim that all members are saints and that their behavior is always impeccable. Yet I basically agree with the assessment of historian David McCullough: "Congress, for all its faults, has not been the unbroken parade of clowns and thieves and posturing windbags so often portrayed. What should be spoken of more often, and more widely understood, are the great victories that have been won here, the decisions of courage and the visions achieved."

Probity in Congress is the rule rather than the exception, and it has increased over the years. When I arrived in Congress, members could accept lavish gifts from special interests, pocket campaign contributions in their Capitol offices, and convert their campaign contributions to personal use. And they were rarely punished for personal corruption. None of that would be tolerated now. Things still aren't perfect, but the ethical climate at the Capitol is well ahead of where it was a couple of decades ago. And, I might add, well ahead of the public's perception of it.

During my 34 years in the House of Representatives, I heard numerous criticisms of Congress. Many seemed to me perceptive; many others were far off the mark—such as when people thought that as a member of Congress I received a limousine and chauffeur, or didn't pay taxes, or was entitled to free medical care and Social Security coverage. When people are upset about Congress, their distress undermines public confidence in government and fosters cynicism and disengagement. In a representative democracy such as ours, what the American people think of the body that's supposed to reflect their views and interests as it frames the basic laws of the land is a matter of fundamental importance. I certainly do not think Congress is a perfect institution, and I have my own list of ways I think it could be improved. Yet often the public's view is based on misunderstanding or misinformation. Here are some of the other criticisms I've heard over the years:

Congress is run by lobbyists and special interests. Americans have differing views of lobbyists and special-interest groups. Some see them as playing an essential part in the democratic process. Others look at them with skepticism but allow them a legitimate role in developing policy. Most, however, see them as sinister forces exercising too much control over Congress, and the cynicism of this majority grew during the recent wave of corporate scandals, when it was revealed how extensively companies such as Enron and Arthur

Andersen had lobbied Congress. The suspicion that Congress is manipulated by powerful wheeler-dealers who put pressure on legislators and buy votes through extensive campaign contributions and other favors is not an unfounded concern, and it will not go away, no matter how fervently some might try to dismiss it.

That said, the popular view of lobbyists as nefarious fat cats smoking big cigars and handing out hundred-dollar bills behind closed doors is wrong. These days, lobbyists are usually principled people who recognize that their word is their bond. Lobbying is an enormous industry today, with billions of dollars riding on its outcomes. Special-interest groups will often spend millions of dollars on campaigns to influence a particular decision—through political contributions, grassroots lobbying efforts, television advocacy ads, and the like—because they know that they'll get a lot more back than they spend if a bill contains the language they want. They're very good at what they do, and the truth is, members of Congress can sometimes be swayed by them.

But the influence of lobbyists on the process is not as simple as it might at first appear. In the first place, "special interests" are not just the bad guys. If you're retired, or a homeowner, or use public transit or the airlines, or are concerned about religious freedom, many people in Washington are lobbying on your behalf. There are an estimated 25,000 interest groups in the capital, so you can be sure your views are somewhere represented. Advocacy groups help Congress understand how legislation affects their members, and they can help focus the public's attention on important issues. They do their part to amplify the flow of information that Thomas Jefferson called the "dialogue of democracy."

Of course, Congress often takes up controversial issues on which you'll find a broad spectrum of opinions. Public attention is strong, a host of special interests weigh in, and the views of both lobbyists and legislators are all over the map. In such circumstances, prospects are very small that any single interest group or lobbyist can disproportionately influence the results. There are simply too many of them involved for that to happen, and the process is too public. It's when things get quiet—when measures come up out of view of the public eye—that you have to be cautious. A small change in wording here, an innocuous line in a tax bill there, can allow specific groups to reap enormous benefits they might never have been granted under close public scrutiny.

The answer, it seems to me, is not to decry lobbying or lobbyists. Lobbying is a key element of the legislative process—part of the free speech guaranteed under the Constitution. At its heart, lobbying is simply people banding together to advance their interests, whether they're farmers or environmentalists or bankers. Indeed, belonging to an interest group—the Sierra Club, the AARP, the Chamber of Commerce—is one of the main ways Americans participate in public life these days.

When I was in Congress, I came to think of lobbyists as an important part of the *public discussion* of policy. I emphasize "public discussion" for a reason. Rather than trying to clamp down on lobbying, I believe we'd be better off ensuring that it happens in the open and is part of the broader policy debate. Our challenge is not to end it, but to make sure that it's a balanced dialogue, and that those in power don't consistently listen to the voices of the wealthy and the powerful more intently than the voices of others. Several legislative proposals have been made over the years that would help, including campaign finance reform, tough restrictions on gifts to members of Congress, prohibiting travel for members and their staffs funded by groups with a direct interest in legislation, and effective disclosure of lobbyists' involvement in drafting legislation. But in the end, something else may be even more important than these proposals: steady and candid conversation between elected officials and the people they represent.

Members of Congress, I would argue, have a responsibility to listen to lobbyists. But members also have a responsibility to understand where these lobbyists are coming from, to sort through what they are saying, and then to make a judgment about what is in the best interests of their constituents and the nation as a whole.

Congress almost seems designed to promote total gridlock. People will often complain about a do-nothing Congress, and think that much of the fault lies in the basic design of the institution. When a single senator can hold up action on a popular measure, when 30 committees or subcommittees are all reviewing the same bill, when a proposal needs to move not just through both the House and the Senate but through their multilayered budget, authorization, and appropriations processes, and when floor procedures are so complex that even members who have served for several years can still be confused by them, how can you expect anything to get done? This feeling is magnified by the major changes American society has undergone in recent decades. The incredible increase in the speed of every facet of our lives has made many people feel that the slow, untidy, deliberate pace of Congress is not up to the demands of modern society.

It is not now, nor has it ever been, easy to move legislation through Congress. But there's actually a method to the madness. Basic roadblocks were built into the process for a reason. We live in a big, complicated country, difficult to govern, with enormous regional, ethnic, and economic differences. The process must allow time for responsiveness and deliberation, all the more so when many issues—taxation, health care, access to guns, abortion, and more—stir strong emotions and don't submit easily to compromise. Do we really want a speedy system in which laws are pushed through before a consensus develops? Do we want a system in which the views of the minority get trampled in a rush to action by the majority? Reforms can surely be made to improve the system, but the basic process of careful deliberation, negotiation, and compromise lies at the very heart of representative democracy. Ours is not a parliamentary system; the dawdling pace comes with the territory.

We misunderstand Congress's role if we demand that it be a model of efficiency and quick action. America's founders never intended it to be that. They clearly understood that one of the key roles of Congress is to slow down the process—to allow tempers to cool and to encourage careful deliberation, so that unwise or damaging laws do not pass in the heat of the moment and so that the views of those in the minority get a fair hearing. That basic vision still seems wise today. Proceeding carefully to develop consensus is arduous and exasperating work, but it's the only way to produce policies that reflect the varied perspectives of a remarkably diverse citizenry. People may complain about the process, but they benefit from its legislative speed bumps when they want their views heard, their interests protected, their rights safeguarded. I recognize that Congress sometimes gets bogged down needlessly. But the fundamental notion that the structure of Congress should contain road blocks and barriers to hasty or unfair action makes sense for our country and needs to be protected and preserved. In the words of former Speaker of the House Sam Rayburn, "One of the wisest things ever said was, 'Wait a minute.'"

There's too much money in politics. When people hear stories about all the fundraising that members of Congress must do today, they come to believe that Congress is a "bought" institution. I've often been told that in our system dollars speak louder than words, and access is bought and sold. By a 4 to 1 margin, Americans believe that elected officials are influenced more by pressures from campaign contributors than by what's in the best interests of the country. But in fact, the problem of money in politics has been with us for many years. It's become so much more serious in recent years because of the expense of television advertising. The biggest portion of my campaign budget in the last election I faced—$1 million, for a largely rural seat in southern Indiana—went for TV spots.

Having experienced it firsthand, I know all too well that the "money chase" has gotten out of hand. A lot of money from special interests is floating around the Capitol—far too much money—and we ignore the problem at our own peril. To be fair, many of the claims that special interests can buy influence in Congress are overstated. Though I would be the last to say that contributions have no impact on a voting record, it's important to recognize that most of the money comes from groups that already share a member's views on the issues, rather than from groups that are hoping to change a member's mind. In addition, many influences shape members' voting decisions—the most important of them being the wishes of their constituents. In the end, members know that if their votes aren't in line with what their constituents want, they won't be reelected. And *that*, rather than a campaign contribution, is what's foremost in their minds.

Still, it's an unusual member of Congress who can take thousands of dollars from a particular group and not be affected, which is why I've come to the view that the influence of money on the political process raises a threat to representative democracy. We need significant reform. We have a campaign finance system today that's gradually eroding the public's trust and confidence. It's a slow-motion crisis, but it is a crisis. It's not possible to enact a perfect, sweeping campaign finance bill today, and perhaps not anytime soon. Yet the worst abuses can be dealt with, one by one.

LEE H. HAMILTON is director of the Wilson Center and director of the Center on Congress at Indiana University. He was U.S. representative from Indiana's Ninth District from 1965 to 1999, and served as chairman of the House Committee on International Relations, the Joint Economic Committee, and several other committees. This essay is adapted from his new book *How Congress Works and Why You Should Care*, published by Indiana University Press.

The Case for Busting the Filibuster

It's time to abolish this undemocratic holdover from the days of slavery and segregation.

THOMAS GEOGHEGAN

This past spring, Senator Claire McCaskill wrote to me asking for $50 to help elect more Democrats, so we could have a filibuster-proof Senate. Now that Al Franken has finally been declared the sixtieth Democratic senator, her plea may seem moot. But even with Franken in office, we don't have a filibuster-proof Senate. To get to sixty on the Democratic side, we'll still have to cut deals with Democrats like Max Baucus, Ben Nelson and others who cat around as Blue Dogs from vote to vote. Whether or not Senator Arlen Specter is a Democrat, the real Democrats will still have to cut the same deals to get sixty votes.

Until we dump the filibuster, Obama's initiatives will strain for the needed sixty votes, allowing the GOP and Blue Dog Dems to stymie reform.

Maybe we loyal Dems should start sending postcards like the following: "Dear Senator: Why do you keep asking for my money? You've already got the fifty-one votes you need to get rid of the filibuster rule." It's true—McCaskill and her colleagues could get rid of it tomorrow. Then we really would have a Democratic Senate, like our Democratic House.

She won't. The Democratic Senatorial Campaign Committee, which paid for her appeal, won't. They use the filibuster threat to hit us up for money. And as long as they do, you and I will keep on kicking in for a "filibuster-proof" Senate, which, with or without Franken, will never exist. Every Obama initiative will teeter around sixty, only the deal-cutting will go on deeper in the back rooms and be less transparent than before.

In the meantime, playing it straighter than Claude Rains, McCaskill and other Democrats tell us how shocked, yes, *shocked* they are that this deal-cutting is going on. May I quote her spring letter? "I'm writing to you today because President Obama's agenda is in serious jeopardy . . ."

It still is, as long as it takes sixty and not fifty-one votes to pass Obama's bills. But no, here's what she says: "Why? Because Republicans in the Senate—the same ones who spent years kowtowing to George W. Bush—are *determined* to block each and every one of President Obama's initiatives."

But why is that a surprise, if there's a rule that lets forty-one senators block a bill? The surprise to people in other countries is that the Senate, already wildly malapportioned, with two senators from every state no matter how big or small the population, does not observe majority rule. Her next line:

"It's appalling really."

It sure is—the way she and other Democratic senators keep the filibuster in place. But let her go on:

"They're the ones who got us into this mess. Now they want to stand in the way of every positive thing the President tries to do to set things right. I'm sure it frustrates you as much as it does me."

Yes, Senator, it frustrates me. But Democratic senators who let this happen and then ask for my money frustrate me even more.

As a labor lawyer, I have seen the Senate filibuster kill labor law reform—kill the right to join a union, freely and fairly—in 1978 and 1994. And, no doubt, in 2010.

And in the end, all we get is a letter from Senator McCaskill asking for more money. Of course, I know there are all sorts of arguments made for the filibuster. For example: "But the filibuster is part of our country's history, and there's much to be said for respecting our history and tradition." Yes, well, slavery and segregation are also part of our history, and that's what the filibuster was used to defend. I'm all in favor of history and tradition, but I see no reason to go on cherishing either the filibuster or the Confederate flag.

Besides, that's not the filibuster we're dealing with. The post-1975 procedural filibuster is entirely unlike the old filibuster, the one Mr. Smith, as played by the unshaven Jimmy Stewart, stayed up all night to mount in his plea for honest government (though usually it was Senator Bullhorn defending Jim Crow). The *old* filibuster that you and I and Frank Capra and the Confederacy love so much was very rare, and now it's extinct. No one has stood up and read recipes for Campbell's Soup for decades. In 1975 Vice President Nelson Rockefeller, in his role as president of the Senate, ruled that just fifty-one senators could vote to get rid of the filibuster entirely. A simple majority of liberals could now force change on a frightened old guard. But instead of dumping the filibuster once and for all, the liberals, unsure of their support, agreed to a "reformed" Rule 22. It was this reform that, by accident, turned the once-in-a-blue-moon filibuster into something that happens all the time. The idea was to reduce the votes needed to cut off debate from sixty-seven, which on the Hill is a big hill to climb, to just sixty. Liberals like Walter Mondale wanted to make it easier to push through civil rights and other progressive legislation. What's the harm in that?

The only problem is that, because the filibuster had rendered the chamber so laughable, with renegade members pulling all-nighters and blocking all the Senate's business, the "reformers" came up with a new procedural filibuster—the polite filibuster, the Bob Dole filibuster—to replace the cruder old-fashioned filibuster of Senate pirates like Strom Thurmond ("filibuster" comes from the Dutch word for freebooter, or pirate). The liberals of 1975 thought they could banish the dark Furies of American history, but they wound up spawning more demons than we'd ever seen before. Because the senators did not want to be laughed at by stand-up comedians, they ended their own stand-up acts with a rule that says, essentially:

"We aren't going to let the Senate pirates hold up business anymore. From now on, if those people want to filibuster, they can do it offstage. They can just file a motion that they want debate to continue on this measure indefinitely. We will then put the measure aside, and go back to it only if we get the sixty votes to cut off this not-really-happening debate."

In other words, the opposing senators don't have the stomach to stand up and read the chicken soup recipes. We call it the "procedural" filibuster, but what we really mean is the "pretend" filibuster.

But the procedural, or pretend, filibuster is an even worse form of piracy, an open invitation to senatorial predators to prey on neutral shipping, to which they might have given safe passage before. After all, why *not* "filibuster" if it's a freebie—if you don't actually have to stand up and talk in the chamber until you're not only half dead from exhaustion but have made yourself a laughingstock? That's what post-1975 senators began to do. In the 1960s, before the procedural filibuster, there were seven or fewer "old" filibusters in an entire term. In the most recent Senate term, there were 138.

At least with the old filibuster, we knew who was doing the filibustering. With the modern filibuster, senators can hold up bills without the public ever finding out their names. No one's accountable for obstructing. No senator runs the risk of looking like a fool. But while they're up there concealing one another's identity, the Republic is a shambles. And now, with a nominal sixty Democratic votes, the need for secrecy as to who has put everything on hold may be even greater than before.

"But just wait till 2010, when we get sixty-two or sixty-three Democrats." I'm sure that's what Senator McCaskill would tell me. "So come on, kick in." But Senator, where will they come from? They could come from bloody border states like yours (Missouri), or from deep inside the South. The problem with the filibuster is not so much that it puts Republicans in control but that it puts senators from conservative regions like the South, the border states and the Great Plains in control. The only true filibuster-proof Senate would be a majority that would be proof against those regions.

An astute book published in 2006, Thomas Schaller's *Whistling Past Dixie,* argued that to craft a presidential majority Democrats don't need the Southern vote. That may be true (although it turned out that Barack Obama made historic inroads in the South, winning three states there). But there is no way to whistle past Dixie when a non-Dixie presidential majority tries to get its program through the Senate. After 2010, we could have sixty-four Democrats in the Senate and still be in bad shape.

A filibuster-proof Senate, then, is a conceptual impossibility. Even with a hundred Democrats, a filibuster would still lock in a form of minority rule. Because among the Democrats there would arise two new subparties, with forty-one senators named "Baucus" blocking fifty-nine senators named "Brown."

Here's another argument for the filibuster: "If we get rid of it, we'll be powerless against the Republicans when they're in charge." That's why we need it, they say: we're waiting for the barbarians, for the nightmare of President Palin. People in the AFL-CIO tell me this even as the filibuster keeps the right to organize a union on ice and union membership keeps shrinking.

Or as a union general counsel said to me: "Everyone here in the DC office would be freaked out completely if we lost the filibuster. They think it's the only thing that saved us from Bush." Inside the Beltway, they all think it's the filibuster that saved those of us who read Paul Krugman from being shipped off to Guantánamo. Really, that's what many people on the left think. "If Bush ever came back, we'd need it."

Of course Bush, or a Bush equivalent, will come back—precisely because Obama and our side will be blocked by the filibuster. Obama is in peril until he gets the same constitutional power that FDR had, i.e., the right to pass a program with a simple majority (at least after Senator Huey Long finally ran out of words). But let's deal with the canard that the filibuster "saved" us from Bush. What's the evidence? Judicial nominations: that's the answer they give. Go ahead, name someone we blocked. Roberts? Alito? Of course there's Bork, whom we blocked in the 1980s. But we didn't block him with a filibuster.

Think seriously about whom we really stopped. Look, I'm all in favor of opposing atrocious right-wing nominations, and I admit that the filibuster, or at least the GOP's refusal to nuke it, did keep some appellate and district courts free of especially bad people. But I can tell you as a lawyer who does appellate work, who has to appear before these judges, it makes little difference to me if we lose the filibuster. All it means is that instead of a bad conservative, I end up with a *really* bad conservative. Either way, I still wind up losing.

I think I can say this on behalf of many liberal lawyers who appear before appellate courts: if we could give up the filibuster and get labor law reform or national health insurance, I'd put up with a slightly more disagreeable group of right-wing judges. We'll take the heat.

The fact is, as long as we have the filibuster, we ensure the discrediting of the Democratic Party and we're more likely, not less, to have a terrible bench.

Sure, sometimes liberal Democrats put the filibuster to good use when Republicans are in power. Sure, sometimes a liberal senator can use the filibuster to stop a piece of corporate piracy. It's impossible to prove that the filibuster *never* does any good. But the record is awfully thin. Look at all the financial deregulation that Senator Phil Gramm and leading Democrats like Larry Summers pushed through only a decade ago. The filibuster did not stop their effective repeal of the New Deal, but it would block the revival of it today.

On the other hand, Republicans and conservative Democrats use their filibusters on labor, health, the stimulus, everything. They can and will block all the change that Obama wanted us to believe in. And even when they lose, they win. For example, when we say that after a major rewriting of the stimulus package—a rewriting that seriously weakened the original bill—it "survived the filibuster," what we really mean is that it didn't.

But let's turn to the final objection: "No one in Washington cares about this. It's not on the agenda. It's a waste of time even to discuss it. What you're talking about is impossible."

What Washington insiders partly mean when they say this is, with a filibuster, any senator can stick up the Senate, and what senator is going to turn in his or her sidearm by giving up the right to demand sixty votes? That's why they're raising a million dollars a day. Otherwise, they'd be peacefully serving in the House. The right to filibuster is what makes each of them a small-town sheriff. That's why it would take massive marches in the streets to force them to give it up.

Indeed, it's hard to imagine how bloody the battle would be. The last time anything so traumatic happened on the Hill was in 1961, when the bigger procedural bar to majority rule was not in the Senate but the House. John Kennedy had just come in, and it was clear that his New Frontier program (we still didn't have Medicare) would go nowhere because of the power of the House Rules Committee chair, the now forgotten "Judge" Howard Smith. Kennedy had to enlist the Speaker of the House, Sam Rayburn, to break Smith's power to stop any bill he disliked from leaving House Rules. In the end, the battle to beat Smith probably killed Rayburn, who died later in the year.

It was an awful power struggle, and many were aghast that Kennedy had thrown away all his capital for this cause. But had he not done it, there probably would not have been a Civil Rights Bill, or certainly not the full-blown version of the Great Society that Lyndon Johnson pushed through after Kennedy's assassination. Imagine having to fight the battle for Medicare today. Without that war on Judge Smith, what we now call the "liberal hour" would not have come.

Nor will any "liberal hour" come in our time, until we bring the filibuster down. I know it seems hopeless. But so did knocking out slavery when the abolitionists first started, or segregation, when civil rights activists began their struggle against Jim Crow. It's a fair enough analogy, since the filibuster is one of the last remnants of racist politics in America: it was a parliamentary tactic used by the Calhounians to make extra certain slavery would stay around.

We should adopt the strategy of the antislavery movement, which in the early stages had three approaches:

1. The laying of petitions on the House. Forgive the archaic legal phrase: I mean petitions to Congress, both houses. In the era of John Quincy Adams—in case you missed the Steven Spielberg movie—there would be mass petitions, with Adams and others reading them on the House floor to the howls of the Southerners. Every group busted by a filibuster should lay on a petition. And start with the House, which is the only place it has a chance of being read.

2. Resolutions by the House, as a warm-up for the Senate. Such resolutions might read: "Resolved, that Congress has no authority to require supermajorities in any chamber except as authorized by the Constitution." Aren't House chairs tired of seeing their bills cast into black holes by senators whose names they never even know?

3. Evangelizing. The most effective tactic in the fight against slavery was the preaching of New England clergy against it. We can start in our battle against the filibuster by enlisting faculty at New England colleges to hold teach-ins. Teach the kids why "Yes, we can" can't happen with the current Senate rules.

By the way, the abolitionists knew the Senate was their enemy, just as it is our enemy today. Let's hope these tactics work for us in getting rid of this last vestige of slavery: Senate Rule 22. What's painful is that we have to cross some of our most sainted senators. But unless we decide to just give up on the Republic, there's no way out. To save the Obama presidency, we may have to fight our heroes.

THOMAS GEOGHEGAN, a lawyer in Chicago, is the author of *In America's Court: How a Civil Lawyer Who Likes to Settle Stumbled Into a Criminal Trial* and *Which Side Are You On? Trying to Be for Labor When It's Flat on Its Back* (both New Press).

Reprinted by permission from the August 31/September 7, 2009, issue of *The Nation*. Copyright © 2009 by The Nation. For subscription information, call 1-800-333-8536. Portions of each week's Nation magazine can be accessed at www.thenation.com

A Bit of Advice, Madam Speaker

CHARLIE COOK

If I were a confidant of House Speaker Nancy Pelosi, my advice to the California Democrat would be, "No more news conferences. No more television appearances. Keep your public profile low. Focus on what you do best." Pelosi is like the student who gets A's in some subjects but D's and F's in others. She needs to avoid the areas where she tends to fail.

No more news conferences. No more TV appearances. Keep your public profile low. Focus on what you do best.

Arguably, Pelosi has amassed and centralized power more successfully than any other speaker in modern history. Committee chairmanships aren't what they used to be. The leadership—specifically, the speaker—now drives this car.

In terms of behind-the-scenes machinations, she is as good as pols come. People who have underestimated Pelosi have done so at their own peril. But her public persona, the way she comes across on television, and the caricatures that have developed around Pelosi do her and her party no good.

First, look at the numbers. In January, CNN/Opinion Research polling pegged Pelosi with a 51 percent approval rating and a 22 percent disapproval rating. By early March, her approval rating had dropped 5 points. It dropped 7 more points in a poll conducted May 14–17, bringing her down to 39 percent. Meanwhile, her disapproval scores soared—from 22 percent in January, to 30 percent in March, to the current 48 percent. While Congress's job-approval rating has gone up, even doubling over some past readings, to 37 percent according to Gallup and 41 percent in Fox News polling, the speaker's popularity has plummeted.

Polling by Research 2000 for the liberal blog *Daily Kos* shows a slightly different pattern in favorability ratings but leads to essentially the same conclusion. In four January surveys, the speaker's favorable ratings, ranging from 39 percent to 42 percent, barely exceeded her unfavorable ones, which were 36 percent to 38 percent. In two surveys this month, she registered 34 percent and 37 percent favorable ratings, with her unfavorables at 46 percent and 50 percent. Considering how few people actually pay attention to Capitol Hill, these are pretty lousy numbers.

Two main caricatures of Pelosi have developed. In the world of conservative talk radio, she is depicted as a lightweight, ultraliberal, San Francisco-socialite-turned-House-speaker, more a source of amusement than of fear, because these adversaries don't respect her enough to fear her. This cartoon image ignores Pelosi's Baltimore roots, however. She learned politics at the knee of her father, Thomas D'Alesandro, who over a 40-year career served as a member of the Maryland House of Delegates, deputy state tax collector, Baltimore City Council member, Charm City mayor, and U.S. representative. His was the era of Big City machine politics when the accumulation and exercise of power was a high art.

His daughter learned her lessons well. Those who dismiss Pelosi's behind-the-scenes political talent do so out of ignorance, not firsthand observation. She has taken down some pretty formidable players in her rise to the top.

However, a second caricature of Pelosi has developed among those who are neither Republican nor conservative. On television, Pelosi often appears treacly and superficial, not the tough, fiercely determined woman she is behind closed doors. Her on-camera performance contributes to the misimpression that she is a lightweight.

Pelosi's disastrous May 14 news conference projected a third negative image, that of a politician caught overreaching and then mishandling the damage control. No matter how opaque the Central Intelligence Agency was in its briefing of Pelosi and other members of Congress in September 2002, after her news conference the score was CIA 1, Pelosi 0.

The speaker's constituents, outside of San Francisco, are the 434 other members of the House, particularly the other Democrats. There is no need for her to be a fixture on television sets across the country, and TV is certainly not her best venue.

When you are very good at one thing, stick to it.

cookreport@nationaljournal.com

Reprinted by permission from *National Journal*, May 23, 2009, p. 64. Copyright © 2009 by National Journal Group Inc. All rights reserved.

Remote Control

The Supreme Court's greatest failing is not ideological bias—it's the justices' increasingly tenuous grasp of how the real world works.

STUART TAYLOR JR.

I've been working on some questions in case the makers of Trivial Pursuit ever decide to put forth a Supreme Court edition: Now that Sandra Day O'Connor has announced her retirement, how many remaining justices have ever held elected office? How many have previously served at the highest levels of the executive branch of government? How many have argued big-time commercial lawsuits within the past thirty-five years? How many have ever been either criminal defense lawyers or trial prosecutors? How many have presided over even a single criminal or civil trial? The answers are zero, zero, zero, one, and one, respectively. (David Souter was a New Hampshire prosecutor once upon a time, and later served as a trial judge.)

The answers would have been starkly different fifty years ago. Five of the nine justices who decided *Brown* v. *Board of Education,* in 1954, had once worked as trial prosecutors, and several had substantial hands-on experience in commercial litigation. More famously, that Court included a former governor, three former senators, two former attorneys general, two former solicitors general, and a former SEC chairman.

That Court, in other words, was intimately familiar with the everyday workings of the political and judicial systems, and with the beliefs and concerns of everyday Americans. Not so the Court that recessed in June, eight of whose members (in addition to their long tenure in the splendid isolation of the Supreme Court's marble palace) have been drawn from judgeships on appellate courts, and sometimes from academic law before that—places already far removed from the hurly-burly of our judicial and political systems. The current justices are smart and dedicated. But they're not like you and me.

Debates over the Court's "balance"—ideological, ethnic, gender—will doubtless heat up as Congress considers the current vacancy. Yet there is likely to be little discussion about the greatest imbalance—the one in the collective real-world experience of its justices. The Court's steady homogenization by professional background has gone largely unremarked.

Should we be concerned? After all, the Supreme Court is supposed to sit above politics and apart from popular whims. But when a large majority of the Court's justices have never cross-examined a lying cop or a slippery CEO, never faced a jury, never slogged through the swamps of the modern discovery process, something has gone wrong. As the Court has lost touch with the real-world ramifications of its decisions, our judicial system has clearly suffered.

The Court's slow disengagement from practicality was visible by the 1970s, when, for example, in a well-intentioned effort to protect students from unwarranted suspension and tenured public school teachers from arbitrary dismissal, the Court issued a series of decisions requiring hearings before such action. The justices presumably imagined simple, cursory hearings to guard against egregious abuses of power. Predictably, that's not what happened. Hearings quickly became clogged with lawyers, witnesses, trial-type formalities, multiple administrative and judicial appeals, and years of delay. To avoid such ordeals, many principals and administrators have simply stopped trying to remove thuggish students and inept teachers from our schools.

Over time the justices have failed ever more conspicuously to understand what messes their decisions might make. In 1997, while forcing Bill Clinton to give a sworn deposition in the Paula Jones sexual-harassment lawsuit, the Court stunned litigators and trial judges by predicting that this was "highly unlikely to occupy any substantial amount of [President Clinton's] time." Only Justice Stephen Breyer seemed to appreciate that the realities of modern discovery practice "could pose a significant threat to the President's official functions." Sure enough, the district court ordered Clinton to answer detailed, tangential questions about his relations with various women. The rest is history.

In a string of decisions since 2000 the Court has thrown the criminal-justice system into utter confusion by repeatedly changing the rules on the roles of judges and juries in sentencing, while providing minimal guidance on how the new rules should be implemented. In response to the rulings, thousands of current inmates have requested re-sentencing, to the consternation of federal trial and appellate judges, who are all over the lot on how to handle these requests. (The judges also have major differences of opinion on how much weight they should now give sentencing guidelines in new cases.) We'll be hearing more about this confusion—it's a clear recipe for an onslaught of additional appeals down the road, which will further tax our already overburdened criminal-justice system.

Then there's the Court's recent Janus-faced pair of rulings on governmental displays of the Ten Commandments. The gist: recently installed, framed copies must be stripped from courthouse walls; forty-year-old, six-foot-high monuments can stay on the grounds outside. The logic: well, for that you'll have to read ten separate opinions totaling 140 pages. In announcing part of this mess, Chief Justice William Rehnquist said, "I didn't know we had that many people on our Court." Chief Justice John Marshall once observed (in *Marbury* v. *Madison*) that "it is the province and duty of the Judicial Department to say what the law is." Government officials and lower-court judges often find the law difficult to ascertain today. But at least they do know—in minute detail—what each justice thinks it ought to be.

As our Supreme Court justices have become remote from the real world, they've also become more reluctant to do real work—especially the sort of quotidian chores done by prior justices to ensure the smooth functioning of the judicial system. The Court's overall productivity—as measured by the number of full, signed decisions—has fallen by almost half since 1985. Clerks draft almost all the opinions and perform almost all the screening that leads to the dismissal without comment of 99 percent of all petitions for review. Many of the cases dismissed are the sort that could be used to wring clear perversities and inefficiencies out of our litigation system—especially out of commercial and personal-injury litigation.

Traditionally the Court decided major questions of federal commercial law, adapting to the changing nature of business and the increasing complexity of litigation. Yet according to Michael Greve, the head of the American Enterprise Institute's Federalism Project, this Court has "resolutely refused to tackle the inconsistencies and absurdities that, after decades of neglect, afflict nearly every area of commercial litigation." One reason, Greve argues, is that with the exception of Justice Breyer, "the Court has absolutely no idea what business litigation in America now looks like."

What accounts for the Court's drift? There are two factors—one political and one biological. Politically the appointment of Supreme Court justices has become more contentious as it has focused on a small number of polarizing issues—most notably abortion. The ideal candidate today is predictable enough to suit the president and his political base, yet not so predictable as to be an easy target for critics. Appellate-court judges simply fit the bill better than other candidates. Their legal opinions signal ideological leanings (providing more of a track record than would exist for, say, a prominent litigator or a prosecutor). But because they are bound to follow Supreme Court precedents, they ordinarily don't say whether they would overturn those precedents if, as justices, they got the chance. (Elected officials, in contrast, must take specific stands on abortion and other hot issues—all but disqualifying them from consideration for the Court.) Past justices took many roads to the Supreme Court. Today, almost invariably, there appears to be just one.

Moreover, that road is receding further in the rear-view mirror. Longer life spans and justices' increasing reluctance to retire have raised their average tenure from fifteen years before 1970 to twenty-five years since then. Until this summer no justice had retired in eleven years. Real-world experiences gained before their years on the appellate and Supreme courts have become distant memories for today's justices.

Will future appointees bring more diversity of experience? Alas, the political incentives to pick appellate judges seem likely to persist. But one proposed reform—which, after a phase-in, would limit judicial terms to eighteen years, and allow each president to appoint a new justice every two years—would create more opportunities to diversify the Court over time.

The proposal, which is backed by some forty-five leading legal scholars, both liberal and conservative, would (among other benefits) ensure frequent and regular infusions of new blood, and with it more recent experience with the practical aspects of judicial decisions. And because more appointments would lower the political stakes for each one, presidents might be willing to look beyond the usual suspects.

That would be welcome. Quietly our Supreme Court has become a sort of aristocracy—unable or unwilling to clearly see the workings, glitches, and peculiarities of the justice system over which it presides from such great altitude.

STUART TAYLOR JR. is a *National Journal* columnist and a *Newsweek* contributor.

Court Approval

Will John Roberts ever get better?

JEFFREY ROSEN

At the end of a bitterly divided Supreme Court term, liberals are by turns fighting mad and full of despair. Although Chief Justice John Roberts began the term by calling for greater consensus, a third of cases were decided by five–four votes, the highest percentage in more than ten years. The polarization inspired the four liberal justices to write some of their most passionate, incisive, and memorable dissents. But how pessimistic should liberals really be about the future of the Court? Just after the term ended, I had an opportunity to interview Justice Stephen Breyer about the Court's role in American democracy at the Aspen Ideas Festival.

Breyer made no bones about his disappointment with the divisions on the Court. He began by discussing his 77-page dissenting opinion in the Seattle case forbidding public schools to use race in student assignments. The dissent is a tour de force. It combines a passionate defense of judicial restraint with blistering criticism of the majority for distorting precedents. "Of course, I got slightly exercised, and the way I show this is that I wrote seventy-seven-page opinions," he joked. "I think the color-blind view is *very* wrong, I think it's *never* been in the law, it's never been accepted by a majority of this Court, and, my goodness, if ever there was a decision that should be made locally, it's this one."

In several of the term's important cases, Roberts and Justice Samuel Alito declined to join Justices Antonin Scalia and Clarence Thomas in calling for the open overruling of previous precedents. Scalia even accused Roberts of "judicial obfuscation" and "faux judicial restraint" for his refusal to overturn the entire structure of campaign finance law rather than dismantling it incrementally. But Breyer, too, seemed unimpressed by conservative incrementalism: He suggested that it was better to overturn precedents cleanly than to pretend to preserve them while distorting them beyond recognition. "There were ten cases listed as important cases in the newspapers. I was in the majority twice—that was better than nothing," he said. "In three of the other cases, the majority of the Court said it was overruling prior precedents, and, in four other cases, the minority of the Court said you are overruling prior precedents. I thought there was quite a lot of precedent overruled, but the people on the other side, who are very good judges, thought they weren't overruling. I do think it's better to be open."

Breyer noted that the number of unanimous opinions has fallen from 32 percent in 2004, Justice Sandra Day O'Connor's last year on the Court, to 22 percent this year, and the five–four decisions rose from about 25 to 33 percent. Moreover, he noted, the number of five–four decisions where what he called "the usual suspects—me and John Stevens and Ruth Ginsburg and David Souter" were joined in a bloc has risen from 55 to 80 percent. He admitted that he had looked up another statistic: "In the 2004 term, I was in the majority eighty percent of the time, and I looked at this term: It's dropped to about thirty-five percent, so I was in dissent quite a lot."

I asked Breyer why Roberts had failed in his efforts to achieve consensus and whether he might ever come closer to achieving these goals. "Will he do better in the future? He can join my dissents!" Breyer replied with a chuckle. But then Breyer said he was always hopeful that new justices will change. "This is a job that people who are appointed have for a long time. . . . It takes a while before you have enough experience with the cases in front of you, before you have a view of what this document is, and a view of the institution." That's why, he said, "[I]t's very hard to predict how a person will decide things five or ten years in the future."

Breyer's cautious hope that the Court might become less polarized in the future, combined with disappointment at the polarization of the present, seems like the right attitude. It is a far more productive model for liberals than self-pity or shock about the unsurprising fact that, now that Alito has replaced O'Connor, the Court has moved right. For example, Emily Bazelon of *Slate* has demanded that liberals and moderates who supported Roberts as a potential unifier (including me) recant. This is premature. Bush won the 2004 election, and the opportunity to replace O'Connor with Alito ensured that he would change the direction of the Court. Those of us who supported Roberts never denied his conservatism. The question was: Who among the candidates President Bush was plausibly inclined to appoint as chief justice would be most likely to avoid the radicalism of Scalia and Thomas and try to unify the Court? In his first term, which began in October 2005, Roberts entirely vindicated these hopes. He embraced bipartisan consensus as his highest goal and presided over more unanimous opinions in a row than at any point in the Court's modern history.

This term, by contrast, Roberts notably failed in his efforts to achieve consensus, although he continued to distinguish himself from Scalia and Thomas with his commitment to incrementalism. The Court's shift to the right was driven by the fact that it took up controversial issues, such as race, abortion, and campaign finance, which it had avoided while waiting for O'Connor's replacement. On all these issues, Alito and Anthony Kennedy are more conservative than O'Connor. And, most important of all, Kennedy, who is less pragmatic than O'Connor, refused to embrace Roberts's invitation to converge around narrow, unanimous opinions. Asked by Stuart Taylor Jr. and Evan Thomas of *Newsweek* what he thought of Roberts's effort after the term ended, Kennedy laughed. "I guess I haven't helped much," he said. "My initial reaction was going to be, 'Just let me write all the opinions.'" Roberts acknowledged from the beginning that he couldn't succeed without his colleagues' support, and he understood that, in the face of resistance to his vision from the median justice, even the most strenuous efforts to achieve consensus would be doomed.

It's too soon, as Breyer suggests, to tell whether Roberts will ultimately be more successful in achieving consensus. But, since he has embraced this as the standard by which his tenure should be judged, Roberts presumably understands that he can't preside over a decade of five–four decisions. Far from going down in history as a unifier in the tradition of John Marshall, he would be perceived as the leader of a partisan conservative Court, one that may be increasingly at odds with a more liberal president and Congress.

For the foreseeable future, however, the political composition of the Court won't likely change. And that has put some liberals in a despairing mood. On *The New Republic's* website, Cass R. Sunstein has lamented "the absence of anything like a heroic vision on the Court's left" to counteract "the existence of such a vision on the Court's right," embodied by Scalia and Thomas. Here I respectfully disagree. There is, in fact, a heroic vision on the Court's left, and it is squarely in the tradition of previous liberal visionaries like Oliver Wendell Holmes and Louis Brandeis. This vision, championed by TNR since its founding in the Progressive era, is rooted in strenuous bipartisan judicial restraint. It is today defended most eloquently and systematically by Breyer and Ginsburg, who have voted to strike down fewer state and federal laws combined than any of their colleagues.

In our conversation, Breyer self-consciously embraced the mantle of restraint. "To a very large measure, judges have to be careful about intruding in the legislative process," he said. "[R]uth and I have been among the ones less likely to strike down laws passed by the legislature, and, by that measure, we're not very activist." Far from being a cautious or defensive posture, bipartisan restraint has always been rooted in liberal self-confidence—confidence that, given a fair opportunity, liberals can fight and win in the political arena. The fact that conservatives now rely on the Court to win their battles for them—striking down democratically adopted campaign finance laws and integration programs—is a sign of their weakness.

Breyer and his liberal colleagues were not unwavering in their restraint this term: They dissented from the partial-birth abortion decision, despite the fact that bans on the procedure are supported by bipartisan majorities in Congress and in most states. When I asked Breyer how he reconciled this dissent with his commitment to judicial deference, he demurred. "The only question for me was, am I suddenly going to overrule a whole lot of precedent? No. That's a strong basis." Liberals, in fact, could have reconciled their commitment to precedent and judicial restraint by upholding the partial-birth law while insisting it include a health exception. But no one is consistent in every case; and the activism of liberals here was an exception, not the rule.

Judged by their willingness to defer to legislatures, liberals are now the party of judicial restraint. Conservatives have responded to this embarrassing turnabout by trying to rob the term of any neutral meaning. In a series of unintentionally hilarious editorials, *The Wall Street Journal* praised the Roberts Court for "restoring business confidence in the rule of law and setting limits on the tort bar and activist judges." Spare us the twistifications. For more than 50 years, conservatives have insisted that judges should defer to legislatures and let citizens resolve their disputes politically. But, at the very moment they consolidated their Supreme Court majority, they have abandoned this principle and embraced the activism they once deplored. I hope that Chief Justice Roberts, over time, will achieve his welcome goal of transcending the Court's divisions and helping conservatives rediscover the virtues of modesty and deference. But, for now, the party of judicial restraint has a convincing spokesman in Justice Breyer.

From *The New Republic*, July 23, 2007. Copyright © 2007 by Jeffrey Rosen. Reprinted by permission of the author.

Marking Time
Why Government Is Too Slow

BRUCE BERKOWITZ

In recent years we have been witness to a portentous competition between two determined but dissimilar rivals on the international scene. In one corner we have al-Qaeda, founded in the early 1990s, the transnational Islamic terrorist organization led by Osama bin Laden. In the other corner, we have the government of the United States of America, established in 1787, at present the most powerful state on the planet. The key question defining this competition is this: Who has the more agile organization? Al-Qaeda, in planning and executing a terrorist attack, or the United States, in planning, developing and executing the measures to stop one?

Let's look at the record. Sometime during the spring of 1999, Khalid Sheikh Mohamed visited bin Laden in Afghanistan and asked if al-Qaeda would fund what came to be called the "planes operation"—the plan for suicide attacks using commercial airliners. (Mohamed had been mulling the plot since at least 1993, when he discussed it with his nephew, Ramzi Yousef, one of the terrorists behind the first World Trade Center bombing and the attempted Philippine-based effort to bring down a dozen U.S. airliners over the Pacific in 1995.) Bin Laden agreed, and by the summer of 1999 he had selected as team leaders four al-Qaeda members—Khalid al-Mihdhar, Nawafal-Hazmi, Tawfiq bin Attash (also known as "Khallad") and Abu Bara al-Yemen.

These four team leaders entered the United States in early 2000 and started taking flying lessons that summer. The so-called "muscle" hijackers, the 15 terrorists tasked with overpowering the crews on the targeted flights, began arriving in April 2001 and spent the summer preparing for the September 11 attack. So from the point in time that a government contracting official would call "authority to proceed" to completion, the operation took approximately 27 months.

Now let's track the U.S. response. U.S. officials began debating options for preventing future terrorist attacks immediately following the September 11 strike. Congress took a year to debate the statute establishing the Department of Homeland Security. George W. Bush, who originally opposed creating a new department, changed his mind and signed the bill into law on November 25, 2002. A joint House-Senate committee finished the first investigation of intelligence leading up to the attack in December 2002. The 9/11 Commission issued its report on July 22, 2004, recommending among other things the establishment of a Director of National Intelligence and a new National Counterterrorism Center. President Bush established the NCTC by Executive Order on August 27, 2004.

Adoption of the Intelligence Reform and Terrorism Prevention Act, which embodied most of the Commission's other proposals, took another three months. The measures it authorized—including the creation of a Director of National Intelligence—lay fallow until a second commission, investigating intelligence prior to the war in Iraq, issued its own report four months later. The new Director was sworn in on April 21, 2005. Total response time, charitably defined: about 44 months, and implementation continues today.

Obviously, planning an attack and adjusting defenses to prevent a subsequent attack are not comparable tasks. Still, it is hard to avoid concluding that organizations like al-Qaeda are inherently nimbler than governments, especially large and highly bureaucratized governments like ours. As things stand now, terrorists can size up a situation, make decisions and act faster than we can. In military terms, they are "inside our decision cycle."

Recall July 7, 2005, for example, when terrorists bombed three London Underground trains and a double-decker city bus, killing 52 commuters. The four bombs exploded within a minute of each other, an operationally and technically challenging feat that is a hallmark of al-Qaeda attacks. A "martyrdom video" proclaiming allegiance to al-Qaeda and taped months earlier by one of the bombers, Muhammad Sidique Khan, soon surfaced on al-Jazeera. Khan apparently made the video during a visit to Pakistan, and investigators concluded that an earlier trip to Pakistan in July 2003 also had something to do with the attack. If so, then the planning of the London attack required two years, possibly less.

Organizations like al-Qaeda are inherently nimbler than governments, especially large ones like ours.

Again, it may seem unfair to compare a government bureaucracy, American or British, with a network of loosely organized, small terrorist cells. But unfairness is the point: Terrorists will *always* make the conflict between us as "unfair" as possible, avoiding our strengths and exploiting our vulnerabilities however they can. So will insurgency leaders and rogue dictators, who also happen to be surreptitious WMD proliferators; narco-traffickers and money launderers, who aid terrorists either wittingly or inadvertently. The U.S. government and similarly arrayed allies will simply lose battle after battle if our adversaries absorb information, make decisions, change tactics and act faster than we can.

Reading the 9/11 Commission Report one cannot help but be struck by how often simple delay and chronic slowness led to disaster on September 11. President Clinton told the Commission that he had asked for military options to get rid of bin Laden in late 1999. But General Hugh Shelton, Chairman of the Joint Chiefs of Staff, was reluctant to provide them. Secretary of Defense William Cohen thought the President was speaking only hypothetically. The one person who could have given a direct order to cut through the resistance and ambiguity, President Clinton himself, did not do so. He thought that raising his temper wouldn't accomplish anything, so he allowed himself to be slow-rolled, and the issue went essentially unaddressed.

The problem wasn't just at the top, however. Down below in the bureaucracy, things were just as bad—case in point, the Predator. The now-famous robotic aircraft was originally built for battlefield reconnaissance and was later modified to carry missiles. The U.S. Air Force had flown Predators in the Balkans since 1996, but Afghanistan was trickier. The aircraft had a limited range and thus needed a remote base and data uplinks to get the information back to Washington. It took until July 2000 to work out these details, and two more months to deploy the Predator over Afghanistan.

Predator operators thought they spotted bin Laden in September 2000, but U.S. officials disagreed over rules of engagement. National Security Advisor Samuel Berger wanted greater confidence in bin Laden's location before approving a strike, and he worried about civilian casualties. At the same time, Air Force leaders were reluctant to carry out what looked to them, not unreasonably, like a covert operation, and the CIA was reluctant to undertake a direct combat operation—or to violate the Executive Order prohibiting assassination.

These disagreements dragged into 2001 as the Bush Administration took office. Then President Bush put everything on hold while National Security Advisor Condoleezza Rice directed a comprehensive plan to eliminate al-Qaeda. George Tenet, the Director of Central Intelligence, deferred the legal over whether the CIA could take part in an attack until the Administration had prepared its new strategy. So it went, until the clock ran out and the terrorists killed nearly 3,000 people.

Or take the inability of the Immigration and Naturalization Service (INS), as it existed on September 11, 2001, to track the whereabouts of known terror suspects and to report relevant information about their attempts to enter the country to other Federal agencies. The INS failed to meet its homeland security responsibilities partly because Congress systematically underfunded it. But even worse, the INS had failed to disentangle its different functions; keeping some people out of the country while letting others in. Meanwhile, everyone—the White House, Congress, the bureaucracy—failed to agree on a solution that both dealt with illegal immigration while also allowing entry to laborers essential to the American economy. The security problem flowing from this failure is obvious: As long as underfunded bureaucrats are unable to regulate the enormous flow of illegal immigrants seeking work, they will never be able to detect and track the few truly dangerous people trying to enter the country.

Of course, the story of the run-up to 9/11 is an oft-told one. Yet almost everyone seems to miss the core problem from which all others followed: There was always time for another meeting, another study, another round of coordination. Virtually no one was worrying about the clock—about whether *time itself mattered*. It's not that every concern raised didn't have some legitimate rationale (at least within the legal-bureaucratic culture that characterizes the U.S. government). It's the fact that, while we were working out legal issues, al-Qaeda was developing and executing its plan.

This same problem surfaced again a year later. Just about everyone agrees now that the United States was unprepared for the insurgency in Iraq, but most overlook that someone else was also unprepared: the insurgents. U.S. analysts who interviewed captured Iraqi officials and military officers for the Defense Department have concluded that Iraqi leaders had not prepared a "stay-behind" or "rope-a-dope" strategy. They had never planned to forfeit the conventional war in order to win a guerrilla war later on. Iraqi military leaders believed they would lose the war and just wanted to get it over with quickly. Saddam Hussein's security services and core Ba'ath Party operatives kept the lid on the various sects, tribes and ethnic groups so that they could not plan a guerrilla war either. The result was that *no one* was prepared for an insurgency. The United States, its coalition partners, Ba'athis who had escaped capture, tribal leaders, religious authorities, foreign fighters—everyone was starting from scratch. So when Saddam's statue came down in Firdos Square on April 9, 2003, the question that mattered most was who could organize and execute faster, the would-be insurgents or the U.S. government?

Alas, we were left in the starting blocks. The insurgents organized much faster than U.S. officials could recognize and respond. We were playing catch-up from the beginning, which is another way of saying we were losing.

Things would perhaps not be so bad if the war on al-Qaeda and the war in Iraq were exceptional. In truth, the problem is pervasive and getting worse. "Organizational agility" sounds abstract, but it really boils down to specific questions: How long does it take to deliver a critical weapon or information system? How fast can an agency bring new people on board? How fast can it change its mix of people if it needs to? In short, *how fast can government agencies act—and is this fast enough to stay ahead of the competition?*

The U.S. government is not always woefully slow. The response to the December 2004 Southeast Asian tsunami, for example, was admirably quick and reasonably effective under the circumstances. So was the relief mission that the United States effectively led following the massive earthquake that rocked northern Pakistan in October 2005. However, these few exceptions aside, the U.S. government has become an increasingly ponderous beast, unable to act quickly or even to understand how its various parts fit together to act at all.

Once, When We Were Fast

It was not always so. After the surprise attack at Pearl Harbor, one of the most heavily damaged ships was the battleship USS *West Virginia*. Most of its port side had been blown away. The ship sank rapidly, but on an even keel on the bottom of the harbor. The Navy needed every 16-inch gun it could muster, so Navy leaders decided to repair the ship. It was not easy, but the USS *West Virginia* steamed into Puget Sound in April 1943 to be refitted and modernized. It rejoined the fleet in June 1944, thirty months after it was sunk, took part in several operations and was present for the surrender ceremonies in Tokyo Bay in September 1945. By comparison, after al-Qaeda agents in Yemen damaged the USS *Cole* far less severely with a single improvised bomb in October 2000, it took 16 months to retrieve the still-floating destroyer and complete repairs in Pascagoula, Mississippi. The ship did not then leave its home port in Norfolk, Virginia, for its first deployment until November 2003—37 months later.

World War II offers many examples like the recovery of the *West Virginia* in which organizations worked with remarkable alacrity. Take the effort to build the first atomic bomb. Albert Einstein wrote to Franklin D. Roosevelt on August 2, 1939, alerting him to the possibilities of nuclear weapons. He met with FDR about a month later, which led Roosevelt to establish the Uranium Committee to research military applications of nuclear fission. Vannevar Bush, Roosevelt's science adviser, persuaded the President to accelerate the project in October 1941, as war with Germany and Japan seemed likely. On September 14, 1942, Brigadier General Leslie Groves was appointed director of the new Manhattan Project, marking the formal start of the project to build the atomic bomb. The Trinity test, the world's first nuclear explosion, took place on July 16, 1945, and Hiroshima was bombed on August 6, less than a month later. The entire effort, costing $21 billion in today's dollars, developed three different means of producing fissile material, two bomb designs and three devices.

Or consider the Office of Strategic Services, the predecessor of today's CIA. President Roosevelt appointed William Donovan as his "Coordinator of Information" in July 1941, and the OSS was itself established in June 1942. Harry Truman disbanded it in September 1945. In other words, the entire history of the OSS—what many consider the Golden Age of American intelligence—spanned just 37 months. In that short time it recruited, trained and deployed a workforce of about 13,000 people. William Casey, directing OSS espionage in Europe, stood up his entire network in about 18 months. By comparison, after 9/11 Tenet said on

Article 27. Marking Time

several occasions that it would require five years to rebuild the CIA's clandestine service.

Or recall the war in the Pacific. The Battle of the Coral Sea was fought in May 1942, the Battle of Midway a month later. Within six months of Pearl Harbor, the U.S. Navy had destroyed five Japanese carriers, along with most of Japan's naval aircraft and aviators. It has taken us longer just to get organized for the so-called War on Terror (to the extent that we *are* organized for it) than it did to fight and win World War II.

Delivering the Product

Everything else today is moving faster, thanks to jet airliners, interstate highways, the computer and the Internet. But government, including the parts responsible for national security, is moving slower, and it's getting worse.

Everyone knows, for example, that weapons have been getting more expensive per unit, but few realize that it now also takes much longer to get a weapon into the hands of the warfighter. In the early 1940s, it took 25 months to get a new fighter like the P-47 Thunderbolt into action from the time the government signed a contract for a prototype. In the late 1940s, this delay had grown to about 43 months for an early jet fighter like the F-86 Sabre. By the 1960s, the F-4 Phantom required 66 months, and its 1970s replacement, the F-15 Eagle, 82 months. The latest fighter to enter service, the F-22 Raptor, traces its development to a prototype built under a contract signed in October 1986. The prototype first flew in September 1990, and the production model entered service in December 2005—a total of 230 months, or about 19 years. Put another way, that comes to slightly longer than the typical career of an officer in the U.S. Air Force. (The new F-35 Lighting II, which will replace the F-16, is slated to require "just" 15 years from signing the contract for the prototype to when it enters service. We'll see.)

One might think the problem with jet aircraft is a result of the growing technical complexity of modern fighter aircraft, but that argument does not hold up. No rule says that the more complex a technology is, the longer it takes to deliver. Government aircraft of *all* kinds take longer to develop, and longer than their commercial counterparts. Compare a military transport, like the C-17 Globemaster III with the new Boeing 787 Dreamliner. The C-17 required 12 years to enter service, while the 787—more complex than the C-17 in many respects—will take just four. And the 787, for example, will require a little *less* time to develop than its predecessor from the early 1990s, the 777.[1]

The problem holds for most weapons other than airplanes, too—ships, tanks, electronic systems and so on. Threats are changing much faster than we can develop the means to counter them. This is why some officials occasionally say we have to anticipate requirements further into the future. But that's simply unrealistic. When you try to forecast two decades ahead because your weapon takes twenty years to develop, it isn't analysis: it's fortune telling.

The ever-slowing pace of government appears in other ways, as well. Simply getting a presidential administration into place is a stellar example. According a 2005 National Academy of Sciences study, every Administration since Kennedy's has taken longer than its predecessor to fill the top 500 jobs in government. In the 1960s it took just under three months; today it is three times as long. A new administration isn't up and running until almost a year after the election that put it in office. How can a team possibly win the Big Game if half the players don't show up until the end of the first quarter?

That is more or less what happened in 2001 as al-Qaeda was preparing 9/11. The Bush Administration's Cabinet Secretaries were confirmed and ready to go when the new President was sworn in on January 20, 2001, but that was about it. The Administration didn't nominate Paul Wolfowitz to be Deputy Secretary of Defense until February 5, and he had to wait until March 2 to be confirmed and sworn in. Wolfowitz's wait was comparatively short; most positions took longer to fill. Richard Armitage, nominated for Deputy Secretary of State, waited until March 23, 2001. Six months passed before the top Defense Department leadership was in place. Douglas Feith, the Under Secretary of Defense for Policy—as in "policy for combating terrorists"—was *last* to be sworn in, in July 2001.

What is so depressing about the National Academy of Science study is that the problem just keeps getting worse. If top officials have to wait two or three months at the beginning of an administration, candidates for positions at the assistant secretary level in the middle of a term can often wait six months or more. Further down the food chain, bringing on new staff is paced largely by how long it takes to obtain a security clearance. For civil servants, this can take almost a year, for government contractors, the average is about 450 days.

Why?

What explains this bureaucratic torpor? In part, government is slowing down because more people insist on getting involved. Ever more congressional committees, lobbyists and oversight organizations vie to get their prerogatives enacted in a law, regulation or procedure. As the participants multiply, workloads expand and everything slows down.

At another level, it's because there is more obligatory paperwork to handle—financial disclosure in the case of officials, cost justification in the case of contracts, quality assurance documentation in the case of hardware. At yet another level, it's because all organizations have standard procedures that never seem to get shorter or more flexible; quite the reverse. New procedures are almost always cumulative, accreting in ever thicker layers of bureaucratic hoariness. Indeed, we may be seeing a classic case of "organizational aging," a phenomenon perhaps first defined by economist Anthony Downs back in 1967.

In his classic book, *Inside Bureaucracy,* Downs observed that when organizations are first established, they have few rules, written or unwritten, and because new organizations tend to be small, they have a flat, short chain of command with little hierarchy. As time goes by, alas, organizations add personnel. Since managers can oversee only a limited number of people, they develop a reporting hierarchy, which adds to the time and difficulty of making a decision. More members are in a position to say "no," and the joint probability of "yes" diminishes. This translates into the well-known bureaucratic adage, "Where there's a will, there's a won't." The fact that people expect promotion to positions with greater responsibility (and pay) also encourages the establishment of more management slots with the selective power to say "no," or just to kibbitz. Either way, the process takes more time.

Also, as organizations mature, they develop dogma—sometimes written, sometimes simply part of the organization's culture. This, of course, is exactly what bureaucracies are supposed to do: simplify decisions and improve efficiency by adopting rules. This is fine, until the rules become cumbersome or no longer appropriate to the situation—which is exactly what is happening today.

But the most insidious problem of all is that as organizations mature their character changes. New organizations with few rules offer lots of challenge and risk, so they tend to attract risk-takers who want to make their own rules. Mature organizations with well-defined rules and missions, on the other hand, attract the "Organization Man"—the sort who wants to plug himself in and carry out tasks as set forth in an official, approved job description.

This is why it is somewhere between ironic and pointless to hear critics complain that this or that long-established government organization needs to become less risk-averse and more innovative. Inevitably, they are speaking to people who, by self-selection, are where they are *precisely because they are risk-averse.* They *like* the way things are; they would not otherwise have joined the organization and stayed with it. Organization Men are no less patriotic, dedicated or capable than risk-takers; they're just temperamentally opposite.

If we are serious about gaining agility, we will clearly have to break some china. Improving agility means more than just rearranging boxes on an organization chart, though that is mostly what we have tried to do. There have been countless studies on how to streamline contracting, speed up background investigations, shorten the process of nominating and confirming appointees, and so on. None of these recommendations will ever amount to anything unless we find a way to produce a new mix of people who can develop new ways of doing things, and attract the kinds of recruits who thrive on doing just that.

It's easy to get lost in the day-to-day specifics of why it takes so long to get anything done in the American national security community today. It is far more important to recognize that the underlying theme connecting all the sources of our sloth is that we are trying to balance risk with speed, and there is rarely a champion for speed. The risks that concern people take many forms—that some group will be underrepresented in a decision, that a design or work task will be flawed, that a secret will be compromised, that someone will cheat the government, that an official will have a conflict of interest. Whatever the specifics, we lose agility every time we manage risk by adding a step to reduce the probability of something bad happening. Rarely does anyone with responsibility, opportunity or power say that we should accept more risks so that we can act faster.

It is easy to argue for doing something to avoid some hypothetical bad thing happening. It is much harder to argue that one can take so many precautions against some kinds of risk that other kinds of risk actually increase due to an organization's diminished capacity to act in a timely fashion. The real question is, or ought to be, how much speed do we want to sacrifice in order to reduce certain kinds of risk? There is no single, objective answer to such a question, but without advocates and mechanisms for greater speed, we will be protected against risk so well that arguably our most dangerous adversaries will beat us every time.

Examples of Speed and Success

Lest we be *too* pessimistic, there are cases—including a few fairly recent ones—in which government organizations moved out smartly on national security missions. These cases show us what we need to do if we want organizations to move fast. Consider, for example:

- *The U-2 aircraft:* In the 1950s, the United States needed a higher-flying airplane to take pictures of Soviet military facilities. The CIA gave Lockheed authority to proceed in December 1954; the aircraft flew its first reconnaissance mission over the Soviet Union in July 1956. Total time required: 18 months.
- *The Explorer 1 satellite:* Desperate to match the Soviet Sputnik I launched in October 1957, the Defense Department authorized the Army Ballistic Missile Agency to prepare a satellite for launch on November 8, 1957. Werner von Braun's team launched it three months later, on January 31, 1958.
- *The GBU-28:* At the start of Operation Desert Storm in 1991, the Air Force discovered it did not have a bomb that could penetrate Iraq's deepest underground shelters. To pack enough kinetic energy, the bomb had to be long, streamlined and heavy. The Air Force Research Laboratory took surplus gun barrels from eight-inch howitzers as a casing, filled them with explosive, bolted an existing laser guidance system to the front end, and—after assigning it an official Air Force designation—delivered a bomb in 27 days.
- *JAWBREAKER:* President Bush asked for options to respond to the September 11 attacks. The CIA presented its plan two days later to use Northern Alliance forces as a surrogate army. CIA units, called "JAWBREAKER," arrived in weeks, and Kabul was taken on November 14, 2001.

These programs are all related to national security, but they are as different from one another as one can imagine. One is an aircraft development program, one a space research mission, one a weapon system and one a covert paramilitary operation. The Army, Air Force and CIA are all represented. Two were in wartime, two in peacetime. Yet they share some common features, the most important of which seems to be that someone was willing to bend rules and take responsibility for getting things done. This is a logical—even a *necessary*—condition for speed.

Every organization has a "natural" maximum speed defined by its standard procedures, which are designed to reduce risk. Some are formal, others implicit. Together they establish the organization's operations—who has to confer with whom, who can approve, what materials have to be prepared and so on. Organizations usually operate well below this optimum speed, but in principle one could analyze any organization and then assess whether it can act faster than its competitors. It is hard to measure maximum speed precisely, but it is easy to identify most of the "hard points" that constitute it, like the one official or office lying in the critical path of workflow. Conversely, when government organizations have moved faster than their normal maximum speeds, it's almost always because someone either bent the rules or managed to evade them. Consider the cases cited above.

In developing the U-2, the CIA avoided the constraining pace of the annual Federal budget cycle by using its special authority to spend money without a specific appropriation—the first time the CIA had used that authority to develop a major system like an aircraft. The CIA also wasn't bound to Defense Department regulations, so rather than use the arduous military acquisition and contractor selection process, the CIA simply chose Lockheed.

Lockheed's famous "Skunk Works," in turn, shortened or eliminated many steps a military contractor would usually take. For example, by having all its people working in one location, an engineer could ask metal workers to adjust the design on the spot with a conversation rather than a meeting, and follow up with documentation later. This would violate normal Defense Department acquisition regulations.

The Army also broke rules in building the Explorer 1 satellite—specifically, the rule saying that the Army wasn't supposed to build satellites. The Defense Department and White House had given the Navy that mission. Major General John Medaris, the Army Ballistic Missile Agency director, "went out on a limb," as he put it, and set aside hardware that later gave the Army the ability to get off a quick shot after the Soviets launched Sputnik.

The U-2 and Explorer 1 also had something in common: They "stole" a lot of technology from other programs, using them in ways that no one had originally intended but that sped up the process. The U-2's design was in many ways just like that of the F-104 Starfighter that Lockheed had designed earlier for the Air Force, but with longer wings and a lot of weight cut out. The rocket that launched Explorer 1 was based on an Army Redstone ballistic missile, which, in turn, was an updated V-2 that the Army's German engineers had developed during World War II.

In the case of the GBU-28, the Air Force Development Test Center team compressed a development program that would ordinarily have taken two years into less than two weeks by taking engineering shortcuts and a more liberal approach to safety. For example, it tested the aerodynamics and ballistics of the weapon with a single drop, rather than the usual thirty.

Note that it required an individual with the *authority* and *inclination* to make the decision on how to interpret a contract or a standard. If a person could not legally give approval, the organization would not have followed his direction. If a person had not been willing to use his authority (and, in the process, accept responsibility), nothing would have happened, either—which brings us to JAWBREAKER.

CIA officers like Gary Schroen, who first went into Afghanistan to prepare the operation immediately after 9/11, had largely acted on their own initiative in the 1990s when they kept up personal contacts with Northern Alliance figures like Ahmed Shah Masoud. After the Soviets were defeated in the U.S. supported guerrilla war from 1980 to 1989, the CIA had turned its interest elsewhere. Schroen's contacts and experience in the region greased the re-establishment of the relationship when the United States decided to retaliate against al-Qaeda and the Taliban.

After the fighting started, the CIA was fortunate to have officers on hand with admitted inclinations for focusing more on results than procedures. Gary Berntsen, who took command of JAWBREAKER as the fighting began, once described himself as a "bad kid" from Long Island who graduated second from the bottom in his high school. Once in the CIA, he bragged about his "grab-'em-by-the-collar" approach.

As Admiral Ernest King supposedly said about wartime, "When they get in trouble, they send for the sons of bitches." If you don't have SOBs on staff and a way to get them to the front line, organizations will plod along at their routine pace. True, if everyone broke the rules all the time, there would be no rules. But one of the keys to a fast organization that can beat its opponent to the punch is almost always a willingness to break the rules. This is nothing new. It was said often in the 19th century that Paris sent officials into the French countryside not to enforce rules, but to decide judiciously when and how to ignore them.

How to Get Faster

If we want more speed and agility, some lessons are clear. We must: Make sure U.S. national security organizations have a legal mechanism for bending or breaking existing rules; make sure they have the means for having such rule-benders at hand; make sure these rule-benders exercise influence; and make sure they don't get out of control. (Even unofficially designated rule-benders need *some* clear lines of accountability.)

We need to allow responsible senior officials to put the government in overdrive when it's really important.

Basically, we need to allow responsible senior officials to put the government into overdrive when it's really important. With the possible exception of the operating forces of the military and their counterparts in the intelligence community, even top officials lack this ability today. This encourages other kinds of risks: workarounds. Cabinet secretaries who need to get decisions fast and begin operations expeditiously know that they cannot entrust such matters to the standing bureaucracy. But workarounds and shortcuts spite the institutional memory of an organization and court disaster from ignorance. Iran-Contra is a good example of a workaround gone wrong. The only way to avoid such dangers is to make the responsible bureaucracies faster only when they really need to be fast.

There is always a tension between orthodoxy and innovation, and between direct command and checks and balances. There is no sure-fire way to ensure the best mix. But we don't seem to be close now, or even trying to get closer. Ultimately, our willingness to balance different sorts of risk must be a political decision, in which voters can turn incumbents out and try something else if they are dissatisfied. But if we don't at least have the foundation for rule-bending, they will never get that choice.

What then, should we do? First, to build agility into the key parts of the U.S. government, Congress will clearly have to cooperate. That's the system; that's the Constitution. It is therefore folly for any administration to try to steamroll the legislators—as the then-popular Bush Administration did from about 2002 to 2004, such as when it shunted aside congressional concerns that the Iraq insurgency was gaining steam rather than entering its "last throes," or that U.S. forces did not have the resources to deal with the worsening situation. Accepting these concerns and criticisms quickly would have both improved the situation and solidified support for the effort by getting Congress' "buy in" on the record.

Second, we should consider establishing a small number of powerful "bottleneck breakers" in the Executive Office of the President. Senior experienced officials could be designated by the White House, formally or informally. The important thing is that officials down the line know that these bottleneck breakers are acting at the behest of the president to make sure his policies are carried out. Unlike the too-familiar "czars" that have been given responsibility for drug enforcement, energy conservation and, most recently, the war in Iraq, these officials would know how, and be given the authority, to work quickly and quietly with the Office of Management and Budget. It would take only a few examples of a sequestered budget line, a dismissed appointee or a transferred senior executive to give these bottleneck-breaker envoys the implicit power they require. The very existence of such EOP envoys, and the only occasional demonstration of their authority, would work wonders with hidebound, risk-averse bureaucrats.

Other measures that would counter the natural tendency of bureaucracies to slow down come readily to mind:

- Requiring senior civil service executives to periodically do a tour in a different Executive Branch department. This would make them more familiar with conditions in other departments, so they could anticipate what might slow down an action. It would also build social networks that could help clear these impediments.
- Create an "up or out" system of promotion for senior executives resembling the approach used in the military to create a dynamic that keeps the bureaucracy from getting too settled.

- Adopt a mandatory, congressionally approved, periodic de-layering of bureaucracies.
- Increase the number of Schedule C appointments to give new administrations a better ability to rattle cages. We need not repeal the Pendleton Act completely, but the trend in most sectors of the economy is toward "at will" employment. As an employee rises higher in the organization, it should be easier to move or remove him or her.

One could think of other measures in the same vein, and some have. The point, however, is that if we do not do *something* to increase the speed of government, we will be sure to fall behind future events, get beaten to the punch, and lose ground to our most ruthless competitors. Given the stakes in today's world, that is a loss we cannot afford.

Note

1. Also consider today's automobiles, which are much more complex than earlier models. Like jet fighters, cars today go faster and handle better. They can also locate their current position and tell you how to reach your destination—all while meeting ever-tougher safety and emissions standards. Yet the time required to develop a car and get it into the showroom *is getting shorter all the time*. Toyota is best at about two years, and it is trying to cut this time to 12 months. Ford and GM are trying to keep up, but still take one to two years longer than Toyota—one reason they have been taking a beating in the market.

BRUCE BERKOWITZ is a research fellow at the Heaver Institution at Stanford University. He was Director of Forecasting and Evaluation at the Department of Defense from 2004–05.

Worse than You Think

What went wrong at Fannie and Freddie—and what still might.

PETER J. WALLISON AND EDWARD PINTO

The government's takeover of Fannie Mae and Freddie Mac in the middle of a presidential race—coupled with the fact that their activities contributed significantly to the current financial crisis—has brought these "government-sponsored enterprises" (GSEs) into unusual prominence. One of the principal elements of the story is its similarity to the savings-and-loan (S&L) collapse of only 20 years ago, and the failure of Congress to understand and apply the lessons of that debacle.

Fannie began life as a government agency, commissioned to add liquidity to the housing-finance system. To perform this function, it borrowed funds in the capital markets and used them to buy mortgages from lenders. For many years it toiled quietly in this routine business.

In 1968, as a budgetary measure, the Johnson administration privatized Fannie by allowing it to sell shares to the public. But the shareholder-owned company retained many of its ties to government, and was given a congressional charter. So despite its private ownership, investors and other creditors continued to believe the government backed it—that taxpayers would come to the rescue if things went wrong.

By the late 1980s, the U.S. financial world was in turmoil. Fed chairman Paul Volcker's effort to curb inflation had resulted in high market interest rates, which in turn had devastated the S&L industry. Unlike commercial banks, S&Ls had a narrow range of permissible activities, focused primarily on housing. Their assets—principally home mortgages—were not diverse enough to keep them alive when the housing market went into one of its frequent tailspins. In a high-interest-rate environment, S&Ls had to pay more to attract and hold deposits than they were receiving in revenue from mortgages. The mismatch—high short-term liabilities, low-yielding long-term assets—was driving the industry toward insolvency.

Deposits in S&Ls, like those in commercial banks, were federally insured, and this enabled them to raise funds despite their weak financial condition. Congress broadened their investment powers, allowing the industry to invest in new and risky ventures as it "gambled for resurrection." This gamble did not pay off, and the losses continued to mount.

In 1989, the first Bush administration recognized that it had to intervene. New legislation established the Resolution Trust Corporation to acquire and sell the assets of failed S&Ls, a process that eventually cost the taxpayers $150 billion. The same legislation also "privatized" Freddie Mac—then a subsidiary agency of the Federal Home Loan Bank Board—under a charter virtually identical to Fannie's.

The prospect of huge losses for taxpayers engendered a bitter debate about causes and blame. On one side were those who argued that greed, fraud, and incompetence among S&L owners and managers were responsible. On the other were those who blamed the government for allowing an industry that was inherently vulnerable to take enormous risks with insured deposits. Both sides were partially right, but only the former explanation seemed to sink in with a Congress eager to deny its culpability.

The Super-S&L

By 1991, James A. Johnson, a politically connected former top aide to Walter Mondale, had become Fannie's chairman and CEO. He stepped into this barren landscape with an idea that would have been rejected out of hand if Congress had correctly diagnosed the S&L problem. Johnson's view was that Fannie could prosper as a super-S&L by using its low-cost, government-backed funds to buy and hold a portfolio of high-yielding mortgages. Fannie and Freddie's activities, as in the case of the S&Ls, were restricted to housing. This business model was different from the S&Ls' in but one important way: This new S&L wouldn't have to limit itself to $100,000 deposits to get government insurance; *all* of Fannie's debt had the implicit backing of the taxpayers.

Fortunately, some in Congress saw that allowing a privately owned company to borrow money with government backing required at least some form of regulation, and in 1991 Congress finally got around to considering revisions to the GSEs' charters and the creation of a regulatory agency to oversee their activities.

At about this time, Fannie, under Johnson's control, committed to loan $10 billion over two years to promote affordable housing. This initiative helped Fannie resist effective regulation in several ways. First, it showed that Fannie would share some of its gains with taxpayers—and thereby created goodwill with lawmakers. Second, members of Congress saw that they could use affordable-housing lending much the way they use earmarks: They could select projects in their states and districts, and politely request that Fannie loan money to them. Unlike the countless banks scattered across the country, Fannie was conveniently centralized in D.C., and talks with it did not require (or receive) much public scrutiny.

In the end, Johnson got a good deal: The regulatory structure that Congress adopted—which, in passing, added an affordable-housing "mission" to Fannie's charter—was seriously deficient. Not two years after the demise of the S&Ls had shown beyond question that government backing (in the form of FDIC insurance) without adequate risk controls was a prescription for disaster and taxpayer loss, Congress repeated its mistake.

The new regulator—the Office of Federal Housing Enterprise Oversight (OFHEO)—had none of the strong authorities routinely given to bank regulators; it was also subject to congressional appropriations, which made it possible for the GSEs to control their own regulator through their congressional supporters. This was an aberration from other congressional activity: The year before, the same Congress had adopted the Federal Deposit Insurance Corporation Improvement Act, which significantly toughened the regulation of banks and gave their regulators more independence.

Jim Johnson lost no time in using the affordable-housing initiatives to cement congressional support into place. The principal element of this bargain was that Congress would allow the GSEs to retain federal backing, and the absence of a strong regulator would permit Fannie and Freddie to grow without serious restriction. The lack of regulation would also make it possible for the GSEs to meet the demands of Congress on the allocation of affordable-housing funds.

In 1994, Johnson announced another affordable-housing initiative, this time with a goal of $1 trillion in loans—intended to enable 10 million families to buy homes by the end of 2000. At the same time, he created local partnership offices (eventually totaling 51) in urban areas across the country. These offices were overtly political, and performed a grassroots lobbying function, assuring congressional backers of Fannie and Freddie that they could tap into supportive local groups when it came time for reelection—or to beat back initiatives that might clip the GSEs' wings.

In 2000, after succeeding Jim Johnson as chairman and CEO of Fannie Mae, Franklin Raines, head of the Office of Management and Budget in the Clinton administration, announced Fannie's "American Dream Commitment," a ten-year, $2 trillion pledge to support affordable housing. It made another huge, taxpayer-backed program available for manipulation and political patronage.

In 2003 and 2004, when Fannie and Freddie were found to have been practicing Enron-style accounting, their friends in Congress rushed to their defense, citing affordable housing. At a House Financial Services Committee meeting in September 2003, Massachusetts Democrat Barney Frank—then ranking minority member and now chairman—observed: "I do think I do not want the same kind of focus on safety and soundness. . . . I want to roll the dice a little bit more in this situation towards subsidized housing." Charles Schumer of New York, then a powerful member of the Senate Banking Committee, stated the next month: "My worry is that we're using the recent safety and soundness concerns, particularly with Freddie, and with a poor regulator, as a straw man to curtail Fannie and Freddie's [affordable-housing] mission."

An Attempt to Regulate

By the end of 2004, things had gotten a great deal bleaker for the GSEs. Their accounting frauds had prompted bad publicity and some serious challenges from within the government. The Bush administration sought the stronger, bank-like regulatory regime that Congress had failed to adopt in the early '90s. Alan Greenspan—then at the height of his authority as Federal Reserve chairman—called for controls on the growth of the GSEs' hugely profitable mortgage portfolios. Fed economists had determined that the GSEs did not, as they'd claimed for years, reduce interest rates for middle-class homebuyers. Franklin Raines had resigned under fire for his participation in Fannie's false accounting. Republicans had introduced stronger regulatory legislation in both the House and the Senate. Drastic steps were needed to rebuild the bond with Congress and prevent the adoption of tough new regulations.

The GSEs made it clear that such regulations would make it harder to get affordable-housing pork to Congress's constituents. A strong regulator could make the GSEs' portfolios less profitable—and without these profits, it would not be possible for Fannie and Freddie to continue to subsidize affordable housing. Worse, a strong regulator might scrutinize their affordable-housing investments, including ones members of Congress had requested.

Beginning in 2005, Fannie and Freddie put more than $1 trillion in junk loans on their books. The unprecedented rate of defaults on this $1 trillion is what precipitated the takeover of Fannie and Freddie by the federal government in September, and will burden taxpayers with tremendous costs. But it worked politically. The GSEs' supporters (and beneficiaries) in Congress held off on any new regulation. The Senate Banking Committee adopted a strong regulatory bill in 2005—with the unanimous support of committee Republicans and over the unanimous opposition of committee Democrats—but it could not be brought to a vote on the Senate floor. Not a single Democrat, including Barack Obama, supported it. The benefits that Fannie and Freddie offered to Congress continued to flow. In 2006, Chuck Schumer's office issued a press release headlined "Schumer Announces up to $100 Million Freddie Mac Commitment to Address Fort Drum and Watertown Housing Crunch." The release boasted that the senator had "urged" the company to "step up" and make this commitment.

Congress thus repeated with Fannie and Freddie the error that had produced the collapse of the S&L industry in the late 1980s. It gave government backing to inadequately supervised private companies. But the case of Fannie Mae and Freddie Mac is far worse than the S&L debacle. First, taxpayers' losses this time will be enormously larger. Second, in the case of the S&Ls, the missteps of Congress can be understood and to some extent excused: It had never encountered anything quite like the S&L collapse, and the banking failures of the Depression were 50 years in the past. Third, while individual lawmakers received favors from the S&L industry, these were the petty graft that tends to go along with political power—not to be condoned, of course, but nothing new. But Congress's failure to create a strong regulatory regime for Fannie Mae and Freddie Mac *was* something new. Coming as it did on the heels of the passage of tough new banking regulation, it had to be a conscious choice by the GSEs' supporters in Congress—most of them liberal Democrats—to continue using the GSEs' financial resources for political purposes.

Perhaps worst of all, the takeover of Fannie and Freddie by a government conservator does not end the problem. In fact, it might open a new and more costly era. In a statement to the House Financial Services Committee on September 25, James B. Lockhart III, director of the agency that serves as both regulator and conservator of Fannie and Freddie, insisted on meeting the affordable-housing goals required by HUD regulations: "The market turmoil of this year resulted in a tightening of underwriting criteria . . . thereby reducing the availability of traditionally goal-rich, high loan-to-value home-purchase loans. . . . I will expect each enterprise to develop and implement ambitious plans to support the borrowers and markets targeted by the goals."

If this is what a Republican administration says about the use to which Fannie and Freddie will be put in conservatorship, one can only imagine what a Democratic administration might do.

MR. PETER J. WALLISON holds the Arthur F. Burns chair at the American Enterprise Institute. **MR. EDWARD PINTO** held various positions at Fannie Mae from 1984 to 1989, and now provides consulting services to the mortgage-finance industry.

From *The National Review*, November 3, 2008, pp. 36–38. Copyright © 2008 by National Review, Inc, 215 Lexington Avenue, New York, NY 10016. Reprinted by permission.

Article 29

Teaching a Hippo to Dance

The most brilliant policies will fail if government does not attract talented people and free them to do their best work.

AMY WILKINSON

Four years ago, I left Silicon Valley to accept a presidential appointment as a White House fellow. After undergoing months of interviews and obtaining a top-secret security clearance, I moved to Washington, D.C., to join a class of 12 nonpartisan White House fellows and to work in the Office of the U.S. Trade Representative. After my fellowship ended I stayed on, caught up in the challenging work of improving the nation's trade policies. My old business-school friends and my colleagues at the consulting firm McKinsey & Company were perplexed. Why would anyone want to serve in the federal government, the epitome of everything that is slow, bureaucratic, and opaque?

There, in a nutshell, is a major problem confronting American government in the 21st century: how to attract talented young people—not just to the prestigious jobs that bring you face to face with a cabinet secretary or the president but to the line jobs that exist across the civil service. It is not just a recruiting challenge. Government will only attract the people it needs when it refashions itself so that public servants can serve the public effectively.

The federal government deserves more credit than it gets, but it is still a slow-moving behemoth. To reinvigorate our federal system and attract fresh talent, we must transform our aged, hierarchical institutions into modern networks of scale and impact. In effect, we must teach a hippopotamus to dance.

Like government, hippos are enormous, weighed down by a heavy mid section and designed with disproportionately big mouth and teeth. Stubby legs, a natural system of checks and balances, support their tremendous bulk. They are powerful, yet slow to change. When perturbed, hippos can move quickly—as the federal government did in passing the $700 billion bailout in just two weeks. Yet usually they plod along, preferring to slumber in murky waters.

In today's networked world, our hippo must dance in sync with private-sector and nonprofit partners. Keeping pace will require a more engaged federal workforce, realignment of out-of-date incentives, and an ability to meet the expectations of modern workers. To succeed, government must get the people piece right.

There are some bright lights in government leadership, and some of the brightest are at the local level. In San Francisco, Mayor Gavin Newsom, a former wine and restaurant entrepreneur, has forged alliances with businesses in housing and other fields, established a 24-hour hotline to promote accountability in city services, and pushed forward on such controversial initiatives as universal health care. In Newark, New Jersey, Mayor Cory Booker has partnered with the Bill & Melinda Gates Foundation and other foundations to jump-start the city's dysfunctional public school system with a $19 million charter school initiative. He has embraced new technologies such as ShotSpotter, an acoustic surveillance system that detects gunshots in seconds, to control crime. "I always say that the biggest problem in America is not a problem of material poverty," Booker said in an interview. "It's a poverty of imagination. It's a poverty of innovation. It's a poverty of action."

Often, what many regard as the very nature of government—its notoriously multilayered bureaucracy—stifles needed innovation and initiative. The average memo originating in a State Department bureau requires between two and 10 sign-offs and five to eight approvals through the chain of command before it reaches the secretary. Beyond whatever sense of public mission individuals bring to their work, there is often little incentive to excel. As one Foreign Service officer I spoke to joked, "At the end of the year I go to the GS schedule, reference my rank and years of service, and poof, there's my promotion cycle and salary."

The high-caliber employees that government does manage to attract are often driven out of public service. Many of the strongest junior people leave government frustrated by mid-level management that is ineffective but will never be fired. Retaining star talent requires replacing our current seniority-based system with merit-based promotions. A close colleague, who distinguished himself while working with Colin Powell, recently left the Foreign Service, discouraged by the bureaucratic mindset. When he was nominated for a fast-track promotion, human resources denied the advancement, stating that there were "already qualified people at that grade level." He is now a partner in an advisory firm.

Today's young professionals expect adaptable work schedules, state-of-the-art technology, and a measure of autonomy. Most of all, we are looking for work that allows us to have an impact. Speed and flexibility define our lives. If we have a question, we Google it. We Skype friends in Poland and instant-message colleagues in Shanghai. These changes have their parallels in organizational life. In the private sector, "flash teams" assemble to tackle specific challenges, disband, and reconfigure as situations evolve. Large companies such as Best Buy allow people at all levels throughout the company to participate electronically and in person in efforts to solve problems. The symbolic apex of this new world may be the professional temp agencies that attract large numbers of workers in high-skills fields, from accounting to graphic design, because these people prefer short assignments and constant change.

In the search for people with talent and ideas, the new field of social entrepreneurship provides stiff competition for government. Rather than work their way up in government or large corporations, many civic-minded leaders in their twenties and thirties now launch nonprofit or business ventures to address social injustices, using business partnerships, grants, and donations.

"Our generation is saying we need private innovation and private initiative to solve big, public problems," Jacqueline Novogratz explained when we met in her New York office. She is the founder and CEO of Acumen Fund, a nonprofit equivalent of a venture capital firm that backs private-sector and nonprofit enterprises that help the poor. "I think that it's a parallel with when John F. Kennedy said we want the best and brightest in government. Today, we want the best and brightest in this field of social enterprise." Bill Drayton, father of the social entrepreneurship movement and founder of a similar organization called Ashoka, told me, "We're in the business of 'everyone a change maker.'" Ashoka has supported some 2,000 social entrepreneurs around the world in launching social start-ups to address ills ranging from domestic violence to water pollution. Half of them, Drayton says, are able to bring about changes in national policy within five years.

The United States is the world's most innovative nation, yet our government is out of sync with today's realities. With more than 2.6 million employees, the federal government is the nation's largest employer. As I can attest after seven years in the corporate world, business does not always escape the problems of bureaucracy. Just ask General Motors, Ford, and Chrysler. But big corporations learn to be nimble in order to compete against agile, new entrants. Government is what is called, in the business world, an incumbent player; it is blind to competition. Change must come from within, beginning at the top. As New York mayor Michael Bloomberg explained, "Part of the government's problem is that it never delegates. In the White House, for example, they control everything."

The antiquated condition of our national government today would have troubled the Founding Fathers.

The antiquated condition of our national government would have troubled the Founding Fathers, who were political entrepreneurs and the creators of revolutionary new public institutions. It is true that they did not design American government to be fast. Our system of checks and balances, along with the diffusion of power among local, state, and federal authorities, is designed to inhibit rapid change. Yet if the Founders were wary of overweening government, they hardly favored *ineffective* government.

Technology offers one route to breaking down barriers and improving productivity. Before the development of Web 2.0 technologies, for example, it would have taken many months to gather information across stovepiped government agencies. Last year, when the Office of Management and Budget needed to compile a database of congressional budgetary earmarks, government personnel were able to bypass normal bureaucratic channels by using a wiki that allowed people from all over the government to report directly on a shared website. They did the job in just 10 weeks, turning up 13,496 earmarks.

Government is clearly in need of such new ideas, but the culture of public institutions is risk averse. Gilman Louie, former CEO of In-Q-Tel, a nonprofit corporation created by the Central Intelligence Agency to promote defense technologies, put the problem in graphic terms when I interviewed him: "The most surprising thing was that if terrorists rolled a hand grenade down the middle of a room, all our CIA employees would jump out of their seats and throw their bodies on it to protect everyone else. They would all give up their lives for one another and their country. However, if someone ran into the room and said, 'I need someone to make a decision, but if it's the wrong one it will be the end of your career, but I need an answer now,' all of them would run toward the door." The problem with public institutions is that the consequence of failure means that there is no reward for risk taking and thus no innovation. Government agencies must change to say that it is all right to fail, just not catastrophically. To do this, they need to evaluate employees not on the success or failure of any particular decision, but on the overall outcome of their performance.

United States Government Policy and Supporting Positions, commonly known as the "Plum Book," lists more than 7,000 available jobs in the new administration. Many of these positions are reserved for cabinet secretaries and other officials to hire their own personal staffs. Barack Obama will award about 3,000 positions, from White House chief of staff to principal deputy under secretary of defense for policy.

There is no shortage of job seekers, but the cumbersome appointment process deters many talented people, and the incoming administration has set up even more hurdles. Prospective Obama appointees are presented with a seven-page questionnaire about their personal and professional lives. They must append copies of all resumés and biographical statements from the past 10 years, list gifts worth more than $50 that they and their spouse have received from anyone other than close friends or relatives, and divulge their and immediate family members' affiliations with Fannie Mae, Freddie Mac, or any other institution receiving government bailout funds. Applicants are also expected to disclose their "Internet presence," including e-mails, Facebook pages, blog posts, and aliases used to communicate online.

Once past the screening, these prospective federal appointees enter a labyrinth of forms, investigations, and intrusive personal and financial disclosures. The process is embarrassing and confusing, and often requires that they seek outside expert advice to process forms and financial information—which applicants pay for out of their own pockets. Senate confirmation proceedings for cabinet secretaries start in January, but subcabinet and Schedule C appointees, the folks who do the nuts-and-bolts work, can wait many months. Only 30 percent of George W. Bush's national security appointees were in place on 9/11, eight months after he took office.

The career civil service faces an even greater challenge. Last year, the Partnership for Public Service estimated that nearly 530,000 personnel—a third of the federal government's workforce—will retire by 2012. "Help wanted" should become Washington's byword if these jobs—many of them critical senior positions—are to be filled by first-rate people. Yet Donna Shalala, the former secretary of health and human services and current president of the University of Miami, said recently at the Woodrow Wilson Center that government recruiters don't even come to her campus: "Kids in Miami are interested in government but have no information about how to apply."

Indeed, a recent Gallup poll found that 60 percent of those under age 30 have never been asked to consider a job in government. Thirty-three percent would give such a request a great deal of consideration if asked by their parents, and 29 percent if asked by the newly elected president. The first challenge government must overcome is ignorance about government opportunities. The nonprofit Teach for America, by contrast, is beating out consulting firms and banks to recruit college graduates. Last year, 25,000 individuals applied to Teach for America and more than 3,700 started teaching in the nation's toughest inner-city schools.

Government must get into the headhunting business. At business schools the pitch could be, *You want to manage complexity and lead a team? Great. We've got big budgets and complex problems. Which would you like to tackle first, health care or Social Security reform?* At law schools, recruiters could ask, *Are you good at negotiating contentious issues and analyzing contradictory information? Perfect. When can you start?* Let's offer undergraduates career tracks that let them quickly rotate through assignments at State, Energy, Defense, and other agencies.

During the recent election campaign, President Obama vowed to "transform Washington" and "make government cool again." And why not? Why shouldn't public service be highly esteemed? Americans rally to support exceptional athletes who compete in the Olympic Games. We applaud extraordinary scientists who work to cure cancer and superior military forces that defend our homeland. We want the best Hollywood talent to entertain us and super computer geeks to invent the next Google. But when it comes to government service we set our sights low.

Last year's election turned ordinary citizens into activists who not only donated money and canvassed door to door in unprecedented numbers but used new media to blog, organize campaign events, and form networks. The question now is how our 44th president will harness civic engagement to govern more effectively. Millions of Americans are waiting by their BlackBerries, iPhones, and laptops to find out.

AMY WILKINSON, a public-policy scholar at the Woodrow Wilson Center, is writing a book about the next generation of leadership.

From *The Wilson Quarterly*, Winter 2009, pp. 59–62. Copyright © 2009 by Amy Wilkinson. Reprinted by permission of Amy Wilkinson and Woodrow Wilson International Center for Scholars.

UNIT 3
Process of American Politics

Unit Selections

30. **Obama's America,** Michael Barone
31. **The 'Enduring Majority'—Again,** Jay Cost
32. **Dr. Dean Regrets Nothing,** James A. Barnes
33. **Direction, Anyone?,** Ramesh Ponnuru
34. **America Observed,** Robert A. Pastor
35. **Can Money Be a Force for Good?,** Mark Schmitt
36. **Vote or Else,** Allison R. Hayward
37. **The American Presidential Nominating Process: The Beginnings of a New Era,** Bruce Stinebrickner
38. **Still the Chosen One?,** Robert Dreyfuss
39. **Don't Call Them Lobbyists,** Theo Francis and Steve LeVine
40. **Born Fighting,** Ronald Brownstein
41. **Why They Lobby,** Winter Casey
42. **The Revolution Will Not Be Published,** Clay Shirky
43. **Build the Wall,** David Simon
44. **A See-Through Society,** Micah L. Sifry

Key Points to Consider

- In comparison with other political systems, how democratic is the American political system?
- How do the political views and behavior of young Americans compare and contrast with those of their parents?
- Do you think that our current procedures for choosing the president are good ones? In light of the Florida controversy in the 2000 presidential election, do you think that electoral reforms are necessary? What do you think about the big influence that voters in Iowa and New Hampshire have in the presidential nomination process? Explain your answers.
- Do you think that interest groups have too much influence in the American political system? Why or why not?
- What do you think about the way elections are financed in the American political system? Do you think that there ought to be limits on how much a presidential candidate can spend to try to get elected? Do you think that the government should provide money ("public financing") to candidates or that they should have to raise money on their own?
- What do you think about candidate Barack Obama pledging in the summer of 2007 to accept public financing for the general election if he were his party's nominee, and then changing his mind in the summer of 2008 and becoming the first presidential candidate to decline public financing (and the accompanying spending limits) because he realized that he could raise a great deal more money from supporters? (As it turned out, Obama spent more than three times as much in the general election campaign as his opponent, John McCain, who accepted public financing.)

Student Website
www.mhhe.com/cls

Internet References

The Gallup Organization
http://www.gallup.com

The Henry L. Stimson Center
http://www.stimson.org

Influence at Work
http://www.influenceatwork.com

LSU Department of Political Science Resources
http://www.lsu.edu/politicalscience

NationalJournal.com
http://nationaljournal.com

Poynter Online
http://www.poynter.org

RAND
http://www.rand.org

Real Clear Politics
http://www.realclearpolitics.com

According to many political scientists, what distinguishes more democratic political systems from less democratic ones is the degree of control that citizens exercise over government. This unit focuses on the institutions, groups, and processes that are supposed to serve as links between Americans and their government.

The first three sections address parties, elections, voters, interest groups, and the role of money in campaigns and governing. Recent changes in these areas will likely affect American politics for decades to come, and these changes are the focus of many of the readings in these sections.

One noteworthy development in the past few decades has been growing polarization between the two major parties. Republicans and Democrats in Congress have both become more likely to toe their party's line in opposition to the other party, with partisan voting increasingly becoming the norm on Capitol Hill. Some decry this increase in partisanship, while others think that sharper and more consistent policy differences between Democrat and Republican officeholders will make elections more meaningful.

The advantages of incumbents in winning re-election in both the House of Representatives and the Senate have also grown in recent years, so much so that, despite Americans' dissatisfaction with President Bush and his Republican supporters in Congress, most observers emphasized how difficult it would be for Democrats to regain majority control of the House and Senate in the 2006 congressional elections. But Democrats *did* win control of both houses, illustrating what many consider a good example of American democracy at work. In the 2008 elections, of course, Democrats won an even larger majority of seats in each house of Congress. Regardless of these results, incumbency advantages—including the way House districts are drawn, name recognition, and easier access to campaign contributions—are likely to remain a concern for those who would like to reform the democratic process in the United States.

Besides the way House district lines are drawn and incumbents' other built-in advantages, American elections suffer from all sorts of shortcomings. Many of these problems became apparent during the controversy over the outcome of the 2000 presidential election, and reform measures were enacted both in Congress and in many states. Despite some improvements in the way elections are conducted in the American political system, many aspects of U.S. election mechanics still seem inferior to the mechanics of elections in many other western democracies.

Campaign financing became a major concern after the 1972 presidential election. Major campaign finance reform laws passed in 1974 and 2002 (the latter is the so-called McCain-Feingold Act) have been aimed at regulating the influence of campaign contributions in the electoral process, but they have met, at best, with only partial success. As recent bribery and corruption scandals make clear, the fundamental challenge of how to reconcile free speech, the freedom of an individual to spend money as he or she wishes, the costs of campaigns, and the fairness of elections remain. In the summer of 2007, Barack Obama publicly pledged to accept public financing—and the

© Getty Images/Lifesize RF

accompanying condition that a candidate who accepts public financing can spend only the sum provided by the government—if he became his party's nominee. A year later, Obama changed his mind, and became the first and only presidential candidate to decline public financing since it became available beginning with the 1976 election. Obama made this decision because he realized that he could expect to raise more than three times as much money from supporters than the sum provided through public financing. As it turned out, candidate Obama *did* raise and spend more than three times as much money as his general election opponent, John McCain, who accepted public financing and the accompanying spending limit. One irony is that Democrats have traditionally been stronger proponents of campaign finance regulation and public financing than Republicans, notwithstanding John McCain's long-standing and much praised leadership in the area.

This unit also treats the roles of interest groups in the American political process and their impact on what government can and cannot do. While "gridlock" is a term usually applied to a situation that some observers think results from "divided government," in which neither major party controls the presidency and both houses of Congress, it seems that gridlock—and perhaps favoritism in policymaking—also may result from the interaction of interest groups and various government policymakers. The weakness of parties in the United States, compared to parties in other Western democracies, is almost certainly responsible for the unusually strong place of interest groups in the American political system. In turn, one can wonder whether the current era of stronger, more disciplined parties in government will eventually contribute to the weakening of interest groups.

The fourth section in this unit addresses news and other media, which play a more important role in the American political system. Television news broadcasts and newspapers are not merely passive transmitters of information. They inevitably shape—or distort—what they report to their audiences, and greatly affect the behavior of people and organizations in politics. Television talk shows, radio talk-back shows, and thirty-minute "infomercials" have entered the political landscape with considerable effect. In 2004, televised attack ads paid for by so-called 527 committees targeted both presidential candidates and seemed to affect voters' views. In 2008, Barack Obama's campaign perfected and improved some of the Internet fund-raising techniques pioneered by Republican candidate John McCain in 2000 and Democratic candidate Howard Dean in 2004, who unsuccessfully sought the Democratic party's presidential nomination. Obama's remarkable run for the presidency included his vanquishing—and outspending—Democratic rival Hillary Clinton, who herself raised and spent more money on her nomination campaign than any candidate in history, *except* Obama. Then, as mentioned above, Obama outspent John McCain by a more than three-to-one margin in the general election campaign.

As already suggested, one key to Obama's extraordinary fundraising prowess in 2007–2008 was the Internet, the medium that has revolutionized so many aspects of American life. In addition to facilitating fundraising, the Internet played another role in the 2008 campaign by hosting political YouTube segments that played to large segments of the population, including some who tended to avoid traditional news media outlets. Finally, as selections in the fourth section of this unit show, online news reports and commentaries are threatening the very existence of traditional hard-copy newspapers.

Selections in the fourth section cover how media, old and new, shape political communication and political behavior in the American political system.

Obama's America

Has the nation entered a new phase in its politics, one that could benefit Democrats for years to come? An excerpt from *The Almanac of American Politics*.

MICHAEL BARONE

On November 4, 2008, Barack Obama was elected president of the United States by 53 percent to 46 percent, the biggest presidential victory since the election of George H.W. Bush 20 years earlier. The achievement was his but also his political party's. Democrats won the popular vote for the House of Representatives by 53 percent to 44 percent and expanded their majority to 257–178. It was the first time since 1988 that either major party had hit 53 percent. In the Senate, the Democrats initially captured seven seats, which put them within reach of a 60-vote majority impervious to the threat of filibusters.

The results of the 2008 election signaled the end of a long period during which both parties appealed to approximately equal segments of the American electorate. After the cliffhanger 2000 election, *The Almanac of American Politics* described America as a 49 percent nation. After the 2008 election, it appears that this is, at least for the moment and possibly for a long time, Obama's nation.

The 2008 campaign was the first since 1952 in which neither a president nor a vice president was a candidate. It produced a dramatic expansion in the size of the electorate from George W. Bush's first election in 2000. The only comparable eight-year growth spurt occurred between 1944 and 1952, when the GI generation first voted in large numbers. After many years in which political analysts bemoaned low voter turnout, the presidential electorate grew from 105 million in 2000 to 131 million in 2008, a 25 percent increase during a period of 8 percent population growth. About 60 percent of eligible voters participated in the 2008 presidential election, a level exceeded only rarely in modern times: in 1952, 1960, 1964, and 1968. America elected its first black president with about the same high level of involvement that it displayed in choosing its first Catholic president in 1960, Democrat John F. Kennedy.

Turnout did not rise evenly across the country. It went up more in target states, those places that were seriously

Points to Consider

- Barack Obama's big victory was a testimony to the organizational strength of his campaign and the shrewdness of his strategists.
- Against the backdrop of fast-changing economic conditions, public opinion can shift quickly.
- Has America reached an inflection point in the balance of opinion on the relationship between government and markets?

contested by the presidential campaigns, and less elsewhere, although it rose by at least 10 percent in every state and the District of Columbia. In Pennsylvania and Ohio, the increase in turnout from 2000 to 2008 was 22 percent, while population growth was only 1 percent. Uncontested California and Texas experienced surges in political participation of 24 percent and 26 percent, respectively, driven only partly by population increases of 8.5 percent and 17 percent.

Nationally, this rush of political adrenaline was fueled by a combination of interest in the candidates and the organizational heft of the two campaigns. Collective enthusiasm worked to the advantage of Republicans in the 2002 midterms and in the 2004 presidential election, but in 2006 and 2008, it worked to the advantage of Democrats even more. Both parties made a concentrated effort to boost turnout, but the Obama campaign's organizing overshadowed Republican operations. In the 2004 exit poll, 26 percent of people said they were contacted by Democratic nominee John Kerry's campaign and 24 percent heard from Republican Bush's campaign. In the 2008 exit poll, 26 percent reported contacts by the Democrats and only 18 percent by the Republicans.

The fact that Obama won in 2008 with nearly the same 7.7-percentage-point margin that gave George H.W. Bush

Democrats Return

Barack Obama's commanding victory in 2008—the largest since the election of George H.W. Bush 20 years earlier—may signal a new era for the Democrats.

Share of the popular vote

Year	Candidate	%
2008	Obama	52.9%
	McCain	45.6%
2004	G.W. Bush	50.7%
	Kerry	48.3%
2000	G.W. Bush	47.9%
	Gore	48.4%
1996	Clinton	49.2%
	Dole	40.7%
1992	Clinton	43.0%
	G.H.W. Bush	37.5%
1988	G.H.W. Bush	53.4%
	Dukakis	45.7%

Source: David Leip's Atlas of U.S. Presidential Elections.

his victory in 1988 has been cited by some scholars as further evidence that the Republican era that began in the 1980s has been superseded by a Democratic era that solidified some time during George W. Bush's second term. Compelling arguments can be made for this view, and Democrats looking forward from 2008 seem to have more reason than Republicans did in 1988 to believe that their party is on its way to an enduring majority. But the 1988 election and the 2008 election happened in markedly different political periods.

In the last quarter-century, the United States experienced relatively long periods of trench-warfare politics, during which the divisions between the parties were stable and the political battles were fought along familiar lines. There were relatively brief periods of open-field politics, in which highly unstable voting behavior produced unlikely electoral outcomes. The period between 1983 and 1991 was one of trench-warfare politics: Americans voted Republican for president and Democratic for Congress to the point that political scientists said the former had a lock on the presidency and political commentators did not even bother to calculate the odds of a Republican majority in Congress.

Then came a period of highly unstable, open-field politics from 1991 to 1995, in which the unthinkable happened. Third-party candidates led in polls for the presidency—Ross Perot in 1992, Colin Powell in 1995—and a Republican president who presided over a successful war was defeated soundly by a young Democrat with no experience in national office. Then, two years later, voters elected a Republican House and a Republican Senate for the first time in 42 years. The turn of events was so dramatic that the term "Republican revolution" was coined to describe the change in control of Congress.

There followed, from 1995 to 2005, another period of trench-warfare politics. This time, the nation was almost evenly divided between the two parties. Democratic President Clinton was re-elected with 49 percent of the vote in 1996. And in the next two presidential elections, the popular vote was divided 48 percent to 48 percent, and 51 percent to 48 percent. In five successive House elections, from 1996 to 2004, Republicans won between 47 percent and 50 percent of the popular vote while Democrats won between 45 percent and 49 percent. Then, starting in 2005, after the public began to sour on the Iraq war, after Hurricane Katrina presented tests that nearly everyone on the political front lines failed, and after Congress wrapped itself in bribery and corruption scandals, Republican Party identification fell, as often happens to the party in power. Democrats won majorities in both chambers of Congress in 2006. The popular vote in House elections was 53 percent to 45 percent in favor of Democrats, almost a precise reversal of the Republicans' 52 percent to 46 percent in their breakthrough year of 1994. In 2008, Democrats won both the House popular vote and the presidency by almost the same numbers.

But the course of the 2008 campaign suggests that these results were not inevitable. In the first place, the two parties' nominations were not won in the usual way. From 1972, when the parties began selecting most of their delegates in primaries, through 2004, contested nominations were won by the candidate who swept the primaries. This was not so in 2008.

Sen. John McCain of Arizona won the Republican nomination by winning narrow pluralities in early primaries—by 5 percentage points in New Hampshire, 3 percentage points in South Carolina, 5 percentage points in Florida, 1 percentage point in Missouri, and 7 percentage points in California. Thanks to Republican winner-take-all delegate allocation rules, he was able to convert those squeaker victories into an insuperable lead by early February. A shift of just 3 percent of the votes from McCain to former Massachusetts Gov. Mitt Romney in all of the primaries up to that point would have left the two of them virtually tied in delegates, with Romney in better financial shape.

The Republican contests showed a party splintered into various warring groups. Former Arkansas Gov. Mike Huckabee carried evangelical Christians, Romney tended to carry affluent suburbanites, and McCain won those betwixt and between. Up through the same-day contests on Super Tuesday, February 5, McCain won 50 percent of the vote only in New Jersey, New York, and Connecticut—hardly the base of the party these days.

On the Democratic side, Sen. Hillary Rodham Clinton of New York actually won more popular votes and more delegates than Obama in the primaries (if you include the results in Florida and Michigan, which were only partially counted by the Democratic National Committee after a dispute with the states over their decision to move up their primary dates). But the Democrats' proportional representation delegate allocation rules left her with fewer delegates than Obama was able to win in his mostly lopsided victories in 12 of the 13 caucus states. That narrow delegate lead persuaded most of the Democrats' numerous superdelegates to endorse Obama. Party officeholders and insiders were not about to deny the nomination to an African-American candidate who, after a spectacular February and a dreary March and April, clung to a narrow but precious lead in pledged (i.e., won in primaries and caucuses) delegates.

Without its superior organizational efforts, the Obama campaign might not have prevailed. The Democratic Party was divided along demographic lines. Clinton consistently carried older voters, downscale voters, Latino voters, and older Jewish voters. And she got her largest majorities in the Appalachian territory stretching from western Pennsylvania southwest through the mountains and west to Arkansas and Oklahoma. Obama consistently won younger voters, upscale voters, and African-American voters. The result was an odd-looking political map, with Clinton carrying most of the northeast and southwest quadrants of the country and Obama winning most of the southeast and northwest quadrants.

A Well-Run Campaign

In the general election campaign, Obama started with great advantages. The Republican president had low job-approval ratings, the Republican Party identification had sharply declined since 2004, and Democrats had a greater share of voter enthusiasm. Despite his protracted battle with Clinton in the primaries, Obama was able to minimize defections in November. The exit poll showed that only 16 percent of Clinton's primary voters moved to McCain. The Obama campaign made brilliant use of the Internet to create and mobilize communities of Obama supporters. And it raised enormous and unprecedented sums of money—so much money that it would have been an act of folly for Obama not to break his pledge to accept federal financing in the fall.

Still, there was some movement in opinion over the course of the campaign. About 14 percent of voters shifted between candidates in the 12 months before the election, with 9 percent switching from McCain to Obama and 5 percent from Obama to McCain, according to a series of AP/Ipsos polls. During the campaign year, opinion moved against the Democrats on two major issues. The perceived success of President Bush's troop surge strategy in Iraq eliminated a major Republican negative, and $4-a-gallon gasoline stirred most Americans to favor offshore oil drilling and energy exploration in the Arctic National Wildlife Refuge. For most of 2008, Obama led McCain in the polls, often by significant margins. But coming out of the two party conventions in September, McCain led Obama for about two weeks. That lead may have just been an unsustainable post-convention bounce or, possibly, a sustainable change in alignment. But events intervened.

The collapse of Lehman Brothers on September 15 led to the crisis in the financial services industry and the subsequent $700 billion government bailout. On September 18, Obama overtook McCain in the *RealClearPolitics* website's average of recent polls. Obama's cool demeanor in response to the crisis contrasted with McCain's relatively impulsive decision to abandon campaigning and return to Washington. McCain's choice of Alaska Gov. Sarah Palin as his vice presidential nominee, initially an asset because of the enthusiasm she aroused among conservatives long indifferent to him, came to seem, through the lens of the financial crisis, as more evidence of impulsiveness. Opinion shifted little after that, and most pre-election polls were very close to the actual results.

Obama carried the electoral vote by 365 to 173. The big spread is testimony to the organizational strength of his campaign and the shrewdness of his strategists. Without the four states he carried with 50 or 51 percent of the vote—Florida, Indiana, North Carolina, and Ohio—he would have had 292 electoral votes, just 22 more than the needed majority.

He carried all 19 states (plus the District of Columbia) that Kerry won in 2004 and he prevailed in two that had been furiously contested in 2000 and 2004—Florida and Ohio—with only 51 percent of the vote. He captured nine states that had gone for Bush in 2004. In Nevada and New Mexico, his campaign did a superb job of registering and turning out newcomers and Latinos, and he won 55 percent and 57 percent, respectively, in what had been exquisitely close states in 2000 and 2004. In Iowa, where the state Democratic Party has had great organizational success and where Obama campaigned extensively before the caucuses, he won 54 percent. He also won 54 percent in Colorado. He received 53 percent in Virginia, where the elections of Mark Warner as governor in 2001 and Tim Kaine in 2005 led to a Democratic resurgence, especially in the Washington suburbs of Northern Virginia.

Obama carried two states that had seemed far out of reach on the basis of the 2004 results. Indiana, a 60 percent to 39 percent Bush state in 2004, went for Obama 50 percent to 49 percent, with the biggest Democratic gains in metro Indianapolis. North Carolina, a 56 percent to 44 percent Bush state even with home-state Sen. John Edwards on the Democratic ticket in 2004, experienced a 10-percentage-point increase in voter turnout, the biggest in the nation and enough to produce a 49.7 percent to 49.4 percent victory for Obama. The Democrat barely missed, by only 3,903 votes, adding Missouri's 11 electoral votes to his tally. In metro Omaha, Neb., he did just well enough to carry the single electoral vote of the 2nd Congressional District.

A comparison of Obama's state percentages with those of Kerry's yields more evidence of his campaign's skill in targeting and turning out voters. The Democratic share of the vote rose 11 percentage points in Indiana; 8 percentage points in New Mexico; 7 percentage points in Colorado,

ANNUAL EDITIONS

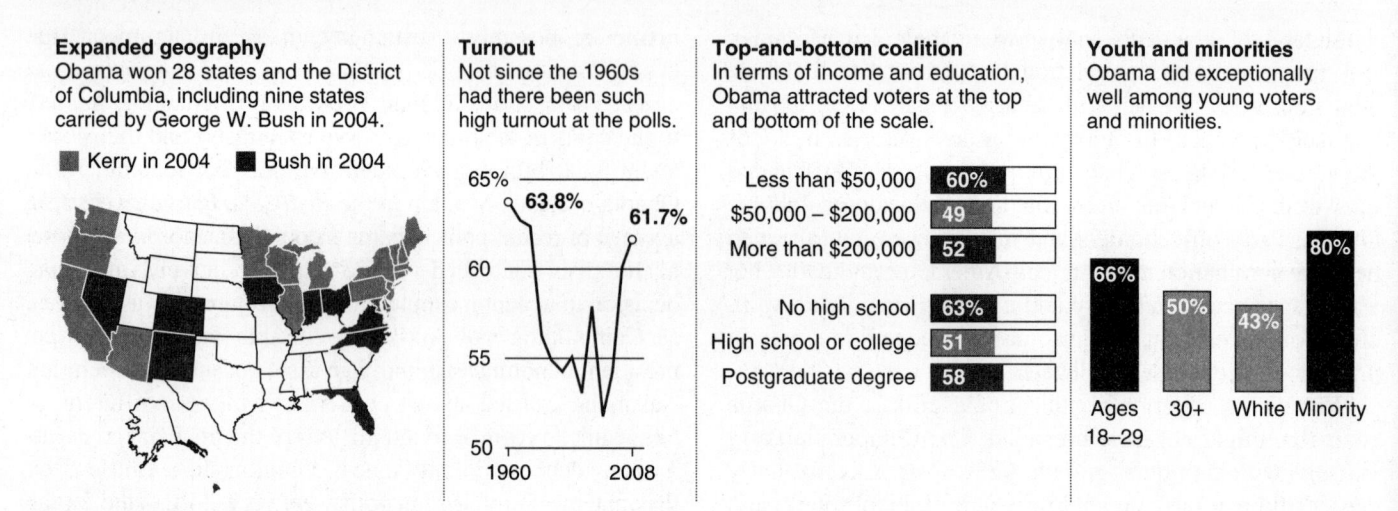

Expanded geography
Obama won 28 states and the District of Columbia, including nine states carried by George W. Bush in 2004.
- Kerry in 2004
- Bush in 2004

Turnout
Not since the 1960s had there been such high turnout at the polls.
63.8% (1960) — 61.7% (2008)

Top-and-bottom coalition
In terms of income and education, Obama attracted voters at the top and bottom of the scale.
- Less than $50,000: 60%
- $50,000 – $200,000: 49%
- More than $200,000: 52%
- No high school: 63%
- High school or college: 51%
- Postgraduate degree: 58%

Youth and minorities
Obama did exceptionally well among young voters and minorities.
- Ages 18–29: 66%
- 30+: 50%
- White: 43%
- Minority: 80%

Keys to Obama's majority coalition.
Sources: Federal Election Commission (election results); Michael McDonald (voter turnout); CNN (exit polls).

Nevada, and Virginia; 6 percentage points in North Carolina; and 5 percentage points in Iowa. It was up 9 percentage points in Montana and North Dakota, states that Bush had won and that Obama targeted. Obama's percentage was below Kerry's in Arkansas, Louisiana, Oklahoma, Tennessee, and West Virginia, as well as in Appalachian counties in western Pennsylvania. Some might be tempted to blame racism, but there is countervailing evidence: In 1989, southwestern Virginia counties voted for a black governor, Douglas Wilder. Turnout in these areas changed only negligibly from 2004 to 2008, suggesting a lack of enthusiasm for both candidates in 2008.

Building Blocs

Several interesting things can be said about the Obama majority coalition. First, he benefited from increased turnout by African-American voters, who were 13 percent of the electorate in 2008, up from 11 percent in 2004. They voted 95 percent for Obama, up 7 percentage points from the level of support they gave Kerry. The Obama campaign seems to have done an excellent job of increasing black turnout, not only in central cities but also in rural counties in Virginia and North Carolina. In addition, black turnout surged in Georgia, which played a role in reducing overall support for the Republican candidate from 58 percent in 2004 to 52 percent in 2008. Overall, Obama's bigger African-American majorities, not to mention his greater support from nonblack voters who were attracted to him in part because of his race, seem to have offset any losses from people who would have voted for a Democrat but not a black Democrat.

The very small percentages of votes cast for Obama by whites in Deep South states, such as Mississippi and Alabama, seem to reflect mostly partisan sentiments. White Democratic candidates in statewide elections there have not done much better among whites in recent years. And the public opinion polls taken before the primary and general election were not wildly out of sync with the election results, as was arguably the case in the 1982 and 1989 gubernatorial races in California and Virginia, which featured black candidates and pre-election polls showing the black candidates with more support than they actually got.

Obama also ran well with Latinos and Asians. The exit poll showed that 9 percent of voters were Latinos, up from 8 percent in 2004, and that they voted 67 percent to 31 percent for Obama. That was a huge increase for the Democrats from 2004, when the split in their favor was 53 percent to 44 percent. Bush ran nearly even with Hispanics in Texas and carried them in Florida; McCain lost Hispanics in both states, and that switch alone could account for Obama's 51 percent to 48 percent victory in Florida. Latinos' lopsided votes for Clinton in the primaries seem not to have represented an aversion to Obama, or, as some suggested, the perception of a rivalry between blacks and Latinos. And McCain's advocacy of a bill to give illegal immigrants a shot at citizenship seems to have won him little of the warm feelings that Latinos had for Bush in some states. Hispanic voters have been especially vulnerable in the real estate bust. The four states with the highest foreclosure rates in 2008 were all states with large Latino populations: Arizona, California, Florida, and Nevada.

Asian voters, heavily concentrated in a few heavily Democratic states, voted 62 percent for Obama. They cast 2 percent of all votes, the same as in 2004. White voters were 74 percent of the electorate, and they voted 43 percent for Obama, 2 percentage points more than for John Kerry. It's safe to assume that switches among whites accounted for about one-third of Obama's 2-percentage-point gain over Kerry, while blacks, Latinos and Asians accounted for about two-thirds of it.

Second, Obama created a top-and-bottom coalition. He carried voters with household incomes under $50,000 and those with household incomes over $200,000, while narrowly losing the 56 percent of voters with incomes in between. Fully 26 percent of voters reported incomes over $100,000, and they were split 49 percent to 49 percent, an astonishing result for those of us old enough to remember when high earners voted heavily Republican. In the 1980s and early 1990s, high earners' opposition to tax increases led them to vote Republican by large margins. By the mid-1990s, cultural issues led many of them to vote Democratic.

There was no sign in 2008 that Obama's promise to raise taxes on households earning more than $250,000 caused him political damage. Obama's 52 percent support among $200,000-plus voters was a huge increase over Kerry's 35 percent. There is an irony here. As the party that typically decries economic inequality, Democrats did well by it electorally in 2008 by carrying the expanding number (at least in this election) of voters from the two income extremes.

Similarly, taking education levels into account, Obama attracted people at the bottom and the top; among those in the middle, he did less well. He won 63 percent of voters who did not graduate from high school, many of them older blacks, and 58 percent of voters with postgraduate degrees. Among the 79 percent in the middle, Obama won a comparatively modest but sufficient 51 percent of the vote. Among white voters, he won 47 percent of college graduates and just 40 percent of noncollege graduates—the best proxy for the white working class of all the exit-poll demographics.

At the Democratic National Convention in August, speaker after speaker talked about the party being in touch with ordinary working families. That message was evidently not entirely persuasive. But white noncollege graduates, once a clear majority of the American electorate, accounted for only 39 percent of all voters, a percentage that is likely to keep declining. They are almost outnumbered already by the 35 percent who are white college graduates and who voted 51 percent to 47 percent for McCain.

The third thing that is striking about the Obama majority coalition is that it is heavily weighted toward the young. Voters age 30 and older favored Obama by only 50 percent to 49 percent. Voters 18 to 29 voted 66 percent (16 percentage points more than their elders) to 32 percent for Obama. This is the biggest difference between the young and the old since the exit poll began in 1972. That year, Republican Richard Nixon carried the under-30 group by 52 percent to 46 percent, and the 30-and-older group by 66 percent to 33 percent. In 2004, voters under 30 preferred Kerry, but only by 54 percent to 45 percent. Put it another way, Obama got about 22 percent of his support from young voters and McCain only about 13 percent.

At the same time, there was no unusually large surge in the young voter turnout. Nationally, young voters made up 17 percent of the electorate in 2004 and 18 percent in 2008.

An examination of county election returns suggests that the Obama campaign did a splendid job of registering and turning out young voters in university towns and in singles' apartment neighborhoods in metropolitan areas. This success is particularly apparent in Indiana, New Mexico, North Carolina, and Virginia—all Bush 2004 states that Obama carried in 2008. Still, young people participated less than their elders. They accounted for 22 percent of the voting-age population but just 18 percent of the electorate.

Gallup polls in May 2009 showed that among voters younger than 35, Democrats had a 10-to-18-percentage-point advantage in party identification, similar to the 12-to-16-percentage-point Democratic advantage in party identification among people 55 to 64, the older half of the Baby Boom Generation. In their youth, Boomers accounted for the unusually high percentages of voters who favored anti-war Democrat George McGovern in 1972. Overall, according to the 2009 Gallup results, the Democratic advantage in party identification was 8 percentage points among seniors (ages 64–85), 10 percentage points among Baby Boomers (45–63), 7 percentage points among Generation X-ers (30–44), and 14 percentage points among what Gallup calls Generation Y and others call the Millennial Generation (18–29).

Trends Favor Democrats

Straight-line extrapolations from the 2008 election results reveal an America in which the Obama majority coalition is slated to grow. Millennial Generation voters will be an increasing part of the electorate, as will, most likely, relatively affluent and highly educated voters, and Latino and Asian voters. African-American turnout and Democratic percentages may, however, have peaked in 2008 (though they could be high again in 2012 if Obama seeks re-election), just as the Democratic percentage among Catholics peaked in 1960 at 78 percent when Kennedy ran for president. McCain carried young voters in only eight states, with 51 electoral votes between them; he did not carry black, Latino, or Asian voters in any state.

Some countervailing data favor the Republicans, but not as strongly. White evangelical Protestants continue to form one-quarter of the electorate; their numbers were actually up from 23 percent in 2004 to 26 percent in 2008, and they continued to vote Republican by 3-to-1. The trend in evangelical churches to take up anti-poverty and environmental protection causes, symbolized by the Rev. Rick Warren of the Saddleback Church in Lake Forest, Calif. (he delivered the invocation at Obama's inauguration), has not yet modified evangelical voting behavior in a major way. And young voters who have no religious commitment may develop one, as members of earlier generations did as they grew older and took on more family obligations.

The fastest-growing parts of the country still voted Republican in 2008, though less so than in 2004. McCain carried 86 of the 100 fastest-growing counties with populations over 10,000 in 2008. Bush won 97 of the fastest-growing counties in 2004. McCain lost three of the five fastest-growing—Kendall County, Ill.; Flagler County, Fla.; and Loudoun County, Va. And he lost the three largest fast-growing counties—Riverside County, Calif.; Clark County, Nev.; and Wake County, N.C. While there is no doubt that party identification changed to the detriment of Republicans—in 2004, 37 percent of voters were Republicans and 37 percent were Democrats, versus 32 percent Republican and 39 percent Democratic in 2008—there has also been a shift of attitude among self-identified independents, who tended to resemble Democrats on many issues in the last years of the Bush presidency. In the first months of the Obama presidency, independents tended to resemble Republicans on some issues, for example, by opposing the massive government bailouts of the financial services industry and the domestic automakers.

Whether the country's period of open-field politics continues or the 2006 and 2008 election results turn out to be the beginning of another period of trench-warfare politics (this time with a small but decisive Democratic majority) is not yet clear. The nation faces new and unfamiliar issues. The continuing troubles of the financial system are unlike anything Americans have experienced since the 1930s, and anyone who was an adult then is older than 90 now. Unprecedented government intervention in the economy has provoked dissatisfaction. The 2008 exit poll showed that 56 percent of respondents opposed the $700 billion bailout for the financial services industry voted by Congress in October 2008, while 39 percent supported it. Continued government infusions of vast sums into banks, mortgage lenders Fannie Mae and Freddie Mac, Detroit's automobile companies, and insurance firms raise questions of propriety and favoritism. And Obama's 2010 budget asks Americans to support or reject a vastly larger and more intrusive government. Moreover, the costly Obama programs to provide government health insurance and to regulate carbon dioxide emissions affect different regions of the country differently, in ways that split both parties' constituencies and potential constituencies.

Voters in November 2008 believed, by 47 percent to 23 percent, that the economy would get better in the coming year, according to the exit poll. Within a few months, those expectations seemed antiquated. Against the backdrop of fast-changing conditions, public opinion can shift quickly, as it did after September 11, 2001.

The United States continues to face major challenges in the world, and in early 2009, Obama decided to continue military operations in Iraq and to step them up in Afghanistan, to the consternation of some on the Democratic left who were so enthusiastic about his candidacy. He decided to continue holding unlawful combatants indefinitely and to try them in military tribunals, both controversial policies with Democrats and some independents during the preceding Bush administration. Obama faces the continuing challenge of dealing with the vicious mullah-cracy of Iran, which has been bent on obtaining nuclear weapons to threaten Israel. The Iranian problem is one that neither the diplomacy nor the aggressive military posture of the previous administration was able to address effectively. Obama also faces a truculent Russia, which seems disinclined to cooperate on any issue from missile defense to the Iranian nuclear program, and a stern China, which provides the United States with a bounty of consumer goods and helps finance its government debt but may not care to do so indefinitely. Any of these challenges could erupt into crisis, with unpredictable repercussions in American public opinion.

The most volatile factor in our politics in the first decade of the 21st century is the balance of enthusiasm. Voter turnout has generally been rising, but the balance of enthusiasm seems to determine which party's supporters increase their turnout most. In 2002 and 2004, that balance favored the Republicans somewhat, and in 2006 and 2008, it favored the Democrats somewhat more.

The question for Republican strategists is how they can excite potential voters. The question for Democratic strategists is how to maintain the level of enthusiasm apparent in the 2008 election results. Off-year and special elections provide some clues. Democratic victories in special elections for House seats in 2007 and 2008 in Illinois, Louisiana, and Mississippi showed the balance of enthusiasm working in the party's favor. Special elections in Georgia, Louisiana, and Virginia from December 2008 to February 2009 showed a bigger drop-off in turnout among Democrats than among Republicans. The 2010 midterm congressional elections will provide more clues.

A Turning Point?

Obama's election and his reform program raise the question of whether America has reached another inflection point in the balance of opinion on the relationship between government and markets. Such inflection points are rare, and seem to have come at 40-year intervals. To oversimplify much, the economic distress of the 1930s, symbolized by the breadlines of the Great Depression, convinced most Americans that markets didn't work very well and that government did. The economic distress of the 1970s, symbolized by the gas lines of the stagflation era, convinced most Americans that government didn't work very well and that markets did.

In this view (with many exceptions and caveats), the 1930s produced a natural Democratic majority for a long generation, and the 1970s produced a natural Republican majority for a long generation, which may now have come to an end. It may be time for another inflection point, for Americans to decide that markets don't work very well and that government does.

But the picture is incomplete. For the change in the balance of opinion owed much not only to the economic distress of the 1930s and 1970s but also to the success, both in economic policy and in America's position in the world, of the 1940s and 1980s. In the 1940s, the United States was the incredibly productive arsenal of democracy in World War II, and then, in the postwar years, it was the engine of world economic growth. In the 1980s, the United States won an almost entirely bloodless victory in the Cold War and embarked on a quarter-century of low-inflation economic growth—"It's morning in America," as Ronald Reagan's 1984 ad proclaimed. Franklin Roosevelt and Reagan both seemed to turn the American economy around, although economists are still arguing to what extent and in what respects. They led the nation to magnificent victories over the fascism of Nazi Germany and the Communism of the Soviet Union. Those triumphs fortified the opinion of the American people that the nation was both great and good.

It is possible to imagine that the American economy may recover sharply and resume its bounteous productivity in another quarter-century of low-inflation economic growth, thanks to, or in spite of, Obama's economic policies. It is more difficult to imagine how the United States can emerge as brilliantly successful against the Islamist terrorists and Iranian mullahs who wish our destruction as it was against Germany and Japan in 1945 and during the fall of the Berlin Wall in 1989. But one must remember that it was difficult to imagine those outcomes when the United States under Roosevelt was aiding a lonely Britain against the alliance of Nazi Germany and Soviet Russia in 1940, and when Reagan was proclaiming to the disdain of almost all supposedly enlightened opinion in 1983 that communism would end up on the "ash heap of history."

America has had great leaders, but they have had a great country to work with. Maybe this will prove true again.

---

mbarone@washingtonexaminer.com.

This article is excerpted from *The Almanac of American Politics, 2010*.

Reprinted by permission from *National Journal*, July 11, 2009, pp. 18–25. Copyright © 2009 by National Journal Group Inc. All rights reserved.

The 'Enduring Majority'—Again

No, the Democrats will not be in power forever . . .

JAY COST

After the Democrats' triumphs in two consecutive elections, left-wing pundits have returned to an old meme: The party's majority will be enduring. In a report published by the Center for American Progress, liberal author Ruy Teixeira boldly proclaimed: "A new progressive America has emerged with a new demography, a new geography, and a new agenda. . . . All this adds up to big change that is reshaping our country in a fundamentally progressive direction. . . . These trends will continue." Other liberals—most notably John Judis of *The New Republic* and Alan Abramowitz of Emory University—have similarly argued that Obama's election ushered in a new, enduring Democratic majority.

This essay will rebut some of the claims made by advocates of this idea. It will also offer a broader perspective on how to understand the 2008 election, and what it means for the Republican party and conservatives in the future.

What makes this task difficult is that it's hard to nail down exactly what the phrase "enduring Democratic majority" is supposed to mean. Which "progressive" policies will be passed? How much control over the government will Democrats have? For how long they will have it? Just how enduring will it be? These questions are typically left unanswered. Recently Judis commented to the *Huffington Post:* "The only circumstances that could bring back the Republicans is Obama's failure to stem the recession." This, of course, would make it indistinguishable from just about every majority in the country's history.

If this sounds like an unfalsifiable hypothesis to you, you're not alone. Judis and Teixeira floated a version of the same argument in their book *The Emerging Democratic Majority* in 2002, just a few months before the Republicans regained control of the Senate and increased their majority in the House. After the 2006 midterm election, they resurrected their thesis in an article for *The American Prospect* titled "Back to the Future" and subtitled "The re-emergence of the emerging Democratic majority." To explain away the years of GOP dominance, they invented a new psychological concept—"de-arrangement." What this means, they explained, is that

> the focus on the war on terror not only distracted erstwhile Democrats and independents but appeared to transform, or de-arrange, their political worldview. They temporarily became more sympathetic to a whole range of conservative assumptions and approaches.

This is a textbook case of special pleading. If creating an *ad hoc* concept out of whole cloth is the only way to salvage a theory, it's time to find a new theory. The concept is not particularly helpful to them, either. After all, couldn't conservatives explain away 2006 and especially 2008 with "dearrangement"? Perhaps our cool, ultra-liberal president bewitched true Republicans with his post-partisan campaign gibberish, and these voters will soon see the error of their ways.

Ultimately, engaging with the advocates of the "enduring Democratic majority" hypothesis is like punching sand. The rules of the game are set up so that the majority is considered enduring even if a recession terminates it or it is interrupted by years of Republican governance. In other words: Heads they win, tails you lose.

It is fairly easy to get away with this kind of unrigorous thinking when you are preaching to the liberal choir. However, this argument has found its way into conservative circles, usually among pundits who blame the party's decline on a lack of attention to their favorite issue. That's misguided, because while the party has been in tough spots before, it has bounced back pretty quickly. Every time the party has suffered a setback, like 1992, it was not long before a comeback, like 1994. Even after Franklin Roosevelt swept the Democrats into office in the 1932 elections, and extended Democratic gains in 1934 and 1936, Republicans came bouncing back in 1938, returning to Capitol Hill with enough numbers to block New Deal legislation with the first of many bipartisan conservative coalitions.

Nevertheless, I sense that many conservatives think the current period in the wilderness will actually last 40 years. This feeling of dread is not a huge surprise, given the attention the "enduring Democratic majority" hypothesis has received from the iron triangle of the mainstream media, the Democratic party, and left-wing interest groups. What follows should help conservatives see that there is a lot more sizzle than steak to this idea.

As we go through the details, it's important to keep the big picture in mind. Analysts like to talk about the movement of this or that group in the last election, but the context is of crucial importance. Voters cast their ballots last fall amid an economy that was shrinking at a 6.3 percent annual rate. This was a dramatic contraction, precipitated by a financial calamity that had struck just weeks before. Additionally, President Bush's job approval had fallen to less than 30 percent due to largely non-ideological concerns like his handling of Iraq and Hurricane Katrina. That's an unwinnable environment for any party. When you're losing, you're losing. Nothing in the data looks particularly good, but this does not mean the data are always going to look bad. The course of politics is not a straight line, and liberal analysts are simply wrong to assume that subsequent elections will look like the previous one.

One point often cited by proponents of the enduring-majority hypothesis is the voting preference of young Americans. There is no doubt that President Obama scored a huge victory among young voters, winning 66 percent of those under 30. Proponents think this group of voters will be important to the party's continuing success.

Perhaps—but this is the same argument we might have heard in 1972, when George McGovern lost the popular vote by 23 points but won voters aged 18 to 24 by a point. In 1976, now aged 22 to 28, this cohort voted for Jimmy Carter roughly in line with the whole country. They went slightly for Ronald Reagan in 1980, and in 1984 and 1988 the GOP had a breakthrough, as they voted for Reagan and then for George H. W. Bush at the same rate as the whole country. By 2008, these voters—most of them now in their late 50s—went for Obama by a point. Given that the whole country voted for Obama by 7 points, we'd have to conclude that they now have a Republican tilt. In other words, though this cohort of voters looked quite Democratic when they were young, the GOP won them over later, when the political pendulum swung its way again.

Past performance is no guarantee of future results. Young voters age, their lives change, and so can their politics.

It's like your financial analyst's disclaimer: Past performance is no guarantee of future results. As young voters age, their lives change, and so can their politics. One big source of change is marriage. Typically, committed conservatives vote Republican and committed liberals vote Democratic, regardless of marital status. But for moderates and the non-ideological, marriage makes a big difference. In 2000 and 2004, George W. Bush did better than Al Gore and John Kerry among moderate voters of nearly all ages if they were married. The big question for the future, which advocates of the enduring-majority view cannot yet answer, is: Will young, unmarried voters follow the older cohorts and trend to the GOP after they marry, or will they stay with the Democrats? None of this is meant to minimize the significance of Obama's accomplishment in bringing young voters to his side, or the work that conservatives will have to do to win over the so-called Millennial Generation. The point is that one cannot simply extrapolate from the 2008 results.

Then there are the "professionals." This is the rather tendentious term typically applied to anybody with a graduate degree. The idea here is that these voters—driving hybrids, shopping at co-ops, hyphenating their last names, and so on—are more sympathetic to progressive views, and are solid Democrats.

Indeed they are. But so what? First of all, the fraction of "professionals" has held fairly constant since 1988, making up 16 to 18 percent of the electorate. They have consistently voted 3 to 7 more points Democratic than the rest of the nation. Given their relatively small size, they have not been decisive. They have not stopped the GOP from winning three of the last six presidential elections, or holding the House of Representatives for twelve years in a row.

It's hard to argue that there's been much of a shift along educational lines. Of all college-educated voters who voted for one of the two major parties, Obama won 53 percent. Ditto non-college voters. In 1992, Bill Clinton performed about the same across education groups, after factoring out the Perot vote: He won 53 percent of college grads and 55 percent of non-college grads. So in 16 years, not much has changed.

Those who expect an enduring Democratic majority also make much of the fact that, in a few decades, the United States will be a minority-majority nation, with whites making up less than half the population. Whether or not this is true, I can say that they tend to overstate the consequences of the underlying trend.

Let's start with black voters. There is no doubt Obama performed very well with them. Typically, the GOP wins about 10 percent of the black vote. In 2008, John McCain won just 4 percent. Obama also brought an unprecedented number of black Americans to the polls. Last year, blacks actually constituted a larger share of the electorate than they do of the population as a whole.

The critical question, as yet unanswerable, is whether these numbers can be sustained. Is this a "personal" vote for Obama, or the beginning of a new trend? It is too soon to say. Nevertheless, we can say that the GOP's performance with blacks has been horrible. George W. Bush won only 26 percent of self-identified *conservative* blacks in 2004. In other words, black Americans who are ideologically sympathetic to the GOP still vote heavily Democratic. The Republicans need to work on this. Minimally, they should strive to make black conservatives comfortable voting for the conservative party.

Hispanics are another matter, though you can't tell that to most advocates of the enduring-majority hypothesis. In a recent article, Abramowitz—arguing that demographic trends will favor the Democrats for decades—allocated white conservatives to the GOP and white liberals to the Democrats, and predicted that white moderates would be swing voters. He then allocated *all* ethnic and racial minorities to the Democrats. This must have come as a shock to the 3.67 million Hispanics who voted for McCain last year. They are a testament to the fact that Hispanic voters cannot be viewed through the same lens as black voters. In fact, they have recently behaved more like white voters, breaking for the party that is closer to their ideology. George W. Bush won 69 percent of Hispanic conservatives and 41 percent of Hispanic moderates in 2004. He did better than any previous Republican by winning about 40 percent of all Hispanics.

Hispanics swung against McCain in 2008, but the Arizona senator still won the same share as George H. W. Bush did in 1988, even though the latter ran in a much more favorable political climate. Additionally, McCain did better than Gerald Ford in 1976 and Bob Dole in 1996. In other words, Hispanics have slowly become more Republican in recent cycles. To place them in the Democratic column so confidently is to ignore this, as well as Bush's breakthrough in 2004. But maybe these deviations can be chalked up to de-arrangement, too.

Nevertheless, conservatives must make outreach to Hispanics a priority—especially if they want to win states such as Nevada, Colorado, and New Mexico. Even though Bush did better with Hispanic conservatives than with black conservatives, too many still "defected" to Kerry. Obama probably won many more Hispanic conservatives, so there is a lot of work to be done. Abramowitz and other Democrats might be content to overlook Bush's performance among Hispanics, but conservatives should not overlook Obama's.

Finally, any discussion about the burgeoning minority vote favoring the Democrats must acknowledge that the GOP has done better with white voters in recent decades. No Democrat has won a majority of whites since Lyndon Johnson in 1964, although Jimmy Carter came close in 1976. Bill Clinton nearly won a plurality in 1992 and 1996. Yet Al Gore lost the white vote to George W. Bush by twelve points in 2000, and Bush improved among whites in 2004, winning 58 percent despite a tough war in Iraq and weak job growth after the 2001 recession. This was about the same share his father pulled in 1988, though the elder Bush had the benefit of running on years of peace and job-creating prosperity.

John McCain won 55 percent of the white vote, the largest share ever to go to a losing presidential candidate, even though President Bush was hugely unpopular and the country was plummeting into a deep recession. Part of McCain's success with whites was probably due to hesitation among some to vote for a black candidate; just as Obama may have won some votes because of his race, he may have lost others. Still, the 2008 result fits with a trend we have seen for 40 years. Whereas Carter and Clinton won Arkansas, Kentucky, Louisiana, Tennessee, and West Virginia thanks to strong showings among white voters, those voters have since flocked to the Republican party, pushing these states out of reach for the Democrats, even in years that favor their party as heavily as 2008 did.

The migration of whites to the GOP has helped counter the advantage the Democrats might otherwise have enjoyed from demographic changes.

This migration of whites to the GOP has helped counter the advantage the Democrats might otherwise have enjoyed from demographic changes. The net effect of all this has been imperceptible to date. Compare the election of 2008 with the last time the Democrats took the White House, in 1992. That year, the Democrats nominated a fresh-faced, 40-something governor promising change amid a weak economy and an unpopular incumbent named Bush. He won 53.5 percent of the two-party vote and 370 Electoral College votes. In 2008, they nominated a fresh-faced, 40-something senator promising change amid a weak economy and an unpopular incumbent named Bush. He won 53.7 percent of the two-party vote and 365 Electoral College votes.

Ultimately, the increasing share of non-whites in the population might tip the scales to the Democrats, as proponents of the enduring-majority hypothesis suggest. But that claim rests on the assumption that the GOP will not match their gains with equal improvements among whites and Hispanics. In other words, those partial to the "enduring Democratic majority" hypothesis are arguing *for* the continuation of some recent trends but *against* the continuation of others.

The comparison between 1992 and 2008 is instructive. From a certain perspective, they are extremely similar: a weak economy, an unpopular incumbent, and so on. The top-line numbers look identical—but underneath them are dramatically different voting coalitions. What conclusions can we draw from this?

First, voting coalitions are in flux. This is the principal reason to question the "enduring Democratic majority" hypothesis—it rests on the false assumption that the parties' electorates are static. Voting coalitions change because the parties work to change them. In 2000 Governor Bush surveyed President Clinton's voting coalition and realized that it was vulnerable in several spots. He exploited those vulnerabilities in his race against Clinton's vice president, Al Gore. Eight years later, Senator Obama found weaknesses in Bush's coalition that he could exploit in his race against Senator McCain. This process is not unique. Each successful challenger finds marginal voters on the other side who can be persuaded to switch. The fact that Obama did this does not mean that the 200-year process is somehow at an end. It means that it is continuing.

This is precisely what we should expect from two broad-based political parties whose objective is to acquire power in our diverse republic: The losers will adapt to the new environment, and the winners will have trouble keeping their voters in the fold. Governing coalitions are stitched together around limited, common goals, and as politicians achieve those goals the coalitions unravel. How was it, for instance, that high earners voted Democratic in 2008? One reason was the GOP's 1980s cuts in tax rates. Those tax cuts have long since come to be taken for granted, removing an issue for the party and thus making it a victim of its own success.

Defeating the party of an unpopular incumbent is the easy part. The hard part is governing to the satisfaction of a majority coalition—which the Democrats have not yet done. Holding his coalition together could be real trouble for Obama. It remains to be seen whether the people who voted for him can be united around some positive goals, or whether they simply voted against Bush and the recession. Candidate Obama was adept at obfuscation during the campaign, trying hard to be all things to

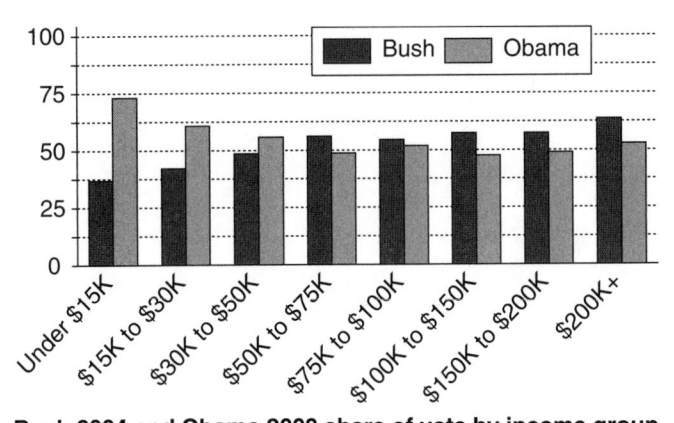

Bush 2004 and Obama 2008 share of vote by income group.
Source: National exit polls.

all people, but you can't do that when you're actually running the government; you have to decide who wins and who loses.

Michael Barone has noted that Obama has a top-bottom voting coalition, which could be unstable. The accompanying chart makes that clear.

The core of Bush's support came from middle earners, with a tilt toward the upper end. Obama's electorate, on the other hand, samples heavily from the poles. This presents an obvious policy problem. The president is promising large increases in government benefits, which will go mostly to lower-income voters. How to pay for it? Heavy tax increases on high earners will damage him among his upper-income voters. If he raises taxes too many times, the wealthy suburbs around Philadelphia and D.C. will suddenly start trending red again. So what to do? It seems the president's solution is $1 trillion budget deficits from here to eternity. Will the middle tolerate that? Those who earn between $50,000 and $100,000 per year were not terribly partial to Obama last November—and their incomes are such that they are already sacrificing important goals as they balance their family budgets. How will they react when they see Obama abandoning the last pretenses of fiscal discipline?

In the final analysis, I'd suggest that the "enduring Democratic majority" theory consists of a few good ideas surrounded by a lot of wind. The liberals who offer it are honest and well intentioned, but their enthusiasm has gotten the best of them. Their thesis appears to be impervious to falsifying evidence. Its empirical claims are overstated and offered without appropriate context. It fails to take into account American electoral history, in particular how and why the parties have shared power over time and why we can expect that to continue into the future. Conservatives should focus on finding a way back to the majority, and ignore those who say it can't be done.

Mr. Jay Cost writes the HorseRaceBlog for RealClearPolitics.com.

From *The National Review*, June 8, 2009, pp. 33–36. Copyright © 2009 by National Review, Inc, 215 Lexington Avenue, New York, NY 10016. Reprinted by permission.

Dr. Dean Regrets Nothing

- No plum Obama post for departing head of the Democratic National Committee.
- As DNC chair, Dean shifted resources to his 50-state party-building project.
- His critics said he spent too little on the most promising Hill races in 2006.

JAMES A. BARNES

Washington has seldom been kind to Howard Dean. And that's one thing that the elevation of Barack Obama didn't change.

The day before Dean, the departing chairman of the Democratic National Committee, headed to American Samoa to check in with party officials there, he learned that the next day, January 8, the president-elect was going to formally announce that Virginia Gov. Tim Kaine would be the next DNC chairman.

Dean's absence from the Obama-Kaine photo-op sparked plenty of comments. "I find it a mystery," said one Democratic operative on K Street, who observed that while plenty of Obama's past rivals and critics "are getting jobs and treated with respect, Howard Dean doesn't get invited to a press conference."

But another Democratic lobbyist, a former Dean fan who requested anonymity to speak candidly, was less charitable toward the exiting party chieftain: "I think his record will be ballyhooed because he was fortunate enough to be the jetsam in the wake of Boat Obama." Two Obama advisers didn't return phone calls seeking comment on Dean.

Whatever one thinks of Dean, he was hardly a bystander as chairman. He shifted the DNC's emphasis from national programs to revitalization of state parties, especially in so-called red states. And he stood his ground when some top Democrats questioned his priorities.

In an exit interview with *National Journal,* Dean, a former governor of Vermont, said that his two most significant accomplishments as chairman were implementing his "50-state" strategy to make his party competitive in all parts of the country and modernizing the DNC. "We basically had not much functioning technology in the building when I got there," Dean recalled.

One tangible product of Dean's innovations was the DNC's "neighbor-to-neighbor" program, which gives grassroots party activists the ability to download information on Democratic or Democratic-leaning neighbors who could be canvassed. Such personal contact is widely regarded as the best way to communicate with potential supporters and to increase the likelihood that they will vote. The Obama campaign eagerly adopted that tool for the general election.

But Dean's emphasis on building up state parties—the DNC transferred more than $66 million to them in the past two years alone—is his most famous and perhaps most lasting initiative. "He's left a tremendous legacy of building the Democratic Party into a national party," said Mark Brewer, chairman of the Michigan Democratic Party and head of the Association of State Democratic Chairs. "Being a revolutionary is not easy, changing the status quo. And we know he did ruffle feathers along the way. But he will go down as one of the best chairs in the history of the party."

And one Democratic political consultant said, "Grudgingly, people think the 50-state strategy worked in helping them recruit [candidates] and establishing a [Democratic] presence in places where not much existed before. It did leave the party cash-poor at points, but it dovetailed nicely with the Obama campaign, which stressed organizing."

Fundraising, often viewed as a party chair's prime responsibility, was never Dean's strength. In the 22-month run-up to the 2008 presidential election, Dean raised $206 million, and the Republican National Committee raised $336 million, according to the most recent analysis by the Federal Election Commission. For the same portion of the 2004 campaign, the DNC took in $299 million.

Dean opted to plow money into helping state parties and boosting the party's technological capabilities rather than into "independent expenditures." In the 2004 campaign cycle, the DNC spent more than $79 million on independent expenditures, much of it on TV spots attacking President Bush. In the 2008 cycle, the DNC devoted just over $1 million to independent expenditures.

That radical change of direction tended not to endear Dean to Washington-based political consultants, especially those whose bread and butter comes from national party ads. But to many of Dean's primary constituents on the national committee, the state party chairs, he was a hero.

"Washington is filled with people who [think they] know all about winning elections [but] have never gone out organizing voters," said South Carolina Democratic Party Chair

Carol Fowler. "Howard Dean disdained their advice and did what he thought was right. And the people out in the states think he did the right thing."

> "Howard Dean disdained [Washington's] advice and did what he thought was right. And the people out in the states think he did the right thing."
>
> —Carol Fowler, chair of South Carolina's Democratic Party

Early on in his chairmanship, Dean was perhaps best known for his verbal blasts at Republicans. In a speech to liberal activists in June 2005, Dean suggested that Election Day should be a national holiday because working-class voters don't have time to stand in long lines but Republicans "can do that because a lot of them never made an honest living in their lives."

A few days later, discussing political outreach with minority leaders at a round-table in San Francisco, Dean declared: "You know, the Republicans are not very friendly to different kinds of people. They're a pretty monolithic party. Pretty much, they all behave the same, and they all look the same. It's pretty much a white, Christian party."

Many fellow Democrats thought Dean was going too far. Then-Sen. Joe Biden of Delaware told ABC's *This Week*, "He doesn't speak for me with that kind of rhetoric. And I don't think he speaks for the majority of Democrats."

But asked if he regrets anything he said as chairman, Dean demurred, adding, "Well, I mean, I'm sure I've always said lively things."

During his second year as chairman, Dean famously tangled with Democratic congressional leaders over fundraising, organizing, and strategy for the 2006 midterm elections. The primary source of tension was money. Dean was adamant about upholding his commitment to the 50-state strategy, while Democrats on Capitol Hill, particularly then-Democratic Congressional Campaign Committee Chairman Rahm Emanuel, thought that Dean was not focusing enough resources on top-priority congressional races. The friction became so great that Emanuel reportedly stopped speaking to Dean for a time.

Although Dean's fundraising skills have often drawn criticism, in the 2006 election cycle, the DNC set a midterm record, collecting more than $118 million—double what it raised during the comparable part of the 2002 campaign.

As he hands over the reins of the DNC, Dean sees the Democratic Party's biggest challenge as fulfilling its campaign promises. "There is no excuse for us not to deliver" now that the party controls both ends of Pennsylvania Avenue, he said. "If we allow health care to be watered down, if we welsh on our promises to labor and to the civil-rights community, then we're in trouble." He quickly added, "I don't expect that to happen."

Party chairmen at the helm when their party wins the White House often get rewarded by the new president. Ron Brown, DNC chairman during the 1992 campaign, became Bill Clinton's first secretary of Commerce. And Jim Nicholson, RNC chairman in 2000, was ambassador to the Vatican in Bush's first term and secretary of Veterans Affairs in his second.

Dean, who is a physician, had his eyes on the Health and Human Services Department. Instead, Obama passed him over entirely.

Dean declined to discuss his disappointment over not becoming HHS secretary but vowed not to disappear. "I intend to stay active in public policy, probably not in the government, but we'll find out," Dean said.

Like other pols in between jobs, Dean plans to cash in on the speech circuit and to travel abroad. His schedule already features three trips to Europe.

Dean said it is important for the Democratic Party to nurture ties with other center-left parties around the globe. "There's a lot to be shared, a lot to be learned, between Americans and others," he explained. "I think we need to be much, much closer than we have been at the political level with foreign leaders, many of whom will go on to be prime minister or other ministers."

As for Washington, a place where he has spent relatively little time because of his travels around the country and frequent weekend visits to his wife at home in Vermont, Dean has mixed feelings. "That is a very different culture than everywhere else in the country, which keeps them out of touch and somewhat self-involved, but the people are pretty good people," he said. "Despite my initial reception, I developed some good friendships and some very good working relationships with the leadership in Congress."

Asked whether he could think of anything he should have done differently and whether he had any disappointments about his chairmanship, Dean paused and replied, "I have to say I don't." He added: "It's been a pretty good record, obviously helped a lot by George Bush and Barack Obama. But, you know, we've won races in places we haven't won races for 30 years, sometimes 40 years."

If neither the party's longtime Washington establishment nor the Obama administration wants to give Dean nearly as much credit for those victories as many Democratic state party chairs do, Dean will happily take his bows beyond the Beltway.

jbarnes@nationaljournal.com

Reprinted by permission from *National Journal*, January 24, 2009, pp. 60–61. Copyright © 2009 by National Journal Group Inc. All rights reserved.

Direction, Anyone?

What the GOP needs is not a leader, but political entrepreneurs.

RAMESH PONNURU

Republicans are looking for a leader. Go to any right-leaning gathering, and at some point the conversation will turn to the party's potential presidential nominee in 2012. Republicans were less consumed by that question in 1993, the first year of the last Democratic presidency. Even when Republicans aren't talking about the 2012 race, they are debating who speaks for the party—sometimes explicitly, as when Rush Limbaugh and Michael Steele feuded this spring. Or they are wondering who will form the next generation of Republican leaders: Eric Cantor? Paul Ryan?

The present-day question can be answered simply: The Republican party has no leader. Nobody should be surprised by this fact. A party without the White House and without either chamber of Congress is unlikely to generate an unquestioned leader. To the extent Newt Gingrich overcame those odds in 1993–94, it was because of highly unusual circumstances. He had led the fight against the previous Republican president's tax increase in 1990, that president had lost his reelection campaign, and the party had concluded both that the tax increase was the most important mistake that had led to the defeat and that it was connected to all the other mistakes.

Ronald Reagan was to some extent the leader of the party after Gerald Ford's 1976 defeat, although we tend to forget how tough a primary campaign Reagan had to fight in 1980. But he would not have earned that status if he had not challenged Ford in a two-man primary and Ford had not then lost the general election.

The present circumstance offers no parallel to either previous set of wilderness years for the Republicans. Nobody ran against Bush in the 2004 primaries, he was reelected, and no single piece of legislation became the organizing principle for an intra-party opposition that ultimately saw its interpretation of events adopted by the party as a whole. Nor did any Republican go mano-a-mano against McCain in 2008.

The search for a leader of the party is therefore destined to be fruitless. The party will not have a leader until it has a presidential nominee or has taken control of a chamber of Congress. The good news is that the party doesn't really need leadership. The bad news is that it also doesn't have what it does need: entrepreneurship.

The situation was quite different in the late 1970s. In today's highly structured, hierarchical GOP it is hard to believe that a congressman who wasn't in the party's leadership, and wasn't even on the House Ways and Means Committee, could become its chief spokesman on economic policy. Yet Jack Kemp came to fill that role even while rejecting many of the party's existing economic tenets—and even though most of the supply-siders around him lacked formal credentials as economists.

Even as late as 1993, the party did not put too much stock in its titular leadership. Bob Michel was, officially, the House minority leader and Bob Dole his Senate counterpart. But it was of course Gingrich who truly led the House Republicans, and such senators as Phil Gramm and Paul Coverdell did more to defeat the Clinton administration's health-care plan than Dole.

The current congressional leaders—Mitch McConnell in the Senate, John Boehner in the House—are more aggressive, and probably more capable, than Dole and Michel. Partly as a result, though, backbench Republicans take fewer actions independent of their leaders. Not much seems to happen among House Republicans, for example, that hasn't been coordinated with Boehner's staff.

So Republicans have a high degree of unity these days, which has been very helpful in opposing liberal initiatives such as the stimulus and the Democrats' healthcare legislation. The downside of that unity is that it is less helpful in generating new ideas, some of which the party will probably need to retake power and will certainly need to exercise it productively. Understandably given their role, the leaders will not embrace an idea unless it has the support of the vast bulk of their followers, or at least does not offend them or compete with their own ideas. But no new idea can pass that test until it gets a thorough airing. Backbenchers can promote those ideas—but only if they are not waiting for someone else to give them direction or, worse, a script.

So opportunities for entrepreneurship abound, unseized. There is no shortage of potentially popular conservative causes. But where is the backbench congressman who will devote himself to publicizing our elite universities' shameful treatment of ROTC programs? Who has the moxie to try to revolutionize the party's economic platform by offering a pro-family tax reform?

What congressman was willing not only to oppose the bailout of Detroit but to advocate that our carmakers instead be released from fuel-economy regulations? Republicans have pounced on the many signs that the Obama administration is distancing itself from Israel. But one could make the case that it has systematically been devaluing our alliances, including our old ones with Britain and Japan and our new one with India. Will anyone make that case?

Among the possible explanations for the decline in entrepreneurship, four stand out. The first has to do with the general tendency of a party to fall in line behind a president who belongs to it. For eight years, the congressional party's agenda was whatever President Bush said it was. That wasn't the case in 1993, since a lot of congressmen had stopped identifying with the first President Bush even before he left office; and it wasn't the case in the late 1970s, since the long-out-of-power congressional GOP had no agenda and wasn't expected to have one. This time there is a habit that has to be unlearnt.

The second is that changes in the way campaigns are financed have changed the psychology of politicians. It has often been observed that Reagan's campaign for governor of California in 1966, and Eugene McCarthy's for president in 1968, would have been impossible under the current campaign-finance laws. A small number of rich people who believed passionately in something had the power to shake up politics; perhaps that ability has been sacrificed to a spurious equality.

The increasing sophistication of gerrymandering may also be partly to blame. (That's my third culprit, if you're counting.) In conversation, Bill Kristol recently described Republican congressmen as exhibiting "a curious mix of dogmatism and timidity." The districts most of them represent encourage both traits. They are packed with conservatives, thus simultaneously reducing conservatives' influence in other districts and relieving the congressmen of any need to learn how to appeal to non-conservatives in order to win and keep their seats. This latter effect could be expected to yield a certain lockstep conformity rather than creativity.

Conservatives have generally resisted the idea of letting nonpartisan commissions draw district lines according to some formula, thinking it a close cousin to campaign-finance regulation and, even more, fearing that it would reduce the number of hardcore conservative congressmen. There are limits to what such a reform could achieve, given that liberals and conservatives over the last generation have tended to move to different neighborhoods and states. But perhaps conservatives should rethink their position on the policy question.

On the other hand, the Republican governors, who provided the party with many of its most successful policy initiatives in the 1990s, do not seem to be brimming with ideas either, with a few exceptions. Gerrymandering cannot explain their passivity.

A final possibility is that the supply of entrepreneurship has fallen because the demand has. Most conservatives have concluded that Republicans fell from power because they fell from grace. Rightworld these days places a considerably higher priority on the maintenance of principles than on finding new ways to apply them. The example of the reigning Democrats, who regained power without coming up with any new ideas, strengthens this inclination.

So we have come to this sorry pass: The party that gives political expression to America's entrepreneurial class has within its number few political entrepreneurs. What Republicans celebrate they do not, alas, exemplify.

From *The National Review*, September 7, 2009, pp. 14, 16. Copyright © 2009 by National Review, Inc, 215 Lexington Avenue, New York, NY 10016. Reprinted by permission.

Article 34

America Observed

Why foreign election observers would rate the United States near the bottom.

ROBERT A. PASTOR

Few noticed, but in the year 2000, Mexico and the United States traded places. After nearly two centuries of election fraud, Mexico's presidential election was praised universally by its political parties and international observers as free, fair, and professional. Four months later, after two centuries as a model democracy, the U.S. election was panned as an embarrassing fiasco, reeking with pregnant chads, purged registration lists, butterfly ballots, and a Supreme Court that preempted a recount.

Ashamed, the U.S. Congress in 2002 passed the Help America Vote Act (HAVA), our first federal legislation on election administration. But two years later, on November 2, more than 200,000 voters from all 50 states phoned the advocacy organization Common Cause with a plethora of complaints. The 2004 election was not as close as 2000, but it was no better—and, in some ways, worse. This was partly because the only two elements of HAVA implemented for 2004 were provisional ballots and ID requirements, and both created more problems than they solved. HAVA focused more on eliminating punch-card machines than on the central cause of the electoral problem, dysfunctional decentralization. Instead of a single election for president, 13,000 counties and municipalities conduct elections with different ballots, standards, and machines. This accounts for most of the problems.

On the eve of November's election, only one-third of the electorate, according to a *New York Times* poll, said that they had a lot of confidence that their votes would be counted properly, and 29 percent said they were very or somewhat concerned that they would encounter problems at the polls. This explains why 13 members of Congress asked the United Nations to send election observers. The deep suspicion that each party's operatives had of the other's motives reminded me of Nicaragua's polarized election in 1990, and of other poor nations holding their first free elections.

Ranking America's Elections

The pro-democracy group Freedom House counts 117 electoral democracies in the world as of 2004. Many are new and fragile. The U.S. government has poured more money into helping other countries become democracies than it has into its own election system. At least we've gotten our money's worth. By and large, elections are conducted better abroad than at home. Several teams of international observers—including one that I led—watched this U.S. election. Here is a summary of how the United States did in 10 different categories, and what we should do to raise our ranking.

1. Who's in Charge? Stalin is reported to have said that the secret to a successful election is not the voter but the vote counter. There are three models for administering elections. Canada, Spain, Afghanistan, and most emerging democracies have nonpartisan national election commissions. A second model is to have the political parties "share" responsibility. We use that model to supervise campaign finance (the Federal Election Commission), but that tends to lead either to stalemates or to collusions against the public's interest. The third, most primitive model is when the incumbent government puts itself in charge. Only 18 percent of the democracies do it this way, including the United States, which usually grants responsibility to a highly partisan secretary of state, like Katherine Harris (formerly) in Florida or Kenneth Blackwell in Ohio.

2. Registration and Identification of Voters. The United States registers about 55 percent of its eligible voters, as compared with more than 95 percent in Canada and Mexico. To ensure the accuracy of its list, Mexico conducted 36 audits between 1994 and 2000. In contrast, the United States has thousands of separate lists, many of which are wildly inaccurate. Provisional ballots were needed only because the lists are so bad. Under HAVA, all states by 2006 must create computer-based, interactive statewide lists—a major step forward that will work only if everyone agrees not to move out of state. That is why most democracies, including most of Europe, have nationwide lists and ask voters to identify themselves. Oddly, few U.S. states require proof of *citizenship*—which is, after all, what the election is supposed to be about. If ID cards threaten democracy, why does almost every democracy except us require them, and why are their elections conducted better than ours?

3. Poll Workers and Sites. Dedicated people work at our polling stations often for 14 hours on election day. Polling sites are always overcrowded at the start of the day. McDonald's hires more workers for its lunchtime shifts, but a similar idea has not yet occurred to our election officials. Poll workers are exhausted by the time they begin the delicate task of counting the votes and making sure the total corresponds to the number who signed in, and, as a result, there are discrepancies. When I asked about the qualifications for selecting a poll worker, one county official told me, "We'll take anyone with a pulse." Mexico views the job as a civic responsibility like jury duty, and citizens are chosen randomly and trained. This encourages all citizens to learn and participate in the process.

4. Voting Technologies. Like any computers, electronic machines break down, and they lose votes. Canada does not have this problem because it uses paper ballots, still the most reliable technology. Brazil's electronic system has many safeguards and has gained the trust of its voters. If we use electronic machines, they need paper-verifiable ballots.

5. Uniform Standards for Ballots, Voting, Disputes. The Supreme Court called for equal protection of voters' rights, but to achieve this, standards need to be uniform. In America, each jurisdiction does it differently. Most countries don't have this problem because they have a single election commission and law to decide the validity of ballots.

6. Uncompetitive Districts. In 2004, only three incumbent members of Congress—outside of House Majority Leader Tom DeLay's gerrymandered state of Texas—were defeated. Even the Communist Party of China has difficulty winning as many elections. This is because state legislatures, using advanced computer technologies, can now draw district boundaries in a way that virtually guarantees safe seats. Canada has a nonpartisan system for drawing districts. This still favors incumbents, as 83 percent won in 2004, but that compares with 99 percent in the United States. Proportional representation systems are even more competitive.

7. Campaign Finance and Access to the Media. The United States spent little to conduct elections last November, but almost $4 billion to promote and defeat candidates. More than $1.6 billion was spent on TV ads in 2004. The Institute for Democracy and Electoral Assistance in Stockholm reported that 63 percent of democracies provided free access to the media, thus eliminating one of the major reasons for raising money. Most limit campaign contributions, as the United States does, but one-fourth also limit campaign expenditures, which the Supreme Court feared would undermine our democracy. In fact, the opposite is closer to the truth: Political equality *requires* building barriers between money and the ballot box.

8. Civic Education. During the 1990s, the federal government spent $232 million on civic education abroad and none at home. As a result, 97 percent of South Africans said they had been affected by voter education. Only 6 percent of Americans, according to a Gallup Poll in 2000, knew the name of the speaker of the House, while 66 percent could identify the host of *Who Wants to Be a Millionaire?* Almost every country in the world does a better job educating citizens on how to vote.

9. The Franchise. The Electoral College was a progressive innovation in the 18th century; today, it's mainly dictatorships like communist China that use an indirect system to choose their highest leader.

10. International Observers. We demand that all new democracies grant unhindered access to polling sites for international observers, but only one of our 50 states (Missouri) does that. The Organization for Security and Cooperation in Europe, a 55-state organization of which the United States is a member, was invited by Secretary of State Colin Powell to observe the U.S. elections, yet its representatives were permitted to visit only a few "designated sites." Any developing country that restricted observers to a few Potemkin polling sites as the United States did would be roundly condemned by the State Department and the world.

On all 10 dimensions of election administration, the United States scores near the bottom of electoral democracies. There are three reasons for this. First, we have been sloppy and have not insisted that our voting machines be as free from error as our washing machines. We lack a simple procedure most democracies have: a log book at each precinct to register every problem encountered during the day and to allow observers to witness and verify complaints.

McDonald's hires extra workers at lunchtime, but this has not yet occurred to our election officials. Poll workers are exhausted by the time they start counting votes.

Second, we lack uniform standards, and that is because we have devolved authority to the lowest, poorest level of government. It's time for states to retrieve their authority from the counties, and it's time for Congress to insist on national standards.

Third, we have stopped asking what we can learn from our democratic friends, and we have not accepted the rules we impose on others. This has communicated arrogance abroad and left our institutions weak.

The results can be seen most clearly in our bizarre approach to Iraq's election. Washington, you may recall, tried to export the Iowa-caucus model though it violates the first principle of free elections, a secret ballot. An Iraqi ayatollah rejected that and also insisted on the importance of direct elections (meaning no Electoral College). Should we be surprised that the Iraqi Election Commission chose to visit Mexico instead of the United States to learn how to conduct elections?

ROBERT A. PASTOR is director of the Center for Democracy and Election Management and a professor at American University. At the Carter Center from 1986–2000, he organized election-observation missions to about 30 countries, including the United States.

Can Money Be a Force for Good?

The revolutionary potential of small-donor democracy.

MARK SCHMITT

Early last year, as the 2008 presidential campaign loomed on the horizon, campaign-finance experts and newspaper editorial boards warned preemptively of a "billion-dollar election." In a February 2007 editorial, The *New York Times* invoked Watergate to warn that such an expensive election would represent a breakdown of campaign-finance regulation and mark a return to the corruption of the Nixon era. If Sen. Hillary Clinton were looking for a clever name for her big fundraisers, something comparable to George W. Bush's "Pioneers," she could, the editorial suggested, call them "Recidivists." (After marveling at the millions that Clinton, Rudy Giuliani, and a few other candidates had already amassed, news stories at the time mentioned in passing that there was also a fellow named Barack Obama who had raised $500,000.)

In the end, more than $1.6 billion was raised for the presidency alone, more than twice as much as was raised four years earlier. A single candidate—Barack Obama—raised and spent $640 million of that total. Candidates for the House and Senate spent more than a billion dollars, even though, as always, most contests were not competitive. All told, the predicted billion-dollar election actually cost $5.3 billion, according to the Center for Responsive Politics.

Only a few presidential candidates participated in the public-financing system for the primaries. One, Obama, was the first candidate since the system was created to opt out of using it in the general election, passing up $85 million in no-strings-attached money in favor of continuing to raise hundreds of millions in private donations. Meanwhile, the other major-party candidate supplemented public financing with $19 million in coordinated funding through the Republican National Committee and at least $36 million through a legal loophole known as a General Election Legal and Accounting Compliance Fund.

Had these staggering circumstances been predicted to campaign-finance reform advocates a few years ago, they would have unanimously described them as a dystopia, a terrifying fate for American democracy and evidence of the collapse of not only the 2002 Bipartisan Campaign Reform Act (the McCain-Feingold law) but the entire edifice of post-Watergate election reforms.

Yet when that day came, many of the same reformers described it as one of the brighter days in the history of American democracy. Voters participated in record numbers, and enthusiasm was palpable, not just for Obama but for other presidential candidates as well as House and Senate candidates. Despite the record number of voters who told pollsters that the country was on the "wrong track" and the unprecedented disapproval ratings for both the president and Congress, there were strong signals that voters were motivated by hope. Unusually high percentages

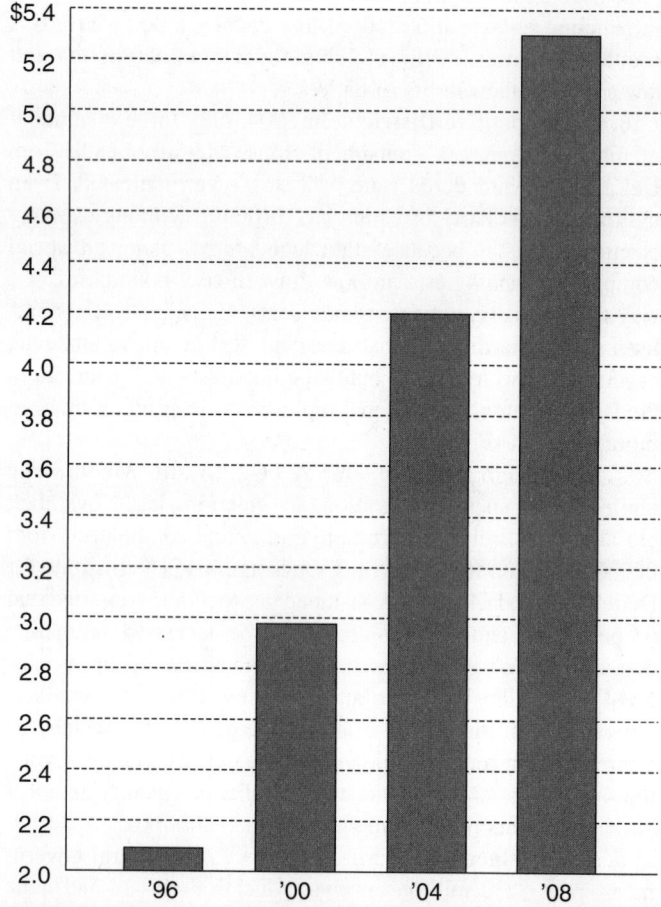

Election money. Total amount spent on all federal races, in billions.
Source: Center for Responsive Politics; Public Citizen

of people told the Pew poll that they were voting, *for* their preferred candidate rather than *against* the other.

And while the amount of money was staggering, so was the number of people involved: More than 3 million donors gave to the Obama campaign alone. Though we don't have good historical data on donors who give less than $200 (the amount required to be reported), we know that in 1996, only 567,000 people gave $200 or more to *any* candidate or party, and only 200,000 people gave to any Democrat or the Democratic Party. By comparison, 322,000 donors gave $200 or more to Obama's campaign, in addition to the roughly 2.7 million who sent smaller amounts. More than 1.2 million people donated $200 or more to campaigns—not only Obama's—in 2008, according to the Center for Responsive Politics. Such a broad and diverse base of donors and the astonishing percentage of small donors (48 percent of Obama's funds and 34 percent of John McCain's came from individuals who gave less than $200) have to significantly alleviate concerns about corruption resulting from the leverage that any individual donor, group of donors, or major fundraiser would hold. In this new world dominated by small donations, no one individual has much sway over the candidate.

Two facts revealed by the 2008 election—the collapse of the campaign-finance regulatory regime and the transformation of small-donor fundraising—call for not just new rules but an entirely new set of assumptions about money in politics. Campaign-finance law treats money in isolation as a bad and corrupting force that should be constrained or eliminated. The authors of the existing laws assumed that small donors were unlikely to play a major part in politics unless constraints on large contributions and on soft-money contributions from corporations and unions forced candidates to go small. And they assumed that money, cynicism, and low participation formed a vicious circle.

These are the assumptions of 1996, when only half a million or so people were involved in politics as contributors and when political participation was at its lowest level ever. (That was the only year in American history when voter turnout fell below 50 percent.) We now know two things we didn't know then: Small donors *can* be drawn to politics, and large sums of money in politics and engaged, participatory democracy are not incompatible; money can, in fact, be an essential form of expression that deepens participation. That is, money, positive engagement with politics and government, and participation can, in certain circumstances, form a virtuous circle.

The election created a paradox: If there were a causal relationship between big money in politics and corruption, public cynicism, and low participation, then a year like 2008—which featured big money but also public enthusiasm and high participation—should not exist. Longtime opponents of reform, such as former Federal Election Commissioner Bradley Smith, jumped on the result as proof that they had been right all along: "Obama's fundraising shows us the emptiness of the arguments for campaign finance 'reform,'" Smith wrote in *The Washington Post* a week before Election Day.

Article 35. Can Money Be a Force for Good?

Obama, who had earlier made a vague pledge to work out an agreement with his opponent whereby both would accept public financing, and was widely criticized for opting out, described his fundraising base as "a parallel public-financing system where the American people decide, if they want to support a campaign, they can get on the Internet and finance it."

He was right in one sense and wrong in another. It is fair to consider his 3 million donors "public financing." A broad base of support, reflecting such enthusiasm that roughly one out of every 30 people who voted for him also made a contribution, can legitimately be called public.

What it cannot be called, however, is a "system." The circumstances that led to Obama's ability to raise almost twice as much money as any previous candidate are not reproducible. And some of the circumstances—such as the extraordinary polarization of the electorate and the passion for change after eight years of George W. Bush—one would never want to reproduce. Certain congressional candidates, especially those who won attention among the online activists of the "netroots," also brought in astonishing levels of small donations. But for the most part there was no change in the price of a competitive congressional race or in the advantage held by incumbents and those with access to larger donors, according to an immediate post-election study by the Campaign Finance Institute.

Indeed, as 14 scholars agreed in the journal *The Forum*, published by the University of California, Berkeley, the regime by which we govern money in politics has "collapsed." The regulations intended to control large contributions and soft money, bolstered by the McCain-Feingold reforms of 2002, were weakened by the Federal Election Commission and finally made irrelevant last year by the Supreme Court's correct ruling that issue advertisements mentioning a candidate near election time cannot be regulated. The 34-year-old public-financing system, an outdated model whose flaws were evident, died from disuse.

Campaign-finance reforms collapsed, but the system was saved by accidental developments outside the legal framework.

While the constructed elements of the campaign-finance system—legal fundraising limits and formal public financing—collapsed, the system was saved by accidental developments outside of the legal framework. The Internet, in particular, made a new kind of small-donor fundraising possible. In the past, asking a donor for a second or third donation was costly, so all the incentives were to ask for a large donation up front. Beginning with Howard Dean's campaign in 2004, campaigns understood that, with a donor's e-mail address in hand, asking for more money was cost-free. Now there was every reason to ask a donor for $5 or $10 to start with and nothing lost if the donor had only $5 or $10 to give. This is not some technological miracle but a small change with huge consequences made possible by technology.

Technology also slashed the transaction costs of organizing to raise money outside the campaigns or parties. A decade ago, the only interests that could organize to raise and contribute money collectively were those with the financial incentive that made it worth the huge costs of organizing to influence government—the large trade associations of Washington's K Street, for example, or a few organized groups of single-issue voters such as gun-rights supporters. Thus a primary goal of reform was to limit such organizations, whether in the form of political action committees (PACs) or the 527 committees that emerged in 2004. Since the ability to organize was distributed unequally, regulating organizing was essential to equality.

But Internet intermediaries such as ActBlue.com, a clearinghouse for individuals or groups to raise money for candidates they favor, have completely transformed the nature of organizing. ActBlue users, acting independently, have raised $83 million for candidates since the site launched in 2004. This, in turn, enabled candidates to raise money without going through the gatekeepers of the big, organized dollars—the lobbyists and financiers—and changed the range of issues that candidates had to respond to. (While the most notable achievements of low-transaction-cost political organizing have been on the left, it is a matter of time before comparable conservative organizations such as Slatecard.com catch up.) Numerous congressional candidacies, such as that of newly elected Rep. Tom Periello in Virginia, would never have been possible, much less victorious, without ActBlue and the thousands who use it to organize.

The challenge in the next wave of reform is not to try to rebuild the post-Watergate campaign-finance regulations but instead to see money as one factor in a larger system and intervene to turn money into a force for good (participation, robust communication) rather than for ill (corruption, massive inequality in the ability of candidates to be heard). Neither the laissez-faire view that opposes reform nor the traditional reform approach based on limiting contributions and closing loopholes recognizes these possibilities. The goal should be to understand the achievements of Obama, ActBlue, and others and institutionalize them into a real system that works for voters and all candidates.

Such a system would seek to create every incentive for small donors to participate and for candidates and parties to seek small donors, especially in the early stages of a campaign. Small-donor democracy is not a single legislative fix. Rather, it is a change of orientation, so that instead of trying to purge politics of big money or organized money, we use the lessons of 2008 to ensure that money can be a force for good. There are a few key ways to fashion a small-donor democracy system that can work for all candidates:

- Change the incentives for candidates to seek small donations. A generous match on small contributions, such as New York City's 6-to-1 public match, is one way to give candidates as much motivation to seek a $50 contribution as a $300 contribution. Even systems of full public financing, such as Arizona's, use small contributions as seed money to prove broad public support. As that state's governor, Janet Napolitano, has said, it led her to approach the same people for money that she approaches for votes.

- Create new ways for small donors to give. Legal scholar Bruce Ackerman has long advocated a system of "patriot dollars"—a voucher given to every citizen to contribute to a candidate or a political organization. The same goals can be achieved through a refundable tax credit for small contributions, especially if it were well publicized. Minnesota's system combines a matching system with a tax credit, appealing to both candidates and contributors.

- Add new incentives for small-dollar organizing. To offset the power of big political organizations, add new incentives for small-donor PACs, such as those organized on ActBlue, by making contributions to certain qualified political organizations eligible for the match or tax credit as well.

These provisions could be combined in various ways so that a public-financing system could have both a matching system for candidates to get started and then full public financing once a certain level of support were reached. Such systems would be flexible, not locking candidates into spending limits or other restrictions that limit their ability to respond if outspent, the core problem of the old presidential system. They respect the role of money as a legitimate expression of enthusiasm and a form of participation. And they build on healthy trends in our politics rather than continuing the futile quest to build a wall against unhealthy trends.

From *The American Prospect*, January/February 2009, pp. A13–A15. Copyright © 2009. Reprinted with permission from Mark Schmitt and The American Prospect, Washington, DC. All rights reserved. www.prospect.org

Vote or Else

A modest proposal for curing election fraud.

ALLISON R. HAYWARD

In the state of Washington, it may be that a governor will serve for the next four years who was not properly elected. Voter registration rolls and election practices are sloppy enough—not just in Washington, mind you, but in many places—that in very close elections it may be impossible to know for sure which candidate has received more properly cast votes. (In three separate counts in Washington, the margins were 261, 42, and 129 votes out of 2.9 million cast.) It is past time we address this problem, and here's a thought: Maybe the United States should require eligible citizens to register to vote, and then to vote.

For most people, this idea is radical and distasteful. Why should we want presumably uninformed, apathetic people voting? Wouldn't they be influenced by caprice, last-minute mud, or improper entreaties? Isn't it a person's right not to vote if he doesn't want to? Only nasty one-party regimes make voting mandatory, right? And Venezuela, for one, requires its citizens to register and vote, showing that mandatory voting and massive fraud can coexist.

The usual defenses for mandatory voting seem tepid in contrast. People would be more "engaged" in government. The underclass would be better represented. "We, the people"—not some motivated subset—would elect representatives. It is not obvious that any of these arguments is true or, if true, is sufficient reason to require voting.

Moreover, it would seem American elections face more urgent challenges, voting fraud and voter intimidation being the most notorious. Yet it is as a palliative to these ills that mandatory voting would have its greatest appeal. That is because a mandatory system would require government to take voter registration—including the issue of fraud—seriously.

Suppose, as in Australia, eligible citizens were required to register and to appear at the polls on Election Day. Election administrators would need to know, first, who among the throng was eligible, and ensure that they registered in the appropriate place. Duplicate registrations and obsolete addresses would have to be purged. At election time, officials would need to ascertain accurately who had voted and who hadn't. No more question of whether precautions, such as requiring identification, would be intimidating. And it would be in the interest of a voter to make sure he was correctly identified. With better records, it would be more difficult to lard the rolls with phony registrations. Nor could the converse scam of "unregistering" valid voters be as easily perpetrated. For those voting absentee, the incentives would be much stronger to make sure their vote was received and cast properly, lest they face a fine for failing to vote.

The significant and sometimes mischievous role partisans now play in our current elections would diminish. Just as we don't see private interests going door to door helping people complete tax or immigration forms, the role special interests and parties now assume in registering and mobilizing voters would fade. There would be no reason to go to elaborate lengths to register or ferret out voters at election time—no more cause to slash the tires or block the phones of the other side's activists, or to pay cash bounties for registrations, subsidizing the duplicative, phony dreck that already clogs our voter rolls.

But isn't mandatory voting a little, um, totalitarian? One could argue that—although arguably no more so than having to file tax forms on a regular basis. A system of mandatory voting does not mean that individuals are forced to vote for any particular candidate, or even any candidate at all. If the United States were to follow a system like Australia's, mandatory registration and voting would be mitigated by the secret ballot. If voters do not care to vote, they can simply take a ballot and not vote it, or "undervote" by choosing some offices and not others.

Would mandatory voting favor liberals and Democrats over conservatives and Republicans? The conventional wisdom for decades has been that making voter registration and voting easier—broadening the "base," as it were—favors the Democratic party. However, people who know much more about this than I tell me that the conventional wisdom no longer necessarily obtains. When the base is broadened in some part by false and duplicative registration, as happens now, the side favored would seem to be the one willing to throw those votes into the pool, i.e., to commit fraud. That can have different partisan implications depending on where you live and what's at stake.

The main obstacle to mandatory voting in the United States is that it is beyond imagination what jurisdiction would implement it. Under the Constitution, election administration and qualifications are for the most part the province of the states.

How could one, or even a handful, of states institute mandatory voting, given the way Americans move about? It would seem impossible to assemble the essential prerequisite—the list of eligible citizens—unless other states could be relied upon to keep good records, too. The federal government might be able to work that miracle nationally (probably not), but whether the federal government could constitutionally institute mandatory voting has yet to be litigated, and would in any case mean a revolution in election jurisdiction that is unlikely to take place.

Still, that need not be the end of the story. As we see from the anti-smoking campaign, people can be made to change their behavior through moral suasion. Following the model of California's antismoking Proposition 99, states could institute taxes to pay for massive voter education efforts, shaming people into self-registering and voting, by associating nonvoting with all things ugly and slothful. Groups could receive grants for crafting an eligible-voter database, or for sanitizing the registration rolls. Hollywood-based consultants could place pro-registration and antifraud references in popular movie and television scripts. State treasuries could reward taxpayers who demonstrate they voted with a tax credit.

Or, in the alternative, states could get serious about cleaning up election rolls, educating voters, and prosecuting election fraud. Ultimately, using mandatory voting to push the system toward reform is a little like punishing the victim.

ALLISON R. HAYWARD is counsel to Commissioner Bradley A. Smith of the Federal Election Commission. The views expressed here are her own, and do not reflect the position of the commission, any of its commissioners, or its staff.

From *The Weekly Standard*, March 21, 2005, pp. 15–16. Copyright © 2005 by Weekly Standard. Reprinted by permission.

Article 37

The American Presidential Nomination Process: The Beginnings of a New Era

BRUCE STINEBRICKNER

Let me start with two points that provide essential context for considering significant changes occurring in the American presidential nomination process today. First, in every presidential election since 1860 (that is, in the last 37 presidential elections) either the Democratic or Republican candidate has won and become president of the United States. Thus, the presidential nomination process serves to identify the *only* two individuals who ultimately have a chance to become president of the United States. Second, since the introduction of presidential primaries in the early twentieth century, the American people have played a much bigger role in the American presidential nomination process than their counterparts in any comparable nomination process in the world.

These two points testify to the importance and uniqueness of the American presidential nomination process. But the process by which major party candidates for president are nominated has not remained static since the introduction of presidential primaries early in the twentieth century, much less since the time of President George Washington. The presidential nominating process has sometimes changed suddenly on account of deliberate and focused reform efforts, and sometimes at a more measured and evolutionary pace.

I begin this article with an overview of the history of the presidential nomination process in the United States, identifying four distinct eras and laying the groundwork for the suggestion that we are entering or about to enter a *fifth* era in the way major party presidential nominees are chosen. Second, from the vantage point of November 2007, I identify the major changes that have arrived—or are arriving—on the scene, tracing their origins back to 2004 or 2000 as needed. Third, by assessing the likely consequences of these changes, I make the case that they represent more than minor revisions or routine evolution of the presidential nomination process. Instead, I argue that a sea change—a major transformation—in the process seems to be at hand.

Four Eras in the Presidential Nomination Process

The First Era: The Congressional Caucus Era (ca. 1800–1828)

Revolutionary War hero George Washington became the first president of the United States, serving two terms in office after having been elected unanimously by the Electoral College in 1788 and again in 1792. After Washington retired, party caucuses in Congress (that is, meetings of all the members of Congress who identified with each party) assumed the function of nominating presidential candidates. In six consecutive presidential elections from 1800 through 1828, every successful candidate had first been nominated by his party's congressional caucus. This first era in the presidential nominating process—the Congressional Caucus era—came to an end in 1831–1832, when parties began to hold national nominating conventions to choose their presidential candidates.

The end of the Congressional Caucus era—which some pejoratively called the "King Caucus" era—is significant. Had members of Congress continued to control the presidential nomination process, a key distinction between the American system of government and the parliamentary system of government would probably not have emerged. At the heart of parliamentary systems such as those in Great Britain, Australia, Japan, Italy, and India lies the relationship between candidates for prime minister (and prime ministers) and members of the lower house of parliament. As these systems have come to operate today, a party's members in parliament choose their leader, and that leader becomes the party's candidate for prime minister. Voters play a decisive role in selecting the prime minister by choosing between the parties, their policy positions, and their prime ministerial candidates in general elections. The end of the Congressional Caucus era in the United States severed the direct link between Congress and presidential nominations. In turn, the relationships between Congress and American presidential candidates, on the one hand, and parliaments and prime ministerial candidates in parliamentary democracies, on the other, developed in fundamentally different ways.[1]

The Second Era: National Conventions of Party Regulars or Activists (ca. 1831–1908)

By ending the direct and controlling role of members of Congress in choosing their parties' presidential candidates, the introduction of national nominating conventions in 1831–1832 marked the beginning of the second era in the history of the nominating process. From 1831 to the early twentieth century, delegates to national nominating conventions were individuals active in party organization affairs at the state and local levels. Party officeholders such as state and county party chairs as well as other party regulars became delegates. The national conventions were gatherings of party organization people—that is, party leaders and other party activists—from all the states, with each state party sending a number of delegates roughly proportional to the population of that state in comparison with other states.

In the twentieth century, two significant changes in the methods for selecting delegates to the parties' quadrennial national conventions gave birth to the third and fourth eras in the history of the presidential nomination process.

The Third Era: The "Mixed System" for Choosing Delegates to National Conventions (ca. 1912–1968)

In the early twentieth century, state governments introduced what has been called "the most radical of all the party reforms adopted in the whole course of American history"—the direct primary.[2] Accompanying the introduction of direct primaries for such offices as member of the United States House of Representatives, governor, state legislator, and mayor, was the introduction of presidential primaries by a number of states. A key objective was to reform, revitalize, and enhance American democracy.

Presidential primaries to choose delegates to national nominating conventions were used by twelve states in 1912. From 1916 through 1968, between thirteen and twenty states used presidential primaries, with roughly 35% to 45% of delegates (a minority, but a significant minority nevertheless) to the national conventions typically being chosen in primaries.[3] Because the remaining delegates were party organization activists, this era in the history of the presidential nominating process has been called the "mixed system."

Although reformers had managed, for the first time, to introduce mass popular involvement in choosing a sizable proportion of delegates to national conventions, their efforts did not result in all delegates being selected by voters in primaries. Even this "mixed system," however, introduced mass involvement in the process for nominating presidential candidates to an unprecedented extent and to a degree unrivalled in the nomination process for any other nation's highest elected government office.

In practice, since no candidate of either party's nomination was likely to win every delegate chosen in presidential primaries and, until 1936, Democratic convention rules required a successful candidate to win two-thirds of the delegates' votes, major party nominees during the "mixed system" era typically had to gain substantial support among those delegates coming from states that did not hold presidential primaries. Even so, "inside" and "outside" strategies for winning a party's nomination were possible. A candidate could concentrate on gaining support directly from the party organization regulars who would be attending the relevant national convention, an "inside" strategy illustrated by Hubert Humphrey's successful 1968 candidacy for the Democratic presidential nomination. Alternatively, a candidate could emphasize the primaries and seek to show sufficient electoral appeal in primary states to convince party leaders and the rest of the delegates to support his candidacy. Candidate Dwight Eisenhower used an "outside" strategy in winning the Republican presidential nomination in 1952, and candidate John F. Kennedy did likewise in winning the Democratic nomination in 1960.

The last year of the "mixed system" era, 1968, was a tumultuous and violent year in American politics. Opponents of the Vietnam War supported the anti-war candidacies of Senators Eugene McCarthy and Robert Kennedy for the Democratic presidential nomination. Kennedy was assassinated in June 1968 and, even though McCarthy or Kennedy had won virtually all the presidential primaries while taking strong anti-war positions, the "mixed system" left McCarthy with substantially less than a majority of delegates at the 1968 Democratic convention in Chicago. Adopting an "inside" strategy in seeking the Democratic party's presidential nomination that year, Vice President Hubert Humphrey did not oppose American involvement in the war being waged by his patron, President Lyndon Johnson, and did not compete in a single presidential primary. Yet Humphrey was duly nominated as his party's presidential candidate. The selection of Humphrey marked the end of the "mixed system" that had made his nomination possible.

The Fourth Era: The Plebiscitary Model for Choosing Delegates to the National Convention (1972–present)

Anti-war opponents of Hubert Humphrey waged vigorous protests in the streets of Chicago outside the 1968 Democratic convention and were violently subdued by Chicago police under the direction of Mayor Richard Daley, a Democrat and a leading supporter of Hubert Humphrey's nomination. As a consolation prize of sorts, the convention voted to establish a reform commission, which came to be known as the McGovern-Fraser Commission, reflecting the names of the two Democratic members of Congress—Senator George McGovern and Congressman Donald Fraser—who, in succession, chaired the commission.

Article 37. The American Presidential Nomination Process: The Beginnings of a New Era

The Commission's charge was to look for ways to make the selection of delegates to future Democratic conventions more transparent and democratic.

The McGovern-Fraser Commission uncovered and reported many interesting—some might say scandalous—points about how delegates were selected in various states and made recommendations about how to reform the system. The recommendations went into effect in 1972 and served to democratize the selection of delegates to the national conventions. (Even though the Commission was a Democratic party body, implementation of its recommendations affected the presidential nomination process for both major parties.) Presidential primaries were used to select a clear majority of delegates to national conventions. Those states not using primaries were required to open their party-run delegate selection procedures to all registered voters identifying with either party. These procedures became known as the "caucus/convention" alternative to presidential primaries, an alternative that Iowa, among other states, adopted. In effect, the McGovern-Fraser reforms completed the work of the early twentieth-century reformers, and a new era in the nominating process—the Plebiscitary Model—began in 1972, four years after the "mixed system" had led to the tumultuous and violence-marred nomination of Democrat Hubert Humphrey in Chicago. The name for this new era emphasizes the newly dominant role that the mass electorate could play in the reformed presidential nomination process, since "plebiscitarian" comes from the Latin word "plebs," which refers to the "common people."

A Closer Look at the Operation of the Plebiscitary Model

My central contention in this article is that changes in the functioning of the presidential nomination process in the first decade of the twenty-first century have been so significant that they signal or foreshadow the pending arrival of a new era, the *fifth*, in the history of the presidential nomination process. A brief examination of selected characteristics of the process in operation under the Plebiscitary Model will provide essential background for subsequently considering the major and noteworthy changes that are becoming apparent in 2007–2008.

My earlier discussion of the "mixed system" (ca. 1912–1968) and the "plebiscitary model" (1972–present) addressed changes in how delegates to national conventions were selected in the states. The "mixed system" began when a sizable minority of states introduced presidential primaries to select delegates to the national convention, thus opening the presidential nomination process to the public to an extent that was unique among the world's democracies. The "plebiscitary model" reformed the "mixed system" in ways that led a majority of states to adopt presidential primaries and required the remaining states to make their party-based caucus/convention systems accessible to all registered voters identifying with the relevant party.

Timing and Scheduling

By the 1950s, New Hampshire had established the "first-in-the-nation" status of its quadrennial presidential primary. Two decades later, Iowa successfully laid claim to scheduling its precinct caucuses, the initial stage of its caucus-convention system that operated over several months, shortly before the New Hampshire primary *and* before any other state started its delegate selection process. This Iowa-New Hampshire sequence has begun the delegate selection processes of the fifty states in every presidential election year since 1972. Candidates, news media, campaign contributors, pollsters, political activists, and the attentive public have all paid disproportionate attention to campaign activities and outcomes in these two states.

The sequence of other states' delegate selection processes has been more variable than the Iowa-first/New Hampshire-second part of the schedule, but a noteworthy phenomenon called "Super Tuesday" emerged in the 1980s. "Super Tuesday" came to refer to a Tuesday in March a few weeks after the New Hampshire primary on which a number of states (initially, mostly Southern states) scheduled their presidential primaries or caucuses. One initial objective was to increase the impact of "moderate" Southern states in the selection of the Democratic presidential nominee. With the introduction of Super Tuesday and ensuing variations in which states participated in Super Tuesday in a given presidential election year, the idea of more deliberately self-conscious and self-serving scheduling seemed to catch on. Some states (like California) that had traditionally held their delegate selection processes "late" (that is, in April, May, or June) began to schedule their selection processes earlier. These movements contributed to a phenomenon called "frontloading," which refers to crowding more and more state delegate selection processes into the months of January, February, and March, rather than having them spread out over the traditional February-through-June period.

After the Plebiscitary Model took hold in 1972, the sequence of delegate selection processes in the states seems to have become more visibly contentious among the states, the bunching of a number of states' primaries and caucuses on a single day became more prevalent (not only on "Super Tuesday," but on other single dates as well), and more delegate selection contests were "front-loaded" to the January-March period, while fewer occurred in April through June.

The "Invisible Primary"

Besides the acceptance of an Iowa–New Hampshire–Super Tuesday sequence in states' delegate selection processes, other expectations about broader matters of timing and scheduling in the presidential nomination process also developed. In the 1970s an observer coined the term "invisible primary" to refer to the activities of candidates and relevant others in the year or so *before* delegate selection processes began in Iowa and New Hampshire early in a presidential election year.[4] The "invisible primary" was, of course, not an actual presidential primary; that is, it was *not* an election run by a state government in which registered voters choose delegates to a national nominating convention. *Nor* was it "invisible." But the term, especially the word "invisible," is helpful in understanding how the presidential nomination process has been changing in the early twenty-first century.

The term "invisible primary" conveyed the largely unnoticed—at least by the general public and to some extent news media—activities in which would-be presidential candidates engaged in the years before presidential general elections.

Would-be candidates met with party leaders, high-ranking government officials, potential campaign contributors, and the like to gain support for their possible candidacy. But typically the would-be candidates did not openly declare their candidacies until late in the year preceding a presidential general election, and media attention was sporadic and not particularly intense. To the average American, these activities were all but "invisible." Even so, the "invisible primary" was hardly irrelevant to the outcome of the presidential nomination process that culminated in the selection of the parties' presidential candidates. The resulting campaign experience, fund-raising, and endorsements, not to mention media commentators' impressions and evaluations, presumably influenced candidates' prospects when the actual state-by-state delegate selection processes began.

Campaign Financing

In 1974, in the aftermath of the Watergate scandal associated with President Richard Nixon and his 1972 re-election campaign, Congress passed the Federal Election Campaign Act, initiating a system of campaign finance regulation that continues in its broad outlines to this day. Subsequent court decisions, legislation (most notably, the Bipartisan Campaign Reform Act of 2002, otherwise known as the McCain-Feingold Act), and administrative regulations (issued mostly by the Federal Election Commission, a six-member government body established by the 1974 Act) have left a tangled and complicated set of rules that apply to the financing of campaigns for presidential nominations.

Campaigns for a presidential nomination became subject to a host of reporting and accounting requirements. The amount that individuals could contribute to a single candidate's campaign was limited, and the government provided "matching" funds to candidates if they met certain conditions in their initial fundraising and agreed to accept limits on their state-by-state and overall campaign spending. The system of matching funds was designed to prevent candidates or would-be candidates who lacked reasonably widespread support in a number of states from receiving government subsidies for their campaigns. To become eligible for matching funds, a candidate had to raise $5000 in contributions of $250 or less in each of twenty states. Thereafter, contributions of up to $250 were matched by an equal amount of government funding. These matching provisions were unique to campaigns for presidential nominations and applied to neither presidential general election nor congressional campaigns. And, to repeat for the sake of emphasis, a candidate's acceptance of matching funds brought restrictions, specifically an overall spending limit for the candidate's nomination campaign and a limit on the amount that s/he could spend in each state (based on each state's population).[5]

The era of the Plebiscitary Model began in 1972, but the matching provisions of the Federal Election Campaign Act of 1974 did not take effect until the 1976 presidential nomination contests. Approximately fifty "serious" candidates sought the Democratic and Republican presidential nominations between 1976 and 1992, and only one—Republican John Connally in 1980, who won only one delegate—did not accept matching funds while campaigning for the presidential nomination.[6] In 1996, the issue of matching funds became significant when a very wealthy but relatively unknown candidate seeking the Republican presidential nomination, Steve Forbes, followed in Connally's footsteps and declined matching funds. In contrast, Republican Bob Dole, the well-known frontrunner for his party's nomination, accepted matching funds and their accompanying spending limits. Forbes poured millions of his own dollars into television advertising, which made Dole spend millions of dollars in response. Dole eventually and somewhat easily prevailed over Forbes and other contenders, but, by late March, 1996, he had spent almost all that he was legally allowed to spend until he was formally nominated by his party's national convention during the summer of 1996. This situation, many observers have noted, left him a sitting duck for several months of effective television advertising launched by the incumbent president, Bill Clinton, who had been unopposed for his party's renomination in 1996. In turn, Dole, who could not buy ads to respond to Clinton's barrage until the summer, fell hopelessly behind his formidable Democratic opponent before being officially nominated.[7]

Recent Changes in the Presidential Nomination Process

Three noteworthy recent changes in the presidential nomination process involve timing and scheduling, campaign financing, and interaction between the two: (1) an earlier start to campaigning and other candidate activities, (2) the introduction of "Super Duper Tuesday" in 2008, and (3) what has been termed the "collapse" of the system of matching funds in the financing of campaigns for the presidential nomination.[8] The first and third changes are not attributable solely to the 2007–2008 nominating cycle; both have their origins in earlier years, most particularly in the 2000 and 2004 contests. The second change, the introduction of "Super Duper Tuesday," stems more specifically from the 2007–08 nominating cycle. What I have termed a *sea change* in the process for nominating presidential candidates has been emerging during at least the two most recent presidential election cycles, while the extent and durability of the changes have become significantly more apparent during the on-going 2007–08 cycle.

An Earlier Start

One change in timing is straightforward and has been much reported: Candidates' serious and visible campaigning for presidential nominations was well under way by the beginning of 2007, a full calendar year before delegate selection processes were scheduled to begin early in the presidential election year of 2008. All sorts of activities associated with candidates' attempts to win their parties' nominations have been occurring earlier than in preceding nomination cycles.

Some candidates seeking to be elected president in 2008 declared their candidacies in late 2006. For example, former two-term Iowa governor Tom Vilsack, more than a political nonentity but less than a putative front-runner in the Democratic party's 2008 presidential nomination competition, announced his candidacy in November 2006 and officially withdrew on 23 February 2007. On the other hand, former Senator Fred

Thompson, whose name surfaced as a potentially formidable candidate for the Republican presidential nomination in the first half of 2007, delayed formal announcement of his candidacy until early September. Commentators wondered why he had waited so long to announce and whether it was too late. Major Democratic contenders John Edwards, Barack Obama, and Hillary Clinton, and major Republican contenders Mitt Romney, Rudy Giuliani, and John McCain all announced their candidacies before March 2007.[9]

Nationally televised debates among Republican and Democratic candidates were in full swing during the first half of 2007. By the summer of 2007, a half-dozen debates among Republican candidates and another half-dozen among Democratic candidates had been aired, with a similar number scheduled to occur in the second half of the year. Six to nine candidates participated in each of these events, which varied in sponsorship (from television stations to labor unions to Howard University) and format (from a single moderator to CNN's YouTube-based venture).

Finally, news media provided extensive coverage of nomination campaigns and the like during the period that used to be called the "invisible primary." Candidates' debate performances, poll results, policy positions, campaign fund-raising efforts, and other "horse race" aspects of the campaign were reported, and systematic comparisons of candidates' proposals on issues such as the Iraq war and health care reform were occasionally provided. In the summer of 2007, *The New York Times* conducted interviews with voters across the United States and reported that they were unusually engaged by the early campaigning as well as "flinching at the onslaught of this early politicking."[10]

The Collapse of the System of Matching Funds

In 2000, Republican candidate George W. Bush was the first presidential nominee of either major party who had not accepted matching funds during his campaign for his party's nomination. In 2003, two leading candidates for the Democratic nomination, Howard Dean and John Kerry, followed Bush's lead of four years earlier and opted out of matching funds. The 1996 predicament of Republican Bob Dole that resulted from his acceptance of matching funds and the accompanying spending limits doubtless influenced later decisions by candidates Bush, Dean, and Kerry. By the start of the 2007–2008 presidential nomination cycle, no major contender for either party's nomination was expected to accept matching funds, although eventually Democrat John Edwards decided to do so. By 2007, the path that Republican nominee Bush had taken in 2000 had become the norm for all but one major candidate. In turn, the system of spending limits that depend on candidates' acceptance of matching funds has been undermined and, in effect, probably ended, at least among major candidates.

Several additional observations about the end of the "old" system of presidential nomination financing are in order. In the absence of spending limits that would have accompanied acceptance of matching funds, fund-raising for 2007–08 presidential nomination campaigns grew enormously. Hillary Clinton's 2007 first quarter total of 26 million dollars and fellow Democrat candidate Barack Obama's close second of 25.6 million can be contrasted with 7.4 million, the total for candidate John Edwards, the leading Democratic fund-raiser in the first quarter of 2003, and 8.9 million, Democratic candidate Al Gore's total in the first quarter of 1999.

The maximum that a candidate could receive in matching funds in the 2007–08 nomination cycle was approximately 21 million dollars. When almost all of the front-running candidates of both parties opted out of the matching system, they were concluding that that amount of partial public funding was not a sufficient reason to accept matching funds. More valuable than 21 million dollars of public funding was the freedom not to abide by the spending limits that accompanied the acceptance of matching funds. Through the end of the third quarter of 2007, Clinton had raised 90.6 million dollars and Obama 80.3 million, while the two candidates who were leading the Republican field in fund-raising, Mitt Romney and Rudy Giuliani, had raised 62.8 million and 45.8 million dollars, respectively.[11]

The demise of the "matching" system for financing campaigns for the presidential nomination cannot be attributed solely to the 2007–08 presidential nomination cycle. Foreshadowed by the predicament in which Republican candidate Bob Dole found himself in March 1996, the "collapse" of the matching system is an early twenty-first century phenomenon that culminated in 2007–08.

The Money Primary

Amidst earlier declarations of candidacy (and, sometimes, withdrawals), earlier and numerous televised debates, earlier extensive media coverage, and the collapse of the system of matching funds, a new term was coined to replace "invisible primary" as a name for the early period of the presidential nomination process—the "money primary." Federal Election Commission (FEC) regulations require quarterly reports of candidates' fund-raising activities in the years preceding presidential general elections (and monthly reports in presidential election years). As 31 March 2007 approached, journalists anticipated the required candidate filings and what they would show in fund-raising prowess and contributors' support. News media reported and analyzed candidates' first-quarter filings with the FEC against a background of different fund-raising expectations for different candidates. On the Democratic side, Barack Obama was judged to have performed especially well, raising 25.6 million dollars, just a little less than front-runner Hillary Clinton and substantially more than John Edward's 14 million. On the Republican side, candidate John McCain fell short of fund-raising expectations and prospects for his candidacy were discounted accordingly, while competitor Mitt Romney's stock rose on account of his first quarter fund-raising total of 20.7 million dollars, six million more than the amount raised by the second-place finisher at that stage of the Republican money primary, Rudy Giuliani.[12]

Through all the changes, news media retained their prominent role as assessors of the nominating competition. Years earlier, when the term *invisible primary* applied, news media had been dubbed the "Great Mentioner" because of their role in identifying candidacies that should be taken seriously. For a candidate not to be mentioned by journalists was like being afflicted with a politically terminal illness. In 2007, news media assessments continued to help the attentive public gauge the ongoing horse race among candidates. Poll results—both national polls and polls in the early caucus and primary states of Iowa, New Hampshire, and South Carolina—and the results of the quarterly "money primaries" were combined with other information and intuitions to make assessments of who was winning, who was gaining or losing ground, and the like. What seemed new in 2007 was the extent of early candidate activity, including the plethora of televised debates in the first half of the year and especially the salience of the "money primary." Campaigns for the two major parties' presidential nominations seemed to be in full swing early in 2007, nearly two years before the November 2008 general election and a year before the states' delegate selection processes were set to begin in Iowa in January 2008.

Super Duper Tuesday and Related Matters

What should probably, because of the earlier start to full-scale campaigning, be called the *2007–2008* presidential nomination process also brought noteworthy change in the clustering of delegate selection processes in the states. During the 1988 presidential nominating process, sixteen mostly Southern states scheduled their delegate selection processes on a single day in early March that was called "Super Tuesday." Such clustering of many states' primaries and caucuses on a single day continued to occur in subsequent years and "Super Tuesday" became a quadrennial event. In 2004, a second, smaller clustering of states on a single Tuesday in March after Super Tuesday was dubbed "mini-Tuesday."

Prior to 2008, the sequence of delegate selection processes in the states during the era of the Plebiscitary Model typically had the following pattern: Iowa; New Hampshire; and, fairly soon thereafter, "Super Tuesday," which grew beyond its original Southern focus to include more non-Southern states. Super Tuesday was sometimes decisive—and sometimes not—in determining eventual presidential nominees, and outcomes in Iowa and especially New Hampshire continued to play disproportionately influential roles.

The phenomenon of Super Tuesday, coupled with a general tendency in the direction of more and more "frontloading," led in 2008 to what was variously dubbed "Super Duper Tuesday," "Tsunami Tuesday," and even "Unofficial National Primary Day." By mid-2007, at least twenty states that together accounted for more than 50% of the delegates to each national convention had scheduled their delegate selection processes for 5 February 2008, a short time after Iowa, New Hampshire, Nevada, and South Carolina were scheduled to hold their delegate selection processes.

As of this writing in November, 2007, the significance of Super Duper Tuesday remains to be seen, but the outcomes of twenty-odd states' delegate selection processes on that day may well be decisive. In other words, 5 February 2008 may become the functional equivalent of a national presidential primary in which, as a consequence of voters casting ballots in at least twenty states *on a single day,* the presidential nominees of both major parties will be determined.

The idea of holding a succession of regional primaries (for example, four of them, each including a contiguous bloc of states in which approximately one-fourth of the population of the United States lives) or a single national primary is not new. Both ideas have been advocated as possible reforms to the presidential nomination process, often with an eye to reducing or eliminating the disproportionate impact of Iowa and New Hampshire. The creation of "Super Duper Tuesday" on 5 February 2008 resulted from decisions by individual states and small groups of states to hold their delegate selection processes on that date, rather than from any single, coordinated reform effort. As the magnitude and implications of "Super Duper Tuesday" came into focus, California, New York, and Florida, among other states, began to re-think the scheduling of *their* 2008 delegate selection processes.

The outline of the Florida story, as of this writing (November, 2007), bears reporting. In May, 2007, the Florida legislature scheduled its presidential primaries for 29 January 2008. Doing so violated both major parties' rule that only Iowa, New Hampshire, Nevada, and South Carolina could hold delegate selection processes before 5 February 2008. In August 2007, the Democratic national party decided that any Florida delegates elected before 5 February 2008 would not be seated at the 2008 Democratic national convention. In late September, the Florida Democratic Party announced its continuing support for holding the Florida presidential primaries on the forbidden 29 January date.[13] The final outcome of this controversy remains to be seen, but one reporter suggested that it might eventually result in the end of Iowa's and New Hampshire's traditional primacy in the presidential nomination calendar.[14]

A Sea Change and a New Era

I have pointed to three recent and significant changes in the presidential nomination process: (1) earlier sustained and public campaigning by candidates, so that public declarations of candidacies and serious campaigning are well underway two years before a presidential general election, (2) the establishment of what may function as an "unofficial national primary" early in February 2008, which reflects the convergence or perhaps even culmination of two earlier trends: (i) increased "frontloading" of the states' delegate selection processes and (ii) growing inclination of states to schedule their delegate selection processes on a single day a few weeks after Iowa and New Hampshire in an attempt to reduce the disproportionate influence of those two states in the outcome of the presidential nomination process, and (3) the demise of the system of matching funds that had anchored the regulation of presidential nomination campaign financing since the passage of the Federal Election Campaign Act in 1974.

What are the implications of these changes? Why might they matter? A simple answer is that these changes will likely affect the sort of individuals who are likely to be nominated and perhaps those who are likely to run. More specifically, the new era, whose beginnings have, in my view, become clearly visible in the 2007–08 cycle, will give the "dark horse," the underdog, the relatively little-known presidential aspirant, less chance to be nominated.

"Dark horses" emerged frequently enough during the "mixed system" era (1912–1968) to make them a staple of political lore. Sometimes such candidates emerged after an unexpectedly strong showing in important primaries, sometimes after party bosses and delegates at a deadlocked convention turned their backs on the two or three leading contenders and sought a "new face" whom supporters of the leading contenders could accept.

Under the Plebiscitary Model, the dramatic increase in the number of delegates chosen by the mass electorate meant that the outcome of early delegate selection processes, especially in Iowa and New Hampshire, led to successful nominations of Democratic dark horse candidates George McGovern and Jimmy Carter in 1972 and 1976, respectively. Little known Democrat Bill Clinton's nomination in 1992 was also a largely unexpected outcome. Yet each won their party's nomination by successfully navigating the sequence of states' delegate selection processes that operated under the Plebiscitary Model. Carter's first-place finish among candidates in Iowa in 1976 ("undecided" was Iowans' first choice), followed by his win in the New Hampshire primary, put the relatively unknown former governor of Georgia on track to be nominated. McGovern's 1972 and Clinton's 1992 successful quests to be nominated followed roughly similar scripts.

Why does the current sea change in the presidential nomination process threaten such dark horse candidacies? Let me begin with the existence of "Super Duper Tuesday," which may function *almost* as a national primary in 2008. So-called retail politics can work in small states such as Iowa and New Hampshire. The little known candidate can, by dint of arduous campaigning, impress attentive Iowa and New Hampshire voters by shaking hands, attending small meetings in people's homes, knocking on doors, and the like. It has been said (almost surely apocryphally) that an Iowa or New Hampshire voter does not take a presidential nomination candidate seriously until the voter has shaken the candidate's hand at least twice! In such a "retail politics" environment, the advantages of initial name recognition, endorsements from leading national political figures, money, and even campaign organization are less important than in the "wholesale politics" required by big state primaries or multiple-state primaries held on a single day. To the extent that "Super Duper Tuesday" approximates a national primary and the wholesale politics that that would entail, the chances of a dark horse or little-known candidate are lessened. Perhaps, as some observers have suggested, the Iowa-New Hampshire-Nevada-South Carolina-Super Duper Tuesday sequence in 2008 will not result in 5 February 2008 functioning as a national presidential primary. Perhaps it will. Regardless, Super Duper Tuesday seems to constitute movement in the direction of a national primary (or at least a series of regional primaries, which would also require wholesale politics), with such a development working to undermine dark horse candidacies.

The collapse of the system of matching funds also seems to disadvantage dark horse or underdog candidacies. Well-known front-runners typically can raise more money than less well-known underdogs. Even so, the matching system worked to narrow the gap between the campaign resources of front-runners and those of underdogs.

The third change in the presidential nomination process that I have identified—the earlier start of full-scale campaigning and resulting news media attention—might on first glance seem to enhance the chances of potential dark horse candidates. The longer the campaigning, it would seem, the more likely an underdog could out-perform better known opponents and overcome their greater resources both over the long haul and in the face of simultaneous contests in a large number of states on "Super Duper Tuesday." In addition, the argument might continue, if such an underdog performed well in the early going, the resource gap between him/her and his/her better known opponents would likely be lessened.

The counter-argument would run in an opposite direction. The superior resources of the front-running candidates and the earlier start to the campaign make it all the more unlikely that an underdog can win. The front-running candidates have more time during which to effectively spend their resources on TV ads and the like, and more time for their larger and better-financed on-the-ground organizations to produce effects. Moreover, news media identification of the top tier of candidates, based partly on the results of the money primary, has longer to sink in with the mass public and, perhaps, become the received wisdom. Finally, the earlier start to serious campaigning means that an underfinanced, underdog candidate needs to compete that much longer against better known, better financed candidates without the prospect of a headline-grabbing victory or at least an unexpectedly strong showing in Iowa or New Hampshire. Instead, the demoralizing effects of the well-publicized money primary undermine underdogs' credibility, often to the point of no return.

As should be clear, I am less certain about the effects of the lengthened nomination campaign season on dark horse candidacies than I am about the effects of an "unofficial national primary" and the demise of the system of matching funds. But, taken as a whole, recent changes in the nomination process that, in my judgment, constitute—or, at the very least, foreshadow—a sea change seem destined to undermine underdog candidacies.

Before closing, let me do one more brief round of "so what?" analysis. Suppose one wanted to change the operation of the Plebiscitary Model to eliminate virtually any chance of underdog candidates such as George McGovern (1972), Jimmy Carter (1976), and, in the 2007–08 cycle, Democrats Tom Vilsack and Chris Dodd and Republicans Tommy Thompson and Sam Brownback, four seasoned politicians with relevant government experience, but little name recognition among the public. To accomplish such an objective, one might introduce the recent changes in the presidential nomination process identified in this article. The latest sea change in the presidential nomination process may relate especially to the sorts of qualities major party presidential nominees need to have. If widespread name recognition and celebrity status—both of which, to be sure, can result from high profile experience in government, a point that sometimes is overlooked—and/or moneyed connections sufficient to raise vast sums of contributions are to be essential characteristics for a presidential nominee, then the nomination process is moving in an accommodating direction.

Perhaps the fifth era in the history of the presidential nomination process will come to be known as "the post-dark horse era," "the celebrity candidate era," "the national (or regional) primary era," or even "the era after the demise of Iowa's and New Hampshire's primacy." Whatever the new era comes to be called and whatever exact shape it takes, please do not say that no one told you it was coming.

Notes

1. The overview of the history of the American presidential nomination process presented here and continued below draws substantially from Bruce Stinebrickner, "The Presidential Nominating Process: Past and Present," *World Review* 19, No. 4 (October 1980), pp. 78–102.

2. The quotation comes from Austin Ranney, as quoted in Stinebrickner, p. 80. Austin Ranney, *Curing the Mischiefs of Faction: Party Reform in America* (Berkeley, California: University of California Press, 1975), p. 121.

3. For a table displaying exact numbers of states using presidential primaries for every presidential election year between 1912 and 2004, see "Table 3-1 Votes Cast and Delegates Selected in Presidential Primaries, 1912–2004," in *Presidential Elections, 1789–2004* (Washington, D.C.: CQ Press, 2005), p. 104.

4. See Arthur T. Hadley, *The Invisible Primary* (Englewood Cliffs, NJ: Prentice Hall, 1976).

5. For more details, see David B. Magleby and William G. Mayer, "Presidential Nomination Finance in the Post-BCRA Era," in William G. Mayer, ed., *The Making of the Presidential Candidates 2008* (Lanham, Maryland: Rowman and Littlefield, 2008), pp. 141–168. The summary of the matching provisions given here is drawn largely from pp. 142–143.

6. Magleby and Mayer, p. 144.

7. This Forbes-Dole-Clinton account is taken largely from Magleby and Mayer, pp. 149–152.

8. Magleby and Mayer use the subtitle "The *Collapse* of the Matching Fund Program" on p. 149 of their chapter (emphasis added). Martin Frost, former member of the U.S. House of Representatives and former chairman of the Democratic Congressional Campaign Committee, observed early in 2007 that it would not be a surprise if the matching system for presidential nomination process financing "simply disappears" after the 2007–08 cycle. "Federal Financing of Presidential Campaigns May Be History," FoxNews.com, 8 January 2007: 23 September 2007, <http://www.foxnews.com>.

9. Announcements signaling a candidacy for a party's 2008 presidential nomination often occurred at more than a single point in time. Several candidates made a combination of announcements, presumably to increase the increments of media attention that such announcements were expected to produce. A single candidate's announcements in 2007 might include the following: that s/he was going to make an "important announcement" in a few days, that s/he was going to begin "exploring" whether to become a candidate (or that s/he was forming an "exploratory committee" to "test the waters"), that s/he had "decided" to become a candidate, and that s/he was "formally" declaring his or her candidacy.

10. Adam Nagourney. "Voters Excited Over '08 Race; Tired of It, Too." *The New York Times*, 9 July 2007, A1.

11. Federal Election Commission: 29 November 2007, http://www.fec.gov/finance/disclosure/srssea.shtml/.

12. "First Quarter 2007 FEC Filings," *Washington Post:* 30 September 2007 <http://projects.washingtonpost.com/2008-presidential-candidates/finance/2007/q1/>.

13. Abby Goodnough, "Florida Democrats Affirm an Early Primary," *The New York Times,* 24 September 2007, A12.

14. "World News", ABC, WRTV, Indianapolis, 24 September 2007, correspondent Jake Tapper: "Democrats are convinced that this is the beginning of the end of the Iowa-New Hampshire monopoly."

I want to thank Luke Beasley, Allison Clem, Annie Glausser, Christina Guzik, Kelsey Kauffman, David Parker, Amy Robinson, and Randall Smith for their helpful comments on an earlier draft of this article. I also want to thank Luke Beasley for his work in locating presidential candidates' announcement dates for the four most recent presidential elections.

An original essay written for this volume. Copyright © 2008 by McGraw-Hill Companies, Contemporary Learning Series.

Still the Chosen One?

For decades, AIPAC has dominated DC's Israel lobby. But a popular president and dissent within the advocacy ranks could lead to a showdown on Middle East policy.

ROBERT DREYFUSS

As two men at the podium called out names in rapid succession, senators and members of Congress rose from their candlelit tables to acknowledge the cheers of 7,000 pro-Israel activists gathered to fete them. The scene was the vast Washington Convention Center; the occasion, the gala banquet capping the annual three-day conference of Washington's most powerful lobbying group, the American Israel Public Affairs Committee. With more than half of Congress attending, and America's top politicians fumbling to score crowd points with awkwardly delivered Hebrew phrases and fulminations concerning Iran, the reading of the names has become a yearly demonstration of AIPAC's clout. Banquet speakers included Joe Biden, Newt Gingrich, and John Kerry, looming on gigantic screens that lined the hall. Representing Israel were President Shimon Peres (whose address was interrupted by a half-dozen Code Pink activists) and, via satellite link, Prime Minister Benjamin Netanyahu. It was a dog and pony show no other group—not the American Medical Association, not the National Rifle Association, not AARP—could hope to match.

For decades, AIPAC—together with Washington's broader Israel lobby, which distributed more than $22 million in campaign contributions during the last election cycle—has had a well-earned reputation for getting what it wants. And many expected the same when, during the May conference, thousands of AIPAC foot soldiers fanned across Capitol Hill to talk up the Iran Refined Petroleum Sanctions Act, a bill designed to throttle Iran's economy by restricting its ability to import gasoline (which it doesn't have much capacity to produce domestically). The legislation is a top priority for AIPAC, which views Iran's nuclear enrichment push as an existential threat to the Jewish state.

But this time, AIPAC was in for a surprise. Rep. Howard Berman, a dependable Israel backer who authored the legislation this past spring, put it on ice just weeks after it was introduced. "I have no intention of moving this bill through the legislative process in the near future," declared the California Democrat, who chairs the powerful House Committee on Foreign Affairs.

"Berman shocked everybody by not moving this bill forward," an official from the Israel lobby told me. "He's essentially put the kibosh on the bill. On his own bill! This is a major, major, *major* problem."

So what happened? The first explanation is obvious: Like many Democrats, Berman is reluctant to stand in the way of President Obama's foreign policy objectives, including his overture to Iran and his push for US leadership toward an Israeli-Palestinian accord. But Berman's action also signaled a deterioration of AIPAC's power. It's begun to appear that "AIPAC is not the 800-pound gorilla everyone says they are," says Dan Fleshier, author of *Transforming America's Israel Lobby*. "They may be just a 400-pound gorilla."

On Capitol Hill, a coalition of groups to the left of AIPAC has been mobilizing Democrats to support Obama's agenda in the Middle East, even if it conflicts with the goals of AIPAC and Netanyahu. "Members of Congress are looking to support the president, and AIPAC hasn't moderated itself as much as it should have," says Patrick Disney, acting legislative director at the National Iranian American Council, which is part of the new coalition.

AIPAC is facing something of a perfect storm. Advocating for stronger ties between the Obama administration and the current right-wing Israeli government would be a difficult chore under any circumstances; on top of that, the megalobby has been weakened by a series of setbacks, including a long-running espionage drama involving two former officials accused of conspiring to pass along classified Pentagon Iran reports to Israel. Charges against the pair were dropped in May, but ripples from the scandal still tainted Rep. Jane Harman (D-Calif.), one of AIPAC's top allies on Capitol Hill, who was caught on a wiretap by the National Security Agency promising a suspected Israeli spy that she would try to get the charges reduced.

Most of all, AIPAC and its allies face a president who is determined to press both Israel and the Palestinians for a deal. He's demanded that Israel halt its expansion of settlements in the West Bank, and in June, alarm bells went off in Israel when Obama, in his long-awaited Cairo speech on US-Muslim relations, expressed sympathy for the plight of the Palestinians in terms rarely used by an American president: "Let there be no doubt: The situation for the Palestinian people is intolerable."

"There is a chance for the most serious dispute between the US and Israel in the entire 61 years of relations between the two," Robert Satloff, executive director of the Israel lobby's chief think tank, the Washington Institute for Near East Policy, told the Israeli newspaper *Haaretz* in May. If Satloff is right, and Obama puts forward a Middle East peace plan that conflicts with the Israeli government's desires, it will prove the severest test yet for AIPAC: Can a popular American president, determined to transform American policy toward West Bank settlements for the first time since 1967, roll over Washington's most powerful lobby?

In a sense, AIPAC and its allies are finding themselves hoist with their own petard. For years, the group has succeeded by gleefully aligning itself with the power of right-wing Republicans and pro-Israel evangelicals, the so-called Christian Zionists, who believe in the end-time and see a role for Israel within their own apocalyptic vision. These alliances proved a winning formula when the Newt Gingrich-led Republicans took over Congress in 1994 and, later, when President George W. Bush unquestioningly backed a series of conservative Israeli governments. But the strategy doesn't look so good anymore. "You do pay a price for having cozied up so intimately and with such apparent relish to the right wing of the Republican Party, to the neocons, and to the Christian right," says Daniel Levy, a senior fellow at the New America Foundation who served as a top negotiator for Israel in 1995 and 2001.

To be sure, it would be a mistake to count AIPAC out. It still has 100,000 members, a $60 million budget, and a $140 million endowment. Some 300 staffers, including an army of lobbyists, work out of 18 AIPAC offices spread across the country; they are tight with State Department and Pentagon bureaucrats, and can call on a vast network of political action committees, campaign contributors, and influentials. At its May conference—event slogan: "Relationships Matter"—AIPAC chose Lee Rosenberg, an Illinois businessman with close ties to Obama, as its next president.

Its name notwithstanding, AIPAC is not a political action committee and does not contribute money directly to political campaigns. The Center for Responsive Politics, however, identifies 31 separate PACs as "pro-Israel" donors. And while independent of AIPAC, many of these organizations look to the mother ship for guidance on which candidates to support. During the 2008 election cycle, according to an analysis conducted for *Mother Jones* by the center, these 31 PACs and their individual donors funneled an eye-popping $22.5 million to various candidates. As detailed in *The Israel Lobby,* a 2007 book by Stephen M. Walt and John J. Mearsheimer that drew withering criticism from Israel hardliners, AIPAC's implicit—if unofficial—endorsement can open the floodgates for these contributions, especially for key candidates in tight races. Last year, Rep. Mark Kirk, a conservative Illinois Republican and AIPAC ally facing a stiff reelection challenge, raked in $407,431 from these sources.

Little surprise, then, that AIPAC is still an agenda setter on Capitol Hill. "If you're looking for a measure of their efficacy," notes a source close to the group, "just take a look at how many members of Congress voted in support of Israel's right to defend themselves from Hamas this January [amid Israel's assault on Gaza]: unanimous in the Senate, and 390-to-5 in the House." In sync with this year's AIPAC conference, 328 House members and three-quarters of the Senate signed the lobby group's letters to Obama, which urged the president to take an Israel-centric approach to Middle East peace and emphasized that "the parties themselves must negotiate the details of any agreement." The letters went on to note that "the proven best way forward is to work closely and privately together" with Israel.

Malcolm Hoenlein—who, as executive vice chairman of the Conference of Presidents of Major American Jewish Organizations, could be described as the unofficial chairman of the Israel lobby—admits that while Obama got three-quarters of the Jewish vote, many influential Jewish activists are upset with the administration's direction. "There are people who are very worried," he says. "I could show you how many emails I get every day, all day long, about all this stuff."

Hoenlein doesn't believe the growing friction between Obama and Netanyahu will lead to a head-to-head test of wills. "It's early," he says of Obama. "The numbers will change. His popularity will go down." That may be true, but AIPAC and its allies face an even broader challenge: The fight over America's Middle East policy is ratcheting up within the Israel lobby itself.

In the tiny, cluttered office warren occupied by the Israel Policy Forum (IPF) in downtown Washington, the group's director of policy analysis, M.J. Rosenberg, waves at a visitor as he wraps up a phone call. Then, slouched on a sofa in shirtsleeves and stocking feet, surrounded by piles of paper, Rosenberg proceeds to blast one of AIPAC's congressional allies, the House minority whip, for the graphic Holocaust imagery he invoked during his speech at the AIPAC convention. "I mean, Eric Cantor gets up there and talks about cattle cars and gas chambers!" Rosenberg tells me. "He's from Virginia! *Virginia!* What the hell is he talking about?"

Rosenberg's organization is one of the pillars of a growing collection of liberal, anti-war Israel policy groups that have emerged to challenge the traditional center-right Israel lobby. Among them are Americans for Peace Now, Brit Tzedek v'Shalom, and a new entry called J Street, founded last year, whose PAC has raised about $600,000 for congressional candidates who are willing to contest the Israeli government's hardline positions.

Of course, compared to the millions of dollars AIPAC can mobilize, the new coalition is far outgunned. But Rosenberg, who worked for AIPAC during the 1980s, argues that it is a paper tiger that capitalizes on perception as much as on reality. "The lobby is kind of like the Wizard of Oz," he explains. "Behind that curtain, there's not very much. It's an illusion." On Capitol Hill, says Rosenberg, support for the group is wide, but not very deep. "They have a couple of people, Jewish members of Congress, who are AIPAC's people on the Hill. Key, respected members—in the current Congress, for instance, Steny Hoyer and Eric Cantor. The broad majority of members look to those

Article 38. Still the Chosen One?

LONESOME DOVES
A Who's who of Holy Land advocacy
—Ben Buchwalter

[Black] = Groups that lobby or hire lobbyists
[Gray] = Other advocacy groups

Hadassah
American Jewish Congress
Rabbinical Assembly
AIPAC
Zionist Organization of America
One Israel Fund
Jewish National Fund
American Jewish Committee
The Israel Project
Ameinu
J Street
Conference of Presidents of Major American Jewish Organizations
Brit Tzedek V'Shalom
New Israel Fund
Republican Jewish Coalition
Jews for Justice for Palestinians
Israel Policy Forum
Friends of the Israel Defense Forces
American Friends of Likud
Jewish Peace Lobby
Jews Against the Occupation
Jewish Voices For Peace
Anti-Defamation League
Americans For Peace Now
Mercaz USA
Jewish Institiue for National Security Affairs
Shalom Center

Dovish ◀──────────────▶ Hawkish

members for guidance: 'Well, this guy is for the resolution; it must be okay with AIPAC, so I'm for it.'" Members reflexively follow AIPAC, says Rosenberg, because they don't want to be hassled by the Israel lobby, and nobody else in the debate carries near the same clout.

The game changer, he says, is Obama. "I don't believe that many members would follow AIPAC rather than the president of the United States if the president of the United States calls," Rosenberg explains. And thanks to decades of gerrymandering, he says, many lawmakers are so secure in their districts that there's not that much AIPAC could do to unseat them, even with its vast contributor network.

Jeremy Ben-Ami, the slight and soft-spoken executive director of J Street, says the change on Capitol Hill is palpable. More and more members of Congress see AIPAC as an obstacle to America's crucial national interest—a durable Middle East peace deal. "Our role is to demonstrate that there is significant and meaningful political support for leadership to achieve peace," Ben-Ami says.

In January, when Obama named former Senate Majority Leader George Mitchell as his special Middle East envoy, J Street got 104 legislators to sign a statement supporting Mitchell. (The traditional Israel lobby views Mitchell, in the words of the Anti-Defamation League's Abraham Foxman, as a little too "even-handed.") In May, when AIPAC's warning letter to Obama began amassing signatures in the House—it ultimately got 328—J Street and its allies put out a competing House letter calling for strong American leadership that accumulated 86 names. "There are a number of members of Congress who are seeking out new voices on the issue," says Rep. Donna Edwards (D-Md.), one of those 86, who visited Israel, the West Bank, and Gaza in May. "There is still a resistance to having open, honest dialogue out of fear about being on the wrong side of AIPAC, but I'm not going to be driven by what one lobby says. What I learned on my trip is that I don't think AIPAC represents even the majority view in Israel."

Netanyahu, who made a pilgrimage to Capitol Hill last spring after meeting with Obama, discovered the emerging new reality firsthand. The *Forward,* a Jewish newspaper based in Manhattan, quoted the prime minister's aides as saying their boss was "stunned" by "what seemed like a well-coordinated attack against his stand on settlements," even from traditional Israel supporters like John Kerry (D-Mass.), who chairs the Senate Committee on Foreign Relations, and Carl Levin (D-Mich.), chair of the Senate Armed Services Committee—as well as representatives Berman and Henry Waxman (D-Calif.). While all have impeccable credentials with the Israel lobby, it's clear that they're increasingly unhappy with Jerusalem's hard-right tilt. And when legislators can point to different views within the Israel policy community, it's harder for groups like AIPAC to accuse them of being anti-Israel.

All the while, Obama has been cementing his Jewish support—as a senior public relations specialist with close ties to the Israeli Embassy groused to me. "I mean, look at the agenda!" the official said. "He went to the Holocaust Museum on Holocaust Memorial Day, and then he declared Jewish Cultural Awareness Month, which is, you know, Bagels Month, and then he had Passover at the White House, which makes all the cultural Jews, the reform Jews, go, 'Oh my God, he's our guy! Seder in the White House, Bagel Month, Passover at the White House!'"

Says Levy, the former Israel negotiator, "I think they're nervous that if there's a showdown, where do the Jews go? And I think it's clear where the majority of the Jews would go. They'd go with Obama."

What happens next with America's Middle East policy will depend on whether Obama can advance an Israel-Palestine compromise as a critical US interest. This would be a sharp break from the past, when US negotiators often ended up in the role of "Israel's lawyer," in the words of Aaron David Miller, who helped oversee the peace process under President Clinton.

This is a key moment in the debate, says Walt, coauthor of *The Israel Lobby.* "It will be important whether he gets enough cover from J Street and the Israel Policy Forum so Obama

ANNUAL EDITIONS

Some Movers and Shakers of America's Israel Policy
Stars of David

Top Dogs

Howard Kohr AIPAC head honcho since 1996, he ranked sixth on *GQ*'s 2007 list of DC's 50 most powerful, besting Hillary Clinton and Karl Rove.

Malcolm Hoenlein Israel lobby's unofficial boss; heads the Conference of Presidents of Major American Jewish Organizations, representing 52 pro-Israel groups.

David Harris Longtime leader of the 103-year-old American Jewish Committee, which took heat in 2007 for an essay claiming liberal Jewish critics of Israel were feeding anti-Semitism.

Other Notables

Matthew Mark Horn and **Marc Stern** took over the American Jewish Congress just before Madoff scandal gutted it.
Abraham Foxman, Anti-Defamation League
John Hagee, Christians United for Israel

The Right

Morton Klein Head of the fringe, 112-year-old Zionist Organization of America. Claimed Obama "may become the most hostile president to Israel ever."

Daniel Pipes Director of Middle East Forum (MEF), Pipes insisted last year that Obama was once a Muslim and that his campaign was "ignorant or fabricating" when it said he'd never prayed in a mosque.

Other Notables

Steve Rosen Blogger for MEF's *Obama Mideast Monitor;* indicted in AIPAC espionage scandal.

The Neocons

Norman Podhoretz At 79, the former editor of neoconservative Jewish magazine—*Commentary* has been called the movement's godfather. In 2007, he told *Politico* he had secretly lobbied President Bush to bomb Iran's nuclear facilities.

Elliott Abrams Podhoretz's son-in-law now works at the Council on Foreign Relations. A Reagan staffer during Iran-Contra, he later pled guilty to withholding information from Congress.

Other Notables

Tom Neumann, Jewish Institute for National Security Affairs
Richard Perle Having cheered the Iraq invasion, an unrepentant Perle now blames Obama for Iran's election fiasco: "When you unclench your fist, it benefits the hardliners."

The Wonks

Robert Satloff Heads Washington Institute for Near East Policy (WINEP), DC's leading pro-Israel think tank. In 2008, called Jimmy Carter America's "most embarrassing ex-somebody" for hugging a senior Hamas official.

Martin Indyk A former AIPAC man, he was ambassador to Israel under President Clinton and is now at the liberal Brookings Institution.

Douglas Feith The Rumsfeld underling whose disastrous oversight of the Iraq War led *Slate* to dub him "Undersecretary of Defense for Fiascos" now directs the Center for National Security Strategies at the Hudson Institute.

Other Notables

Danielle Pletka, American Enterprise Institute (AEI)
Paul Wolfowitz, AEI

The Left

Jeremy Ben-Ami His grandparents were among the first Jewish settlers in Tel Aviv. Last year, Ben-Ami cofounded J Street, DC's leading liberal Israel policy lobby.

M.J. Rosenberg A former AIPAC official turned critic, he has been with Israel Policy Forum since 1998.

Other Notables

Debra DeLee, Americans for Peace Now
Daniel Levy, New America Foundation

The Pols

Sen. Carl Levin (D-Mich.) Since 1989, has received more cash from pro-Israel groups than any senator except Joe Lieberman.

Rep. Gary Ackerman (D-N.Y.) In 2007, crossed party lines to stop Congress from limiting the president's ability to attack Iran.

Sen. Chuck Schumer (D-N.Y.) Tight with AIPAC, Schumer strongly criticized Chas Freeman, Obama's first National Intelligence Council nominee, as not pro-Israel enough—until Freeman withdrew his name. "I repeatedly urged the White House to reject him, and I am glad they did the right thing," Schumer later said.

Other Notables

Senators Joe Lieberman (I-Conn.) and **John Kerry (D-Mass.); representatives Steny Hoyer (D-Md.), Jane Harman (D-Calif.), Eric Cantor (R-Va.), Howard Berman (D-Calif.), and Henry Waxman (D-Calif.)**

The Obama Team

Dennis Ross WINEP alum and diplomat under Clinton and H.W. Bush, Ross now sits on the National Security Council and serves as Obama's special assistant.

Rahm Emanuel Attended camp in Israel as a kid and briefly volunteered on an Israeli base during the Gulf War. Emanuel made a point of endorsing Obama just after the candidate's AIPAC speech, and, as White House chief of staff, has met with AIPAC high rollers to sell them on his boss' policies. "Obviously, he will influence the president to be pro-Israel," said his Jerusalem-born father. "What is he, an *Arab?*"

Article 38. Still the Chosen One?

Stars of David (continued)

Other Notables
George Mitchell, special Middle East envoy
  Dan Shapiro, National Security Council
  Jeff Feltman A senior US diplomat who works with Shapiro on Syria relations

The Opposition
James Zogby A former Jesse Jackson adviser, he founded the Arab American Institute in 1985 and is still its president. In 2007, he was targeted by a midlevel US diplomat whose career ended after he left the institute abusive voice mails and emails: "Fuck the Arabs and fuck James Zogby and his wicked Hezbollah brothers."

Other Notables
Mary Rose Oakar, American-Arab Anti-Discrimination Committee
Samar Assad, Jerusalem Fund/Palestine Center
Ziad Asali, American Task Force on Palestine

The Media
Bill Kristol Founding editor of the *Weekly Standard,* he favors a hardball approach. "It's all fair and nice to talk about this peace process," he said of Obama's Cairo speech, "but he has increased the chances of an Israeli strike on Iran, and sooner rather than later."

Other Notables
Marty Peretz, WINEP board member and editor of *The New Republic*
  Fred Hiatt, *Washington Post* op-ed page editor
  Charles Krauthammer, *Washington Post* columnist
  Bret Stephens, *Wall Street Journal* columnist

---

can say, 'AIPAC is not representative of the American Jewish community.' But I must say, I'm not wildly optimistic about this. I don't know if Obama is really ready to buck them."

The power struggle comes down to "who will do a better job of interfering in the other's politics," says David Mack, a deputy assistant secretary of state under George H.W. Bush who spent decades as a diplomat in the region. "Bibi [Netanyahu] is very good at this. He really knows how to play the American game. He knows how to line up various groups, right-wing hawks, right-wing evangelicals, the military industrial complex, and the right wing of the American Jewish community."

But Mack suggests that Obama might have a few tricks up his own sleeve—including an array of allies with solid Israel contacts who can be deployed to muster support in Israeli politics and media. Among them, Mack says, are former ambassadors to Israel Samuel Lewis, Daniel Kurtzer, and Martin Indyk, as well as Rahm Emanuel, Obama's chief of staff, who volunteered on an Israeli supply base during the Gulf War, and Dennis Ross, a White House adviser who spent years at the hawkish Washington Institute for Near East Policy.

In the six decades of Israel's existence, there have been few full-fledged confrontations between an American president and the Israel lobby. In the early 1980s, after Ronald Reagan decided to sell an advanced airborne radar system to Saudi Arabia, he won a showdown with AIPAC. A decade later, George H.W. Bush and James Baker, his secretary of state, threatened to withhold loan guarantees for Israel to pressure the Jewish state over the peace process; they stared down AIPAC, contributing to the collapse of a right-wing government in Israel.

But those were only skirmishes. What's at stake today is what many observers believe is the last best hope for a peace accord, one that will require Israel to remove hundreds of thousands of settlers, withdraw from the West Bank, and accept at least some Palestinian authority in now occupied East Jerusalem. The nation's most formidable lobby can huff and it can puff, but if it resists, it may be its own house that gets blown down.

From *Mother Jones*, September/October 2009, pp. 43–47. Copyright © 2009 by Mother Jones. Reprinted by permission of the Foundation for National Progress.

Article 39

Don't Call Them Lobbyists

The Obama Administration aimed to reduce the power of K Street, but Washington's influence brokers have proved adept at adapting their tactics to the shifting landscape.

THEO FRANCIS AND STEVE LEVINE

Despite the rhetoric of the past 18 months, few in the nation's capital really believed the Beltway lobbyist would disappear overnight just because a new President vowed to change business-as-usual in Washington and Congress heightened scrutiny. Yes, lobbyists now must heed stringent new disclosure rules; the gift-giving and golf outings have largely vanished. But the influence game rolls on in Obama's Washington.

That isn't to say, of course, that nothing has changed. The Democrats have set in motion a landslide of potentially transformative legislation: an overhaul of the U.S. health-care system; a sweeping energy and climate-change bill; new regulations to rein in the financial markets; and more. "There are a lot of challenges for business," says Steve Elmendorf, a longtime aide to former House Democratic Leader Dick Gephardt who now runs his own lobbying firm. "When there are challenges, they hire help."

Elmendorf says businesses are hiring lobbyists to help with "a lot of challenges."

With so much legislation and so many new rules, many K Streeters are adjusting their playbooks. One lobbyist says that where a client once hired two firms—one Republican, one Democrat—it now may hire five, including specialists for each house of Congress and at least one big-picture strategist. Twitter, Facebook, and sophisticated Web sites have become de rigueur tools of influence. And lobbyists are looking to cooperate more often with lawmakers—or at least appear to be doing so—rather than simply training their guns on bills they deem hostile.

At a time when lobbying is under assault, the most effective practitioner is sometimes someone who technically isn't a lobbyist. The rules say lobbyists must register with the feds if they call or visit lawmakers, staff, or key Administration officials to influence policy at least twice in a quarter—and also spend at least 20% of their time for any given client on "lobbying-related" activities. Registering as a lobbyist nowadays is "like walking around with a scarlet letter," says a lobbying-law specialist. That helps explain why more lobbyists are deregistering and setting up shop as arm's-length strategists. These people don't contact lawmakers or Administration officials on behalf of clients, but instead offer an insider's insight into which lawmakers are likely to be most receptive to what arguments and how procedural battles could play out. Such advice is in demand as companies and business groups sort out how to tackle multiple issues at once. "There's more of a premium on strategic thinking now," says John Jonas, a registered lobbyist who established the health-care practice at lobbying powerhouse Patton Boggs.

Thomas A. Daschle, the former Senate majority leader, now serves as a "special policy adviser" and strategist at Alston & Bird, focusing in part on health care and financial services. He never registered as a lobbyist. Former Bush Administration counselor Ed Gillespie, a lobbyist for most of the past decade, opted not to reregister this year. Instead he has started Ed Gillespie Strategies, offering companies "strategic planning," "message development," and "crisis management." He declined to comment for this story. Daschle says he doesn't lobby directly but lends others insight into legislative terrain and the tendencies of lawmakers he knows well.

Sometimes these "strategic" lobbyists suggest that their clients do the schmoozing themselves, as meeting with a company CEO is often more palatable to lawmakers than lunching with lobbyists. The Managed Funds Assn., which represents hedge funds, has stepped up its fly-ins. The National Association of Manufacturers recently brought in more than 300 executives. 3M is also among those sending executives more often, says John Woodworth, who oversees the company's supply chain. "It sends more of a message if you're willing to spend your time," Woodworth says.

Lobbyists are increasingly taking the fight to the people—or, at least, to their own people. This month the American Farmland Trust, a relatively small farm lobby focused on conservation,

Lobbying's Big Spenders

Percentage change in lobbying expenditures by top U.S. organizations, first-half 2008 vs. first-half 2009

Company/organization	Increase
American Wind Energy Assn.	403%
Dow Chemical	119
ConocoPhillips	108
CVS/Caremark	108
Chevron	104

Data: Center for Responsive Politics

plans to mobilize its 30,000 members to urge Farm Belt senators to support the cap-and-trade bill. Using articles in trade publications, talk-radio appearances, Twitter, and Facebook, the group aims to win the backing of rural-state senators, some of whom are concerned about how the measure would affect fuel costs as well as electricity prices in states heavily dependent on coal power.

Bipac, the country's oldest business lobby, says interest in grassroots campaigns has picked up sharply of late. "To the degree this town becomes more difficult for lobbyists to have face time with policymakers, there's going to have to be another way for them to make their message known," says President and CEO Gregory S. Casey. Murphy Oil, an El Dorado (Ark.) oil and gas company, has affixed tear-off leaflets to its gas pumps. The leaflets warn that the "current legislative proposals could cause gas prices to increase at least 60%" and direct customers to a Web site operated with Bipac's help. The site offers arguments against the cap-and-trade bill—and Casey says half its visitors click to e-mail lawmakers on the issue.

Tried-and-true tactics still work, of course. In late June, power industry lobbyists managed to get a last-minute amendment slapping tariffs on steel and other carbon-intensive imports into climate-change legislation. But the K Street crowd is less likely now to try killing legislation outright. "The smart strategy is getting taken care of, or getting [lawmakers] to go in a different direction," says Jonas, the Patton Boggs lobbyist. By signing on to White House health-reform efforts, he says, the pharmaceutical industry transformed itself "from Public Enemy No. 1 to the tolerated in-law." One by one, other health-care organizations have followed suit. Appearing cooperative is the new name of the game.

"There's a fair amount of rhetoric around things that all of us think are important, like climate change, health care, the economy. The actual content is completely different than what most of us are hearing. Most of this is generating incredible deficits for our children; most of it is happening much too quickly in the wrong ways. On fiscal stimulus, on climate change, on health care, we don't like what's happening. It's not just against the oil industry. It's doesn't make sense for America."
—James Hackett, CEO, Anadarko Petroleum

"I would say Obama's health-care reform is making more progress than a lot of people would have predicted. We're on the verge of a bill coming out of the House that's clearly going to happen. Nobody seems to have walked away from the table yet. Well, some have walked away from the table. But there's still a lot of people working."
—Jeffrey B. Kindler, CEO, Pfizer

"For the near-term crisis, the Treasury and Federal Reserve actions have been very good. We were staring into the abyss. The possibility of Armageddon was there. [Yet] the stimulus package they put through, which was crucial to the turnaround, is failing. It is embarrassing when China does a stimulus package more effectively than we can, and we are a free enterprise system."
—Mike Jackson, CEO, AutoNation

CEO reporting was organized and led by chief of correspondents Joseph Weber and Los Angeles correspondent Chris Palmeri. Other contributors: Michael Arndt, Amy Barrett, Matthew Boyle, Peter Burrows, Nanette Byrnes, Kerry Capell, John Carey, Tania Chen, Roger Crockett, Cliff Edwards, Peter Elstrom, Dean Foust, Ron Grover, Burt Helm, Arik Hesseldahl, Rob Hof, David Kiley, Jena McGregor, Arlene Weintraub, Lauren Young

---

With Jane Sasseen, Elise Craig, and Keith Epstein in Washington.

From *BusinessWeek*, August 10, 2009, pp. 43–44. Copyright © 2009 by BusinessWeek. Reprinted by permission of the McGraw-Hill Companies.

Article 40

Born Fighting

RONALD BROWNSTEIN

Apart from his political skills, two forces above all have propelled Barack Obama in his once-improbable quest for the presidency.

One is on vivid display this week: a wave of dissatisfaction with the country's direction that has created a visceral demand for change. That wave has reached towering heights amid the financial crisis roiling Wall Street and consuming Washington. No other candidate has drawn more power than Obama has from that desire to shift course.

With much less fanfare, this week also marked a milestone in the evolution of the second force that has lifted Obama: the rise of the Internet as a political tool of unparalleled power for organizing a vast activist and donor base.

Ten years ago this week, Wes Boyd and Joan Blades, two California-based software developers (their company created the "Flying Toaster" screensaver), posted an online petition opposing the drive by congressional Republicans to impeach President Clinton. The one-sentence petition urged Congress instead to censure Clinton and "move on." Within days the couple had collected hundreds of thousands of names. Thus was formed MoveOn.org, the first true 21st-century political organization.

Born fighting, MoveOn has become the point of the spear for the Democratic Left through eight years of combat with President Bush over issues from Iraq to Social Security. No group has been more influential, innovative, or controversial in devising the Internet-based organizing strategies that are precipitating the new age of mass political participation symbolized by Obama's immense network of contributors and volunteers. "In the evolution of this, they were there at the very beginning," says veteran Democratic strategist Joe Trippi.

MoveOn's political impact must be measured on two levels: message and mechanics. The group's techniques draw praise in both parties. Boyd and Blades, and later Eli Pariser, a young organizer who has become MoveOn's leading force, recognized that the Internet created unprecedented opportunities for organizing. Traditionally, causes and candidates faced daunting expenses in trying to find like-minded people through advertising, direct mail, or canvassing. But the Internet reversed the equation: Once MoveOn established itself at the forefront of liberal activism, millions of people who shared its views found it at little (or no) cost to the group.

"Our observation was: Whenever we fight, we get stronger."

—Wes Boyd, MoveOn.org founder

Indeed, MoveOn quickly discovered that the more fights it pursued, the more names it collected—and the more it increased its capacity to undertake new campaigns. "There's this old model of political capital: Every time you fight, you are spending something," Boyd says. "Our observation was: Whenever we fight, we get stronger."

Fueled by this dynamic, MoveOn routinely generates levels of activity almost unimaginable not long ago. Since 1998, it has raised $120 million; it mobilized 70,000 volunteers for its get-out-the-vote effort in 2004, and might triple that number this year. It now stands at 4.2 million members, after adding 1 million, mostly through social-networking sites, this year.

The purposes to which MoveOn applies these vast resources are more debatable. The group has become a favored target for Republicans and a source of anxiety for some Democratic centrists, who worry that it points the party too far left. On domestic issues, it fits within the Democratic mainstream. But on national security, it defines the party's left flank. MoveOn resisted military action not only in Iraq but also in Afghanistan. And on both foreign and domestic concerns, it often frames issues in terms so polarizing that it risks alienating all but the most committed believers. The group's lowest moment came in 2007 when it bought a newspaper ad disparaging Gen. David Petraeus, the U.S. commander in Iraq, as "General Betray Us" on the grounds that he would attempt to mislead Congress about the war. Petraeus's brilliant subsequent progress in stabilizing

Iraq has only magnified the unseemliness of that accusation. "I wouldn't have done the headline the exact same way," Pariser now concedes.

Still, as candidates and groups in both parties adapt its strategies for online organizing, MoveOn can justly claim a central role in igniting the surge in grassroots activism that is transforming American politics. "Regardless of your political convictions, you have to feel like this is a very healthy thing for democracy," Pariser says. MoveOn's causes may divide, but Democrats and even many Republicans are increasingly uniting around the bottom-up vision of political change that these ardent activists have helped to revive.

Reprinted by permission from *National Journal,* September 27, 2008, p. 78. Copyright © 2008 by National Journal Group Inc. All rights reserved.

Article 41

Why They Lobby

WINTER CASEY

Thank You for Smoking, the 2005 film based on a novel by Christopher Buckley, follows the life of Nick Naylor, a chief spokesman for Big Tobacco with questionable morals, who makes his living defending the rights of smokers and cigarette-makers and then must deal with how his young son, Joey, views him. Naylor may have been a fictitious character, but Washington has its share of lobbyists arguing for the interests of industries with a perceived darker side.

The cynical response in Washington is that career decisions and political give-and-take revolve around money: Greenbacks triumph over ethics. There is little argument from lobbyists that their profession's financial rewards have an undeniable allure. But those who represent socially sensitive industries such as tobacco and alcohol have a lot more to say about why, out of all the potential job opportunities, they chose and often "love" what they do.

> Representing "sin" industries, such as tobacco, alcohol, or gambling, can provide a challenge like no other.

For some, the job is a result of personal history or connections. For others, lobbying on behalf of a difficult industry provides a challenge like no other. They all make it a point to note that the First Amendment sanctions lobbying: "the right of the people . . . to petition the government for a redress of grievances."

Tobacco

In the film, Naylor works for the Academy of Tobacco Studies, which Buckley based on the Tobacco Institute, the industry's former trade association. Andrew Zausner, a partner at the firm Dickstein Shapiro (which occupies some of the Tobacco Institute's old space), is a registered lobbyist for Lorillard Tobacco, the Cigar Association of America, and Swisher International. He has been working on behalf of tobacco clients for nearly 30 years, ever since he fell into the industry when he was a partner at a New York City law firm that represented Pinkerton Tobacco.

Zausner feeds off the challenge of lobbying for tobacco interests. "The more unpopular the client, the better you have to be as a lobbyist," he declares. "Believing in your client's position makes you a more forceful advocate." Although Zausner doesn't want his children to use tobacco, he notes that the "product has been continuously used in the United States before the United States existed" and says that the industry has a legitimate point of view and a constitutional right to express it.

Beau Schuyler lobbies for UST Public Affairs, a subsidiary of the holding company that owns U.S. Smokeless Tobacco and Ste. Michelle Wine Estates. A former congressional aide to two Democratic House members from his native state of North Carolina—in the heart of tobacco country—Schuyler says that the "opportunity to work internally at one of the oldest continually listed companies on the New York Stock Exchange was just too good to pass up."

Gambling

James Reeder, a lobbyist at Patton Boggs, has spent about half his time over the past decade representing the gambling industry. He insists he didn't seek out this niche, adding, "I tell my grandchildren that gambling is a bad habit . . . and to go fishing."

Shortly after Reeder joined Patton Boggs, a client named Showboat called the firm looking for someone who knew about Louisiana because the company was interested in building a casino there. Reeder happened to be from the Pelican State and was put on the case. He reasoned that Louisiana has always been a home to illegal gambling, and "if the culture of the state supports the industry, [the state] might as well make it legal and reap the benefits and get more tax money." Reeder eventually lobbied in about 17 states to get legislation passed to allow casinos—then mostly on riverboats.

"Whenever you take on one of these vices like booze or gambling and you just pass a law to say it is illegal," Reeder says, "you end up like in Prohibition, when the mob took over the liquor business."

Reeder excelled at lobbying for the gambling industry even though he avoids games of chance. "I don't gamble, because I am not a good card player," he says. "My friends would die laughing because I would go to offices to talk to clients on gambling and I would never go into a casino." If a lawmaker was morally opposed to gambling, Reeder wouldn't argue with him, he says.

John Pappas began working for the industry as a consultant for the Poker Players Alliance while at Dittus Communications. Then the alliance asked him to open its own Washington office.

Pappas calls poker a game of skill that has a rich history in America. He grew up playing cards with family members and friends, and noted during an interview that he would be playing poker with 20 lawmakers that evening at a charity tournament. "Responsibility in all aspects of life is paramount," he says.

Firearms

Richard Feldman's book, *Ricochet: Confessions of a Gun Lobbyist*, has been gaining the former National Rifle Association employee some attention recently. Feldman says that the gun control issue, like most, is not black and white. Working for the NRA, he says, "was the best job I ever had." The "huge power" he was able to wield "in the middle of major political battles" was more attractive to him at the time than the money he earned.

Feldman says he would sometimes play hardball but "didn't hit below the belt" in his pursuit of the gun industry's objectives. "Lobbying an issue that you have some special passion on (guns) is like waking up every day already having consumed a triple espresso," he said in an e-mail to *National Journal*. "On the other hand, if you can empathize with your client's position regardless of the issue, one can be a more convincing advocate, which I've always viewed as the more critical aspect of truly effective lobbying."

John Velleco ran his own painting company before he took a job in 1993 as an intern at the Gun Owners of America. Today, he is director of federal affairs for the 350,000-member group. "Most people, no matter what side of any particular issue they're on, don't always have the time to sort through what's happening in the D.C. sausage factory, so they depend on groups like GOA to keep them informed," he says. "Politicians may not like it, but my job is not to represent the views of the Congress to the people, but the views of American gun owners to the Congress."

Video Games

Because many video games contain a fair share of gunplay and other violence, Entertainment Software Association President Michael Gallagher has had to address complaints that playing violent games causes psychological harm such as increased aggression.

His group lobbies against "efforts to regulate the content of entertainment media in any form, including proposals to criminalize the sale of certain video games to minors; create uniform, government-sanctioned entertainment rating systems; or regulate the marketing practices of industry."

Gallagher, a former assistant Commerce secretary for communications and information in the Bush administration, calls video games a great form of family entertainment. The titles are responsibly rated, he says, and the gaming consoles have easy-to-use parental controls.

"I have been playing video games all my life," Gallagher says, including with his children. He contends that his industry "leads all forms of media when it comes to disclosure on what's in the game" and says that it works with retailers to "make sure minors can't buy games that are inappropriate for them."

Alcohol

Lobbyists who work for the beer, wine, and spirits industries have to deal with a host of negative images, among them drunk-driving accidents, underage drinking, and the effects of alcohol on health.

> **Lobbyists say their work is protected by the First Amendment—the right to "petition the government for a redress of grievances."**

Mike Johnson, a lobbyist for the National Beer Wholesalers Association, acknowledges that alcohol is a "socially sensitive product" and says that is why the industry operates under strict government guidelines.

"I am blessed. I get to represent some great family-owned and -operated businesses that are very active in their communities and provide some really great jobs," Johnson says. "I am completely comfortable one day having a conversation with my son about who I work for, because I can tell him what a great job that beer distributors do in ensuring a safe marketplace and in protecting consumers from a lot of the problems we see with alcohol in other places in the world."

Craig Wolf, president of the Wine & Spirits Wholesalers, calls alcohol a "great social lubricant" that "creates great environments." Wolf got involved in wine-industry issues when he was counsel for the Senate Judiciary Committee. As his job there was ending, Wolf was offered the post of general counsel at the association; he took over as president in 2006.

"The key to advocating for a socially sensitive product is doing business responsibility," Wolf says. "We spend more time and resources [on the issue of] responsible consumption of alcohol then all other issues combined."

Distilled Spirits Council President Peter Cressy says, "I was interviewed for this position precisely because the Distilled Council wanted to continue and increase its very serious approach to fighting underage drinking." As chancellor of the University of Massachusetts (Dartmouth), Cressy says, he was active in "fighting binge drinking on campuses." The opportunity to join the council, which has lobbyists in 40 states, gave him the chance to have a national audience, he says. After nine years with the council, Cressy notes, he "has not been disappointed."

Snack Foods

Nicholas Pyle stands at the policy divide where junk food meets America's bulging waistlines. "I love my job," says Pyle, a lobbyist for McKee Foods, the makers of Little Debbie, America's leading snack-cake brand.

Many of the brand's affordable treats contain a dose of sugar, along with corn syrup, partially hydrogenated oil, bleached flour, and artificial flavor. Little Debbie "has been the target of a number of folks out there who want to paint people as a victim of the foods they eat," says Pyle, who is also president of the Independent Bakers Association. Little Debbie is a "wonderful food, great product, wholesome," with a wonderful image, he says. Pyle explains that he and his children enjoy the snacks.

"The big question of obesity is all about personal responsibility and people balancing [snacking] with a healthy and active lifestyle," Pyle insists. He contends that McKee, a family-owned business, doesn't target children in its marketing. "We market to the decision makers in the household," he says, adding that the company doesn't advertise on Saturday morning cartoon shows.

Snack Food Association President and CEO Jim McCarthy says that lobbying is one of his many duties as head of the organization. "Our belief is that all foods fit into the diet," McCarthy says, and "we don't like the term 'junk food.'" Products made by his segment of the industry—which include potato chips, party mix, corn snacks, snack cakes, and cookies—all contain natural ingredients such as vegetables, nuts, and fruit, he says.

The industry has developed healthier products over the years, McCarthy says, but at "certain times consumers haven't bought these products." He attributes the obesity problem to a lack of exercise and shortcomings in educating people about the need for a balanced diet.

Challenging Stereotypes

No matter what industry they represent, lobbyists interviewed for this article said that a good practitioner of their profession knows all sides of an issue, enabling lawmakers and their staffs to make the best-informed decision. "The system weeds out the bad actors, and the honest folks are the most successful and the longest-lasting," one lobbyist says.

Although many of the lobbyists acknowledge some familiar situations in *Thank You for Smoking,* they insist that the stereotypes are not altogether fair. "I think people don't understand the importance of lobbying to the system. If I don't explain what we do and I am not here to explain it to people, Congress will make uninformed decisions without understanding the consequences to the industry," a former liquor lobbyist says.

"Everyone draws the line in the sand about what they will or will not work on," says Don Goldberg, who leads the crisis communications practice at Qorvis Communications and was a key player on President Clinton's damage-response team. "The line is not set in stone.

"If you don't believe the points you are arguing are the best argument for your client and also that it's truthful, then you shouldn't be in this business," Goldberg continues. "I strongly believe in the First Amendment, [but] I don't believe the First Amendment is the reason to take on clients. The reason to take on clients is, they have a good story to tell and they are honest and reputable organizations."

But James Thurber, director of the Center for Congressional and Presidential Studies at American University, says that at the end of the day, money is a good explanation for why many lobbyists end up in their positions. This is especially true when it comes to tobacco, which was the leading preventable cause of disease and death in the United States in 2007, according to the Centers for Disease Control and Prevention.

For consumers, the message that lobbyists appear to be sending is that the individual is responsible for making the right choices in life. Yet the profusion of advertising, marketing ploys, political rhetoric, and seemingly conflicting studies can be bewildering. And although the financial incentive is ever-present, lobbyists believe they fill a fundamental role in society and deserve some relief from the negative stereotypes.

Reprinted by permission from *National Journal,* May 31, 2008, pp. 46–48. Copyright © 2008 by National Journal Group Inc. All rights reserved.

Article 42

The Revolution Will Not Be Published

Why we must shift our attention from "save newspapers" to "save society."

CLAY SHIRKY

In 1993 the Knight-Ridder newspaper chain began investigating piracy of Dave Barry's popular column, which was published by the *Miami Herald* and syndicated widely. In the course of tracking down the sources of unlicensed distribution, they found many things, including the copying of his column on usenet; a 2,000-person mailing list also reading pirated versions; and a teenager in the Midwest who was doing some of the copying himself, because he loved Barry's work so much he wanted everybody to be able to read it.

One of the people I was hanging around with online back then was Gordy Thompson, who managed Internet services at the *New York Times*. I remember Thompson saying something like, *When a 14-year-old kid can blow up your business in his spare time, not because he hates you but because he loves you, then you got a problem.*

I think about that conversation a lot these days.

The problem newspapers face isn't that they didn't see the Internet coming. They not only saw it miles off, they figured out early on that they needed a plan to deal with it, and during the early '90s they came up with not just one scheme but several.

One was to partner with companies like America Online, a fast-growing subscription service that was less chaotic than the open Internet. Another approach was to educate the public about the behaviors required of them by copyright law. New payment models such as micropayments were proposed. Alternatively, newspapers could pursue the profit margins enjoyed by radio and TV, if they became purely ad-supported. Still another plan was to convince tech firms to make their hardware and software less capable of sharing, or to partner with the businesses running data networks to achieve the same goal. Then there was the nuclear option: educate the public about copyright law and sue those who break it, making an example of them.

In all this conversation, there was one scenario that was widely regarded as unthinkable: that the ability to share content wouldn't shrink, it would grow.

Walled-off content would prove unpopular. Digital advertising would reduce inefficiencies, and therefore profits. Dislike of micropayments would prevent widespread use. People would resist being educated to act against their own desires. Old habits of advertisers and readers would not transfer online. Even ferocious litigation would be inadequate to constrain massive, sustained law-breaking.

Revolutions create a curious inversion of perception. In ordinary times, people who describe the world around them are seen as pragmatists, while those who imagine fabulous alternative futures are viewed as radicals. The last couple of decades haven't been ordinary, however. Inside the papers, the pragmatists were the ones simply looking out the window and noticing that the real world was increasingly resembling the unthinkable scenario. These people were treated as if they were barking mad. Meanwhile, the people envisioning micropayments and lawsuits, visions unsupported by reality, were regarded not as charlatans but as saviors.

When reality is labeled unthinkable, it creates a kind of sickness in an industry. Leadership becomes faith-based, while employees who have the temerity to disagree are herded into Innovation Departments, where they can be ignored enmasse. This shunting aside of the realists in favor of the fabulists has different effects on different industries at different times. One of the effects on newspapers is that many of their most passionate defenders are unable, even now, to plan for a world in which the industry they knew is visibly going away.

The curious thing about the various plans hatched in the '90s is that they were, at base, all the same plan. The details differed, but the core assumption behind all imagined outcomes was that the organizational form of the newspaper, as a general-purpose vehicle for publishing a variety of news and opinion, was basically sound, and only needed a digital facelift. As a result, the conversation has degenerated into enthusiastic grasping at straws, pursued by skeptical responses.

"The *Wall Street Journal* has a paywall, so we can too!" (Financial information is one of the few kinds of information whose recipients don't want to share.) "Micropayments work for iTunes, so they will work for us!" (Micropayments work only where the provider can avoid competitive business models.) "The *New York Times* should charge for content!" (They've tried, with qPass and later TimesSelect.) "*Cook's Illustrated* and

Consumer Reports are doing fine on subscriptions!" (Those publications forgo ad revenues; users are paying not just for content but for unimpeachability.)

Round and round this goes, with the people committed to saving newspapers demanding to know "If the old model is broken, what will work in its place?" To which the answer is: Nothing. There is no general model with which newspapers can replace the one the Internet just broke.

With the old economics destroyed, organizational forms perfected for print production have to be replaced with structures optimized for digital data. It makes increasingly less sense even to talk about a publishing industry, because the core problem it solves—the difficulty, complexity, and expense of making something available to the public—has stopped being a problem.

Elizabeth Eisenstein's magisterial treatment of Gutenberg's invention, *The Printing Press as an Agent of Change,* first published in 1979, opens with a recounting of her research into the early history of the printing press. She was able to find many descriptions of life in the early 1400s, the era before movable type. Literacy was limited, the Catholic Church was the pan-European political force, Mass was in Latin, and the average book was the Bible. She was also able to find endless descriptions of life in the late 1500s, after Gutenberg's invention had started to spread. Literacy was on the rise, as were books written in contemporary languages, Copernicus had published his epochal work on astronomy, and Martin Luther's use of the press to reform the Church was upending both religious and political stability.

What Eisenstein focused on, however, was not a description of what the world looked like before and after the spread of print—that's child's play, and all too typical in most historical texts on the subject. She chose instead to analyze how we got from one era to the next.

It was, as it turns out, chaotic. When the Bible was translated into local languages some people saw it as an educational boon, others as the work of the devil. Erotic novels appeared, prompting the same sort of response. Copies of Aristotle and Galen circulated widely, but direct encounter with the relevant texts revealed that the two sources clashed, tarnishing faith in the Ancients. As novelty spread, old institutions seemed exhausted while new ones seemed untrustworthy; as a result, people almost literally didn't know what to think. If you can't trust Aristotle, who can you trust?

Only in retrospect were experiments undertaken during the wrenching transition to print revealed to be turning points. Aldus Manutius, a Venetian printer and publisher, invented the smaller octavo volume. What seemed like a minor change—take a book and shrink it—was in retrospect a key innovation in the democratization of the printed word. As books became cheaper, more portable, and therefore more desirable, they expanded the market for all publishers, heightening the value of literacy still further.

That is what real revolutions are like. The old stuff gets broken faster than the new stuff is put in its place. The importance of any given experiment isn't apparent at the moment it appears; big changes stall, small changes spread. Ancient social bargains, once disrupted, can be neither mended nor quickly replaced, since any such bargain takes decades to solidify.

And so it is today. When people demand to know how we are going to replace newspapers, they are really demanding to be told that we are not living through a revolution. They are demanding to be told that old systems won't break before new systems are in place. They are demanding to be told that ancient social bargains aren't in peril, that core institutions will be spared, that new methods of spreading information will improve previous practice rather than upending it. They are demanding to be lied to.

There are fewer and fewer people who can convincingly tell such a lie.

If you want to know why newspapers are in such trouble, the most salient fact is this: Printing presses are terrifically expensive to set up and to run. This bit of economics, normal since Gutenberg, limits competition while creating positive returns to scale for the press owner, a happy pair of economic effects that feed on each other.

In a notional town with two perfectly balanced newspapers, one paper would eventually generate some small advantage—a breaking story, a key interview—at which point both advertisers and readers would come to prefer it, however slightly. That paper would in turn find it easier to capture the next dollar of advertising, at lower expense, than the competition. This would increase its dominance, which would further deepen those preferences, repeat chorus.

For a long time, longer than anyone in the newspaper business has been alive, in fact, print journalism has been intertwined with these economics. The expense of printing created an environment where Wal-Mart was willing to subsidize the Baghdad bureau. This wasn't because of any deep link between advertising and reporting, nor was it about any real desire on the part of Wal-Mart to have its marketing budget go to international correspondents. It was just an accident. Advertisers had little choice other than to have their money used that way, since they didn't really have any other vehicle for display ads.

The competition-deflecting effects of printing cost got destroyed by the Internet, where everyone pays for the infrastructure, and then everyone gets to use it. And when Wal-Mart, and the local Maytag dealer, and the law firm hiring a secretary, and that kid down the block selling his bike, were all able to use that infrastructure to get out of their old relationship with the publisher, they did. They'd never really signed up to fund the Baghdad bureau anyway.

Newspaper people argue that their labor benefits society as a whole. This is true. But "you're gonna miss us when we're gone" has never been much of a business model.

People in the newspaper business often note that their labor benefits society as a whole. This is true, but irrelevant to the problem at hand; "you're gonna miss us when we're gone" has never been much of a business model.

It's true that the print media do much of society's heavy journalistic lifting, from teasing out every angle of a huge story to the grind of attending the city council meeting, in case something happens. This coverage is beneficial even for people who aren't newspaper readers, because the work of print journalists is used by everyone from politicians to district attorneys to talk radio hosts to bloggers.

So who will cover that city council meeting when the newspaper reporter on that beat loses her job?

I don't know. Nobody knows. The Internet turns 40 this fall. Public access is less than half that age. Web use, as a normal part of life for a majority of the developed world, is less than half *that* age. We just got here. Even the revolutionaries can't predict what will happen.

Imagine, in 1996, asking some Net-savvy soul to expound on the potential of craigslist, then just a year old and not yet incorporated. The answer you'd almost certainly have gotten would be extrapolation: "Mailing lists can be powerful tools," "Social effects are intertwining with digital networks," etc. What no one would have told you, could have told you, was what actually happened: Craiglist became a critical piece of infrastructure. Not the idea of craigslist, or the business model, or even the software driving it. Craigslist itself spread to cover hundreds of cities and has become a part of public consciousness about what is now possible. Only in retrospect are experiments revealed to be turning points.

Society doesn't need newspapers. What we need is journalism. For a century, the imperatives to strengthen journalism and to strengthen newspapers have been so tightly bound together as to be indistinguishable. That's been a fine accident, but when that accident stops, as it is stopping before our eyes, we're going to need lots of other ways to strengthen journalism.

When we shift our attention from "save newspapers" to "save society," the imperative changes from "preserve current institutions" to "do whatever works"—and what works today isn't the same as what used to work.

We don't know who the Aldus Manutius of the current age is. It could be Craig Newmark, or Caterina Fake. It could be Martin Nisenholtz, or Emily Bell. It could be some 19-year-old kid few of us have heard of, working on something we won't recognize as vital until a decade hence. Any experiment, though, designed to provide new models for journalism is going to be an improvement over hiding from the real, especially in a year when, for many papers, the unthinkable future is already in the past.

For the next few decades, journalism will be made up of overlapping special cases. Many of these models will rely on amateurs as researchers and writers. Many of these models will rely on sponsorship or grants or endowments instead of revenues. Many of these models will rely on excitable 14-year-olds distributing the results. Many of these models will fail. No one experiment is going to replace what we are now losing with the demise of news on paper, but over time, the collection of new experiments that do work might give us the journalism we need.

CLAY SHIRKY, an adjunct professor at New York University's graduate program in interactive telecommunications, has written extensively about the Internet since 1996. His essays on the online experience have been featured in publications such as the *New York Times, Wired,* and *Harvard Business Review.* His critically acclaimed book *Here Comes Everybody: The Power of Organizing Without Organizations* was published by Penguin in 2008. Excerpted from a post on the author's website (March 13, 2009); www.shirky.com.

Article 43

Build the Wall

Most readers won't pay for news, but if we move quickly, maybe enough of them will. One man's bold blueprint.

DAVID SIMON

To all of the bystanders reading this, pardon us. The true audience for this essay narrows necessarily to a pair of notables who have it in their power to save high-end journalism—two newspaper executives who can rescue an imploding industry and thereby achieve an essential civic good for the nation. It's down to them. The rest of the print journalism world is in slash-and-burn mode, cutting product and then wondering why the product won't sell, rushing to give away what remains online and wondering further why that content is held by advertisers to be valueless. The mode is full-bore panic.

And yet these two individuals, representing as they do the two fundamental institutions that sit astride the profession, still have a card to play, and here's a shard of good news: it's the only card that ever really mattered. Arthur Sulzberger Jr. and Katharine Weymouth, publishers of *The New York Times* and *The Washington Post,* are at the helms of two organizations trying to find some separate peace with the digital revolution, though both papers have largely failed to do so, damaging their own still-formidable institutions and, on a deeper level, eviscerating more vulnerable regional newspapers and newspapering as whole. Yet incredibly, they delay, even though every day of inertia means another two dozen reporters somewhere are shown the door by a newspaper chain, or another foreign bureau closes, or another once-precise and competent newsroom decides it will make do without a trained city editor, an ombudsman, or a fully staffed copy desk.

This then, is for Mr. Sulzberger and Ms. Weymouth:

Content matters. And you must find a way, in the brave new world of digitization, to make people pay for that content. If you do this, you still have a product and there is still an industry, a calling, and a career known as professional journalism. If you do not find a way to make people pay for your product, then you are—if you choose to remain in this line of work—delusional.

I know that content wants to be free on the Internet. I know that the horse was long ago shown the barn door and that, belatedly, the idea of creating a new revenue stream from online subscriptions seems daunting and dangerous. I know that commentary—the froth and foam of print journalism—sells itself cheaply and well on thousands of blogs. I know that the relationships between newspapers and online aggregators—not to mention The Associated Press and Reuters—will have to be revisited and revised. True, all true.

Most of all, I know that here you are being individually asked to consider taking a bold, risk-laden stand for content—that antitrust considerations prohibit the *Times* and the *Post,* not to mention Rupert Murdoch or the other owners, from talking this through and acting in concert. Would that every U.S. newspaper publisher could meet in a bathroom somewhere and talk bluntly for fifteen minutes, this would be a hell of a lot easier. And yes, I know that if one of you should try to go behind the paywall while the other's content remains free, then, yes, you would be destroyed. All that is apparent.

But also apparent is the fact that absent a radical revisiting of the dynamic between newspapering and the Internet, there will be little cohesive, professional, first-generation journalism at the state and local level, as your national newspapers continue to retrench and regional papers are destroyed outright.

You must act. Together. On a specific date in the near future—let's say September 1 for the sheer immediacy of it—both news organizations must inform readers that their websites will be free to subscribers only, and that while subscription fees can be a fraction of the price of having wood pulp flung on doorsteps, it is nonetheless a requirement for acquiring the contents of the news organizations that spend millions to properly acquire, edit, and present that work.

No half-measures, either. No TimesSelect program that charges for a handful of items and offers the rest for free, no limited availability of certain teaser articles, no bartering with aggregators for a few more crumbs of revenue through microbilling or pennies-on-the-dollar fees. Either you believe that what The *New York Times* and *The Washington Post* bring to the table every day has value, or you don't.

You must both also individually inform the wire-service consortiums that unless they limit membership to publications, online or off, that provide content only through paid subscriptions, you intend to withdraw immediately from those consortiums. Then, for good measure, you might each make a voluntary donation—let's say $10 million—to a newspaper trade group to

156

establish a legal fund to pursue violations of copyright, either by online aggregators or large-scale blogs, much in the way other industries based on intellectual property have fought to preserve their products.

And when the Justice Department lawyers arrive, briefcases in hand, to ask why America's two national newspapers did these things in concert—resulting in a sea change within newspapering as one regional newspaper after another followed suit in pursuit of fresh, lifesaving revenue—you can answer directly: We never talked. Not a word. We read some rant in the *Columbia Journalism Review* that made the paywall argument. Blame the messenger.

Truth is, a halting movement toward the creation of an online subscription model already exists; at this writing, internal discussions at both the *Times* and the *Post* are ongoing, according to sources at both papers. And one small, furtive, and cautious meeting of newspaper executives took place in Chicago in May to explore the general idea of charging for online distribution of news. As for Rupert Murdoch, his rethought decision not to freely offer *The Wall Street Journal* online speaks volumes, as do his recent trial balloons about considering an online subscription model for less unique publications. Where the *Times* and the *Post* lead, Murdoch and, ultimately, every desperate and starving newspaper chain will simply follow. Why? Because the need to create a new revenue stream from the twenty-first century's information-delivery model is, belatedly, apparent to many in the industry. But no one can act if the *Times* and the *Post* do not; the unique content of even a functional regional newspaper—state and municipal news, local sports and culture—is insufficient to demand that readers pay online. But add to that the national and international coverage from the national papers that would no longer be available on the Internet for free but could be provided through participation in the news services of the *Times* and the *Post* and, finally, there is a mix of journalism that justifies a subscription fee.

Time is the enemy, however, and the wariness and caution with which the *Times* and the *Post* approach the issue reveal not only how slow industry leaders have been to accurately assess the realities, but how vulnerable one national newspaper is to the other. Should the *Times* go behind a pay curtain while the Post remains free, or vice versa, the result would be a short-term but real benefit to the newspaper that fails to act, and fiscal bleeding for the newspaper attempting to demand recompense for work that is elsewhere being provided free of charge. Neither the *Times* nor the *Post* can do this alone.

Will it work? Is there enough demand for old-line, high-end journalism in the age of new media? Will readers pay for what they have already accepted as free? And can industry leaders claw their way back in time to the fateful point when they mistook the Internet as a mere advertising opportunity for their product?

Perhaps, though the risks are not spread equally. Given the savage cutting that has been under way at regional, chain-owned newspapers over the last decade or more, it may be too late for some metro dailies; they may no longer have enough legitimate, unique content to compel their readership to pay. But for the *Times* and the *Post*—entities that are still providing the lion's share of journalism's national, international, and cultural relevance—their reach has never been greater.

The proof is that while online aggregation and free newspaper websites have combined to batter paid print circulation figures, more people are reading the product of America's newspapers than ever before. Certainly more of them are reading the *Times* (nearly 20 million average unique visitors monthly) and the *Post* (more than 10 million monthly unique visitors), though they are doing it online and not paying for the privilege. And tellingly, the *Times*—its product still unmatched in print or online by other mainstream publications or anything that new media has yet offered—has transformed its print circulation into a profit center for the first time in years, merely by jacking up the price, with newsstand prices rising in June to $2 and up to $6 on Sunday.

Clearly, the product still moves. But to what purpose, when more and more readers rightly identify the immediate digitized version as superior, yet pay nothing for that version, and online advertising simply doesn't deliver enough revenue? If the only way to read the *Times* is to buy the *Times,* online or off, then readers who clearly retain a desire for that product will reach for their wallets. And those comfortable acquiring their news at a keyboard will be happy to pay much less than they do for home delivery.

No doubt some mavens of new media who have read this far have spittle in the corners of their mouths at the thought of the dying, tail-dragging dinosaurs of mainstream journalism resurrecting themselves by making the grand tool of the revolution—the Internet—less free. There is no going backward, they will declare, affronted by the idea that a victory already claimed can even be questioned. The newspaper is all but dead, they will insist. Long live the citizen journalist.

Not so fast. While their resentment and frustration with newspapers—given the industry's reduced editorial ambitions—are justified, their reasoning and conclusions are not. A little history:

For the first thirty years of its existence as America's primary entertainment medium, television was—after the initial purchase of the set itself—provided at no cost to viewers, instead subsidized by lucrative ad revenues. The notion of Americans in 1975 being asked to pay a monthly bill for their television consumption would have seemed farcical. Yet in the ensuing thirty years, we have become a nation that shells out $60, $70, or $120 in monthly cable fees; indeed, whole vistas of programming exist free of advertising revenue, subsidized entirely by subscriptions.

How did this happen?

Again, content is all. The move to the pay-cable model was preceded by an expansive effort to create additional programming to justify the upgrade from network fare to multichannel packaging. In the beginning, some of that new content amounted to little more than feature-film purchases, additional sports, and twenty-four-hour news and weather. But ultimately, the quantitative increase in programming was accompanied by a qualitative improvement in television fare. You paid more, you got more: HBO, Showtime, Cinemax, and, ultimately, a string of niche channels catering to specific audiences and interests. One can critique American TV however ruthlessly one wishes, but the industry is doing something right. More channels, more programming, more revenue—indeed, a revenue stream where none had existed.

By contrast, we have American newspapering, an industry that a quarter century ago was—pound for pound—as lucrative as television, with Wall Street commanding profit margins of 25 and 30 percent. As with television, circulation was accepted as a loss leader, strongly subsidized so that the money it cost to deliver content was more than made up by advertising dollars.

But unlike television, in which industry leaders were constantly reinvesting profits in research and development, where a new technology like cable reception would be contemplated for all its potential and opportunity, the newspapering world was content to send its treasure to Wall Street, appeasing analysts and big-ticket shareholders. There was no reinvestment in programming, no intelligent contemplation of new and transformational circulation models, no thought beyond maximized short-term profit.

Incredibly, and in direct contrast to the growth of television, the remaining monopoly newspapers in American cities—roped together in unwieldy chains and run by men and women who had, by and large, been reared in boardrooms rather than newsrooms—spent the last of their profitable days *cutting* product, scaling back news holes, shedding veteran reporters, and reducing the scope of coverage. Hiring freezes and buyouts were ongoing in the early and mid-1990s, all of this happening amid the unspoken assumptions that the advertising base was everything, that content didn't really matter, that news was the stuff troweled into the columns next to the display ads, that there was more profit producing a half-assed, mediocre paper than a good one.

In the 1970s, American auto manufacturing was complicit in its own marginalization through exactly the same mindset: Why not churn out Pacers and Gremlins and Vegas, providing cheap, shoddy vehicles that would be rapidly replaced with newer cheap, shoddy vehicles? What would captive American consumers do? Buy a car from Japan? Germany? South Korea?

Well, yes, as it turns out. But the analogy doesn't quite capture the extraordinary incompetence exhibited by the newspaper industry. After all, a Toyota is a good car and all that was required for Detroit to begin its agonizing decline was for consumers to be offered a legitimate choice.

In the newspaper industry, however, the fledgling efforts of new media to replicate the scope, competence, and consistency of a healthy daily paper have so far yielded little in the way of genuine competition. A blog here, a citizen journalist there, a news website getting under way in places where the newspaper is diminished—some of it is quite good, but none of it so far begins to achieve consistently what a vibrant newspaper, staffed with competent, paid beat reporters and editors, once offered. New-media entities are not yet able to truly cover—day after day—the society, culture, and politics of cities, states, and nations. And until new models emerge that are capable of paying reporters and editors to do such work—in effect becoming online newspapers with all the gravitas this implies—they are not going to get us anywhere close to professional journalism's potential.

Detroit lost to a better, new product; newspapers, to the vague suggestion of one.

Beyond Mr. Sulzberger and Ms. Weymouth—and yes, get cracking, you two; September comes fast—there is, in retrospect, a certain wonderment that so many otherwise smart people in newspapering could have so mistaken the Internet and its implications. A lot has been written on this phenomenon and more will follow, but three factors are worth noting—if only because of their relevance to the online subscription model that is clearly required:

First, there is the familiar industrial dynamic in which leaders raised in one world are taken aback to find they have underestimated the power of an emerging paradigm.

When I left my newsroom in 1995, the Internet was a mere whisper, but even five years later, as its potential was becoming a consideration in every other aspect of American life, those in command of *The Baltimore Sun* were explaining the value of their free website in these terms: this is advertising for the newspaper. Young readers will see what we do by "surfing the Web" and finding our site, and they will read some, and then settle down and buy the newspaper.

Looking back, it sounds comical. Absent the buyouts and layoffs and lost coverage of essential issues, it would be buggy-whip-maker funny. But as it stands, the misapprehension of men and women who spent their lives believing in the primacy of newsprint is as tragic as the strategists who built battleships even after Billy Mitchell used air power to bomb one to the ocean floor in 1921. Regardless, it was industry-wide in newsrooms. On the business side, they were a little busy hurling profits at Wall Street to pay much attention.

Second, the industry leaders on both the business and editorial sides came of age in an environment in which circulation had long been a loss leader, when newspapers never charged readers what it actually cost to get the product to their doorstep. Advertising, not content, was all.

This specific dynamic maximized everyone's blindness to the real possibilities of a subscription model. Every reader who can be induced to accept an online subscription to a newspaper—at even a half or a third the price of doorstep delivery—represents the beginning of a new and quite profitable revenue stream.

For example, if *The Baltimore Sun*'s product isn't available in any other fashion than through subscription—online or off—and if there is no profit to be had in delivering the paper product to homes at existing rates, then by all means, jack up those rates—raise hard-copy prices and drive as many readers as possible online, where you charge less, but at a distinct profit.

Yes, you would lose readers. But consider: 10 percent of the existing 210,000 *Baltimore Sun* readers, for example, who pay a subscription rate less than half the price of home delivery, or roughly $10, would represent about $2.5 million a year. Absent the cost of trucks, gas, paper, and presses, money like that represents the beginnings of a solid revenue stream. In the same fashion, the first handful of subscribers to HBO watched bad movies and boxing, but as the revenue grew, it paid for original programming and, ultimately, a vast expansion of product. First, someone had to dream it. At newspapers, no one did. Newspaper dreams of the last fifty years involved luscious department-store display ads and fat classified sections—visions that can no longer be.

Last, and perhaps most disastrous, the rot began at the bottom and it didn't reach the highest rungs of the profession until far too much damage had been done.

As early as the mid-1980s, the civic indifference and contempt of product inherent in chain ownership was apparent in many smaller American markets. While this was discussed in some circles, usually as a matter of mild rumination, little was done by the industry to address a dynamic by which men in Los Angeles or Chicago or New York, at the behest of Wall Street, determined what sort of journalism would be practiced in Baltimore, Denver, Hartford, or Dallas. If you happened to labor at a newspaper that was ceding its editorial ambition to the price-per-share, it may have been agony, but if you were at the *Times*, the *Post*, *The Wall Street Journal*, or the *Los Angeles Times*, you were insulated. As the Internet arrived, profit margins were challenged and buyouts began at even the largest, most viable monopoly papers in regional markets. But only when the disease reached their own newsrooms did it really matter to the big papers.

Last year at *The Washington Post*, the paper's first major buyout arrived at about the time of its six Pulitzer victories. The day the prizes were announced, newsroom staffers publicly predicted that such winning journalism would likely not be replicated at the *Post* in an era of cutbacks. This, they moaned, might be the newspaper's last great prize haul. But of course the buyout of one hundred reporters at the *Post*, while painful and damaging, represented a bit more than a 10 percent reduction in force. At that point, the loss of the same number of reporters at *The Baltimore Sun* would have been a 30 percent reduction. The *Sun*, at this point, has had about eight rounds of buyouts and layoffs, beginning well before the arrival of the Internet, dropping the editorial staff from 500 to 160. Given that kind of carnage, there was no need for the *Post* to have any prize-based worries. In the end, the *Times*, the *Post*, and the *Journal* will be taking up more seats at the Pulitzer luncheon, not fewer. With whom, after all, do they think they are still competing?

The cancer devouring journalism began somewhere below the knee, and by the time the disease reached the self-satisfied brain of the Washington and New York newsrooms, the prognosis was far worse. Or to employ another historical metaphor: when they came for the Gannett papers, I said nothing, because I was not at a Gannett paper.

For the industry, it is later than it should be; where a transition to online pay models would once have been easier with a healthy product, now the odds for some papers are long. But given the timeline, here are a few possible outcomes, if the *Times* and the *Post* go ahead and build that wall.

First scenario: The *Times* and the *Post* survive, their revenue streams balanced by still-considerable print advertising, the bump in the price of home delivery and newsstand sales, and, finally, a new influx of cheap yet profitable online subscriptions.

And reassured that they can risk going behind the paywall without local readers getting free national, international, and cultural reporting from the national papers, and having seen that the paid-content formula can work, most metro dailies will follow suit. As they do, they re-emphasize that which makes them unique: local coverage, local culture, local voices—coupled with wire-service offerings from the national papers otherwise available only through paid sites.

In our scenario, metro papers re-emphasize that which makes them unique: local coverage, local culture, local voices.

Some of the chain dailies may well make the mistake of taking the fresh revenue and rushing it back to Wall Street. We need to worry that although readers, like television viewers, might be convinced to pay online for a strong, unique product, there is little in the last twenty years to suggest that newspaper chains would reinvest to create such a product. For those papers, it's likely that a thin online subscriber base will reflect the hollowness of their product.

But in our scenario, others do reinvest in their newsrooms, hiring back some of the talent lost. Coverage expands, becomes more local, even neighborhood-based, which in turn leads to more online subscriptions, as well as additional online advertising lured by those subscribers.

Second scenario: In those cities where regional papers collapse, the vacuum creates an opportunity for new, online subscription-based news organizations that cover state and local issues, sports, and finance, generating enough revenue to maintain a slim—but paid—metro desk. Again, given the absence of circulation costs, such an outcome becomes, by conservative estimates, entirely possible.

Here is a back-of-the-envelope plan. In a metro region the size of Baltimore, where 300,000 once subscribed to a healthy newspaper, imagine an initial market penetration of a tenth of that—30,000 paid subscribers (in a metro region of more than 2.5 million), who are willing to pay $10 per month. This is less than half their previous *Sun* home-delivery rate for the only product in town that covers local politics, local culture, local sports, and financial news—using paid reporters and paid editors to produce a consistent, professional product.

That's $300,000 a month in revenue, or $3.6 million a year, with zero printing or circulation costs. Moreover, that total doesn't include whatever money online advertising might generate. Advertisers—considering a *paid* circulation base rather than meaningless Web hits—might be willing to once again pay a meaningful rate.

Round it up to $4 million in total revenue, then knock off a half million in operating and promotional costs. At $100,000 a position for editors and reporters, that's a metro desk of some thirty-five paid souls, enough to provide significant coverage of a city and its suburbs. If the reporters are on $50,000 contracts and benefits are not initially included, it's a newsroom of seventy—larger than the *Sun*'s metro staff in the nineties.

And if that online-only, paid-subscription daily were a locally-run *nonprofit,* with every increase in subscriptions going to fund additional coverage, well, what more does professional journalism require to survive at the state and local level?

Third scenario: Except for one in which professional journalism doesn't endure in any form, this is the worst of all worlds. The *Times* and the *Post* survive because their coverage is unique and essential. But the regional dailies, too eviscerated to offer a credible local product, cannot entice enough online subscriptions to make do. They wither and die. And further, new online news ventures are stillborn because both national papers become exactly that—national.

Imagine major American cities without daily newspapers, and further imagine the *Times* or the *Post* employing just enough local journalists in regional markets to produce zoned editions—*The New York Times* with, say, a ten-person St. Louis bureau, giving readers two or three pages of metro, sports, and local business coverage. Or a *Washington Post* edition for the Baltimore region, using a dozen ex-*Sun* staffers to create a thin but viable product, where once a comprehensive metro daily once stood.

The joke then would be on the Justice Department lawyers as well. The longer it takes for the newspaper industry to get its act together, the more likely it is that regional dailies will be too weak and hollow to step through the online-subscription portal. Even localized Internet startups—the fledgling, digitized versions of professional newsrooms—will find themselves competing with, or bought out by, national monoliths. More monopoly, not less, for as long as we continue to fret the antitrust issues.

But all of this is, of course, academic. Because at this moment, Mr. Sulzberger and Ms. Weymouth have yet to turn that last card. Until they find the will and the courage to do so, no scenario other than the slow strangulation of paid, professional journalism applies. Meanwhile, we dare to dream of a viable, online future for American newsrooms.

DAVID SIMON is a writer, author, and television producer. He is the creator of HBO's *The Corner, Generation Kill,* and *The Wire.* From 1982 to 1995, he was a reporter at *The Baltimore Sun.*

From *Columbia Journalism Review,* July/August 2009, pp. 36–40. Copyright © 2009. Reprinted by permission of Columbia Journalism Review.

A See-Through Society

How the Web is opening up our democracy.

MICAH L. SIFRY

It may be a while before the people who run the U.S. House of Representatives' Web service forget the week of September 29, 2008. That's when the enormous public interest in the financial bailout legislation, coupled with unprecedented numbers of e-mails to House members, effectively crashed www.house.gov. On Tuesday of that week, a day after the House voted down the first version of the bailout bill, House administrators had to limit the number of incoming e-mails processed by the site's "Write Your Representative" function. Demand for the text of the legislation was so intense that third-party sites that track Congress were also swamped. GovTrack.us, a private site that produces a user-friendly guide to congressional legislation, had to shut down. Its owner, Josh Tauberer, posted a message reading, "So many people are searching for the economic relief bill that GovTrack can't handle it. Take a break and come back later when the world cools off."

Once people did get their eyes on the bill's text, they tore into it with zeal. Nearly a thousand comments were posted between September 22 and October 5 on PublicMarkup.org, a site that enables the public to examine and debate the text of proposed legislation set up by the Sunlight Foundation, an advocacy group for government transparency (full disclosure: I am a senior technology adviser to Sunlight). Meanwhile, thousands of bloggers zeroed in on the many earmarks in the bill, such as the infamous reduction in taxes for wooden-arrow manufacturers. Others focused on members who voted for the bill, analyzing their campaign contributors and arguing that Wall Street donations influenced their vote.

The explosion of public engagement online around the bailout bill signals something profound: the beginning of a new age of political transparency. As more people go online to find, create, and share vital political information with one another; as the cost of creating, combining, storing, and sharing information drops toward zero; and as the tools for analyzing data and connecting people become more powerful and easier to use, politics and governance alike are inexorably becoming more open.

We are heading toward a world in which one-click universal disclosure, real-time reporting by both professionals and amateurs, dazzling data visualizations that tell compelling new stories, and the people's ability to watch their government from below (what the French call *sousveillance*) are becoming commonplace. Despite the detour of the Bush years, citizens will have more opportunity at all levels of government to take an active part in understanding and participating in the democratic decisions that affect their lives.

Log On, Speak Out

The low-cost, high-speed, always-on Internet is changing the ecology of how people consume and create political information. The Pew Internet & American Life Project estimates that roughly 75 percent of all American adults, or about 168 million people, go online or use e-mail at least occasionally. A digital divide still haunts the United States, but among Americans aged eighteen to forty-nine, that online proportion is closer to 90 percent. Television remains by far the dominant political information source, but in October 2008, a third of Americans said their main provider of political information was the Internet—more than triple the number from four years earlier, according to another Pew study. Nearly half of eighteen-to-twenty-nine-year-olds said the Internet was their main source of political info.

Meanwhile, we're poised for a revolution in participation, not just in consumption, thanks to the Web. People talk, share, and talk back online. According to yet another study by Pew, this one in December 2007, one in five U.S. adults who use the Internet reported sharing something online that they created themselves; one in three say they've posted a comment or rated something online.

People are eager for access to information, and public officials who try to stand in the way will discover that the Internet responds to information suppression by routing around the problem. Consider the story of a site you've never seen, ChicagoWorksForYou.com. In June 2005, a team of Web developers working for the city of Chicago began developing a site that would take the fifty-five different kinds of service requests that flow into the city's 311 database—items like pothole repairs, tree-trimming, garbage-can placement, building permits, and restaurant inspections—and enable users to search by address and "map what's happening in your neighborhood" The idea was to showcase city services at the local level.

ChicagoWorks was finished in January 2006, with the support of Mayor Richard Daley's office. But it also needed to be reviewed by the city's aldermen and, according to a source who worked on the project, "they were very impressed with its functionality, but they were shocked at the possibility that it would go public." Elections were coming up, and even if the site showed 90 percent of potholes being filled within thirty days, the powers-that-be didn't want the public to know about the last 10 percent. ChicagoWorksForYou.com was shelved.

But the idea of a site that brings together information about city services in Chicago is alive and kicking. If you go to EveryBlock.com, launched in January 2008, and click on the Chicago link, you can drill down to any ward, neighborhood, or block and discover everything from the latest restaurant-inspection reports and building permits to recent crime reports and street closures. It's all on a Google Map, and if you want to subscribe to updates about a particular location and type of report, the site kicks out custom RSS feeds. Says Daniel O'Neil, one of Every Block's data mavens, "Crime and restaurant inspections are our hottest topics: Will I be killed today and will I vomit today?"

EveryBlock exists thanks to a generous grant from the Knight News Challenge, but its work, which covers eleven cities, including New York, San Francisco, and Washington, D.C., offers a glimpse of the future of ubiquitous and hyperlocal information. EveryBlock's team collects most of its data by scraping public sites and spreadsheets and turning it into understandable information that can be easily displayed and manipulated online.

It may not be long before residents of the cities covered by EveryBlock decide to contribute their own user-generated data to flesh out the picture that city officials might prefer to hide. EveryBlock founder Adrian Holovaty tells me that his team is figuring out ways for users to connect directly to each other through the site. Forums that allowed people to congregate online by neighborhood or interest would enable EveryBlock users to become their cities' watchdogs. If city agencies still won't say how many potholes are left unfilled after thirty days, people could share and track that information themselves.

Such a joint effort is no stretch to young people who have grown up online. Consider just a couple of examples: since 1999, RateMyTeachers.com and RateMyProfessors.com have collected more than sixteen million user-generated ratings on more than two million teachers and professors. The two sites get anywhere from half a million to a million unique visitors a month. Yelp.com, a user-generated review service, says its members have written more than four million local reviews since its founding in 2004. As the younger generation settles down and starts raising families, there's every reason to expect that its members will carry these habits of networking and sharing information into tracking more serious quality-of-life issues, as well as politics.

Cities Lead the Way

Recognizing this trend, some public officials are plunging in. In his "State of the City" speech in January 2008, New York Mayor Mike Bloomberg promised to "roll out the mother of

> ### A Sunshine Timeline
>
> **1966**
> FOIA passes. Without the votes to sustain his threatened veto, and with Bill Moyers, his press secretary, urging him on, LBJ signs the bill. But he nixes a press release announcing the new law, and forgoes a signing ceremony, the only time in his tenure he did so. (Ironic footnote: Donald Rumsfeld co-sponsored the bill.)

all accountability tools." It is called Citywide Performance Reporting, and Bloomberg promised it would put "a wealth of data at people's fingertips—fire response times, noise complaints, trees planted by the Parks Department, you name it. More than five hundred different measurements from forty-five city agencies." Bloomberg, whose wealth was built on the financial-information company he built, says he likes to think of the service as a "Bloomberg terminal for city government—except that it's free."

Bloomberg's vision is only partly fulfilled so far. A visitor to the city's site (nyc.gov) would have a hard time finding the "Bloomberg terminal for city government" because it's tucked several layers down On the Mayor's Office of Operations page, with no pointers from the home page.

Still, the amount of data it provides is impressive. You can learn that the number of families with children entering the city shelter system is up 31 percent over last year, and that the city considers this a sign of declining performance by the system. Or you can discover that the median time the city department of consumer affairs took to process a complaint was twenty-two business days, and that that is considered positive! Another related tool, called NYC*SCOUT, allows anyone to see where recent service requests have been made, and with a little bit of effort you can make comparisons between different community districts. New York's monitoring tools still leave much to be desired, however, because they withhold the raw data—specific addresses and dates-of-service requests—that are the bones of these reports. This means the city is still resisting fully sharing the public's data with the public.

Compare that to the approach of the District of Columbia. Since 2006, all the raw data it has collected on government operations, education, health care, crime, and dozens of other topics has been available for free to the public via 260 live data feeds. The city's CapStat online service also allows anyone to track the performance of individual agencies, monitor neighborhood services and quality-of-life issues, and make suggestions for improvement. Vivek Kundra, D.C.'s innovative chief technology officer, calls this "building the digital public square." In mid-October, he announced an "Apps for Democracy" contest that offered $20,000 in cash prizes for outside developers and designers of websites and tools that made use of the city's data catalog.

In just a few weeks, Kundra received nearly fifty finished Web applications. The winners included:

- iLive.at, a site that shows with one click all the local information around one address, including the closest places to go shopping, buy gas, or mail a letter; the locations of recently reported crimes; and the demographic makeup of the neighborhood;
- Where's My Money, DC?—a tool that meshes with Facebook and enables users to look up and discuss all city expenditures above $2,500; and
- Stumble Safely, an online guide to the best bars and safe paths on which to stumble home after a night out.

The lesson of the "Apps for Democracy" contest is simple: a critical mass of citizens with the skills and the appetite to engage with public agencies stands ready to co-create a new kind of government transparency. Under traditional government procurement practices, it would have taken Kundra months just to post a "request for proposals" and get responses. Finished sites would have taken months, even years, for big government contractors to complete. The cost for fifty working websites would have been in the millions. Not so when you give the public robust data resources and the freedom to innovate that is inherent to today's Web.

The Whole Picture

So, how will the Web ultimately alter the nature of political transparency? Four major trends are developing.

First, the day is not far off when it will be possible to see, at a glance, the most significant ways an individual, lobbyist, corporation, or interest group is trying to influence the government. Here's how Ellen Miller, executive director of the Sunlight Foundation and a longtime proponent of open government, sees the future of transparency online: "If I search for Exxon, I want one-click disclosure," she says. "I want to see who its PAC is giving money to, who its executives and employees are supporting, at the state and federal levels; who does its lobbying, whom they're meeting with and what they're lobbying on; whether it's employing former government officials, or vice versa, if any of its ex-employees are in government; whether any of those people have flown on the company's jets. And then I also want to know what contracts, grants, or earmarks the company has gotten and whether they were competitively bid."

She continues: "If I look up a senator, I want an up-to-date list of his campaign contributors—not one that is months out of date because the Senate still files those reports on paper. I want to see his public calendar of meetings. I want to know what earmarks he's sponsored and obtained. I want to know whether he is connected to a private charity that people might be funneling money to. I want to see an up-to-date list of his financial assets, along with all the more mundane things, like a list of bills he's sponsored, votes he's taken, and public statements he's made. And I want it all reported and available online in a timely fashion."

This vision isn't all that far away. In the last three years, thanks in large measure to support from Sunlight, OMB Watch (a nonprofit advocacy organization that focuses on budget issues, regulatory policy, and access to government) created

A Sunshine Timeline

1986
In the wake of India's Bhopal disaster, the Emergency Planning and Community Right-to-Know Act mandates development of national and local systems to respond to leaks of dangerous chemicals. Included is the requirement, for the first time, that computerized regulatory information be made public.

FedSpending.org, a searchable online database of all government contracts and spending. The Center for Responsive Politics (OpenSecrets.org), meanwhile, has developed searchable databases of current lobbying reports, personal financial disclosure statements of members of Congress, sponsored travel, and employment records of nearly ten thousand people who have moved through the revolving door between government and lobbying. Taxpayers for Common Sense (Taxpayer.net) is putting the finishing touches on a complete online database of 2008 earmarks.

The National Institute on Money in State Politics, headed by Ed Bender, is filling in the picture at the state level, aiming to give the public "as complete a picture as possible of its elected leaders and their actions, and offer information that helps the public understand those actions," he says. "This would start with the candidates running for offices, their biographies and their donors, and would follow them into the statehouses to their committee assignments and relationships with lobbyists, and finally to the legislation that they sponsor and vote for, and who benefits from those actions."

The incoming Obama administration, meanwhile, has expressed a commitment to expanding government transparency, promising as part of its "ethics agenda" platform (change.gov/agenda/ethics_agenda) to create a "centralized Internet database of lobbying reports, ethics records, and campaign-finance filings in a searchable, sortable, and downloadable format," as well as a "'contracts and influence' database that will disclose how much federal contractors spend on lobbying, and what contracts they are getting and how well they complete them."

To insure that all citizens can access such a database, we can hope that Obama pushes universal Internet access as part of his investment in infrastructure. As Andrew Rasiej and I argued in *Politico* in December, "Just as we recognized with the Universal Service Act in the 1930s that we had to take steps to ensure everyone access to the phone network, we need to do the same today with affordable access to high-speed Internet. Everything else flows from this. Otherwise, we risk leaving half our population behind and worsening inequality rather than reducing it."

3-D Journalism

A second trend propelling us toward a greater degree of political transparency is data visualization. The tools for converting boring lists and lines of numbers into beautiful, compelling images get more powerful every day, enabling a new kind of 3-D journalism: dynamic and data-driven. And in many cases, news consumers can manipulate the resulting image or chart, drilling into its layers of information to follow their own interests. My favorite examples include:

- The Huffington Post's Fundrace, which mapped campaign contributions to the 2008 presidential candidates by name and address, enabling anyone to see whom their neighbors might be giving to;
- The *New York Times*'s debate analyzer, which converted each candidate debate into an interactive chart showing word counts and speaking time, and enabled readers to search for key words or fast forward; and
- The Sunlight Foundation and Taxpayers for Common Sense's Earmarks Watch Map (earmarkwatch.org/mapped), which layered the thousands of earmarks in the fiscal 2008 defense-appropriations bill over a map of the country allowing a viewer to zero in on specific sites and see how the Pentagon scatters money in practically every corner of the U.S.

The use of such tools is engendering a collective understanding of, as Paul Simon once sang, the way we look to us all. As news consumers grow used to seeing people like CNN'S John King use a highly interactive map of the United States to explain local voting returns, demand for these kinds of visualizations will only grow.

Little Brother Is Watching, Too

The third trend fueling the expansion of political transparency is *sousveillance,* or watching from below. It can be done by random people, armed with little more than a camera-equipped cell phone, who happen to be in the right place at the right time. Or it can be done by widely dispersed individuals acting in concert to ferret out a vital piece of information or trend, what has been called "distributed journalism." In effect, Big Brother is being watched by millions of Little Brothers.

For example, back in August, San Francisco Mayor Gavin Newsom was having coffee at a Starbucks in Malibu when he was spotted by a blogger who took a couple of photos and posted them online. The blogger noted that Newsom was "talking campaign strategy" with someone, but didn't know who. The pictures came to the attention of *San Francisco Chronicle* reporter Carla Marinucci, who identified that person as political consultant Garry South. Soon political bloggers were having a field day, pointing out that the liberal mayor was meeting with one of the more conservative Democratic consultants around. This is *sousveillance* at its simplest.

The citizen-journalism project "Off the Bus," which ultimately attracted thousands of volunteer reporters who posted their work on The Huffington Post during the 2008 election, was *sousveillance* en masse. Much of their work was too opinionated or first-person oriented to really break news, but Mayhill Fowler's reporting of Barack Obama's offhand remarks at a San Francisco fundraiser about "bitter" blue-collar workers

---

A Sunshine Timeline

2003

World Bank begins supporting FOI-related conditions in agreements with some developing countries, but stops short of making right-to-know laws mandatory. According to Privacy International, today roughly eighty-one governments worldwide have some form of FOI law.

---

at least briefly changed the course of the campaign. And there are numerous examples of bloggers and their readers acting in concert to expose some hidden fact. The coalition of bloggers known as the "Porkbusters" were at the center of an effort to expose which senator had put a secret hold on a bill creating a federal database of government spending, co-sponsored by none other than Barack Obama and Tom Coburn. Porkbusters asked their readers to call their senators, and by this reporting process, discovered that Senator Ted Stevens of Alaska was the culprit. Soon thereafter, he released his hold. Likewise, Josh Marshall has frequently asked readers of Talking Points Memo to help him spot local stories that might be part of a larger pattern. It was this technique that helped him piece together the story of the firings of U.S. Attorneys around the country, for which he won the Polk Award.

The World's A-Twitter

The final trend that is changing the nature of transparency is the rise of what some call the World Live Web. Using everything from mobile phones that can stream video live online to simple text message postings to the micro-blogging service Twitter, people are contributing to a real-time patter of information about what is going on around them. Much of what results is little more than noise, but increasingly sophisticated and simple-to-use filtering tools can turn some of it into information of value.

For example, in just a matter of weeks before the November election in the U.S., a group of volunteer bloggers and Web developers loosely affiliated with the blog I edit, techPresident.com, built a monitoring project called Twitter Vote Report. Voters were encouraged to use Twitter, as well as other tools like iPhones, to post reports on the quality of their voting experience. Nearly twelve thousand reports flowed in, and the result was a real-time picture of election-day complications and wait times that a number of journalistic organizations, including NPR, PBS, and several newspapers, relied on for their reporting.

Nothing to Hide

The question for our leaders, as we head into a world where bottom-up, user-generated transparency is becoming more of a reality, is whether they will embrace this change and show that they have nothing to hide. Will they actively share all that is relevant to their government service with the people who, after all, pay their salaries? Will they trust the public to understand the complexities of that information, instead of treating them like children who can't handle the truth?

The question for citizens is, Will we use this new access to information to create a more open and deliberative democracy?

The question for citizens, meanwhile, is, Will we use this new access to information to create a more open and deliberative democracy? Or will citizens just use the Web to play "gotcha" games with politicians, damaging the discourse instead of uplifting it?

"People tend not to trust what is hidden" write the authors of the November 2008 report by a collection of openness advocates entitled "Moving Toward a 21st Century Right-to-Know Agenda." "Transparency is a powerful tool to demonstrate to the public that the government is spending our money wisely, that politicians are not in the pocket of lobbyists and special-interest groups, that government is operating in an accountable manner, and that decisions are made to ensure the safety and protection of all Americans." In the end, transparency breeds trust. Or rather, transparency enables leaders to earn our trust. In the near future, they may have to, because more and more of us are watching.

MICAH L. SIFRY is co-founder of the Personal Democracy Forum, an annual conference on how technology is changing politics; editor of its group blog techPresident.com; and a senior technology adviser to the Sunlight Foundation.

From Columbia Journalism Review, January/February 2009, pp. 43–47. Copyright © 2009. Reprinted by permission of Columbia Journalism Review.

UNIT 4
Products of American Politics

Unit Selections

45. **The Tax-Cut Con,** Paul Krugman
46. **The Realities of Immigration,** Linda Chavez
47. **The Health of Nations,** Ezra Klein
48. **The *Real* Infrastructure Crisis,** Burt Solomon
49. **Speculators, Politicians, and Financial Disasters,** John Steele Gordon
50. **A Flimsy Trust: Why Social Security Needs Some Major Repairs,** Allan Sloan
51. **How Globalization Went Bad,** Steven Weber et al.
52. **Are Failed States a Threat to America?,** Justin Logan and Christopher Preble
53. **Worth Fighting—or Not,** Burt Solomon
54. **The Abandonment of Democracy,** Joshua Muravchik

Key Points to Consider

- What do you think is the single most important social welfare or economic policy issue facing the American political system today? The single most important national security or homeland security issue? What do you think ought to be done about them?
- What factors increasingly blur the distinction between foreign and domestic policy issues? How does "homeland security" fit into this context?
- How would you compare President Obama's performance in the areas of social welfare and economic policies with the way he has handled national security and diplomatic affairs? What changes has he tried to make in each of these areas?
- What policy issues currently viewed as minor matters seem destined to develop into crisis situations?
- How important a policy issue for Americans is climate change or global warming? How important is it for you?
- What short-term and long-term effects did the events of September 11, 2001 have on the U.S. policy process and the direction of U.S. government policies?
- What do you think about the idea of devolution, which means giving state and local governments more responsibility for policymaking and policy implementation, and the national government less? What reasons are there to expect that state and local governments will do a better—or worse—job than the national government in such areas as welfare and access to health-care for the old and the poor?
- How and why would you prioritize the following list of policy challenges facing American government? Which do you think need to be addressed quickly and forcefully, even if that means delaying on others? List of policy challenges: economic recovery, global warming, health care reform, homeland security, education, the budget deficit and the national debt, and rapidly increasing Social Security and Medicare costs associated with the coming retirements of the baby boomer generation.

Student Website
www.mhhe.com/cls

Internet References

American Diplomacy
http://www.unc.edu/depts/diplomat/

Cato Institute
http://www.cato.org/research/ss_prjct.html

Foreign Affairs
http://www.foreignaffairs.org

International Information Programs
http://usinfo.state.gov

STAT-USA
http://www.stat-usa.gov/stat-usa.html

Tax Foundation
http://www.taxfoundation.org/index.html

"Products" refers to the government policies that the American political system produces. The first three units of this book have paved the way for this fourth unit, because the products of American politics are very much the consequences of the rest of the political system.

The health of the American economy is almost always a prominent policy issue in the American political system. One of the most remarkable consequences of twelve years (1981–1993) under President Reagan and the first President Bush was enormous growth in budget deficits and in the national debt. During the Clinton presidency, the country enjoyed the longest period of continuous economic growth in U.S. history, accompanied by low unemployment and low inflation rates. Continuing economic growth increased tax revenues to such an extent that the long-sought goal of a balanced budget was reached in 1998 amid predictions that the entire national debt would be eliminated within a decade or so. In the last months of the Clinton administration, however, some signs of an economic slowdown appeared. President George W. Bush pushed tax cuts through Congress early in his presidency, the country entered a recession in the second half of President Bush's first year in office, and the September 11 terrorist attacks accelerated the economic downturn. Large budget deficits returned and the national debt grew accordingly. By 2007, with the costs of the war in Iraq continuing to mount and the retirement of baby boomers drawing ever nearer, the country's fiscal situation was a cause for serious concern.

In 2008, home mortgage and other financial market problems shook the foundations of the nation's credit and banking systems, bringing Wall Street woes and a recession. Meanwhile, the national government's budget deficit soared, and growth in the national debt exceeded even that which had occurred during the Reagan administration and the first Bush presidency. By late 2008, it was unclear whether the traditional mainstays of American industry, the Big Three automakers, would avoid bankruptcy, as they publicly sought a "bail-out" from Washington in order to survive. Economic problems in the United States reverberated around the globe and many observers suggested that the economic downturn was going to be the worst since the Great Depression.

In its first months in office, the Obama administration concentrated on the country's economic woes. Besides using the second half of the $700-billion dollar Troubled Asset Relief Program (TARP) to try to prop up failing financial institutions as well as General Motors and Chrysler, President Obama pushed Congress for a stimulus package to try to get the economy growing again. The result was a stimulus bill providing $787 billion to try to combat the recession. By late 2009 economic growth had returned, but amidst high unemployment rates that threatened "a jobless recovery." TARP and stimulus spending, combined with the costs of America's wars in Iraq and Afghanistan, and other costs associated with the recession made national government budget deficits reach the highest levels since the end of World War II. While Obama supporters claimed that his policies had saved the country from another great depression, Obama critics expressed concern about the mounting national debt, the continuing huge budget deficits, and when prosperity would return to the United States.

© S. Meltzer/PhotoLink/Getty Images RF

Domestic public policy usually involves "trade-offs" among competing uses of scarce resources. During his 1992 campaign, Bill Clinton called attention to many such trade-offs in the area of health care. As president, Clinton introduced a comprehensive health care reform proposal late in 1993. Congress never voted on that proposal, and, while various minor changes were made in the nation's health care delivery system during the Clinton administration, no comprehensive overhaul was ever achieved. In his 2007 State of the Union address, President Bush presented several proposals relating to health care, including a change in relevant tax code provisions. Health care reform was a major priority of the two leading candidates for the Democratic presidential nomination in 2008, Hillary Clinton and Barack Obama, and change-oriented Obama's victory over John McCain would, under ordinary circumstances, have suggested that some action would be taken.

As this is written in early November 2009, the U.S. Congress seems reasonably close to passing a major health care reform package. But passage is hardly a certainty, and, if a health care reform bill is passed, its exact shape cannot be predicted, even after months and months of public debate in both the House and Senate and in the nation as a whole. There are still trade-offs to be made among competing ideas about what ought to be in the bill and about how much the final price tag can be and how to pay for it. Moreover, by urging Congress to work on passing a health care reform bill as priority matter, President Obama and congressional leaders have accepted inevitable trade-offs: efforts to pass cap-and-trade legislation to reduce greenhouse gas emissions and to enact immigration reform will be delayed in favor of getting health care reform enacted.

For most of the last half of the twentieth century, the United States and the Soviet Union each had the capacity to end human existence as we know it. Not surprisingly, the threat of nuclear war often dominated American foreign policy and diplomacy. During that same period, however, the United States used conventional military forces in a number of places, including Korea, Vietnam, Grenada, and Panama.

The demise of the Soviet Union in 1991 left the United States as the world's sole superpower, profoundly affecting world politics and U.S. foreign policy ever since. Questions about the appropriateness of U.S. intervention in such disparate places as Bosnia-Herzegovina, Somalia, Haiti, Iraq, Kosovo, and even Russia were at the forefront of foreign policy concerns during the Clinton administration. The George W. Bush administration and the nation as a whole, of course, became preoccupied with antiterrorism efforts and homeland and national security after the September 11 terrorist attacks.

The foreign and defense policy process in the United States raises a host of related issues, including continuing struggle between legislative and executive branches for control. In 1991, Congress authorized war with Iraq, which was the first time since World War II that there has been explicit and formal congressional approval before commencement of U.S. military hostilities. In late 1995, President Clinton committed the United States to sending troops to Bosnia-Herzegovina as part of a multinational peacekeeping force. Despite some opposition, Congress passed resolutions supporting the troops. Toward the end of 1997, President Saddam Hussein of Iraq obstructed UN weapons inspection teams in his country, and President Clinton responded by increasing the readiness of U.S. military forces in the Persian Gulf. In late 1998, several days of U.S. air strikes on Iraq followed what was viewed as further provocation.

In the aftermath of the 9/11 terrorist attacks in 2001, Congress supported President George W. Bush in pursuing the perpetrators and launching an assault on Al Qaeda sites in Afghanistan. In the fall of 2002, Congress authorized President Bush to wage war against Iraq if he deemed it necessary to safeguard American security. Early in 2003, U.S. forces invaded Iraq, and critics in Congress and elsewhere suggested that President Bush had made insufficient attempts to gain international support. The initial military success in toppling Saddam Hussein's government has been followed by years of violent insurgency that threatened the legitimacy of Iraqi self-government, killed more than 4,000 U.S. troops and many multiples of that number of Iraqis, and cost billions and billions of dollars. Americans' dissatisfaction with the Iraq war led to the Democratic takeover of the House and Senate in November 2006, which in turn set the stage for a sharp debate between President Bush and Congress about what to do next and about the proper role of each branch in shaping national security policy.

Barack Obama made his early opposition to the Iraq war a cornerstone of his 2008 presidential candidacy and promised to remove American troops from Iraq in a timely manner if he became president. By late 2008, the Iraqi government declared that American troops should be removed from Iraq within three years. During the transition period between his election and his taking the oath of office on January 20, 2009, Obama announced that he would keep President Bush's Secretary of Defense, Robert Gates, one of whose responsibilities would be to oversee the safe withdrawal of American troops from Iraq. This move suggested that, at long last, American policy-makers and the American public were moving toward a consensus about ending American military involvement in Iraq. In the second month of his presidency, President Obama announced his plan to withdraw American combat troops from Iraq by August 2010, a process that was underway by the end of 2009. But even as his Iraq withdrawal plan was being met with approval by most Americans, in the fall of 2009 President Obama found himself wrestling with various military options in Afghanistan, which ranged, according to some observers, from "bad" to "worse." U.S. military forces in Afghanistan faced a resurgent Taliban insurgency and the corrupt Afghanistan government led many Americans to wonder whether mounting American casualties in Afghanistan were justified.

The traditional distinction between domestic and foreign policy is becoming more and more difficult to maintain, since so many contemporary policy decisions have important implications on both fronts. President Clinton's emphasis on the connection between domestic and international economic issues in maintaining what he called national economic security reinforced this point. In turn, he worked hard to pass the NAFTA accord of 1993, which dramatically reduced trade barriers among Canada, Mexico, and the United States. Similarly, President George W. Bush has repeatedly noted the connection between, on the one hand, military and diplomatic activities with respect to faraway places like Afghanistan, Iraq, Iran, and North Korea and, on the other, homeland security in the post-September 11 era. In his second inaugural address in 2005, President Bush declared that the liberty and security of Americans at home depends on the "expansion of freedom in all the world."

Two prominent policy challenges facing the Obama administration, economic recovery and global warming, further illustrate the convergence between domestic and foreign policy. With an increasingly globalized economy, the economic health of the United States is inevitably tied to economic conditions around the world. Similarly, no unilateral action by the United States to fight global warming can be successful; strategies to combat climate change can succeed only if pursued on a multilateral, or global, level.

Article 45

The Tax-Cut Con

PAUL KRUGMAN

1. The Cartoon and the Reality

Bruce Tinsley's comic strip, "Mallard Fillmore," is, he says, "for the average person out there: the forgotten American taxpayer who's sick of the liberal media." In June, that forgotten taxpayer made an appearance in the strip, attacking his TV set with a baseball bat and yelling: "I can't afford to send my kids to college, or even take 'em out of their substandard public school, because the federal, state and local governments take more than 50 percent of my income in taxes. And then the guy on the news asks with a straight face whether or not we can 'afford' tax cuts."

But that's just a cartoon. Meanwhile, Bob Riley has to face the reality.

Riley knows all about substandard public schools. He's the governor of Alabama, which ranks near the bottom of the nation in both spending per pupil and educational achievement. The state has also neglected other public services—for example, 28,000 inmates are held in a prison system built for 12,000. And thanks in part to a lack of health care, it has the second-highest infant mortality in the nation.

When he was a member of Congress, Riley, a Republican, was a staunch supporter of tax cuts. Faced with a fiscal crisis in his state, however, he seems to have had an epiphany. He decided that it was impossible to balance Alabama's budget without a significant tax increase. And that, apparently, led him to reconsider everything. "The largest tax increase in state history just to maintain the status quo?" he asked. "I don't think so." Instead, Riley proposed a wholesale restructuring of the state's tax system: reducing taxes on the poor and middle class while raising them on corporations and the rich and increasing overall tax receipts enough to pay for a big increase in education spending. You might call it a New Deal for Alabama.

Nobody likes paying taxes, and no doubt some Americans are as angry about their taxes as Tinsley's imaginary character. But most Americans also care a lot about the things taxes pay for. All politicians say they're for public education; almost all of them also say they support a strong national defense, maintaining Social Security and, if anything, expanding the coverage of Medicare. When the "guy on the news" asks whether we can afford a tax cut, he's asking whether, after yet another tax cut goes through, there will be enough money to pay for those things. And the answer is no.

But it's very difficult to get that answer across in modern American politics, which has been dominated for 25 years by a crusade against taxes.

I don't use the word "crusade" lightly. The advocates of tax cuts are relentless, even fanatical. An indication of the movement's fervor—and of its political power—came during the Iraq war. War is expensive and is almost always accompanied by tax increases. But not in 2003. "Nothing is more important in the face of a war," declared Tom DeLay, the House majority leader, "than cutting taxes." And sure enough, taxes were cut, not just in a time of war but also in the face of record budget deficits. Nor will it be easy to reverse those tax cuts: the tax-cut movement has convinced many Americans—like Tinsley—that everybody still pays far too much in taxes.

A result of the tax-cut crusade is that there is now a fundamental mismatch between the benefits Americans expect to receive from the government and the revenues government collect. This mismatch is already having profound effects at the state and local levels: teachers and policemen are being laid off and children are being denied health insurance. The federal government can mask its problems for a while, by running huge budget deficits, but it, too, will eventually have to decide whether to cut services or raise taxes. And we are not talking about minor policy adjustments. If taxes stay as low as they are now, government as we know it cannot be maintained. In particular, Social Security will have to become far less generous; Medicare will no longer be able to guarantee comprehensive medical care to older Americans; Medicaid will no longer provide basic medical care to the poor.

How did we reach this point? What are the origins of the antitax crusade? And where is it taking us? To answer these questions, we will have to look both at who the antitax crusaders are and at the evidence on what tax cuts do to the budget and the economy. But first, let's set the stage by taking a look at the current state of taxation in America.

2. How High Are Our Taxes?

The reason Tinsley's comic strip about the angry taxpayer caught my eye was, of course, that the numbers were all wrong. Very few Americans pay as much as 50 percent of their income in taxes; on average, families near the middle of the income distribution pay only about half that percentage in federal, state and local taxes combined.

In fact, though most Americans feel that they pay too much in taxes, they get off quite lightly compared with the citizens of other advanced countries. Furthermore, for most Americans

ANNUAL EDITIONS

tax rates probably haven't risen for a generation. And a few Americans—namely those with high incomes—face much lower taxes than they did a generation ago.

To assess trends in the overall level of taxes and to compare taxation across countries, economists usually look first at the ratio of taxes to gross domestic product, the total value of output produced in the country. In the United States, all taxes—federal, state and local—reached a peak of 29.6 percent of G.D.P. in 2000. That number was, however, swollen by taxes on capital gains during the stock-market bubble.

By 2002, the tax take was down to 26.3 percent of G.D.P., and all indications are that it will be lower still this year and next.

This is a low number compared with almost every other advanced country. In 1999, Canada collected 38.2 percent of G.D.P. in taxes, France collected 45.8 percent and Sweden, 52.2 percent.

Still, aren't taxes much higher than they used to be? Not if we're looking back over the past 30 years. As a share of G.D.P., federal taxes are currently at their lowest point since the Eisenhower administration. State and local taxes rose substantially between 1960 and the early 1970's, but have been roughly stable since then. Aside from the capital gains taxes paid during the bubble years, the share of income Americans pay in taxes has been flat since Richard Nixon was president.

Of course, overall levels of taxation don't necessarily tell you how heavily particular individuals and families are taxed. As it turns out, however, middle-income Americans, like the country as a whole, haven't seen much change in their overall taxes over the past 30 years. On average, families in the middle of the income distribution find themselves paying about 26 percent of their income in taxes today. This number hasn't changed significantly since 1989, and though hard data are lacking, it probably hasn't changed much since 1970.

Meanwhile, wealthy Americans have seen a sharp drop in their tax burden. The top tax rate—the income-tax rate on the highest bracket—is now 35 percent, half what it was in the 1970's. With the exception of a brief period between 1988 and 1993, that's the lowest rate since 1932. Other taxes that, directly or indirectly, bear mainly on the very affluent have also been cut sharply. The effective tax rate on corporate profits has been cut in half since the 1960's. The 2001 tax cut phases out the inheritance tax, which is overwhelmingly a tax on the very wealthy: in 1999, only 2 percent of estates paid any tax, and half the tax was paid by only 3,300 estates worth more than $5 million. The 2003 tax act sharply cuts taxes on dividend income, another boon to the very well off. By the time the Bush tax cuts have taken full effect, people with really high incomes will face their lowest average tax rate since the Hoover administration.

So here's the picture: Americans pay low taxes by international standards. Most people's taxes haven't gone up in the past generation; the wealthy have had their taxes cut to levels not seen since before the New Deal. Even before the latest round of tax cuts, when compared with citizens of other advanced nations or compared with Americans a generation ago, we had nothing to complain about—and those with high incomes now have a lot to celebrate. Yet a significant number of Americans rage against taxes, and the party that controls all three branches of the federal government has made tax cuts its supreme priority. Why?

3. Supply-Siders, Starve-the-Beasters and Lucky Duckies

It is often hard to pin down what antitax crusaders are trying to achieve. The reason is not, or not only, that they are disingenuous about their motives—though as we will see, disingenuity has become a hallmark of the movement in recent years. Rather, the fuzziness comes from the fact that today's antitax movement moves back and forth between two doctrines. Both doctrines favor the same thing: big tax cuts for people with high incomes. But they favor it for different reasons.

One of those doctrines has become famous under the name "supply-side economics." It's the view that the government can cut taxes without severe cuts in public spending. The other doctrine is often referred to as "starving the beast," a phrase coined by David Stockman, Ronald Reagan's budget director. It's the view that taxes should be cut precisely in order to force severe cuts in public spending. Supply-side economics is the friendly, attractive face of the tax-cut movement. But starve-the-beast is where the power lies.

The starting point of supply-side economics is an assertion that no economist would dispute: taxes reduce the incentive to work, save and invest. A businessman who knows that 70 cents of every extra dollar he makes will go to the I.R.S. is less willing to make the effort to earn that extra dollar than if he knows that the I.R.S. will take only 35 cents. So reducing tax rates will, other things being the same, spur the economy.

This much isn't controversial. But the government must pay its bills. So the standard view of economists is that if you want to reduce the burden of taxes, you must explain what government programs you want to cut as part of the deal. There's no free lunch.

What the supply-siders argued, however, was that there was a free lunch. Cutting marginal rates, they insisted, would lead to such a large increase in gross domestic product that it wouldn't be necessary to come up with offsetting spending cuts. What supply-side economists say, in other words, is, "Don't worry, be happy and cut taxes." And when they say cut taxes, they mean taxes on the affluent: reducing the top marginal rate means that the biggest tax cuts go to people in the highest tax brackets.

The other camp in the tax-cut crusade actually welcomes the revenue losses from tax cuts. Its most visible spokesman today is Grover Norquist, president of Americans for Tax Reform, who once told National Public Radio: "I don't want to abolish government. I simply want to reduce it to the size where I can drag it into the bathroom and drown it in the bathtub." And the way to get it down to that size is to starve it of revenue. "The goal is reducing the size and scope of government by draining its lifeblood," Norquist told *U.S. News & World Report*.

What does "reducing the size and scope of government" mean? Tax-cut proponents are usually vague about the details. But the Heritage Foundation, ideological headquarters for the movement, has made it pretty clear. Edwin Feulner, the foundation's president, uses "New Deal" and "Great Society" as terms of abuse, implying that he and his organization want to do away with the institutions Franklin Roosevelt and Lyndon Johnson created. That means Social Security, Medicare, Medicaid—most of what gives citizens of the United States a safety net against economic misfortune.

The starve-the-beast doctrine is now firmly within the conservative mainstream. George W. Bush himself seemed to endorse the doctrine as the budget surplus evaporated: in August 2001 he called the disappearing surplus "incredibly positive news" because it would put Congress in a "fiscal straitjacket."

Like supply-siders, starve-the-beasters favor tax cuts mainly for people with high incomes. That is partly because, like supply-siders, they emphasize the incentive effects of cutting the top marginal rate; they just don't believe that those incentive effects are big enough that tax cuts pay for themselves. But they have another reason for cutting taxes mainly on the rich, which has become known as the "lucky ducky" argument.

Here's how the argument runs: to starve the beast, you must not only deny funds to the government; you must make voters hate the government. There's a danger that working-class families might see government as their friend: because their incomes are low, they don't pay much in taxes, while they benefit from public spending. So in starving the beast, you must take care not to cut taxes on these "lucky duckies." (Yes, that's what *The Wall Street Journal* called them in a famous editorial.) In fact, if possible, you must *raise* taxes on working-class Americans in order, as *The Journal* said, to get their "blood boiling with tax rage."

So the tax-cut crusade has two faces. Smiling supply-siders say that tax cuts are all gain, no pain; scowling starve-the-beasters believe that inflicting pain is not just necessary but also desirable. Is the alliance between these two groups a marriage of convenience? Not exactly. It would be more accurate to say that the starve-the-beasters hired the supply-siders—indeed, created them—because they found their naive optimism useful.

A look at who the supply-siders are and how they came to prominence tells the story.

The supply-side movement likes to present itself as a school of economic thought like Keynesianism or monetarism—that is, as a set of scholarly ideas that made their way, as such ideas do, into political discussion. But the reality is quite different. Supply-side economics was a political doctrine from Day 1; it emerged in the pages of political magazines, not professional economics journals.

That is not to deny that many professional economists favor tax cuts. But they almost always turn out to be starve-the-beasters, not supply-siders. And they often secretly—or sometimes not so secretly—hold supply-siders in contempt. N. Gregory Mankiw, now chairman of George W. Bush's Council of Economic Advisers, is definitely a friend to tax cuts; but in the first edition of his economic-principles textbook, he described Ronald Reagan's supply-side advisers as "charlatans and cranks."

It is not that the professionals refuse to consider supply-side ideas; rather, they have looked at them and found them wanting. A conspicuous example came earlier this year when the Congressional Budget Office tried to evaluate the growth effects of the Bush administration's proposed tax cuts. The budget office's new head, Douglas Holtz-Eakin, is a conservative economist who was handpicked for his job by the administration. But his conclusion was that unless the revenue losses from the proposed tax cuts were offset by spending cuts, the resulting deficits would be a drag on growth, quite likely to outweigh any supply-side effects.

But if the professionals regard the supply-siders with disdain, who employs these people? The answer is that since the 1970s almost all of the prominent supply-siders have been aides to conservative politicians, writers at conservative publications like *National Review*, fellows at conservative policy centers like Heritage or economists at private companies with strong Republican connections. Loosely speaking, that is, supply-siders work for the vast right-wing conspiracy. What gives supply-side economics influence is its connection with a powerful network of institutions that want to shrink the government and see tax cuts as a way to achieve that goal. Supply-side economics is a feel-good cover story for a political movement with a much harder-nosed agenda.

This isn't just speculation. Irving Kristol, in his role as co-editor of *The Public Interest*, was arguably the single most important proponent of supply-side economics. But years later, he suggested that he himself wasn't all that persuaded by the doctrine: "I was not certain of its economic merits but quickly saw its political possibilities." Writing in 1995, he explained that his real aim was to shrink the government and that tax cuts were a means to that end: "The task, as I saw it, was to create a new majority, which evidently would mean a conservative majority, which came to mean, in turn, a Republican majority—so political effectiveness was the priority, not the accounting deficiencies of government."

In effect, what Kristol said in 1995 was that he and his associates set out to deceive the American public. They sold tax cuts on the pretense that they would be painless, when they themselves believed that it would be necessary to slash public spending in order to make room for those cuts.

But one supposes that the response would be that the end justified the means—that the tax cuts did benefit all Americans because they led to faster economic growth. Did they?

4. From Reaganomics to Clintonomics

Ronald Reagan put supply-side theory into practice with his 1981 tax cut. The tax cuts were modest for middle-class families but very large for the well-off. Between 1979 and 1983, according to Congressional Budget Office estimates, the average federal tax rate on the top 1 percent of families fell from 37 to 27.7 percent.

So did the tax cuts promote economic growth? You might think that all we have to do is look at how the economy performed. But it's not that simple, because different observers read different things from Reagan's economic record.

Here's how tax-cut advocates look at it: after a deep slump between 1979 and 1982, the U.S. economy began growing rapidly. Between 1982 and 1989 (the first year of the first George Bush's presidency), the economy grew at an average annual rate of 4.2 percent. That's a lot better than the growth rate of the economy in the late 1970s, and supply-siders claim that these "Seven Fat Years" (the title of a book by Robert L. Bartley, the longtime editor of *The Wall Street Journal*'s editorial page) prove the success of Reagan's 1981 tax cut.

But skeptics say that rapid growth after 1982 proves nothing: a severe recession is usually followed by a period of fast growth, as unemployed workers and factories are brought back on line. The test of tax cuts as a spur to economic growth is whether they produced more than an ordinary business cycle recovery. Once the economy was back to full employment, was it bigger than you would otherwise have expected? And there Reagan fails the test: between 1979, when the big slump began, and 1989, when the economy finally achieved more or less full employment again, the growth rate was 3 percent, the same as the growth rate between the two previous business cycle peaks in 1973 and 1979. Or to put it another way, by the late 1980s the U.S. economy was about where you would have expected it to be, given the trend in the 1970s. Nothing in the data suggests a supply-side revolution.

Does this mean that the Reagan tax cuts had no effect? Of course not. Those tax cuts, combined with increased military spending, provided a good old-fashioned Keynesian boost to demand. And this boost was one factor in the rapid recovery from recession that developed at the end of 1982, though probably not as important as the rapid expansion of the money supply that began in the summer of that year. But the supposed supply-side effects are invisible in the data.

While the Reagan tax cuts didn't produce any visible supply-side gains, they did lead to large budget deficits. From the point of view of most economists, this was a bad thing. But for starve-the-beast tax-cutters, deficits are potentially a good thing, because they force the government to shrink. So did Reagan's deficits shrink the beast?

A casual glance at the data might suggest not: federal spending as a share of gross domestic product was actually slightly higher at the end of the 1980s than it was at the end of the 1970s. But that number includes both defense spending and "entitlements," mainly Social Security and Medicare, whose growth is automatic unless Congress votes to cut benefits. What's left is a grab bag known as domestic discretionary spending, including everything from courts and national parks to environmental cleanups and education. And domestic discretionary spending fell from 4.5 percent of G.D.P. in 1981 to 3.2 percent in 1988.

But that's probably about as far as any president can shrink domestic discretionary spending. And because Reagan couldn't shrink the belly of the beast, entitlements, he couldn't find enough domestic spending cuts to offset his military spending increases and tax cuts. The federal budget went into persistent, alarming, deficit. In response to these deficits, George Bush the elder went back on his "read my lips" pledge and raised taxes. Bill Clinton raised them further. And thereby hangs a tale.

For Clinton did exactly the opposite of what supply-side economics said you should do: he raised the marginal rate on high-income taxpayers. In 1989, the top 1 percent of families paid, on average, only 28.9 percent of their income in federal taxes; by 1995, that share was up to 36.1 percent.

Conservatives confidently awaited a disaster—but it failed to materialize. In fact, the economy grew at a reasonable pace through Clinton's first term, while the deficit and the unemployment rate went steadily down. And then the news got even better: unemployment fell to its lowest level in decades without causing inflation, while productivity growth accelerated to rates not seen since the 1960s. And the budget deficit turned into an impressive surplus.

Tax-cut advocates had claimed the Reagan years as proof of their doctrine's correctness; as we have seen, those claims wilt under close examination. But the Clinton years posed a much greater challenge: here was a president who sharply raised the marginal tax rate on high-income taxpayers, the very rate that the tax-cut movement cares most about. And instead of presiding over an economic disaster, he presided over an economic miracle.

Let's be clear: very few economists think that Clinton's policies were primarily responsible for that miracle. For the most part, the Clinton-era surge probably reflected the maturing of information technology: businesses finally figured out how to make effective use of computers, and the resulting surge in productivity drove the economy forward. But the fact that America's best growth in a generation took place after the government did exactly the opposite of what tax-cutters advocate was a body blow to their doctrine.

They tried to make the best of the situation. The good economy of the late 1990s, ardent tax-cutters insisted, was caused by the 1981 tax cut. Early in 2000, Lawrence Kudlow and Stephen Moore, prominent supply-siders, published an article titled "It's the Reagan Economy, Stupid."

But anyone who thought about the lags involved found this implausible—indeed, hilarious. If the tax-cut movement attributed the booming economy of 1999 to a tax cut Reagan pushed through 18 years earlier, why didn't they attribute the economic boom of 1983 and 1984—Reagan's "morning in America"—to whatever Lyndon Johnson was doing in 1965 and 1966?

By the end of the 1990s, in other words, supply-side economics had become something of a laughingstock, and the whole case for tax cuts as a route to economic growth was looking pretty shaky. But the tax-cut crusade was nonetheless, it turned out, poised for its biggest political victories yet. How did that happen?

5. Second Wind: The Bush Tax Cuts

As the economic success of the United States under Bill Clinton became impossible to deny, there was a gradual shift in the sales strategy for tax cuts. The supposed economic benefits of tax cuts received less emphasis; the populist rationale—you, personally, pay too much in taxes—was played up.

I began this article with an example of this campaign's success: the creator of Mallard Fillmore apparently believes that typical families pay twice as much in taxes as they in fact do. But the most striking example of what skillful marketing can accomplish is the campaign for repeal of the estate tax.

As demonstrated, the estate tax is a tax on the very, very well off. Yet advocates of repeal began portraying it as a terrible burden on the little guy. They renamed it the "death tax" and put out reports decrying its impact on struggling farmers and businessmen—reports that never provided real-world examples because actual cases of family farms or small businesses broken up to pay estate taxes are almost impossible to find. This campaign succeeded in creating a public perception that the estate tax falls broadly on the population. Earlier this year, a poll found that 49 percent of Americans believed that most families had to pay the estate tax, while only 33 percent gave the right answer that only a few families had to pay.

Still, while an insistent marketing campaign has convinced many Americans that they are overtaxed, it hasn't succeeded in making the issue a top priority with the public. Polls consistently show that voters regard safeguarding Social Security and Medicare as much more important than tax cuts.

Nonetheless, George W. Bush has pushed through tax cuts in each year of his presidency. Why did he push for these tax cuts, and how did he get them through?

You might think that you could turn to the administration's own pronouncements to learn why it has been so determined to cut taxes. But even if you try to take the administration at its word, there's a problem: the public rationale for tax cuts has shifted repeatedly over the past three years.

During the 2000 campaign and the initial selling of the 2001 tax cut, the Bush team insisted that the federal government was running an excessive budget surplus, which should be returned to taxpayers. By the summer of 2001, as it became clear that the projected budget surpluses would not materialize, the administration shifted to touting the tax cuts as a form of demand-side economic stimulus: by putting more money in consumers' pockets, the tax cuts would stimulate spending and help pull the economy out of recession. By 2003, the rationale had changed again: the administration argued that reducing taxes on dividend income, the core of its plan, would improve incentives and hence long-run growth—that is, it had turned to a supply-side argument.

These shifting rationales had one thing in common: none of them were credible. It was obvious to independent observers even in 2001 that the budget projections used to justify that year's tax cut exaggerated future revenues and understated future costs. It was similarly obvious that the 2001 tax cut was poorly designed as a demand stimulus. And we have already seen that the supply-side rationale for the 2003 tax cut was tested and found wanting by the Congressional Budget Office.

So what were the Bush tax cuts really about? The best answer seems to be that they were about securing a key part of the Republican base. Wealthy campaign contributors have a lot to gain from lower taxes, and since they aren't very likely to depend on Medicare, Social Security or Medicaid, they won't suffer if the beast gets starved. Equally important was the support of the party's intelligentsia, nurtured by policy centers like Heritage and professionally committed to the tax-cut crusade. The original Bush tax-cut proposal was devised in late 1999 not to win votes in the national election but to fend off a primary challenge from the supply-sider Steve Forbes, the presumptive favorite of that part of the base.

This brings us to the next question: how have these cuts been sold?

At this point, one must be blunt: the selling of the tax cuts has depended heavily on chicanery. The administration has used accounting trickery to hide the true budget impact of its proposals, and it has used misleading presentations to conceal the extent to which its tax cuts are tilted toward families with very high income.

The most important tool of accounting trickery, though not the only one, is the use of "sunset clauses" to understate the long-term budget impact of tax cuts. To keep the official 10-year cost of the 2001 tax cut down, the administration's Congressional allies wrote the law so that tax rates revert to their 2000 levels in 2011. But, of course, nobody expects the sunset to occur: when 2011 rolls around, Congress will be under immense pressure to extend the tax cuts.

The same strategy was used to hide the cost of the 2003 tax cut. Thanks to sunset clauses, its headline cost over the next decade was only $350 billion, but if the sunsets are canceled—as the president proposed in a speech early this month—the cost will be at least $800 billion.

Meanwhile, the administration has carried out a very successful campaign to portray these tax cuts as mainly aimed at middle-class families. This campaign is similar in spirit to the selling of estate-tax repeal as a populist measure, but considerably more sophisticated.

The reality is that the core measures of both the 2001 and 2003 tax cuts mainly benefit the very affluent. The centerpieces of the 2001 act were a reduction in the top income-tax rate and elimination of the estate tax—the first, by definition, benefiting only people with high incomes; the second benefiting only heirs to large estates. The core of the 2003 tax cut was a reduction in the tax rate on dividend income. This benefit, too, is concentrated on very high-income families.

According to estimates by the Tax Policy Center—a liberal-oriented institution, but one with a reputation for scrupulous accuracy—the 2001 tax cut, once fully phased in, will deliver 42 percent of its benefits to the top 1 percent of the income distribution. (Roughly speaking, that means families earning more than $330,000 per year.) The 2003 tax cut delivers a somewhat smaller share to the top 1 percent, 29.1 percent, but within that concentrates its benefits on the really, really rich. Families with incomes over $1 million a year—a mere 0.13 percent of the population—will receive 17.3 percent of this year's tax cut, more than the total received by the bottom 70 percent of American families. Indeed, the 2003 tax cut has already proved a major boon to some of America's wealthiest people: corporations in which executives or a single family hold a large fraction of stocks are suddenly paying much bigger dividends, which are now taxed at only 15 percent no matter how high the income of their recipient.

It might seem impossible to put a populist gloss on tax cuts this skewed toward the rich, but the administration has been remarkably successful in doing just that.

One technique involves exploiting the public's lack of statistical sophistication. In the selling of the 2003 tax cut, the catch phrase used by administration spokesmen was "92 million Americans will receive an average tax cut of $1,083." That sounded, and was intended to sound, as if every American family would get $1,083. Needless to say, that wasn't true.

Yet the catch phrase wasn't technically a lie: the Tax Policy Center estimates that 89 million people will receive tax cuts this year and that the total tax cut will be $99 billion, or about $1,100 for each of those 89 million people. But this calculation carefully leaves out the 50 million taxpayers who received no tax cut at all. And even among those who did get a tax cut, most got a lot less than $1,000, a number inflated by the very big tax cuts received by a few wealthy people. About half of American families received a tax cut of less than $100; the great majority, a tax cut of less than $500.

But the most original, you might say brilliant, aspect of the Bush administration's approach to tax cuts has involved the way the tax cuts themselves are structured.

David Stockman famously admitted that Reagan's middle-class tax cuts were a "Trojan horse" that allowed him to smuggle in what he really wanted, a cut in the top marginal rate. The Bush administration similarly follows a Trojan horse strategy, but an even cleverer one. The core measures in Bush's tax cuts benefit only the wealthy, but there are additional features that provide significant benefits to some—but only some—middle-class families. For example, the 2001 tax cut included a $400 child credit and also created a new 10 percent tax bracket, the so-called cutout. These measures had the effect of creating a "sweet spot" that could be exploited for political purposes. If a couple had multiple children, if the children were all still under 18 and if the couple's income was just high enough to allow it to take full advantage of the child credit, it could get a tax cut of as much as 4 percent of pretax income. Hence the couple with two children and an income of $40,000, receiving a tax cut of $1,600, who played such a large role in the administration's rhetoric. But while most couples have children, at any given time only a small minority of families contains two or more children under 18—and many of these families have income too low to take full advantage of the child tax credit. So that "typical" family wasn't typical at all. Last year, the actual tax break for families in the middle of the income distribution averaged $469, not $1,600.

So that's the story of the tax-cut offensive under the Bush administration: through a combination of hardball politics, deceptive budget arithmetic and systematic misrepresentation of who benefits, Bush's team has achieved a major reduction of taxes, especially for people with very high incomes.

But where does that leave the country?

6. A Planned Crisis

Right now, much of the public discussion of the Bush tax cuts focuses on their short-run impact. Critics say that the 2.7 million jobs lost since March 2001 prove that the administration's policies have failed, while the administration says that things would have been even worse without the tax cuts and that a solid recovery is just around the corner.

But this is the wrong debate. Even in the short run, the right question to ask isn't whether the tax cuts were better than nothing; they probably were. The right question is whether some other economic-stimulus plan could have achieved better results at a lower budget cost. And it is hard to deny that, on a jobs-per-dollar basis, the Bush tax cuts have been extremely ineffective. According to the Congressional Budget Office, half of this year's $400 billion budget deficit is due to Bush tax cuts. Now $200 billion is a lot of money; it is equivalent to the salaries of four million average workers. Even the administration doesn't claim its policies have created four million jobs. Surely some other policy—aid to state and local governments, tax breaks for the poor and middle class rather than the rich, maybe even W.P.A.-style public works—would have been more successful at getting the country back to work.

Meanwhile, the tax cuts are designed to remain in place even after the economy has recovered. Where will they leave us?

Here's the basic fact: partly, though not entirely, as a result of the tax cuts of the last three years, the government of the United States faces a fundamental fiscal shortfall. That is, the revenue it collects falls well short of the sums it needs to pay for existing programs. Even the U.S. government must, eventually, pay its bills, so something will have to give.

The numbers tell the tale. This year and next, the federal government will run budget deficits of more than $400 billion. Deficits may fall a bit, at least as a share of gross domestic product, when the economy recovers. But the relief will be modest and temporary. As Peter Fisher, under secretary of the treasury for domestic finance, puts it, the federal government is "a gigantic insurance company with a sideline business in defense and homeland security." And about a decade from now, this insurance company's policyholders will begin making a lot of claims. As the baby boomers retire, spending on Social Security benefits and Medicare will steadily rise, as will spending on Medicaid (because of rising medical costs). Eventually, unless there are sharp cuts in benefits, these three programs alone will consume a larger share of G.D.P. than the federal government currently collects in taxes.

Alan Auerbach, William Gale and Peter Orszag, fiscal experts at the Brookings Institution, have estimated the size of the "fiscal gap"—the increase in revenues or reduction in spending that would be needed to make the nation's finances sustainable in the long run. If you define the long run as 75 years, this gap turns out to be 4.5 percent of G.D.P. Or to put it another way, the gap is equal to 30 percent of what the federal government spends on all domestic programs. Of that gap, about 60 percent is the result of the Bush tax cuts. We would have faced a serious fiscal problem even if those tax cuts had never happened. But we face a much nastier problem now that they are in place. And more broadly, the tax-cut crusade will make it very hard for any future politicians to raise taxes.

So how will this gap be closed? The crucial point is that it cannot be closed without either fundamentally redefining the role of government or sharply raising taxes.

Politicians will, of course, promise to eliminate wasteful spending. But take out Social Security, Medicare, defense, Medicaid, government pensions, homeland security, interest on the public debt and veterans' benefits—none of them what people who complain about waste usually have in mind—and you are left with spending equal to about 3 percent of gross domestic product. And most of that goes for courts, highways, education and other useful things. Any savings from elimination of waste and fraud will amount to little more than a rounding-off error.

So let's put a few things back on the table. Let's assume that interest on the public debt will be paid, that spending on defense and homeland security will not be compromised and that the regular operations of government will continue to be financed. What we are left with, then, are the New Deal and Great Society programs: Social Security, Medicare, Medicaid and unemployment insurance. And to close the fiscal gap, spending on these programs would have to be cut by around 40 percent.

It's impossible to know how such spending cuts might unfold, but cuts of that magnitude would require drastic changes in the system. It goes almost without saying that the age at which Americans become eligible for retirement benefits would rise, that Social Security payments would fall sharply compared with average incomes, that Medicare patients would be forced to pay much more of their expenses out of pocket—or do without. And that would be only a start.

All this sounds politically impossible. In fact, politicians of both parties have been scrambling to expand, not reduce, Medicare benefits by adding prescription drug coverage. It's hard to imagine a situation under which the entitlement programs would be rolled back sufficiently to close the fiscal gap.

Yet closing the fiscal gap by raising taxes would mean rolling back all of the Bush tax cuts, and then some. And that also sounds politically impossible.

For the time being, there is a third alternative: borrow the difference between what we insist on spending and what we're willing to collect in taxes. That works as long as lenders believe that someday, somehow, we're going to get our fiscal act together. But this can't go on indefinitely. Eventually—I think within a decade, though not everyone agrees—the bond market will tell us that we have to make a choice.

In short, everything is going according to plan.

For the looming fiscal crisis doesn't represent a defeat for the leaders of the tax-cut crusade or a miscalculation on their part. Some supporters of President Bush may have really believed that his tax cuts were consistent with his promises to protect Social Security and expand Medicare; some people may still believe that the wondrous supply-side effects of tax cuts will make the budget deficit disappear. But for starve-the-beast tax-cutters, the coming crunch is exactly what they had in mind.

7. What Kind of Country?

The astonishing political success of the antitax crusade has, more or less deliberately, set the United States up for a fiscal crisis. How we respond to that crisis will determine what kind of country we become.

If Grover Norquist is right—and he has been right about a lot—the coming crisis will allow conservatives to move the nation a long way back toward the kind of limited government we had before Franklin Roosevelt. Lack of revenue, he says, will make it possible for conservative politicians—in the name of fiscal necessity—to dismantle immensely popular government programs that would otherwise have been untouchable.

In Norquist's vision, America a couple of decades from now will be a place in which elderly people make up a disproportionate share of the poor, as they did before Social Security. It will also be a country in which even middle-class elderly Americans are, in many cases, unable to afford expensive medical procedures or prescription drugs and in which poor Americans generally go without even basic health care. And it may well be a place in which only those who can afford expensive private schools can give their children a decent education.

But as Governor Riley of Alabama reminds us, that's a choice, not a necessity. The tax-cut crusade has created a situation in which something must give. But what gives—whether we decide that the New Deal and the Great Society must go or that taxes aren't such a bad thing after all—is up to us. The American people must decide what kind of a country we want to be.

PAUL KRUGMAN is a *Times* columnist and a professor at Princeton. His new book is *"The Great Unraveling: Losing Our Way in the New Century."*

From *The New York Times Magazine*, September 14, 2003. Copyright © 2003 by Paul Krugman. Distributed by the New York Times Special Features. Reprinted by permission.

The Realities of Immigration

LINDA CHAVEZ

What to do about immigration—both legal and illegal—has become one of the most controversial public-policy debates in recent memory. But why it has occurred at this particular moment is something of a mystery. The rate of immigration into the U.S., although high, is still below what it was even a few years ago, the peak having been reached in the late 1990s. President Bush first talked about comprehensive immigration reform almost immediately after assuming office, but he put the plan on hold after 9/11 and only reintroduced the idea in 2004. Why the current flap?

By far the biggest factor shaping the popular mood seems to have been the almost daily drumbeat on the issue from political talk-show hosts, most prominently CNN's Lou Dobbs and the Fox News Channel's Bill O'Reilly and Sean Hannity (both of whom also have popular radio shows), syndicated radio hosts Rush Limbaugh, Laura Ingraham, Michael Savage, and G. Gordon Liddy, and a plethora of local hosts reaching tens of millions of listeners each week. Stories about immigration have become a staple of cable news, with sensational footage of illegal crossings featured virtually every day.

Media saturation has led, in turn, to the emergence of immigration as a wedge issue in the still-nascent 2008 presidential campaign. Several aspiring Republican candidates—former House Speaker Newt Gingrich, Senate Majority Leader Bill Frist, and Senator George Allen—have worked to burnish their "get tough" credentials, while, on the other side of the issue, Senator John McCain has come forward as the lead sponsor of a bill to allow most illegal aliens to earn legal status. For their part, potential Democratic candidates have remained largely mum, unsure how the issue plays with their various constituencies.

And then there are the immigrants themselves, who have shown surprising political muscle, especially in response to legislation passed by the House that would turn the illegal aliens among them into felons. Millions of mostly Hispanic protesters have taken to the streets in our big cities in recent months, waving American flags and (more controversially) their own national flags while demanding recognition and better treatment. Though Hispanic leaders and pro-immigrant advocates point to the protests as evidence of a powerful new civil-rights movement, many other Americans see the demonstrators as proof of an alien invasion—and a looming threat to the country's prosperity and unity.

In short, it is hard to recall a time when there has been so much talk about immigration and immigration reform—or when so much of the talk has been misinformed, misleading, and ahistorical. Before policy-makers can decide what to do about immigration, the problem itself needs to be better defined, not just in terms of costs and benefits but in relation to America's deepest values.

Contrary to popular myth, immigrants have never been particularly welcome in the United States. Americans have always tended to romanticize the immigrants of their grandparents' generation while casting a skeptical eye on contemporary newcomers. In the first decades of the 20th century, descendants of Northern European immigrants resisted the arrival of Southern and Eastern Europeans, and today the descendants of those once unwanted Italians, Greeks, and Poles are deeply distrustful of current immigrants from Latin America. Congressman Tom Tancredo, a Republican from Colorado and an outspoken advocate of tighter restrictions, is fond of invoking the memory of his Italian immigrant grandfather to argue that he is not anti-immigrant, just anti-illegal immigration. He fails to mention that at the time his grandfather arrived, immigrants simply had to show up on American shores (or walk across the border) to gain legal entry.

With the exception of the infamous Alien and Sedition Acts of 1798, there were few laws regulating immigration for the first hundred years of the nation's history. Though nativist sentiment increased throughout the later decades of the 19th century, giving rise to the 1882 Chinese Exclusion Act, it was not until 1917 that Congress began methodically to limit all immigration, denying admission to most Asians and Pacific Islanders and, in 1924, imposing quotas on those deemed undesirable: Jews, Italians, and others from Southern and Eastern Europe. These restrictions remained largely in effect until 1952, when Congress lifted many of them, including the bar on Asians.

The modern immigration era commenced in 1965 with the passage of the Immigration and Nationality Act, which abolished all national-origin quotas, gave preference to close relatives of American citizens, refugees, and individuals with certain skills, and allowed for immigrants from the Western hemisphere on a first-come, first-served basis. The act's passage drew a huge wave, much of it from Latin America and Asia. From 1970 to 2000, the United States admitted more than 20 million persons as permanent residents.

By 2000, some 3 million of these new residents were formerly illegal aliens who had gained amnesty as part of the 1986 Immigration Reform and Control Act (IRCA). This, Congress's first serious attempt to stem the flow of illegal immigration, forced employers to determine the status of their workers and imposed heavy penalties on those hiring illegal entrants. But from the beginning, the law was fraught with problems. It created huge bureaucratic burdens, even for private individuals wanting to hire someone to cut their lawn or care for their children, and spawned a vast new document-fraud industry for immigrants eager to get hold of the necessary paperwork. The law has been a monumental failure. Today, some 11.5 million illegal aliens reside in the U.S.—quadruple the population of two decades ago, when IRCA was enacted—and the number is growing by an estimated 500,000 a year.

The status quo has thus become untenable, and particularly so since the attacks of 9/11, which prompted fears of future terrorists sneaking across our sieve-like borders as easily as would-be busboys, janitors, and construction workers. Though virtually all Americans agree that something must be done, finding a good solution has proven elusive. The Bush administration has significantly increased border enforcement, adding nearly 30-percent more border-patrol agents since 2001 and increasing funding by 66 percent. The border patrol now employs nearly as many agents as the FBI, over 12,000 by the end of this fiscal year (not counting the additional 6,000 proposed by the President in May). But with some 6,000 miles of land border to monitor, that figure represents only one agent per mile (assuming eight-hour, 'round-the-clock shifts). Still, there has been progress: illegal immigration has actually slowed a bit since its peak during the boom economy of the late 1990s—a fact rarely noted in the current debate—though it has begun climbing again.

The latest suggestion is to build a wall along the border with Mexico. Some sections of the border already have 10-foot-high steel fences in place, and bills recently passed by the House and Senate authorize the construction of hundreds of additional miles of fencing along the border in California, Arizona, New Mexico, and Texas. The President, too, has endorsed the idea of a more formidable barrier. The Minuteman Project, a group that fashions itself a citizens' patrol, has volunteered to build the fence on private property along the Arizona/Mexico border. But unless the United States is prepared to build fences on its southern and northern borders, illegal entry will continue, albeit in diminished numbers. (Some 200,000 illegal immigrants—the equivalent of 1.8 million in U.S. terms—now live in Canada; most are Asians, but they are increasingly being joined by Latin Americans who in many cases are hoping to make the United States their ultimate destination.) More problematic for advocates of a fence is that an estimated 45 percent of all illegal aliens enter lawfully and simply overstay the terms of their visas.

So what might alleviate the current situation? Restrictionists claim that better internal enforcement, with crackdowns on employers who hire illegal aliens, would deter more from coming. This might work if we were willing to adopt a national identification card for every person in the country and a sophisticated instant-check system to verify the employment eligibility of each of the nation's 150 million workers. But concern over immigration seems unlikely on its own to spark sufficient support for such a system. Even after 9/11, when some experts recommended national ID's as a necessary security measure, Americans were reluctant to endorse the idea, fearing its implications for privacy.

President Bush has now proposed a tamper-proof card that all foreign workers would be required to carry, though one can envision grave "profiling" difficulties with this, not least when native-born Hispanic and Asian workers are selectively asked to produce such identification. Moreover, an experimental version of a program to require instant checks of work eligibility—now included in both the House and the Senate immigration bills—produced a nearly 30-percent error rate for legal immigrants who were denied employment.

The real question is not whether the U.S. has the means to stop illegal immigration—no doubt, with sufficient resources, we could mostly do so—but whether we would be better off as a nation without these workers. Restrictionists claim that large-scale immigration—legal and illegal—has depressed wages, burdened government resources, and acted as a net drain on the economy. The Federation for American Immigration Reform (FAIR), the most prominent of the pressure groups on the issue, argues that, because of this influx, hourly earnings among American males have not increased appreciably in 30 years. As the restrictionists see it, if the U.S. got serious about defending its borders, there would be plenty of Americans willing to do the jobs now performed by workers from abroad.

Indeed, FAIR and other extremists on the issue wish not only to eliminate illegal immigration but drastically to reduce or halt legal immigration as well. Along with its public-policy arm, the Center for Immigration Studies (CIS), FAIR has long argued that the U.S. should aim for a population of just 150 million persons—that is, about half the current level. If such an agenda sounds suspiciously like views usually found on the Left, that is no accident.

One of the great ironies of the current immigration debate is the strange ideological bedfellows it has created. The founder of the modern anti-immigration movement, a Michigan physician named John Tanton, is the former national president of Zero Population Growth and a long-time activist with Planned Parenthood and several Left-leaning environmentalist groups. Tanton came to the issue of immigration primarily because of his fears about overpopulation and the destruction of natural resources. Through an umbrella organization, U.S. Inc., he has created or funded not only FAIR and CIS but such groups as NumbersUSA, Population-Environment Balance, Pro-English, and U.S. English.[1] The Social Contract Press, another of Tanton's outfits, is the English-language publisher of the apocalyptic—and frankly racist—1975 novel *Camp of the Saints,* written by the French right-wing author Jean Raspail. The book, which apparently had a considerable influence in shaping Tanton's own views, foretells the demise of Europe at the hands of hordes of East Indians who invade the continent, bringing with them disease, crime, and anarchy.

As for the more conventional claims advanced by restrictionists, they, too, are hard to credit. Despite the presence in our workforce of millions of illegal immigrants, the U.S. is currently creating slightly more than two million jobs a year and boasts an unemployment rate of 4.7 percent, which is lower than the average in each of the past four decades. More to the point perhaps, when the National Research Council (NRC) of the National Academy of Sciences evaluated the economic impact of immigration in its landmark 1997 study The New Americans: Economic, Demographic, and Fiscal Effects of Immigration, it found only a small negative impact on the earnings of Americans, and even then, only for workers at lower skill and education levels.

Moreover, the participation of immigrants in the labor force has had obvious positive effects. The NRC estimated that roughly 5 percent of household expenditures in the U.S. went to goods and services produced by immigrant labor—labor whose relative cheapness translated into lower prices for everything from chicken to new homes. These price advantages, the study found, were "spread quite uniformly across most types of domestic consumers," with a slightly greater benefit for higher-income households.

Many restrictionists argue that if Americans would simply cut their own lawns, clean their own houses, and care for their own children, there would be no need for immigrant labor. But even if this were true, the overall economy would hardly benefit from having fewer workers. If American women were unable to rely on immigrants to perform some household duties, more of them would be forced to stay home. A smaller labor force would also have devastating consequences when it comes to dealing with the national debt and government-funded entitlements like Social Security and Medicare, a point repeatedly made by former Federal Reserve Board Chairman Alan Greenspan. As he told a Senate committee in 2003, "short of a major increase in immigration, economic growth cannot be safely counted upon to eliminate deficits and the difficult choices that will be required to restore fiscal discipline." The following year, Greenspan noted that offsetting the fiscal effects of our own declining birthrate would require a level of immigration "much larger than almost all current projections assume."

The contributions that immigrants make to the economy must be weighed, of course, against the burdens they impose. FAIR and other restrictionist groups contend that immigrants are a huge drain on society because of the cost of providing public services to them—some $67 to $87 billion a year, according to one commonly cited study. Drawing on numbers from the NRC's 1997 report, FAIR argues that "the net fiscal drain on American taxpayers [from immigration] is between $166 and $226 a year per native household."

There is something to these assertions, though less than may at first appear. Much of the anxiety and resentment generated by immigrants is, indeed, a result of the very real costs they impose on state and local governments, especially in border states like California and Arizona. Providing education and health care to the children of immigrants is particularly expensive, and the federal government picks up only a fraction of the expense. But, again, there are countervailing factors. Illegal immigrants are hardly free-riders. An estimated three-quarters of them paid federal taxes in 2002, amounting to $7 billion in Social Security contributions and $1.5 billion in Medicare taxes, plus withholding for income taxes. They also pay state and local sales taxes and (as homeowners and renters) property taxes.

Moreover, FAIR and its ilk have a penchant for playing fast and loose with numbers. To support its assessment of immigration's overall fiscal burden, for instance, FAIR ignores the explicit cautions in a later NRC report about cross-sectional analyses that exclude the "concurrent descendants" of immigrants—that is, their adult children. These, overwhelmingly, are productive members of the workforce. As the NRC notes, when this more complete picture is taken into account, immigrants have "a positive federal impact of about $1,260 [per capita], exceeding their net cost [$680 per capita on average] at the state and local levels." Restrictionists also argue that fewer immigrants would mean more opportunities for low-skilled native workers. Of late, groups like the Minuteman Project have even taken to presenting themselves as champions of unemployed American blacks (a curious tactic, to say the least, considering the views on race and ethnicity of many in the anti-immigrant camp[2]).

But here, too, the factual evidence is mixed. Wages for American workers who have less than a high-school education have probably been adversely affected by large-scale immigration; the economist George Borjas estimates a reduction of 8 percent in hourly wages for native-born males in that category. But price competition is not the only reason that many employers favor immigrants over poorly educated natives. Human capital includes motivation, and there could hardly be two more disparately motivated groups than U.S.-born high-school dropouts and their foreign-born rivals in the labor market. Young American men usually leave high school because they become involved with drugs or crime, have difficulty with authority, cannot maintain regular hours, or struggle with learning. Immigrants, on the other hand, have demonstrated enormous initiative, reflecting, in the words of President Reagan, "a special kind of courage that enabled them to leave their own land, leave their friends and their countrymen, and come to this new and strange land."

Just as important, they possess a strong desire to work. Legal immigrants have an 86-percent rate of participation in the labor force; illegal immigrant males have a 94-percent rate. By contrast, among white males with less than a high-school education, the participation rate is 46 percent, while among blacks it is 40 percent. If all immigrants, or even only illegal aliens, disappeared from the American workforce, can anyone truly believe that poorly skilled whites and blacks would fill the gap? To the contrary, productivity would likely decline, and employers in many sectors would simply move their operations to countries like Mexico, China, and the Philippines, where many of our immigrants come from in the first place.

Of equal weight among foes of immigration are the cultural changes wrought by today's newcomers, especially those from Mexico. In his book *Who Are We? The Challenges to National Identity* (2004), the eminent political scientist Samuel P. Huntington warns that "Mexican immigration is leading toward the demographic reconquista of areas Americans took from Mexico by force in the 1830s and 1840s." Others have fretted about the aims of militant Mexican-American activists, pointing to "El Plan de Aztlan," a radical Hispanic manifesto hatched in 1969, which calls for "the control of our barrios, campos, pueblos, lands, our economy, our culture, and our political life," including "self-defense against the occupying forces of the oppressors"—that is, the U.S. government.

To be sure, the fantasy of a recaptured homeland exists mostly in the minds of a handful of already well-assimilated Mexican-American college professors and the students they manage to indoctrinate (self-described "victims" who often enjoy preferential admission to college and subsidized or free tuition). But such rhetoric understandably alarms many Americans, especially in light of the huge influx of Hispanic immigrants into the Southwest. Does it not seem likely that today's immigrants—because of their numbers, the constant flow of even more newcomers, and their proximity to their countries of origin—will be unable or unwilling to assimilate as previous ethnic groups have done?

There is no question that some public policies in the U.S. have actively discouraged assimilation. Bilingual education, the dominant method of instruction of Hispanic immigrant children for some 30 years, is the most obvious culprit, with its emphasis on retaining Spanish. But bilingual education is on the wane, having been challenged by statewide initiatives in California (1998), Arizona (2000), and Massachusetts (2004), and by policy shifts in several major cities and at the federal level. States that have moved to English-immersion instruction have seen test scores for Hispanic youngsters rise, in some cases substantially.

Evidence from the culture at large is also encouraging. On most measures of social and economic integration, Hispanic immigrants and their descendants have made steady strides up the ladder. English is the preferred language of virtually all U.S.-born Hispanics; indeed, according to a 2002 national survey by the Pew Hispanic Center and the Kaiser Family Foundation, 78 percent of third-generation Mexican-Americans cannot speak Spanish at all. In education, 86 percent of U.S.-born Hispanics complete high school, compared with 92 percent of non-Hispanic whites, and the drop-out rate among immigrant children who enroll in high school after they come here is no higher than for the native-born.

It remains true that attendance at four-year colleges is lower among Hispanics than for other groups, and Hispanics lag in attaining bachelor's degrees. But neither that nor their slightly lower rate of high-school attendance has kept Hispanic immigrants from pulling their economic weight. After controlling for education, English proficiency, age, and geographic location, Mexican-born males actually earn 2.4 percent more than comparable U.S.-born white males, according to a recent analysis of 2000 Census data by the National Research Council. Hispanic women, for their part, hold their own against U.S.-born white women with similar qualifications.

As for the effect of Hispanic immigrants on the country's social fabric, the NRC found that they are more likely than other Americans to live with their immediate relatives: 88.6 percent of Mexican immigrant households are made up of families, compared with 69.5 percent of non-Hispanic whites and 68.3 percent of blacks. These differences are partially attributable to the age structure of the Hispanic population, which is younger on average than the white or black population. But even after adjusting for age and immigrant generation, U.S. residents of Hispanic origin—and especially those from Mexico—are much more likely to live in family households. Despite increased out-of-wedlock births among Hispanics, about 67 percent of American children of Mexican origin live in two-parent families, as compared with 77 percent of white children but only 37 percent of black children.

Perhaps the strongest indicator of Hispanic integration into American life is the population's high rate of intermarriage. About a quarter of all Hispanics marry outside their ethnic group, almost exclusively to non-Hispanic white spouses, a rate that has remained virtually unchanged since 1980. And here a significant fact has been noted in a 2005 study by the Population Reference Bureau—namely, that "the majority of inter-Hispanic children are reported as Hispanic." Such intermarriages themselves, the study goes on, "may have been a factor in the phenomenal growth of the U.S. Hispanic population in recent years."

It has been widely predicted that, by mid-century, Hispanics will represent fully a quarter of the U.S. population. Such predictions fail to take into account that increasing numbers of these "Hispanics" will have only one grandparent or great-grandparent of Hispanic heritage. By that point, Hispanic ethnicity may well mean neither more nor less than German, Italian, or Irish ethnicity means today.

How, then, to proceed? Congress is under growing pressure to strengthen border control, but unless it also reaches some agreement on more comprehensive reforms, stauncher enforcement is unlikely to have much of an effect. With a growing economy and more jobs than our own population can readily absorb, the U.S. will continue to need immigrants. Illegal immigration already responds reasonably well to market forces. It has increased during boom times like the late 1990's and decreased again when jobs disappear, as in the latest recession. Trying to determine an ideal number makes no more sense than trying to predict how much steel or how many textiles we ought to import; government quotas can never match the efficiency of simple supply and demand. As President Bush has argued—and as the Senate has now agreed—a guest-worker program is the way to go.

Does this mean the U.S. should just open its borders to anyone who wants to come? Hardly. We still need an orderly process, one that includes background checks to insure that terrorists and criminals are not being admitted. It also makes sense to require that immigrants have at least a basic knowledge of English and to give preference to those who have advanced skills or needed talents.

Moreover, immigrants themselves have to take more responsibility for their status. Illegal aliens from Mexico now pay significant sums of money to "coyotes" who sneak them across the border. If they could come legally as guest workers, that same money might be put up as a surety bond to guarantee their return at the end of their employment contract, or perhaps to pay for health insurance. Nor is it good policy to allow immigrants to become welfare recipients or to benefit from affirmative action: restrictions on both sorts of programs have to be written into law and stringently applied.

A market-driven guest-worker program might be arranged in any number of ways. A proposal devised by the Vernon K. Krieble Foundation, a policy group based in Colorado, suggests that government-licensed, private-sector employment agencies be put in charge of administering the effort, setting up offices in other countries to process applicants and perform background checks. Workers would be issued tamper-proof identity cards only after signing agreements that would allow for deportation if they violated the terms of their contract or committed crimes in the U.S. Although the Krieble plan would offer no path to citizenship, workers who wanted to change their status could still apply for permanent residency and, ultimately, citizenship through the normal, lengthy process.

Do such schemes stand a chance politically? A poll commissioned by the Krieble Foundation found that most Americans (except those with less than a high-school education) consider an "efficient system for handling guest workers" to be more important than expanded law enforcement in strengthening the country's border. Similarly, a CNN tracking poll in May found that 81 percent of respondents favored legislation permitting illegal immigrants who have been in the U.S. more than five years to stay here and apply for citizenship, provided they had jobs and paid back taxes. True, other polls have contradicted these results, suggesting public ambivalence on the issue—and an openness to persuasion.

Regardless of what Congress does or does not do—the odds in favor of an agreement between the Senate and House on final legislation are still no better than 50–50—immigration is likely to continue at high levels for the foreseeable future. Barring a recession or another terrorist attack, the U.S. economy is likely to need some 1.5 to 2 million immigrants a year for some time to come. It would be far better for all concerned if those who wanted to work in the U.S. and had jobs waiting for them here could do so legally, in the light of day and with the full approval of the American people.

In 1918, at the height of the last great wave of immigrants and the hysteria that it prompted in some circles, Madison Grant, a Yale-educated eugenicist and leader of the immigration-restriction movement, made a prediction:

The result of unlimited immigration is showing plainly in the rapid decline in the birth rate of native Americans because the poorer classes of colonial stock, where they still exist, will not bring children into the world to compete in the labor market with the Slovak, the Italian, the Syrian, and the Jew. . . . The man of the old stock is being crowded out of many country districts by these foreigners, just as he is today being literally driven off the streets of New York City by the swarms of Polish Jews. These immigrants adopt the language of the native American, they wear his clothes, they steal his name, and they are beginning to take his women, but they seldom adopt his religion or understand his ideals, and while he is being elbowed out of his own home, the American looks calmly abroad and urges on others the suicidal ethics which are exterminating his own race.

Today, such alarmism reads as little more than a historical curiosity. Southern and Eastern European immigrants and their children did, in fact, assimilate, and in certain cases—most prominently that of the Jews—they exceeded the educational and economic attainments of Grant's "colonial stock."

Present-day restrictionists point to all sorts of special circumstances that supposedly made such acculturation possible in the past but render it impossible today. Then as now, however, the restrictionists are wrong, not least in their failure to understand the basic dynamic of American nationhood. There is no denying the challenge posed by assimilating today's newcomers, especially so many of them in so short a span of time. Nor is there any denying the cultural forces, mainly stemming from the Left, that have attenuated the sense of national identity among native-born American elites themselves and led to such misguided policies as bilingual education. But, provided that we commit ourselves to the goal, past experience and progress to date suggest the task is anything but impossible.

As jarring as many found the recent pictures of a million illegal aliens marching in our cities, the fact remains that many of the immigrants were carrying the American flag, and waving it proudly. They and their leaders understand what most restrictionists do not and what some Americans have forgotten or choose to deny: that the price of admission to America is, and must be, the willingness to become an American.

Notes

1. I was briefly president of U.S. English in the late 1980s but resigned when a previously undisclosed memo written by Tanton was published. In it, he warned of problems related to the "educability" of Hispanics and speculated that an influx of Catholics from south of the border might well lead the U.S. to "pitch out" the concept of church-state separation. Tanton was forced to resign as chairman of U.S. English and no longer has any affiliation with the group.

2. As the author and anti-immigration activist Peter Brimelow wrote in his 1995 book *Alien Nation,* "Americans have a legitimate interest in their country's racial balance . . . [and] a right to insist that their government stop shifting it." Himself an immigrant from England, Brimelow wants "more immigrants who look like me."

LINDA CHAVEZ, the author of *Out of the Barrio* (1991), among other books, is the chairman of the Center for Equal Opportunity in Washington, D.C. She is at work on a new book about immigration.

From *Commentary,* July/August 2006, pp. 34–40. Copyright © 2006 by Commentary. Reprinted by permission of Commentary and Linda Chavez.

Article 47

The Health of Nations

How Europe, Canada, and our own VA do health care better.

EZRA KLEIN

Medicine may be hard, but health insurance is simple. The rest of the world's industrialized nations have already figured it out, and done so without leaving 45 million of their countrymen uninsured and 16 million or so underinsured, and without letting costs spiral into the stratosphere and severely threaten their national economies.

Even better, these successes are not secret, and the mechanisms not unknown. Ask health researchers what should be done, and they will sigh and suggest something akin to what France or Germany does. Ask them what they think can be done, and their desperation to evade the opposition of the insurance industry and the pharmaceutical industry and conservatives and manufacturers and all the rest will leave them stammering out buzzwords and workarounds, regional purchasing alliances and health savings accounts. The subject's famed complexity is a function of the forces protecting the status quo, not the issue itself.

So let us, in these pages, shut out the political world for a moment, cease worrying about what Aetna, Pfizer, and Grover Norquist will say or do, and ask, simply: What should be done? To help answer that question, we will examine the best health-care systems in the world: those of Canada, France, Great Britain, Germany, and the U.S. Veterans Health Administration (VHA), whose inclusion I'll justify shortly.

Putting aside the VHA, America's annual per person health expenditures are about twice what anyone else spends. That actually understates the difference, as our 45 million uninsured citizens have radically restricted access to care, and so the spending on the median insured American is actually quite a bit higher. Canada, France, Great Britain, and Germany all cover their entire populations, and they do so for far less money than we spend. Indeed, Canada, whose system is the most costly of the group, spends only 52 percent per capita what we do.

While comparing outcomes is difficult because of various lifestyle and demographic differences in the populations served, none of the systems mentioned betray any detectable disadvantage in outcomes when compared with the United States, and a strong case can be made that they in fact perform better. Here, however, I largely restrict myself to comparisons of efficiency and equity. With that said, off we go.

Oh, Canada!

As described by the American press, Canada's health-care system takes the form of one long queue. The line begins on the westernmost edge of Vancouver, stretches all the way to Ottawa, and the overflow are encouraged to wait in Port Huron, Michigan, while sneering at the boorish habits of Americans. Nobody gets to sit.

Sadly for those invested in this odd knock against the Canadian system, the wait times are largely hype. A 2003 study found that the median wait time for elective surgeries in Canada was a little more than four weeks, while diagnostic tests took about three (with no wait times to speak of for emergency surgeries). By contrast, Organisation for Economic Co-operation and Development data from 2001 found that 32 percent of American patients waited more than a month for elective surgery, and 5 percent waited more than four months. That, of course, doesn't count the millions of Americans who never seek surgery, or even the basic care necessary for a diagnosis, because they lack health coverage. If you can't see a doctor in the first place, you never have to wait for treatment.

Canada's is a single-payer, rather than a socialized, system. That means the government is the primary purchaser of services, but the providers themselves are private. (In a socialized system, the physicians, nurses, and so forth are employed by the government.) The virtue of both the single-payer and the socialized systems, as compared with a largely private system, is that the government can wield its market share to bargain down prices—which, in all of our model systems, including the VHA, it does.

A particularly high-profile example of how this works is Canadian drug reimportation. The drugs being bought in Canada and smuggled over the border by hordes of lawbreaking American seniors are the very same pharmaceuticals, made in the very same factories, that we buy domestically. The Canadian provinces, however, bargain down the prices (Medicare is barred from doing the same) until we pay 60 percent more than they do.

Single-payer systems are also better at holding down administrative costs. A 2003 study in *The New Great Britain Journal of Medicine* found that the United States spends 345 percent more per capita on health administration than our neighbors up north. This is largely because the Canadian system doesn't have to employ insurance salespeople, or billing specialists in every doctor's office, or underwriters. Physicians don't have to negotiate different prices with dozens of insurance plans or fight with insurers for payment. Instead, they simply bill the government and are reimbursed.

The downside of a single-payer system in the Canadian style is that it constructs a system with a high floor and a low ceiling. If you don't like the government's care options, there's no real alternative. In this, Canada is rare. As we'll see with both France and Germany, other countries are able to preserve a largely nationalized system with universal access while allowing private options at the upper levels.

France

It's a common lament among health-policy wonks that the world's best health-care system resides in a country Americans are particularly loath to learn from. Yet France's system is hard to beat. Where Canada's system has a high floor and a low ceiling, France's has a high floor and no ceiling. The government provides basic insurance for all citizens, albeit with relatively robust co-pays, and then encourages the population to also purchase supplementary insurance—which 86 percent do, most of them through employers, with the poor being subsidized by the state. This allows for as high a level of care as an individual is willing to pay for, and may help explain why waiting lines are nearly unknown in France.

France's system is further prized for its high level of choice and responsiveness—attributes that led the World Health Organization to rank it the finest in the world (America's system came in at No. 37, between Costa Rica and Slovenia). The French can see any doctor or specialist they want, at any time they want, as many times as they want, no referrals or permissions needed. The French hospital system is similarly open. About 65 percent of the nation's hospital beds are public, but individuals can seek care at any hospital they want, public or private, and receive the same reimbursement rate no matter its status. Given all this, the French utilize more care than Americans do, averaging six physician visits a year to our 2.8, and they spend more time in the hospital as well. Yet they still manage to spend half per capita than we do, largely due to lower prices and a focus on preventive care.

That focus is abetted by the French system's innovative response to one of the trickier problems bedeviling health-policy experts: an economic concept called "moral hazard." Moral hazard describes people's tendency to overuse goods or services that offer more marginal benefit without a proportionate marginal cost. Translated into English, you eat more at a buffet because the refills are free, and you use more health care because insurers generally make you pay up front in premiums, rather than at the point of care. The obvious solution is to shift more of the cost away from premiums and into co-pays or deductibles, thus increasing the sensitivity of consumers to the real cost of each unit of care they purchase.

This has been the preferred solution of the right, which has argued for a move toward high-deductible care, in which individuals bear more financial risk and vulnerability. As the thinking goes, this increased exposure to the economic consequences of purchasing care will create savvier health-care consumers, and individuals will use less unnecessary care and demand better prices for what they do use.

Problem is, studies show that individuals are pretty bad at distinguishing necessary care from unnecessary care, and so they tend to cut down on mundane-but-important things like hypertension medicine, which leads to far costlier complications. Moreover, many health problems don't lend themselves to bargain shopping. It's a little tricky to try to negotiate prices from an ambulance gurney.

A wiser approach is to seek to separate cost-effective care from unproven treatments, and align the financial incentives to encourage the former and discourage the latter. The French have addressed this by creating what amounts to a tiered system for treatment reimbursement. As Jonathan Cohn explains in his new book, *Sick:*

> In order to prevent cost sharing from penalizing people with serious medical problems—the way Health Savings Accounts threaten to do—the [French] government limits every individual's out-of-pocket expenses. In addition, the government has identified thirty chronic conditions, such as diabetes and hypertension, for which there is usually no cost sharing, in order to make sure people don't skimp on preventive care that might head off future complications.

The French do the same for pharmaceuticals, which are grouped into one of three classes and reimbursed at 35 percent, 65 percent, or 100 percent of cost, depending on whether data show their use to be cost effective. It's a wise straddle of a tricky problem, and one that other nations would do well to emulate.

Great Britain

I include Great Britain not because its health system is very good but because its health system is very cheap. Per capita spending in Great Britain hovers around 40 percent what it is in the United States, and outcomes aren't noticeably worse. The absolute disparity between what we pay and what they get illuminates a troublesome finding in the health-care literature: Much of the health care we receive appears to do very little good, but we don't yet know how to separate the wheat from the chaff. Purchasing less of it, however, doesn't appear to do much damage.

What's interesting is that many of the trade-offs that our health-care system downplays, the English system emphasizes. Where our medical culture encourages near-infinite amounts of care, theirs subtly dissuades lavish health spending, preferring to direct finite funds to other priorities.

This sort of national prioritizing is made easier because Great Britain has a socialized system, wherein the government directly employs most of the providers. Great Britain contains costs in part by paying doctors through capitation, which gives doctors a flat monthly sum for every patient in their practice. Since most patients don't need care in a given month, the payments for the healthy subsidize the needs of the sick. Crucially, though, the fixed pool of monthly money means doctors make more for offering less treatment. With traditional fee-for-service arrangements, like ours, doctors gain by treating more. The British system, by contrast, lowers total costs by lowering the quantity of prescribed care. As University of San Francisco professors Thomas Bodenheimer and Kevin Grumbach write, "British physicians simply do less of nearly everything—perform fewer surgeries, prescribe fewer medications, and order fewer x-rays."

That may sound strange, but it also means that society pays for fewer of those surgeries, fewer of those medications, and fewer of those x-rays—and as far as we can tell, the English aren't suffering for it. Indeed, a 2006 study published in *The Journal of the American Medical Association* found that, on average, English people are much healthier than Americans are; they suffer from lower rates of diabetes, hypertension, heart disease, heart attack, stroke, lung disease, and cancer. According to the study's press release, the differences are vast enough that "those in the top education and income level in the U.S. had similar rates of diabetes and heart disease as those in the bottom education and income level in Great Britain."

Great Britain's example proves that it is possible to make economy a guiding virtue of a health system. We could do that on the supply side, through policies like capitation that would change the incentives for doctors, or on the demand side, by making patients pay more up front—or both, or neither. Americans may not want that system, in the same way that the owner of a Range Rover may not want a Corolla, but we should at least recognize that we have chosen to make health care a costly priority, and were we to decide to prioritize differently, we could.

Germany

The German system offers a possible model for those who want to retain the insurance industry but end its ability to profit by pricing out the sick and shifting financial risk onto individuals. The German system's insurers are 300 or so different "sickness funds" that act both as both payers and purchasers for their members' care. Originally, each fund covered only a particular region, profession, or company, but now each one has open enrollment. All, however, are heavily regulated, not for profit, and neither fully private nor publicly owned. The funds can't charge different prices based on age or health status, and they must continue covering members even when the members lose the job or status that got them into the fund in the first place. The equivalent would be if you could retain membership in your company's health-care plan after leaving the company.

The move toward open enrollment was an admission that interfund competition could have some positive effects. The fear, however, was that the funds would begin competing for the healthiest enrollees and maneuvering to avoid the sickest, creating the sort of adverse selection problems that bedevil American insurance. To avoid such a spiral, the government has instituted exactly the opposite sort of risk profiling that we have in the United States. Rather than identifying the unhealthy to charge them higher rates, as our insurers do, the government compels sickness funds with particularly healthy applicants to pay into a central fund; the government then redistributes those dollars to the funds with less-healthy enrollees. In other words, the government pays higher rates to sickness funds with unhealthy enrollees in order to level the playing field and make the funds compete on grounds of price and efficiency. In this way, the incentive to dump the sick and capture the well is completely erased. The burdens of bad luck and ill health are spread across the populace, rather than remaining confined to unlucky individuals.

The system works well enough that even though Germans are allowed to opt-out of the sickness funds, they largely don't.

Those with incomes of more than $60,000 a year are not required to join a sickness fund; about 10 percent of these citizens purchase private insurance and .02 percent choose to eschew coverage entirely. The retention of a private insurance option ensures that Germans have an escape hatch if the sickness funds cease providing responsive and comprehensive coverage; it also clears a channel for experimentation and the rapid introduction of new technologies. And the mix of private-public competition works to spur innovation: By 2005, Germany had spent $21.20 per capita wiring its system with health-information technology; America, meanwhile, had spent a mere 43 cents per capita, and most U.S. hospitals still have no systems to speak of.

What the German system has managed to achieve is competition without cruelty, deploying market forces without unleashing capitalism's natural capriciousness. They have not brought the provision of health care completely under the government's control, but neither have they allowed the private market, with its attendant and natural focus on profits, to have its way with their health system. It's a balance the United States has been unable to strike.

The Veterans Health Administration

The mistreatment and poor conditions at the Walter Reed Army Medical Center were a front-page story recently, and they were rather conclusive in showing the system's inadequacy. But don't be confused: Walter Reed is a military hospital, not a VHA hospital. Poor reporting inaccurately smeared the quietly remarkable reputation of the best medical system in America.

Over the last decade or two, the VHA system has become a worldwide leader in both the adoption and the invention of health-information technology, and it has leveraged its innovations into quantifiable gains in quality of care. As Harvard's Kennedy School noted when awarding the VHA its prestigious Innovations in American Government prize:

> [The] VHA's complete adoption of electronic health records and performance measures have resulted in high-quality, low-cost health care with high patient satisfaction. A recent RAND study found that VHA outperforms all other sectors of American health care across the spectrum of 294 measures of quality in disease prevention and treatment. For six straight years, VHA has led private-sector health care in the independent American Customer Satisfaction Index.

Indeed, the VHA's lead in care quality isn't disputed. *A New Great Britain Journal of Medicine* study from 2003 compared the VHA with fee-for-service Medicare on 11 measures of quality. The VHA came out "significantly better" on every single one. The *Annals of Internal Medicine* pitted the VHA against an array of managed-care systems to see which offered the best treatment for diabetics. The VHA triumphed in all seven of the tested metrics. The National Committee for Quality Assurance, meanwhile, ranks health plans on 17 different care metrics, from hypertension treatment to adherence to evidence-based treatments. As Phillip Longman, the author of *Best Care Anywhere,* a book chronicling the VHA's remarkable transformation, explains: "Winning

NCQA's seal of approval is the gold standard in the health-care industry. And who do you suppose is the highest ranking health care system? Johns Hopkins? Mayo Clinic? Massachusetts General? Nope. In every single category, the veterans health care system outperforms the highest-rated non-VHA hospitals."

What makes this such an explosive story is that the VHA is a truly socialized medical system. The unquestioned leader in American health care is a government agency that employs 198,000 federal workers from five different unions, and nonetheless maintains short wait times and high consumer satisfaction. Eighty-three percent of VHA hospital patients say they are satisfied with their care, 69 percent report being seen within 20 minutes of scheduled appointments, and 93 percent see a specialist within 30 days.

Critics will say that the VHA is not significantly cheaper than other American health care, but that's misleading. In fact, the VHA is also proving far better than the private sector at controlling costs. As Longman explains, "Veterans enrolled in [the VHA] are, as a group, older, sicker, poorer, and more prone to mental illness, homelessness, and substance abuse than the population as a whole. Half of all VHA enrollees are over age 65. More than a third smoke. One in five veterans has diabetes, compared with one in 14 U.S. residents in general." Yet the VHA's spending per patient in 2004 was $540 less than the national average, and the average American is healthier and younger (the nation includes children; the VHA doesn't).

The VHA's advantages come in part from its development of the health-information software VistA, which was created at taxpayer expense and is now distributed for free to any health systems that wish to use it. It's a remarkably adaptive program that helps in virtually every element of care delivery, greatly aiding efforts to analyze symptoms and patient reactions in order to improve diagnoses and treatments, reduce mistaken interventions, and eliminate all sorts of care redundancies.

The VHA also benefits from the relative freedoms of being a public, socialized system. It's a sad reality that in the American medical system, doctors make money treating the sick, not keeping patients well. Thus, we encourage intervention-based, rather than prevention-based, medicine. It's telling, for instance, that hospital emergency rooms, where we handle traumas, are legally required to treat the poor, but general practitioners, who can manage conditions and catch illnesses early and cheaply, can turn away the destitute.

Moreover, patients are transient, so early investments in their long-term health will offer financial rewards to other providers. And which HMO wants to be known as the one that's really good at treating diabetes? Signing up a bunch of diabetes patients is no way to turn a profit.

As Longman details, the VHA suffers from none of these problems. Its patients are patients for life, so investing early and often in their long-term health is cost-effective; the system was set up to deal with the sick, so the emphasis is on learning how to best manage diseases rather than avoid the diseased; and the doctors are salaried, so they have no incentives to either over- or undertreat patients. Moreover, the VHA is not only empowered to bargain down drug costs; it also uses formularies (lists of covered drugs), and so is actually empowered to walk away from a pharmaceutical company that won't meet its offer.

The results have been clear. "Between 1999 and 2003," writes Longman, "the number of patients enrolled in the VHA system increased by 70 percent, yet funding (not adjusted for inflation) increased by only 41 percent. So the VHA has not only become the health-care industry's best quality performer, it has done so while spending less and less on each patient." Pretty good for socialized medicine.

The goal of health care is to get everyone covered, at the lowest possible cost, with the highest possible quality. But in the United States, there is another element in the equation that mucks up the outcome: Our system seeks to get everyone covered, at the lowest possible cost, with the highest possible quality, while generating the maximum possible profits. Within that context, the trade-offs and outcomes all seem to benefit the last goal, and so we tolerate 45 million uninsured Americans, unbelievably high prices, and a fractured system that lacks the proper incentives to deliver high-quality care.

This makes it hard to move toward a preventive system, as Canada has, because preventive medicine pays less. It makes it hard to address moral-hazard issues wisely, as the French have, because it's unprofitable to insure diabetics, and less profitable still to make their care essentially free. It makes it hard to institute the cost savings that Great Britain has, because with less money flowing into the system, there would be far less profit to be made. It makes it hard to harness market forces while protecting against individual risk, as Germany has, because insurer business models are predicated on shifting risk to employers and individuals, and profits are made when insurers can keep that risk from being shifted back onto them. And it is impossible to implement the practices that have so improved the VHA, because doing so would require a single, coherent health system that stuck with its members through their life cycles rather than an endlessly fractured structure in which insurers pawn off their members as they grow old, ill, or unemployed.

That's not to say that there's no room for profit within the American health-care system, but that it's time the discussion stopped focusing on how to preserve the interests of moneyed stakeholders and started asking how to deliver the best care, for the lowest cost, at the highest quality—to every American. Such a system will probably still have private insurers (at least at the high end of care), pay enough to encourage pharmaceutical innovation, and allow for choice and competition and market pressures. But it will take as its guiding principle the health of the populace, rather than that of the providers. That, in the end, is what all the model health-care systems have in common. Except ours.

From The American Prospect, May 2007. Copyright © 2007. Reprinted with permission from Ezra Klein and The American Prospect, Washington, DC. All rights reserved. www.prospect.org

Article 48

The *Real* Infrastructure Crisis

The nation's roads and bridges are in pretty good shape. It's the national will that is suspect.

BURT SOLOMON

It's a frighteningly familiar catastrophe to imagine. An earthquake in Northern California ruptures 30 levees along the converging Sacramento and San Joaquin rivers, and 300 billion gallons of saltwater rush inland from San Francisco Bay, flooding 16 islands and ruining the supply of fresh water across two-thirds of the nation's most populous state. Or picture this: In southern Kentucky, the 55-year-old Wolf Creek Dam (where water has seeped through the foundations for years) gives way. The breach lets loose the largest man-made reservoir east of the Mississippi River, flooding the communities along the Cumberland River and shorting out the electric guitars in Nashville.

These were the top two horror stories—"5 Disasters Coming Soon If We Don't Rebuild U.S. Infrastructure"—that *Popular Mechanics* conjured up for its readers last fall, after the collapse of a bridge in Minnesota killed 13 innocents on their way home from work. The stunning sight of an interstate highway plunging into the Mississippi River, just two weeks after a steam pipe exploded beneath Lexington Avenue in Midtown Manhattan—and less than two years after Hurricane Katrina brought New Orleans to its knees—dramatically brought the nation's fallible infrastructure to the public's attention. So, too, did the overwhelmed levees along the Midwestern rivers during the recent rains. And so did the garden-variety failures, such as the water main break on June 16 in Montgomery County, Md., bordering Washington that forced some of the capital's bigwigs to boil water before brushing their teeth.

In the mammoth but aging networks of roads, bridges, railroads, air traffic, sewers, pipelines, supplies of fresh water, and electricity grids that helped turn the United States into the world's economic superpower, other dangers lurk. All over the country, clean-water and wastewater facilities are wearing out. The combined sewers that 40 million people in 772 cities use could disgorge their raw contents into waterways when the next storm passes through. Every summer brings the possibility of blackouts.

Traffic gridlock has become a fact of life, jamming the highways and airways and creating bottlenecks of goods through the ports, especially around Los Angeles and New York City. The American Society of Civil Engineers has classified 3,500 of the nation's 79,000 dams as unsafe; in a 2005 report card

How Bad Is It?

- The total amount of money spent on infrastructure has **consistently been increasing,** mainly because of state and local investments.
- Even so, on a global scale, American infrastructure is **no longer on the cutting edge.**
- Both John McCain and Barack Obama have highlighted **infrastructure spending as an issue** in the presidential campaign.

on the nation's infrastructure, the society assigned grades that ranged from C+ (for the proper disposal of solid waste) down to D− (for the supply of drinking water and the treatment of wastewater).

Talk of the "crisis" in the nation's physical infrastructure has leapt beyond think-tank forums and earnest editorials. It has quickened legislators' interest, generated heartfelt lobbying on Capitol Hill—expected to climax next year when Congress must reauthorize the pork-laden highway program—and nosed its way into the presidential campaign.

Experts, however, consider "crisis" an overblown description of the perils that America's infrastructure poses. Federal investigators have tentatively concluded that the ill-fated Interstate-35W in Minnesota collapsed not because it was structurally deficient—although it was—but because of a design defect: The gusset plates connecting the steel beams were half as thick as they should have been. Nationwide, bridges are in better structural condition than they were 20 years ago, and the most critical of the nation's 4 million miles of roadways are in pretty good shape. In the transportation system, "the physical condition has not noticeably deteriorated . . . in the past two decades," said Katherine A. Siggerud, the managing director of physical infrastructure issues at the determinedly nonpolitical Government Accountability Office. "The condition of the most-traveled roads and bridges in the United States, the interstates and the national highways, [has] improved in quality."

Article 48. The *Real* Infrastructure Crisis

The more serious problem is the lack of roads and the traffic congestion that this shortage creates, especially around major cities. In the nation's airways, too, congestion has become chronic, especially at airports in the Northeast. But Gerald Dillingham, the GAO's director of civil aviation issues, doesn't see a crisis in the near- or midterm, and he is hopeful that better technology and new ways of structuring the airways can stave off disaster for at least the next 15 years. The Transportation Department has calculated the overall economic cost of congestion at $200 billion a year, surely a drag on the nation's commerce, not to mention a vexation to anyone stuck in traffic. Still, in a $14 trillion economy, that amounts to 1.4 percent—a pittance.

Fixing the nation's infrastructure is "a matter of fine-tuning the economic production system," said Kenneth A. Small, an economist who specializes in transportation at the University of California (Irvine), "not a matter of moral outrage." Rudolph G. Penner, a senior fellow at the Urban Institute, said, "I'd call it a problem, not a crisis." Even the lobbyists who urge more spending on the nation's infrastructure acknowledge that the assertions of impending doom are an exaggeration. Janet F. Kavinoky, the director of transportation infrastructure at the U.S. Chamber of Commerce, is the executive director of Americans for Transportation Mobility, an alliance of construction companies and labor unions. "If you don't say it's a crisis," she explained, "nobody shows up at your press conference."

> **Even the lobbyists who urge more spending acknowledge that the assertions of impending doom are an exaggeration. "If you don't say it's a crisis, nobody shows up at your press conference."**
>
> —Janet F. Kavinoky, director of transportation infrastructure at the U.S. Chamber of Commerce

Nor is the country ignoring the issue. The nation's spending on infrastructure continues to rise; New Orleans is rebuilding the levees that Katrina breached. "The things that need to get done are getting done, by and large," said Timothy P. Lynch, the American Trucking Associations' senior vice president for federal relations and strategic planning.

This isn't to say, of course, that all is hunky-dory. The future of U.S. infrastructure could be grim indeed if too little is done. At the core, it's a question of cost. Bridges and roads are expensive—to build or to fix—and so are mass transit, airport runways, and almost everything else. The civil engineers issued a widely invoked price tag of $1.6 trillion over five years to do what needs to be done, but even champions of a strong infrastructure find such a number inflated—"a compilation of a wish list," the ATA's Lynch said.

Moreover, investment bankers say that plenty of capital is available for work that is critical to the nation's well-being. What may be missing, however, is the political will to spend this capital. Increasingly, legislators and local governments are trying to arrange infrastructure financing in ways that conceal the true costs from taxpayers, who are reluctant to foot the bill, and that may transfer the financial burdens to future generations. If the measure of a society's responsibility is its willingness to invest for the long run, then the crisis in infrastructure is this: Do Americans possess the national will to pay for what their children and their children's children are going to need?

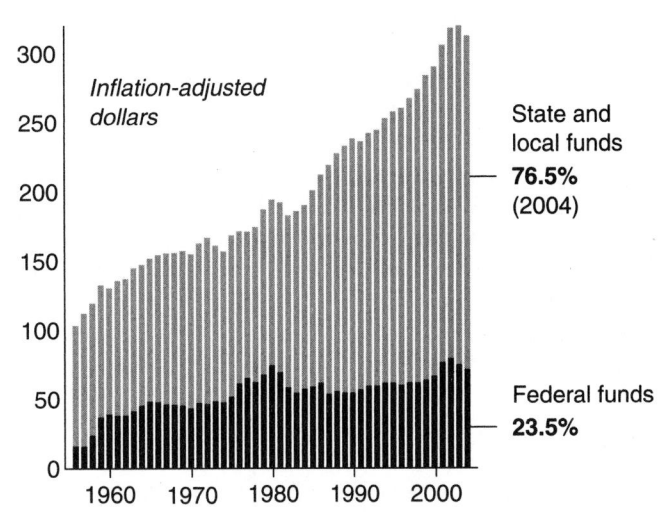

The Big Picture Spending on the nation's infrastructure has increased, but state and local governments are footing a larger share of the bill.

Total Public infrastructure Spending, 1956–2004.

Source: Congressional Budget Office.

Ancient Rome Meets Reagan

Only occasionally has a civilization made its infrastructure an emblem of its ambition or greatness. Consider, notably, the marvels of ancient Rome—its roads, its aqueducts, its public baths and lavatories, its Colosseum and other sites of public entertainment. Conceived as a military necessity to assure the movement of troops through a far-flung empire, Rome's extravagant and enduring infrastructure took on other functions, too. As a public benefaction, it gave the state a way to justify its own existence, according to Garrett G. Fagan, a historian at Pennsylvania State University, and the many amenities that wealthy families financed served as "a kind of social compact between the upper classes and the poorer classes." The boldness and breadth of Roman infrastructure, Fagan said, "go a long way to explain why the empire lasted so long."

The United States has often shown a similar ambition. In 1808, after Thomas Jefferson's Louisiana Purchase added a vast wilderness that stretched as far as the future Montana, Treasury Secretary Albert Gallatin proposed a national transportation network of roads, rivers, and ports.

In the following decades, Henry Clay of Kentucky lent his legislative weight in the House, and then in the Senate, to the "internal improvements" of canals and railroads. Abraham Lincoln, even as he struggled to win the Civil War, pursued plans for a transcontinental railroad. Theodore Roosevelt, so fond of proclaiming the needs of "future generations," convened a conference of governors that resulted in water projects that irrigated the West and generated electricity cheaply; his list of ventures-still-undone gave TR's fifth cousin, Franklin D. Roosevelt, a starting point when he tried to spend the nation out of the Great Depression. Then, in the postwar boom of the 1950s, President Eisenhower pressed for a system of interstate highways that knitted the nation together and bolstered its economy. As late as the 1970s, after the Cuyahoga River in Cleveland caught fire in 1969, the federal government invested tens of billions of dollars in sewer systems and wastewater treatment plants.

Taxpayers' generosity toward the nation's infrastructure, however, took a dive during the 1980s. President Reagan's aversion to using taxes for domestic spending, exacerbated by Wall Street's obsession with quarterly earnings, encouraged a shortsightedness in assessing the public good. According to Sherle R. Schwenninger, the director of the New America Foundation's economic growth program, the money that government at all levels has devoted to infrastructure, as a proportion of the nation's total economic output, slipped from 3 percent during the 1950s and 1960s to only 2 percent in recent years.

"We've just not reinvested," former Council of Economic Advisers Chairman Martin N. Baily complained at a Brookings Institution forum last fall, "because nobody wanted to raise the taxes to do that." Even in Katrina-devastated Louisiana, when the Army Corps of Engineers announced in 2006 that its estimate for fixing the levees had ballooned from $3.5 billion to $9.5 billion, the state's politicians and editorial writers wailed.

Not to Worry

It wouldn't take many years, or so it is said, before the weeds poked up through a neglected interstate highway. Not to worry. Even as the nation's enthusiasm for long-term investments has flagged, the total amount of money spent on its infrastructure has continued to grow. As the federal share has shrunk (from 32 percent in 1982 to less than 24 percent in 2004, according to the Congressional Budget Office), state and local governments have picked up the slack. Counting all levels of government, public entities spent $312 billion on the nation's transportation and water infrastructure in 2004, three times as much—after taking inflation into account—as in 1956, when Eisenhower's heyday began. *(See chart.)*

Has the U.S. underfunded its infrastructure, on which its economy rests? "Compared to what we really need, I think so," said Penner, a former CBO director, "but relatively slightly."

Consider, for example, the state of the nation's bridges. Last summer's tragedy in Minnesota cast a spotlight on the Federal Highway Administration's alarming conclusion that, as of last December, 12 percent of the nation's bridges were structurally deficient. But less attention was paid to the fact that this proportion had shrunk from 13 percent in 2004 and nearly 19 percent in 1994. Nor was it widely noticed that the label of "structurally deficient" covered a range of poor conditions, from serious to far less so. Fewer than a tenth of the tens of thousands of bridges deemed deficient are anywhere close to falling down. (A Federal Highway Administration spokeswomen said the agency does not have summary information about the location and size of the worst bridges.)

The surge of bridge inspections that followed the disaster in Minnesota turned up a second bridge with bowed gusset plates across the Mississippi in Minneapolis-St. Paul—it was immediately closed and slated for repairs—and another one in Duluth. The Minnesota Legislature found numerous shortcomings in the state inspectors' work on the I-35 bridge that had been tagged as structurally deficient for some cracking and fatigue. According to the National Transportation Safety Board's investigators, however, the inspectors were not the problem. Indeed, the investigators cited the effort to repair the bridge, which entailed piling construction supplies and equipment on its overburdened deck, and the thin gusset plates as the likely leading causes of the I-35 collapse. The more that they have learned about the disaster, the less it has served as a morality tale.

As for a fear of falling bridges, "I don't really think we're in a crisis," said economist Small. He also mentioned the "pretty strong" system of bridge inspections and placed the 13 deaths in Minnesota into the context of all U.S. traffic fatalities, which average 120 a day. "If you plot the statistics," he noted, "you might not notice the bump."

On the roads, too, drunk drivers or malfunctioning vehicles cause many more deaths than potholes or crumbling concrete. The roads are OK, but there aren't enough of them to hold the traffic, and building more will only increase demand. The gridlock is worst of all around Los Angeles, the San Francisco Bay area, Chicago, New York City, Atlanta, and Washington, but it has also spread into unlikelier venues. A third lane is being built along certain truck-clogged stretches of Interstate 80 in Iowa and Nebraska. The GAO's Siggerud pointed to "bottlenecks in every mode of transportation," which stand to get worse. The Federal Aviation Administration has predicted that air traffic may triple during the next two decades, and the American Road & Transportation Builders Association has forecast that the volume of cargo on U.S. roads will double. In Los Angeles, the freight volume is expected to triple as the population grows by 60 percent, producing strains that the U.S. chamber's Kavinoky warned "will paralyze the city."

Ian Grossman, the FHWA's associate administrator for public affairs, lamented the Little League games unattended and the volunteerism in decline because of congestion. "It shouldn't be a fact of life," he said.

The economic impact of the bottlenecks has been "woefully understudied," according to Robert Puentes, an expert in infrastructure at the Brookings Institution, who regards transportation policy as "a fact-free zone." But Clifford Winston, an economist at Brookings, has tried. His calculation of the annual economic cost of congestion is just a third of DOT's—$15 billion in air traffic and nearly $50 billion on the roads, counting the shipping delays, the higher inventories required, the wasted fuel, the value of gridlocked motorists' time, and other not-quite-tangible factors. The impediments are numerous, Winston said, but "none of them are big. That's why they persist."

The problem of congestion is, to a degree, self-limiting. It could injure the economy of a gridlocked metropolis, but by no more than 5 to 10 percent, according to Small, by driving business to the suburbs, exurbs, and smaller cities that stand to benefit from the big cities' pain.

Nor has congestion in the air been neglected. The air traffic system, in which 25 percent of last year's flights arrived late, has added runways in recent years in Atlanta, Boston, Cincinnati, Minneapolis, and St. Louis; starting this November it will add another runway at Chicago's O'Hare. The $13 billion that the FAA spends annually on infrastructure development for civil aviation falls a mere $1 billion short—pocket change, really—of what GAO analyst Dillingham believes it should spend. The next generation of air traffic control, based on a global positioning system instead of on radar, has been delayed—not because of the immense cost or the technology, Dillingham said, but because of the difficulty of integrating it into the existing system.

Scarier, perhaps, for the nation's economic future is the possibility that congestion or other strains on an elderly infrastructure will damage America's already shaky competitive position in global markets. The American business executives who leave South Korea's luxurious Incheon International Airport or Shanghai's modern, half-empty airport to arrive at New York's seedy JFK are bound to feel repulsed. Today, that is nothing more than inconvenience, but eventually, economists say, it could count.

"In a globalized economy," the New America Foundation's Schwenninger said, "there are only a few ways you can compete." Asian countries can claim lower wage rates and taxes, and Europe boasts governmental subsidies and an educated workforce. This leaves infrastructure, Schwenninger ventured, as American businesses' best hope for a competitive edge—more so than 20 to 30 years ago, and more important than education. Silicon Valley, he reported, has lost some of its silicon-wafer manufacturing to Texas and countries overseas because producers fear brownouts in California.

Yet the threat to U.S. competitiveness shouldn't be exaggerated, for other countries face similar problems with congestion. Gaining permission to build a new road or runway is even harder in cramped, environmentally conscious Europe. China and India are spending 9 percent and 5 percent, respectively, of their gross domestic product on infrastructure. The U.S., however, has an overwhelming advantage: Its elaborate infrastructure—4 million miles of roads, 600,000 bridges, 26,000 miles of commercially navigable waterways, 11,000 miles of transit lines, 500 train stations, 300 ports, 19,000 airports, 55,000 community drinking water systems, and 30,000 wastewater plants—is already built.

Ducking the Costs

Still, on matters of infrastructure, the United States is losing ground. "It would be an overstatement to say our system is in crisis," Brookings's Winston said. "At the same time, the annual costs of the inefficiencies [because of congestion] are large, growing, and unlikely to be addressed by the public sector."

No longer is American infrastructure on the cutting edge. "I think we are falling behind the rest of the world," Rep. Earl Blumenauer, an earnest veteran Democrat from Portland, Ore., said in an interview. He is pushing legislation to create a blue-ribbon commission that would frame a coherent national vision for dealing with the country's disparately owned and operated infrastructure, variously the responsibility of federal, state, or local governments or—for a majority of dams and many recent water systems—private owners. Besides the existing bottlenecks in the movement of goods, Blumenauer foresees "real problems with the backlog of projects"—for sewers, roads, water, bridges, etc.—within five to 10 years. And deferring maintenance, he noted, increases the costs, which is one reason he thinks that the astronomical price tags "tend to be understated, not overstated."

America was once on the cutting edge of infrastructure, but no more. "I think we are falling behind the rest of the world. . . . In the end, there's no substitute for making systematic investment."

—Rep. Earl Blumenauer, D-Ore., who wants to create a blue-ribbon commission on infrastructure

The GAO, among others, is more skeptical, not only of the civil engineers' $1.6 trillion, $300-billion-plus-a-year cost projection but also of a congressionally created panel's recommendations. The National Surface Transportation Policy and Revenue Study Commission announced in January that the nation must spend $225 billion annually—$140 billion more than at present—on its roads, waterways, and railroads. "Most of the needs assessments," the Urban Institute's Penner explained, "are very much influenced by special interests," using unrealistic assumptions and self-serving estimates.

How much the nation must spend, however, is certain to rise. For fresh water and wastewater alone, by the GAO's calculations, the infrastructure costs over the next 20 years will range between $400 billion and nearly $1.2 trillion to correct past underinvestment. The existing facilities, if not repaired or replaced, would probably take 10 to 20 years to deteriorate, an offical said, not two or three.

Given the presumed reluctance of American taxpayers to pay up front, such projections have quickened the search for politically palatable alternatives to financing infrastructure projects—artful ways of ducking the costs. Hence the rising popularity of public-private partnerships, "or as we called them, business deals," Everett M. Ehrlich, an expert on infrastructure financing, told the House Transportation and Infrastructure Committee in June. On May 19, Pennsylvania Gov. Ed Rendell had announced the winning $12.8 billion bid (submitted by a Spanish toll-road company and a division of Citigroup) for a 75-year lease of the Pennsylvania Turnpike. The idea wasn't original. The city of Chicago signed a $1.8 billion lease for the Chicago Skyway in 2005 and has received a half-dozen bids for privatizing Midway Airport. The Indiana Toll Road was leased in 2006 for $3.8 billion. A private company built and runs the Dulles Toll Road in Northern Virginia, and the Texas Legislature has imposed a two-year moratorium on a planned network of private toll roads out of concern that the deals were too lucrative for the operators.

A private operator, the thinking goes, can raise tolls with an abandon that would give politicians the willies, and investment banks are salivating at the prospect of jumping in. But the criticism has mounted. "Deferred maintenance will become a big part of creating profits for shareholders," Allen Zimmerman, a resident of South Whitehall Township, Pa., warned about leasing the turnpike, in a letter to *The Morning Call* of Allentown, Pa. Economists worry that a private operator might milk the drivers along the popular routes while ignoring the boondocks.

By the GAO's lights, the value of any given deal depends on the particulars, such as the quality of the management, the assurances of proper maintenance, and the uses to which a state will put the newfound revenues. Indiana is spending its bump in revenue on a 10-year transportation plan; Chicago, on the other hand, has pointedly refrained from any allocation. Pennsylvania officials have vowed to spend their windfall on transportation but have been "evasive," the ATA's Lynch said, about specifics.

At least so far, the greatest hindrance to an influx of private capital for the nation's infrastructure, according to Penner of the Urban Institute, is the paucity of investment opportunities. He also lacks faith in the other ideas being pitched on Capitol Hill that seek to lure capital while dodging the costs—notably, proposals to establish an infrastructure "bank" to leverage private investments and to institute a separate capital budget for the federal government. Nor does the direct approach—the possibility of federal appropriations—give him reason to hope. He fears that the entitlement programs (Social Security, Medicare, and Medicaid) will squeeze the budget, shrinking the discretionary spending on infrastructure projects.

Where, then, will the money come from? At Brookings, infrastructure expert Puentes thinks that relatively small, targeted investments can relieve the worst bottlenecks—those of national importance, such as the congestion at the port of Long Beach, Calif. In any event, simply relying on the construction of new highways and airport terminals won't suffice, in Small's view: "It's just too expensive."

Many economists favor another solution—congestion pricing. London, Stockholm, and Singapore now charge vehicles that drive into the central cities at busy times of the day. Michael Bloomberg, New York City's businessman-turned-mayor, pursued the idea until the state Legislature shot it down. Pure congestion pricing, a high-tech means of raising or lowering the toll depending on the traffic, is being tested on a highway north of San Diego, where the price of driving changes every few minutes. Such pricing would be one way for Americans to pay their way.

The Political Marketplace

On the night that Sen. Barack Obama of Illinois claimed the Democratic nomination for the presidency, he spoke to the nation about, among a litany of intentions, "investing in our crumbling infrastructure." Of course, he happened to be in Minnesota, less than 10 miles from where the I-35 bridge had collapsed. But then he spoke of the problem again two days later while campaigning in Virginia and, later, at a roundtable with 16 Democratic governors. In trying to bolster his appeal to working-class voters in Flint, Mich., on June 16, Obama promised to use the money he would save from ending the war in Iraq on a National Infrastructure Reinvestment Bank that would spend $60 billion over 10 years. Stressing the issue helps Obama look sober and serious about the nation's long-term needs, which is useful for a candidate who is criticized for being inexperienced.

24% of infrastructure spending in 2004 was federally funded.

Sen. Hillary Rodham Clinton of New York, whom Obama bested for the nomination, demonstrated the versatility of infrastructure as a political issue. A week after the bridge fell in Minnesota, she delivered a speech in New Hampshire on infrastructure as "a silent crisis." She showed a thorough understanding of the issue ("Today nearly half the locks on our waterways are obsolete.") and offered a detailed plan of attack, including a $10 billion emergency repair fund, $1.5 billion for public transit, $1 billion for intercity passenger railways, and sundry other millions for additional projects. Nine months later, however, facing political death as Indiana Democrats readied to vote, she climbed onto the back of a pickup truck and appealed to voters beleaguered by the soaring price of fuel. Her idea? Suspend the federal gasoline tax, which pays for the upkeep on the nation's pivotal highways. Economists gagged at the thought, but Indiana Democrats rewarded her with a narrow victory.

The presumed Republican nominee, Sen. John McCain of Arizona, who agreed with Clinton on the gasoline tax, has also used infrastructure as a political football. It's a word he reveres. In campaign speeches, he has applied "infrastructure" to public health, alternative fuels, "the infrastructure of civil society," and "the Republican infrastructure." But in the conventional sense, he has linked it to one of his trademark issues. "The problem with roads and infrastructure and bridges and tunnels in America can be laid right at the doorstep of Congress," he said in May, four months after federal investigators blamed the Minnesota bridge collapse on a design flaw, "because the pork-barrel, earmark spending, such as the 'Bridge to Nowhere' in Alaska, has diverted people's hard-earned tax dollars that they pay at the gas pump." This charge drew a public rebuke from Tim Pawlenty, Minnesota's Republican governor, who is a national co-chairman of McCain's campaign and is often mentioned as a possible running mate. "I don't know what he's basing that on," Pawlenty said, "other than the general premise that projects got misprioritized throughout time."

One legislator's pork, of course, is another's infrastructure. Such criticism of "pork," as a result, has not dampened Congress's enthusiasm for spending money on highways and such. The 2005 highway legislation (known, improbably, as SAFETEA-LU) authorized $286 billion over six years, $32 billion more than the Bush administration wanted. But this amount was miserly compared with the House-approved $380 billion.

Members of Congress earmarked just one-tenth of the money for particular projects back home, and not all of those were considered boondoggles. An earmark, for instance, funded the newly built Woodrow Wilson Bridge along the Capital Beltway between Virginia and Maryland.

The lobbyists for the labor unions and the contractors that stand to benefit from road construction are already gearing up for next year's effort to reauthorize the highway bill. The pot will surely grow bigger—reportedly to $500 billion over six years—especially if a Democratic president works with a Democratic Congress. Spending on infrastructure has recently been touted by Rockefeller Foundation President Judith Rodin, among others, as a Keynesian response to an impending recession. And even if earmark-happy highway bills inevitably waste money, they may be worthy of praise for paying up front for whichever roads and bridges—to nowhere or to somewhere—the democratic system has deemed worthy. "In the end, there's no substitute for making systematic investment," Rep. Blumenauer said.

As a political issue, infrastructure is the kind that democracies have a hard time with—a chronic, usually invisible problem that only occasionally becomes acute. For better or worse, however, politics has become inseparable from the battles over infrastructure, sometimes to the point of amusement. When members of the House Transportation and Infrastructure Committee discussed the fateful gusset plates in Minnesota, the Republicans stressed the arbitrary nature of such a failure, which money would never have averted, while the Democrats kept mentioning the bridge's wear and tear, for which more money would have mattered. Partisan positions on gusset plates—who knew?

Still, the politics of infrastructure are far from straightforward. Earmarks and pork find enthusiasts and critics within both political parties. Congestion pricing has produced odd bedfellows. Both Bush administration conservatives and environmental activists approve of such a market mechanism that would save fuel and improve economic efficiency, while some Democrats worry about the effect of "Lexus lanes" on the poor.

The true political divide may lie between Americans who'll be willing and able to pay up front for the nation's needs—whether through taxes or tolls—and those who would rather skimp or burden their children. This sort of decision, between a world-class infrastructure and muddling through, will be made in the political marketplace. If Americans get disgusted enough, they'll do what it takes. Otherwise, they won't.

Reprinted by permission from *National Journal*, July 5, 2008, pp. 14–20. Copyright © 2008 by National Journal Group Inc. All rights reserved.

Speculators, Politicians, and Financial Disasters

JOHN STEELE GORDON

Fueled by easy credit, the real-estate market had been rising swiftly for some years. Members of Congress were determined to assure the continuation of that easy credit. Suddenly, the party came to a devastating halt. Defaults multiplied, banks began to fail. Soon the economic troubles spread beyond real estate. Depression stalked the land.

The year was 1836.

The nexus of excess speculation, political mischief, and financial disaster—the same tangle that led to our present economic crisis—has been long and deep. Its nature has changed over the years as Americans have endeavored, with varying success, to learn from the mistakes of the past. But it has always been there, and the commonalities from era to era are stark and stunning. Given the recurrence of these themes over the course of three centuries, there is every reason to believe that similar calamities will beset the system as long as human nature and human action play a role in the workings of markets.

Let us begin our account of the catastrophic effects of speculative bubbles and political gamesmanship with the collapse of 1836. Thanks to a growing population, prosperity, and the advancing frontier, poorly regulated state banks had been multiplying throughout the 1830's. In those days, chartered banks issued paper money, called banknotes, backed by their reserves. From 1828 to 1836, the amount in circulation had tripled, from $48 million to $149 million. Bank loans, meanwhile, had almost quadrupled to $525 million. Many of the loans went to finance speculation in real estate.

Much of this easy-credit-induced speculation had been caused, as it happens, by President Andrew Jackson. This was a terrific irony, since Jackson, who served as President from 1829 until 1837, hated speculation, paper money, and banks. His crusade to destroy the Second Bank of the United States, an obsession that led him to withdraw all federal funds from its coffers in 1833, removed the primary source of bank discipline in the United States. Jackson had transferred those federal funds to state banks, thereby enabling their outstanding loans to swell.

The real-estate component of the crisis began to take shape in 1832, when sales by the government of land on the frontier were running about $2.5 million a year. Some of the buyers were prospective settlers, but most were speculators hoping to turn a profit by borrowing most of the money needed and waiting for swiftly-rising values to put them in the black. By 1836, annual land sales totaled $25 million; in the summer of that year, they were running at the astonishing rate of $5 million a month.

While Jackson, who was not economically sophisticated, did not grasp how his own actions had fueled the speculation, he understood perfectly well what was happening. With characteristic if ill-advised decisiveness, he moved to stop it. Since members both of Congress and of his cabinet were personally involved in the speculation, he faced fierce opposition. But in July, as soon as Congress adjourned for the year, Jackson issued an executive order known as the "specie circular." This forbade the Land Office to accept anything but gold and silver (i.e., specie) in payment for land. Jackson hoped that the move would dampen the speculation, and it did. Unfortunately, it did far more: people began to exchange their banknotes for gold and silver. As the demand for specie soared, the banks called in loans in order to stay liquid.

The result was a credit crunch. Interest rates that had been at 7 percent a year rose to 2 and even 3 percent a month. Weaker, overextended banks began to fail. Bankruptcies spread. Even several state governments found they could not roll over their debts, forcing them into default. By April 1837, a month after Jackson left the presidency, the great New York diarist Philip Hone noted that "the immense fortunes which we heard so much about in the days of speculation have melted like the snows before an April sun."

The longest depression in American history had set in. Recovery would not begin until 1843. In Charles Dickens's *A Christmas Carol,* published that same year, Ebenezer Scrooge worries that a note payable to him in three days might be as worthless as "a mere United States security."

Modern standards preclude government officials and members of Congress from the sort of speculation that was rife in the 1830's. But today's affinities between Congressmen and lobbyists, affinities fueled by the largess of political-action committees, have produced many of the same consequences.

Consider the savings-and-loan (S&L) debacle of the 1980's. The crisis, which erupted only two decades ago but seems all but forgotten, was almost entirely the result of a failure of government to regulate effectively. And that was by design. Members of Congress put the protection of their political friends ahead of the interests of the financial system as a whole.

After the disaster of the Great Depression, three types of banks still survived—artifacts of the Democratic party's Jacksonian antipathy to powerful banks. Commercial banks offered depositors both checking and savings accounts, and made mostly commercial loans. Savings banks offered only savings accounts and specialized in commercial real-estate loans. Savings-and-loan associations ("thrifts") also offered only savings accounts; their loan portfolios were almost entirely in mortgages for single-family homes.

All this amounted, in effect, to a federally mandated cartel, coddling those already in the banking business and allowing very few new entrants. Between 1945 and 1965, the number of S&L's remained nearly constant at about 8,000, even as their assets grew more than tenfold from almost $9 billion to over $110 billion. This had something to do with the fact that the rate of interest paid on savings accounts was set by federal law at .25 percent higher than that paid by commercial banks, in order to compensate for the inability of savings banks and S&L's to offer checking accounts. Savings banks and S&L's were often called "3-6-3" institutions because they paid 3 percent on deposits, charged 6 percent on loans, and management hit the golf course at 3:00 P.M. on the dot.

These small banks were very well connected. As Democratic Senator David Pryor of Arkansas once explained:

> You got to remember that each community has a savings-and-loan; some have two; some have four, and each of them has seven or eight board members. They own the Chevy dealership and the shoe store. And when we saw these people, we said, gosh, these are the people who are building the homes for people, these are the people who represent a dream that has worked in this country.

They were also, of course, the sorts of people whose support politicians most wanted to have—people who donated campaign money and had significant political influence in their localities.

The banking situation remained stable in the two decades after World War II as the Federal Reserve was able to keep interest rates steady and inflation low. But when Lyndon Johnson tried to fund both guns (the Vietnam war) and butter (the Great Society), the cartel began to break down.

If the government's first priority had been the integrity of the banking system and the safety of deposits, the weakest banks would have been forced to merge with larger, sounder institutions. Most solvent savings banks and S&L's would then have been transmuted into commercial banks, which were required to have larger amounts of capital and reserves. And some did transmute themselves on their own. But by 1980 there were still well over 4,500 S&L's in operation, relics of an earlier time.

Why was the integrity of the banking system not the first priority? Part of the reason lay in the highly fragmented nature of the federal regulatory bureaucracy. A host of agencies—including the Comptroller of the Currency, the Federal Reserve, the FDIC and the FSLIC, state banking authorities, and the Federal Home Loan Bank Board (FHLBB)—oversaw the various forms of banks. Each of these agencies was more dedicated to protecting its own turf than to protecting the banking system as a whole.

Adding to the turmoil was the inflation that took off in the late 1960's. When the low interest rates that banks were permitted to pay failed to keep pace with inflation, depositors started to look elsewhere for a higher return. Many turned to money-market funds, which were regulated by the Securities and Exchange Commission rather than by the various banking authorities and were not restricted in the rate of interest they could pay. Money began to flow out of savings accounts and into these new funds, in a process known to banking specialists by the sonorous term "disintermediation."

By 1980, with inflation roaring above 12 percent—the highest in the country's peacetime history—the banks were bleeding deposits at a prodigious rate. The commercial banks could cope; their deposit base was mostly in checking accounts, which paid no interest, and their lending portfolios were largely made up of short-term loans whose average interest rates could be quickly adjusted, not long-term mortgages at fixed interest. But to the savings banks and S&L's, disintermediation was a mortal threat.

Rather than taking the political heat and forcing the consolidation of the banking industry into fewer, stronger, and more diversified banks, Washington rushed to the aid of the ailing S&L's with quick fixes that virtually guaranteed future disaster. First, Congress eliminated the interest-rate caps. Banks could now pay depositors whatever rates they chose. While it was at it, Congress also raised the amount of insurance on deposits, from $40,000 to $100,000 per depositor.

At the same time, the Federal Home Loan Bank Board changed the rules on brokered deposits. Since the 1960's, brokers had been making, on behalf of their customers, multiple deposits equal to the limit on insurance. This allowed wealthy customers to possess insured bank deposits of any cumulative size—an end-run around the limit that should never have been tolerated in the first place. Realizing that these deposits were "hot money," likely to chase the highest return, the Home Loan board forbade banks to have more than five percent of their deposit base in such instruments. But in 1980 it eliminated the restriction.

With no limits on interest rates that could be paid and no risk of loss to the customers, the regulators and Congress had created an economic oxymoron: a high-yield, no-risk security. As money flowed in to take advantage of the situation, the various S&L's competed among themselves to offer higher and higher interest rates. Meanwhile, however, their loan portfolios were still in long-term home mortgages, many yielding low interest.

As a result, they went broke. In 1980 the S&L's had a collective net worth slightly over $32 billion. By December 1982 that number had shrunk to less than $4 billion.

To remedy the disaster caused by the quick fixes of 1980, more quick fixes were instituted. The FHLBB lowered reserve requirements—the amount of money that banks must keep in highly liquid form, like Treasury notes, in order to meet any demand for withdrawals—from 5 to 3 percent of deposits. "With the proverbial stroke of the pen," the journalist L.J. Davis wrote, "sick thrifts were instantly returned to a state of ruddy health, while thrifts that only a moment before had been among the dead who walk were now reclassified as merely enfeebled."

For good measure, the Bank Board changed its accounting rules, allowing the thrifts to show handsome profits when they were, in fact, going bust. It was a case of regulators authorizing the banks they regulated to cook the books. Far worse, the rule that only locals could own an S&L was eliminated. Now anyone could buy a thrift. High-rollers began to move in, delighted to be able to assume the honorific title of "banker."

And Congress, ever anxious to help the Chevy dealers and shoe-store owners, lifted the limits on what the thrifts themselves could invest in. No longer were they limited to low-interest, long-term, single-family mortgages. Now they could lend up to 70 percent of their portfolios for commercial real-estate ventures and consumer needs. In short, Congress gave the S&L's permission to become full-service banks without requiring them to hold the capital and reserves of full-service banks.

Now came the turn of state-chartered thrifts, whose managers understandably wanted to enjoy the same freedoms enjoyed by federally-chartered S&L's. State governments from Albany to Sacramento were obliging. California, which had the largest number of state-chartered S&L's, allowed them to invest in anything from junk bonds to start-up software companies—in effect, to become venture-capital firms using government-guaranteed money. The consequence, as predictable as the next solar eclipse, was a collapse of the S&L's en masse. Between 1985 and 1995, over a thousand were shut down by the government or forced to merge. The cost to the public is estimated to have run $160 billion.

As the sorry tale of the S&L crisis suggests, the road to financial hell is sometimes paved with good intentions. There was nothing malign in attempting to keep these institutions solvent and profitable; they were of long standing, and it seemed a noble exercise to preserve them. Perhaps even more noble, and with consequences that have already proved much more threatening, was the philosophy that would eventually lead the United States into its latest financial crisis—a crisis that begins, and ends, with mortgages.

A mortgage used to stay on the books of the issuing bank until it was paid off, often twenty or thirty years later. This greatly limited the number of mortgages a bank could initiate. In 1938, as part of the New Deal, the federal government established the Federal National Mortgage Association, nicknamed Fannie Mae, to help provide liquidity to the mortgage market.

Fannie Mae purchased mortgages from initiating banks and either held them in its own portfolio or packaged them as mortgage-backed securities to sell to investors. By taking these mortgages off the books of the issuing banks, Fannie Mae allowed the latter to issue new mortgages. Being a government entity and thus backed by the full faith and credit of the United States, it was able to borrow at substantially lower interest rates, earning the money to finance its operations on the difference between the money it borrowed and the interest earned on the mortgages it held.

Together with the GI Bill of 1944, which guaranteed the mortgages issued to veterans, Fannie Mae proved a great success. The number of Americans owning their own homes climbed steadily, from fewer than 15 percent of non-farm families in the 1930's to nearly 70 percent by the 1980's. Thus did Fannie Mae and the GI Bill prove to be powerful engines for increasing the size of the middle class.

It can be argued that 70 percent is about as high a proportion as could, or should, be hoped for in home ownership. Many young people are not ready to buy a home; many old people prefer to rent. Some families move so frequently that home ownership makes no sense. Some people, like Congressman Charlie Rangel of New York, take advantage of local rent-control laws to obtain housing well below market rates, and therefore have no incentive to buy.

And some families simply lack the creditworthiness needed for a bank to be willing to lend them money, even on the security of real property. Perhaps their credit histories are too erratic; perhaps their incomes and net worth are lower than bank standards; or perhaps they lack the means to make a substantial down payment, which by reducing the amount of the mortgage can protect a bank from a downturn in the real-estate market.

But historically there was also a class, made up mostly of American blacks, for whom home ownership was out of reach. Although simple racial prejudice had long been a factor here, it was, ironically, the New Deal that institutionalized discrimination against blacks seeking mortgages. In 1935 the Federal Housing Administration (FHA), established in 1934 to insure home mortgages, asked the Home Owner's Loan Corporation—another New Deal agency, this one created to help prevent foreclosures—to draw up maps of residential areas according to the risk of lending in them. Affluent suburbs were outlined in blue, less desirable areas in yellow, and the least desirable in red.

The FHA used the maps to decide whether or not to insure a mortgage, which in turn caused banks to avoid the redlined neighborhoods. These tended to be in the inner city and to comprise largely black populations. As most blacks at this time were unable to buy in white neighborhoods, the effect of redlining was largely to exclude even affluent blacks from the mortgage market.

Even after the end of Jim Crow in the 1960's, the effect of redlining lingered, perhaps more out of habit than of racial prejudice. In 1977, responding to political pressure to abolish the practice, Congress finally passed the Community Reinvestment Act, requiring banks to offer credit throughout their marketing areas and rating them on their compliance. This effectively outlawed redlining.

Then, in 1995, regulations adopted by the Clinton administration took the Community Reinvestment Act to a new level. Instead of forbidding banks to discriminate against blacks and black neighborhoods, the new regulations positively forced banks to seek out such customers and areas. Without saying so, the revised law established quotas for loans to specific neighborhoods, specific income classes, and specific races. It also encouraged community groups to monitor compliance and allowed them to receive fees for marketing loans to target groups.

But the aggressive pursuit of an end to redlining also required the active participation of Fannie Mae, and thereby hangs a tale. Back in 1968, the Johnson administration had decided to "adjust" the federal books by taking Fannie Mae off the budget and establishing it as a "Government Sponsored Enterprise" (GSE). But while it was theoretically now an independent corporation, Fannie Mae did not have to adhere to the same rules regarding capitalization and oversight that bound most financial institutions. And in 1970 still another GSE was created, the Federal Home Loan Mortgage Corporation, or Freddie Mac, to expand further the secondary market in mortgage-backed securities.

This represented a huge moral hazard. The two institutions were supposedly independent of the government and owned by their stockholders. But it was widely assumed that there was an implicit government guarantee of both Fannie and Freddie's solvency and of the vast amounts of mortgage-based securities they issued. This assumption was by no means unreasonable. Fannie and Freddie were known to enjoy lower capitalization requirements than other financial institutions and to be held to a much less demanding regulatory regime. If the United States government had no worries about potential failure, why should the market?

Forward again to the Clinton changes in 1995. As part of them, Fannie and Freddie were now permitted to invest up to 40 times their capital in mortgages; banks, by contrast, were limited to only ten times their capital. Put briefly, in order to increase the number of mortgages Fannie and Freddie could underwrite, the federal government allowed them to become grossly undercapitalized—that is, grossly to reduce their one source of insurance against failure. The risk of a mammoth failure was then greatly augmented by the sheer number of mortgages given out in the country.

That was bad enough; then came politics to make it much worse. Fannie and Freddie quickly evolved into two of the largest financial institutions on the planet, with assets and liabilities in the trillions. But unlike other large, profit-seeking financial institutions, they were headquartered in Washington, D.C., and were political to their fingertips. Their management and boards tended to come from the political world, not the business world. And some were corrupt: the management of Fannie Mae manipulated the books in order to trigger executive bonuses worth tens of millions of dollars, and Freddie Mac was found in 2003 to have understated earnings by almost $5 billion.

Both companies, moreover, made generous political contributions, especially to those members of Congress who sat on oversight committees. Their charitable foundations could be counted on to kick in to causes that Congressmen and Senators deemed worthy. Many of the political contributions were illegal: in 2006, Freddie was fined $3.8 million—a record amount—for improper election activity.

By 2007, Fannie and Freddie owned about half of the $12 trillion in outstanding mortgages, an unprecedented concentration of debt—and of risk. Much of the debt was concentrated in the class of sub-prime mortgages that had proliferated after the 1995 regulations. These were mortgages given to people of questionable credit standing, in one of the attempts by the federal government to increase home ownership among the less well-to-do.

Since banks knew they could offload these subprime mortgages to Fannie and Freddie, they had no reason to be careful about issuing them. As for the firms that bought the mortgage-based securities issued by Fannie and Freddie, they thought they could rely on the government's implicit guarantee. AIG, the world's largest insurance firm, was happy to insure vast quantities of these securities against default; it must have seemed like insuring against the sun rising in the West.

Wall Street, politicians, and the press all acted as though one of the iron laws of economics, as unrepealable as Newton's law of universal gravity, had been set aside. That law, simply put, is that potential reward always equals potential risk. In the real world, unfortunately, a high-yield, no-risk investment cannot exist.

In 2006, after an astonishing and unsustainable climb in home values, the inevitable correction set in. By mid-2007, many sub-prime mortgages were backed by real estate that was now of lesser value than the amount of debt. As the market started to doubt the soundness of these mortgages, their value and even their salability began to deteriorate. So did the securities backed by them. Companies that had heavily invested in sub-prime mortgages saw their stock prices and their net worth erode sharply. This caused other companies to avoid lending them money. Credit markets began to tighten sharply as greed in the marketplace was replaced by fear.

A vicious downward spiral ensued. Bear Stearns, the smallest investment bank on Wall Street, was forced into a merger in March with JPMorgan Chase, with guarantees from the Federal Reserve. Fannie and Freddie were taken over by the government in early September; Merrill Lynch sold itself to Bank of America; AIG had to be bailed out by the government to the tune of $85 billion; Lehman Brothers filed for bankruptcy; Washington Mutual became the biggest bank failure in American history and was taken over by JPMorgan Chase; to avoid failure, Wachovia, the sixth largest bank in the country, was taken over by Wells Fargo. The most creditworthy institutions saw interest rates climb to unprecedented levels—even for overnight loans of bank reserves, which are the foundation of the high-functioning capitalist system of the West. Finally it became clear that only a systemic intervention by the government would stem the growing panic and allow credit markets to begin to function normally again.

Many people, especially liberal politicians, have blamed the disaster on the deregulation of the last 30 years. But they do so in order to avoid the blame's falling where it should—squarely on their own shoulders. For the same politicians now loudly proclaiming that deregulation caused the problem are the ones who fought tooth and nail to prevent increased regulation of Fannie and Freddie—the source of so much political money, their mother's milk.

To be sure, there is more than enough blame to go around. Forgetting the lessons of the past, Wall Street acted as though the only direction that markets and prices could move was up. Credit agencies like Moody's, Standard & Poor's, and Fitch gave high ratings to securities that, in retrospect, they clearly did not understand. The news media did not even try to investigate the often complex economics behind the housing market.

But remaining at the heart of the financial beast now abroad in the world are Fannie Mae and Freddie Mac and the mortgages they bought and turned into securities. Protected by their political patrons, they were allowed to pile up colossal debt on an inadequate capital base and to escape much of the regulatory oversight and rules to which other financial institutions are subject. Had they been treated as the potential risks to financial stability they were from the beginning, the housing bubble could not have grown so large and the pain that is now accompanying its end would not have hurt so much.

Herbert Hoover famously remarked that "the trouble with capitalism is capitalists. They're too greedy." That is true. But another and equal trouble with capitalism is politicians. Like the rest of us, they are made of all-too-human clay and can be easily blinded to reality by naked self-interest, at a cost we are only now beginning to fathom.

JOHN STEELE GORDON is the author of, among other books, *An Empire of Wealth: The Epic Story of American Economic Power* (2004). His "Look Who's Afraid of Free Trade" appeared in the February *Commentary*.

Article 50

A Flimsy Trust
Why Social Security Needs Some Major Repairs

ALLAN SLOAN

In Washington these days, the only topics of discussion seem to be how many trillions of dollars to throw at health care and the recession, and whom on Wall Street to pillory next. But watch out. Lurking just below the surface is a bailout candidate that may soon emerge like the great white shark in "Jaws"—Social Security.

Perhaps as early as this year, Social Security, which at $680 billion is the nation's biggest social program, will be transformed from an operation that's helped finance the rest of the government for 25 years into a cash drain that will need money from the Treasury. In other words, a bailout.

I've been writing about Social Security's problems for more than a decade, arguing that having the government borrow several trillion dollars to bail out the program so it can pay its promised benefits would impose an intolerable burden on our public finances. But I've changed my mind about what "intolerable" means. With the government spending untold trillions to bail out incompetent banks and the auto industry, it should damn well bail out Social Security recipients, too. But in a smart way.

Why am I talking about Social Security now, when health care is sucking up nearly all the oxygen in our nation's capital? Because Social Security is a big deal, providing a majority of the income for more than half of Americans 65 and up and also supporting millions of people with disabilities and survivors of deceased workers. And because the collapse of stock prices and home values makes Social Security retirement benefits far more important than they were during the highs of a few years ago. And because the problems aren't that hard to solve if we look at Social Security realistically instead of treating it as a sacred, untouchable program (liberals) or a demonic plot to make people dependent on government (conservatives).

Finally, this is a good time to discuss Social Security because the Obama folks say it's next on the agenda, after health care. No one at the White House, the Treasury Department or the Social Security Administration would discuss specifics, however.

It ought to tell you something that Peter Orszag, director of the White House Office of Management and Budget, is a noted Social Security scholar. Alas, he wouldn't tell me what he plans to propose. "Health care first" was all he'd say.

I'd like to show you that Social Security has a real and growing cash problem even as its trust fund is getting bigger than ever, explain how the program really works, and—immodest though it may seem—propose a few solutions.

Social Security has a real—and growing—cash problem.

The Cash Problem

How can Social Security possibly need a bailout when, by Washington rules, it's "solvent" for another 26 years? To understand the problem, look at me. I'll turn 66 next year, which makes me and my wife eligible for full Social Security benefits. They'll be about $42,000 a year for the both of us starting Jan. 1, 2011, and are scheduled to rise as the consumer price index does.

Social Security, which analyzed my situation, values those promised (but not legally binding) benefits at a bit more than $600,000. That is a lot of money, but Social Security is way ahead of us because the value of our benefits is far less than the Social Security taxes we and our employers will have paid by the end of next year, plus the interest Social Security will have earned on that money in the decades since we started working. Those taxes and interest will total more than $800,000 by Dec. 31, 2010. For example, the $5.18 my employer and I paid in 1961—the year I got my card—will have grown to $140 by next year.

I don't have a problem with this disparity. One of the principles of Social Security is that higher-paid folks like me support the lower-paid. That's as it should be, given that the Social Security tax (12.4 percent of covered wages, split equally between employer and employee) is regressive, far more costly as a percentage of income to a $40,000-a-year worker than it is to me. According to the Tax Policy Institute, five of six U.S. workers pay more in Social Security tax (including the employer's portion) than in federal income tax—something that makes it especially important (and only fair) to preserve the program for lower earners, who get old-age benefits of up to 90 percent of their covered wages, while I get only 28 percent.

How can my wife and I pose a problem to Social Security when our benefits are valued at $600,293, while our tax payments plus interest will total $804,686? Answer: Because the obligation is real, but the $800,000-plus asset is illusory, consisting solely of government IOUs to itself.

Now, let's step back a bit—to 1935, actually—to see how we got into this mess. President Franklin D. Roosevelt set up Social Security as an intergenerational social-insurance plan, under which today's workers support their parents (and those with disabilities and workers' survivors) in the hope that their children will in turn support them. It's not a pension fund. It's not an insurance company.

Social Security exists in its own world. In this world, taxes are called "contributions," though they're certainly not voluntary. "Trust funds," which in the outside world connote real wealth bestowed on beneficiaries, are nothing but IOUs from one arm of the government (the Treasury) to another (the Social Security Administration). And "solvency," which in the real world means that assets are greater than liabilities, means only that the Social Security trust fund has a positive balance.

Alas, the trust fund is a mere accounting entry, albeit one with a moral and political claim on taxpayers. It currently holds about $2.5 trillion in Treasury securities and is projected to grow to more than $4 trillion, even as Social Security begins to take in far less cash in taxes than it spends in benefits. For instance, it projects a cash deficit of $234 billion for 2023. But the trust fund will grow—on paper—because it will get $245 billion in Treasury IOUs as interest. The Treasury pays its interest tab with paper, not cash.

"The trust fund has no financial significance," says David Walker, former head of the Government Accountability Office and now president of the Peter G. Peterson Foundation, which advocates fiscal responsibility. "If you did [bookkeeping like] that in the private sector, you'd go to jail."

Let me show you why the Social Security trust fund isn't social or secure, has no funds, and can't be trusted, by returning to my favorite subject: myself.

The cash that Social Security has collected from me and my wife and our employers isn't sitting at Social Security. It's gone. Some went to pay benefits, some to fund the rest of the government. Since 1983, when it suffered a cash crisis, Social Security has been collecting more in taxes each year than it has paid out in benefits. It has used the excess to buy the Treasury securities that go into the trust fund, reducing the Treasury's need to raise money from investors. What happens if Social Security takes in less cash than it needs to pay benefits? Watch.

Let's say that late next year, Social Security realizes that it's short the $3,486 it needs to pay me and my wife for our Jan. 1, 2011, benefit. It gets that money by having the Treasury redeem $3,486 in trust-fund Treasury securities. The Treasury would get the necessary cash by selling $3,486 in new Treasury securities to investors. That means that $3,486 has been moved from the national debt that the government owes itself, which almost no one cares about, to the national debt it owes investors, which almost everyone—and certainly the bond market—takes very seriously.

This example shows you that the trust fund is of no economic value to the government as a whole (which is what really matters), because the government has to borrow from private investors the money it needs to redeem the securities. It would be the same if the trust fund sold its Treasury securities directly to investors—the government would be adding to the publicly held national debt to fund Social Security checks.

Social Security's "solvency" calculations—and the insistence by the status quo's supporters that there's "no problem" until 2036 because the trust fund will have assets until then—assumes that the Treasury can and will borrow the necessary money to redeem the trust fund's Treasury securities. There is also the assumption that our children, who by then will be running the country, will allow all this money to be diverted from other needs. I sure wouldn't assume that.

This whole problem of Social Security posting huge surpluses for years, using proceeds from a regressive tax to fund the rest of the government and then needing a Treasury bailout to pay its bills, is an unanticipated consequence of the 1983 legislation that supposedly fixed the system.

In order to show 75 years of "solvency" as required by law, Congress, using the bipartisan 1983 Greenspan Commission report as political cover, sharply raised Social Security taxes, cut future benefits and boosted the retirement age (then 65, currently 66, rising to 67).

The changes transformed Social Security from an explicitly pay-as-you-go program into one that produced huge cash surpluses for years followed by huge cash deficits. No one in authority seems to have realized that the only way to really save the temporary surpluses was to let the trust fund invest in non-Treasury debt securities, such as high-grade mortgages (yes, such things exist) or corporate bonds. That way, interest and principal repayments from homeowners and corporations would have been covering Social Security's future cash shortfalls, rather than the Treasury's having to borrow money to cover them.

This problem has been metastasizing for 25 years. Now I'll show you why the day of reckoning may finally be here.

Just last year, Social Security was projecting a cash surplus of $87 billion this year and $88 billion next year. These were to be the peak cash-generating years, followed by a cash-flow decline, followed by cash outlays exceeding inflows starting in 2017.

But in this year's Social Security trustees report, the cash flow projections for 2009 and 2010 have shrunk by almost 80 percent, to $19 billion and $18 billion, respectively. How did $138 billion of projected cash go missing in one year? Stephen Goss, Social Security's chief actuary, says the major reason is that the recession has cost millions of jobs, reducing Social Security's tax income below projections.

But $18 billion is still a surplus. So why do I say Social Security could go cash-negative this year? Because unemployment is far worse than Social Security projected. It assumed that unemployment would rise gradually this year and peak at 9 percent in 2010. Now, of course, the rate is 9.5 percent and rising—and we're still in 2009.

Social Security's having negative cash flow this year would be a relatively minor economic event—what's a few more billion dollars when the government's already borrowing more than $1 trillion?—but I think it would be a really important psychological and political event.

Orszag pooh-poohed my thinking when I met with him. He says I'm wrong to harp on Social Security's near-term cash flow—a term, by the way, that he won't use. "I think the real question of Social Security is how we bring long-term revenues in line with long-term expenses," he said, "not whether the primary surplus within Social Security turns negative within the next few years." I guess we'll see.

When you look back at numbers from previous years, you suddenly realize that Social Security's finances have been deteriorating for a long time. Social Security's cash flow (and thus its trust fund balances) has fallen well below earlier projections. Seven years ago, the projected 2009 cash flow was $115 billion. That fell to $87 billion by last year and is now $19 billion. Ten years ago, the trust fund was projected to be $3 trillion at the end of this year, rather than the currently projected $2.56 trillion.

In 1983, the system was projected to be "solvent" until the 2050s. This year it's only until 2036. Social Security's Goss says the major reason is that over the past two decades, the wages on which Social Security collects taxes have grown more slowly than projected. He said Social Security projected them to grow at 1.5 percent above inflation, but they've been growing at only 1.1 percent above it.

The scariest thing, at least to me, is that even as its financials erode, Social Security is as important as ever—maybe more so. Let me elaborate on what I said earlier, about how older people depend heavily on Social Security. It accounts for more than half the income of 52 percent of married couples over 65, and 72 percent of that of 65-and-up singles, according to the Social Security Administration.

What's more, this dependence—which Goss says isn't projected to change—comes despite 30 years of broadly popular self-directed retirement accounts such as 401(k)s, IRAs, 403(b)s and such.

Why haven't those savings accounts reduced dependence on Social Security? Part of the reason is that it takes a lot of money to generate serious retirement income: about $170,000 for a $1,000-a-month lifetime annuity. Inflation protection, if you can find it, is ultra-expensive. Vanguard, which offers a lifetime inflation-adjusted annuity in conjunction with an AIG insurance company called American General, quoted me a staggering price for an annuity mimicking my wife's and my Social Security benefit. Would you believe $774,895?

Another problem is that the stock market has been stinko. Stocks are below their level of April 2000, when the great bull market (August 1982 to March 2000) ended. It's hard to make money in stocks when they've been down for nine years. The Employee Benefit Research Institute estimates that the average retirement account balance of people 65 to 74 was $266,000 in 2007 but had fallen to $217,000 as of mid-June.

Then there's the problem of lost home equity. According to a study conducted for Fortune by the Center for Economic and Policy Research, people in the lower-income to upper-middle-income ranges have lost a far greater proportion of their net worth as a result of the housing bust than the most wealthy people have.

The bottom line is that many older people who felt reasonably well fixed for retirement a few years ago now need Social Security more than ever. That makes it even more important to come up with a way to sustain it and to show our children a realistic plan to give them benefits, rather than to rely on the trust fund and the supposed political clout of the geezer class to keep benefits flowing when cash flow goes negative.

So how do we fix these problems? Let me divide it into three categories: what to do, what to change and what not to do.

What to Do

Many of the old standbys: raising the "covered wage" limit, but not to outrageous levels; tweaking the benefit formulas so that high-end people like me get a little less bang for the buck; modifying cost-of-living increases for us high-end types; and,

---

Good Numbers Gone Bad

Social Security will soon take in less cash than it spends, partly because of rising unemployment. Its cash flow will shrink to a projected $19 billion this year, compared with the $115 billion predicted seven years ago.

Shrinking projections of Social Security cash flow for 2009 (in billions)

2009 cash flow as projected in 2002

$115

$87 ... as projected in 2008

$19 ... as projected in 2009

Number of Social Security beneficiaries per 100 workers

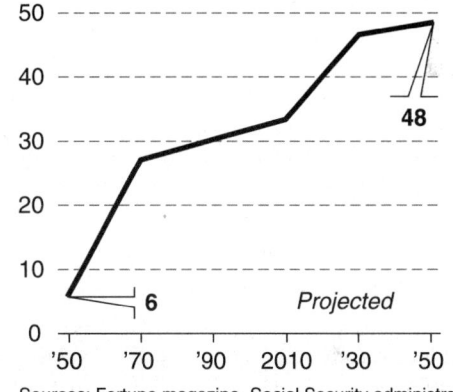

[Line graph showing values rising from 6 in 1950 to 48 projected in 2050, with axis marks at '50, '70, '90, 2010, '30, '50]

Sources: Fortune magazine. Social Security administration

most important, raising the retirement age to 70, with a special earlier-retirement provision for manual laborers, who can't be expected to work that long.

What to Change

- **The law requiring 75-year solvency.** It's hard to predict what will happen 75 days from now, let alone 75 years from now. But the obsession with 75-year solvency and the status of the trust fund has obscured what's really going on.

This requirement forces Social Security's actuaries—who are among the best and smartest public servants I know—to make all sorts of impossible projections. As we've seen, even one faulty projection—such as overestimating wage growth—can cause substantial problems.

- **The trust fund.** Before the Greenspan Commission-related changes in 1983, the trust fund was a checking account. The workings of Social Security since 1983 have turned it into something it was never intended to be: an investment account. Let's gradually draw down the trust fund by having the Treasury redeem $100 billion or so annually (less than the current interest the fund earns) by giving the fund cash rather than Treasury IOUs, gradually increasing the redemptions. That will let the fund buy assets that will be useful when serious cash-flow deficits hit, assets such as high-grade mortgage securities and high-grade bonds.

That way we'll be bailing out Social Security a bit at a time, which is realistic, rather than in huge chunks, which isn't. Combine that with the lower costs and higher revenues, and today's kids could see that there really is a way they'll get benefits someday.

What Not to Do

- **Depend on taxing "the rich."** One solution you hear in Washington is restoring "covered wage" levels to the good old Greenspan Commission days, when 90 percent of wages were subject to Social Security tax, compared with 83 percent now. Sounds simple and fair, doesn't it? But that would increase the Social Security wage base to about $170,000 from the current $106,800, according to Andrew Biggs of the American Enterprise Institute—at 12.4 percent, a huge new tax to middle-class workers.

(And yes, that's middle-class income, not rich-person income, in large parts of the country.)

During his campaign, President Obama proposed (and then dropped) a plan to leave the Social Security wage cap where it is but to apply the 12.4 percent Social Security tax to all wages above $250,000. That—like the 90-percent-level-of-income idea—would be a huge new tax that would weaken support for Social Security among higher-income people. I'm not saying "rich people," because truly rich people generally have huge amounts of investment income, which isn't subject to Social Security tax.

- **Means-test benefits.** It's being done. We'd be making a terrible mistake to means-test Social Security by saying that people above a certain income level can't get it. That would violate the social compact that everyone pays Social Security taxes and everyone gets something.

Besides, Social Security is already means-tested, indirectly. That's because if you have enough non-Social Security income—about $23,000 a year in my case—you pay federal income tax on 85 percent of your benefit.

Given the three pensions I stand to collect from previous employers, I think I hit that level. So, for the final time, let's run my numbers. If my wife and I are in the 28 percent federal tax bracket when we start collecting benefits, we'll be giving almost a quarter of our benefit right back to Social Security.

It would also mean that the $600,000 benefit I talked about earlier would cost Social Security only about $450,000—just 55 percent or so of the $800,000-plus value of our taxes.

I don't mind that big haircut, but I'd be furious if the government decided to just confiscate all the money my wife and I put in over the decades by saying we were "rich" and had no right to any benefits. And I wouldn't be alone.

Given the way health-care reform has bogged down, Social Security may not make it onto the agenda until next year. But it's going to show up sooner or later, probably sooner, because the numbers are so bad that something's going to have to be done. As I hope I've shown, we're going to have to bail out Social Security or risk hurting a lot of low-income older people or putting the whole program at risk by gouging and alienating upper-income Social Security sympathizers like me.

So let's fix this already. By the numbers. And by the right numbers, not fantasy ones.

With reporting by Doris Burke of *Fortune*. **ALLAN SLOAN** is *Fortune* magazine's senior editor at large. His e-mail address is asloan@fortunemail.com.

From *The Washington Post*, Business section, August 2, 2009, pp. G1, G5. Copyright © 2009 by Fortune Magazine. Reprinted by permission via PARS International Corp.

Article 51

How Globalization Went Bad

From terrorism to global warming, the evils of globalization are more dangerous than ever before. What went wrong? The world became dependent on a single superpower. Only by correcting this imbalance can the world become a safer place.

STEVEN WEBER ET AL.

The world today is more dangerous and less orderly than it was supposed to be. Ten or 15 years ago, the naive expectations were that the "end of history" was near. The reality has been the opposite. The world has more international terrorism and more nuclear proliferation today than it did in 1990. International institutions are weaker. The threats of pandemic disease and climate change are stronger. Cleavages of religious and cultural ideology are more intense. The global financial system is more unbalanced and precarious.

It wasn't supposed to be like this. The end of the Cold War was supposed to make global politics and economics easier to manage, not harder. What went wrong? The bad news of the 21st century is that globalization has a significant dark side. The container ships that carry manufactured Chinese goods to and from the United States also carry drugs. The airplanes that fly passengers nonstop from New York to Singapore also transport infectious diseases. And the Internet has proved just as adept at spreading deadly, extremist ideologies as it has e-commerce.

The conventional belief is that the single greatest challenge of geopolitics today is managing this dark side of globalization, chipping away at the illegitimate co-travelers that exploit openness, mobility, and freedom, without putting too much sand in the gears. The current U.S. strategy is to push for more trade, more connectivity, more markets, and more openness. America does so for a good reason—it benefits from globalization more than any other country in the world. The United States acknowledges globalization's dark side but attributes it merely to exploitative behavior by criminals, religious extremists, and other anachronistic elements that can be eliminated. The dark side of globalization, America says, with very little subtlety, can be mitigated by the expansion of American power, sometimes unilaterally and sometimes through multilateral institutions, depending on how the United States likes it. In other words, America is aiming for a "flat," globalized world coordinated by a single superpower.

That's nice work if you can get it. But the United States almost certainly cannot. Not only because other countries won't let it, but, more profoundly, because that line of thinking is faulty. The predominance of American power has many benefits, but the management of globalization is not one of them. The mobility of ideas, capital, technology, and people is hardly new. But the rapid advance of globalization's evils is. Most of that advance has taken place since 1990. Why? Because what changed profoundly in the 1990s was the polarity of the international system. For the first time in modern history, globalization was superimposed onto a world with a single superpower. What we have discovered in the past 15 years is that it is a dangerous mixture. The negative effects of globalization since 1990 are not the result of globalization itself. They are the dark side of American predominance.

The world is paying a heavy price for the instability created by globalization and unipolarity, and the United States is bearing most of the burden.

The Dangers of Unipolarity

A straightforward piece of logic from market economics helps explain why unipolarity and globalization don't mix. Monopolies, regardless of who holds them, are almost always bad for both the market and the monopolist. We propose three simple axioms of "globalization under unipolarity" that reveal these dangers.

Axiom 1: Above a certain threshold of power, the rate at which new global problems are generated will exceed the rate at which old problems are fixed.

Power does two things in international politics: It enhances the capability of a state to do things, but it also increases the number of things that a state must worry about. At a certain point, the latter starts to overtake the former. It's the familiar law of diminishing returns. Because powerful states have large spheres of influence and their security and economic interests touch every region of the world, they are threatened by the risk of things going wrong—anywhere. That is particularly true for the United States, which leverages its ability to go anywhere and do anything through massive debt. No one knows exactly when the law of diminishing returns will kick in. But, historically, it starts to happen long before a single great power dominates the entire globe, which is why large empires from Byzantium to Rome have always reached a point of unsustainability.

That may already be happening to the United States today, on issues ranging from oil dependency and nuclear proliferation to pandemics and global warming. What Axiom 1 tells you is that more U.S. power is not the answer; it's actually part of the problem. A multipolar world would almost certainly manage the globe's pressing problems more effectively. The larger the number of great powers in the global system, the greater the chance that at least one of them would exercise some control over a given combination of space, other actors, and problems. Such reasoning doesn't rest on hopeful notions that the great powers will work together. They might do so. But even if they don't, the result is distributed governance, where some great power is interested in most every part of the world through productive competition.

Axiom 2: *In an increasingly networked world, places that fall between the networks are very dangerous places—and there will be more ungoverned zones when there is only one network to join.*

The second axiom acknowledges that highly connected networks can be efficient, robust, and resilient to shocks. But in a highly connected world, the pieces that fall between the networks are increasingly shut off from the benefits of connectivity. These problems fester in the form of failed states, mutate like pathogenic bacteria, and, in some cases, reconnect in subterranean networks such as al Qaeda. The truly dangerous places are the points where the subterranean networks touch the mainstream of global politics and economics. What made Afghanistan so dangerous under the Taliban was not that it was a failed state. It wasn't. It was a partially failed and partially connected state that worked the interstices of globalization through the drug trade, counterfeiting, and terrorism.

Can any single superpower monitor all the seams and back alleys of globalization? Hardly. In fact, a lone hegemon is unlikely to look closely at these problems, because more pressing issues are happening elsewhere, in places where trade and technology are growing. By contrast, a world of several great powers is a more interest-rich environment in which nations must look in less obvious places to find new sources of advantage. In such a system, it's harder for troublemakers to spring up, because the cracks and seams of globalization are held together by stronger ties.

Axiom 3: *Without a real chance to find useful allies to counter a superpower, opponents will try to neutralize power, by going underground, going nuclear, or going "bad."*

Axiom 3 is a story about the preferred strategies of the weak. It's a basic insight of international relations that states try to balance power. They protect themselves by joining groups that can hold a hegemonic threat at bay. But what if there is no viable group to join? In today's unipolar world, every nation from Venezuela to North Korea is looking for a way to constrain American power. But in the unipolar world, it's harder for states to join together to do that. So they turn to other means. They play a different game. Hamas, Iran, Somalia, North Korea, and Venezuela are not going to become allies anytime soon. Each is better off finding other ways to make life more difficult for Washington. Going nuclear is one way. Counterfeiting U.S. currency is another. Raising uncertainty about oil supplies is perhaps the most obvious method of all.

Here's the important downside of unipolar globalization. In a world with multiple great powers, many of these threats would be less troublesome. The relatively weak states would have a choice among potential partners with which to ally, enhancing their influence. Without that more attractive choice, facilitating the dark side of globalization becomes the most effective means of constraining American power.

Sharing Globalization's Burden

The world is paying a heavy price for the instability created by the combination of globalization and unipolarity, and the United States is bearing most of the burden. Consider the case of nuclear proliferation. There's effectively a market out there for proliferation, with its own supply (states willing to share nuclear technology) and demand (states that badly want a nuclear weapon). The overlap of unipolarity with globalization ratchets up both the supply and demand, to the detriment of U.S. national security.

It has become fashionable, in the wake of the Iraq war, to comment on the limits of conventional military force. But much of this analysis is overblown. The United States may not be able to stabilize and rebuild Iraq. But that doesn't matter much from the perspective of a government that thinks the Pentagon has it in its sights. In Tehran, Pyongyang, and many other capitals, including Beijing, the bottom line is simple: The U.S. military could, with conventional force, end those regimes tomorrow if it chose to do so. No country in the world can dream of challenging U.S. conventional military power. But they can certainly hope to deter America from using it. And the best deterrent yet invented is the threat of nuclear retaliation. Before 1989, states that felt threatened by the United States could turn to the Soviet Union's nuclear umbrella for protection. Now, they turn to people like A.Q. Khan. Having your own nuclear weapon used to be a luxury. Today, it is fast becoming a necessity.

North Korea is the clearest example. Few countries had it worse during the Cold War. North Korea was surrounded by feuding, nuclear-armed communist neighbors, it was officially at war with its southern neighbor, and it stared continuously at tens of thousands of U.S. troops on its border. But, for 40 years, North Korea didn't seek nuclear weapons. It didn't need to, because it had the Soviet nuclear umbrella. Within five years of the Soviet collapse, however, Pyongyang was pushing ahead full steam on plutonium reprocessing facilities. North Korea's founder, Kim Il Sung, barely flinched when former

U.S. President Bill Clinton's administration readied war plans to strike his nuclear installations preemptively. That brinkmanship paid off. Today North Korea is likely a nuclear power, and Kim's son rules the country with an iron fist. America's conventional military strength means a lot less to a nuclear North Korea. Saddam Hussein's great strategic blunder was that he took too long to get to the same place.

How would things be different in a multipolar world? For starters, great powers could split the job of policing proliferation, and even collaborate on some particularly hard cases. It's often forgotten now that, during the Cold War, the only state with a tougher nonproliferation policy than the United States was the Soviet Union. Not a single country that had a formal alliance with Moscow ever became a nuclear power. The Eastern bloc was full of countries with advanced technological capabilities in every area except one—nuclear weapons. Moscow simply wouldn't permit it. But today we see the uneven and inadequate level of effort that non-superpowers devote to stopping proliferation. The Europeans dangle carrots at Iran, but they are unwilling to consider serious sticks. The Chinese refuse to admit that there is a problem. And the Russians are aiding Iran's nuclear ambitions. When push comes to shove, nonproliferation today is almost entirely America's burden.

The same is true for global public health. Globalization is turning the world into an enormous petri dish for the incubation of infectious disease. Humans cannot outsmart disease, because it just evolves too quickly. Bacteria can reproduce a new generation in less than 30 minutes, while it takes us decades to come up with a new generation of antibiotics. Solutions are only possible when and where we get the upper hand. Poor countries where humans live in close proximity to farm animals are the best place to breed extremely dangerous zoonotic disease. These are often the same countries, perhaps not entirely coincidentally, that feel threatened by American power. Establishing an early warning system for these diseases—exactly what we lacked in the case of SARS a few years ago and exactly what we lack for avian flu today—will require a significant level of intervention into the very places that don't want it. That will be true as long as international intervention means American interference.

> **If there were rival great powers with different cultural and ideological leanings, globalization's darkest problem of all—terrorism—would look different.**

The most likely sources of the next ebola or HIV-like pandemic are the countries that simply won't let U.S. or other Western agencies in, including the World Health Organization. Yet the threat is too arcane and not immediate enough for the West to force the issue. What's needed is another great power to take over a piece of the work, a power that has more immediate interests in the countries where diseases incubate and one that is seen as less of a threat. As long as the United States remains the world's lone superpower, we're not likely to get any help.

Even after HIV, SARS, and several years of mounting hysteria about avian flu, the world is still not ready for a viral pandemic in Southeast Asia or sub-Saharan Africa. America can't change that alone.

If there were rival great powers with different cultural and ideological leanings, globalization's darkest problem of all—terrorism—would also likely look quite different. The pundits are partly right: Today's international terrorism owes something to globalization. Al Qaeda uses the Internet to transmit messages, it uses credit cards and modern banking to move money, and it uses cell phones and laptops to plot attacks. But it's not globalization that turned Osama bin Laden from a small-time Saudi dissident into the symbolic head of a radical global movement. What created Osama bin Laden was the predominance of American power.

A terrorist organization needs a story to attract resources and recruits. Oftentimes, mere frustration over political, economic, or religious conditions is not enough. Al Qaeda understands that, and, for that reason, it weaves a narrative of global jihad against a "modernization," "Westernization," and a "Judeo-Christian" threat. There is really just one country that both spearheads and represents that threat: the United States. And so the most efficient way for a terrorist to gain a reputation is to attack the United States. The logic is the same for all monopolies. A few years ago, every computer hacker in the world wanted to bring down Microsoft, just as every aspiring terrorist wants to create a spectacle of destruction akin to the September 11 attacks inside the United States.

Al Qaeda cells have gone after alternate targets such as Britain, Egypt, and Spain. But these are not the acts that increase recruitment and fundraising, or mobilize the energy of otherwise disparate groups around the world. Nothing enhances the profile of a terrorist like killing an American, something Abu Musab al-Zarqawi understood well in Iraq. Even if al Qaeda's deepest aspirations lie with the demise of the Saudi regime, the predominance of U.S. power and its role supporting the house of Saud makes America the only enemy really worth fighting. A multipolar world would surely confuse this kind of clear framing that pits Islamism against the West. What would be al Qaeda's message if the Chinese were equally involved in propping up authoritarian regimes in the Islamic, oil-rich Gulf states? Does the al Qaeda story work if half its enemy is neither Western nor Christian?

Restoring the Balance

The consensus today in the U.S. foreign-policy community is that more American power is always better. Across the board. For both the United States and the rest of the globe. The National Security Strategy documents of 2002 and 2006 enshrine this consensus in phrases such as "a balance of power that favors freedom." The strategy explicitly defines the "balance" as a continued imbalance, as the United States continues "dissuading potential competitors . . . from challenging the United States, its allies, and its partners."

In no way is U.S. power inherently a bad thing. Nor is it true that no good comes from unipolarity. But there are significant downsides to the imbalance of power. That view is hardly revolutionary. It has a long pedigree in U.S. foreign-policy thought. It was the perspective, for instance, that George Kennan brought to the table in the late 1940s when he talked about the desirability of a European superpower to restrain the United States. Although the issues today are different than they were in Kennan's time, it's still the case that too much power may, as Kennan believed, lead to overreach. It may lead to arrogance. It may lead to insensitivity to the concerns of others. Though Kennan may have been prescient to voice these concerns, he couldn't have predicted the degree to which American unipolarity would lead to such an unstable overlap with modern-day globalization.

America has experienced this dangerous burden for 15 years, but it still refuses to see it for what it really is. Antiglobalization sentiment is coming today from both the right and the left. But by blaming globalization for what ails the world, the U.S. foreign-policy community is missing a very big part of what is undermining one of the most hopeful trends in modern history—the reconnection of societies, economies, and minds that political borders have kept apart for far too long.

America cannot indefinitely stave off the rise of another superpower. But, in today's networked and interdependent world, such an event is not entirely a cause for mourning. A shift in the global balance of power would, in fact, help the United States manage some of the most costly and dangerous consequences of globalization. As the international playing field levels, the scope of these problems and the threat they pose to America will only decrease. When that happens, the United States will find globalization is a far easier burden to bear.

STEVEN WEBER is professor of political science and director of the Institute of International Studies at the University of California, Berkeley. **NAAZNEEN BARMA, MATTHEW KROENIG,** and **ELY RATNER** are PhD candidates at U.C., Berkeley, and research fellows at its New Era Foreign Policy Center.

Reprinted in entirety by McGraw-Hill with permission from *Foreign Policy,* January/February 2007, pp. 48+. www.foreignpolicy.com. © 2007 Washingtonpost.Newsweek Interactive, LLC.

Article 52

Are Failed States a Threat to America?

The Bush administration's nation-building efforts are a big mistake.

JUSTIN LOGAN AND CHRISTOPHER PREBLE

Throughout the 1990s, conservatives castigated the Clinton administration for conducting foreign policy like social work, taking on vague, ill-defined missions in remote locales from Haiti to Bosnia. Although the editors of *The Weekly Standard* enthusiastically supported the Clinton administration's interventions in the Balkans, most on the right were encouraged when George W. Bush and his senior foreign policy adviser, Condoleezza Rice, came out strongly against such missions during the 2000 presidential campaign. In 2000 Rice famously declared that "we don't need to have the 82nd Airborne escorting kids to kindergarten." Bush was equally blunt. During one of his debates with Al Gore, he said: "I don't think our troops ought to be used for what's called nation building.... I mean, we're going to have some kind of nation-building corps from America? Absolutely not."

We agree. That's why we're alarmed that the Bush administration has created a nation-building corps from America: the State Department's new Office of the Coordinator for Reconstruction and Stabilization, which was established by Congress in July 2004. The office's mandate is to "help stabilize and reconstruct societies in transition from conflict or civil strife, so they can reach a sustainable path toward peace, democracy, and a market economy." Meanwhile, a November 2005 Defense Department directive makes stability operations a "core U.S. military mission." Such operations would involve on-the-ground assistance, not unlike the provisional reconstruction teams in Iraq; Secretary of State Condoleezza Rice says the office is presently looking at action in Haiti, Liberia, and Sudan. Beyond that, the details are unclear.

Bush and Rice's change of heart regarding nation building is usually attributed to 9/11. But while the terrorist attacks on the World Trade Center and the Pentagon certainly underscored the dangers that nontraditional threats can pose, they did not transform every poorly governed nation into a pressing national security concern. Nor did 9/11 change the dismal track record of past nation-building efforts. This debate has obvious relevance in Iraq, where the absence of a functioning state following the U.S. invasion is the most widely accepted argument against withdrawing American forces. But it has much wider implications for America's post-Cold War, post-9/11 foreign policy, pitting nation builders who want to protect the United States by fixing failed states against skeptics who believe such a strategy is unnecessary, impractical, and dangerous.

Depending on how you count, the U.S. is currently involved in as many as 10 nation-building missions—arguably more. Most of these—from Djibouti to Liberia to Kosovo—are far removed from America's national security interests, just as they were in the '90s. Taking on such missions in conflicted environments is even more worrisome today because it would threaten to embroil Americans in an array of foreign conflicts for indefinite periods of time with vague or ambiguous public mandates and little likelihood of success at a time when we should be focused on defeating Al Qaeda and other Islamic terrorist groups that intend to attack the United States. This approach to security policy squanders American power, American money, and American lives. Unless events in a failed state are genuinely likely to dramatically affect the lives of Americans, we should have normal diplomatic relations with their governments, assess potential threats discretely, and otherwise leave them alone.

Getting in on the Coming Anarchy

The idea that state failure is inherently threatening to the United States has been circulating for some time. In an influential 1994 article, *The Atlantic Monthly*'s Robert Kaplan sounded the alarm about "the coming anarchy," urging Western strategists to start worrying about "what is occurring ... throughout West Africa and much of the underdeveloped world: the withering away of central governments, the rise of tribal and regional domains, the unchecked spread of disease, and the growing pervasiveness of war." He warned that "the coming upheaval, in which foreign embassies are shut down, states collapse, and contact with the outside world takes place through dangerous, disease-ridden coastal trading posts, will loom large in the century we are entering." He argued that insecurity and instability in remote regions should be high on the list of post-Cold War foreign policy concerns because the damage and depredations of the Third World would not always be contained, and would inevitably—though he doesn't really explain how—touch the lives of those in America and Western Europe. Although humanitarianism was the most frequently heard justification for the Clinton administration's attempts at nation building, the president's defenders in and out of government also offered a Kaplanesque rationale that fixing failed states would make the U.S. safer.

Despite his initial skepticism toward Clinton-era nation building, President Bush changed course dramatically after September 11, 2001. The United States National Security Strategy, released in September 2002, made "expand[ing] the circle of development by opening societies and building the infrastructure of democracy" a central plank of America's response to the 9/11 attacks. Part of the administration's new security policy would be to "help build police forces, court systems, and legal codes, local and provincial government institutions, and electoral systems." The overarching goal was to "make the world not just safer but better."

According to the administration's October 2005 National Intelligence Strategy, "the lack of freedom in one state endangers the peace and freedom of others, and . . . failed states are a refuge and breeding ground of extremism." The strategy therefore asks our overworked intelligence services not just to gather information on America's enemies but to "bolster the growth of democracy and sustain peaceful democratic states." The premise is, as the former Cato foreign policy analyst Gary Dempsey put it, that "if only we could populate the planet with 'good' states, we could eradicate international conflict and terrorism."

Many foreign policy pundits agree with the Bush administration's goal of making the world safe through democracy. Lawrence J. Korb and Robert O. Boorstin of the Center for American Progress, for example, warn in a 2005 report that "weak and failing states pose as great a danger to the American people and international stability as do potential conflicts among the great powers." A 2003 report from the Center for Strategic and International Studies agrees that "as a superpower with a global presence and global interests, the United States does have a stake in remedying failed states." In the course of commenting on a report from the Center for Global Development, Francis Fukuyama, a professor at the Johns Hopkins School of Advanced International Studies, argued that "it should be abundantly clear that state weakness and failure [are] the single most critical threat to U.S. national security."

Even foreign policy specialists known for their hard-nosed realism have succumbed to the idea that nation building is a matter of self-defense. A 2005 Council on Foreign Relations task force co-chaired by Brent Scowcroft, national security adviser in the first Bush administration and a critic of the current war in Iraq, produced a report that insists "action to stabilize and rebuild states marked by conflict is not 'foreign policy as social work,' a favorite quip of the 1990s. It is equally a humanitarian concern and a national security priority." The report says stability operations should be "a strategic priority for the armed forces" and the national security adviser should produce an "overarching policy associated with stabilization and reconstruction activities."

Those arguments suffer not so much from inaccuracy as from analytical sloppiness. It would be absurd to claim that the ongoing state failure in Haiti poses a national security threat of the same order as would state failure in Indonesia, with its population of 240 million, or in nuclear-armed Pakistan. In fact, the overwhelming majority of failed states have posed no security threat to the United States. Take, for example, the list of countries identified as failed or failing by *Foreign Policy* magazine and the Fund for Peace in 2005. Using 12 different indicators of state failure, the researchers derived state failure scores, and then listed 60 countries whose cumulative scores marked them as "critical," "in danger" or "borderline," ranked in order. If state failure is itself threatening, then we should get very concerned about the Democratic Republic of the Congo, Sierra Leone, Chad, Bangladesh, and on and on.

In short, state failure ranks rather low as an accurate metric for measuring threats. Likewise, while the lists of "failed states" and "security threats" will no doubt overlap, correlation does not equal causation. The obvious nonthreats that appear on all lists of failed states undermine the claim that there is something particular about failed states that is necessarily threatening.

The dangers that can arise from failed states are not the product of state failure itself. They are the result of other factors, such as the presence of terrorist cells or other malign actors. Afghanistan in the late 1990s met anyone's definition of a failed state, and the chaos in Afghanistan clearly contributed to Osama bin Laden's decision to relocate his operations there from Sudan in 1996. But the security threat to America arose from cooperation between Al Qaeda and the Taliban government, which tolerated the organization's training camps. Afghanistan under the Taliban was both a failed state and a threat, but in that respect it was a rarity. More common are failed states, from the Ivory Coast to Burma, that pose no threat to us at all.

It's true that Al Qaeda and other terrorist organizations can operate in failed states. But they also can (and do) operate in Germany, Canada, and other countries that are not failed states by any stretch of the imagination. Rather than making categorical statements about failed states, we should assess the extent to which any given state or nonstate actors within it intend and have the means to attack America. Afghanistan is a stark reminder that we must not overlook failed states, but it does not justify making them our top security concern.

That Fixer-Upper Isn't as Cheap as It Looks

If state failure does not in itself pose a threat to U.S. security, an ambitious program of nation building would, in turn, be a cure worse than the disease. One particularly troubling prospect is the erosion of internationally recognized sovereignty. As Winston Churchill said of democracy, sovereignty may be the worst system around, except for all the others. A system of sovereignty grants a kernel of legitimacy to regimes that rule barbarically; it values as equals countries that clearly are not; and it frequently enforces borders that were capriciously drawn by imperial powers. But it's far from clear that any available alternative is better.

Yet in his previous life as an academic, Stephen Krasner, the director of policy planning at the U.S. State Department, flatly declared that the "rules of conventional sovereignty no longer work." A stroll through the work of scholars who support nation building reveals such alternative concepts as "shared sovereignty," "trusteeships," even "postmodern imperialism." (The latter is supposed to mean an attempt to manipulate domestic politics in foreign countries without all that old-fashioned imperial messiness.)

If the United States proceeds on a course of nation building, based largely on the premise that sovereignty should be de-emphasized, where will that logic stop? Who gets to decide which states retain their sovereignty and which states forfeit it? Will other powers use our own rhetoric against us to justify expansionist foreign policies? It's not hard to envision potential flashpoints in eastern Europe and East Asia.

An American exceptionalist might reply that the United States gets to decide, because we're different. But such an argument is unlikely to prevent other countries from using our own logic against us. If we tug at the thread of sovereignty, the whole sweater may quickly unravel.

An aggressive nation-building strategy would also detract from the struggle against terrorism, by diverting attention and resources, puncturing the mystique of American power, and provoking anger through promiscuous foreign intervention. A prerequisite for nation building is establishing security in the target country, which requires the presence of foreign troops, something that often inspires terrorism. In a survey of suicide terrorism between 1980 and 2003, University of Chicago political scientist Robert A. Pape concluded that almost all suicide attacks "have in common . . . a specific secular and strategic goal: to compel modern democracies to withdraw military forces from territory that the terrorists consider to be their homeland."

Such risks might be justified if the chances of success were high. But history suggests they're not. In the most thorough survey of American nation-building missions, the RAND Corporation in 2003 evaluated seven cases: Japan and West Germany after World War II, Somalia in 1992–94, Haiti in 1994–96, Bosnia from 1995 to the present, Kosovo from 1999 to the present, and Afghanistan from 2001 to the present. Assessing the cases individually, the authors count Japan and West Germany as successes but all the others as failures to various degrees. They then try to determine what made the Japanese and West German operations succeed when all the nation-building efforts since have failed.

Their answer is complex and not entirely satisfying. To the extent that any clear conclusion can be drawn from this research, the report says, it is that "nation building . . . is a time- and resource-consuming effort." Indeed, "among controllable factors, the most important determinant is the level of effort—measured in time, manpower, and money."

In its 2004 Summer Study on Transition to and from Hostilities, the Defense Science Board, a panel that advises the Defense Department on strategy, reached a similar conclusion. Although "postconflict success often depends on significant political changes," it said, the "barriers to transformation of[an] opponent's society [are] immense." And in the absence of a decisive outcome between warring parties (such as happened in World War II), there is always a danger that violence will continue.

Not surprisingly, successful nation building is highly contingent on security within the target country. The non-war-fighting roles a nation-building military has to play would be tremendously taxing for both the armed services and the U.S. treasury.

By the Defense Science Board's calculations, achieving "ambitious goals" in a failed state requires 20 foreign soldiers per 1,000 inhabitants. Applying this ratio to a few top-ranked failed states yields sobering results. Nation building in the Ivory Coast would require 345,000 foreign troops. Sudan would take 800,000. Iraq, where the U.S. and its allies currently have 153,000 troops, would need 520,000. And if history is any guide, effective execution would require deployments of 10 years or longer.

All this means that nation-building missions are extremely expensive, regardless of whether they succeed or fail. Zalmay Khalilzad, former U.S. ambassador to Afghanistan and current ambassador to Iraq, believes that in the case of Afghanistan, "it will take annual assistance [of $4.5 billion] or higher for five to seven years to achieve our goals." Operation Uphold Democracy in Haiti, which restored a government and installed 8,000 peacekeepers but left that country in its perpetual state of chaos, cost more than $2 billion. Operations Provide Relief and Restore Hope in Somalia, which provided tons of food as humanitarian relief (which were in turn looted by warlords) and eventually got dozens of Americans killed and injured, leading to a hasty and disastrous American retreat, ended up costing $2.2 billion. As of 2002 the United States had spent more than $23 billion intervening in the Balkans since the early '90s. In Iraq, we have already crested the $300 billion mark, having decided that the vagaries of Iraqi sectarian politics should decide our future mission in that country.

Even Francis Fukuyama, a staunch advocate of nation building, admits such efforts have "an extremely troubled record of success." As Fukuyama wrote in his 2005 book *State Building: Governance and World Order in the 21st Century*, "It is not simply that nation building hasn't worked; in cases like sub-Saharan Africa, many of these efforts have actually eroded institutional capacity over time." Put simply, there is no "model" for nation building. The few broad lessons we can draw indicate that success depends on a relentless determination to impose a nation's will, manifested in many years of occupation and billions of dollars in spending.

In this light, the position of the more extreme neo-imperialists is more realistic than that of nation builders who think we can fix failed states on the cheap. The Harvard historian Niall Ferguson argues that a proper approach to Iraq would put up to 1 million foreign troops on the ground there for up to 70 years. If resources were unlimited, or if the American people were prepared to shoulder such a burden, that might be a realistic suggestion. But the notion that such enterprises can be carried out quickly and inexpensively is badly mistaken.

A Really Distant Mirror

People who believe that failed states pose a threat to U.S. security and that nation building is the answer see the world as both simpler and more threatening than it is. Failed states generally do not represent security threats. At the same time, nation building in failed states is very difficult and usually unsuccessful.

There is certainly a point at which Robert Kaplan's "coming anarchy," if it were to materialize, would threaten American interests. Here's how Ferguson, in *Foreign Policy* magazine, describes a world in which America steps back from its role as a global policeman: "Waning empires. Religious revivals. Incipient anarchy. A coming retreat into fortified cities. These are the Dark Age experiences that a world without a hyperpower might quickly find itself reliving."

It's telling that to find a historical precedent on which to base his argument, Ferguson has to reach back to the ninth century. His prediction of a "Dark Age" hinges on a belief that America will collapse (because of excessive consumption, an inadequate army, and an imperial "attention deficit"), the European Union will collapse (because of an inflexible welfare state and shifting demographics), and China will collapse (because of a currency or banking crisis). There is little reason to believe that if America refuses to administer foreign countries, the world will go down this path. The fact that advocates of fixing failed states have to rely on such outlandish scenarios to build their case tells us a good deal about the merit of their arguments.

JUSTIN LOGAN (jlogan@cato.org) is a foreign policy analyst at the Cato Institute. **CHRISTOPHER PREBLE** (cpreble@cato.org) is director of foreign policy studies at the Cato Institute.

From *Reason* Magazine and Reason.com, July 2006, pp. 32–38. Copyright © 2006 by Reason Foundation, 3415 S. Sepulveda Blvd., Suite 400, Los Angeles, CA 90034. www.reason.com

Worth Fighting—or Not

In judging which of its dozen major wars America should have fought, *unintended consequences* often outweigh the intended ones.

BURT SOLOMON

War is hell, but it can also be useful as hell. Even if that isn't always obvious at the time. Ponder, for a moment, the War of 1812. When the fledgling United States of America repulsed the British—again—in 1815, the war "felt like a loss or a tie," according to Allan Millett, a military historian at the University of New Orleans. The torch had been put to the Capitol and the White House, and the Battle of Baltimore produced the lyrics of a National Anthem that generations of Americans would struggle to sing. The Americans hadn't won; the British had lost.

Only as the years passed did it become clear that the war had truly served the United States as a Second War of Independence. It forced Britain to respect its former colony's sovereignty; helped to nudge the Spanish out of Florida; persuaded the European colonial powers to accept the Louisiana Purchase and to stop aiding the Indians, thereby opening the way to Western expansion; and prepared the geopolitical groundwork for the Monroe Doctrine. Not for another 186 years, until September 11, 2001, would the continental United States suffer a foreign attack.

"In the long run," Millett judged, "it worked out."

Unintended consequences can also work in the other direction, of course. Consider the following zigzag of events. The humiliating American defeat in the Vietnam War may have encouraged the Soviet Union's adventurism, notably its invasion of Afghanistan in 1979, four years after North Vietnamese troops seized control of South Vietnam. The Afghan mujahedeen eventually drove the Soviets out, with the covert support of the United States, as dramatized in the 2007 movie *Charlie Wilson's War*. The playboy member of Congress, a Texas Democrat, prevailed upon Israel, Egypt, Saudi Arabia, Pakistan, and the U.S. Congress to cough up billions of dollars and untraceable weaponry.

But recall the movie's penultimate scene, when Wilson fails to persuade his fellow House appropriators to spend a pittance to rebuild Afghan schools, in hopes of reconstructing a land left broken by war and occupation. The resulting power vacuum allowed the Taliban to emerge as the mountainous nation's militantly Islamic rulers, offering sanctuary and succor to Al Qaeda as it prepared its terrorist attacks on New York City and Arlington, Va., on 9/11. Surely, the best and brightest who botched the Vietnam War hadn't given the slightest thought to backward Afghanistan or to the World Trade Center's twin towers, which were dedicated just six days after the last U.S. troops withdrew from Vietnam in 1973.

Bunker Hill to Baghdad

Revolutionary War
War of 1812
Mexican War
Civil War
Spanish-American
WWI
WWII
Korean War
Vietnam War
Persian Gulf War
War in Afghanistan
War in Iraq

- All wars, in a sense, are **wars of choice**.
- The smaller wars the U.S. has fought often turned out pretty well: **low cost with high impact**.
- Vietnam is the war from which the **fewest benefits** seem to have flowed, historians say.

Sometimes, the desirability of a particular war will rise and fall over time. When Chou En-lai, the Chinese premier, was asked to assess the French Revolution fought nearly two centuries before, he famously replied: "It is too early to say." Consider the oscillating historical verdicts on the Mexican War. President Polk and Mexican dictator Santa Anna "were as combustible a combo as [Bush] 43 and Saddam," said Philip Zelikow, a historian at the University of Virginia who was a foreign-policy adviser for both Presidents Bush. When the war ended in 1848, it was counted as a clear-cut American success, assuring that Texas would remain part of the United States and adding territories that became the states of Arizona, California, and New Mexico. But after 1850, this territorial expansion reignited the political battles over slavery that the war's opponents (including a one-term member of Congress named Abraham Lincoln) had feared, thereby accelerating the descent into civil war. But that was then. Now, with the Civil War long past, it is hard to imagine the United States without the former chunks of Mexico. At least it was—until Texas Gov. Rick Perry, a Republican, raised the possibility recently that his state might want to secede from the U.S.

With occasional exceptions, the minor wars that the United States has waged from time to time have worked out pretty much as hoped. From the Barbary pirates to Grenada to Bosnia and Kosovo, clear objectives and a sufficiency of military force led to success at a low cost. But in America's 12 major wars during its 233 years of independence, things have rarely played out as expected, in the aftermath of the conflicts if not during them.

Historians, probably wisely, are wary of balancing the costs and benefits of America's past wars and delivering a bottom-line judgment. But if pressed, they'll divide them into a few "good" wars, especially the American Revolution, the Civil War, and World War II; several muddled wars; and a real stinker, Vietnam, the only one that America has lost outright.

Which brings us, of course, to the two wars that the United States is fighting now. There are reasons for hope and reasons for skepticism about the likely outcome of both. The war in Afghanistan, which President Obama has escalated, threatens to become the first war of necessity that the United States loses, especially if the nation next door, nuclear-armed Pakistan, devolves into chaos. In Iraq, the prospect of a reasonably stable, tolerably democratic regime has grown. But even in the unlikelier event that Iraq becomes a beacon of democracy for a mostly despotic Middle East, because of the high costs—including the encouragement of a nuclear-armed Iran and an ebb in American influence—some foreign-policy experts doubt that history will ever judge the Iraq war as worth the fight.

Apples and Oranges

How to judge a war? Let us count the ways.

Thucydides, the historian of ancient Greece who chronicled the Peloponnesian War, categorized wars by the aggressor's motivation for starting them—namely, fear, honor, and interests. In judging the importance of the national interest, "most people put it first, and they're mostly wrong," said Donald Kagan, a professor of classics and history at Yale University. "It's way down the list." Alarm at foreigners' intentions and, especially, feelings of dishonor are more often the main reasons that nations go to war, he says.

Another way of judging the usefulness of a war is by assessing the need for it. In *War of Necessity, War of Choice: A Memoir of Two Iraq Wars,* published in May, Richard Haass distinguishes between a necessary Persian Gulf war, in 1991, when he served on the staff of President George H.W. Bush's National Security Council, and an unnecessary invasion of Iraq begun in 2003, while he directed the State Department's policy planning. A war of necessity, in his thinking, is one that involves a vital national interest and in which military force is the only option that might succeed—judgments that entail "elements of subjectivity," Haass, who is now president of the Council on Foreign Relations, noted in an interview. Rare, after all, is the war that its proponents don't try to sell to the public as essential, even when it isn't. Zelikow, who served as the executive director of the bipartisan commission that examined 9/11, is skeptical of the distinction. "It takes a post facto argument and makes it sound like objective history," he said. "The only war we did not choose is the one that was brought to New York City on 9/11."

Maybe the purest way of judging a war is to contemplate whether it is just or unjust to fight, an exercise most usefully pursued before the shooting starts. Michael Walzer, a political philosopher and professor emeritus at the Institute for Advanced Study in Princeton, N.J., is the author of *Just and Unjust Wars,* published in 1977 in the wake of Vietnam. The factors in figuring a war's justice are a mix of morality and fact, taking into account whether a nation was attacked or is (credibly) about to be attacked; its efforts to find peaceful solutions; the international or legal legitimacy of its military response; its likelihood of success; and, once a war has begun, the conduct of the fighting.

But these judgments, too, are "different," Walzer acknowledged in an interview, from the practical considerations—measured in lives, treasure, territory, security, and power—that determine whether a nation benefits, on balance, from starting or entering a war. Indeed, neither the justice nor the necessity of a war bears more than an incidental correlation to whether, in hindsight, it was worth fighting. Walzer regards the Mexican War, for instance, as an "unjust war that worked out well," for the United States at least. In Haass's mind, the American Revolution probably ought to be counted as a war of choice, though a "warranted" one that should have been fought. Even a war of choice can be worth fighting—it's just that "the standards are higher," he said—if its benefits sufficiently exceed its costs, measured both in the short and longer term.

"Each had benefits," said Mackubin Owens, a professor of strategy and force planning at the U.S. Naval War College, referring to the major wars that the United States has fought. The problem for decision makers, of course, is that neither costs nor benefits can be known with any certainty—or even good guesswork—in advance. A war's consequences, more often than not, are unfathomable. Even afterward, as any fair-minded historian will attest, it is no easy task to judge. Start with the impossibility of placing a value on the lives lost and disrupted; take into account the improbability of divining the future; and imagine the necessarily speculative character of the counterfactuals—what would have happened had the war not broken out. This is far beyond the reach of any mathematical or actuarial formulation.

Worse, weighing the costs and benefits of a war is an exercise in comparing apples and oranges. Consider the war in Korea, which lasted from 1950 to '53. The U.S.-led combat to repel Communist North Korea's invasion of anti-communist (though autocratic) South Korea proved popular with the American public at first. But that support soured, especially when an armistice settled on virtually the same boundary between the two Koreas that existed when the war began, at the cost of 36,574 American lives. Nonetheless, as the Cold War went on, it became clear that in this first test of resolve after World War II, the U.S. willingness to stand up to Communist aggressiveness cooled Soviet strongman Joseph Stalin's geopolitical ambitions and kept South Korea—and Japan—allied with the West. "I thought it was a just war at the time," Walzer recounted, and "I think it probably helped in the eventual victory over communism."

Andrew Bacevich, a professor of international relations at Boston University, agrees—up to a point. "The initial U.S. response to Korea was a war that we needed to fight," he said. But a crucial mistake was made in conducting it: President Truman's decision to acquiesce in Gen. Douglas MacArthur's desire to invade the North drew Communist China into the war and ultimately produced a stalemate. The consequences, Bacevich said, went beyond the estimated 30,000 additional American Millet to include two decades of enmity between the United States and China—until President Nixon opened the door in 1972—and a failure to exploit the Sino-Soviet schism in a manner that might have weakened the Soviet

U.S. Wars: Worth Fighting?

Historians, if pressed, will divide America's wars into a few "good" wars—especially the American Revolution, the Civil War, and World War II; several muddled wars; and a real stinker, Vietnam.

	Revolutionary War (1775–83)	War of 1812 (1812–15)	Mexican War (1846–48)	Civil War (1861–65)	Spanish-American War (1898–99)	World War I (1917–18*)	World War II (1941–45*)	Korean War (1950–53)	Vietnam War (1964–73)	Persian Gulf War (1990–91)	War in Afghanistan (2001–)	War in Iraq (2003–)
Strategic Benefits	Won independence	Gained recognition of Louisiana Purchase, lessened Indian threat, laid groundwork for Monroe Doctrine	Assured Texas as a state, seized New Mexico, Arizona, California	Preserved the Union, ended slavery	Incorporated Puerto Rico and Hawaii, assured U.S. predominance in Americas	Emerged as world power	Defeated Nazi Germany and Japan	Discouraged Communist aggression, kept Japan and South Korea as U.S. allies	None	Blocked Saddam Hussein from threatening Saudi oil	Ousted Al Qaeda from camps	Created U.S. ally in Arab Middle East
Strategic Cost	Tories punished, Indians harmed	Failed to gain control of Canada	Inflamed debate over slavery	Devastation	Annexation of the Philippines brought conflict with Japan	Diplomatic aftermath led to World War II	Enabled Soviet hegemony in Eastern Europe, Cold War	Led to two decades of antipathy with mainland China	First U.S. defeat, reduced diplomatic influence, caused domestic discord	Left Saddam in power	Destabilized Pakistan	Diminished American influence, emboldened Iran
American Deaths (total serving)	25,324 (290,000)	2,260 (286,730)	13,283 (78,718)	498,332 (3,713,363)	2,446 (306,760)	116,516 (4,734,991)	405,399 (16,112,566)	36,574 (1,789,000**)	58,209 (3,403,000**)	382 (694,550**)	685† (More than 1.9 million troops have served in these wars since 9/11)	4,294†
Financial Cost (in billions of constant 2008 dollars)	$1.8	$1.2	$1.8	$60.4	$6.8	$253	$4,114	$320	$686	$96	$189††	$642††

* Duration of U.S. involvement.
** In war zone only.
† As of May 30, 2009.
†† Does not include $75.5 billion in supplemental war funding requested in April 2009.

Sources: Oxford Companion to American Military History; Defense Department; Congressional Research Service.

Union and bolstered the West. "It sent us down a path," he pointed out, "that cast the decision to go in in a different light." Bacevich cautioned against trying to arrive at "concise judgments" about the desirability of the Korean—or any—War.

The "Good" Wars

The nation's first war, for its independence, was probably its most essential—and successful. King George III had committed "a long Train of Abuses and Usurpations," as Thomas Jefferson detailed in the Declaration of Independence, even as the Founding Draftsman glossed over perhaps the most threatening of the British monarchy's tyrannical acts. Yale's Kagan cited Britain's efforts, from 1763 on, to impose taxes and restrictions that suppressed the commercial ambitions of an entrepreneurial people. Hence the impulse for independence.

Still, only a third of the colonists, historians estimate, supported a rebellion against their British masters; a third remained loyal to the Crown and the rest were ambivalent or indifferent. Many of the Tories paid a price for their loyalty, Bacevich noted, in having to knuckle under or flee. The continent's aboriginal inhabitants likewise did not fare well. Conceivably, the colonists might have acted like their neighbors to the north—Canada waited until 1867 to obtain self-government from Britain without shedding blood—although it is daunting to find anyone who would make that case today.

The Civil War, pitting brother against brother, produced a more vehement diversity of opinion, at the time and ever since. The war was probably unavoidable, most historians say, given the conflicts between the North and the South in their economies—with or without slavery—and their cultures. Had the conflict not broken out in 1861, they suppose, it would have happened later. And by the time the Civil War ended, it accomplished more than its participants had imagined. Early on, President Lincoln declared that he was willing to keep slavery or to end it, in whole or in part, as long as the Union was preserved; the Emancipation Proclamation referred to abolition in the rebellious states as a matter of "military necessity."

Had the South successfully seceded, historians debate whether slavery would have faded out on its own as the soil in the cotton fields was depleted, or, rather, would have spread to states farther west and into Latin America. A popular theme in counterfactual histories posits that the Confederacy and the Union would have reunited eventually. In any event, slavery would presumably have ended sometime (Brazil became the last country in the Western Hemisphere to abolish it, in 1888), although maybe not quickly enough for a slow-changing electorate to choose an African-American president in 2008. But was an earlier end of slavery "worth 600,000 deaths? It's hard to say," concluded Max Boot, a senior fellow at the Council on Foreign Relations. "There wasn't a lot of whooping for joy in 1865. Wars look better when the human costs have faded into history."

> **"There wasn't a lot of *whooping for joy* in 1865. Wars look better when the human costs have faded into history."**
>
> —Max Boot

The classic "good" war, fought by the Greatest Generation, was good ol' Double-U-Double-U-Two. The United States had to be dragged into the Second World War—until the Japanese bombed Pearl Harbor—over the isolationists' objections that the fighting in Europe and Asia was, for a nation protected by oceans, a war of choice. Before it ended, the human costs were staggering, estimated at more than 72 million deaths worldwide, including 405,399 Americans. But the benefits, historians say, were mightier still: the defeat of Hitler's Germany, with its ambitions to control Europe and beyond, and the end of Japan's brutal imperialism across the Far East.

Nonetheless, World War II can be blamed for an unintended consequence—and it was a biggie. The defeat of Nazi Germany left a power vacuum, especially in Eastern Europe, that for nearly a half-century allowed the Soviet Union to have its way. A strong Germany, BU's Bacevich said, would have restrained Soviet aggression, but America's entry ensured Germany's defeat. The United States was drawn into the Cold War, featuring an Iron Curtain, a nuclear arms race, the Berlin airlift, hot wars in Korea and Vietnam, the Cuban missile crisis, and decades of living on the brink of World War III. So which would have better served U.S. interests after World War II: victory by a hegemonic Stalin, or by a genocidal Hitler? Pick your poison.

Wars of Confusion

Something else troubles historians in recounting World War II: It might have been avoided. Winston Churchill, Britain's wartime prime minister and a historian in his own right, described it as a necessary war that shouldn't have been fought.

But it was, and historians blame the sloppy diplomacy that marked the end of World War I. The United States, had it accepted the Treaty of Versailles, would have joined with Britain and France in policing the European peace, presumably to block Hitler from remilitarizing the Rhineland in 1936. That would have prompted the German generals to fire him as chancellor, Kagan said, and "Hitler would never have risen to power." An intransigent President Wilson, unwilling to accept Senate skeptics' reservations about the treaty, is usually accorded the bulk of the blame.

For historians with a taste for slapstick, World War I is the classic case of diplomatic bungling that leads to an unnecessary war. In Lenin's view, both sides were engaged in an imperialist war, trying to carve up spheres of influence. For the European powers, the war proved pointlessly destructive.

But not necessarily for the United States. "The U.S. might have limited the damage of World War I if it had credibly prepared to intervene in 1916 and used that threat to mediate negotiations that leaders on both sides wanted," according to Zelikow. It didn't. But by entering the war in 1917, almost three years after it started in Europe, American troops ended the military stalemate, defeating Kaiser Wilhelm's aggressiveness and bringing the conflict to a triumphal conclusion.

Historians disagree over what might have happened had Germany prevailed. Years later, a German historian found archival evidence that the kaiser's ambitions for a "Greater Germany" extended into Russia and France. The power of a militarily mighty, scientifically advanced, boldly affluent Germany might have blocked—or at least complicated—the emergence of America as a world power. But Walter McDougall, a professor of history and international relations at the University of Pennsylvania, contends that it also would have meant "no Bolshevism, no Holocaust, perhaps no World War II, atomic weapons, or Cold War."

As it happened, WWI fell laughably short of Wilson's idealistic hopes for a war that would end all wars and would make the world safe for democracy. Yet America benefited greatly. Its 19 months at war "gave the U.S. more diplomatic leverage than it probably deserved," military historian Millett said. The war's devastation in Europe held an extra benefit for the United States: It ensured an economic superiority over Germany and Britain, the strongmen of the prewar world, that America has never relinquished.

America's emergence onto the international scene had begun during its previous war. As with World War I, the Spanish-American War of 1898 has given historians fits. Driven by domestic politics in the United States as well as in Spain, it was set off by the typically American blur between idealism and naked self-interest. The Spanish brutalities in Cuba spurred William Randolph Hearst to sell his newspapers by inspiring American intervention in a situation on its doorstep. On a Friday afternoon, after his boss had knocked off for the weekend, the imperialist-minded assistant Navy secretary—Theodore Roosevelt, by name—ordered some battleships moved closer to the Philippines. The result was a quick and relatively bloodless conflict that was "clearly a war of expansion," said Edward (Mac) Coffman, a retired military historian at the University of Wisconsin. It freed Cuba from Spanish rule and, according to Owens at the Naval War College, "basically made it clear that we're the dominant power in the Western Hemisphere. Now we had a seagoing Navy capable of projecting power and an ability to defend the Monroe Doctrine."

The war against Spain probably benefited, on balance, the inhabitants of Puerto Rico and Hawaii by bringing them under U.S. control. But some historians discern a downside in America's trophy of the war. "The annexation of the Philippines created a 'hostage' that the Japanese could attack at will," Millett said. "Long-term, it was a political and strategic disaster," one that put the United States "crosswise" with Japan, fueling an antipathy that exploded on December 7, 1941. The Bataan Death March, in 1942, was another unintended consequence.

Julian Zelizer, a historian at Princeton University, posits a longer-term cost of the Spanish-American War. It was a turning point for the United States, he said, in establishing an "expansionist model" for wielding its influence overseas. He sees in it the roots of another, sadder war seven decades later in Vietnam.

> "The annexation of the Philippines created a 'hostage' that the Japanese could attack at will. Long-term, it was a *political and strategic disaster*."
>
> —Allan Millett, on the Spanish-American War

The Ugliest War

The widely ridiculed "domino effect," so often invoked by Lyndon Johnson in making his case for the Vietnam War, wasn't in itself a stupid idea. "A number of dominoes fell," Graham Allison, a professor of government at Harvard University and former Pentagon adviser, pointed out. Communism's advance in Vietnam ushered in a Communist regime in Laos (which remains in power, as it does in Vietnam) and another, far more virulent version in Cambodia.

Yeah, so? Even if the United States had won in Vietnam, historians say, the benefits wouldn't have been worth the costs. A pro-Western regime in South Vietnam wouldn't have mattered. Thailand and Indonesia would be just about the same. "I lost 58,000 colleagues," said Owens, a Marine veteran of Vietnam who was wounded twice. Tallying up the economic costs and the turmoil in the streets at home, he now concludes that the war probably wasn't worth fighting. ("Though who could say that [the turmoil] wouldn't have happened anyway?") Internationally, the defeat in Vietnam contributed to the image of the United States, which had never lost a war, as a paper tiger.

The miscalculations made in conducting the war are legendary, starting with the "ludicrous" assumption (as Allison put it) among U.S. decision makers that North Vietnam was acting as an agent for China, its enemy of many centuries' standing. A tour of the Hanoi Hilton that showcases John McCain's Navy uniform at the end begins with a guillotine dating from the 19th-century days of French colonial rule. The Americans who decided on the war failed to understand the enemy, a mistake they would make again in Iraq.

"The threat was not real, the death toll was so big, and it affected the U.S. role in the world," Princeton's Zelizer said. "A pretty big catastrophe."

Who was to blame? President Eisenhower comes in for the greatest share from historians. By backing the French as they were being driven out of Vietnam and committing Washington to support a corrupt and unpopular government in Saigon, Yale's Kagan said, Eisenhower made it politically dangerous for Presidents Kennedy and Johnson to back away from Vietnam without seeming soft on communism. In private (though taped) conversations with Sen. Richard Russell, D-Ga., who was a friend, Johnson sounded far more ambivalent about a war that ultimately ruined his presidency and drove him from the White House.

Two Iraq Wars

After the moral morass of Vietnam came the clarity of the Persian Gulf War. When Iraqi troops invaded Kuwait in 1990 and British Prime Minister Margaret Thatcher prevailed on Bush 41 not to go "wobbly," the carefully planned and well-executed war fulfilled Bush's vow: "This will not stand." Kuwait regained its freedom, and Saddam Hussein's forces were forced back across the border into Iraq. With only 382 Americans killed, the United States accomplished a lot at a relatively low cost.

"It would have been a disaster if Saddam Hussein had kept Kuwait," because it would have furthered his progress toward development of a nuclear bomb and destabilized the Middle East, according to Boot of the Council on Foreign Relations. For the United States, something even more vital was at stake. "It was about oil," said Harvard's Allison, citing the fear that the Iraqi dictator would march his troops beyond Kuwait and into Saudi Arabia, in hopes of manipulating the world's—and America's—oil supply. The invasion did not stand. Threat undone.

Yet Bush's famed prudence, reflected in his decision not to chase the Iraqi army back to Baghdad or to oust Saddam from power, took on a different cast during his son's presidency a dozen years later. With a half-million U.S. troops already on the scene, the elder Bush might have had an easier time changing the Baghdad regime than George W. Bush did. The unfinished business of the first Iraq war led, as events (and perhaps a father-and-son psychodrama) unfolded, to the second, harder war.

The two military ventures showed that the political appeal of a war bears little relationship to its utility. "Iraq I passed the Senate by only five votes and was absolutely right," Zelikow said. "Iraq II passed the Senate by 50 votes and was iffy."

The younger Bush might have tried other, less costly ways to alter Iraqi behavior. An assassination or a coup could have sufficed to change the leadership. Or, Haass wrote, "the United States could well have accomplished a change in regime behavior and a change in regime threat without regime change." The costs of the six-year-long war have exceeded 4,300 American military deaths, a price tag of nearly $1 trillion or beyond—and something less tangible but perhaps more consequential. "Iraq contributed to the emergence of a world in which power is more widely distributed than ever before," Haass maintained, "and U.S. ability to shape this world much diminished."

So, will the potential benefits of the second Iraq war ever be judged worth the price? On that, the jury is out. It could take 10 or 20 or 30 years, foreign-policy experts say, to determine whether the Iraqi government functions as a democracy that is able to bring stability, without a dictator's iron hand, to a nation of sectarian hatreds. Proponents say that the odds of a tolerably good outcome are about even.

But *how* good an outcome is still possible seems harder to gauge. The neoconservative enthusiasts for the Iraq war (along with the likes of *New York Times* columnist Thomas Friedman) envisioned a shining democracy in a reborn nation that would inspire the undoing of Islamic autocracies across the Middle East. Haass believes that such a goal has become "unreachable." Whether anything less would produce enough benefits to make the war ultimately worth fighting will depend, at least in part, on the price. Haass said he sees no plausible scenario by which the direct and indirect costs of the war wouldn't outweigh its benefits. U.S. mistreatment of Iraqi insurgents at Abu Ghraib prison and the indefinite detention of accused enemy combatants at Guantanamo Bay sullied America's good-guy image across the Muslim world (and elsewhere) and surely led to the recruitment of additional terrorists.

Potentially, the most perilous of these costs extend beyond Iraq's borders. The chaos of war and the rise to power of Iraq's Shiite majority have emboldened the imperial ambitions of Shiite-dominated Iran. Moises Naim, the editor of *Foreign Policy*, fears that the Iraq war has encouraged Iran to develop nuclear weaponry, which in turn could inspire Egypt, Saudi Arabia, and possibly Arab Gulf states to do the same. "Is a shining, democratic Iraq," he asked, "worth a neighborhood full of nuclear bombs?"

War(s) of Necessity

Another cost of the Iraq war has been the distractions it has caused, not only in Iran and North Korea, which is pursuing a nuclear program of its own, but also Afghanistan. Barack Obama repeatedly leveled such a charge about the neglect of America's other ongoing war during his 2008 campaign. As president, he has announced the deployment of an additional 17,000 troops to Afghanistan, ousted his top general on the scene, and—in next year's budget, for the first time—has proposed to spend more Defense Department money in Afghanistan than in Iraq. Invading Afghanistan after 9/11 was widely considered necessary, not only to clean out Al Qaeda's camps but also to ensure a stable government that wouldn't give terrorists safe haven again.

"We had to do it, no matter what," Boot said. "Even if it doesn't work, no one will fault Bush [for invading], though maybe for how he fought it." Experts on all sides say that the war is "losable," as Kagan put it, but they're hopeful that it isn't too late to change tactics and win. This was evidently the Obama administration's motivation in recently replacing the cautious American commander in the field with an advocate of counterinsurgency.

Haass, for one, no longer regards the war in Afghanistan as essential to U.S. national security. As long as the American military continues to strike at terrorist-related targets, the United States could accept a "messy outcome" in Afghanistan, he said, one that allows the Taliban to make some political inroads in a civil war. Afghanistan has evolved from a war of necessity, Haass said, into "Mr. Obama's war of choice."

But there is plenty of reason to worry about the deteriorating situation just beyond Afghanistan's borders. In the muddled Afghan war, "what's at stake is Pakistan anyway," military historian Millett said. The nuclear-armed nation, with its shaky democratic government, is facing the Taliban on the doorstep of Islamabad, the Pakistani capital. Should Pakistan's government collapse or if any of its nuclear weapons fall into the wrong hands, the United States could well find itself in yet another war of necessity, one that would prove treacherous to lose.

---

bsolomon@nationaljournal.com.

Reprinted by permission from *National Journal*, June 13, 2009, pp. 30–37. Copyright © 2009 by National Journal Group Inc. All rights reserved.

Article 54

The Abandonment of Democracy

How Obama's philosophy of moral equivalence took the place of promoting freedom and human rights.

JOSHUA MURAVCHIK

The most surprising thing about the first half-year of Barack Obama's presidency, at least in the realm of foreign policy, has been its indifference to the issues of human rights and democracy. No administration has ever made these its primary, much less its exclusive, goals overseas. But ever since Jimmy Carter spoke about human rights in his 1977 inaugural address and created a new infrastructure to give bureaucratic meaning to his words, the advancement of human rights has been one of the consistent objectives of America's diplomats and an occasional one of its soldiers.

This tradition has been ruptured by the Obama administration. The new president signaled his intent on the eve of his inauguration, when he told editors of the *Washington Post* that democracy was less important than "freedom from want and freedom from fear. If people aren't secure, if people are starving, then elections may or may not address those issues, but they are not a perfect overlay."

Secretary of State Hillary Clinton followed suit, in opening testimony at her Senate confirmation hearings. As summed up by the *Post*'s Fred Hiatt, Clinton "invoked just about every conceivable goal but democracy promotion. Building alliances, fighting tenor, stopping disease, promoting women's rights, nurturing prosperity—but hardly a peep about elections, human rights, freedom, liberty or self-rule."

A few days after being sworn in, President Obama pointedly gave his first foreign press interview to the Saudi-owned Arabic-language satellite network, Al-Arabiya. The interview was devoted entirely to U.S. relations with the Middle East and the broader Muslim world, and through it all Obama never mentioned democracy or human rights.

A month later, announcing his plan and timetable for the withdrawal of American forces from Iraq, the president said he sought the "achievable goal" of "an Iraq that is sovereign, stable, and self-reliant," and he spoke of "a more peaceful and prosperous Iraq." On democracy, one of the prime goals of America's invasion of Iraq, and one toward which impressive progress had been demonstrated, he was again silent.

While drawing down in Iraq, Obama ordered more troops sent to Afghanistan, where America was fighting a war he had long characterized as more necessary and justifiable than the one in Iraq. But at the same time, he spoke of the need to "refocus on Al Qaeda" in Afghanistan, at least implying that this meant washing our hands of the project of democratization there. The *Washington Post* reported that "suggestions by senior administration officials . . . that the United States should set aside the goal of democracy in Afghanistan" had prompted that country's foreign minister to make "an impassioned appeal for continued U.S. support for an elected government."

In early April, former *New York Times* correspondent Joel Brinkley summed up the administration's initial performance:

> Neither President Obama nor Secretary of State Hillary Clinton has even uttered the word democracy in a manner related to democracy promotion since taking office more than two months ago. The State Department's Bureau of Democracy, Human Rights and Labor has put out 30 public releases, so far, and not one of them has discussed democracy promotion. Democracy, it seems, is banished from the Obama administration's public vocabulary.

At a glance, Obama's motives seemed readily apparent. Former State Department official J. Scott Carpenter observed that it was "obvious and understandable" that "the Obama administration wanted to distance itself from the tone and perceived baggage of the Bush administration." But there were two reasons why this explanation did not satisfy.

For one, Obama might have put his own stamp on the issue without turning so sharply away from the goals of human rights and democracy. In 1981, Ronald Reagan came to the presidency with a mandate analogous to Obama's, namely, to undo the works of an unpopular predecessor. At first, Reagan was inclined to eschew human rights as just another part of Jimmy Carter's wooly-minded liberalism. In an early interview Secretary of State Alexander Haig announced that the Reagan administration would promote human rights mostly by combating terrorism. But soon Reagan had second thoughts: instead of jettisoning the issue, he put his own distinctive spin on it by shifting the rhetoric and the program to focus more on fostering democracy.

Obama might have put his own stamp on the issue of democracy promotion without turning so sharply away from the overall idea. In 1981, upon assuming office, Ronald Reagan did just that.

In a similar vein, Obama could have faulted the Bush administration for its ineffectiveness in promoting democracy and promised that his own team would do it better. Indeed, Michael McFaul, who handled democracy issues in the Obama campaign, declared after the election that the new administration would "talk less and do more" about democratization than Bush had done. But when McFaul was appointed to the National Security Council staff, he was given the Russia portfolio rather than the job of overseeing democracy promotion. The latter task, which had been entrusted to senior staff during the Bush years, was given to no one.

The other reason why Obama's tack cannot be understood merely by his impulse to be unlike Bush is that his disinterest in democracy and human rights is global. The idea of promoting these values did not originate with Bush but with Carter and Reagan, reinforced by Bill Clinton. Bush's innovation was to apply this to the Middle East, which heretofore largely had been exempted. Repealing Bush's legacy would have meant turning the clock back on America's Middle East policy. But Obama scaled back democracy efforts not only there; he did it everywhere.

Thus for example, Clinton, on a first state visit to China, told reporters she would not say much about human rights or Tibet because "our pressing on those issues can't interfere with the global economic crisis, the global climate change crisis and the security crisis." Amnesty International declared it was "shocked and extremely disappointed" by her words. Unfazed, Clinton moved on to Russia, where she glibly presented its dictator, Vladimir Putin, with a toy "reset button" even while the string of unsolved murders of independent journalists that has marked his reign continued to lengthen.

To be sure, China and Russia are powerful countries with which Washington must do business across a range of issues, and because of their importance, all U.S. administrations have been guilty of unevenness in lobbying them to respect human rights. However, the Obama administration has downplayed human rights not only with the likes of Beijing and Moscow but also with weak countries whose governments have no leverage over America.

For example, Clinton ordered a review of U.S. sanctions against the military dictatorship of Burma because they haven't "influenced the Burmese government." This softening may have emboldened that junta to place opposition leader Aung San Suu Kyi on trial in May after having been content to keep her under house arrest most of the last eighteen years. The government of Sudan is even weaker and more of an international pariah than Burma's, but the Obama administration also let it be known that it was considering easing Bush-era sanctions applied against Khartoum in response to the campaign of murder and rape in Darfur. According to the *Washington Post:*

Many human rights activists have been shocked at the administration's apparent willingness to consider easing sanctions on Burma and Sudan. The Obama presidential campaign was scornful of Bush's handling of the killings in Sudan's Darfur region, which Bush labeled as genocide, but since taking office, the administration has been caught flat-footed by Sudan's recent ousting of international humanitarian organizations.

While it is hard to see any diplomatic benefit in soft-pedaling human rights in Burma and Sudan, neither has Obama anything to gain politically by easing up on regimes that are reviled by Americans from Left to Right. Even so ardent an admirer of the President as columnist E. J. Dionne, the first to discern an "Obama Doctrine" in foreign policy, confesses to "qualms" about "the relatively short shrift" this doctrine "has so far given to concerns over human rights and democracy."

Whether or not there is something as distinct and important as to warrant the label "doctrine," the consistency with which the new administration has left aside democracy and human rights suggests this is an approach the president has thought through. Following his meeting with the Organization of American states in April, Obama told a press conference: "What we showed here is that we can make progress when we're willing to break free from some of the stale debates and old ideologies that have dominated and distorted the debate in this hemisphere for far too long." His secretary of state echoed the thought: "Let's put ideology aside," she said. "That is so yesterday."

This begs the question of exactly which ideologies are passé or whether all are equally so. Communism, which so roiled the twentieth century is certainly on its deathbed. Democracy, on the other hand, has flourished and spread in recent decades as never before, to the point where more than sixty percent of the world's governments are chosen in bona fide elections. To lump together these "ideologies" is gratuitously to belittle democracy.

Obama seems to believe that democracy is over-rated, or at least overvalued. When asked about the subject in his pre-inaugural interview with the *Washington Post,* Obama said that he is more concerned with "actually delivering a better life for people on the ground and less obsessed with form, more concerned with substance." He elaborated on this thought during his April visit to Strasbourg, France:

We spend so much time talking about democracy—and obviously we should be promoting democracy everywhere we can. But democracy, a well-functioning society that promotes liberty and equality and fraternity, does not just depend on going to the ballot box. It also means that you're not going to be shaken down by police because the police aren't getting properly paid. It also means that if you want to start a business, you don't have to pay a bribe. I mean, there are a whole host of other factors that people need . . . to recognize in building a civil society that allows a country to be successful.

Article 54. The Abandonment of Democracy

Whether or not the President was aware of it, he was echoing a theme first propounded long ago by Soviet propagandists and later sung in many variations by all manner of Third World dictators, Left to Right. It has long since been discredited by a welter of research showing that democracies perform better in fostering economic and social well being, keeping the peace, and averting catastrophes. Never mind that it is untoward for a President of the United States to speak of democracy as a mere "form," less important than substance.

The trend of downgrading democracy and human rights has already been evident in some important actions abroad. When Venezuela's would-be dictator, Hugo Chavez, held a referendum to set aside the country's long tradition of presidential term limits, the U.S. government went out of its way to endorse the process. The Associated Press reported:

> The Obama administration says the referendum that cleared the way for Venezuelan President Hugo Chavez to run for re-election was democratic. It was rare praise for a U.S. antagonist after years of criticism from the Bush administration. U.S. State Department spokesman Gordon Duguid noted "troubling reports of intimidation." But he added Tuesday that "for the most part this was a process that was fully consistent with democratic process."

While focusing on lack of irregularities in the polling, this response studiously ignored the larger issue. Term limits have been a pillar of democracy across Latin America, where there is a lamentable history of elected leaders holding onto office by unscrupulous means.

However punctilious the procedure, this constitutional maneuver on the part of Chavez, who makes no secret of his ambition to serve as president for life, posed a dire threat to the preservation of democracy in that country.

Perhaps the clearest shift in U.S. policy has been toward Egypt. By far the largest of the Arab states, and the most influential intellectually, Egypt has also been the closest to Washington. Thus, the Bush administration's willingness to pressure the government of Hosni Mubarak was an earnest sign of its seriousness about democracy promotion.

For their part, Egyptian reformers urged the U.S. to make its aid to Egypt conditional on reforms. The Bush administration never took this step, but the idea had support in Congress, and it hung like a sword over the head of Mubarak's government. Obama has removed the threat. As the Associated Press reported: "Egypt's ambassador to the U.S., Sameh Shukri, said last week that ties are on the mend and that Washington has dropped conditions for better relations, including demands for 'human rights, democracy and religious and general freedoms.'"

"Conditionality" with Egypt "is not our policy," Secretary of State Clinton said in an interview with Egyptian TV earlier this month. "We also want to take our relationship to the next level."

While promising unimpeded assistance to the regime, the Obama administration backed away from aiding independent groups, something the Bush administration had insisted on doing despite objections from the authorities. Announcing the elimination of programs directly supporting Egyptian civil-society organizations, the U.S. ambassador, Margaret Scobey, explained that this would "facilitate" smoother relations with the Egyptian government. The *New York Times* summarized the Obama administration's steps:

> The White House has accommodated President Mubarak by eliminating American funding for civil society organizations that the state refuses to recognize, and by stating publicly that neither military nor civilian funding will be conditioned on reform. This has provoked alarm from liberals, from scholarly experts and from activists in the region.

As the popular young Egyptian blogger, "Sand-monkey," irrepressibly irreverent and scatological, put it: "Let's face it, [Obama] ain't going to push on human rights and democracy. That era is gone. We are all about diplomacy and friendship now, and that's what the American people want, even if the price is that the democracy activists in Egypt get f—ed."

This formed the backdrop to the president's much-anticipated speech to the Muslim world delivered in Cairo on June 4. Of the many thorny issues he was expected to address, the setting necessitated that he spell out his views on democracy and human rights in Middle East more explicitly than before. In the *New York Times,* James Traub formulated the question this way:

> Egypt was the central target of President Bush's Freedom Agenda. . . . But when an opposition Islamist party did well at the polls, Egypt's security apparatus cracked down. The Bush administration, concerned about pushing a key ally too far, responded meekly. . . . President Obama's words in Cairo are presumably being framed in the context of that episode. Should Mr. Bush have pushed harder for democratic reform in Egypt and with other allies? Should his administration have spoken more softly, less publicly? Should he, like his father, have devoted less attention to the way regimes treat their citizens, and more to winning cooperation on America's national security objectives?

In the speech, Obama tackled the issue head-on, making "democracy," "religious freedom," and, "women's rights" three of the seven "specific issues" that he said "we must finally confront together." On democracy, he spoke with eloquence:

> All people yearn for certain things: the ability to speak your mind and have a say in how you are governed; confidence in the rule of law and the equal administration of justice; government that is transparent and doesn't steal from the people; the freedom to live as you choose. These are not just American ideas; they are human rights. And that is why we will support them everywhere.

Strong as this was, its ultimate import remained elusive. Obama followed these words immediately with the caveat that "there is no straight line to realize this promise." And while he asserted his belief in "governments that reflect the will of the people," he added, "Each nation gives life to this principle in its own way, grounded in the traditions of its own people. America does not presume to know what is best for everyone."

> "America," the president said, "does not presume to know what is best for everyone." This, alas, is very much the claim advanced by many authoritarian regimes, among them Saudi Arabia.

This, alas, is very much the claim advanced by many authoritarian regimes, including the absolute monarchy of Saudi Arabia, which Obama had visited the day before. Nowhere did the president make the critical point that elections are the only known way to determine the will of the people. That, apparently, would have been "presumptuous."

When he turned to women's rights, Obama's strongest words were that women should be educated and free to choose whether or not to live in a traditional manner. Here, too, he was at pains to avoid sounding as if America had a worthier record than the nations he was addressing or had something to teach them. To the contrary: "Women's equality [is] by no means simply an issue for Islam. In Turkey, Pakistan, Bangladesh, Indonesia, we've seen Muslim-majority countries elect a woman to lead. Meanwhile, the struggle for women's equality continues in many aspects of American life, and in countries around the world."

At three different points in the speech, Obama defended a woman's right to wear the hijab, apparently as against the restrictions in French public schools or Turkish government offices or perhaps in the U.S. military which insists on uniform headgear. But he said not a word about the right *not* to wear head covering, although the number of women forced to wear religious garments must be tens of thousands of times greater than the number deprived of that opportunity. This was all the more strange since he had just arrived from Saudi Arabia, where *abbayas*—head-to-toe cloaks put on over regular clothes—are mandatory for women whenever they go out. During Obama's stop in Riyadh the balmy spring temperature was 104 degrees; in the months ahead it will be twenty or thirty degrees hotter. The *abbayas* must be black, while the men all go around in white which, they explain, better repels the heat.

Nor did Obama mention either directly or indirectly that all Saudi women are required to have male "guardians," who may be a father, husband, uncle or brother or even a son, without whose written permission it is impossible to work, enroll in school or travel, or that they may be forced into marriage at the age of nine. Speaking on women's rights in Egypt, he might—but did not—also have found something, even elliptical, to say about genital mutilation, which is practiced more in that country than almost anywhere else.

On religious freedom, Obama invoked Islam's "proud tradition of tolerance." In one of his more prodding passages, he declared that "the richness of religious diversity must be upheld—whether it is for Maronites in Lebanon or the Copts in Egypt." One of the two institutions co-hosting his speech was Al-Azhar University, which Obama saluted in his opening paragraph as "a beacon of Islamic learning." This may be so, but Al-Azhar admits only Muslims. Foreign as well as native adherents to the message of the Prophet may attend, but Egyptian Christians are excluded. Perhaps this could be understood if it were only a school of Islamic learning (although, even then, why?), but today Al-Azhar offers degrees in medicine, engineering, and a panoply of subjects. Its tens of thousands of students are subsidized by state funds provided by Egyptian taxpayers, ten percent of whom are Copts, barred from Al-Azhar.

In these passages, as throughout the speech, Obama's method was to induce his audience to swallow a few perhaps-unwelcome truths by slathering them over with a thick sauce of soothing half-truths, distortions, omissions and false parallels.

Thus, the Cairo oration was a culmination of the themes of Obama's early months. He had blamed America for the world financial crisis, global warming, Mexico's drug wars, for "failure to appreciate Europe's role in the world," and in general for "all too often" trying "to dictate our terms." He had reinforced all this by dispatching his Secretary of State on what the *New York Times* dubbed a "contrition tour" of Asia and Latin America. Now he added apologies for overthrowing the government of Iran in 1953, and for treating the Muslim countries as "proxies" in the Cold War "without regard to their own aspirations."

Toward what end all these mea culpas? Perhaps it is a strategy designed, as he puts it, to "restor[e] America's standing in the world." Or perhaps he genuinely believes, as do many Muslims and Europeans, among others, that a great share of the world's ills may be laid at the doorstep of the United States. Either way, he seems to hope that such self-criticism will open the way to talking through our frictions with Iran, Syria, China, Russia, Burma, Sudan, Cuba, Venezuela, and the "moderate" side of the Taliban.

This strategy might be called peace through moral equivalence, and it finally makes fully intelligible Obama's resistance to advocating human rights and democracy. For as long as those issues are highlighted, the cultural relativism that laced his Cairo speech and similar pronouncements in other places is revealed to be absurd. Straining to find a deficiency of religious freedom in America, Obama came up with the claim that "in the United States, rules on charitable giving have made it harder for Muslims to fulfill their religious obligation." He was referring, apparently, to the fact that donations to foreign entities are not tax deductible. This has, of course, nothing to do with religious freedom but with assuring that tax deductions are given only to legitimate charities and not, say, to "violent extremists," as Obama calls them (eschewing the word "terrorist").

Consider this alleged peccadillo of America's in comparison to the state of religious freedom in Egypt, where Christians may not build, renovate or repair a church without written authorization from the President of the country or a provincial governor (and where Jews no longer find it safe to reside). Or compare it to the practices at the previous stop on Obama's itinerary, Saudi Arabia, where no church may stand, where Jews were for a time not allowed to set foot, and where even Muslims of non-Sunni varieties are constrained from building places of worship.

In short, while it may be possible to identify derogations from democracy and human rights in America, those that are ubiquitous in the Muslim world are greater by many orders of magnitude. If democracy and human rights are held as high values, then all societies are not morally equal. This is a thought that cuts sharply against Obama's multicultural sensibilities.

America not only embodies these values, it is also more responsible than any other country for their spread. Many peoples today enjoy the blessings of liberty thanks to the influence of the United States, thanks to its aid, its example, and its leading role in bringing down the Axis powers, the Soviet Union and European colonialism. Moreover, the advancement of human rights and democracy requires the exercise of American influence and in turn may serve to strengthen that influence—neither of these, it seems, processes to be welcomed by apostles of national self-abnegation.

In Cairo, once again, President Obama criticized the Bush administration for having acted "contrary to our ideals" when it infringed rules of due process in the course of the war against terror and authorized "enhanced interrogation techniques" that many believe are tantamount to torture. At worst, these infringements were bad answers to questions to which there were no good ones. Some of these practices may have been wrong, but there has not been a single serious allegation that any official employed them for any ulterior purpose, that is, for anything other than the goal of protecting our country in a time of war and national peril.

To dwell on this subject, as Obama has done, is to place great emphasis on humane values. How odd, then, to remove human rights and dernocracy from the agenda of our foreign policy. This is not the place to enter the debate about torture, but even if Khaled Sheikh Mohammed—the mastermind of the 9/11 attacks who was the main victim of waterboarding—and others were abused, there is little doubt that they were up to evil. It is hard to understand vociferating over their treatment even while silencing America's voice on behalf of such brave liberals as Ayman Nour and Sa'ad Edin Ibrahim, persecuted by the government that hosted Obama in Cairo for the peaceful advocacy of democracy. In this can be found neither strategic nor moral coherence.

JOSHUA MURAVCHIK is a fellow at the Foreign Policy Institute of the Johns Hopkins University School of Advanced International Studies. His new book, *The Next Founders: Voices of Democracy in the Middle East,* has just been released by Encounter.

From *Commentary,* July/August 2009, pp. 21–26. Copyright © 2009 by Commentary. Reprinted by permission of Commentary and Joshua Muravchik.

Test-Your-Knowledge Form

We encourage you to photocopy and use this page as a tool to assess how the articles in *Annual Editions* expand on the information in your textbook. By reflecting on the articles you will gain enhanced text information. You can also access this useful form on a product's book support website at *http://www.mhhe.com/cls*.

NAME: DATE:

TITLE AND NUMBER OF ARTICLE:

BRIEFLY STATE THE MAIN IDEA OF THIS ARTICLE:

LIST THREE IMPORTANT FACTS THAT THE AUTHOR USES TO SUPPORT THE MAIN IDEA:

WHAT INFORMATION OR IDEAS DISCUSSED IN THIS ARTICLE ARE ALSO DISCUSSED IN YOUR TEXTBOOK OR OTHER READINGS THAT YOU HAVE DONE? LIST THE TEXTBOOK CHAPTERS AND PAGE NUMBERS:

LIST ANY EXAMPLES OF BIAS OR FAULTY REASONING THAT YOU FOUND IN THE ARTICLE:

LIST ANY NEW TERMS/CONCEPTS THAT WERE DISCUSSED IN THE ARTICLE, AND WRITE A SHORT DEFINITION:

We Want Your Advice

ANNUAL EDITIONS revisions depend on two major opinion sources: one is our Advisory Board, listed in the front of this volume, which works with us in scanning the thousands of articles published in the public press each year; the other is you—the person actually using the book. Please help us and the users of the next edition by completing the prepaid article rating form on this page and returning it to us. Thank you for your help!

ANNUAL EDITIONS: American Government 10/11

ARTICLE RATING FORM

Here is an opportunity for you to have direct input into the next revision of this volume.
We would like you to rate each of the articles listed below, using the following scale:

1. **Excellent: should definitely be retained**
2. **Above average: should probably be retained**
3. **Below average: should probably be deleted**
4. **Poor: should definitely be deleted**

Your ratings will play a vital part in the next revision.
Please mail this prepaid form to us as soon as possible.
Thanks for your help!

RATING	ARTICLE	RATING	ARTICLE
	1. The Declaration of Independence		27. Marking Time: Why Government Is Too Slow
	2. The History of The Constitution of the United States		28. Worse than You Think
			29. Teaching a Hippo to Dance
	3. The Size and Variety of the Union as a Check on Faction: Federalist No. 10		30. Obama's America
			31. The 'Enduring Majority'—Again
	4. Checks and Balances: Federalist No. 51		32. Dr. Dean Regrets Nothing
	5. Can America Fail?		33. Direction, Anyone?
	6. The Right Bite		34. America Observed
	7. Progressivism Goes Mainstream		35. Can Money Be a Force for Good?
	8. The Hazard of Moral Hazard		36. Vote or Else
	9. Not So Popular Where It Counts		37. The American Presidential Nominating Process: The Beginnings of a New Era
	10. It Is Time to Repair the Constitution's Flaws		
	11. Pursuit of Habeas		38. Still the Chosen One?
	12. Is Judicial Review Obsolete?		39. Don't Call Them Lobbyists
	13. Two Takes: Pulpit Politics Is Free Speech/ Campaigns Can Split Churches		40. Born Fighting
			41. Why They Lobby
	14. Misremembering Reagan		42. The Revolution Will Not Be Published
	15. Small Ball after All?		43. Build the Wall
	16. The Founders' Great Mistake		44. A See-Through Society
	17. Happy Together?		45. The Tax-Cut Con
	18. Veto This!		46. The Realities of Immigration
	19. A Political Odyssey		47. The Health of Nations
	20. The Shuffle President		48. The *Real* Infrastructure Crisis
	21. When Congress Stops Wars: Partisan Politics and Presidential Power		49. Speculators, Politicians, and Financial Disasters
			50. A Flimsy Trust: Why Social Security Needs Some Major Repairs
	22. The Case for Congress		
	23. The Case for Busting the Filibuster		51. How Globalization Went Bad
	24. A Bit of Advice, Madam Speaker		52. Are Failed States a Threat to America?
	25. Remote Control		53. Worth Fighting—or Not
	26. Court Approval		54. The Abandonment of Democracy

ANNUAL EDITIONS: AMERICAN GOVERNMENT 10/11

BUSINESS REPLY MAIL
FIRST CLASS MAIL PERMIT NO. 551 DUBUQUE IA

POSTAGE WILL BE PAID BY ADDRESSEE

McGraw-Hill Contemporary Learning Series
501 BELL STREET
DUBUQUE, IA 52001

NO POSTAGE
NECESSARY
IF MAILED
IN THE
UNITED STATES

ABOUT YOU

Name _____ Date _____

Are you a teacher? ☐ A student? ☐
Your school's name _____

Department _____

Address _____ City _____ State _____ Zip _____

School telephone # _____

YOUR COMMENTS ARE IMPORTANT TO US!

Please fill in the following information:
For which course did you use this book?
_____

Did you use a text with this ANNUAL EDITION? ☐ yes ☐ no
What was the title of the text?
_____

What are your general reactions to the Annual Editions concept?
_____

Have you read any pertinent articles recently that you think should be included in the next edition? Explain.
_____

Are there any articles that you feel should be replaced in the next edition? Why?
_____

Are there any World Wide Websites that you feel should be included in the next edition? Please annotate.
_____

May we contact you for editorial input? ☐ yes ☐ no
May we quote your comments? ☐ yes ☐ no